BOUND FOR THE
BACKCOUNTRY

A HISTORY OF IDAHO'S
REMOTE AIRSTRIPS

RICHARD H. HOLM JR.

Bound for the Backcountry
A History of Idaho's Remote Airstrips

by Richard H. Holm Jr.

To purchase copies of *Bound for the Backcountry* please contact Richard H. Holm Jr. at
boundforthebackcountry@gmail.com *or* visit www.coldmountainpress.com

Published by Cold Mountain Press
McCall, Idaho

Front Cover: Johnson Flying Service Travel Air NC450N sitting at the top of the Shearer
airfield in the late 1930s. (J. Renshaw)

Back Cover: A Johnson Flying Service Cessna 206 (N29024) departing Campbell's Ferry
in the fall of 1974. (Fogg collection)

Cover and Interior Design by Cari Campbell Design, LLC

ISBN: 978-0-615-68112-2

Second Edition

Printed in the United States of America

CONTENTS

PREFACE
ACKNOWLEDGEMENTS

CHAPTER 7

CLEARWATER MOUNTAINS AND VICINITY... 346

CHAPTER 8

SELWAY-BITTERROOT WILDERNESS... 370

SELWAY RIVER... 373

MOOSE CREEK... 394

AN ADDITIONAL AIRSTRIP... 429

CHAPTER 9

MORE ON BACKCOUNTRY AVIATION... 436

PREFACE

To plan and write a book can be a precarious and time-consuming venture. However, after I published several articles and another book, and collected information on backcountry aviation for nearly ten years, I figured the project would be a challenging but feasible endeavor. When I scanned through old and new aviation sectional charts of central Idaho, I found the list of backcountry airstrips lengthy but not intimidating. It was not until about a year into the actual writing of this book that I realized the magnitude of the endeavor.

As I dove further and further into the history of each individual airstrip, researching through oral interviews, libraries, government agencies, and peoples' personal files, more and more historical aircraft landing areas emerged. At one point I even became reluctant to call certain people who were helping me, as they too were discovering airstrips lost to regenerating forests. With an overwhelming amount of ground to cover, I slowly narrowed the scope of the book. Because geographic features so distinctively divide Idaho it was a thorny task deciding which airstrips to include.

One idea that often came to my mind and to others trying to approach this cantankerous subject was to explore the definition of "backcountry." It is a term synonymous with Idaho or even Montana, similar to Alaska and its "bush" country. Commonly the term "backcountry" was used in early twentieth century literature by foresters, wildlife managers, and government agencies to distinguish the difference between those areas without roads, compared to areas with roads that were called "front country." Although the original meaning is rarely used in this context anymore, I first thought it had validity; maybe true backcountry airstrips are those that lie within federally designated roadless or wilderness areas? Many friends kidded me that I was being too precise and recommended the use of a dictionary. One buddy kindly laughed, "You writers know what those are, right?" I thoughtfully took the advice, but quickly discovered that definitions such as "a sparsely inhabited rural region," could define most of Idaho. I rapidly dismissed the idea because many of the airstrips I consider as backcountry do not fit this description.

Returning to the dilemma time and time again throughout the project I eventually decided that I would leave the notion or idea of what the "backcountry" is to the reader and simply clarify the boundaries for the airstrips included. The most southerly airstrips incorporated in this book are those at the headwaters of the Middle Fork of the Salmon River, such as Bear Valley and Marsh creeks, along with all of the Middle Fork's tributaries. Moving northward I covered airstrips within the watersheds of the South Fork and the East Fork of the South Fork of the Salmon River, the Main Salmon River from Colson Creek to Island Bar, the Clearwater Mountain area of Dixie and Elk City, and the Selway-Bitterroot Wilderness area.

Even within this narrowed scope, the number of airstrips promptly mounted to over ninety individual landing areas. To be considered a landing area it had to be a location where a runway was once under construction, or a locality where both ski-equipped airplanes and fixed-wing aircraft mounted on wheels have landed. **I want to be very clear that this is not a "guide book" or a "how to book." It is a history book. Many of the airstrips included in this publication are PRIVATE, meaning: Please respect the landowner's privacy and DO NOT land without prior permission from a property-owner.** A few private property owners opposed the inclusion of their airstrip in this book. However, with the goal of compiling a complete history, I did incorporate these.

With each airstrip I made the greatest effort to obtain information related to its use, construction, owners, and anything else pertinent. Information for places such as Moose Creek and Chamberlain was plentiful, while information about short-lived airstrips like Butts Creek Point or Hoodoo Meadows was meager.

Due to the lack of primary documents related to many of the privately owned airstrips, I had to rely more on oral histories. I interviewed many individuals and recorded the resulting information as accurately as possible. When practicable, I used primary documents to verify dates and references. I obtained these documents from the Bureau of Land Management (BLM), United States Census Bureau, the United States Forest Service (USFS), various county courthouses, the Federal Aviation Administration (FAA), and the National Transportation Safety Board (NTSB).

Throughout the course of writing, I struggled with which stories to include and which ones to exclude. People bombarded me with information about a specific wreck or accident that they knew of. I pored through NTSB reports. At one point I started to include every wreck I found and could verify. Part way through this attempt, on a revision of the entire manuscript, most of these were scratched. I told myself I was straying from the topic of the book. Recording all of these events made for some down right depressing days of writing. I decided to keep stories that were important to a particular airstrip or the general history of the Idaho backcountry. In spite of the hundreds of accidents and thousands of incidents that have occurred since wings first took flight over this primitive and rugged section of the state, I continually reminded myself of the thousands of airplanes that come and go in this region each year. Taking the statistics into account, the safety record is actually good. However, accidents continued to enter into conversations about the book. I began to tell people I was not writing a "crash book," but rather a history of the airstrips.

Another focus of mine was to include and highlight information on many of the extremely skilled and professional pilots who have flown or continue to fly in the backcountry. One thing I noted when interviewing people, especially pilots, was a degree of bias. Aviators from areas such as Boise, McCall, Challis, Salmon, Grangeville, and Missoula boasted of themselves as being the best or the real pioneers. As a result, variations in how history became perceived in each of these locales varied widely. In such cases I did my best to interpret and record as fairly as possible.

As with any book, one of the most common questions asked was: How had I become interested in this topic? It really is a question for which I have no easy answer. My first brush with the subject occurred in college while writing an article about the Army Air Force Douglas B-23 that crashed in January 1943 on the shore of Loon Lake. Two of the many heroes in the story, unbeknownst to me at the time, were famous backcountry pilots. Fascinated with the event, I researched every angle of the saga, including these pilots. Although both figures had long been dead, I discovered a trail of books and articles, which led me to develop a friendship with their families.

Through several of their connections, I found subjects for more articles and read everything I could get my hands on concerning the backcountry. The other attraction for me was the ever-evolving personal connection to the land as I began to experience the country on foot and as a private and commercial aviator. After I visited place after place and met many of the legends involved with the development of the airstrips, I thought an accurate history needed to be written. I started the manuscript for the book several years ago, but quickly became so frustrated that I shelved it until a pilot who was steeped in the history himself offered his help and encouragement. It was an offer I'm sure he came to regret as he received a telephone call or a knock on his hangar door about once a week with a list of questions.

Another incentive for writing the book also developed from meeting many of the people tied to the backcountry. For example, shaking the hand of a man who had lived in the wilds of Idaho since 1938 was a powerful feeling. Sitting in a person's living room along the Middle Fork of the Clearwater River, spending hours watching a chronological tour of his eighty years in the Selway-Bitterroot area through a slide show was pure inspiration. These once-in-a-lifetime experiences became frequent and remain unforgettable.

Although my findings are now bound herein, I also came to understand during the journey of writing this book that the subject is similar to flying the backcountry – it is a lifelong passion of enjoyment, discovery, and constant learning.

ACKNOWLEDGEMENTS

I would like to thank the following people for their help and contributions to this publication:

Jim and Holly Akenson, Ed Allen, Tor Andersen, Sue Anderson, Ted Anderson, Pat Armstrong, Carol Arnold, Ray Arnold, Skip Atkinson, Jim Babb, Dennis Baird, Ron Bayok, Glen Baxter, Willy Beebe, Bill Bernt, Bob Black, Bill Blackmore, Hal Blegen, Arnie Brandt, Kirk Braun, Doran Bricker, Rolla Briggs, Frank Brown, Mary Jane Brown, Norm Brown, Amie-June Brumble, Jane Bruesch, Barry Bryant, Ed Burnet, Jean Carroll, Becky Cawley, Travis Christensen, Norm Close, Cort Conley, Dave Cook, Don Chapman, Charlotte Coombes, Linda Cross, Frank Crowe, Jerry Deal, Judd and Diane DeBoer, Mike and Lynn Demerse, Tom Demorest, Don Denton, Dave and Chris Dewey, Robert Diers Jr., Eleanor Dixon, Gayle Dixon, Preston Dixon, Earl Dodds, Allen and Mary Dee Dodge, Bob Dodge, George Dorris, Mike and Leslee Dorris, Harold Dougal, Daryl Drake, Jim Duren, Bob Dustman, Lloyd and Joan Dyer, Ty Edling, Jim Eldredge, Warren Ellison, Frances Ellsworth, Scott Farr, Rick Fereday, Scott Findlay, Bill Fogg, Gloria Freeborg, Chad Frei, Berend Friehe, Craig Fuller, Gary Gadwa, Hank Galpin, Glenn Gemelli, Catherine Gillihan, Bob and Robin Griffiths, Mel Guerrera, Ron Gustin, Bill Guth Jr., Norman Guth, Ray Hamell, Bud Hamilton, the Robert Hansberger family, Sue Hanson, Dennis Hardy, Deanna Harkleroad, Hank Harris, J. Mark Hatch, Bonnie Hathaway, Grant Havemann, Brian Hawkes, Stan Hepler, Deane Hess, Jay and Floy Hester, Marty Hibbs, Kathy Deinhardt Hill, Jerry Hinkle, Amy Holm, Rich and Ellen Holm, Dr. Maurice Hornocker, Brian Howard, Dick Hughes, Tim Hull, Jim Huntley, Mike Jager, Leila Jarvis, Bill Jeffs, Nels Jensen, Wayne Johnson, Robbin Johnston, Dick Karr, Steve Kammeyer, Penny Keck, Larry Kingsbury, Mike Koeppen, Herman Konrad, Ted Koskella, Cathy Kough, Tom Kovalicky, Jim Larkin, Billie Orr Larson, Frank Lester, Dan LeVan Jr., Bill Little, Brent Lloyd, Lorren Loewen, Nick Long, Mike Lorenzi, Joaquin Lowe, Joyce Lukecart, Ramona McAfee, Jerry McCauley Sr., Jerry McCullough, Sandy McRae, Greg Metz, Pat Metzler, Don Micknak, Dr. G. Wayne Minshall, Jim Mizer, Julie Monroe, Jim Moorhead, Marty Morache, Peter Mourtsen, Gloria Mozingo, Steve Mulberry, Edith Mullins, Pete Nelson, Steve Nelson, Jim Newcomb, Russ Newcomb, Loren Newman, Bob Nicol , Rod Nielsen, Dana Odessey, Dr. Bob Olsen, Greg Painter, Steve Passmore, Fred Porter, Brad Potts, Stan Potts, Bruce Reichert, Allen Renshaw, Jim Renshaw, Virginia Rhinehart, David Richards, Alice Rickman, Tom and Jeanette Roberts, Steve Robertson, Jerry Robinson, Ken Roth, Cindy Schacher, Bill Scherer, Joe Rimensberger, Mady Rothchild Schmitt, Julie Schwane, Dan and Laura Scott, Dr. John Seidensticker, Rob Shellworth, Dick Shotwell, Steve Shotwell, Jeraldine Smith, Steve Smith, Walt Smith, Rod Snider, Dr. Adam Soward, Liter Spence, Bill Statham, Dan Stohr, Penn Stohr Jr., Roland Stoleson, Ted Strickler, Zach and Annie Stuckey, Phil Sullivan, Tom Sullivan, Larry Swan, Marilyn Sword, Mark Tabor and Marge Kuehn-Tabor, Harold Thomas, Rick Thomas, Gar Thorsrude, Bob Tice, Dick Tice, Doug and Phyllis Tims, Jack Trueblood, Harry and Gerry Turner, Ray Vadnais, Pat Vance, Alan Virta, Dick Waite, Doug Walberg, Mike Wallace, Leonard Wallace, Ken Walters, William Wardwell, Zeke West, Wilbur Wiles, Dick Williams, Bill Wilson, Charles and Karen Wilson, Dean Wilson, Richa Wilson, Melissa Wolff, Randy Woods, and Bert Zimmerly Jr.

Nick Mamer with an early fire patrol plane at the Chamberlain Ranger Station airstrip circa 1930.

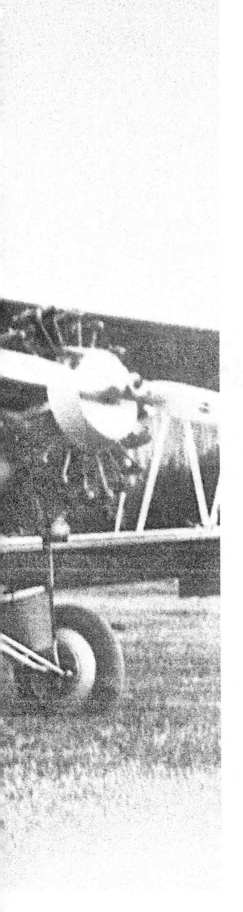

CHAPTER 1

An Overview

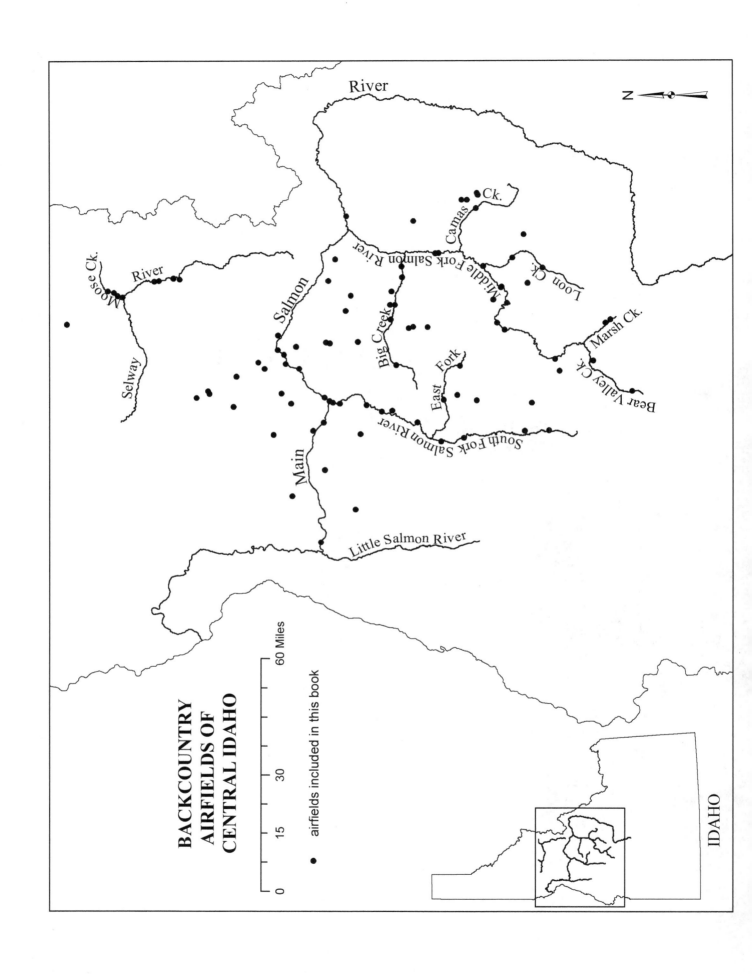

BACKCOUNTRY AIRFIELDS OF CENTRAL IDAHO

River

Moose Ck.

River

Selway

Salmon

Middle Fork Salmon River

Camas Ck.

Loon Ck.

Marsh Ck.

Bear Valley Ck.

Big Creek

East Fork

South Fork Salmon River

Main

Little Salmon River

IDAHO

N

0   15   30   60 Miles

• airfields included in this book

ISHS MS #269-22

Members of Shellworth's 1927 Idaho backcountry trip on lower Big Creek. This particular outing was where the idea of designating a large portion of the area as "primitive" was forged (l to r): unknown, unknown, R. H. Rutledge, Harry Shellworth, Dave Lewis, "Goldie" Moore, "Jeff" Jeffries, Andy Casner, Governor Clarence Baldridge, and Stanly Easton.

The Pioneering and Primitive Area Years (1920s–45)

Nick Mamer first landed an airplane in the Idaho backcountry circa 1925 at the Stonebraker Ranch hayfield in Chamberlain Basin. Mamer, a World War I veteran, returned to the United States at the war's end and in 1924 joined the Washington National Guard based at Spokane, Washington's Felts Field. Mamer along with several other pilots in the Guard, began to work with the local USFS, using aircraft to detect wildland fire. The idea had actually originated a few years earlier in regions of California.

Mamer teamed up with Region 1 (Northern Rocky Mountain) forester Howard Flint and developed a system of fire patrols in western Montana and central Idaho. Flint, an innovator, was fascinated with the potential for air travel and the advancements it could bring to forestry. Mamer and Flint created a close working relationship and developed some of the first aerial photographs of National Forests (NF) in the region. *National Geographic Magazine* published several of these early images.

In the midst of Mamer's work with the Guard, he started his own aviation business, which eventually turned into full-time work. However, it was through his connection with Flint and the aerial fire patrols that he became primarily responsible for pioneering air transportation in the Idaho and Montana backcountry.

By the fall of 1925 Mamer advertised in local papers his ability to fly hunters to Chamberlain Basin. Mamer and other pilots urged the USFS to develop landing fields in remote roadless areas for better access. With the goal of fire suppression and timber protection, the agency was impressed with

the efficiency of aircraft to get men and equipment into the backcountry in a timely manner. The USFS particularly took notice when airplanes were used in suppression efforts during the 1931 Salmon River Breaks Fire. In this case they used the airstrips at the Chamberlain Ranger Station and Stonebraker Ranch. Again airstrips such as Moose Creek and Shearer proved vital in the Selway Fires of 1934. The USFS was sold on the idea of air transportation and on average built at least one backcountry airstrip per year prior to World War II.

At one point federal individual foresters believed airstrips were the wave of the future to combat wildland fire. For example, in 1935 the Idaho National Forest (NF) (now encompassed within the Payette NF) managers proposed the construction of forty-five additional airfields. The author of the report, Ranger A. E. Briggs, commented: "After several years experience with air transportation in fire control the airplane has quite definitely established its practicability and has been given a very important place in our fire control set-up on the Idaho Forest. We depend on the airplane in the same degree of

13

Idaho Senator William Borah (left) and Harry Shellworth (right) on their August 1927 trip to the upper Big Creek area.

to establish policies to protect areas that had not yet been affected by roads, extensive mining, or widespread logging. Agreeing that some type of preservation was needed, the USFS created the L-20 Regulations in 1929. These allowed lands to be designated as "Primitive Areas." Land use restrictions were established under the designation, but industrial use was not totally eliminated.[3] Primitive areas were defined by the L-20 Regulations as, "To prevent the unnecessary elimination or impairment of unique natural values, and to conserve, so far as controlling economic considerations will permit, the opportunity to the public to observe the conditions which existed in the pioneer phases of the Nation's development, and to engage in the forms of outdoor recreation characteristic of that period; thus aiding to preserve national traditions, ideals, and characteristic, and promoting a truer understanding of historical phases of national progress . . . "[4]

With the new L-20 Regulations in place, forest managers looked for regions where they could be applied. One glance at an Idaho map and it was evident that the primitive area description applied to a large center portion of the state. A group of Idaho politicians and businessmen who annually frequented the Middle Fork country on hunting and fishing trips spearheaded a campaign to designate the relatively untouched Salmon River Mountains as a primitive area.

The driving force among the group was Harry Shellworth, an executive with the Boise Payette Lumber Company. Starting in the 1920s he organized annual trips throughout the remote region that became a tradition in his life. Shellworth was well connected politically and a cadre of people joined him over the years on the three to four week outings. It was on these excursions that he voiced the idea of creating a primitive area designation for the region to help protect it from future development. Shellworth

confidence that we do our ever faithful pack strings and trucks."[1] Even with the USFS's enthusiasm, only two of the proposed airstrips were actually completed. One other was partially constructed, but never finished.

However, not all USFS personnel in the remote regions of the Idaho backcountry supported the construction of airfields. One critic in particular was Elers Koch, a forest ranger from Missoula, Montana. Koch felt some areas should remain inaccessible and unprotected from wildfire. His controversial thoughts were published in a 1935 edition of the *Journal of Forestry* in the article, "The Passing of the Lolo Trail." Airfields in the Selway-Bitterroot area were only some of many improvements that he warned would result in a loss of wild places.[2]

Although Koch's thinking was radical for 1930s Idaho, there were other land managers who also held the same view. Concerns rose with the increasing threat of industrial development on a majority of the nation's public lands in the early part of the twentieth century, most notably those managed by the USFS. Many foresters fought back, urging preservation of the country's National Forests.

Koch looked to colleagues like Arthur Carhart who in 1920 established a management plan that prohibited road building around Trappers Lake in Colorado. He also looked to Aldo Leopold who in 1924 accomplished something similar in the Gila NF of New Mexico. A few land managers sought adored the isolated country so much that he labeled his personal files on the subject, "My Dreamland."[5]

While Shellworth had promoted the concept for many years it was not until 1927 when Idaho Governor Clarence Baldridge joined the trip that "new life and impetus" was brought to the movement.[6] Shellworth's friend "Cougar Dave" Lewis of Big Creek hosted the group of roughly eleven people for a majority of their expedition, working as a packer and hunting guide. In addition to those mentioned the group included District Forester Richard H. Rutledge, accomplished Idaho photographer Ansgar Johnson Sr., Boise lawyer Jess Hawley, mining executive Stanly Easton, and forester Andy Casner.[7] In August the same year, prior to the governor's trip, Shellworth organized a special auto tour of the backcountry for Senator William Borah. On the outing the group took in views of the prospective primitive area, while fishing Elk Creek and upper Big Creek.[8]

With support from these prominent Idaho figures the USFS created the 1,087,744 acre Idaho Primitive Area in March 1931 (later increased to 1,232,744 acres).[9] Next came the creation of the 1,239,840 acre Selway-Bitterroot Primitive Area and the 216,870 acre Salmon River Breaks Primitive Area in 1936. With the exception of the latter the other two had a well-established history of aircraft use and developed landing fields. Three years later the Selway-Bitterroot Primitive Area was re-classified under the more restrictive U Regulations. The U Regulations, unlike the L-20, limited timber harvesting and did not permit road construction for fire protection and mining, but allowed the use of aircraft.

From the beginning, the USFS viewed airfields as an economic asset for fire suppression and general management purposes. Even with the tightening of the U Regulations in the Selway-Bitterroot Primitive Area, an influential segment of the public was supportive of aircraft use. While several less powerful parties opposed the inclusion of aircraft, the USFS overruled, creating accommodating language in the *Idaho Primitive Area Report* of 1931.

At the same time the USFS began to incorporate aircraft into the campaign against wildland fire, an economic shift took place in the backcountry. Homesteads in the region that had originally relied on selling goods and services to miners began to slowly fade away. No longer were people passing through these remote areas to claims at places such as Thunder Mountain, wanting to buy meat or produce. In an effort to make the homesteads profitable landowners transformed the properties into destinations for hunting, fishing, and other outdoor activities. To overcome the obstacle of getting customers into the isolated region many turned to aviation and constructed landing fields. Eventually over half the homesteads along the roadless river corridors built runways. Early examples include: W. A. Stonebraker at his Chamberlain Basin ranch (1925), Merl "Blackie" Wallace at the Flying W Ranch on Cabin Creek (1931), and Alvin Renshaw at the 51 Ranch on the Selway who utilized neighbor Phil Shearer's airstrip (1934).

Other remote areas in central Idaho used aircraft as well. For example the surviving mining industries at Stibnite (1930), Warren (1931), and Mackay Bar (1933) built airfields. As a result of these activities there was a demand for pilots and airplanes in the area and aviation companies sprang up to serve those choosing to recreate or work in these less-populated regions.

Robert "Bob" Johnson the founder of Johnson Flying Service.

The Golden Era (1946–63)

While many airstrips were never finished or abandoned due to the start of World War II, the USFS and private landowners took advantage of the postwar technology. Proprietors constructed airstrips in places once thought to be impossible, while the USFS enlarged many of their facilities to accommodate bigger airplanes to move men and equipment. The period between 1946 and 1963 saw the most active use of backcountry airstrips in Idaho. By 1963 roughly seventy airstrips were functional.

The fight against wildfire in National Forests also increased during this period. Technology from the war was again enlisted, and included new uses such as the aerial applications of chemicals. Many of the chemical refueling stations were located at airstrips like Moose Creek Ranger Station, Bruce Meadows, Chamberlain Ranger Station, and Dixie Ranger Station. The USFS stepped up its prewar experimental smokejumping program. Top-notch smokejumper bases popped up around the Northwest. Serving the Northern Rocky Mountain Region was the Missoula base and serving the Intermountain Region (Region 4) was the McCall base. Connected to these operations as well as the development of many of the airstrips, was Johnson Flying Service, headquartered in Missoula with a satellite base in McCall.

Well before the war, Robert "Bob" Johnson, his pilots, planes, and company had become a permanent fixture in the Idaho and Montana backcountry. Johnson started his business in 1928 and it grew to a sizable operation within a few years. The company single-handedly became the expert the USFS relied on for anything aviation-related in the Northern and Intermountain Regions. It was Johnson aircraft and pilots who dropped the first smokejumpers in both management areas.

A 1964 meeting of the IOGA. Seated (l to r): Rolla Briggs – Selway Lodge, Rex Lanham – Flying W Ranch, Max Walker – Peck, Lois Menett – Secretary, Bill Guth Sr. – Salmon. Standing (l to r): Gordon Stimmel – Kooskia, Don Smith – North Fork, Loren Gillman – Lochsa Lodge, Pat Reed – Boise, Bill Guth Jr. – Salmon, Paul Filer – Shepp Ranch, Bob Cole – Middle Fork Lodge, Eddie Bennett – Trail Creek Lodge, and Eggs Beckley – Sulphur Creek Ranch.

In the postwar years Johnson bought numerous aircraft to fulfill and expand his operations. He also helped to extend services to private residences along river corridors by offering assistance in laying out airstrips. With most of the airfields in place by the late 1950s, the United States Postal Service put mail delivery contracts out to bid. Johnson appropriately held the Salmon River Star Route for twenty years. Other contractors bid on similar routes that covered other drainages, such as the Middle Fork of the Salmon River.

The recreation industry in the Idaho backcountry came to rely greatly on aviation. The Idaho Outfitters and Guides Association (IOGA), founded in 1954, began to license outfitters who ran commercial businesses tied to hunting, fishing, boating, and other outdoor activities. Many of the IOGA members began using aircraft in their businesses. The new sport of floating rivers created demand for aircraft, especially on the Middle Fork of the Salmon River, where water levels on the upper reaches diminish to flows too shallow for boating later in the year. Aircraft enabled delivery of boats, people, and supplies to remote areas where groups could float the navigable part of the rivers.

River floaters were not the only groups to become reliant on aircraft, but also hunters, hikers, and fisherman. Outfitters and private sportsman were also granted greater access to public lands, particularly state owned properties, when the Idaho Department of Fish & Game (IDFG) purchased between 1946 and 1949 fifteen backcountry homesteads totaling over 2,000 acres. Some of these old ranches were then leased to the public and several included pre-existing runways. The acreage acquired through Pittman-Robertson funding had the goal of restoring wildlife habitat and providing public access to improve game management.[10]

N. Long

Senator Frank Church.

Wilderness and Aircraft (1964–80)

The postwar boom in the backcountry connected to aircraft came to a crossroad in the early 1960s when Idaho's Democratic Senator Frank Church backed a wilderness bill that had been rejected previously. The generally conservative people from his state did not support wilderness, but he pressed on, gaining national support. In 1964 Senator Church sponsored The Wilderness Act on the floor of the United States Senate. The bill passed and instantly designated nine million acres of federal land as wilderness. The bill, ghost-written by Howard Zahniser, defined the term wilderness – "A wilderness, in contrast with those areas where man and his own works dominate the landscape, is hereby recognized as an area where the earth and community of life are untrammeled by man, where man himself is a visitor who does not remain."[11] By literal definition the heavily restricted wilderness areas no longer allowed motorized or mechanical equipment, including the basics such as bicycles or even a wheelbarrow, let alone an airplane.

Most early wilderness areas had previously been designated as primitive areas under the more restrictive U Regulations. As a result when President Lyndon Johnson signed The Wilderness Act, the Selway-Bitterroot Primitive Area instantly earned wilderness status. At the time it was the largest single contiguous wilderness area covering 1,243,659 acres. Debate arose on whether or not airfields were going to remain open as access points within wilderness locales. Management plans drafted for the new areas in Idaho had a grandfather clause that allowed existing airfields to remain open. In contrast the Bob Marshall Wilderness in Montana placed a closure on all of its backcountry airstrips. However, the Selway-Bitterroot Management Plan did call for the acquisition of private in-holdings when feasible and possible. Once the properties were obtained, the airfields were to be closed, a provision consistently executed.[12]

The notion of retaining the use of aircraft in wilderness areas enraged many wilderness "purists," while other more moderate supporters accepted their use. After the landmark year of 1964, the wilderness movement swept the nation. In 1973 Idaho resident, conservationist, author, and avid outdoorsman, Ted Trueblood formed the River of No Return Wilderness Council. This grassroots council sought permanent wilderness status for the already existing Salmon River Breaks Primitive Area and the Idaho Primitive Area. The group also pushed for inclusion of the Main Salmon River in the Wild and Scenic Rivers System. Trueblood, being an author not only of outdoor books, but also for *Field & Stream*, along with several other national media magazines, had a perfect avenue to reach readers in hopes of rallying support. The efforts of this small group caught the eye of Senator Church, who became a huge voice and leader of the cause.

The USFS agreed that the two primitive areas, which comprised about 1.5 million acres, should be changed to wilderness status. However, Trueblood and Church felt that this was not enough to protect the watersheds of the areas involved and thought the acreage should be doubled. The two understood the necessity for compromise on the issue of aircraft access, one of the largest deal breakers.

Idaho Senator Jim McClure was a wary supporter of the wilderness movement and saw the complexities of the issue surrounding the designation and aircraft. To better understand the situation he and a member of his staff chartered an airplane and flew to many of the airstrips to have a firsthand look. On his return he was adamant that the remote landing strips remain open. McClure's biographer, William L. Smallwood, paraphrased his thoughts on the subject and wrote, "[G]etting into the 'backcountry' by airplane was not only essential for Idaho's booming tourist industry, it was one of those rights considered inalienable by Western private pilots, especially those in Idaho who had the highest per-capita ownership of general aviation airplanes outside of Alaska."[13]

Trueblood and Church knew that with the inclusion of aircraft they could achieve about 2.3 million acres of wilderness in central Idaho.[14] Although less acreage than they wanted, it exceeded the originally-proposed 1.5 million acres. Trueblood often pointed out that the Wilderness Act Section 4 (d) clearly provided for aircraft in wilderness, stating: "Within the wilderness areas designated by this Act the use of aircraft or motorboats, where these uses have already become established, may be permitted to continue . . ."[15]

As expected, the decision to allow aircraft created controversy with some sectors of wilderness advocates. Senator Church and his staff developed a general response to the anti-aircraft citizen. One extensive response letter to Clem L. Pope of McCall clearly and succinctly written by Church himself remains as one of the best examples of his view on the subject. "Dear Mr. Pope: I have received your two letters expressing your opposition . . . However, I would like to say a word about the provisions in the bill which relate to the landing strips, in the light of your objection. . . . Because of the vastness of the River of No Return area, without continued access by air, few people could see and enjoy the remote and less accessible parts of the region. Therefore, in the Senate bill we provided that the landing of aircraft shall be permitted to continue. We also prohibited the Forest Service from closing airstrips in regular use . . . The history of man goes back over 8,000 years in this area, but even today the region – – with the airstrips and other rustic facilities – – is largely 'wilderness' under the definition of the 1964 Wilderness Act . . . As the floor manager of the 1964 Wilderness Act, I recall quite clearly what we were trying to accomplish by setting up the National Wilderness Preservation System, and I make no apologies for my commitment to assuring that this spectacular area can be seen and enjoyed, whether the access is by horseback, on foot, via jetboat, or small plane. I hope, after reviewing this material and my letter, you too will believe that the legislation passed recently by the Senate does justice to this region of rugged beauty and remoteness. With best wishes for the holiday season, Sincerely, Frank Church."[16]

Without Church, Trueblood, and McClure reaching a compromise with various agencies, user groups, and citizens concerning the inclusion of aircraft, the second-largest designated wilderness in the lower forty-eight would not have come to fruition. In 1980 Congress designated the wilderness area under Trueblood's suggested title, "The River of No Return Wilderness." The Lewis and Clark Expedition coined this term after discovering the Main Salmon to be un-navigable in 1805.

Also designated in 1980 as "Wild and Scenic River" were 125 miles of the Main Salmon River. This Act, established by Congress in 1968 was another of Church's accomplishments. One of the original rivers to be included was the Middle Fork of the Salmon.

Four years after the creation of the massive River of No Return Wilderness, Church at the age of fifty-nine was diagnosed with cancer. To honor his efforts in preserving land in Idaho and also across the country, Church's name was added to the title at the urging of Senator McClure. A few weeks later, in April 1984, Church died.

Senator Jim McClure standing with a McCall Air Taxi Cessna 206 at McCall in the late 1980s.

Post-Wilderness Designation (1981–present)

Even though Church and his constituents agreed on the inclusion of aircraft in central Idaho's wilderness areas, some minority wilderness extremists could not accept the compromise. In the early 1980s the USFS, without the proper authority, closed a handful of well-established landing fields that were acquired in the 1970s. Although these strips originally had been built for access to private homesteads, many in the aviation community advocated for public use.

A series of successful airfield closures in the Selway-Bitterroot started first in 1966 with the obliteration of Moose Creek Ranches. This action created a fear of eventually losing all air access to central Idaho wilderness areas, no matter what had been agreed-upon by Congress. Panicked, many aviation-minded people protested the 1980s closings. One person in particular was McCall pilot Bill Dorris, who contacted none other than Senator McClure. Again, McClure's office flew to many of the questionable airstrips such as Simonds, Dewey Moore, Vines, Mile High, and Cabin Creek to investigate the situation in person. Within a short time McClure was able to persuade the USFS to keep the airfields open for public access.

Over the next few years some of those opposed to the re-opening of the airfields did not sit idle. Several individuals, most likely acting alone, began a course of eco-terrorist acts by sabotaging specific landing fields. The placement of salt that attracted game, which in return caused substantial damage and erosion, created several forced closures based on questions of safety. The damage caused by these illegal activities was corrected at the cost of thousands of dollars. The next several attempts at destroying airfields included the practice of digging trenches across runway surfaces to create washouts during spring runoff. Another documented attempt cited the intentional plugging of runway culverts, also causing washouts. Fortunately commercial aircraft operators noted the damages and repaired the causes.

It is ironic that individuals who believed strongly in eliminating the use of airstrips for the "betterment" of wilderness were willing to do so at the cost of destroying other wilderness values. Take for example the continued efforts in the 1980s and 1990s at the Dewey Moore airstrip on upper Big Creek. In all instances water was forced down the runway, washing silt, soil, and debris straight into a fragile river ecosystem. Such counter-productive activities have consistently been defeated.

As a consequence of wilderness designations in central Idaho, only six airstrips were closed between 1966 and 2012. Many veteran backcountry pilots continued to exercise what they believed was their "right of use," even after certain closures. Most have since been reclaimed and in some cases are barely visible today, making them far from usable.

The post-wilderness years are distinguished from the other eras by three major changes. First, the number of flight hours for commercial air taxi operators escalated during the summer months. This was caused by the booming rafting industry on the Main and Middle Fork of the Salmon River starting in the mid to late 1970s. In order to meet the demand, air taxis began to fly from sunup to sundown, often flying in high-risk conditions; in prior eras, commercial operators obeyed the unwritten rule of flying the backcountry before mid-morning and wrapping up additional flights in the calm of the evening. It is also interesting to note that for a few years during this period the FAA designated both Alaska and the Idaho backcountry as "remote geographic areas" and allowed commercial air taxi pilots to fly without instrument ratings. Secondly, commercial operators began utilizing aircraft that enabled pilots to overcome conditions and situations that were once limited by less capable airplanes. Of these planes, the 310 horsepower (turbo) equipped Cessna 206 was the most significant. Thirdly, private sector pilots began using the area more and more. This resulted in mountain-flying instruction courses that were initiated to improve safety. Dick Williams of Salmon, Idaho, offered one of the first courses in flying the Idaho backcountry in the early 1980s, called "Mountains to Canyons Flying School." He later teamed up with a group of seasoned mountain pilots, Gridley Rowles, Frank Giles, and Bill Dorris. This group taught an FAA-sponsored backcountry school annually in Challis under the title of "River of No Return Mountain Flying Seminar," which Bob Plummer eventually took over.[17] Other organizations followed and have made learning to fly the mountains and canyons of the backcountry a must for aviation enthusiasts seeking more technical flying.

Fly-in events and gatherings helped to increase use by private aircraft. Since more people come to the backcountry to recreate via airplanes, organizations have evolved to promote the area. In spite of the increased use, the Idaho backcountry is arguably one of the most unique, rugged, and remote areas that offers challenging flying found no where else in the lower forty-eight states. The region's rich aviation history, lore, and legend are a fascinating subject to anyone traveling into the area.

A typical view of the Idaho backcountry from the pilot's seat - the most remote undeveloped land found in the lower forty-eight states, encompassing thousands of acres of roadless land and several nearly contiguous federally designated wilderness areas.

Looking downstream at the original Crandall airfield in February 1939 with a Zimmerly owned Travel Air 6000 (NC9844) in the foreground.

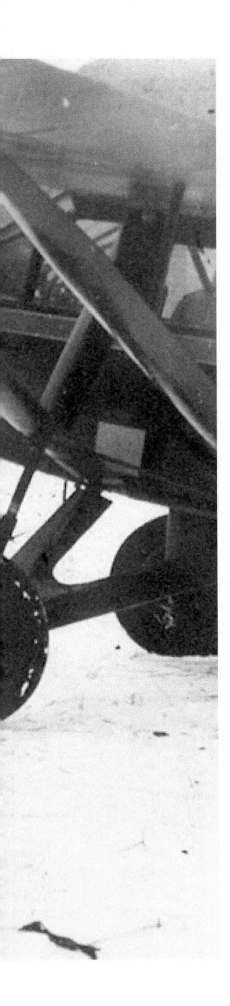

Middle Fork of the Salmon River

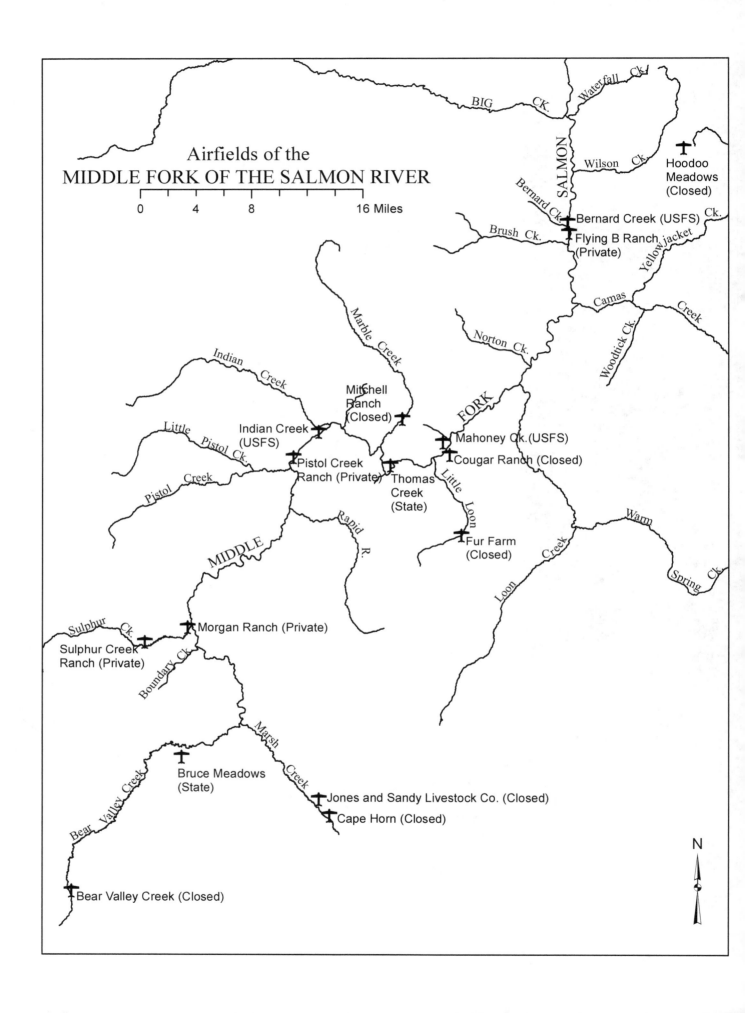

Airfields of the
MIDDLE FORK OF THE SALMON RIVER

0   4   8   16 Miles

BIG   CK.   Waterfall   Ck.

Wilson   Ck.

Hoodoo
Meadows
(Closed)

SALMON

Bernard Ck.

Brush Ck.

Bernard Creek (USFS)   Ck.

Flying B Ranch
(Private)

Yellowjacket

Camas

Norton Ck.

Woodtick Ck.

Creek

Marble   Creek

Indian   Creek

Little   Pistol Ck.

Pistol   Creek

Pistol

Mitchell
Ranch
(Closed)

FORK

Indian Creek
(USFS)

Mahoney Ck.(USFS)

Cougar Ranch (Closed)

Pistol Creek
Ranch (Private)

Thomas
Creek
(State)

Little Loon

Warm

MIDDLE

Rapid R.

Fur Farm
(Closed)

Loon   Creek

Spring   Ck.

Sulphur   Ck.

Morgan Ranch (Private)

Sulphur Creek
Ranch (Private)

Boundary Ck.

Marsh

Creek

Bruce Meadows
(State)

Jones and Sandy Livestock Co. (Closed)

Cape Horn (Closed)

Bear Valley Creek

Bear Valley Creek (Closed)

N

Looking north at the former site of the Bear Valley Group mining claims.

The abandoned north-south runway in 2009.

BEAR VALLEY CREEK

The sizeable open areas and meadows along this large tributary were popular for sheep grazing beginning at the turn of the twentieth century. In about 1907 a grazing dispute occurred between two large sheep outfits, the Van Deusen and a competitor from Wyoming. The two groups fortified themselves on opposite ends of a big meadow armed with Winchester rifles and were prepared for a shootout. The USFS dispatched a ranger to the area to investigate the problem. The ranger set up his camp in the middle of the meadow and was able to help them reach a solution.[1]

Bear Valley Creek was not only popular for livestock grazing, but also for its rich minerals. Mining in various forms has occurred over the years, including a large dredging operation on the upper end at the confluence of Bear Valley and Casner creeks. In 1910 six parties claimed this land under the names: Big Meadow Group Placer, White Hawk Placers, Bear Valley Group, Monazite Group, Gold Eagle Group Placer, and War Eagle Group Placer. These entities, owned by several individuals who had connections with other backcountry operations, made many improvements to the claims. By the late 1940s a large 40' X 100' framed lodge was constructed along with a shop, apartment complex, pump house, and several other buildings. Enormous dredges operated by Porter Brothers were used to extract euxenite, columbite, and monazite, all used in the production of metals. These operations continued at least into the 1950s.[2]

In 1962 Leo and Madge Cram, James Harris, Jack Howard, Helen Casner, and Edna Harris patented the claims under the name of Bear Valley Group. With this approval they set out to further develop the 910.13 acre claim.[3] One of the improvements was the leveling of the old dredge tailings to create a 1700' runway. The crude north-south airstrip is still visible and parallels the Bear Valley Road. Little is known about its use, but airplanes were landing on the airfield through the early 1980s.

The dredges were eventually dismantled and the claim sat idle. Bill Harris, the son of James Harris, owned an interest in the then Bear Valley Minerals Inc., and headed the selling of the claim to the USFS. Harris, similar to his father, had many ties to the backcountry as a surveyor of remote properties. Harris worked a deal with the agency that was finalized in 1989.[4] Much of the area has since gone through the reclamation process.

BERNARD CREEK

A downstream view of the 1900' Bernard airstrip.

Native Americans used this flat along the Middle Fork for fishing and hunting. When soldiers arrived at the area in 1879 in search of Indians they found a winter camp consisting of six wickiups (pole and brush structures).[5] Some soldiers even camped here under a large protective tree.[6] General Reuben F. Bernard's name was later added to the site, as he commanded one of the military units that passed through the location.

An Airstrip and a Guard Station

Fifty years after the discovery of the Indian encampment by the military the USFS packed in horse-drawn equipment to construct an airfield at the site. By the end of 1932 Wayne O'Conner and Dutch Morrison had finished the airstrip to a total length of 1400'. The same year the USFS withdrew 91.76 acres for administrative purposes. The Laing family had previously occupied the acreage as early as 1900. The next inhabitant of the property was A. D. Clark who in 1916 built a log cabin at the site. In 1933 the USFS used the remains of the cabin foundation to construct a guard station. In 1960 the USFS had thought about developing the location into a large administrative complex, but the plans did not materialize. However, the next year the agency did build a new dwelling at the site and converted the old station into a storage facility.[7]

Early Pilots

In the early years of the airstrip's use it was expanded to a total length of 1900' and further smoothed. Other than being in the steep canyon, USFS officials considered the runway to be one of the best in the area during the 1930s. Little has been done to the airstrip since its construction other than routine grading.

Many early pilots used this field including Bob Johnson, A. A. Bennett, and Bill Hamner. Hamner made many early flights to Bernard, flying in supplies such as groceries and dynamite for trail crews along the river.[8] He and his father built the first airport in their hometown of Salmon. The field proved inadequate for needed expansion, so Hamner's father, a local Salmon doctor, sold land to the city where the current airport is located today.[9] Hamner later became the postmaster in Salmon, but maintained an interest in aviation by leasing an airplane and ground to Eldredge Flying Service.[10]

An Intermountain Twin Otter parked at Bernard circa 1970 with a Cessna 206 on short final.

Denis Morgan and wife Dorothy with their Maule.

Owner Grant Eldredge returned from World War II, where he flew the Hump with C-54s and C-109s. He operated the postwar business through the mid-1950s, flying much of the Middle Fork country, mainly using Stinsons.[11]

Aircraft Troubles with Bridge Equipment

In the summer of 1956, Aircraft Service Company owned by the Bradley Mining Company and located at their field in Boise, bid a contract with the USFS to haul bridge parts for the current Bernard Creek Bridge. Flying the majority of the parts was pilot Harold Dougal in Travel Air 6000 NC8865. The parts were flown primarily from Challis to Bernard, as well as a few trips from Salmon. Dougal made over thirty-seven round trips to finish the contract.[12]

One of the flights from Challis proved memorable for Dougal. Several minutes after takeoff the old Travel Air was climbing well, even with a thousand pounds of timber for the bridge. All of a sudden he heard and felt a massive burst of air come through the cockpit. It did not take long for him to figure out what had happened as he was bathed in sunlight. Looking straight up he could see the blue morning sky. This all happened within a matter of seconds. He then noticed the plane handling oddly. Dougal tried kicking the rudder, but obtained no reaction. He was able to make a shallow turn with just the ailerons and nursed the plane back to the Challis airport. After getting out of the airplane he quickly recognized what had happened. The fabric from the top of the fuselage had ripped from the windshield and tore its way down the length of the airplane. It then started flapping in the wind and wrapped itself around the vertical stabilizer and rudder.[13]

Creative Runway Work

In the early 1980s the Salmon NF decided the Bernard airfield was in need of maintenance. Wanting to keep the work within wilderness parameters they looked for a contractor who could drag the field with horse-drawn equipment. The cheapest bid came from Denis Morgan of Salmon, who operated a charter business called Alpine Air. The USFS and other people who bid on the project could not figure out how he was going to complete the job and make any money. In an effort to keep annual budgets to a minimum, the USFS awarded the bid to Morgan.[14]

When the USFS showed up to see how Morgan was doing at Bernard, they found him taxiing back and forth along the runway with his yellow de Havilland Beaver, dragging a homebuilt apparatus for leveling the field. Expecting to find horses performing the labor the USFS was shocked but could not renege on the contract, as he was technically within the guidelines of wilderness operations. Morgan completed the required work and in a short time, loaded up his equipment, and was back flying.[15]

A few years after Morgan's innovative wilderness airfield maintenance contract he bought a new yellow Maule (N121A). In June 1985 while flying the plane close to Gibbonsville, Idaho, four miles up Pierce Creek he was caught in a severe downdraft crossing a ridge at a low altitude. The plane was forced into the hillside, killing Morgan and two passengers.[16]

27

BRUCE MEADOWS

Early Occupants

The current 5000' Bruce Meadows runway.

At the turn of the twentieth century this area, similar to others in the upper Middle Fork watershed, was known for its abundant open ground and plentiful grasses that make it ideal for grazing. One of the earliest known stockmen to utilize the lush meadow was John C. Bruce.[17] The expansive high-altitude open terrain and meandering waterways also made for excellent salmon spawning grounds, which attracted many Native Americans during the summer. Later it also attracted early Euro-Americans to the area, not only for the fisheries but also for trapping.

In the 1930s the USFS constructed a north-south runway measuring 1952' long that was used into the 1950s. This runway was later abandoned and the present airstrip was constructed nearly perpendicular through the center of the original. Maintenance at the newer 5000' airstrip, also built by the USFS, was transferred under a special use permit in the mid-1970s to the Idaho State Department of Aeronautics. The state continues to maintain the airstrip.[18] For many years this airfield was used as an auxiliary air tanker refueling location. More recently the airstrip's primary use comes from commercial operators shuttling river rafters to Indian Creek when the water levels become too low to launch below Dagger Falls.

Airplane Adventures

On November 23, 1948 Ronald Campbell departed the McCall Ranch at Thomas Creek along the Middle Fork in a blue Taylorcraft en route to Boise. He battled his way through several snow squalls and soon became surrounded by poor visibility. Not able to go any farther or turn back, he made a forced landing at Bruce Meadows, and badly damaged his airplane because of the deep snow. However, he was able to find shelter in a nearby log cabin. Three days later Bill Woods flew from Boise in search of the plane, which he located. Due to the deep snow conditions he could not land his wheeled airplane and instead contacted his friend Bob Fogg at Johnson Flying Service in McCall.[19]

Fogg then loaded some rations in a ski-equipped Piper Cub to rescue Campbell. Fogg thought he had the rescue made, but then broke an axel on takeoff and was also stranded at Bruce Meadows. The two had to wait until another plane came looking for them. The following day Woods and Chet Moulton flew over again and spotted the two marooned planes. Fogg stomped out a message in the snow. In response Moulton tied a note to a heavy object and threw it down to the men on the ground, saying something to the effect that they would be back.[20]

The next day Del Crone, a volunteer with the state, flew from Boise with a small ski-equipped aircraft. After landing, his plane became mired in the deep snow as well and broke a ski. By November 28 they had stomped out a message indicating what equipment was needed for repairs. Les Randolph, the

28

Bob Fogg's message requesting parts.

One of the marooned airplanes at Bruce Meadows in November 1948.

manager of Bradley Field in Boise, flew in a pair of skis with his company's ski-equipped Travel Air 6000 (NC8865). Crone's plane was repaired and he safely flew out with Campbell, returning to Boise. Bob Johnson, Fogg's boss, also flew in with a Travel Air 6000 on skis and retrieved Fogg. The two downed airplanes were later flown out.[21]

Welcoming Fogg back to McCall were the owners of the recently opened Shore Lodge. The hotel bought the Fogg family and Johnson a free meal and ran a publicity story in the local paper.[22]

A similar event occurred in the early 1980s when Pat Dorris and Steve Passmore were out flying on a nice sunny winter day. Passmore, flying a ski-equipped Stinson 108-2 (N876D) with his wife, decided to land at Bruce Meadows. Dorris in a Cessna 170 wearing skis as well, watched Passmore break through the snow on landing. Knowing he was badly stuck, Dorris circled and flew back to McCall for help.

Pat consulted with his brother Mike and they determined that only one should return in order to keep the weight to a minimum. Mike was looking for an adventure and elected to go, throwing in a sleeping bag and a pair of snowshoes. As suspected, he too sunk on landing. All three began stomping the snow out ahead of the airplanes, but the aircraft would only go a few feet, before a ski would bury. Abandoning the idea of getting out that day, they spent the remainder of the afternoon packing the runway hoping it would freeze hard over night for an easy departure the next morning.

The three located the same old cabin used by Fogg thirty-some years earlier and settled in for the night. The cabin was sparsely furnished, having only a small sheepherder stove, a pile of dry wood, and a few apple crates. The next morning they tried again with no luck. However, Pat and Bill Dorris flew over in a Cessna 206 to assess the situation. On the final pass with Pat hanging out the back door he attempted to kick out a survival pack with food, but it caught on a seat rail. By the time he untangled the mess from the plane it dropped a fair distance from the runway. The group on the ground had no complaints and were just happy to have some nourishment.

Throughout the flyover Mike talked with his father on the radio and it was determined that the only chance of getting out was to have friends from Stanley come over with snowmobiles to pack down the runway. This idea worked and by the end of the following day they were able to get back to McCall by nightfall.

After the whole event was over Bill noted that the snow conditions in that area were often a bit odd. He had almost spent the night there a few times himself while flying roof-shoveling crews to the nearby Elk Creek Ranger Station west of Bear Valley. Ski landings were occasionally made near the ranger station in the right conditions, but no field was ever developed.

1 *Steve Passmore's Stinson stuck at Bruce Meadows.*
2 *Passmore attempting to pack-down the runway.*
3 *Aircraft on packed pathways – waiting for an overnight freeze to harden the surface for a takeoff back to civilization.*
4 *The Bruce Meadows sheepherder cabin.*
5 *Looking down Bear Valley Creek at one of the stranded airplanes.*

B. Scherer

A late 1960s photograph of the entrance to the Cape Horn airstrip.

CAPE HORN

In 1929 the USFS built the Cape Horn cross-runways for fire suppression activities and quicker access to the nearby guard station.[23] The administrative site was developed in 1910 and expanded in 1933 by the Civilian Conservation Corps (CCC).[24] The landing facility was also improved about the same time and the north-south runway measured 1834'. Bisecting this runway was the longer northwest-southeast strip measuring 3232'.[25] Sometime later the USFS added a longer 4000' east-west runway intersecting both the original airstrips.[26]

Eventually the road from the Cape Horn Guard Station to Stanley was realigned and cut through the upper end of the north-south strip and bisected the center of the large 4000' runway. When this was first done road graders would carefully avoid putting ridges across the runway surfaces. Generally the runways were graded at the same time. However, this courtesy did not last long and in 1972 the facility was closed. Within a few years several individuals objected, requesting that it be reopened. One of the more adamant protesters was the Jones and Sandy Livestock Company. The company happened to own a small ranch between the airport and the guard station and used the strip in association with their summer sheep grazing operation. The reopening request was denied.[27] The company eventually built a small airstrip perpendicular to the road on their ranch.

The guests of the Cape Horn Lodge located four miles to the north also frequently used the airstrips. In 1921 William T. Burns homesteaded the 57.15 acre lodge property. Moving onto the land at the turn of the twentieth century he built numerous buildings at the ranch, including several log cabins, two barns, and a main house.[28] His work became the foundation

for the development of a dude ranch by Harry and Janette LeMoyne. The LeMoynes operated the guest ranch for several years, but could not make ends meet during the Depression. Dr. Earl Fox of Hailey, a frequent guest, did not want to lose access to the ranch and purchased it from the LeMoynes, who were his relatives.[29]

Dr. Fox further improved the place by constructing a large main lodge, a swimming pool piped with natural hot water, and several more guest cabins. At the height of his ownership he had several employees, forty head of horses, two wranglers, and a year-round caretaker. It was a busy place in the summer and guests were regularly taken to Stanley on Saturday nights for dancing and gambling.[30]

Although Dr. Fox and his family thoroughly enjoyed spending time at the lodge during the summers, the venture had run its course and they sold the property. The Boy Scouts of America ultimately acquired the ranch in 1956 and named it the Cape Horn Scout Reservation. Honoring a major donor the name was later changed to Camp Bradley at the Cape Horn Scout Reservation.

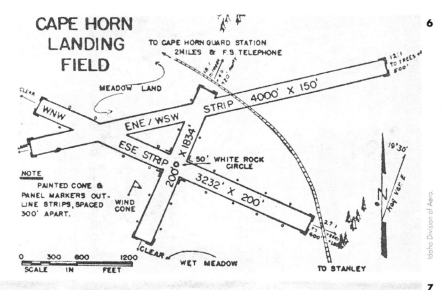

CAPE HORN LANDING FIELD

6 A 1968 diagram of the Cape Horn airfields.

7 An expansive view of the Stanley Basin looking south. The Cape Horn airfield (center) is between the two trees on the north side of the old Stanley Road (currently USFS 203). The outline of Marsh Creek flowing to the Middle Fork can be seen on the right.

8 An aerial view of the Boy Scout Camp facility in the foreground with the Cape Horn Lakes to the north.

The Cougar Ranch airstrip ran parallel to the Middle Fork, downstream from the IDFG patrol cabin. The runway end markers of the Mahoney airstrip can be seen on the opposite side of the river.

| COUGAR RANCH

In 1908 John Helmke settled on the Cougar Ranch property. During the early years the location was called the Dutch John Place. Helmke made a modest living here growing hay and selling produce from his garden. He died at the property and his grave remains here with two others.[31]

In 1924 Charles and Wilma Warnock bought the acreage. The two moved to the ranch the following year with their daughter Amey. Warnock was a well-known Snake River area stockman and recognized by many for his skills as a packer. In fact Warnock was hired by Elmer Keith to help pack famous writer Zane Grey and his entourage from Meyers Cove to the Mormon Ranch (see Ramshorn Ranch for more information).[32]

In 1948 the Warnocks sold the 67 acre ranch to the IDFG. To help cover costs the department leased the acreage to various outfitters and guides.[33] For several years in the early 1960s the partners at the Middle Fork Lodge leased the Cougar Ranch along with the Mitchell Ranch for pasture ground. The additional properties were needed, as the USFS would no longer allow them to graze on federal land.[34]

To maintain the property and the stock animals at the Cougar Ranch, Norman and Bill Guth, whose parents were partners in the lodge, cleared a little landing area for their Super Cub (N1652P) in the hayfield. The two would fly down from the lodge and change the water about every other week from spring through fall.[35]

The improvised airstrip continued to be used by Joe Peck who acquired the lease after the Guths. Peck leased the property for a few years and used pilot Jim Searles of Challis for his flying needs. Searles landed many times at the Cougar Ranch, bringing in hunting supplies with his de Havilland Beavers. The field was used a couple more times with the next leaseholders after Peck and then abandoned.[36] The ranch is no longer leased, but the IDFG continues to use the little cabin for patrol work.

For a few years Air Unlimited of Challis operated their orange and brown de Havilland Beavers at Cougar Ranch delivering supplies for outfitter Joe Peck.

Flying B Ranch

The Early Years and the Crandalls

Looking up the Middle Fork at the Flying B airstrip.

Shoshone Indians used the site of the Flying B Ranch frequently and when Captain Bernard's troops came through the Middle Fork area in 1879 there were six large lodges at the location. After the military campaign a few miners came and went from the open acreage. Around 1912 Albert Kurry arrived and was the first to stay any length of time. In 1920 Kurry patented 160 acres here and was later joined by his brother who in 1926 homesteaded another 160 acres. The two created a large orchard of nectarines, peaches, plums, and apples. In addition to the orchard they ran cattle for a short time.[37] By the 1930s the ranch sold to George Crandall and his wife and became known as the Crandall Ranch.

The Crandalls made many improvements to the property including the construction of a rough runway in the lower hayfield. The strip was built using horse-drawn equipment.[38] The crude field not only allowed for quicker access to the outside, but it also facilitated the construction of the Bernard Creek Bridge, which was flown in piece by piece by Zimmerly Brothers Air Transport Service of Lewiston. Bert Zimmerly Sr. did most of the flying for the job during the winter, using a Travel Air 6000 (NC9844) from the original Salmon City airport. Zimmerly bundled up to counter well-below freezing temperatures, wearing long johns and heavy winter clothing. He stripped the airplane of all unnecessary parts, even the landing light, to compensate for the heavy weight of the bridge cables.[39]

By the early 1940s the Crandalls sold their ranch to backcountry pilot Almer Acie "Ben" Bennett. Bennett named the property the Flying B Ranch and had the vision of turning the place into a hunting and fishing resort much like it is today. The dream did not materialize for Bennett, but he did spend a fair amount of time at the ranch and made several improvements. In June 1944 he flew a portable sawmill and bull-rake to the ranch from Salmon. At the same time he made plans to fly a dismantled bulldozer to the property to improve the runway and lengthen it to 2300'.[40]

Bert Zimmerly Sr.'s Travel Air 6000 parked at the old Salmon airport with a spool of bridge cable bound for the Crandall Ranch.

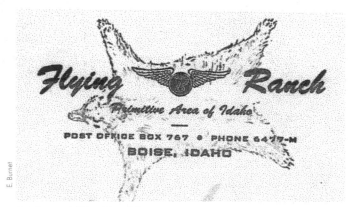

A group of people at the Crandall Ranch associated with building the Bernard Creek Bridge in February 1939.

A. A. Bennett's Flying B Ranch logo.

Bennett's main 1930s operation in Boise with a Travel Air 6000 and a Zenith Z6B.

Bennett at the controls of a Zenith (NC392V) in 1937 hauling freight and passengers from McCall.

A. A. "Ben" Bennett of the Flying B Ranch

Bennett was originally from a small town near San Diego, California, and learned to fly in the early 1920s.[41] With dreams of becoming a professional pilot he moved to Fairbanks, Alaska, where he formed a partnership with Jimmy Rodebaugh under the name of Bennett-Rodebaugh Company. Bennett flew in Alaska until 1931 when he and Rodebaugh sold their business to Wien Alaska Airways owned by well-known Alaska pilot Noel Wien. He had worked for them for a few years prior to starting his own operation.[42] Before leaving Alaska, Bennett consulted with the Zenith Company of Midway, California, about building the ultimate mountain airplane. Although the company specialized in producing farm implements they wanted to break into the flourishing aviation business. Based on many of his suggestions, seven Zenith Z6B cabin bi-wing planes were built prior to the economic downturn of the Depression. The Bennett-Rodebaugh Company flew one of the first Zeniths in Alaska.

In 1931 Bennett moved to Montana, scrounging up flying work with Bob Johnson in Missoula. Bennett flew for Johnson Flying Service into the fall and then moved to Boise, flying mail contracts. Their business relationship curdled over financial matters and the two became competitors.[43] By this time Bennett had started Bennett Air Transport Company by purchasing, not surprisingly, two Zeniths, NC134W and NC392V. Over the years he added more airplanes and hired pilots such as Bob King, Chick Walker, and Tom Staker. Also while living in Boise he married Hattie Burnet, whom he had rescued in Atlanta, Idaho, after she suffered injuries from a gas lantern explosion. Hattie and Ben had one daughter, Marion, and the family moved to Boise. Hattie became the shrewd business end of the company and also obtained her pilot's license. Bennett's son Earl, from one of his two previous marriages, joined the family company as a pilot. Bennett had taught him to fly at the age of eleven in Alaska. Earl went on to fly in the Ferry Command during World War II and then for the airlines. He unfortunately got on the wrong side of the law and in 1953 died in a Texas prison.[44]

Bennett flew the backcountry for many years from Boise. About the same time he bought the Flying B Ranch he capitalized on the war-effort boost to the aviation industry by starting two Civilian Pilot Training Programs (CPTP) in Idaho Falls and Pocatello. During this time he also had two short stints as the Idaho Director of Aeronautics. Not long after the war he sold Bennett Air Transport and went back to chasing flying jobs around the western United States and Alaska. He also consulted with CallAir based in Afton, Wyoming, on their new line of postwar aircraft. His daughter and wife continued to spend time at the ranch entertaining guests.[45]

By the 1950s Bennett and his family moved to California, where he eventually added a helicopter rating to his license, before his death in 1970. He and his wife are both buried in Las Vegas, Nevada.[46]

Bennett Teaches Ranch Hands – Carol Jarvis

In the summer of 1945 Bennett hired the two Jarvis brothers from Challis to help at the ranch. The boys' parents thought the opportunity was great as it would be difficult for them to get into any trouble at the remote location. Over the course of the summer Beryl, age thirteen, and Carol, age twelve, both took up initial pilot training from Bennett. With Bennett's World War II background in running CPTPs he was able to instruct with a light touch.[47]

Most of the early instruction took place at or around the Challis airport, but Carol remembered that some instruction was done from the Flying B Ranch. They both eventually earned their private licenses. After Carol graduated from high school he worked as an assayer for the Cobalt Mine. While at Cobalt he once gave rides to friends in a Piper Cub over the Fourth of July holiday from a small makeshift landing area. Eventually he earned

Bennett and wife Hattie (Burnet) in the late 1930s.

Carol Jarvis flying a Salmon Air Taxi Cessna 206 in 1977.

several commercial ratings and became an instructor in 1965 at Bradley Field in Boise. While working in Boise he met his wife, Leila, who was also employed at the airfield. The two left Boise in 1968, having purchased Salmon Air Taxi. Living in Salmon they built the business up and ultimately sold it in the spring of 1980 to Richard Disney.[48]

Before retiring, Jarvis and his operation were featured in the article, "Flying Idaho's Back Country," published in the November 1977 issue of *Private Pilot*. Flying the author, Michael Parfit, on an aerial tour of the Middle Fork for the article, Jarvis was sure to point out where his aviation career started at the Flying B Ranch. Prior to selling his business, Jarvis hired Dick Williams who eventually became the chief pilot of the company. Shortly after selling, Javis died. After the funeral services Leila and her daughter asked Williams to take Carol for one last flight. The three took off from Salmon one autumn morning in a Salmon Air Taxi Cessna 182 (N475L) and scattered his ashes across the Salmon River Mountains near Cobalt. It was an honor for Williams as he respected Jarvis as a great mentor.[49]

A Business Women and DC-3 Landings

In the early 1950s Ruth Vernon of Boise bought the Flying B Ranch. At the time of her purchase the place was fairly run down. Like Bennett she wanted to turn the place into a first-class backcountry hunting and fishing resort. Going to work quickly, her main focus was to expand the runway so that it could handle bigger aircraft to bring in materials and supplies to improve the place. To make this all possible she leased and bought several airplanes and hired Bill Woods of Boise as her pilot. Over time she leased a 10D Travel Air (N518N), a Travel Air 6000 (NC9084), and purchased a de Havilland Beaver.

Among pilots who worked for the ranch during these years she was known as a very demanding woman. On one occasion she put in a call to Boise for an order of ten pounds of sugar. They told her it would be on the next cargo flight in. Vernon in anger responded that she needed it now and wanted it flown in immediately. The only one of her planes available

Ruth Vernon's Flying B emblem.

for the trip was Travel Air NC9084. After making one very expensive delivery of sugar, the pilots nicknamed the plane "Sugar." Playing off of the name, the other Travel Air became known as "Spice."[50]

These airplanes could haul a respectable amount of freight, but by 1955 the items she needed required a bigger aircraft. The oversized items included a generator, bulldozer, and several other pieces of equipment. The only business flying in the backcountry that was able to handle the order was Johnson Flying Service.

Johnson accepted the challenge, knowing the load would fit in a DC-3. The pilots assigned to the job were Ed Thorsrude and Dick Karr, flying DC-3 N49466. Thorsrude flew C-46s and C-47s from England to France during World War II. His main assignment in the military was transporting fuel in C-47s for General George Patton's tanks, which often required landing on undeveloped strips in the French countryside. As a result he had perfected a unique skill that not many pilots had at the time, of being able to fly a DC-3 low and slow. Later several Johnson pilots adopted his technique.[51]

A few days after the call, Thorsrude flew a company Cessna 180 to the Flying B Ranch and accessed the situation. Determining it was possible to land the DC-3 he and Karr flew the DC-3 to Boise from Missoula and loaded the generator.[52] They spent the night and flew the heavy load to the Flying B the next morning. Karr, riding in the right seat, caught the event on a handheld 8 mm Kodiak movie camera. The footage still in existence today shows Thorsrude weaving the wide DC-3 through the walls of the Middle Fork canyon and landing at the ranch. While crews

The Flying B Ranch in 1964.

B. Scherer

unloaded the generator the two spent some time fishing and then headed back to Boise for another load.[53]

Karr also filmed the second trip the following day. This flight brought in a wide assortment of building material for the new lodge. Meeting them with another load from Missoula was Johnson pilot Ken Roth, flying a Ford Tri-Motor. While the planes were being unloaded they again took part in some fishing before taking to the sky. With the camera rolling once more Karr filmed Roth departing the strip. It did not take long for the big DC-3 to pass Roth in the old Ford en route to Missoula. Thorsrude wanted to let his wife know he was back in town and made a low pass over the house, nearly tearing the roof off. Coincidently a Civil Aeronautics Authority (CAA – now known as the FAA) inspector was giving a flight check nearby and saw the whole event. The inspector came by the Johnson hangar asking questions. They swore up and down they were at a legal altitude. Nothing ever came of it except a few laughs.[54]

Johnson Flying Service's successful trip led them to land at the Flying B Ranch several more times. Other pilots such as Roth took the controls of the DC-3 on these trips. Cargo freighted-in on these flights included parts for the Big Creek Bridge. Interestingly, Ralph Smothers was contracted by the USFS to transport the items down to the bridge site from the ranch with his jet boat, powered with outboard motors. Smothers drove the boat in from the Main Salmon River. Once everything was transferred, USFS crews then assembled the bridge.

With the materials that were brought in Vernon had crews build a new lodge and several other cabins. The original structures left from the Crandall era were also remodeled. With everything in place by 1956 and guests regularly visiting via her fleet of airplanes, Vernon set her sights on improving the Root Ranch property, which she had acquired a few years earlier from Howard Elkins (for more information see Root Ranch).

The Flying Resort Ranches

After finishing the projects at the Root Ranch, financial woes plagued the operations and Vernon ultimately lost both to the Idaho First National Bank. Seeing an opportunity, Andy Anderson came up with the idea to start a membership organization that would own and operate the ranch. Anderson first started spending time on the Middle Fork in 1938, leasing property on Lower Loon Creek. After World War II he began experimenting with the use of military surplus rubber rafts to float fishing parties down the river. With mildly successful runs he started one of the first commercial boat operations on the river.

Even though Anderson was a very innovative person he was pushed out of his membership idea, but it was used by a group of southern Idaho businessmen made up of doctors, lawyers, farmers, and contractors under the name of Flying Resort Ranches. Not all of them were pilots or aircraft owners, but all enjoyed the Idaho backcountry. Over time this group grew and was also able to buy the Root Ranch circa 1964 from the bank.

By the early 1960s the ranch was never completely solvent, but survived. Peewee Holmes, a contractor from Burley, Idaho, assumed the role of secretary. He often flew in with his Cessna 180 to lend a helping hand along with the others. As time wore on the lodge was updated, and a few other cabins were added.

Bill Sullivan of Stanley managed the ranch during the first part of the decade. He had been outfitting and guiding in the Middle Fork country since the late 1930s and was a good fit for the job. He and his wife lived here nearly year-round with their youngest son Terry and were joined frequently by

A Loening Air Cessna Skymaster at the Flying B in 1964 (l to r): Bill Scherer, Dale Erickson, Mike Loening, and Bill Sullivan.

their other two boys, Phil and Tom. The two older sons, especially Tom, spent summers helping on the ranch.[55]

In the beginning of Sullivan's career he either owned or leased saloons during the winter, and by the time steelhead season started he and his clients were headed to the river. He would often be busy guiding fishing trips and then transition to hunting season, staying in the country until fall snows pushed him out. His hunting guests were generally packed in on twenty-day trips coming in through Seafoam and ultimately setting up base camp at either the Tappan or Mormon Ranch. From here they hunted the Norton Ridge area.

In 1958 Sullivan purchased the Dutch Charlie mining claim located on Little Loon Creek. He used this location mainly as a hunting camp. By the mid-1960s Sullivan gave up his claim after pressure from the USFS.[56]

While Sullivan was managing the Flying B Ranch he packed and guided for members and their guests, which was his true passion. Sullivan was familiar with the ranch since he had visited it at the age of twelve on one of his first hunting trips with his father and brother, Cornelius. He remembered thinking he was a "man" until he was greeted by Mrs. Crandall who apparently had not seen a child in years. It was well known that they lived a solitary life and had not left the ranch in nearly fifteen years. She thought young Sullivan was quite "cute," which really deflated his ego.[57]

Phil Sullivan, like his father, also had memories of the ranch prior to their tenure as managers. He had visited there many times on hunting trips with his father, but most memorable was his first flight to the ranch in 1951 with A. A. Bennett. His parents had arranged for him to miss a few days of school to join them on a hunting trip that began at the Flying B. As they flew over the field Bennett turned to young Phil and asked, "Can you see the windsock? I need to know what the winds are doing down there." Looking out the window from the right seat he started scanning the ground for the sock. Bennett then took another turn over the ranch and told Phil what to look for. A short discussion ensued and it was determined the wind was not a problem. Bennett cranked the airplane around and landed. It was later understood that Bennett in his older years had poor eyesight.[58]

Pilots, Guests,
and a One-Man Shootout

By the early 1960s most of the flying was done by members of the ranch, who were attracted to the idea of flying, family, friends, and goods in on their own. As a result, a wide variety of people from all walks of life came through, also flying a wide range of aircraft. One interesting episode with a member occurred on a hot summer day. A typical afternoon thunderstorm brewed over the backcountry and just as it was getting really nasty a Beech Bonanza came in and landed. Spilling out of the airplane were several young children and their father. This member had previously been to the ranch and really liked Bill Sullivan. Over the course of a few days he followed Sullivan around while he tended to the various chores on the ranch.[59]

Sullivan did not like the attention and became concerned. His uneasiness was justified as gunshots were heard from the man's cabin one evening. It was known at this point that the fellow was going through a divorce, which sparked a midlife crisis. It was also known that he kept guns with him. Concerned, several ranch employees headed for the cabin to investigate all the commotion. The guy then burst out of the cabin. All the kids were accounted for but obviously scared. Sullivan tried to calm the fellow down but he insisted on packing up his kids and flying home. Sullivan followed him down toward the airport, trying to dissuade him from leaving the ranch.[60]

Sullivan was no pilot, but he knew with hundred-degree temperatures and a heavy load that the fellow's Bonanza would not even get off the strip. Meanwhile his son Tom was on the backcountry radio trying to get word out for help. The confrontation became ugly at the corrals and the guy turned around firing two shots with his pistol at Sullivan. Both bullets luckily missed and imbedded in a fence rail. It had become a serious situation and Sullivan let the man head for his plane while he went and grabbed a rifle.[61]

At this point Sullivan wanted to shoot the man, but Tom calmed him down. They then spotted the fellow over at his Bonanza draining gas out of it to reduce the weight giving him a better chance to get airborne. Sure enough he loaded his kids into the plane and somehow forced the aircraft into the air. Sullivan knew that his gas supply would limit his range, and local law authorities were notified. He only had enough gas to reach Challis, where he was arrested.[62]

By the mid-1960s the Sullivan's youngest son was of school age and they decided to leave the Flying B Ranch. Sullivan semi-retired but continued to spend time hunting and fishing, eventually retiring to Clayton, Idaho. Starting in 1969 Tom took up flying the Idaho backcountry seasonally from Challis. He flew for eighteen years before moving to Alaska.[63]

Recent Years

Several managers followed Sullivan, including Bill Kornell, Roger Thompson, Howard Jones, and Bill Guth Jr. Guth and his wife managed the lodge from 1985 through 2005. Guth had sold his interest in the family outfitting business in 1982. Having his commercial pilot's license, he went to work for Richard Disney, who owned Salmon Air Taxi, until the Flying B position opened. Guth did not give up flying as he leased his Cessna 206 (N58441) to the Flying Resort Ranches. It was used for two years hauling freight and passengers until it was replaced with another Cessna 206 (N7233N) which was used for the same type of work. In his twenty years of management he did enough flying between the 206s to go through four motors. In 2005 he retired and in March 2006 sold the airplane.[64]

During his years of managing the ranch several buildings were added: a shop, laundry facility, tack shed, generator building, and cabins. Many other structures were remodeled. Some of these construction projects replaced buildings burned in the wildfires of 1990 and 2000.

HOODOO MEADOWS

Holm

The closed Hoodoo Meadows runway in April 2010.

Plans for the airfield were first drafted in 1936 and two years later the CCC finished the northeast-southwest runway measuring 2200' in length. It was the highest airstrip ever used in the Idaho backcountry at an average runway surface elevation of 8233'. The airstrip saw active use from the 1940s though the late 1960s. The location provided easy access to the Bighorn Crags and the Yellowjacket Mountains. By the early 1970s the runway had received little maintenance and the USFS opted to close the airstrip in 1974.[65]

Many outfitters and backcountry pilots, including Bill Dorris and Eric Ryback, rallied to reopen the runway on many occasions in the 1970s and 1980s. However, they met resistance. The main arguments against reopening the strip were high repair costs and that access was already provided to the area by nearby roads.[66] Despite the closure, pilots with Piper Cubs used the airfield into the early 1980s.[67]

During these years Salmon Air Taxi had inquiries about hauling hunters into the area via airplane. Chief Pilot Dick Williams thought it was possible, but wanted to inspect it before making a commitment. The strip had been technically closed and he did not want to risk a public incident. To insure the usability of the runway he flew Super Cub N8480H from Salmon early one morning and landed. He carried with him a small saw to remove any obstructions. His suspicions were correct as saplings growing along each side of the runway brushed the bottom of his wings. However, the centerline was clear and the surface was decent.[68]

After a successful test run and a little maintenance, he returned a few days later with a load of bighorn sheep hunters and their gear in a company Cessna 185 (N4772Q). Williams made several similar trips for about a two-year period. Even in the cool fall air with a highly capable airplane he made a rule that he would not use the strip any later than nine o'clock in the morning. Not only was he fighting density altitude, but also the air on takeoff and landing was peculiar every time he operated at the field. Perhaps this is one reason Hoodoo Meadows was never overly popular or widely used.[69] Since these landings, trees have grown too large for aircraft use, even with ski-equipped planes and high snow accumulations.

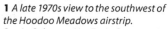

1 A late 1970s view to the southwest of the Hoodoo Meadows airstrip.

2 A Salmon Air Taxi Cessna 185 (N4772Q) at Hoodoo in the early 1980s.

3 As seen in this early 1980s photograph the well-graded surface of the runway remained in good condition after it was closed.

4 The original windsock pole still stands.

5&6 Both of these photos were taken from the upper end of the airstrip looking toward the southwest. The first image was taken in the early 1980s and the second image in August 2011.

Looking upstream at the Indian Creek strip.

INDIAN CREEK

Homestead, USFS, and the Airfield

Circa 1914 Eleck Watson first settled the site around the present Indian Creek airfield. He and his grandchildren built several small buildings and made a living prospecting. The USFS later took over the location and made it an administrative site.[70]

Starting in the early 1920s the USFS leased a corner of George Risley's property (present day Pistol Creek Ranch) about three miles upstream from the current Indian Creek complex. They then bought some acreage from Risley in 1928 and developed it into a small administrative site first known as the Risley Ranger Station and later named the Middle Fork Ranger Station. By the late 1930s the facility had several buildings. When the Indian Creek administrative site became substantially developed in 1936, the need for the Middle Fork Ranger Station diminished. From 1958 through 1968 three structures were relocated from the latter site and rebuilt at Indian Creek.[71]

One of the main reasons for focusing the efforts on the Indian Creek location was the proximity of the airfield there.[72] The airstrip was finished by 1936 and like many other early strips its primary use was for fire suppression and administrative activities. Over time the USFS further improved the airfield and other facilities at the site.[73] By 1950 the field measured 2300' long. In 1954 a Johnson Flying Service DC-3 flew in a six-ton bulldozer broken into several pieces for airfield improvements. The dozer was reassembled and put to work. By the end of 1955 the runway was extended to roughly 4650' and the trees on the approach end

and along each side were cleared for the use of larger airplanes.[74] By the early 1960s the USFS no longer allowed employees to use the bulldozer and did not want to spend the money to fly or walk it out. As a result it was buried to the north of the present administrative buildings.[75]

Fishing Parties, Boating, and Airplanes

In the early 1950s a foreshadowing event occurred when outfitter and guide Andy Anderson started using the airstrip in connection with his river boating business. When the water became too low to float the upper portion of the river's headwaters at Marsh or Bear Valley creeks he launched clients from Indian Creek for weeklong trips. Prior to this he had moved the boats and clients to the river with packstrings down Camas Creek. From there parties departed from the old Tappan Ranch. Anderson mainly used pilot Paul Abbott of Challis to fly the gear and people to the river. He hated to fly and in the beginning he had to have several drinks before he would get into the airplane. His son Ted would then blindfold him and back him into the aircraft so he could not see what kind of crate was going to carry him over the rough mountain terrain. Eventually Anderson became used to it.[76] Don Smith, another early boat operator, started taking his clients to Indian Creek as well, chartering Johnson Flying Service and their Ford Tri-Motors.[77]

Looking downstream at the present runway from the parking area.

In 1958–59 some of the access problems were solved when the IDFG built a road down to the Middle Fork at the bottom of Dagger Falls for the construction of the fish ladder. This road was to be removed once the project was finished, but public pressure kept it open.[78] The road allowed rafters to launch a little later in the season, however the river below the road can become un-navigable, depending on the snowpack. Consequently, launching from Indian Creek became a mainstay in the business. With the development and popularity of rafting the river, Indian Creek can be one of the busiest airstrips in the backcountry after the upper Middle Fork becomes too shallow to run. Most of the summer traffic here is from commercial operators shuttling boats, gear, and people for various rafting companies.

In the early 1970s Intermountain Aviation used the airstrip with their de Havilland Caribou.

Scheduled Air Service

The rise in rafting popularity throughout the 1970s caused several in the aviation business to re-think flight operations. One group wanting to capitalize on the rafter clientele was Key Transportation, Inc. who owned Sun Valley Key Airlines. In the 1970s the airline was already running scheduled flights from Sun Valley to various regional airports. Looking to grab the Middle Fork traffic from local Part 135 Air Taxi operators they applied to the Idaho Public Utilities Commission to run a seasonal scheduled airline connecting Indian Creek into their routes, starting May 1 and ending October 10 each year.[79]

The Commission must have been a little surprised when they received the application – a scheduled airline operating in the Idaho backcountry? Following the correct procedures, the Commission posted the application and waited the twenty-day period for written objections from possible opposing parties. Only one protest was received, which was from Challis NF Supervisor Richard Benjamin. He strongly complained stating, "The Indian Creek landing field is located on National Forest Land . . . This airfield is within the Idaho Primitive Area and has been recommended for inclusion in the wilderness system. I do not believe that daily scheduled air service is compatible with wilderness use. Therefore, I recommend that your office not approve."[80]

Amazingly the Commission did approve.

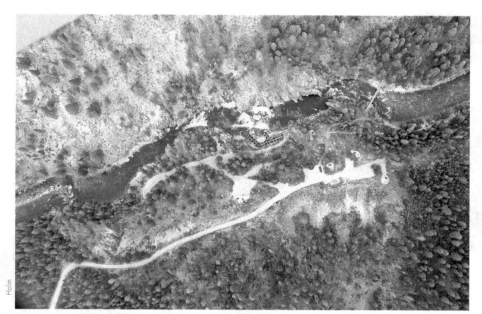

The Dagger Falls fish ladder and access road from the air.

An advertisement for Sun Valley Key Airlines.

The airline was then required to obtain a special use permit from the USFS, which was also issued. In 1975 the airline tried to make a go of the Indian Creek venture, operating two Twin Otters and offering flights practically at cost to attract customers. They had two routes, one between Boise and Salmon, Stanley, Indian Creek, and McCall and the second between Hailey and Salmon, Stanley, Indian Creek, and McCall.[81]

However, the whole arrangement was doomed for many reasons. The airline had a difficult time acquiring customers even at dirt-cheap rates, as outfitters and guides were loyal to their 135 Air Taxi operators. Another issue arising was the "scheduled" part. It simply took too long at Stanley to load all

the gear, food, and people into the Twin Otter and fly twenty minutes to Indian Creek. Once at Indian Creek the reverse process also took a large chunk of time. This alone was not time-efficient for an airline, nor could they judge exactly how long it was going to take them to complete this process on both ends of the trip, so the "scheduled" part was a joke. The airline then often had to fly a repositioning flight (empty) to the next destination. The outfitters then encountered further issues after the plane left Indian Creek, as they were stuck trying to ready the boats and gear, which takes several hours, and had to entertain the clients instead of having them all ready to go at their arrival. As predicted by many, Sun Valley Key Airlines scheduled flights to Indian Creek were short-lived.

A Salmon Air Taxi/McCall Aviation Islander unloading rafting supplies at the boat ramp.

Boise Air Service - A New Airplane for the Backcountry

Boise Air Service also saw an opportunity to attract more clientele with the rafting business tied to Indian Creek. Pilot Harold Dougal figured a bigger plane was the answer to the operation. Cessna 206s and 207s were great airplanes and worked, but he thought more space and a higher useful load was the answer. After much research he determined the Britten-Norman Islander would be an excellent

CRASH SITE
BEHIND RIDGE

FIRE ➡

FIRE

⊕ ← CRASH SITE

Rafters at the Indian Creek boat ramp.

Both photographs show the location of where Skip Knapp crashed the Johnson Flying Service C-45 Twin Beechcraft.

fit. He pitched the idea to his boss and located one (N688JA). The plane was rough looking, but they hung two new engines and it became a mainstay in their Indian Creek rafting charters.[82] This may have been the first Islander used in the Idaho backcountry. A few other operators followed suit and it has become a fixture in the business for the last thirty years.

Several years after Boise Air Service's introduction of the Islander they closed their doors, due partially to a fatal crash en route from Boise to Indian Creek with a group of rafters in 1979. The pilot Max Sandborn of Boise was flying a company Cessna 210 (N6286B) and had some issues with extending the landing gear. Wanting to ensure that it had dropped completely, he overflew the field where someone on the ground with a radio could verify the gear's status. Sandborn then headed back upriver to turn around near Pistol Creek. It was extremely smoky because of the Mortar Creek Fire and with the low visibility he accidently turned up Garden Creek. Unable to outmaneuver the terrain the plane crashed.

The accident killed all five passengers and started a small forest fire. Smokejumpers were dispatched to the blaze and found Sandborn still alive. He was transported to the University of Utah Medical Center, but only lived for a short time.[83]

A Twin Beech Crash

North of the runway above the guard station is the grave of Byron "Skip" Knapp. Knapp's family requested he be buried at Indian Creek after he was killed in an airplane wreck downstream on July 9, 1965. Knapp who was a first-season pilot with Johnson Flying Service based in McCall, was flying a C-45H Twin Beechcraft (N9327E) when he was killed. The plane was loaded with four McCall smokejumpers and spotter Kenneth "Moose" Salyer.

The Twin Beech's two engines were the only recognizable pieces of the aircraft at the crash site.

Knapp was flying the jumpers to a fire north of the Middle Fork near Norton Creek. The four jumpers included Jim Tracy, Ron Maki, Gary Watts, and Mike Kohlhoff.[84]

Once over the fire the four jumpers bailed out of the Beech and made it to the ground safely. A cargo drop was made, which included two of the four fire packs needed to fight the fire. Smokejumper Maki reported seeing the plane right after the drop and he went to retrieve the two packs that had landed in the fire. He then yelled to Tracy to put out more streamers to indicate the need for more cargo and four more jumpers. However, the plane had already crashed at this point and never saw the ground communications.[85]

The jumpers spotted the new smoke on the next ridge and thought the fire had spotted or a sleeper had flared up. The crew of four began digging fireline and then noticed two TBMs dropping retardant on the new smoke. Later the two planes returned and dropped retardant on the fire they were working on. Wanting more help they put out a ground signal requesting

a radio. Soon thereafter the Idaho City-based Twin Beech spotted the signal and responded. When the radio came alive they heard the voice of Idaho City Smokejumper Foreman Smokey Stover, who told the group what had happened.[86]

After the information was relayed, four Idaho City jumpers were put on the cleanup of the wreck, while the McCall crew was instructed by Wayne Webb to stay put and work the fire. The following evening they were all carried out by helicopter.[87]

The result was the loss of both Knapp and Salyer. It was determined that Knapp lacked mountain flying time. In a letter to the USFS, Bob Fogg, the manager of Johnson Flying Service's McCall operation, explained what he believed caused the accident. Fogg thought that Knapp had the aircraft in a down canyon turn with downdraft air, low, slow, and with a tailwind. Even though the aircraft was probably well above stalling speeds this situation created no room for recovery in rough air with heavy downdrafts.[88]

Jones and Sandy Livestock Company/Silva

The east-west Jones and Sandy Livestock Company airstrip. Notice the current road bisecting the runway.

In the early 1980s the Jones and Sandy Livestock Company built the small northwest-southeast airstrip because of the Cape Horn airstrip closure in 1974. During the lag time several landings were made at the property in the pasture, but it was rough. The strip was originally only about 800' long, but was later extended over the bisecting road by several hundred feet. The company used the property and runway throughout the summer grazing season as a satellite to their ranches in southern Idaho.

Similar to the Jones and Sandy runway is the Silva airstrip located a few miles to the southeast on Valley Creek. This strip was used in connection with the Silva brothers' grazing activities. Floyd and Corwin Silvas's father, Arthur, purchased the property where they built the 2500' northwest-southeast airstrip in the 1930s. The Silvas constructed the airstrip mainly for access during the summer, when they were utilizing their ranch and nearby grazing permits. The crude runway was merely leveled pasture ground. The brothers also built a small strip along the lower end of the Yankee Fork to access another grazing allotment. This strip was nothing more than leveled mine tailings from the Yankee Fork dredge.[89] Their main sheep operation near Shoshone, Idaho, was known as the Bar S Ranch. At Corwin's Shoshone property he built a small airstrip and hangar to store his Aeronca Champ (NC81443). Floyd also flew the Champ, but had his own Stinson 108.[90]

In the fall of 1945 Corwin acquired the Champ in an unusual way. With the end of World War II, both brothers wanted to purchase airplanes and Corwin placed an order with Piper for a new J-3 Cub. However,

Looking north at the runway with Knapp Creek winding through the meadow in the background.

The Silva airstrip was situated at the divide between the headwaters of the Middle Fork and the Main Salmon. The runway was positioned parallel and east of Valley Creek. Although no longer visible in this southern facing vantage, the former airstrip was sandwiched between the road and the creek.

one day while at the Gooding, Idaho, airport the Champ flew in and a young man was fueling it. Corwin inquired about the plane and asked the fellow if he could sit in it. The young man insisted that he give it a try, explaining that he was merely flying it to a dealer in Oregon. Comfortably lounging in the plane, Corwin looked at the guy and said, "Well looks like you need to buy yourself a train or bus ticket early because I just bought this airplane."[91]

The Silva brothers have both since died and the property sold. The Silvas's favorite little Champ was later acquired by Hailey pilot Dale Mizer. Their old airstrip also received occasional use into the 2000s by local commercial operators. The late Bob Danner, who owned Stanley Air Taxi, sporadically tied an airplane or two down at the location during the summer. This often allowed him to beat the morning fog out of the basin.

MAHONEY CREEK

The Homestead

Little remains of Ray Mahoney's homestead located between the airstrip and the south side of Mahoney Creek. Notice the dying orchard trees in the center of the photograph.

Ray Mahoney first occupied the flat area north of the airstrip after the turn of the twentieth century. Mahoney built a small operation, mainly selling fruit from his orchard to miners at Thunder Mountain. He later relocated several miles upstream from the confluence of the Middle Fork and the Main Salmon Rivers.

Following Mahoney to the property was Kenneth Cameron, who in 1924 homesteaded the 147.2 acre parcel. At this time the place had a well-constructed log house, barn, and other outbuildings.[92] Although maps of the era continued to call it the Mahoney Ranch, others dubbed it the Cameron Ranch. Cameron sold to neighbor Charles Warnock, and moved to a parcel of land at the mouth of Loon Creek.[93] Warnock used the property in connection with his Cougar Ranch in-holding. Both of these parcels were ultimately sold in October 1948 to the IDFG for $6,000 each.[94] Little remains of the old homestead other than a few flat spots where the buildings once stood and a few fruit trees.

was erected on the north side of the airstrip to house the machine. The little outfit was used to maintain the field into the 1960s, but maintaining and servicing the dozer was inconvenient. Circa 1970 Sherrill Benham, owner of Valley Flying Service in Challis, purchased the Cletrac. Using a company Cessna 206 he hauled the device out in several trips with the idea that he would reassemble it and sell it for a profit. Never finding time to work on the project, the broken down machine sat in his Challis hangar for some time before he sold it as parts.[96]

Several outfitters have operated from the Mahoney location over the years. Most of them were connected to the IDFG's Cougar Ranch lease.

The Airfield

Circa 1932 the USFS scraped-in a runway on the high river bench south of Mahoney Creek and the homestead property. By 1933 many successful landings had been made at the strip. The original intent, as with others in the area, was to provide the USFS with speedy access to the remote area for fire suppression.[95]

Initially the runway measured 1700' long. After 1950 the airstrip was expanded to 2050' with a small Cletrac Caterpillar bulldozer that the USFS had broken down and flown to the airstrip in pieces. A shed

Rebuilding the Airstrip

By the mid-1980s the strip was in need of repair. To keep within wilderness parameters, the USFS had a horse-drawn grader rebuilt in Challis. New babbitt bearings and zerc fittings were installed and the old machine was painted primer gray. Bob Plummer flew the grader pieces to the airstrip with a Cessna 206, where it was reassembled.[97]

The USFS originally intended to reconstruct the runway in-house, but problems arose concerning knowledgeable staff and the availability of stock animals. The project was then put out to bid. Pat

1 *1970s Salmon Air Taxi owner Carol Jarvis unloading supplies from a Cessna 206 at the Mahoney airstrip.*
2 *Looking upstream at the Mahoney airfield.*
3 *Looking downstream at the Mahoney runway.*
4 *Pat Armstrong (on grader) and team rebuilding the airstrip*

Armstrong of McCall successfully bid the project and in April 1988 started the work. Joining Armstrong was friend Shannon Platt and the Armstrong family dog, a Queensland heeler. Pratt brought the mule team in from Meyers Cove and Armstrong, flying a Cessna 180 (N2486C), hauled supplies in, including camp equipment, a slip scraper, a Fresno, and water pipe.[98]

The pipe was used to bring water to the site for the workers, horses, and to run a pair of sprinklers. At first a piston-powered pump was used, drawing water from Mahoney Creek, but because of problems with spring runoff plugging the system, more pipe was flown in and a gravity feed system was located farther up the creek.[99]

Armstrong, not wanting to wear his mule team out, custom built a Fresno with airplane wheels on each end, making it much easier to pull. Over the course of several weeks a large hump in the middle of the runway was excavated. The material removed from this area was then used to extend the lower end of the airstrip to a total length of 2150'. Toward the end of the project, Armstrong's family joined him to complete the job. The USFS also came to film parts of the renovation, and produced a short film about repairing wilderness airstrips with the proper techniques.[100]

A Broken Wheel and an Electrocuted Dog

During the first part of the summer only half of the airstrip was usable at times and this caused one of two incidents. One morning Armstrong finished moving and stacking several large boulders near the center of the airstrip when one of Bob Plummer's pilots radioed to them that he was landing. With a handheld radio they told the pilot in the Super Cub to land short to avoid the rocks. However, he landed a little too long and knocked a main wheel off. Armstrong and Platt helped the pilot prop the aircraft up and devise a plan. In the end the wheel was wired on and the pilot flew the Cub back to Challis without any problems.[101]

The second incident took place on an abnormally hot day in April. The heat in the canyon brought to life many rattlesnakes. As luck would have it Armstrong's dog was bitten on the leg. Not having any antivenom Armstrong decided to fly the dog out

to Challis for help. However, the rapid heating over the Salmon River Mountains resulted localized storms. Realizing he could not make it to Challis, he tried for a route to Salmon and when that did not work he flew to Thomas Creek.[102]

At Thomas Creek he made contact with the caretaker of the Middle Fork Lodge and asked him if he had antivenom. Regrettably he did not, but told Armstrong of a recent article he had read about the use of applying electrical shocks around the area of the snakebite. The shocks needed to be administered with a source of electricity that had high voltage but low amperage, such as a basic automobile electrical system. The shocks were supposed to nullify the copper ions of the venom.[103]

Armstrong decided there were no other options left and the caretaker gave him a few feet of insulated wire and he was back in the air headed for Mahoney. Once at Mahoney he relayed the story to Platt. Armstrong then popped the front cowling door open on his plane and pulled a sparkplug wire off a plug end. He then attached a length of wire to a sparkplug lead and then rigged a ground line to the main landing gear. Platt, clear of the propeller, then held the dog down and the two wires to the area of the snakebite. Sitting in the cockpit Armstrong took all precautions such as shutting the fuel off. He only planned on giving the starter a quick burst, with the hope the engine would not start. The motor fired and in the midst of trying to shut it down he looked out the window and saw Platt's eyes pulsing with the beat of the engine's ignition system. The dog was yelping and by the time the propeller blades stopped spinning the dog was long gone.[104]

Over the next two days eight inches of snow fell on the airstrip and the two men thought the dog was dead. Another day passed and the sun began shining, melting the snow. As they geared up for work, the little dog was found huddled under the Fresno. The swelling on the outside of the leg where the electricity was applied had gone down, but on the inside the muscles were badly damaged. The dog did eventually heal, but it took a while for her to warm back up to Armstrong.[105]

Hornback/Vance

The Morgan Ranch lodge in the early 1950s.

MORGAN RANCH

Early Homestead and the Morgans

Starting in 1904 James and Annazie Fuller settled here at the confluence of Sulphur Creek and the Middle Fork.[106] In 1930 the two received their official homestead papers for 160 acres and at that time had a cabin, barn, and an enclosed structure over some nearby hot springs for bathing.[107] In 1947 the Fullers sold to Dr. Ben Morgan of Chicago, Illinois.[108]

Dr. Morgan, a successful surgeon and anesthesiologist, was a pioneer in ether anesthesia. He is credited by some in the medical community for creating the position of an anesthesiologist. His wife Freda, also interested in the field, was an anesthesiologist.[109]

Morgan was originally from The Dalles, Oregon, and grew up with horses and spent time outdoors. Wanting to get back to his roots and the West, during the mid-1940s he booked a pack trip with Marvin Hornback. While on the trip he was shown a piece of backcountry property at the top of Sulphur Creek. Shortly thereafter he bought the place, with Hornback originally as a manager and later a partner. Then Morgan sold Sulphur Creek Ranch completely to Hornback and concentrated his money and effort on improving the lower property.[110]

A New Lodge, Improvements, and an Airstrip

What remained of the original homestead was fairly dilapidated. Morgan decided to build a new lodge similar to what he had built with Hornback at Sulphur Creek Ranch. The structure was constructed on concrete footings with concrete floors, and the exterior was finished with vertical logs. Morgan even took advantage of the nearby natural hot water and piped it through the floors, circulating it to heat the place. He also added a swimming pool.[111]

Making much of the construction possible was a small wagon trail between the property and the Sulphur Creek Ranch. However, having air support was also necessary as materials could then be brought directly to the ranch from the Treasure Valley. Hornback walked a bulldozer down from his ranch and constructed a landing field. This first airstrip included the existing south end, but had a dogleg that continued southwest off the deeded land onto USFS property. The USFS forbade the use of the airstrip and told Morgan he needed to realign it so the whole runway was on private ground. One other problem with the dogleg end was that it was extremely swampy.[112]

About the same time the battle over the runway occurred, the USFS was contracting with heavy equipment operators to terrace an old burned area for replanting on nearby Morehead Mountain. Morgan went to Morehead Mountain and hired equipment operator Hy Dailey to revamp the airstrip at the ranch. Dailey walked a piece of equipment down and realigned the runway, splitting the property in half. Boise area pilot John Peterson was involved with setting up the layout and approach. Once it was completed the equipment was walked out and Peterson was the first to land there with his Piper Super Cruiser.[113]

Hornback/Vance

Dr. Ben Morgan, son Benny, and wife Freda in the late 1940s pose with a Sulphur Creek Ranch airplane.

Learning to Fly, Airplanes, Fall Snowstorms, and Crackups

With an airstrip on their property, the Morgans wanted to learn how to fly. They purchased a 135 horse Piper Tri-Pacer and were given lessons by Peterson. Freda developed her flying skills quickly, while her husband struggled. Interestingly, some of the flight instruction was done from the ranch, while the rest was given at the Strawberry Glenn Airport near Boise. Freda went on to get her license and flew regularly to the ranch until the late 1960s. Ben threw in the towel after he flipped their Tri-Pacer over at the ranch on a landing. The family was watching the landing and ran to the airplane thinking the worst. As they approached the plane Morgan, who was hanging upside down, popped the window open and tossed his hat out letting everyone know he was fine. Retelling the story years later, the anecdote about the hat was Morgan's punch line. The plane was ultimately replaced with an upgraded 150 horsepower Tri-Pacer (N1791P).[114]

Friend and instructor Peterson remained closely connected to the Morgans. He was the ranch caretaker until the early 1990s; Parkinson's Disease claimed his life a few years later. The Morgans commonly spent May through September at the ranch and generally returned once during hunting season.[115]

One year after a late fall hunting trip Peterson and Freda returned to the ranch in November to fly out elk meat and close the cabin for the winter. Part of the winterization process was to remove the hydro dam from Sulphur Creek, preventing ice or flood damage. Peterson flew his Super Cruiser in and Freda flew her Tri-Pacer. They planned on only staying one night, but temperatures plummeted to thirty below freezing. By mid morning they had a mess on their hands. Pipes had frozen and the airplanes were ice cubes. It was quickly realized they were going nowhere.[116]

As the two spent the day working at the ranch the thermometer crept to about thirty degrees and it began snowing. Over the next few days it snowed constantly. On about the fifth day it started to rain, followed by a morning with a weather break. At this time, the two loaded into the Super Cruiser and headed for home. The runway was soft, but Peterson thought a takeoff was possible. The plane became airborne, but as they came over the end of the runway the tail

Dr. Morgan cooking in the backcountry.

Freda with her trick horse Prince in the early 1950s.

wheel snagged a stump, bringing the plane back to the ground. Freda sustained minor injuries to her face.[117] Peterson was able to move the damaged Cruiser to a safe area. The two then readied the Tri-Pacer for an early morning departure, waiting for the runway to freeze. The plan worked and when they flew back to Boise the tower at the airport was elated to hear from them.[118]

Peterson had plans to go back for his airplane, but he waited too long. When he returned to the ranch for the Cruiser, he found it crushed by heavy snow. The plane was a complete loss. To prevent a similar incident from happening, the Morgans built a hangar on the property.[119]

In need of a replacement airplane, Peterson purchased a Piper J-3 Cub, which he jokingly called a "J-3 and a half." The new airplane became a well-used workhorse at the property. Peterson even flew the lodge's eight-foot wide dining table in, strapped to the bottom of the plane. The event, caught in a Morgan family home movie, shows Dr. Morgan giving Peterson the wave to go around again so he can try and get a better shot for the camera.[120]

Only two other accidents have claimed planes at the ranch. The first was a Cessna 120 being operated by two men sightseeing along the upper Middle Fork. Maneuvering in steep turns, the plane ran out of gas on the selected tank. Low in the canyon and unable to react quickly enough to reposition the fuel selector, the pilot crashed the plane into some trees near the river above the Morgan Ranch. The two walked away and were able to salvage a few pieces of the plane for resale, but the wings are still at the ranch.[121]

The second accident occurred when a fellow from Utah ran into some weather and left his Cessna 180 at the Morgans. No one was at the ranch, but he was courteous and let the family know his airplane was there. The pilot returned to retrieve his plane and attempted to takeoff uphill. About halfway down the runway he chopped the power, realizing he was not going to clear the trees at the end. Unable to get the plane stopped in time, he smashed it into some trees. Again the pilot called the family and apologized for the accident. He returned a final time to the Morgan Ranch, this time with a helicopter.[122]

More Recent Events

Following in her mother's footsteps, the Morgan's daughter Mary Dee learned how to fly, along with her husband Allen Dodge. The two even received instruction from Peterson in the family Tri-Pacer. They both flew for many years and became involved with the flying community around their home in Coeur d'Alene. On one occasion they flew local pilot Gladys Buroker to the ranch for a visit. Buroker, a woman pioneer in the field of aviation, was also a member of the Idaho Chapter of the Ninety-Nines (a women's flying organization) as was Freda. Many of her flying experiences were included in her autobiography *Wind in My Face*.[123]

The Dodges flew regularly to the ranch from the 1970s through the early 1980s, mainly using a Piper J-5 (N35412). A routine route from Coeur d'Alene was to fly to Slate Creek along the Main Salmon and camp for the night. Early the following morning they would then fly the remaining leg to the ranch.[124]

Dr. Morgan and Freda enjoyed the ranch throughout their lives. Dr. Morgan died in 1974 and Freda in 2002. Allen and Mary Dee spend as much time as possible at the place during the summer. A great effort has been made to keep the ranch as original as possible, with the exception of the 1961 A-frame and a relatively new barn. Although they are no longer active pilots, they continue to enjoy the flying aspect of getting to the ranch with Arnold Aviation based in Cascade.[125]

A view of the Morgan Ranch and airstrip (center) looking up the Middle Fork.

The current Morgan Ranch airstrip. The cut from the original dogleg is still visible bending to the left off the upper end of the strip.

Hornback/Vance

Pistol Creek Ranch founder Marvin Hornback in 1960 with a bear and a Cessna 182 advertising his ranches.

PISTOL CREEK RANCH

The Early Years

In 1910 Sam Hoppins settled on the property now known as Pistol Creek Ranch. Hoppins arrived in the Middle Fork country in 1892, first filing for a homestead on Loon Creek. After moving to Pistol Creek, Hoppins made a living hauling supplies for various miners in the area. In 1914 he sold to Eleck Watson, and eventually moved to the Big Creek area to start his own mining operation at Copper Camp. A hunting accident later took his life.[126]

Watson and his wife sold the land to George Risley, who in 1923 homesteaded 144.33 acres at the location.[127] The property during his ownership was known as the Risley Ranch.

The Bill Wayne Ownership

In the early 1950s Bill and Adelaide Wayne bought the place from the Risleys with the intention of turning it into a hunting lodge. Wayne was not a pilot, but knew an aircraft would be crucial for easier access from Boise. Wayne hired Boise-based pilot Harold Dougal, not only to find an airplane suited for the job, but also to be his personal pilot.[128] Dougal was up to the challenge and in August 1955 located a Stinson Detroiter (N11166) for Wayne in Pocatello, Idaho. A 220 horse, nine-cylinder radial powered the airplane, which was often not enough muscle for the available cargo space, but it worked.[129]

During Wayne's ownership of the property it did not have an airstrip, so all the materials were flown from Boise to Indian Creek and then hauled upriver by trail. One of the first items flown to Indian Creek was a small Farmall Cub tractor, along with the pieces to build a homemade trailer. This little machine was used to move people and material between the airstrip and the property. The heavy parts of the tractor were flown in with a Ford Tri-Motor (NC8407) and the remaining components in a Travel Air 6000 (NC8865). Dougal used the same Travel Air to haul in parts of a portable sawmill and building materials. When not flying, Dougal also helped Wayne and his brother work on the lodge. When staying at the property prior to the completion of the lodge, the crew used a few very small log cabins; structures later burned.[130]

By the spring of 1956 Dougal had became too busy with his other flying jobs to work solely for Wayne. Needing someone full-time, Wayne hired pilot Joe Monaghan to fly his plane and to work as a helper at the property. Not long after being hired, Monaghan flew Wayne and some supplies to the property from Boise. On May 14 the two returned to Indian Creek, got in the Stinson and headed for Boise. However, the plane never arrived and no word was heard from Monaghan or Wayne.[131]

Worried that Wayne had not shown up as planned, his wife called Dougal. Dougal told her not to fret and that he would take a look for him as he had a flight to Indian Creek the next day. When he and copilot Glenn Higby arrived at the airstrip in the Ford Tri-Motor he noted the Stinson was gone. He confirmed with Wayne's brother that they had left the day before for Boise.[132]

At this point Dougal knew they were in trouble and he began to search. Shortly after leaving Indian Creek, Higby spotted the downed aircraft along the Middle Fork in some rocks across from the mouth of Elk Creek, between Pistol Creek and Sulphur Creek. Unable to do anything, they circled and headed back to Boise for help.[133]

Helicopters and smokejumpers responded quickly, and Dougal followed closely behind in one of his company's Navions to watch. In the end Monaghan suffered a few non-fatal injuries, but Wayne was killed. The most likely cause of the accident was carburetor icing. After the funeral in Boise, Dougal spread Wayne's ashes over the ranch from an airplane.[134]

The Start of Pistol Creek Ranch

After her husband's death, Adelaide sold the property in 1957 to Sulphur Creek Ranch owners Marv and Barbara Hornback. The Hornbacks renamed the place Pistol Creek Ranch. A landing strip was an early improvement to the property.[135] Hornback first attempted construction with a team of horses. Then the same fall he leased the USFS dozer located at Indian Creek. Bill Watson helped Hornback walk the dozer up to Pistol Creek at low water. The project was completed and the machine returned.[136] This was the same piece of equipment that built the present Indian Creek airfield in 1954–55.

The property was then split into several lots that were put up for sale to create much-needed revenue. Many of the lots sold to frequent customers of their Sulphur Creek Ranch. When the individual parcels were sold, the buyer had the option of whether to build a one-, two-, or three-bedroom cabin. Once purchased, the cabins were guaranteed to be built, furnished, and ready to occupy within thirty days. Hornback hired caretaker Dewey Heater and his son Don, along with seasonal help, to construct most of the cabins. The Heaters stayed involved, building most of the cabins through 1978. In the beginning the development of Pistol Creek was made possible by floating certain items downriver from Sulphur Creek. Objects brought in this way included a John Deere tractor, Pelton wheel generator, septic tank systems, a portable sawmill, and propane systems. Once the airstrip was built most things were brought in by airplane, even large items such as Jeeps.[137]

One of the only setbacks occurred early in 1958 when clothing hung near a stovepipe in the Wayne-built lodge caught on fire. Hornback employee's Bill Watson, Glen Baxter, and Tom Chaloupka were sitting downstairs in the lodge when the fire started. The group tried putting the fire out at first, but it was ineffective. Then one person began disconnecting the propane, another began getting the water system going, and the other started to carry out valuables. The water system started to work, but they could not get enough pressure to the

second floor. Before long the whole lodge was engulfed in flames. Despite the unfortunate loss of the structure, a new one was rebuilt bigger and better than before.[138]

Once underway, the Hornbacks found the business venture successful. Pistol Creek Ranch, similar to their Sulphur Creek Ranch, attracted national attention in magazines. It also caught the eye of Cessna, as the Hornback's purchased a new airplane from the company nearly every year, ranging from 175s to 182s and ultimately 206s. The company featured the ranch and the Hornbacks in the fall 1962 edition of their magazine, *The Cessna Pennant*, and titled the spread, "Pistol Creek – – Fly-In Shangri-LA."

An Aviation Destination, Airline Captains, Clay Lacy, and Allen Paulson

The folks at Cessna were not the only ones in the aviation industry who took notice of Pistol Creek Ranch. In fact many of the initial lot owners were people heavily involved in the aviation profession who had met the Hornbacks on fly-in vacations at Sulphur Creek in the mid-1950s. While Hornback did sell lots to Idahoans such as Joe Albertson, Ferris Lind, Buzz Cheney, and Warren Anderson, the majority of the early cabins were purchased by out-of-state residents attracted to the ranch, in part because of the flying aspect.

Several airline employees bought places, including Richard DeLong with United, Lanier Turner with PanAm, and Bill Pecora with Horizon. Another in the aircraft industry was John "Jack" Conroy, a cofounder of Aero Spacelines, a company that created large aircraft conversions and was most recognized for producing the Super Guppy used in NASA's space program.

Clay Lacy was another early cabin owner tied to the aviation industry. An avid aviation enthusiast and successful businessman, Lacy began flying for United Airlines in 1952 when he was nineteen years old. After spending time in the Air Force he returned to the airline before starting Clay Lacy Aviation, the first private jet charter company on the West Coast. Over the course of his career he logged over 50,000 hours of flight time and flew over 300 different types of aircraft. To access

his place at Pistol Creek he generally used a Pilatus Turbo Porter or a North American T-6. However, he occasionally would buzz the ranch in a Learjet, letting Hornback know he was ready to be picked up at the McCall airport.

Originally Lacy shared a cabin with good friend and business partner Allen "Al" Paulson. The two later had separate cabins next to one another. Paulson had introduced Lacy to the world of business aviation when his company became a distributor for Learjets. Needing a sales manager, Paulson hired Lacy to cover eleven western states. Paulson, like Lacy, had a background in the airlines and started his own business after World War II, wholesaling military aircraft surplus parts. By the early 1970s his company, California Airmotive Corporation, grew to be the largest dealer of secondhand aircraft in the world. The company also became involved with the development of Gulfstream jets, of which Paulson remained a part until the early 1990s. Paulson generally flew to the ranch in the early years with light twins, such as a Beechcraft 50, and later primarily used a green and white Aero Commander.

While at Pistol Creek, all of these professionals simply had fun – fishing, hunting, socializing, relaxing, and flying. The biggest gathering of the year was at Fourth of July. Most of the owners brought in their families and the children generally entertained themselves. For example, it was not uncommon for the kids to gather several cheap rafts and spend the day floating down the river to Thomas Creek. Once at the Thomas Creek airfield, the adults would fly down and pick them up. Many fond memories were created during these years at the ranch, much of which was captured by the Hornbacks in still photographs and in 8 mm home movies. The footage in existence today reveals a stereotypical atmosphere for the era, except for the wild flying, which included contests of who could buzz the airfield better, along with Lacy's aerobatic demonstrations.

It was during these wonderful summers that one of the Hornback's daughters, Patricia, became acquainted with one of Paulson's four sons, Robert. The two were eventually married and had one daughter, Crystal. In 1970 Robert lost his life in an aircraft accident near Eagle, Idaho. After Allen Paulson died in 2000, Crystal inherited the family cabin.

1 *The Pistol Creek lodge built by the Hornbacks in 1958–59. This lodge burned in a 2000 wildfire and has since been replaced by a private residence.*
2 *A load of chickens for the ranch in one of Hornback's Cessna 206s.*
3 *Clay Lacy at Pistol Creek with his North American T-6 in the early 1960s.*
4 *Allen Paulson (far right) and Barbara Hornback (center) smiling with Paulson's Beechcraft 50 at Pistol Creek in the late 1950s.*

Paulson's Aero Commander arriving at Pistol Creek in the early 1960s.

A Corporation, A New Lodge, and the Hornback Legacy

In October 1965 tragedy struck the operation and family when Hornback was killed in an airplane accident at the Strawberry Glenn Airport near Boise. Hornback was offered a ride in a Stinson Mule V-77 (N60361) by an ex-Air Force pilot. To show the airplane's performance the pilot made several touch-and-goes at the airport. On the final approach to landing, the plane's tail wheel clipped a high berm that caused the airplane to crash, killing both Hornback and the pilot.

After Hornback's death, the family sold their portion of the ranch to the lot owners, who created a non-profit corporation known as Middle Fork Ranch Inc. Barbara Hornback died in 1971. The Hornback's main lodge became privately owned by Jack Thornton and was remodeled. The corporation built a new main lodge in the 1980s to serve members and guests. In 2000 a large wildfire swept the subdivision and burned seventeen of the twenty-two original Hornback era cabins. Fourteen of these owners rebuilt. Several of the cabins are co-owned, while others are individually owned. A handful of these property owners maintain private aircraft to access the ranch.[139]

A String of Them...

In late July 2000 Arnold Aviation pilot John Lancaster flew a routine trip to the ranch picking up several hundred pounds of garbage with a Cessna 206 (N206RA). After loading the airplane he took off downriver and then came back upstream. As the plane passed over the ranch heading to Cascade, people on the ground heard the plane sputtering. With an engine failure on his hands, Lancaster cranked the plane into a left downwind leg for an emergency upstream landing. As he turned base to final, smoke was trailing behind the airplane. With the runway nearly made, he came up short by about fifty feet and crashed into a large tree northwest of the airstrip. Lancaster was killed on impact.

Just three years later in April 2003, longtime backcountry pilot Mike Lorenzi was flying supplies to Pistol Creek from Boise in a Cessna 206 (N756WZ). As he came down the Middle Fork he inspected the strip and noted no obstructions other than a small amount of work being done on the downstream end of the runway. Already anticipating the shortened length of the airstrip, he adjusted his approach accordingly. As Lorenzi was on short final about to set down, a

The current Pistol Creek Ranch Lodge used by members.

young boy drove a tractor out onto the field right where he intended to land. Over the noise of the river and the tractor the kid did not hear the airplane and failed to even look.

Making a go-around was out of the question, but Lorenzi also did not want to kill himself or the person on the vehicle. Without hesitation and a little finesse he shoved enough power to the 206 to hop over the top of the tractor. But with the already shortened runway, plus the ground lost from clearing the tractor, Lorenzi knew he could not make a clean landing on the strip. He quickly chose an alternative spot at the end of the runway. The plane touched down in a rocky area with a ditch and rolled a few hundred feet before the nose gear was ripped off. The aircraft was destroyed, but Lorenzi survived.

Only one year passed before another accident was linked to Pistol Creek. On September 13, 2004 Bob Danner, owner and operator of Stanley Air Taxi left the ranch to return to Stanley. Flying alongside Danner in another Cessna 206 on the job was Karl Urquhart of Grangeville. Poor weather plagued the area as the two departed. Edging their way south toward Stanley they kept getting blocked by low

ceilings. With Danner in the lead over Dagger Falls he reported that he was going to go around though Bear Valley. Both Urquhart and Danner tried several times at varying altitudes.

Unable to find an opening they turned around and Danner split off. Urquhart radioed to Danner that he was going to try the Middle Fork again and if that failed he was headed to Sulphur Creek to wait the weather out. Danner responded back while working his way up Marsh Creek that the ceilings were low. Urquhart was concerned, as his own visibility toward Sulphur Creek also worsened. Worried about Danner's progress, he asked Danner if he was able to turn around and come back down the river with him. Danner's last transmission was that he was unable to turn and the fog was extending to the ground. Meantime Urquhart landed safely at Sulphur Creek Ranch. Knowing something had gone wrong he contacted authorities as soon as possible.

The wreckage of Danner's 206 (N20GV) was found the following evening on Cape Horn Mountain. Danner, at age sixty-three a highly respected and experienced pilot, did not survive.

1 Landing upstream at Pistol Creek.
2 A view of the ranch from the manager's house.
3 Mike Lorenzi flying a Cessna 206.
4 Looking down the Pistol Creek Ranch runway in October 2011.

Photos by Holm

Holm

M. Dorris

Holm

SULPHUR CREEK RANCH

Early Occupants, Homestead, and Aircraft

Sulphur Creek Ranch in the early 1950s.

At the turn of the twentieth century Sam Phillips settled at the property now known as Sulphur Creek Ranch, and in 1923 homesteaded the 160 acres. Phillips had a nice, well-built cabin and raised a family here, often leasing the ground to his downstream neighbor, Jim Fuller, for cattle grazing. The place then sold to Ed P. Parker. Parker and his son hunted, trapped, and sold moonshine during the 1930s from the remote location.[140] The ranch saw the first use of small aircraft on an unimproved landing area during the Parkers's ownership. Johnson Flying Service of McCall and Missoula made frequent trips to the property in the 1930s on both skis and wheels, hauling freight in Travel Air 6000s.[141]

In the winter of 1938 Parker sent a bill to the IDFG. He wanted to be reimbursed for several Johnson Flying Service trips he had paid-for where hay was hauled in. He claimed that because of the harsh winter he was forced to feed the area elk herd. He told one reporter, "We have cared for these elk since 12 years ago when four straggled in from somewhere. Now the herd has grown to 150. If something isn't done to pay us for feeding them during a hard winter we've got to destroy them."[142] It is unknown if Parker received the money for transporting the hay to his ranch.

New Owners, a Guest Ranch, and a Developed Airfield

In the mid-1940s Dr. Ben Morgan of Chicago bought the property from the Parker family. Included in the sale was a Zenith bi-plane which he traded to Boise-based pilot Bill Woods for flying freight to the ranch. Morgan hired Marvin Hornback as a manager and then brought him in as a partner. The two named it Sulphur Creek Ranch and set out to make it a fly-in dude ranch. Work to improve the property began

with a new lodge. In 1947 Morgan bought the lower Fuller homestead at the mouth of Sulphur Creek near the Middle Fork. He then sold his interest in the ranch to Hornback and his wife Barbara, but remained as a financial backer until Dave and Signe Callender of Boise became involved.[143]

The Hornbacks continued with the goal of making it a first-class dude ranch. They added a barn, several smaller cabins for guests, and a Pelton wheel generator for power. The husband and wife team worked extremely hard to make a go of the ranch, in addition to raising a family of two girls, Patricia and Jackie.[144]

Aircraft were a crucial element to the success and operation of the Sulphur Creek Ranch. At the time the Hornback's purchased the place they were flying a Piper Cub, which they used frequently to fly back and forth from Boise. They had both learned to fly with Bill Woods. Barbara later earned a commercial rating in 1954 and was an active member in the Idaho Chapter of the Ninety-Nines, serving as the Idaho charter president in 1954–56. During her time in the backcountry she flew regularly from the various ranches to Boise. Barbara was also very influential on getting other women in the backcountry to become pilots and join the Ninety-Nines.[145]

Wanting to build a formal runway that would accommodate a wide variety of larger aircraft, Hornback bought a Cletrac bulldozer and walked it in from Bear Valley. After a long trip and the ranch in sight he unfortunately rolled it over. With a few repairs he had it up and running and built the present 3300' airstrip.[146]

By 1951 Sulphur Creek was on the map as a destination fly-in dude ranch. The Hornbacks hosted many flying clubs and fly-ins from all over the country. The couple also advertised frequently in California, particularly at the annual sportsmen show held at the Cow Palace near San Francisco, which brought in well-known clientele. Some of the guests included Fred MacMurray, Rod Cameron, the Crosby family, Warren Nelson of the Club Cal Neva, Johnny Ascuaga of the Nugget Casino, and Howard Hughes.[147] Also attracting clientele was the fact that the ranch was featured in several national magazines. The article "Wanta Go to Heaven?," which appeared in the July 1948 copy of *The Air Traveler* promoted the ranch extensively to the flying public. The title alone was a good enough review of the operation, not to mention that it earned a place on the cover and a several-page spread that raved about the place.

A New Era

In 1957 the Hornbacks expanded their operation and bought what is now Pistol Creek Ranch. They eventually sold the Sulphur Creek property in 1960 to Robert Dees of Nevada and moved permanently to Pistol Creek. Gene Barton and Les MacGray from Minnesota, who owned a construction business, acquired the property from Dees.[148]

For the next seventeen years Eggs and Catherine Beckley managed the ranch and ran an outfitting business. Beckley was a good friend and employee of the Hornbacks. He had been involved with the ranch starting in the early 1950s and was also a pilot.[149] Tom Allegrezza of Boise, along with Bill George and George Truppi purchased the property in 1977.[150] The ranch was then sold to Sulphur Creek LLC of Belleview, Washington. The popular backcountry location still serves as a guest ranch and destination for pilots.

Bill Woods and a Floating Airplane

Bill Woods of the Floating Feather Airport near Boise had a reputation of making more crash landings than any other pilot in the backcountry. In March 1955, one of his better-known crashes occurred when he lost an engine in a Travel Air 6000 after clearing Sulphur Creek Summit. At the time he was powering the engine back for a gentle descent to the Flying B Ranch. The motor seized, and Woods was forced to put the ship down on the ice covered Middle Fork. He and the plane both fared the accident amazingly well. Safe on the ground he somehow was able to contact Billie Oberbillig on the radio and she placed a call to Johnson Flying Service in McCall to rescue him.

Meantime Woods gathered his two Wirehaired Terriers and emergency rations and started to walk downriver toward the Indian Creek airstrip. Bucking through a consistent three feet of snow without snowshoes and having to ford the river once, the traveling was difficult and slow. At times the snow was too deep for his dogs and he developed a rhythm of tossing one then the other in front of him to keep moving. Luckily the weather permitted and several aircraft combed the area and spotted him.[151]

The next afternoon more planes circled the area between snowstorms. Warren Brown of McCall along with passenger Wayne Webb dropped a package from Brown's Super Cub containing socks, boots, a radio, food, and snowshoes. Following a much-needed lunch, Woods strapped on the snowshoes and continued downstream. A few minutes later Johnson pilot Jim Larkin met Woods on the trail, as he had landed a ski-equipped airplane at Indian Creek. On the second day of hiking with Larkin the two were met by Brown and Webb and they all hiked back to the airstrip with a quick stop at Pistol Creek, where friend Eggs Beckley had prepared them a warm meal.[152]

After the accident many people wanted to know why Woods had not stayed with the airplane. In response Woods noted, "I was not injured in any way whatever, I was not lost, and I had to get to

1 Barbara and Marvin Hornback circa 1950 at Sulphur Creek in a Piper Cub.
2 Barbara at a sportsman show in the 1950s.
3 A company Stinson at Sulphur Creek in the late 1940s.
4 One of the Hornback's daughters, Patricia at Sulphur Creek with her horse Dusty, and dog Mike. In the background is a Cessna 170.
5 Big band leader Bob Crosby (adult on left) frequented the ranch on fishing trips.
6 One of Johnson Flying Service's DC-3s (NC24320) preparing for takeoff at Sulphur Creek in the early 1950s.
7 Guests relaxing at the lodge.
8 A 1950s Sulphur Creek brochure.
9 Looking up the Sulphur Creek drainage at the ranch.

Hornback/Vance

66

5

6

7

9

8

Indian Creek before I could get out. No one could have picked me up where the ship was located . . . I knew the country and I am a firm believer in the principle that a man that will not try to help himself, doesn't deserve help anyhow . . . Actually this canyon is narrow, twisting, full of trees a hundred and fifty feet high, and there are darned few places where anything could be dropped from a plane to a man in three feet of snow, and that man would ever stand much chance either finding it or getting to it."[153]

While he was able to get out rather painlessly considering the situation, Woods knew it was not going to be easy to move his Travel Air. He had very little time as spring runoff was nearing, so he had the idea of floating the airplane down to Indian Creek, where he could then work on it. He contacted friend Carl Kriley of Salmon who had boats for outfitting fishing trips. Kriley agreed it could be done.

Not long thereafter, Johnson Flying Service pilots Bob Fogg and Ken Roth with a Ford Tri-Motor met Kriley and his crew at the Salmon airport. The group loaded a twenty-eighty foot rubber military-surplus bridge boat into the Ford and all the associated gear. They took off and landed at Sulphur Creek where Hornback met the plane with a little tractor pulling a wagon. The men transferred the gear to the wagon and piled on for the put-in location near the confluence of Sulphur Creek and the Middle Fork.

Floating the river went without incident, and after running Big Bar Rapid the wrecked Travel Air came into view. Woods's crew had the plane disassembled as much as possible. The two groups strapped parts of the airplane onto the boat and started down the river. The first day they negotiated Sheepeater Rapid and then camped. The following day they had some difficulty getting through Pistol Creek Rapid, but made it. At the Indian Creek airfield, Woods met the crew and prepared a big feast. It is unclear how many trips it took to float the complete airplane down to Indian Creek. However, at the airstrip Woods erected a tent serving as a shop and also flew in the items needed to repair the aircraft, including a new engine. They borrowed the USFS's tractor and skidded the wrecked airplane sections up to the shop with long lengths of lumber. The plane was slowly repaired and later flown out.

A Cessna 175 Explodes

Prior to selling Sulphur Creek, Hornback was busy flying back and forth between the property and his new Pistol Creek Ranch. During the summer he kept a full-time caretaker to help run the operation, but in the winter he frequented both places. In December 1959 Hornback and employee Wayne Rowe were working at Pistol Creek when a cold snap settled in. They managed to get through the cold temperatures, but needed a battery charger left at Sulphur Creek to complete a project. At three o'clock in the afternoon it warmed up enough that the two decided to make a quick trip in Hornback's Cessna 175 to retrieve the charger.[154]

It was not known at the time, but when they took off from Pistol Creek, wet mud packed into the wheel skirts and froze during the flight, locking all three wheels. When the plane touched down at Sulphur Creek it skidded forty feet, before being thrown off center, at which point the left wing tore off. The 175 then flipped over on its back and fuel began to leak everywhere.[155]

Through the accident Rowe remained conscious, but the impact knocked Hornback out. As Rowe escaped from the wreckage a small fire ignited. Realizing the danger he quickly returned to the aircraft and pulled Hornback from the cockpit and carried him about 150' from the accident. As they reached safe ground Hornback came to, just in time to see his airplane explode. In the annual Hornback family Christmas letter Barbara recounted the rest of the story, "Neither one of the fellows were hurt a speck, but the plane was little bits of nothing. It scared me to death when we flew over and found the plane, but the boys had written o.k. in the snow and what a relief to everyone. Sent in a helicopter and brought them on back to Pistol Creek and then on to Boise."[156]

M. Dorris collection

The Thomas McCall Ranch.

THOMAS CREEK
The Early Years and the Airstrip

The name Thomas Creek is derived from a miner who worked the area in the 1880s. Jim Voller later moved to the area and made a humble living. In 1913 Voller homesteaded the 80.53 acres that is now known as the Middle Fork Lodge. With the help of friends, Voller created an irrigation system that permitted him to grow dozens of acres of alfalfa and timothy clover. With the available feed, he and his associates raised all types of animals. They built a log cabin, decent sized barn, and a log tramway across the river.[157]

Voller's health failed and he moved to Lewiston where he eventually died. The property then sold to a group of cattlemen that included Freeman Nethkin, Ed Osborn, and Henry Clay. Nethkin was also associated with several properties on the lower portion of the South Fork of the Salmon River in cattle operations. Prior to 1919 this crowd sold to another cattle company. The new group's venture was hit hard in the harsh winter of 1919–20. Most of the cattle moved from Thomas Creek to Cascade died before they were brought to slaughter. Unable to pay, the property reverted back to Nethkin and Osborn. With the place on the market and no offers, the two rented the Voller cabin to the IDFG and then in the 1930s to Milt and Mary Hood. The Hoods established the first commercial hunting and fishing operation on the river. Circa 1936 the Thomas Creek airstrip was built on a state-owned section of land across the river from the Voller homestead. The first person reported to have landed here was Boise-based pilot Bob King in a Waco. Many pilots referred to the strip during this time as the Hood Ranch. Bob and Dick Johnson of Johnson Flying Service operated a Ford Tri-Motor (NC435H) on this strip as early 1937.[158]

Hollywood Aviatrix - Bernadine King

In October 1937 Bernadine Lewis King flew solo to the Hood Ranch from Hollywood. King, who is often compared to her contemporary Amelia Earhart, was also respected in the aviation field, not only as a woman, but also as a professional. However, unlike Earhart she was often a target for tabloids, stemming from her early barnstorming career when she admitted to sunbathing in her open cockpit airplane. She was thus often known as "The Flying Godiva."

Although not quite of national fame, King was known in the West and particularly the Southwest, often appearing at regional air shows. She piloted a wide variety of aircraft including a Lockhead Vega. She began flying in 1934 at age twenty-three after graduating from a Chicago music school.

Also an avid outdoorswoman, King enjoyed hunting throughout the West. Hearing of the large game in central Idaho, she booked a trip to the Hood Ranch. Unaccompanied by a guide, she scouted the Middle Fork country for several days looking for a

Hollywood aviatrix Bernadine Lewis King about the time she visited Thomas Creek on a hunting trip in October 1937.

Holm collection

large buck. On the fourth day she took a shot with her .30-30 rifle and reported back to Milt Hood to have him pack the carcass out. In an interview with *The Idaho Statesman* she commented, "You can be certain I'll display his antlers in a prominent place when I get back home."[159]

Prior to leaving the Middle Fork her bounty was checked by local Game Warden Lee Clark who found she did not have verification of a hunting license or a deer tag. King's explanation to the charge was quoted in *The Challis Messenger*, "I lost my $50 non-resident hunting license and the $1 deer tag . . . of course I couldn't put the tag on the deer because I had lost it and consequently I was arrested. The whole matter is cleared up now, however, and I'm once more on my way."[160]

King returned to Hollywood and continued flying until her career ended rather abruptly. While performing at an air show in Utah her brakes failed. The airplane wheeled into the crowd and killed a spectator. Although she survived unharmed, her reputation did not.

The McCall Ranch

In 1938 Nethkin and Osborn finally sold the property to Thomas and Nell McCall. McCall was the grandson of the man for whom the city of McCall, Idaho, is named. The property at this time became known as the McCall Ranch. With the sale the

Hoods moved downriver to nearby Sunflower Creek, although they still used the airstrip. They continued this operation until late 1943.

It was rumored on the river that McCall and Hood were bitter enemies. Apparently Hood even took a couple of shots at McCall when he would land at the strip with his airplane. It was even suggested that the feud between the two is what eventually ran the Hoods off the river.[161] Prior to the purchase of the ranch, McCall operated his own air service, known as Intermountain Air Transport Company, based in McCall. The business owned a few Travel Air 6000s and a Stearman.

After the sale of the ranch to McCall, the Idaho Bureau of Aeronautics (Idaho Department of Aeronautics) leased the airstrip from the state of Idaho. Backed by House Bill No. 307 the Bureau was able to retain the lease only if the runway was maintained as a public airport. Trying to obtain additional funding, the Bureau of Aeronautics released the airstrip to the IDFG. The IDFG wanted not only to maintain the airport, but also wanted to develop a recreation area at the site. The recreation area was platted on the property acquired by the IDFG in 1946 and used by Milt Hood from 1938–43. By 1950 these plans had not materialized and the Idaho Department of Aeronautics regained the lease of the airstrip.[162]

The Start of the Middle Fork Lodge

In November 1954 McCall sold the ranch to a group of outfitters and guides including Ken Roundy, Bill Guth Sr., and Dr. Hugh Dean. Roundy owned a flying service based in Burley, Idaho, and after two years sold his portion to Rex Lanham. It was under this group of partners that the property was named the Middle Fork Lodge. Guth then sold his portion to the other two partners and leased it back for running his outfitting business with sons Norman and Bill Jr.[163]

The Guth family had a lot of good memories from their time on the Middle Fork. Bill Sr. was an old-fashioned horse-and-mule man and had little interest

The Thomas Creek airstrip (center).

in airplanes. However, when Norman was of age, his dad encouraged him to be a pilot. When Norman graduated from high school he bought a 1951 Aeronca Sedan 15AC (N1471H). Lanham helped him in his early flying career and one of Norman's first jobs was hauling cement sacks from the Cape Horn airstrip near Stanley to the lodge for the building of the swimming pool. The Aeronca could haul up to six sacks in the morning and the heat of the day reduced the load to four sacks. Lanham on the other hand was able to transport about eight sacks per load all day long in his 1954 Cessna 180. Between the two planes they took in 550 sacks.[164]

Lanham provided the money for the whole pool project. He also found just about every available kid in Boise to carry rocks, as no heavy equipment was used for the project. It does seem a bit outlandish to build a 60' X 20' pool 8' deep in the middle of nowhere, but the owners were simply taking advantage of the 118-degree natural hot water springs. Norman said in reference to the water, "It is the best, most pure water in the world. It was a wonderful place to swim."[165]

Norman put over 2,000 hours on the Aeronca flying various jobs for the lodge. Norman's brother, Bill Jr., was also hooked on flying. The two each owned various airplanes during their time on the Middle Fork. Bill Jr. operated a 135 horsepower Super Cub (N1652P) with tandem landing wheels, which he bought from Lanham. Bill Jr. flew this particular airplane to the Billy Mitchell Ranch on Marble Creek, which the lodge leased from the IDFG in the early 1960s. The old Mitchell Ranch was used only to pasture extra stock, but it was necessary to

salt, irrigate, and check on the various animals.[166]

For a landing area, the Guths filled in a few old ditches in the hayfield and called it good. However, braking was difficult with the tandem wheel setup. The rear wheels were the only ones with brakes attached, which caused insufficient stopping power. After several landings in 1962 and 1963 Bill Jr. decided it was too hard on the airplane. Wanting to save the aircraft they reverted back to the hour and fifteen minute horseback ride from the lodge to the old ranch.[167]

Earlier the Guths had built another landing field on Little Loon Creek. Norman packed a slip scraper on a horse, going downriver and up Little Loon Creek about seven miles to the Dutch Charlie mining claim. This claim was often called the Fur Farm and was acquired by family friend Bill Sullivan. Norman had permission from Sullivan to rough out a 600' airstrip with the horse-drawn scraper. The project did not take long and he returned several days later with the Super Cub and a rather large hired hand from the lodge.[168]

The approach and landing were easy, but when Norman taxied to the top of the runway and pointed the plane down the field, the trees on the end looked a little too tall, especially with the rather large passenger. Norman shut the plane down and the two went to work with a crosscut saw. They removed twenty-seven trees, clearing the departure end of the runway.[169]

The Dutch Charlie claim was used about six times during one hunting season, as they tended to hunt the Thomas Creek drainage earlier on, which

1 *Dr. Hugh Dean (left) and pilot Ridd Solomon (right) at Thomas Creek with Dean's Cessna 182A in the late 1950s.*
2 *Middle Fork Lodge owners in a pickup driven by Bill Guth Sr. leaving the Thomas Creek airfield in the late 1950s.*
3 *The landing site at the Mitchell Ranch used by the Guth brothers.*
4 *Looking up Marble Creek at the Billy Mitchell Ranch.*
5 *Looking north at the landing site used by the Guth brothers that was known as the Fur Farm or the Dutch Charlie mining claim at the confluence of Little Loon and Blue Lake creeks. The Guths used the long field in the upper portion of the photograph running parallel to Little Loon from the cabin to the creek. A bridge was built over Corley Creek to connect the fields together (currently where the brush crosses the runway perpendicularly).*
6 *A 1963 advertisement for the Guth's outfitting business.*
7 *Paul Abbott of Challis with the Fairchild 71 that he used to fly a D2 Caterpillar into Thomas Creek for runway repairs.*

6

Middle Fork Lodge

On the Middle Fork of the Salmon River
in the Idaho Primitive Area

MODERN LODGE AND CABINS

HUNTING	FISHING
Elk, Deer, Bear, Mt. Sheep from Lodge and Spike Camps	Steelhead, Salmon, Trout

BOAT TRIPS

Down the Middle Fork, 3-4-5-7 days
Best of Equipment — Experienced Guides
Licensed and Bonded, Members of Idaho Outfitters and Guides Assos.

BILL GUTH & SONS

18 Years Experience Outfitting and Guiding in this Area

For Reservations Write or Call — Bill Guth, Box 308, Challis, Idaho
Phone 344-0497, Boise, Idaho
(WE HAVE TWO-WAY RADIO COMMUNICATION WITH BOISE, IDAHO)

IOGA

7

J. M. Hatch

drove a majority of the game over into Little Loon. The claim had a beautifully built cabin that was intact from the old days and included a whipsaw setup. Toward the end of the hunting season the USFS noticed the cut trees while on a fly over. The Guths admitted to the landing activities but never had to pay a fine; although a crew from the lodge did have to go to the site, buck, limb, and pile the downed trees.[170]

Beyond the little strips at the Dutch Charlie claim and the Mitchell Ranch, they also cleared a landing area at the Cougar Ranch, which the lodge leased from the IDFG as well (see Cougar Ranch). Norman, laughing about their impromptu landing strips, mentioned that they landed the Super Cub all over the Middle Fork country asking, "What else would you expect two kids to do with a their own Super Cub?"[171]

The Guth family used the lodge extensively for their outfitting and guiding services, starting in the spring of 1955, taking people fishing and boating in the summers and hunting in the fall. One of the more popular trips in the early years was a three day float and fishing trip from the Middle Fork Lodge downriver to the Flying B Ranch, where guests could either be flown back to the lodge or out to civilization.[172] One frequently returning guest and fisherman was potato giant Jack Simplot. The Guths would take the Simplot party from the lodge on a one-day fishing trip to his property at the confluence of Loon Creek and the Middle Fork. Then the group was either flown out by Simplot pilot Bob Whipkey or by one of the Guths.[173]

Another repeated guest group was the Don Vest family. Vest started what became Univair Aircraft Incorporated, a large used-aircraft parts dealer. During the time he was a guest at the lodge, around 1955–60, he advertised himself as the largest used-aircraft dealer in the world. He generally flew his family to Thomas Creek in the latest V-tail Bonanza.[174]

Early on the Guths worked hard to better the Thomas Creek airfield. As kids, Norman and Bill Jr. were hired by Idaho Division of Aeronautics Director Chet Moulton to improve the runway. The two used a Fresno pulled behind a horse. The main problem with the airstrip was a large hump in the middle that could make a novice pilot think the airplane was flying before it really was. This false jolt into the air caused several early accidents. Regardless of the Guth's efforts their non-motorized equipment would not quite move the big runway hump.[175]

Eventually the lodge hired Paul Abbott of Challis to fly a dismantled D2 Caterpillar in with a Fairchild 71. Abbott was famous in his own right as a pilot involved with the 1928 Byrd Expedition to the Antarctic, run by Admiral Richard E. Byrd. With the D2 they were able to take the hump out of the runway for good.[176]

Among some of the most interesting airplanes to land at Thomas Creek during the early days of the Middle Fork Lodge were a Boeing 247 and a Lockheed 12. The 247 was piloted by Bob King, and owned by well-known Ford Tri-Motor pilot Rex Williams. King also piloted the Lockheed 12.[177]

After the sale of the Middle Fork Lodge in 1965, Lanham moved his operations permanently to Cabin Creek on the Big Creek drainage. Bill Guth Sr. became involved on the Selway River at the Selway Lodge, and his two sons also moved on. Bill Jr. and Norman continued to operate a successful outfitting business on the Middle Fork and the Main Salmon Rivers. In 1979 the Guths took President Jimmy Carter on a float trip down the Middle Fork. Norman retired from the outfitting and guiding business in 1997 and Bill Jr. in 2005.

The entrance to the re-modeled Harrah lodge.

The Harrah Era

In 1965 Bill Harrah of Harrah's Reno and Lake Tahoe made a trip to Idaho on the suggestion of his physician. Harrah's doctor told him that he needed to quit all of his bad habits, slow down, and find a healthy outlet in his life. The doctor set Harrah up with Stanley fishing guide Bob Cole. He really took to the country and made some inquires about area real estate. The Middle Fork Lodge was at the top on his list of available realty.[178]

Harrah assigned the task of purchasing the lodge to Harrah Club Vice President of Real Estate and Finance, Lloyd Dyer. Dyer was largely in charge of the acquisition of items for Harrah personally and for his company. Dyer contacted Lanham and explained the situation. Lanham said it was too late as they had given the USFS the option to buy it three days earlier. Not accepting no for an answer, Dyer said Harrah still wanted to buy the lodge, and that he would be right up to Idaho to work out a deal.[179]

The next day Dyer arrived in Boise and was met at the airport by Lanham in one of his Cessnas. Dyer had never been around small aircraft before, let alone a real workhorse of the Idaho backcountry that looked like a well-used pickup truck. He took one look at the inside of the plane and wanted to know where he could sit as it was full of lumber. Lanham assured him there was plenty of room and cleared off the one remaining seat in the airplane behind the pilot.[180]

Bill Harrah and Lloyd Dyer.

The Middle Fork Lodge in 1972.

The two flew to Cabin Creek and spent the night. The following day Lanham gave Dyer a tour of the backcountry, landing at various places along the route. Later in the afternoon they returned to Cabin Creek, had a drink, and talked. Dyer told him that he was willing to do whatever it took to close the deal. The USFS had offered $175,000. Dyer casually said how about $200,000 and you can have anything you want (personal items, outfitting privileges, etc). Lanham agreed to the transaction, figuring he would be the head contractor for any improvements.[181]

The whole agreement worked out well over the years and many of the Harrah folks became great friends with Lanham. Not long after the purchase, the ranch was given a facelift and Lanham's crews performed much of the work. Construction teams built a new bridge, spruced up the swimming pool, added separate guest cabins, remodeled the main lodge, restored the original homestead cabin, and brought in all the modern convinces imaginable. At the same time, Harrah hired Bob Cole as lodge manager, and for several years McCall also came back to work his old ranch.

At roughly the same time of the sale to Harrah, the Idaho Department of Aeronautics had a growing concern about the deterioration of the runway. The department's plan was to walk a dozer to the site to realign and lengthen the runway. The idea was never executed as they came to an agreement in 1968 with Harrah that he would help maintain the airfield.[182]

Harrah had a wide variety of fine aircraft that his staff of pilots flew in and out of the lodge over the years, including a Beechcraft Model 80 Queen Air with JATO, a DHC-6-100 Twin Otter, two different DHC-6-300 Twin Otters, a Cessna 337, two different Cessna 206s, and a completely restored Ford Tri-Motor (NC9645). With the exception of registration numbers on vintage aircraft, all of his other airplanes were registered with a single leading number followed by "711H." The "711" portion was derived from dice and the "H" stood for "Harrah." The most common way to reach the lodge was for his various jets or twin turbine aircraft to fly guests to Boise, and then the Twin Otter would fly the final leg to the Middle Fork.[183]

To accommodate the Queen Air used early on in Harrah's ownership, the dogleg in the runway was extended as much as possible. Bill Blackmore a Harrah pilot, 1964–76, almost always landed the big plane on the exact same spot each time, and it became evident. The plane created a set of ruts about ten feet from the bank of the river through the brush and on to the end of the runway.[184]

The local FAA caught wind that Harrah was using the Queen Air at Thomas Creek and asked him to stop. Blackmore felt the plane was very capable because of the JATO system. If an engine was lost after rotation at gross weight and in takeoff configuration with flaps and gear down, the JATO switch could be flipped and it was as if you had gained the lost engine back for over thirteen seconds. This extra precaution allowed for safe operation of the aircraft in and out of the strip.[185]

76

7

L. Dyer

9

B. Blackmore

10

B. Blackmore

11

M. Jager

8

B. Blackmore

1 *The Middle Fork Lodge and pool in 1977.*
2 *An early Harrah owned 206 at Thomas Creek.*
3 *Pilot Bill Blackmore (left) with the company's Beechcraft Model 80 Queen Air, known as the "Tahoe Queen," in 1966 at Thomas Creek.*
4 *Outfitter Bob Cole and pilot Bill Blackmore.*
5 *The Harrah Ford Tri-Motor at Thomas Creek in the fall of 1970. Johnson Flying Service pilot Bob Fogg (center) is standing with Harry Volpi, (left) the head of Harrah's restoration shops. Sitting in the vehicle next to the airplane is former lodge owner Thomas McCall.*
6 *A 1967 photograph of hauling supplies for the lodge in Harrah's 100 series Twin Otter.*
7 *Early Harrah aircraft at Thomas Creek.*
8 *The 100 series Twin Otter on skis at Thomas Creek. The aircraft was dubbed "The Middle Fork Otter."*
9 *The second Harrah Otter used at the lodge.*
10 *Hauling propane to the lodge in June 1972 from the Challis office/hangar.*
11 *The Middle Fork Lodge automobile collection.*

Greeting Middle Fork Lodge guests at the airfield.

The third Harrah Twin Otter (N3H) used at the lodge.

During the mid-1960s Harrah's prized Ford Tri-Motor was completely rebuilt by his restoration shop in Reno. Ken Roth, of Johnson Flying Service, who was a highly respected Ford pilot, initially flew the airplane in Reno and checked out Harrah's pilots on the vintage ship.[186] In the fall of 1970 the plane was flown from Reno to McCall, and Bob Fogg, also of Johnson Flying Service, flew with the Harrah pilots to the lodge and helped certify them with the Ford.[187]

Once the first Twin Otter came on the scene in 1967, it became the main aircraft used for the lodge. From 1967 through 1969 Blackmore and the other pilots would fly from sunup to sundown, making eight to twelve trips per day from Challis. Most of the supplies, including fuel, were hauled from Challis, as Harrah had a small office and hangar at the airport. The trip to the lodge could be made one way in fifteen minutes. In the winter the plane was outfitted with retractable skis and worked quite well. However, the skis weighed about 600 pounds, which cut into the useful load. In spite of that, the skis made operations at the lodge and Stanley possible. The later model

Harrah's passion for his Middle Fork property was often the subject of his company magazine.

Twin Otters were purchased with heavier nose gears and bigger tires, and then the snow-covered runways were rolled, thus the skis were discarded.[188]

Harrah was meticulous about all of his operations, particularly the Middle Fork Lodge. He did not want anything unnecessarily disturbed. As a consequence, all of the aggregate for anything built of concrete had to be hauled in along with the cement sacks. One day Blackmore came in for another load of aggregate at Challis and a fellow asked him what he was hauling. Blackmore just smiled and replied, "Haul'n rock." A full load was thirty-four bags at one hundred pounds each.[189]

The Twin Otter was also outfitted at times with a removable military rubber bladder that could haul over 300 gallons of fuel. When the second Twin Otter, a new 300 series model, was purchased circa 1977, it was outfitted with a custom metal tank on tracks that could haul about 250 gallons. Both setups carried diesel fuel that was needed to operate the lodge's generators.[190]

After many of the improvements were made to the runway and the lodge property, Harrah went about outfitting his remote getaway with the finest décor possible. Being a serious collector of antique automobiles, he loaded several of his vintage vehicles in car transporters and had them driven to the Bruce Meadows airfield at the headwaters of the Middle Fork. From Bruce Meadows a helicopter carried the cars in slings to the lodge. These vehicles were used for general transportation around the property, but were mainly show pieces to carry guests to and from the airfield.

The lodge and guest quarters were also decked out in the best that money could buy. Any type and brand of liquor ever desired could be ordered. The interior of the main lodge even featured a collection of famous Charles Russell western paintings. During the Middle Fork Lodge's heyday, Harrah himself was in residence for at least two weeks a year, particularly during the steelhead run. The remainder of the time the caretakers were kept busy

Mr. Bill Blackmore
Reno, Nevada

Friend, Bill

I have tried my hand at putting your Airoplane ride in verse – It's a humble attempt at comparison, with a tough old Salmon River Bronc – I tried to ride. I appreciated your and Dave's kindness, it was quite a shock to me, after all the years I've traveled the Salmon River country. We send you our sincere thanks. Hope you cross our range sometime on the ground. Will see you some day – so stay on the trail Bill.

Your friend
John Carrey

THE FLYING OTTER
– a wild ride – through – eternity with Bill Blackmore – – and Dave Davis

by John Carrey - Riggins, Ida

In the beautiful month of October
Bob Cole gave me a call;
He hired me to come to Loon Creek,
To guide throughout the fall.

So gather around me old-packers,
And listen to this story close
While I tell you about a mustang,
Part Otter, part airplane, and ghost.

You might have heard tell of Bill Blackmore
And that airship he calls a steed;
Well, he spends his time with the eagles,
And only comes down for his feed.

He works for a man called Bill Harrah
They have hired him to fly;
Bill eats and drinks in the badlands
And ranges around in the sky.

For years Bill has worked for this outfit;
Dave's a co-pilot – they say.
He keeps an eye on the dashboard
So the darn thing won't get away.

I swore for the love of my sister, I'd mount it
If the engine kept running free;
But his guide had too many clothes on,
And it was almost the finish of me.

If you'll listen, because
I don't know where to begin,
A twin engine Otter is awful
And at times it goes higher than a sin.

Well, I crawls in just like he was gentle,
I'm a little bit nervous, you bet,
But I feel pretty sure I can ride him
'Cause the motor ain't running, just yet.

Very easy, I sat down in the saddle,
The seatbelt I cinched deep in my hide,
I took the slack out of my spur straps
'Cause it looked like a pretty tough ride.

Bill wound up the motor and it snorted . . .
Moved off like he was walking on eggs
It grunted, then exploded like a pistol
And I see he's at home, without legs.

Hard winters, cougars, and grizzlies,
Centipedes, rattlers, and such.
Scorpions, hunters, and bad whiskey,
Compared to this ride, wasn't much.

Well, I thought of Bob Cole, who's the ramrod,
If I could just get my hands round his throat;
I thought of my poor old Mother
And the last long letter she wrote.

Well I had a deep seat in the saddle,
My spurs both socked in the cinch;
I don't aim to take any chances,
And I won't let it budge me an inch.

It soon started acting plumb loco . . .
I buggared and was losing my sense;
It was weaving and flying so crooked
That I thought of a rimrock fence.

Now we're high in a rimrock country,
I think over Deadwood Springs,
And I like to fell out of my saddle
When he started a dipping his wings.

I'm riding my best and I'm busy,
I'm troubled at keeping my seat;
He don't need wings for flying
And, handy when off of his feet.

He's got me half blind and I weaken,
We're flying around in big rings;
Besides he keeps me a guessin'
I'm a ducking and dodgin' his wings.

I grabs me both hands full of leather
When a hole in the clouds she went through;
By golly, he starts getting rougher . . .
He's spinning and sunfishing too.

We dove to the ground like a twister,
My eardrums were busted right there;
Before I could turn loose and quit him
Bill shot her back up in the air.

Then he smoothes out and keeps on a climbin'
Till away down Marble Creek below
I take a good look at the mountains,
The peaks were all covered with snow.

Then up through the clouds he shot it
I'm plumb white round the gills to boot;
I sure was a wishin' I had me
That thing called a parachute.

And then I sorta went loco . . .
Passed out in the darndest sleep
'Cause when I wakes up I'm laying
At Middle Fork Lodge in a heap.

Well I knew I'd been up with the angles
But I wasn't very light on my feet;
I think I got horns like the devil
And a mouth fit for eating raw meat.

I've shrunk off five pounds of leaf lard
But I'm here on the job with my things
But I'm sure glad to be here to tell you,
Stay off of those horses with wings – –

John Carrey's thank you letter and poem written to Bill Blackmore after receiveng a ride in the Harrah Twin Otter.

An advertisement for Middle Fork Charters.

Dick Williams served not only as the lodge's general manager, but also as the chief pilot under the McCaw ownership. Here Williams stands with the Twin Otter at Soldier Bar.

hosting Harrah family members, personal guests, and employees. With the lodge being the premier piece of real estate on one of the most famous whitewater rivers in the world, it attracted an amazing group of visitors and famous guests. Some of the more well-known people that drifted through the lodge include: Bill Cosby, Loretta Lynn, William O. Douglas, John Denver, Steve McQueen, Jim Nabors, Glen Campbell, President Jimmy Carter, Vice President George Bush, Sammy Davis Jr., Dick Smothers, Parnelli Jones, Lawrence Welk, Daryl Lamonica, Bobby Kennedy, Peggy Fleming, along with several Idaho governors, senators, representatives, and many others.

John Carrey, locally famous at the time as a writer and historian of the Salmon River country, also spent time at the lodge visiting and occasionally working for Harrah. For a short stint Carrey ran a guiding service from Lower Loon Creek for Harrah. One afternoon Blackmore flew down to pick Carrey up and fly him back to the lodge. "The old cowboy did not know quite what to think of riding in an airplane like the Twin Otter." Carrey later wrote a poem about the experience and sent a copy to Blackmore as a thank you.[191]

Another piece of literature connected to the lodge was a history book of the area entitled, *The Middle Fork Lodge*, by Joe Midmore. Harrah, being an enormous history buff, had the orange hardbound pocket-sized book prepared. The little book was then placed around the lodge and handed out to guests.

In 1978 Bill Harrah died at the age of sixty-six during an operation to repair an aortic aneurism. The lodge continued on in fine fashion for a few more years and merged with Holiday Inn. Under the new operation the flight department was re-organized. Hoping to cover some of the operating costs of the flying associated with the lodge, a 135 Air Taxi certificate was acquired under the name of Harrah's Middle Fork Charters and based in Boise. The 300 series Twin Otter (N3H) was transferred to the certificate and joined by a Cessna 206 (N9H). The spin-off business did not really work out, but continued to provide the needed services to the lodge.[192] In December 1989 the lodge was sold to the Nature Conservancy. The group's main goal was to place scenic easements on the property. The Conservancy quickly turned the real estate, selling it to wilderness enthusiast John McCaw. At the time of the sale, Middle Fork Charters was dissolved and McCaw acquired the Twin Otter.

The most recent lodge at the property constructed by the Farrs.

The Lodge Today

McCaw along with his father and brothers founded McCaw Cellular Communications. He and his family have made billions in recent decades as forerunners in the development of cellular telephones. McCaw retained Middle Fork Charters pilot Dick Williams to fly the Twin Otter and also serve as the lodge's general manager.

McCaw then sold to New York City investment banker Charles Stevenson. Stevenson uses the lodge both privately and as a commercial venture. Outfitter Scott Farr has operated from the lodge since 1995 and in more recent years has served as the lodge's general manager. Farr and his son Jerrod tore down the Harrah era lodge and rebuilt an amazing new structure over the previous footprint.

The current 2100' long Thomas Creek airstrip continues to have use related to the lodge along with commercial and private activity as well. In 1998 the Middle Fork Management Company (operators of the lodge) agreed to maintain the runway under the direction of the Idaho Department of Aeronautics. The state along with the help of the Idaho Aviation Association annually maintains the airstrip.

The current lodge's great room.

The only remaining Charles Russell painting (right) at the lodge.

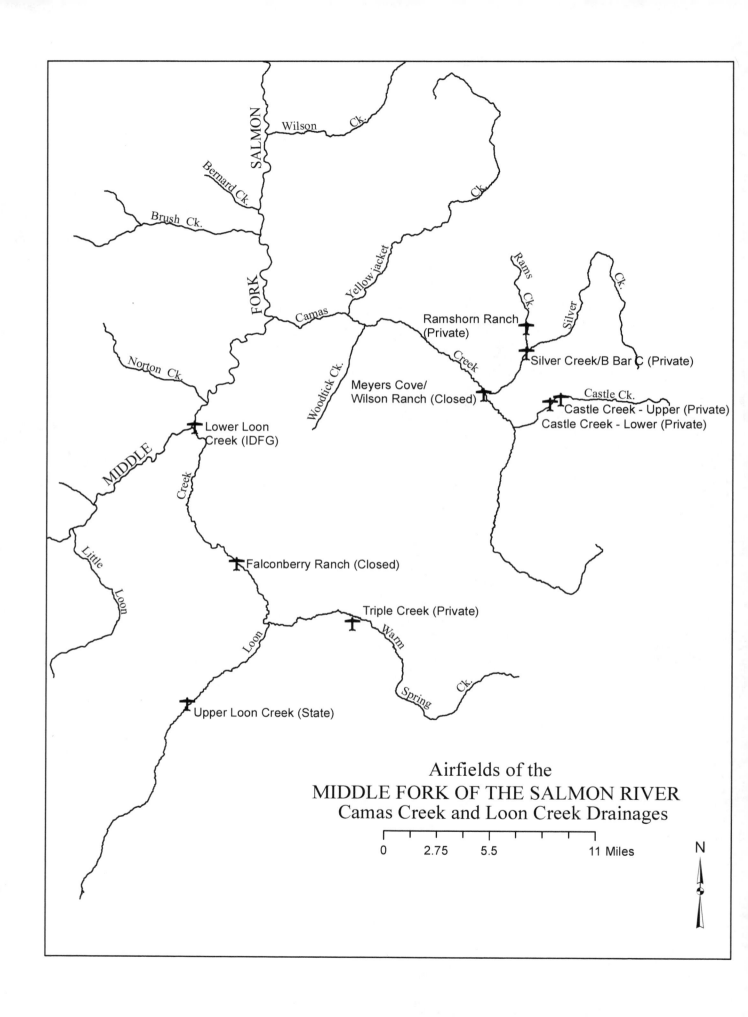

Airfields of the
MIDDLE FORK OF THE SALMON RIVER
Camas Creek and Loon Creek Drainages

0   2.75   5.5   11 Miles

N

MIDDLE FORK OF THE SALMON RIVER
LOON CREEK

FALCONBERRY RANCH

Early Homesteads

The original Falconbery Loon Creek Lodge complex in the late 1940s. The main lodge structure was later removed by Dr. Hatch to lengthen the runway.

What became known as the Falconberry Ranch, owned for over thirty years by Dr. John Hatch of Idaho Falls, was originally three separate homesteads. In the early 1910s Rupert L. Falconbery first began occupying the upper parcel, and in March 1922 received homestead approval for 78.77 acres.[193] In 1911 Jack Ferguson proved up on 81.82 acres forming the middle homestead. At the time of approval Ferguson had built a corral, barn, cabin, and an access bridge across Loon Creek.[194] A few years later Falconbery purchased the property from Ferguson, and although not connected, operated the two places as one ranch and made several improvements.[195] In 1924 George Frinklin homesteaded 38.41 acres on the lower property. Frinklin, like Falconbery, grew crops, trapped, and hunted.[196]

Lodge, Airfield, and Dr. Hatch

Falconbery sold his two parcels in 1937 to a group of businessmen from southern Idaho who renamed it the Falconbery Loon Creek Lodge.[197] Falconbery, who was nearly seventy years old at the time, retained the right to live in one of his cabins. In October 1939, while gathering winter supplies in Challis, he died in a rented cabin owned by Chas Jenson.[198] Falconbery's name continues to be associated with the property, a USFS facility, a nearby peak, and a high mountain lake. Although at some

point the spelling was officially changed to include an additional "r" making it Falconberry.

Many southern Idaho businessmen came and went as partners on the ranch. At one time seventeen individuals were involved.[199] By 1942 a field at the original Ferguson homestead was leveled to facilitate airplane landings.[200]

After World War II Dr. John Hatch joined the group of southern Idaho owners. Hatch grew up in a medically-oriented family in Idaho Falls. He and three of his four brothers followed in the family line of work and became doctors. After graduating from Harvard Medical School he joined the Navy as

1 The Hatch built lodge with one of his CallAirs in the foreground.
2 Longtime Falconberry Ranch owner Dr. John Hatch.
3 The lower portion of the Falconberry Ranch homesteaded by Frinklin and later occupied by the Biggs family. Hatch eventually burned these buildings because of varmint infestation.
4 Looking down Loon Creek at the lower end of the rebuilt 1700′ runway.
5 Hatch's "Cart Trail" along Jack Creek from the ranch to the Indian Springs Guard Station.

86

5

J.M. Hatch

he needed, which he traded for medical attention.[203]

Charles Wilson and his family were a prime example of patients who traded work for doctor bills. Wilson, a general contractor from southern Idaho, built a majority of the structures at the ranch, starting in the late 1950s through the 1970s. He and friends such as Bud Price and Arlow Coleman constructed a sawmill, bathhouse, several guest cabins, milk barn, water system, and numerous other features on the property. Commonly whole families would go in and work, hunt, and fish during the course of the projects. Wilson's wife Karen commented, "We never even knew what a doctor or medical bill was until after Dr. John passed away. He was a wonderful man, and we all had marvelous times at his ranch."[204]

a doctor. Discharged at the end of the war, Hatch returned to his hometown to open a practice. He had multiple business ventures on the side, such as owning a local diary, raising horses, and buying a share of the Falconbery Loon Creek Lodge.[201]

It did not take Hatch long to figure out that all of the owners had different ideas concerning the future of the ranch. He then put together a plan that they all agreed on. Hatch proposed to buy them out over the next ten years. Within the buyout period the other owners could continue using the property.[202]

When Hatch gained sole ownership of the place in the 1950s he began spending a lot of time and money at the ranch. He also obtained the downstream Frinklin homestead and simply called them collectively the Falconberry Ranch. Shortly after acquiring the lower property, which was then known as the Biggs Ranch he burned the original buildings because they were infested with rats and varmints. He then set his sights on improving the middle property and hired Curly Angel and his wife to build a new main house. Angel was also involved in improving the runway. Hatch and Angel used several horse-drawn implements pulled with two draft horses. Through this process the airfield was leveled and extended to 1700'. In order to gain more length Hatch removed the original lodge building. Over the remainder of his life he continually enhanced the ranch. Generally he worked on a barter system, hiring patients with the skills

At the same time improvements were being made at the ranch, Hatch agreed with the USFS to improve the trail from the Indian Springs Guard Station via Jack Creek to his property, in exchange for the use of more ground on his upper parcel.[205] Starting in 1940 the USFS obtained a lease for 7.3 acres from the collective Falconbery Loon Creek Lodge owners to build a guard station at the location that was originally called Indian Creek (the name was changed later to Falconberry to prevent confusion with the Indian Creek complex on the Middle Fork). In the end Hatch gave up 52 acres of land to the USFS.[206] The route he had built became dubbed the "Cart Trail," as Hatch had the agency widen it for a pair of horses to pull a wheeled cart up and down the path. He purposefully did not want it broad enough or overly improved to prevent four-wheel drive vehicles from using it. This trail provided better and shorter access to the ranch instead of having to come down the longer trail along Loon Creek. Timber for many of the structures was obtained along this route and many of the building supplies were hauled in this way.

Hatch juggled spending time at the ranch

with his busy life and family commitments in Idaho Falls. His wife Ruth and three kids spent weekends and vacations at the ranch through the years. His son Mark worked many summers helping with stock, haying, painting, and general chores. Hatch made an effort to make the ranch venture solvent and also hired people from time to time to help him run an outfitting and guiding business. Folks were put up in the guest cabins and taken on fishing and hunting trips. It was not uncommon for Hatch to join these excursions, guiding his guests. He eventually gave up on the outfitting business, and when it was still legal he leased his hunting area to various outfitters.[207]

Son Mark Hatch at Falconberry with the second CallAir.

Aviation, Airplanes, and Wrecks

Hatch, similar to others involved in the ranch, was a pilot and in 1949 purchased a new model A-3 CallAir (N2909V). Although not an ideal mountain airplane, Hatch liked getting a "deal" on things he bought, and had a connection at the small company. Hatch even flew the plane home from the factory located in Afton, Wyoming. Along with the acquisition came a set of skis that permitted him to access the ranch during the winter.[208]

The CallAir was used for many years. Hatch's pilot days came to an end after he wrecked the airplane attempting to land at the ranch on a hot summer afternoon. On approach to the airstrip he hit a bad downdraft and was unable to overcome the situation and stalled the plane into the upper field. He was badly injured, but recovered. The damaged aircraft was replaced with a 1951 model A-2 CallAir (N2916V), which Hatch flew several times to Falconberry. It then became evident to him that he simply did not fly enough to be piloting his own aircraft in and out of the ranch. The CallAir was sold and he began chartering with various companies.[209]

One of the first pilots he used to fly to the

Lawrence Johnson's wrecked Bellanca Skyrocket at the Falconberry Ranch.

J. M. Hatch

Repairing the Bellanca at the ranch shop. The tail of L. Johnson's Staggerwing Beech can also be seen.

ranch was Lawrence Johnson, who operated a small flying business from Hailey. Johnson primarily used a Beechcraft Model D-17S (N18V) Staggerwing and a Bellanca CH-400 Skyrocket (N6707) for his backcountry work.[210] Hatch used his services for several years until the early 1960s. The relationship ended when Hatch hired Johnson to fly himself, along with his friend Dr. Davis and his family, to the ranch. Because they had a large load of people and groceries Johnson used his Bellanca. Johnson came in too fast and attempted a small slip to bleed some airspeed off. The plane sunk more quickly than expected and the slip caused him to be misaligned with the touchdown area. The aircraft skidded off the runway into the rocks. The Bellanca came to an abrupt stop, catapulting a large watermelon forward that hit one of Davis's kids on the head. Other than a small, bruised, screaming child, no one was hurt.[211]

Mark Hatch watched the event unfold and rushed over to help people out of the plane. He then hitched up a pair of draft horses and assisted Johnson in pulling the plane back onto the runway. Assessing the damage, Johnson noted the prop was trashed and one wing was completely totaled. Mark pulled the plane to the shop. Meantime, another one of Johnson's pilots was notified and he flew in to pick Johnson up in the Staggerwing.[212] Later some crude field repairs were made to the Bellanca, which were rumored to have entailed plywood nailed to the wing spar.

Being shaken by the second aircraft accident at the ranch within a short time, Hatch began hiring other charter businesses. Pilots flying him frequently included Pete Hill of Idaho Falls, Paul Abbott of Abbott Aviation Inc. (Challis), Carol Jarvis of Salmon Air Taxi, Jim Searles of Air Unlimited (Challis), and Ed Browning and Vard Hendricks of Red Baron Flying Service (Idaho Falls).

Hatch also chartered with Johnson Flying Service of McCall when the new house was completed. In need of an airplane to fly large pieces of furnishings, Johnson brought a Ford Tri-Motor to the ranch. Commercial operators were not the only ones to use the airstrip, as Hatch had many friends who were pilots with their own airplanes. One fellow who flew frequently to the ranch was Ed Gregory. He was an engineer at the Idaho National Laboratory (INL) from the early days when it was called the Atomic Energy Commission. He mainly flew his Piper Cub back and forth from Idaho Falls to the ranch. Mark remembered riding with him several times. Just for amusement and to test the radar system at INL, he would maneuver the Cub on a route over the no-fly zone about twenty feet off the ground through a labyrinth of gullies. It was all in fun and he was never reprimanded. In July 1968 Gregory was killed while flying his Pitts Special over the Craters of the Moon lava beds.[213]

A Remote Tennis Court

One of the things that Hatch enjoyed about his ranch was "projecting" around the property – deciding which new project to undertake. It was his way of winding down and forgetting about the real world. By the mid-1970s this became a bit of dilemma when the Falconberry Ranch was in good condition and his "projects" completed. In need of a mission he somehow came up with the idea of building a tennis court. Doesn't every backcountry ranch need a tennis

A 1971 view of the Falconberry Ranch near the height of its development.

court? His family thought he was crazy, but their opinion mattered little and they understood his need for projects.[214]

Hatch again enlisted Charles Wilson for the job. Wilson not only helped him figure out the necessary materials, but he also walked in a Cletrac bulldozer and a Ford 8N tractor from Indian Springs for the job.[215] Sacks of cement were transported by truck to the Upper Loon Creek airstrip and then shuttled by Steve Mulberry in the fall of 1977 with his Cessna 185 (N2785J).[216] Hatch delighted in the activity brought about by the tennis court venture, despite the fact that he had never lifted a tennis racket in his life.[217]

The Mulberrys were family friends of the Hatchs and Steve Mulberry had returned from flying Cessna 185s out of Bethel, Alaska, for the summer. While in Alaska he saved enough money to purchase his own 185. Mulberry then leased the aircraft to Ed Browning's Red Baron Flying Service, with the agreement that he was the only pilot who could fly it. In the two weeks that Mulberry worked for Hatch, he made 149 landings at Falconberry while moving the cement. When late fall weather loomed in the forecast, an operator from Challis came in to help with a Cessna 206. Mulberry wore out a set of tires and brakes moving the heavy loads. The runway also had to be repaired as he had made a pair of ruts in the process.[218]

Looking back on the project, Mulberry, now a pilot for United Airlines, commented, "I was not too smart about the business side of it, I only charged Dr. John for the hours on the airplane. But my time flying in Idaho and out of the Falconberry are one of the highlights of my career." However after the project, Hatch was always generous with letting Mulberry spend time at the ranch. He lived there for a few months one winter, studying for FAA exams, and commuted to the outside with the 185. Also, when he and his wife were married in 1980 they honeymooned at the ranch. While there he even received a wedding gift delivery from pilot friend Clyde Ritter. Unannounced, Ritter flew in and left a brand new pair of 850X6 tires with a bow wrapped around them on the runway.[219]

As Mulberry flew the cement mix to the ranch, crews stacked the barn full of the bags. The following spring crews returned under the direction of Hatch and the real labor began. Hatch had workers haul gavel from Loon Creek to the site where it was mixed with the cement. Once the court was finished he spent time

Hatch standing on his property during the late 1980s Loon Creek flood. For the aging ranch owner the damage caused by the event was overwhelming.

Looking down Loon Creek at the former Falconberry Ranch in 2010 where the main building complex and airfield were located.

keeping it clean. In the early 1980s Hatch invited Fred Glimp and his family to the ranch for a vacation. Glimp, the Dean of Harvard College and an old Idaho friend of Hatch's, enjoyed tennis and brought along some rackets. Glimp and his son played the first and possibly the only match on the court.[220] Oddly enough the court remains one of the most visible remnants of the ranch.

Hatch Sells to the USFS

Shortly after the completion of the tennis court, Hatch understood he could not continue to keep up with the maintenance that he once found mentally relaxing. Although his son had a passion for the ranch, Hatch was a businessman and viewed it more as an asset rather than a family legacy. Acting on this, he quietly searched for a buyer. Several private individuals and corporations became interested, including the Nature Conservancy. The USFS also showed interest and offered the most money. Wrangling for the highest dollar, Hatch flew a group of appraisers from Las Vegas to the ranch, and countered on the agency's offer. The USFS agreed to the price, justifying the expenditure as an opportunity to naturalize the developed property.[221]

In 1980 after more than thirty years of owning the property, Hatch sold the over 190 acre parcel to the USFS with the reservation of a lifetime use. In the sale agreement it was clearly stated that the airstrip would be closed to the public and permanently closed after Hatch's death. In a letter to the Idaho Department of Aeronautics, Hatch asked for the field to be removed from all aeronautical charts and reference materials.[222]

With the lifetime use arrangement, he spent time at the ranch through the 1980s. As he aged and struggled with health issues, he spent less and less time at the place. During a tremendous spring runoff in the late 1980s Loon Creek flooded, sweeping away twenty to thirty feet of the stream's bank along the property. Along with the washout it flooded parts of the ranch, destroying buildings and the sawmill. It was the final breaking point. Unable to repair the damages, he lost interest. Hatch last visited his much-adored ranch in 1989 and died three years later.[223]

The ranch sat vacant for many years. In 1998 Travis Bullock received a contract from the USFS to pack everything out. Bullock packed the remnants on packstrings to the end of the road at Tin Cup Camp. From here it was hauled out over the road past the Diamond D Ranch. Prior to this the USFS had gutted the buildings and put debris in big piles. One outfitter in the area said for a few years it was so ugly that he was embarrassed to trail clients by the place. In August 2003 the remaining building shells burned in a wildfire. The USFS continues to use the upstream Falconberry Guard Station and an occasional airplane lands illegally at the ranch runway.

LOWER LOON CREEK

The Early Years, Simplots, Andy Anderson, and a Crash

Looking up the Middle Fork at the ranch with Loon Creek flowing in from the left.

In 1914 Robert Lee Ramey homesteaded the flat.[224] Ramey came to the Salmon River country in 1909 after hearing about it from his uncle, John Ramey. His uncle was a guide with Captain Bernard during the Sheepeater Campaign of 1879. Jack McGiveny had previously occupied the location, living in a small cabin. Ramey improved the place immensely, running cattle and cultivating the property. The acreage during this time was known as the Ramey Ranch. His brother Oscar joined him about the same time, and he expanded his operation by buying the downstream Mormon Ranch.[225]

Later owners of the ranch included Ray Mahoney, Sam Lovell, and Bob Simplot.[226] Simplot bought the property, along with the Tappan Ranch, in the mid-1940s at the urging of outfitter and guide acquaintance Andy Anderson. The two met in southern Idaho, and at the time the property had a decent shop and log cabin.[227]

A few years prior to Simplot's purchase a rough airfield was constructed. In June 1942 one of the backcountry's first fatal airplane accidents occurred here. Abraham Knowles, of Webb's Flying Service based in Boise, flew to the ranch in an open cockpit biplane. Knowles was flying out Harvey Jones, a twenty-two year old trapper who lived in a cabin three miles up Pungo Creek. Harvey had fallen ill and was going to Pocatello for medical attention. Shortly after takeoff the plane stalled in an attempt to miss a tree at the end of the airfield. The plane spun into the terrain on the other side of the river.[228]

Rescuers helped Knowles and Harvey out of the wreckage. Both were still alive, and Penn Stohr Sr. of Johnson Flying Service in Cascade flew into pick

the injured men up at the developed Mahoney airstrip upriver. Before they could get to the airfield, Harvey died.[229] Stohr, in Travel Air NC655H flew Knowles, who still needed medical help, from Mahoney along with Harvey's body to Cascade.[230]

The airstrip continued in use, and was later lengthened under Simplot's ownership while Andy Anderson was leasing it. In 1947 Anderson assigned the task to his son Ted and hired hand Shorty Waite. The two used a Fresno pulled by a pair of workhorses to complete the project. The runway was improved to its present length of 1200'.[231]

One day Waite was in the cabin lying in bed and noticed a rat stealing his matches out of a box that was sitting on a shelf. He reached over and grabbed his .22 caliber pistol and started shooting. It is not known if a bullet actually hit the critter or not, but the bullets miraculously hit the matches and sparked a fire. Waite jumped out of bed, pulled some shoes on, and ran outside. Climbing on the roof with a pail of water, he tried to douse the flames. In his haste he did not tie his bootlaces. While crawling off the roof

A Johnson Flying Service Travel Air 6000 landing at the Lower Loon Creek airstrip in the late 1940s.

The original log cabin at the ranch that was accidentally burned by Shorty Waite.

Ranch worker Shorty Waite.

for more water the laces caught on a nail and Waite got flipped upside down and was hanging off the burning building. Telling the story around a campfire years later, he created a colorful account of how he pulled himself out of the jam, "I says to myself said I – I got to do somethin or I'm a gonna be a goner. So I wrangled in my pocket, found my cuttin' knife, and cut the strings." Falling to the ground with a thud he was able to escape before the whole place burned to the ground.[232]

Along the way Bob Simplot signed the place over to his successful brother Jack. When Bob sold the Tappan Ranch in 1948 for $5,000, Jack also sold most of the acreage at Loon Creek for $8,500, keeping a few acres where the cabin and shop were located.[233] He also maintained use of the airstrip, located off the portion he retained. The Jack Simplot family continues to own the property and has leased it to various outfitters over the years. Most of the leaseholders also have leased the surrounding IDFG land to keep stock.

Middle Fork Lodge Lease

After Bill Harrah bought the Middle Fork Lodge he began leasing the Simplot property. The location was used for hunting parties, but mainly as a pick up point for river rafters. It was common for guests of the lodge to take a one-day float trip from Thomas Creek to Loon Creek. Here they were loaded into planes along with the boats and flown back to the lodge. Making it more efficient, Harrah pilot Blackmore introduced the idea of using the Twin Otter

The Lower Loon Creek airstrip in 1964.

Harrah's second Twin Otter parked at Lower Loon in July 1972.

Flying low and slow, the pilot caused a cross control stall and the plane fell out of the air. It crashed into a bench on the northwest side of the river, killing all four occupants. Evidence at the accident site indicated the aircraft had little to no forward velocity on impact.

The crash was the final straw, breaking Jim Searles's Air Unlimited flying business based in Challis. The year before, he had lost a matching orange de Havilland Beaver (N5157G), also on the Middle Fork. The pilot, carrying one other person, had a heart attack while on a downwind leg to land at the Mahoney airstrip. Prior to this accident, in 1979 he had lost a Cessna 182 (N3158Y) on the East Fork of the Salmon River.

Recent Years

In 1995, longtime Idaho outfitter and guide Scott Farr returned to the backcountry from a decade in Canada. Wanting to reenter the business he acquired both the Cougar and Loon Creek hunting areas and leased the Simplot property for his operation. As in his prior outfitting operations he needed an airplane that would haul decent loads, so he sold the float equipped Super Cub (C-GHYK) that he had been flying in British Columbia and bought a Cessna 206 (N8530Q).[236]

After a few seasons Farr kicked the idea around of trying to purchase the roughly ten acre Simplot property. Realizing you never know until you ask, he told Simplot of his interest in the place, if he ever thought of selling. Less than four weeks later a helicopter landed and Simplot himself stepped off, wanting to talk with Farr. Simplot commented that he would never sell the property as he wished he had never sold the other portion of it to the IDFG years ago. He did make the observation that the place had never looked better.[237]

Capitalizing on the compliment, Farr asked if he could make some improvements. Simplot told him

to shuttle people and gear back upriver. In 1967, wanting to make sure it was possible, he and another company pilot, Jack Usher, flew the lodge's first 100 series Twin Otter to the short strip. Pilots used the strip regularly thereafter.[234]

The use of Twin Otters at Loon Creek lasted through the early 1990s. The last 300 series Twin Otter owned by Harrah was part of the sale when John McCaw bought the Middle Fork Lodge. Dick Williams flew the plane during these final years when he also served as the lodge manager.[235]

Another Crash

In November 1983 one of Jim Searles orange de Havilland Beavers (N9006) departed Lower Loon Creek with three hunters aboard, headed to the Mahoney airstrip. Instead of continuing downriver to gain adequate altitude and space to maneuver upriver, the pilot made a quick 180-degree turn.

Jim Searles's de Havilland Beaver (N9006) that crashed following takeoff from the ranch in November 1983.

Part of the lease agreement is to maintain the state owned runway.[241]

Nearly up until his death in May 2008, Simplot made at least an annual trip to the property. While in his later years he flew to the place by helicopter, earlier he had always kept an airplane specifically for flying in the backcountry. His favorite and the plane he owned for the longest time was a Cessna 185 (N8414Q), which he bought new. Kirk Braun, who married one of the Simplot granddaughters, later acquired the plane. Starting in the early 1980s Simplot primarily flew with Braun and his McCall-based charter company, Pioneer Aviation, when traveling in the backcountry.[242]

to do whatever he wanted. For the next several years Farr did just that, first by remodeling the main cabin by extending the living space over the existing porch and by adding a bigger patio in front of the new addition. He then built a duplex for added living space, and tore apart the Harrah-built bunkhouse, utilizing the wood to construct a tack shed. At the same time he improved the water system.[238]

The final additions to the ranch were more guest quarters, which were acquired from upriver Middle Fork Lodge in 2001, when builder Ron Fry was hired to replace the old Harrah cabins at the lodge with custom log structures. Not wanting the Harrah cabins to go to waste, Farr worked a deal to obtain them. Farr then contacted Dave Handy of the Flying B who owned a rubber sweep boat. The buildings were taken apart and Handy floated them down the Middle Fork to Loon Creek. It took a total of eight trips to move four cabins, with three of them going to the Simplot property and one going to the IDFG section. After each trip the boat was collapsed and flown back to Thomas Creek in Farr's Cessna 206.[239]

Farr continued to operate from the Loon Creek property while also working at the Middle Fork Lodge. He eventually left for full-time work at the lodge. The lease on the Simplot property has changed hands a few times in recent years, but is currently held by Middle Fork Outfitters, owned by Ron and Karla Ens.[240] Ens also has the lease with the IDFG, which is the only remaining state lease in the backcountry.

Searles's de Havilland Beavers in Challis shortly after he took delivery of them in 1979. The Beaver in the background is still in military colors awaiting a new paint scheme.

The 1200' Lower Loon Creek airstrip and ranch.

95

TRIPLE CREEK RANCH

The Early Years

Looking down Warm Springs Creek at the Triple Creek airstrip and ranch in 2011.

Horace Johnson occupied the property in the early 1900s and in July 1909 filed a homestead claim. Within the next four years he built a log house and barn and had land under cultivation. In April 1914 he received approval on his claim for 102.81 acres.[243] The place was then purchased by Mr. Foster and became known as the Foster Ranch.

Harold McKean and Clark Heiss then bought the place in the 1950s. McKean was a pilot and roughed-in a workable airstrip for easier access. The owners split a chunk of land off the southeast corner and then sold the rest of the property to Charles Carte. Carte had dreams of making Triple Creek a fly-in hunting and fishing destination similar to Marv Hornback's Pistol Creek Ranch. He made some small improvements to the airstrip and planned on dividing the operation into shares.

Loening - Triple Creek Ranch

In 1964 Mike Loening bought Carte's part of the old ranch. Loening discovered the Idaho backcountry after arriving in the state on his honeymoon with first wife, Elaine DuPont. The two were flying the western United States in a 1937 Gullwing Stinson and ended up in Salmon. In 1953 they purchased land eighteen miles south of Salmon on Rattlesnake Creek and named it Twin Peaks Ranch. Originally, the Loenings ran it as a cattle operation and later as a dude ranch.[244] Since they were both pilots, a modest 800′ strip was constructed on the property and the Stinson

was replaced with a Cessna 195 and a Piper Super Cub.[245]

In addition to Twin Peaks, the Loenings started Salmon Air Taxi circa 1955 and based it at the Salmon airport.[246] Loening became an Idaho aviation icon in his own right, not to mention that he was from a family entrenched in America's aviation history. His father, Grover, was a well-known aeronautical engineer who had an impressive career. He managed the Wright Company in Dayton, Ohio, for Orville Wright, became the United States military's first civilian aeronautical engineer, designed many aircraft, founded his own aircraft company, and authored several aviation-related books. Mike quickly became accomplished in aviation as well, earning the 1970 National Point Champion title with his modified P-51, served multiple terms as president of the National Pilots Association, and started an air taxi business.

With Salmon Air Taxi up and running, he expanded to Boise in 1963, buying Roberts Flying Service and renaming it Loening Air Inc. Loening was innovative, as he was one of the first people to bring modern equipment to the Idaho backcountry by buying one of the area's first Cessna 185s (N185ML) and one of the first Cessna 206s (N206LA).[247] He

The initial hangar in Salmon that Mike Loening used for the Salmon Air Taxi business. Loening (left) and pilot Bill Scherer (right) are standing in front of a Piper Cub and a Cessna 185.

Mike Loening and Bill Scherer at the Boise operation in 1963.

Loening's P-51 Mustang.

even outbid big names like Johnson Flying Service for smokejumper contracts. In 1967 he sold the Salmon operation to Carol Jarvis.

Loening ran an outfitting and guiding business at the Root Ranch in the early 1960s in connection with his flying company. When he and Elaine divorced, the Twin Peaks Ranch was sold. Loening then moved full-time to Boise and married Marilyn Borup. By the late 1960s he began to spend more time on improving the Triple Creek property. He started outfitting from the new location under the name of Raw Hide Camps Inc., and obtained help from packer Arch Marsing.[248]

Wanting to add accommodations for himself and guests, he hired one of his pilots, Bill Scherer, and a crew to build a small lodge, tack shed, and outhouse. At about the same time, Loening bought an International T-9 bulldozer from local Challis rancher Bud L. Nelson. Part of the sale agreement was that Nelson would deliver the dozer to the ranch. Nelson's son Steve flew him over the area in a Cessna 172 (N8363X) to scout the best route. Coincidentally Steve had recently taken a check ride for his license with Loening and landed at the ranch during the exam.[249]

Based on the information gathered from the flight, Nelson walked the bulldozer in over the Sleeping Deer Road along Mahoney Creek Ridge, and then followed a drainage down to the ranch.[250] The machine was then used to expand the airstrip an additional 200' on the east end, bringing it to a total

The Bill Scherer family at Triple Creek in the early 1970s.

Landing upstream at Triple Creek in 1970.

based in Boise for Aero Union of Chico, California.[252]

In February 1977 Loening was killed flying his son Scott and the son's friend Linda Winter in the rugged Uinta Mountains near Duchesne, Utah.[253] The 206 (N72308) he was flying crashed en route from Colorado to Boise near frozen Betsy Lake. The plane was not found until two days after the accident occurred, leaving all three to die of exposure in a severe winter storm at high elevation.[254]

While newspapers speculated about causes of the accident, pilots and friends who knew Loening's knowledge and skills, deduced water in the gas was the primary reason for the engine failure. It is not known whether he was flying above an overcast layer, or if he was scud running below a layer, when the engine quit. But it is believed that he spotted the snow-covered lake and planned to make an emergency landing there. His effort to reach the lake dead stick was hindered when one of the plane's wings struck something on the top of a cirque above the lake. The wing severed, causing the plane to barrel roll. Loening amazingly maintained some forward control and the plane made it to the lake fairly intact, but upside down on the lake's surface. The well-below freezing temperatures at the scene were too harsh for the three to endure.

Following services, Loening's ashes were spread over his Triple Creek Ranch. Wanting to create a memorial for him, Marilyn, daughter Lynne, Joe Cenaurrusa, and Frank Giles worked hard to have a mountain in the Middle Fork country named in his honor. The group wanted the prominent land feature, which Loening used as a navigation point when flying from Boise to Triple Creek, to bear his name. Thus Mount Loening stands east of Horseshoe Lake at the

of 2600'. Most of the large building materials were driven to the small Silva airstrip north of Stanley and flown in under contract with Harrah's Twin Otter. Clay Lacy in his personal Turbo Porter also flew in smaller loads. Scherer and Loening also hauled loads with 206s.[251]

While Loening was making changes at Triple Creek, adjustments were being made to his Boise operation. He sold it to Don Watkins, who renamed it Boise Air Service. Loening remained with the company for a short time and eventually started his own aircraft brokerage business using the Loening Air title. Supplementing his business, he flew TBMs for Milt Smilanich and later piloted a B-17 tanker headwaters of Loon Creek in the Tango Peaks. In the early 1980s after the landmark was named, a large fly-in was held at the Smiley Creek airport, and attended by Loening's family and friends.[255]

After his untimely death at age forty-four, his family continued to enjoy Triple Creek. Family friend's John Jeffcoat and Frank Giles looked after the place. For many years Giles ran an outfitting business from the ranch, often helped by Loening's son, Mark. Through these years the ranch remained under his first wife's name. However, in 1990 she was killed in a car accident and their daughter Lynne Loening inherited it. Lynne and her husband Sage Dorsey continue to enjoy the place along with other family members. The couple has a private strip at their regular residence near Bend, Oregon, and the Dorseys own a Cessna 182 (N91753) to commute to the ranch property.

Patrick Property and SP Aircraft |

In the early 1990s Scott Patrick of Boise acquired the parcel McKean and Heiss split off from the original homestead. Patrick envisioned building a cabin on the property, but due to legal conflicts could not obtain regular use of the airstrip. Unfortunately on September 25, 2011, he died at age fifty-nine, when he did not recover from a scheduled heart surgery.

Patrick was a well-known pilot in the Idaho backcountry and respected by many. In 1982, after flying for several operators, he established SP Aircraft in Boise. One of his four children, Andy, who flew regularly for the family operation, continues in his father's footsteps with the business.

Holm

A current look at the Triple Creek Ranch.

UPPER LOON CREEK/ DIAMOND D RANCH

The State Builds an Airstrip

Looking upstream at the Upper Loon Creek airstrip in 2010.

Chet Moulton, director of the Idaho Department of Aeronautics, pushed for public access in this area, starting in the early 1960s. Working with the USFS, Moulton chose the location of the current Upper Loon Creek airstrip. With all parties in agreement, the USFS issued "a special use permit for the purpose of constructing and maintaining a public use airport." Preliminary work was started in 1964 and the following year it was finished to a total length of 2500'.[256] The state continues to maintain this airstrip.

Former Townsites and the Diamond D Ranch

Several historical features dot the landscape to the south of the airfield along an access road, including the mining townsites of Oro Grande and Casto. Oro Grande was founded in 1869 after gold deposits were found nearby. The small area boomed and busted within three years. However, a small Chinese population inhabited the community, reworking old claims. In February 1879 five of these Chinese were brutally murdered and the killers were believed to be hostile Native Americans, which sparked the Sheepeater Indian Campaign.[257] After the campaign ended, the Indians denied having any involvement.

While small remnants can still be seen of both towns, interpretive signs are also in place. Several larger ruins stand at the late-1800s era Casto site that was burned by a wildfire in 2006. The stone basement and living area of the former Casto hotel is the most visible.

Three miles south of the Upper Loon Creek airstrip sits the beautiful Diamond D Ranch. The Coleman family originally homesteaded the ranch at the turn of the twentieth century. Neighboring them to the west was another smaller place occupied by the Metcalf family. One of the Coleman's daughters, Lillian, married John Boyle, who worked for the USFS, and the two acquired their own land on the east side of Mayfield Creek. Boyle was then drafted during World War I. With the belief that he would not return from the war, the land was deeded to his mother.[258]

To Boyle's surprise he returned from military duty and by 1933 combined all three homesteads into one and it became known as the Boyle Ranch. Sometime thereafter Boyle's brother Joe acquired the ranch.[259]

Joe Boyle worked as the Idaho state manager for Hiram Walker, a major liquor company known for creating Canadian Club whiskey. His boss in the company was John Demorest, who in 1951 visited the ranch with his family while in the process of moving from Michigan to California. Demorest was taken with the beauty of the place, and the following year became a partner with Boyle in the property. The Demorests only lived out West one year and returned

100

An Intermountain Aviation Twin Otter at Upper Loon Creek in the late 1960s.

suited for a landing area. In the early 1960s, prior to the construction of the Upper Loon Creek strip, he graded out an 1800' runway with an International TD-9. The first person to land here was Ed Osterman of Challis with a Cessna 182. The field saw minimal use and has not been used for many years.[264]

A day in November 1995 was one of the last times the impromptu airstrip was used, when Scott Patrick of SP Aircraft flew to the field with a Cessna 180 (N52095). Patrick was

to Michigan, spending summer vacations at the ranch.[260]

At the urging of his son, Tom, who had recently graduated from the University of Michigan, John Demorest became sole owner of the ranch in 1960. Tom moved to Idaho and began building the ranch into a full-time business that he still operates today. Under their complete control the property was renamed the Diamond D Ranch.[261]

Over a lifetime Demorest has developed the secluded property into an impressive backcountry operation. In 1960 the property only contained the Coleman homestead house and barn along with a few 1930s era cabins constructed by the Boyles. Demorest was able to save and renovate the original Coleman buildings. Since then he has added a generator house, shop, recreation building, swimming pool/hot tub, an executive cabin, and bunkhouse with private living quarters and an office for the business.[262]

The Diamond D Ranch offers a wide variety of accommodations and activities throughout the year. Annual outfitting and guiding during the summer and fall has been a mainstay.[263]

Even with a road to the property, Demorest wanted the conveniences provided by aircraft. In the 1940s aircraft landed in a hayfield located on the west side of the ranch. However, Demorest felt a large flat spot on the eastern portion of the ranch was better

attempting to fly two passengers and some gear to the Flying B Ranch, but due to weather was unable to reach the destination or turn back to Boise. He opted to land at the Diamond D Ranch where he and his clients spent the night.

The next morning they boarded the plane and prepared for a flight to the Flying B. Patrick firewalled the 180 and as the plane bounced down the field he could tell he was not going to make it and safely aborted the takeoff. He turned around and gave it another try. The aircraft came off the ground this time, but barely. In an effort to build his airspeed he nosed it over, putting it into ground effect. Unfortunately, as the plane came over the bottom end of the pasture, the left main wheel caught a fence and was torn off along with the tail wheel. As pieces broke away from the plane it dipped downward and the left wing tip struck a tree.

Astoundingly, Patrick kept the plane in the air. Assessing the damage the best he could, he decided that the plane was flying well enough to continue. Patrick ruled out landing at any of the close airstrips and diverted to Challis where he had the best chance of making a safe emergency landing, which he did.

1

Holm

2

T. Demorest

3

T. Demorest

5

T. Demorest

4

CLAYTON

IDAHO

BIG GAME
HUNTING

DIAMOND D RANCH

Holm collection

1 *The entrance to the Diamond D Ranch.*
2 *The main Coleman built structure that now serves as the main lodge.*
3 *A 1930s photograph of the current lodge.*
4 *A 1960s promotional brochure for the ranch.*
5 *Diamond D Ranch owners John Demorest and son Tom relax on the porch in the early 1960s.*
6 *The renovated Coleman lodge and surrounding buildings at the ranch in 2011.*
7 *The interior of the main lodge.*
8 *In the 1940s a field on the western portion of the ranch was used as a landing site.*
9 *Current owner Tom Demorest taking a break at the ranch in the 1960s.*
10 *In the early 1960s Demorest smoothed out an 1800' landing area in a lower field on the east side of the ranch (center). The site is no longer active.*

MIDDLE FORK
OF THE SALMON RIVER
CAMAS CREEK

CASTLE CREEK –
UPPER AND LOWER

Looking down Castle Creek at the Upper Castle Creek airstrip. The Lower Castle Creek strip can be seen paralleling the drainage on the far side of the creek.

In December 1919 Ernest R. Splettstosser homesteaded 160 acres after living for five years at the location. At that time the upstream end of the property had a cabin, storehouse, barn, and cultivated fields.[265] In Splettstosser's later years his neighbors, the Wilsons and the Andersons, frequently checked in on him.[266] Worth Boggeman, who bought the Anderson's Bar X Ranch on Silver Creek, eventually acquired Splettstosser's land. The property was then split into four sections. The center parcels were rather small, while the extreme ends were large enough for their own airstrips. These two properties with runways are commonly known to pilots as "Upper" and "Lower" Castle creeks.

Boggeman sold the upper property to Mr. Reddekopp who was a pilot and is believed to have built the airstrip. Reddekopp then sold it to a group of four men from California. In 1972 two of the men backed out, leaving Dick McAfee and Dan Drake as the sole owners of the property. McAfee, the owner of Cycleland Speedway near Chico, California, enjoyed the great outdoors, most of all hunting and fishing. His brother, Hugh, had found the piece of property advertised in an issue of *United Farm Catalog*. Drake was a land developer from the same area and served more as a silent partner.[267]

In the beginning, McAfee and his wife Ramona only spent time at the ranch seasonally until new accommodations could be built. The first year at the property they lived in Splettstosser's original cabin. Recalling the rough conditions Ramona remarked, "It was the wrong introduction to the Idaho backcountry for a person from San Francisco. Rats and mice were crawling around at night and it was not much of a cabin. This later changed and I grew to love spending time at the ranch." Within a few years McAfee replaced several logs on the old place and built his wife a new cabin.[268]

Tired of commuting back and forth, they moved permanently to the ranch in 1977. Living at Castle Creek full-time, they added a personal cabin for Drake and his wife, and other structures for guest

The original Splettstosser cabin as it appeared in 1973.

Ramona and Dick McAfee with their dog Starr, at the Castle Creek property in 1998.

Del Mallan and McAfee (on backhoe) cutting grass on the Upper Castle Creek airstrip in 1995.

quarters. McAfee also improved the runway with a small dozer, lengthening it to a total of 2000' with an estimated 1800' usable.[269]

At about the same time the airstrip was improved, McAfee built a 1500' runway on the opposite end of the old homestead for neighbors Jerry and Evelyn Williams, which became known as Lower Castle Creek. These two built a new cabin and used it primarily as a second residence.[270]

In the midst of the all the improvements, McAfee acquired neighbor Ken Stickler's hunting area in 1976 and started Castle Creek Outfitters. He used the upper airstrip to fly clients in. He did a fair amount of the flying himself, generally using a Cessna 182 (N9138R), but also used commercial operators. Drake was also a pilot and accessed the property mainly with a Cessna 210.[271]

Ramona devised a business plan of her own to bring supplemental income to the operation, by advertising the ranch for backcountry fly-in breakfasts. Later she created a bed-and-breakfast for pilots. Her

venture was well received and the McAfee's hosted a wide variety of pilots and people over the years. When she first opened the operation she made an effort to photograph customers with their airplanes. Her large collection of photographs papered the walls of the dining area for years and was a local attraction. In fact many of the folks in the pictures continue to stay in touch with her.[272] The largest airplane to show up at the ranch during a fly-in breakfast was the Middle Fork Lodge's Twin Otter flown by Dick Williams. Williams also landed the plane at the lower airstrip.[273]

1 *Final approach to the 2000' Upper Castle airstrip.*
2 *Dick McAfee with his Cessna 182 at the ranch in 1998.*
3 *Salmon Air Taxi owner Dan Schroeder (left) and family (right) at the property in the 1980s with a ski-equipped Cessna 185. Dick McAfee is kneeling on the far right.*
4 *The Middle Fork Lodge's Twin Otter at Castle Creek for a visit. Standing (l to r): Dick Williams, McAfee, Hank, Ken Jones, and Sam Davis.*
5 *Looking up the Castle Creek drainage in 2011. The lower 1500' runway is in the foreground, while the longer upper airstrip is in the background to the right.*

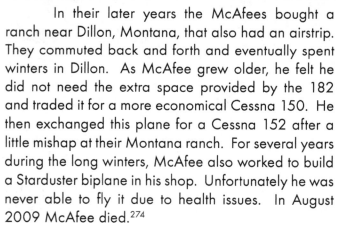

In their later years the McAfees bought a ranch near Dillon, Montana, that also had an airstrip. They commuted back and forth and eventually spent winters in Dillon. As McAfee grew older, he felt he did not need the extra space provided by the 182 and traded it for a more economical Cessna 150. He then exchanged this plane for a Cessna 152 after a little mishap at their Montana ranch. For several years during the long winters, McAfee also worked to build a Starduster biplane in his shop. Unfortunately he was never able to fly it due to health issues. In August 2009 McAfee died.[274]

Six years earlier the McAfees had sold their portion of the Castle Creek property to John Gregory. After McAfee's death his ashes were spread over the property and Ramona placed a memorial at the top of the runway honoring him. In September 2010 Ramona sold his Cessna 152 and donated the Starduster to the local Missoula chapter of the Experimental Aircraft Association. Her son continues to operate Castle Creek Outfitters from Salmon.[275]

A view down Camas Creek with the Meyers Cove property center. The former airstrip remains visible paralleling the creek on the left side of the drainage in the open area above the West Fork of Camas Creek, which flows in from the left.

MEYERS COVE/ WILSON RANCH

Early Homesteads

This area, located at the confluence of Camas Creek, Silver Creek, and West Fork of Camas Creek, was settled after the turn of the twentieth century. In August 1912 Andrew E. Lee was the first to homestead a parcel in the area.[276] Five more homesteads were approved over the next two decades. The last one of the five was granted in 1936 to William "Bill" Wilson for 119.81 acres along Camas Creek north of the others.[277] Wilson later married the daughter of a neighboring rancher and eventually acquired all the properties.[278]

Wilson worked hard cultivating the land, running cattle, and working as an outfitter in the Middle Fork area. Because of the large operation, most referred to the area as the Wilson Ranch. However, after the Meyers Cove Post Office closed, Wilson adopted the name "Meyers Cove," as the mail was then delivered to his ranch because of its central location to his neighbors.[279]

Stricklers, Simplot, and an Airstrip

Wilson sold the ranch in the early 1950s to Ken and Guy Strickler. The brothers already owned property eight miles up Camas Creek at Goat Creek, called Hidden Valley Ranches. Ken Stickler ran a mobile home and transport business in California and often spent summers in Idaho. Stickler, always looking to make money, saw the purchase as an opportunity to run more cattle and acquire an outfitting and guiding business.[280]

Ken Strickler's son, Ted, ran the ranch through the late 1950s. During this time they had several employees and continued to maintain what the Wilsons had worked hard to build. The Stricklers added a few bunkhouses for guests, moved a couple of buildings, and removed a barn. At the height of the operation the ranch had 480 head of cattle.[281]

Not long after they purchased the ranch, Jack Simplot approached them about landing on the northern part of their property that paralleled the east side of Camas Creek to access his Fluorspar Mine. The mine was located between Fluorspar and Duck creeks. The Stricklers gave him permission but the small narrow uphill landing spot was difficult. After a company pilot and Piper Cub made two landings on the crude airstrip, the pilot voiced his dissatisfaction.

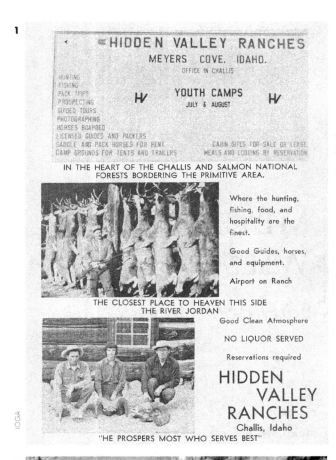

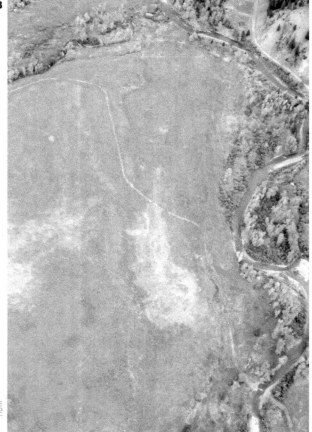

He considered the landing strip too risky for himself and the aircraft.

Simplot then found a second location for an airfield that also happened to be on the Strickler's property. Strickler again agreed and Ted mowed one of their hayfields located on a small bench, paralleling the west side of Camas Creek and perpendicular to the south side of the West Fork of Camas Creek. The roughly 800' strip was then combed for rocks with a tractor and lined with a few log markers. Simplot's pilots, flying a Cub, used the runway starting in about 1953 through the early 1960s. They only had one incident at the strip when a wheel was ripped off the main gear on landing. Fortunately the wheel broke loose at a low speed and did little damage to the aircraft.[282] Dick Williams made the last known landing here in the early 1980s with a Piper Super Cub (N8480H). Williams was not even sure it was an official airstrip, but had seen it from the air for many years and just could not resist giving it a try.[283]

The Striklers continued to use the ranch into the 1960s as part of their upper Hidden Valley Ranch property until Ted moved back to California. For several years the ground was leased to local cattlemen for grazing during the summer. Strickler began to see the property as a business loss and debated selling. Ted objected, wanting him to at least keep some of the property for future cabin sites.[284] However, Hidden Valley Ranches sold all 476.24 acres to the USFS in April 1970.[285] The Strickler family did retain their original parcel at the mouth of Goat Creek and continue to use it each summer for recreation.[286]

Holm

A view down Rams Creek at the Ramshorn Ranch.

RAMSHORN RANCH

In 1919 Frank Allison homesteaded the 152 acre property, which he named the Ramshorn Ranch. By the time it was approved he had built a house, barn, cellar, and was cultivating a sizable portion of the land.[287] In the summer of 1931 Allison hosted famous writer Zane Grey at the ranch. It was a common practice for Grey to travel for book research by visiting places he was going to write about. Interested in developing a story loosely based on the Thunder Mountain Gold Rush of the early 1900s he wanted to gain a feel for the country.[288]

Grey hired renowned Salmon, Idaho, outfitter Elmer Keith to take him and his entourage, which included his son and daughter with their spouses, a family friend, two stenographers, and his Japanese cook, though the Idaho Primitive Area hunting and fishing. The trip was ultimately planned to end in the Thunder Mountain Mining District and then return to Salmon.[289]

To manage the large party Keith hired two additional packers, Charles Warnock and Jerry Ravndal, who also provided their own personal packstrings.[290] The group met some delays early in the trip because of forest closures caused by wildland fires. Once the travel restrictions were lifted the crew trucked everything to the confluence of Silver and Camas creeks. They stayed the night with Allison at the ranch and then departed down Camas Creek to the Middle Fork.[291]

Several days were spent at a camp below the mouth of Camas Creek near Bear Creek. While at this location Grey received a telegram delivered by a USFS employee. After reading it he decided to leave the trip. Ravndal later noted, "I don't know what it said, but I've often wondered about that telegram. I think he could see the trip was going to get too rough for him to enjoy, and had sent it himself."[292]

A few of Grey's friends stayed on to perform the needed research. From here the remaining group rode down to the Mormon Ranch, then to Waterfall Creek, where they crossed the Middle Fork and headed up Big Creek. The crew then camped in the Cold Meadows area before departing for Monumental Creek and Thunder Mountain. After seeing all the sights in the old mining district, the outfit returned through Marble and Camas creeks to the Ramshorn Ranch. The two-month trip had its problems, the biggest being that Grey's first check to Keith bounced. Only half of the trip was ever paid for, which only allowed Keith to compensate his guides and cover some of the costs. However, in 1935 when the book *Thunder Mountain* was released, Keith was sent an autographed copy from the wealthy author.[293] Ravndal summed up the 1931 event, "I've always been a great fan of Zane Grey. His books actually made the West famous. But the one on Thunder Mountain, I think was the poorest he ever wrote – he didn't even finish it, in my opinion. Just like he didn't finish the trip. At any rate, that trip was sure quite an experience for me! I'll never forget it!"[294]

In memory of Grey visiting the ranch, Allison named the little cabin he stayed in the "Zane Grey Cabin" – a sign still hangs over the door. Allison sold the ranch to Red Kopp and he transformed it into a dude ranch operation called Ramshorn Guest

The current building complex at the property owned by the Ramshorn Limited Partnership LLP. The unfinished lodge is located in the upper left of the photograph.

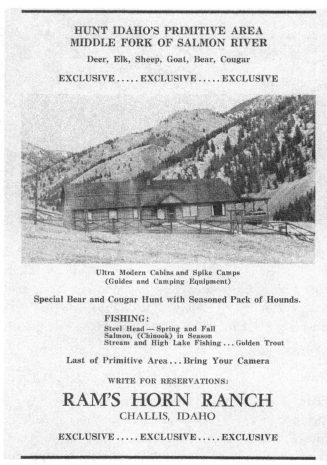

A 1963 advertisement for the ranch.

Ranch. Kopp added several buildings and updated the already existing lodge. By the 1950s the ranch was purchased by Don French, a co-founder of Cactus Pete's Casino, in Jackpot, Nevada. Originally French had his gaming operations located in Idaho, but when the state outlawed gambling he and his partner, "Cactus Pete" Piersanti, moved across the state line. Piersanti is credited with founding the town of Jackpot.[295]

Rumor in the backcountry was that French was hiding out from the mob and figured the Ramshorn Ranch was a safe place to lay low. During French's tenure he had a private four-room cabin built about one hundred yards below the main lodge. It was not uncommon for him to be accompanied by several bodyguards while at the ranch. It is unlikely that he was really under a threat from the mob as in the late 1950s he subdivided the lower part of the property into 128 parcels and advertised them for sale. However, he kept a 90 acre tract of land for his own use on the upper end where the lodge was located. Most of the lots were sold through his connections at the casino or to close friends. The lots were so small that in order to feasibly build a structure, customers generally had to purchase at least three.[296]

About the same time the subdivision was platted, a 2200' airstrip was constructed on the upper portion of the ranch. French's son-in-law Joe Smith was the main equipment operator for the job. Smith used a scraper and a Terex bulldozer to build the runway and by 1960 it was smoothed and completed.[297]

A few years after airplanes began using the property, the place was sold to Clarence Pheachy who ran it as a dude ranch into the 1970s under the name Ram's Horn Ranch. He built his own cabin about forty yards below the main lodge. Pheachy sold the ranch to a doctor from Boise who only owned it for a short time after becoming involved in a malpractice lawsuit. At the time the legal issues arose, the doctor had started construction on a 7,200 square foot, four-story lodge. In the end the doctor had no insurance and the property defaulted back to Pheachy.[298] The new lodge was abandoned and never finished.

In 1982 a conglomerate came together under the title of Ramshorn Limited Partnership LLP and purchased the ranch. Twenty-one shares were created and sold. It is a very casual organization, where shareholders make reservations on a first-come, first-served, basis. Owners are from all over the country including some from Ohio, Illinois, California, Washington, and a few as close as Salmon. The private airport has some use from shareholders and is regularly maintained.[299]

Looking up Rams Creek at the Ramshorn Ranch airstrip.

SILVER CREEK/
B BAR C

The main lodge at the ranch while under the ownership of Andy and Joe Anderson.

This area near the junction of Rams and Silver creeks was widely utilized by Native Americans. It was an annual summer camp used for fishing and hunting through the early 1900s. In 1913 Robert Lee Ramey attempted to homestead the property. Three years before, he had also applied for a 121 acre spread at the mouth of Loon Creek, which was approved in 1914. At this point he moved full-time to the Loon Creek property.[300] Several others came and went from the place until March 1936, when Max Oyler homesteaded 103 acres at the location.[301]

Oyler set out to improve the property and built a sizable lodge in addition to the already-existing cabin, as well as blacksmith shop and corrals. Beginning in 1938 Oyler allowed acquaintance Andy Anderson to take clients hunting and fishing while he stayed at the lodge. Anderson liked the ranch so much that he and his brother Joe bought the place in about 1942 and named it the Bar X Ranch. It became a fully functioning ranch for several years until he sold it in about 1952.[302]

A view up the Silver Creek drainage at the current B Bar C property.

Worth Boggeman of Jacksboro, Texas, bought the property from Anderson. Boggeman, a large boat dealer and marina owner in Texas, made his own improvements to the place, adding a summer cabin, barn, and a good-size dam that now bears his name for water storage. In the late 1970s Boggeman wanted to increase his property value and hired neighbor Dick McAfee to rough in a 1400' airstrip. Boggeman also renamed the ranch the B Bar C. The "B" signified his name, while the "C" represented his partner Lew Carlisle. Carlisle was originally an airline pilot who left the business to fly for the Los Angeles Dodgers baseball team. The Dodgers were the first professional sports team to have their own airplane. Carlisle became the second pilot to hold the position, generally flying the team's Boeing 720 Fan Jet. He was killed in a car accident in France while on vacation.

As Boggeman aged he and his wife spent more and more time in Texas to be with family. He sold the ranch in the mid-1990s to local real estate agent Preston Dixon. Under Dixon's ownership the ranch was mainly used as a second home or a place to hold retreats. By the end of the decade Berend Friehe of Washington had bought the property.[303]

Unlike Dixon, Friehe occasionally uses the airstrip to reach the ranch. Since his purchase he has rebuilt Oyler's lodge located at the mouth of Ramshorn Creek. One of the more interesting buildings on the property was used to house the Meyers Cove Post Office. Although not easily identifiable because of multiple remodels, it is at the center of one structure. Friehe leases the B Bar C to Middle Fork Outfitters owned by Ron and Karla Ens. The Ens also hold leases on the Middle Fork at Lower Loon Creek.[304]

Looking down Silver Creek at the ranch. The 1400' airstrip is located between and parallel to the creek and the road.

An early 1960s advertisement for Boggeman's ranch.

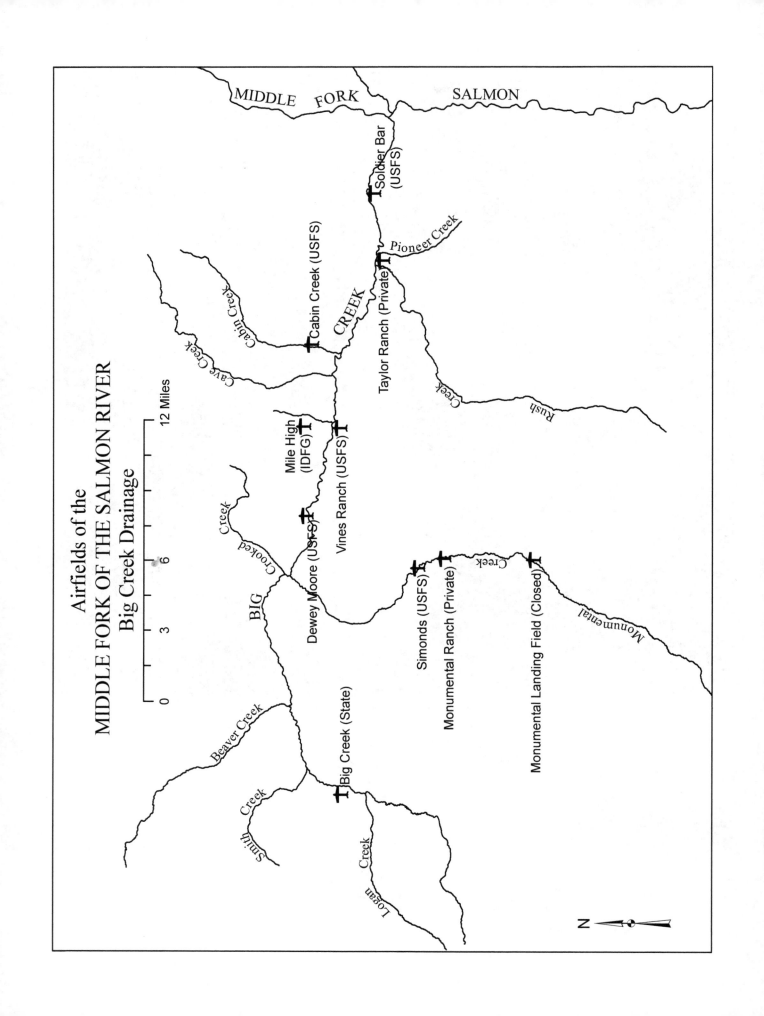

Airfields of the
MIDDLE FORK OF THE SALMON RIVER
Big Creek Drainage

MIDDLE FORK OF THE SALMON RIVER
BIG CREEK

BIG CREEK

Edwardsburg and the USFS

Looking down the Big Creek airfield in the early 1930s. The original USFS complex can be seen on the right. Notice the unaltered lower meadow that makes up the majority of the current runway.

The Big Creek drainage, which is one of the largest tributaries to the Middle Fork, attracted many people during the Thunder Mountain Gold Rush. William and Annie Edwards traveled to the area and in 1904 founded the small town of Edwardsburg located at the headwaters of Big Creek. Edwards, a mining attorney, sought to profit from the gold rush by opening a small law practice along with a general store and post office, mainly run by his wife. Edwardsburg served as a year-round hub for area residents into the mid-1940s, until mining activity tapered off. The Edwards's operation was somewhat taken over by their only son Napier, who lived at the townsite until his death in 1965. The ruins of their original house/store can still be seen behind Gillihan's Lodge near Logan Creek. Edwardsburg is now mainly comprised of well-kept private cabin sites that are used during the summers.

In 1920 the area around the current airfield became a ranger station. Fred Williams served as the first Big Creek District ranger, operating from a tent. Over the years the site became a major USFS headquarters. The first permanent buildings were built on the southeast side of the present runway. The original ranger station has since burned down, but the beautifully-built commissary remains. In the 1930s the CCC had a seasonal camp on the northwest side of the approach end of the runway. By the 1940s and into the 1950s the main USFS facilities were moved across the runway to the west side, where they remain today.

The Big Creek Hotel

To the south of the airstrip and current USFS buildings was the Big Creek Hotel/Store. For decades the hotel was an Idaho backcountry attraction for many travelers, particularly for pilots who enjoyed a good cup of coffee and a home-style country breakfast.

In the mid-1930s Dick Cowman and brother-in-law Joe Bayok built the lodge and the other early associated structures. The modest outfit, operated by Cowman and his wife Sophie, had several rooms

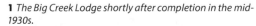

1 *The Big Creek Lodge shortly after completion in the mid-1930s.*
2 *Johnson Flying Service pilots Warren Ellison (left) and Bob Fogg (second from left) on a supply flight to Big Creek circa 1946 with a Travel Air 6000. Big Creek Lodge owner Dick Cowman is third from left with friend Wilmer Shaver (far right).*
3 *The Big Creek Lodge in the 1970s.*
4&5 *A chimney or electrical fire destroyed the Big Creek Lodge in September 2008. Arnold aviation pilot Walt Smith happened to be flying by and captured the event on film.*

for rent and a nice-sized dining area for guests and other passing customers. In addition to the lodging business they sold goods and ran a post office at various times. The function of the place remained the same, but went through many owners. In 1947 the Cowmans sold it to the Weymouths, who turned it over in 1951 to Horace Fereday, who sold it to Carl Whitmore. The Harpers then purchased the lodge and sold it to Harry Eaton and two partners. In 1973 Bruce Minter acquired the place. He and a partner sold time-shares, which turned into a messy situation. In the mid 2000s Scott and Trudy Fodor obtained the

A fire patrol airplane landing at Big Creek during the summer of 1936.

lodge. Unfortunately, in the fall of 2008 while under their ownership, a chimney or electrical fire burned the place down. The historic lodge and outbuildings were constructed on USFS leased land and were not rebuilt.[305]

The Airstrip

Starting in 1926 the USFS began using the land where the current upper portion of the airfield is located, for grazing pack animals. In 1929 the pasture developed into an aircraft-landing site.[306] James Hornberger a mining foreman in the Big Creek area, worked with the USFS on the project and utilized his crews from the Golden Hand and Werdenhoff Mines to do the initial clearing.[307] The runway was later smoothed out with equipment and measured 1300' long. It was not until the early 1940s that the airstrip was further improved with drainage pipe and material brought in to eliminate soft areas.[308] The more-upgraded runway made it possible to operate aircraft as large as Ford Tri-Motors.

In 1957 the D7 Caterpillar that was used at Chamberlain and Cold Meadows was walked back to

Landing upstream at Big Creek circa 1950 with a Johnson Flying Service Travel Air 6000. Notice the CCC building in the lower right corner of the photograph.

the Big Creek Ranger Station. This Cat was used along with other large equipment to completely rebuild the airfield. During the field seasons of 1958 and 1959 major areas downstream from the original runway were improved by installing culverts, moving 28,000 cubic yards of material, and extending the runway to 3550'.[309] By September 1958 the field had been lengthened enough that Bob Fogg of Johnson Flying Service executed the first upstream takeoff. Fogg performed this maneuver in a Travel Air 6000 (N9038).[310]

A late 1930s view of the Big Creek airfield and vicinity.

Johnson Flying Service Travel Air 6000 NC9038 delivering mail to Big Creek circa 1950.

Johnson Flying Service Travel Air 6000 NC9038 parked at the upper end of the airstrip in June 1949 with snowcapped Goat Mountain in the background.

In 1960 Chet Moulton with the Idaho Department of Aeronautics became involved and supplied state funds to help finish the project. The following year the USFS issued a special use permit to the state. The state became heavily involved with maintenance over the years, particularly with irrigation and surface reseeding.[311] The Big Creek facility, along with Johnson Creek, is one of the department's premiere airstrips in the backcountry. The field has been used extensively for USFS fire suppression activities, as well as by the public. The largest aircraft known to have landed here is a DC-3.

Even without the Big Creek Hotel as a destination, the airfield continues to be popular with pilots, hunters, fisherman, campers, and hikers. The runway not only offers a great entry point to the area for recreation, but also provides access for cabin owners in the surrounding Edwardsburg and Big Creek areas. Many of the cabin owners are pilots and aviation enthusiasts who operate their own aircraft.

1 By the 1940s Johnson Flying Service used their Ford Tri-Motors at Big Creek. The picture of this Ford (NC8419) was taken circa 1953.

2 In September 1958 Bob Fogg executed the first upstream takeoff at Big Creek with the newly expanded runway in a Travel Air 6000. Equipment for the project can still be seen in the background on the lower portion of the runway.

3 Hanging a new engine on a Cessna 195 at Big Creek in 1972.

4 McCall Aviation pilot John Ugland delivering freight to the USFS using a Cessna 206 (N7520N) in the spring of 2009.

USFS

E. Dodds

USFS

Holm

119

R. McRae/G. Short

CABIN CREEK

The Early Years

Merl "Blackie" Wallace the founder of the Flying W Ranch.

The Cabin Creek area was the location of a critical encounter between the United States military and the Shoshone Indians during the Sheepeater Campaign of 1879. A skirmish played out south of what most maps label as Vinegar Hill. A few years later two squatters built a small cabin on the lower part of the drainage and were most likely prospecting. Perhaps this small log structure lent to the naming of the creek. Fifteen years after the Shoshone were forced out of the Salmon River Mountains the Caswell brothers settled the Cabin Creek area. The Caswells lived here from 1895–1902, hunting, trapping, and prospecting. Upon finishing a cabin in 1898 they hung elk antlers above the porch and one of the brothers named the place Elk Horn Ranch. The group struck it rich and sparked the Thunder Mountain Gold Rush, one of the last gold rushes in the West.

After the Caswells sold their Thunder Mountain claims to Colonel W. M. Dewey and became wealthy, they departed the area. John Conyers then occupied the place for a short time, developing a small farm. Over time this tributary of Big Creek attracted numerous people and was split into three official 160 acre homesteads. In January 1918 Orlando M. Abel patented the southern portion of the property.[312] Abel's sister Elizabeth Bellingham homesteaded the far northern segment and had a home site at the confluence of Cabin and Cow creeks.[313] The third homestead sat west of Abel's property and was patented in September 1918 by Archie C. Bacon.[314] However, a small 40 acre parcel in the center of these other properties remained unclaimed. In 1928 Merl "Blackie" Wallace laid claim on the unpatented area and eventually purchased the Bacon place.

In April 1931 the first airplane landed at Cabin Creek to rescue injured trail crew worker Noel Routson. Here Routson is being loaded into Gowen's Travel Air 6000 parked on the upper bench.

The Beginning of the Flying W Ranch and the First Airplane

Wallace operated a ranch at the location during the winters and was joined by his wife, Jean, during the other parts of the year. Wallace knew the area well after working for the USFS as the Cold Meadows District ranger. He utilized the property to run an outfitting and guiding business and eventually left the USFS to run the ranch full-time. His outfitting operation was one of the first in the Idaho Primitive Area with airplane service for guests and supplies.[315]

Pilot Bill Gowen, flying a Travel Air 6000 (NC9846), made the first landing at Cabin Creek in the upper field to the north of the present-day airstrip, on the Bellingham place. On April 21, 1931 the USFS was building a trail along lower Big Creek, between Dunce and Snake creeks. In an effort to navigate a route through the narrow canyon the crew attempted to drill a tunnel through the rock. While constructing the passageway a cave-in occurred that pinned trail crewmember Noel Routson down in debris. Routson was knocked unconscious, and was rescued by his coworkers. In time he came to, but then went into complete shock.[316]

Noel's brother, Emmit, was also on the trail crew and he rushed to Wallace's ranch for help. At the ranch he was also able to make a telephone call to the Werdenhoff Mine for further assistance. By early afternoon several men arrived at Wallaces. It was decided to clear a small, elevated bench just north of Cow Creek so an airplane could land. A plane was dispatched from Boise in hopes of getting Noel to a hospital.[317]

Meantime, while Noel was packed to the Wallace ranch, Gowen had flown from Boise to Weiser to pick up another Routson brother, John, so he could guide the plane to Cabin Creek. All went as planned and at four o'clock on April 23 Gowen and Noel were back in the air headed for Boise.[318]

After two months of recovery Noel resumed work with the USFS as the Big Creek fire dispatcher. Upon his return, the main topic of conversation remained the landing of the first plane in the Big Creek area. The day the plane was flying out of the Big Creek canyon, an old prospector named Charles "Mattie" Mahan, who had a cabin near the top of Ramey Ridge, spotted the small plane. Mahan, who had been eavesdropping on the telephone chatter throughout the day's events, immediately called Big Creek Dispatcher Harold "Slim" Vasser. Mahan excitedly said, "Slim it's all over for that plane! It's going to crash. The wings are just barely flapping!" Vasser had to explain that airplanes did not fly like birds – no flapping was required.[319]

Prior to Gowen's departure to Boise, Big Creek rescuers pose for a quick picture with the first airplane to land at the ranch.

121

A 1952 aerial of the lower Cabin Creek drainage showing the upper airstrip located on the original Bellingham homestead and the lower airstrip constructed by Wallace.

Looking down the upper bench runway toward Big Creek.

Looking north on the upper bench strip in February 1947.

A New Airstrip

After the successful airplane landing, Wallace continued to use the upper bench location, as indicated in a letter to his wife dated August 14, 1932, "Mr. Scribner, Woods, Shank, Nick Mamer the Spokane flying man and another state commerce man from Washington D.C. was in here to look at the landing field and Mamer said he could land here with his big tri-motored Ford and he would like to do my freighting. He will do it for 4 cents a pound from McCall or a like distance so you see when we make some money I am going to quit packing. I think I could get him to bring it from Boise or Spokane for that."[320]

It is not known if Mamer ever flew one of his large Fords to Cabin Creek, but Wallace noted in a letter to his wife a week later that improvements were being made. "The man that bought Jake's mine [Snowshoe] has got two men here cutting the timber up Cabin Creek for a two-way landing. They have engaged all of the spuds and onions and four beefs. They figure on using this field next winter."[321]

By April the next year the field was still in use and Wallace reported to his wife that the first airplane accident occurred at the place. A ski plane overshot the runway, landed midway and "nearly climbed a tree at the far end." The pilot had not flown with skis before and misjudged the distance required to slow down. Apparently the pilot walked away and only minor damage was caused to the aircraft.[322]

During the first week of May 1933 Wallace sought additional advice on enhancing the airstrip, this time consulting with pilot A. A. Bennett. Bennett and Wallace decided to relocate the strip at roughly its current location, calling it the "Big Meadow." In a letter to his wife after working ten days on the "Big Meadow" airstrip, he commented, "It is a 2-way field and sure looks good."[323]

Even though successful landings were made at the new location, Wallace had some setbacks with the lower runway and in late June 1933 was forced to use the upper bench, which was used on and off through the late 1940s. He wrote to his wife about the trouble, remarking: "The high water washed a big hole in the new landing field so they are using the old one. I don't know when I will get time to fix it."[324]

Wallace's brochure promoting his Flying W Ranch.

A Johnson Flying Service Travel Air 6B (NC447W) parked on the lower end of the upper airstrip in February 1947 (l to r): pilot Ken Huber, property owner Joe Mabee, and area resident Shorty Granger.

Carole Mabee at Cabin Creek with an elk nicknamed, "Judy."

The Close of the Wallace Era

It is clear that within the next few years Wallace had the lower strip well established, as in 1938, Francis Woods a USFS land surveyor, measured the runway to be roughly 900' long.[325] Sometime during the creation of air service to Cabin Creek, Wallace named his place the Flying W Ranch. Included with the name was the simple slogan, "The most remote cattle ranch in America." In an early 1930s brochure for the ranch, Wallace explained the naming of the property, "We call it the Flying W because that is our brand, and also in compliment to that pioneer of the skies, the airplane, by which we plan to link our wilderness home with the outside world."[326]

In 1940 the Wallaces ended their operation of the ranch and the following year Blackie moved to Alaska. The property was then leased to several different outfitters. The northern portion of the Cabin Creek drainage was also sold during this period to Joe and Carole Mabee, who then sold it to Gordon Ray.[327] Under these owners the acreage was known as The Pinto Dude Ranch, most likely because of its stock of pinto horses.

Former Cabin Creek land owner Gordon Ray (left), Dewey Moore (center), and Loren Hollenbeak (right) with Hollenbeak's Cessna 180 at Cabin Creek circa 1957.

Hollenbeak - Cabin Creek Ranch

In the autumn of 1956 Loren Hollenbeak bought the upper property from Ray. Hollenbeak was a logger from Redding, California, who owned L. K. Hollenbeak Logging Company along with a mill based in Hayfork, California. He and his wife Diana purchased the place after meeting Ray through a business deal. The two thoroughly enjoyed spending time from May through September at the property with their four daughters.[328]

At about the same point Hollenbeak bought his place, Rex Lanham purchased the Wallace in-holdings from Wallace's ex-wife Jean, making the final payment in 1959. Lanham, an owner of a commercial construction business in Pocatello, was involved at this time with several partners on the ownership of Middle Fork Lodge. During Lanham's early years at Cabin Creek, the land at the stream's mouth was naturally being washed away by Big Creek. Wanting to prevent the ever-changing course of the river he went about devising plans to put a dike in place. Lanham also knew from his experiences at the Middle Fork Lodge that having good air access was essential to a backcountry ranch. However, the Cabin Creek airstrip was located on Hollenbeak's property.

Hollenbeak, like Lanham, was also a pilot and wanted to improve the short runway. As a result the two property owners bought a D8 Caterpillar from

Hollenbeak's logging company. The owners hired a cat skinner to walk it in with the help of upstream residents Dewey Moore and Bob Gillihan, who both used packstrings to support the effort.[329]

The cat skinner walked the machine down Big Creek from the ranger station to Crooked Creek, up to the Snowshoe Mine, around the north side of Acorn Butte to Crescent Meadows, then down Cave Creek to Cabin Creek. Hollenbeak and Lanham carried out several projects with the D8 while under their ownership, including work on the Cabin Creek airstrip, construction of a dike along Big Creek, and the construction of the Vines airstrip upriver.[330]

Hollenbeak added several structures to his property, including a barn, hangar, guest cabins, and a large addition to the main house. Most of the timber for these projects was skidded off USFS land and processed through a portable sawmill that was erected at various places north of the main building complex. The mill worked well, but occasionally produced irregular boards and thus the operation was named T & T Logging Company – "thick and thin."[331] The mill was one of many items Hollenbeak transported to the ranch with an airplane. Shortly after his initial purchase of the property he hired Johnson Flying Service of McCall, as well as Jim Larkin with his spacious Cunningham-Hall, to fly in several loads of oversized items. Included in these big loads were a broken down Jeep, wagon, hay baler, and gas-powered generator. On one of the Johnson

Flying Service flights a Travel Air 6000 was damaged at the airstrip, requiring a new propeller and repair to the landing gear.[332]

Hollenbeak primarily used the property for personal enjoyment and to operate his outfitting business, known simply as Cabin Creek Ranch. He enjoyed the location for the primitive aspects it offered and viewed it as a place to escape his busy life. Friends from Redding regularly flew in for visits. Many of them eventually bought property in the backcountry. Hollenbeak accessed the ranch with a Cessna 180 (N2408C). His friends flew a wide variety of aircraft to the ranch, ranging from Cessna 182s to Beechcraft 50s.[333]

Diana was also a pilot and flew often in and out of the ranch with the Cessna 180. In fact when the barn was being constructed, Loren fell off the roof breaking an arm and several ribs. Several men carefully loaded him in the airplane and Diana flew him to Boise for medical attention. With a family of six, it was customary to remove the backseat in the plane to help provide room for the four children and luggage, while the parents sat in the front. All of the Hollenbeak children viewed it as an adventure to travel and spend time at their backcountry ranch, and have many fond memories.[334]

1 *The Cabin Creek D8 Caterpillar hard at work above the ranch.*
2 *Repairing a spun track on the D8 dozer during the building of the dike along Big Creek.*
3 *The Hollenbeak's main house at Cabin Creek with the large addition (right) that they constructed shortly after their purchase.*
4 *The building of the Hollenbeak barn in the summer of 1958.*

125

5

Kough/Hollenbeak

6

Kough/Hollenbeak

7

Kough/Hollenbeak

8

Kough/Hollenbeak

9

Kough/Hollenbeak

10

Kough/Hollenbeak

5 *One of Hollenbeak's friends visiting with a Cessna 180.*
6 *Hollenbeak family friend Ruby Glassburn with her husband's (Ray) airplane in front of one of the newly constructed guest cabins.*
7 *A Beechcraft 50 in front of the Hollenbeak's hangar.*
8&9 *Cutting lumber for the various building projects on the ranch.*
10 *Baling hay at the ranch.*

126

11 *A Johnson Flying Service Travel Air 6000 damaged during the transportation of large items to the ranch.*
12 *Loren Hollenbeak at the controls of his Cessna 180.*
13 *Hollenbeak's Cessna 180 on the lower end of the airstrip.*
14 *Many of Hollenbeak's friends often flew their own airplanes in to help work on the various ranch projects. The larger airplane at the upper end of the parking area was Jim Larkin's Cunningham-Hall.*
15 *The Hollenbeak complex of buildings in September 1964.*
16 *Diana Hollenbeak (right) and her sister Alice "Patty" Patton with a string of trout from Big Creek.*

The Lanham Years -
Continuing the Flying W Ranch

In 1963 Hollenbeak sold his portion of Cabin Creek to Lanham.[335] Hollenbeak retained a residence in McCall and after retiring had places at Riggins and Lucille along the Main Salmon River. He and his wife eventually settled in Lewiston and when she died he moved to Boise where he passed away in May 1999.[336]

As the sole owner, Lanham continued to make improvements and collectively called the place the Flying W Ranch. Lanham was originally from the Midwest and made his way to Idaho after graduating from Omaha Tech. While working as a miner in the Hells Canyon area he bought land in Council and Cascade. Living in Cascade during the early 1940s he took flying lessons at Johnson Flying Service, mainly receiving instruction from Penn Stohr Sr.[337]

Lanham lost his Cascade property to the construction of the Cascade Reservoir after World War II and moved to Pocatello. In southern Idaho he developed a large commercial contracting company. His main focus was building power lines throughout the western United States. Many aircraft were used in connection with his construction projects and he started his own flying company called Gate City Flying Service, also located in Pocatello. In 1958 he and his wife, Hazel, moved their family of four kids to Emmett along with the business headquarters. At this time he sold Gate City Flying Service and started another operation from his own private airstrip outside of Emmett.[338]

The move also put him within a shorter reach of his properties in the backcountry. With the faster commute and exclusive ownership of Cabin Creek, along with the sale of the Middle Fork Lodge to Bill Harrah, he directed all his spare energy to the Cabin Creek property and focused on more outfitting.

One of the key elements to the Cabin Creek operation was the expansion and further development of the airfield. The airstrip that was mainly situated on the original Bellingham portion of the complex was extended considerably upstream to 1750'. The larger field enabled him to bring in materials for more

Rex Lanham at Cabin Creek with one of his Cessna 206s.

buildings such as a private house, guest cabins, and main lodge. Much of the ranch's equipment including several tractors, a backhoe, and a Jeep were delivered in pieces by airplane.

Through the sale of the Middle Fork Lodge, Lanham kindled a relationship with Harrah. One of the more interesting flights to the ranch was the delivery of a restored Model A Ford pickup gifted to Lanham by Harrah. A Harrah pilot with the Middle Fork Lodge's Twin Otter flew the vehicle in partially disassembled. Harrah also sent some business to the Flying W Ranch. A few times a year, starting in 1967, Harrah pilots would fly Middle Fork Lodge guests over to Cabin Creek for dinner. After a great meal everyone was loaded back into the Otter and flown to the lodge. It made for a fun adventure with the flight and entertainment on each end. Harrah also flew a few hunting clients over to Cabin Creek from the lodge so they could hunt with Lanham's outfit.[339]

Lanham operated various aircraft at Cabin Creek including several Piper Cubs, a Cessna 170, 180, 182, and a couple of 206s. He eventually narrowed it down to three main airplanes after seeing friend Marv Hornback of Pistol Creek fly in part of a Jeep with a Cessna 206. Lanham cottoned to the plane's capabilities and made it a mainstay at the ranch, complimented by a 182 and a Super Cub. He thoroughly enjoyed flying the Idaho backcountry and liked being able to link it to his business.[340] In regards to Lanham's flying, Norman Guth, longtime outfitter, guide, and backcountry pilot, commented, "Rex was probably the best pilot in the country during his time, even though he was never given credit for it."[341]

Kough/Hollenbeak

USFS

USFS

1 *A 1965 advertisement for Lanham's Flying W Ranch.*

2 *Lanham's Cessna 180 landing at Cabin Creek.*

3 *The Lanham constructed guest quarters. In 1990 this building was disassembled and moved to the Taylor Ranch with a helicopter.*

4 *A 1971 view of the Cabin Creek runway and upper ranch complex. Notice the old dam in the lower right corner of the photograph.*

Lanham at his Cabin Creek property looks onward during sale negotiations with the USFS.

Lanham Sells

After Lanham decided to sell his Cabin Creek property, the USFS instantly became interested. After government appraisers viewed the property the negotiations began. Lanham felt that with the number of improvements, the parcel size, and the location, that the government's offer was low. Wanting his own land appraisal for comparison, he contacted Harrah who arranged to have several appraisers come in and write up a much higher counteroffer to the USFS.[342]

In 1974 a final sale agreement was made and for some odd reason a USFS employee with purchasing authorities was assigned the job from the Region 1 headquarters in Missoula instead of Region 4. USFS pilot Nels Jensen was assigned to the flight and flew the purchasing agent from Missoula to Cabin Creek one morning in a USFS Cessna 185 (N193Z). After landing, Lanham served coffee at the lodge and was quite jovial. Jensen took his coffee and drifted about the property, admiring the remote complex. A short time later a check was cut and the two were back in the air bound for Missoula.[343]

After the sale of Cabin Creek Lanham hauled out most of his personal items by airplane. Bill Harrah offered the use of his Twin Otter to move the bigger items, which included the Model A Ford pickup. Overlapping his time at Cabin Creek, he also purchased and developed land up Big Creek along Logan Creek in Edwardsburg. He spent the remainder of his time in the backcountry at this location. Lanham

continued to fly and work from his private airstrip in Emmett. He suffered a setback in 1979 when his hangar full of airplanes, equipment, and parts burned. The loss was devastating but he moved on and acquired another Cessna 206. Lanham died in January 1981.[344]

The USFS Years

Even though the Idaho Primitive Area had not been designated wilderness, the USFS's intent with the property was to "restore the area to wilderness condition to the fullest possible extent." Many federal employees were anxious to act on their wilderness beliefs. One of many examples of the agency's objectives at Cabin Creek is exemplified in a March 20, 1975 letter from Payette NF Supervisor W. B. Sendt to the Director of the IDFG stating, "We propose to work with the Department of Aeronautics to close the airstrip as soon as possible, hopefully before July 1, 1975. There will be some administrative flights to the ranch by the USFS for completion of site cleanup and restoration. Building removal will begin as soon as manpower is available . . . we do not intend leaving any facilities, nor anticipate any interim use of the facilities . . ."[345]

When the Washington and regional offices of the USFS became aware of the Payette NF's Cabin Creek plans they quickly, advised the forest not to act hastily on removing anything or closing the airstrip. They warned them that local public support concerning

Several of the Lanham constructed buildings burned by the USFS.

M. Dorris

The burying of the D8 Caterpillar by the USFS circa 1990 on the north side of Cow Creek.

wilderness was already shaky enough. There was no need to disrupt the progression of the River of No Return Wilderness designation that was in the works at the time the property was acquired. In addition, they were reminded that Idaho's senior senator, Frank Church, was leading the wilderness movement and it would be doubly awkward for the agency to attract what could be perceived as negative attention.

The advice was taken into account and the Big Creek District proceeded with caution. Al and Rita Romine were hired to watch over the place, along with performing regular guard station duties. The two lived in Lanham's old private house near the creek, working trails and greeting visitors for several years. During this period no regular maintenance was carried out at the ranch. As things slowly began to deteriorate, the guard position was cut, and the ranch became more of satellite location for trail crews and administrative work connected to the Big Creek Ranger Station.

In 1988 after several years of managing the site as wilderness, the USFS began to eradicate structures and improvements. In 1990, many of the buildings were burnt to the ground. However, the University of Idaho salvaged one of the Lanham log structures. The building was completely disassembled and flown by helicopter to the Taylor Ranch, where it was rebuilt. Also about this time the old D8 Cat was coaxed back to life and used to bury what could not be burned. The Cat was then walked across Cow Creek, opposite the current tie down area, and buried

in a shallow grave.

The only items left at the ranch were those deemed as historic. Several of these have burned over the years. In the large 2000 wildfire season log ruins associated with Caswell and Bellingham were lost. Then in the summer of 2008 an accidental fire set by a seasonal USFS employee claimed another historic structure, leaving only two in place today. The first is the original Caswell cabin that was relocated by Wallace to the present day location. This cabin is believed to be the oldest surviving structure in the River of No Return Wilderness. The second building has functioned in several roles throughout the years including bunkhouse, tack shed, and tool shed. In 1990 these remaining buildings were listed on the National Register of Historic Places and continue to be used by the USFS for housing trail crews and wilderness rangers. Two excellent books that detail much of Cabin Creek's history are *Wilderness Brothers* and *Cabin Creek Chronicles* by Dr. G. Wayne Minshall.

The Washout

In the spring of 1996 the USFS received reports from air taxi pilots that Cow Creek was flooding over the runway. Forest officials also knew about the problem, as a trail crew was living at the Cabin Creek administrative site while working on the Big Creek Trail. When the crew reported the potential flooding conditions to their superiors they were told not to take action. Substantial damage resulted to the runway, washing out sections as big as 24' wide and 8' deep. A controversy then arose between the aviation community and the Payette NF, as several government employees were opposed to rebuilding the airstrip. Political pressure eventually forced the hand of the Payette NF to commit resources to rebuild it. Pat Armstrong of McCall obtained the contract and planned to start work quickly, but he and the

Little remains at Cabin Creek but the airstrip (center) and the two buildings in the lower right corner of the photograph. The Cabin Creek drainage is entering on the left, while the Cow Creek drainage is entering on the upper right.

USFS then become blocked by Wilderness Watch. Ultimately the latter group's only accomplishment was to cause a delay.[346]

In early April 1998, almost two years after the runway was closed, Armstrong started work. With the airfield unsuitable for landing, Armstrong made arrangements with then manager Jim Akenson to land his Cessna 180 (N2486C) at the Taylor Ranch Field Station. From the Taylor Ranch Armstrong packed some rations, a shovel, and a disassembled wheelbarrow to Cabin Creek. Within five days he had the lower 500' on the west side filled in. He worried about one large tree off the approach end of the strip and pleaded with the USFS to allow removal. They adamantly denied his request in spite of the safety concerns. Armstrong, undeterred, later returned with his airplane and was forced to snake around the tree, but landed safely.[347]

The USFS designated several borrow-pit areas and material was moved from these locations. Much of the work was carried out just as Armstrong had done over ten years earlier while rebuilding the Mahoney airstrip on the Middle Fork. With the help of his family he used a team of mules and a wheeled Fresno. To level the runway he used a land planer constructed of logs and sections of chain link fence. After eight months of work the airstrip was finished in December, before the snow began sticking. In the end Armstrong had to move over 2,200 cubic feet of material, far more than the 1,200 cubic feet estimated by the USFS. The discrepancy caused a conflict over the contract. Armstrong was forced to take legal action and the USFS eventually owned up to the error.[348]

4

5

6

7

1&2 *Runway damage incurred from the spring 1996 washout of Cow Creek.*
3 *Contractor Pat Armstrong rebuilding the Cabin Creek airstrip in the summer of 1998.*
4 *Looking downstream at the progress on the Cabin Creek airfield restoration project.*
5&6 *Installing water bars on the rebuilt airstrip in the fall of 1998.*
7 *Armstrong's 1954 Cessna 180 at Cabin Creek with some of the equipment used to rebuild the airstrip.*

DEWEY MOORE

The Early Years and Homestead

Walter Estep at his Acorn Creek property circa 1930.

Circa 1911 George Yardley first settled the property at the confluence of Acorn Creek. Then John Routson purchased the place and named it the Routson Ranch. Routson was a prospector, packer, rancher, and area postman on the Big Creek mail route. He and his wife, Lettie, raised six children on the place. It was a modest outfit with a 20' X 24' log house, 16 'X 20' barn, commissary, and a chicken coop. As the children became older they started spending more time in Weiser, particularly during the winters, although the family held the Idaho backcountry close to them and returned often.[349]

Two of the Routson kids wrote detailed accounts of their time living and visiting in the Big Creek area. Adelia Routson Parke wrote *Memoirs of An Old Timer* published in 1955, and Noel wrote *Memoirs of An Old Prospector* published in 1980. Routson Creek and Routson Peak were named after the family, memorializing their contributions to the rugged country. Routson Peak stands prominently to the southeast, across Big Creek from the property, and is easily visible from the upper end of the airstrip.

In 1925 the Routsons sold the property to Walter Estep. Estep, a former ranger on the then Idaho NF, homesteaded 33.25 acres at the location in 1929. Estep was later murdered in December 1935 several miles below his property along Big Creek. He was shot by area resident Frank Lobear after being confronted about having an affair with Lobear's wife. In early 1932 Phil Beal, of the Chamberlain Basin, bought the Acorn property. Beal renamed the place the Rhubarb Ranch after the numerous rhubarb plants growing in the garden. Many of these plants can still be seen on the property today.

The Routson Ranch circa 1925.

The George Dewey Moore Years

Lee Avery acquired the property from Beal, then sold it a short time later to Shirley McLaughlin. In 1947 a Texan, George Dewey Moore purchased the ranch from McLaughlin.[350] Moore improved the property over the years, adding on to the main house along with general maintenance. By the early 1950s he named his acreage the Hanging H Ranch.[351] The name was derived from Moore's registered brand.[352]

Circa 1952 he hired Lawrence Johnson, a pilot from Hailey, Idaho, to walk an International bulldozer to his property to build an airstrip.[353] The dozer was hauled to the end of the Big Creek Road at Monumental Creek and then walked down the river to Moore's property.[354] Once completed, the runway measured about 1000' long with an average slope of six to eight percent. However, the layout only afforded about 700' usable. The downstream terrain of the river canyon dictates the reduced takeoff length. If the full length of the field were used on takeoff, the pilot would be unable to negotiate the necessary departure turn downriver. The first plane to land here was a Piper Tri-Pacer with a power prop piloted by Johnson. The main purpose behind putting an airstrip in was for better access and to get aerial mail delivery. After the runway was finished Moore also brought in a Jeep and later a small tractor. He used the dozer

John Routson working in the Idaho backcountry.

George Dewey Moore (right) at his ranch with a visitor in the late 1960s.

The Moore Ranch in October 1972.

A 1960s view of the mowed 1000' runway at the Moore Ranch.

to widen several trails from his property, making it possible to use these vehicles for such activities as firewood collection. Several of these scars remain visible on the landscape.

Moore touted himself as a big game outfitter and guide until the fall of 1965 when he retired.[355] He often outfitted from his ranch, but also ran a regular hunting camp near the south end of Cold Meadows. People either got along with Moore or they did not. He was known for his loathing of the USFS and his inability to get along with some of his Big Creek neighbors. However, some of his guests returned year after year. He supposedly had treasure maps that showed the locations of the "real" Sheepeater Indian

Campaign of 1879, different from those published in books and on USFS maps. The maps enabled people to find buried artifacts. Moore's one-of-a-kind maps were only available for purchase to his clients.

When Moore's health began to deteriorate in the late 1960s, he decided he should sell the ranch. The USFS became interested but Moore refused to sell the parcel to the government and in September 1972 sold the property to Walter C. Gerlach. One month later Gerlach turned the place over to the USFS for $65,000.[356] Moore moved to New Plymouth, Idaho, where he died four years later at the age of seventy-six.[357]

Flying the approach to the Dewey Moore airstrip.

A Johnson Flying Service 185 (N4546F) parked on the strip during the USFS property cleanup.

The USFS and Conflict

The USFS was relieved that Moore was out of the country and immediately tacked yellow and black metal signs reading, "Property of the United States Government" on all the buildings. Although the site was not considered historic at the time, the USFS had the goal of removing all the rundown buildings and burying the remaining junk. The key to the project was getting Moore's old International dozer running, so that large pits could be dug to hold trash.

137

The Big Creek USFS crew was unable to get the old machine operating. However, Big Creek Ranger Earl Dodds knew just the man for the job, Francie Wallace. USFS Maintenance Foreman, Bill Jeffs, who was also a pilot, flew Wallace to the Moore Ranch in his personally owned Cessna 182 to assess the situation. Bill Dorris of Johnson Flying Service carried out the remainder of the flying for the project with a Cessna 185 (N4546F).

After a flight or two back and forth to McCall for parts and gas, Wallace had the old machine running. The crew burned what they could and then buried what remained, such as the small farm tractor, trailers, and Jeep. On the last day Wallace, who stayed around as the equipment operator, was digging a large hole for the dozer and was almost done when it quit. Calmly he unbolted the fuel tank and waved for Dodds to come over and help him. He told Dodds to hold the tank up high above the engine and sure enough it started. It was just enough fuel to finish the job. The dozer remains buried in its own grave on the east side of the airstrip.

The runway at the Acorn property, referred to by most pilots as "Dewey Moore" has come under threat of closure many times. In the early 1980s the USFS actually placed a closure on the airstrip along with others in the Big Creek drainage. However, the actions were later reversed.[358]

About the same time the closure was lifted, a USFS trail crew cut a new trail through the former hay meadow below the existing trail. Many pilots instantly became suspicious as the new trail was dug early in the year across the airstrip below the runway culvert. A heavy rainstorm could have washed the entire airstrip into the delicate Big Creek ecosystem. Pilot Mike Dorris documented the incident and reported it to officials. The runway was eventually repaired and the trail moved toward the upper end of the airfield.

Since the reopening of the airstrip several more accounts of sabotage have been noted. One year large rocks were piled in the turnaround area, perfectly camouflaged by the tall grass, at the right height to cause prop damage. In May 2000 another incident of sabotage occurred when two higher-level USFS employees were working along Big Creek and noticed water pouring down the runway. Upon further investigation they found two huge chunks of

Burning the historic Routson built barn in the spring of 1975.

Photos by USFS

USFS mechanic Francie Wallace burying Moore's old Jeep at the ranch in the fall of 1974

Wallace using the International dozer to dig its own grave about half way down the east side of the runway.

The illegally constructed trail across the runway below the airstrip's upper culvert.

An aerial photograph showing the illegally constructed trail about two-thirds the way up and across the top of the runway. The original trail followed the river below the airstrip and was then relocated above the runway, which can be seen in the lower center of the photograph. However, the third unnecessary trail was directed through the meadow and across the runway.

sod placed in the streambed of Acorn Creek, diverting the water down the runway in hopes of washing it out. Both men were very irritated and removed the sod bundles. When they hiked through the old ranch a day later, a newly erected tent was noticed and the sod was placed back in the stream. No occupants could be found, but they again removed the sod.

Days later, while on a routine flight, Mike Dorris flew over the ranch and noticed the same thing observed by the two USFS employees. Not wanting the strip to wash out, he took a calculated risk and landed. Dorris found the runway culvert stuffed full of compacted sod that had been carefully cut with a sharp tool. After confronting a trail crew camped nearby he returned to McCall and contacted the Payette NF supervisor and local law enforcement. An investigation ensued and the malicious damage was corrected.

MILE HIGH RANCH

Elliott Homestead and Lafe Cox

Looking south toward the Big Creek canyon at the Mile High Ranch building complex.

In May 1920 Joseph Elliott homesteaded 160 acres on the land now known as the Mile High Ranch. It is believed that he worked the ranch with his brothers Roy, Ernest "Hardrock," and Bert, running cattle and farming much of the acreage into the 1930s. The brothers built a unique house, several outbuildings, and a springhouse. The Elliotts eventually went their separate ways. Roy moved to a ranch located at the confluence of Monumental and Holy Terror creeks, which he homesteaded in 1928. Hardrock ended up taking over the Mile High operation but died unexpectedly in May 1934 of spotted fever. He was buried on a knoll above the main house with an incredible view of the Big Creek drainage. Elliott's grave is still visible, but the concrete headstone was damaged in a 2000 wildfire.

The origin of the name "Mile High Ranch," is not clearly known. One version notes the name was derived from the mile-long telephone line that extended from the primary cabin to the main line along Big Creek. The other more likely reason for the name is that the actual elevation of the ranch's airstrip (5,680') is just a little over a "mile high." Another unknown about the name is the actual intended spelling. Starting in the 1940s the United States Geologic Survey (USGS) and USFS documentation began using "Mile Hi," while the IDFG has consistently used "Mile High Ranch."

In the fall of 1937 the Elliott family sold the property to Carroll Tarwater, who turned around and sold it in late 1939 to Lafe and Emma Cox.[359] The Coxs enhanced the property and lived at the ranch until 1942 when Lafe's parents no longer wanted to operate the family dude ranch on Johnson Creek.[360] One of the biggest improvements the Coxs made at the ranch was finishing the interior of the main lodge. Over the course of one winter Lafe skidded in 3,000 feet of lumber behind a horse. The lumber was first trucked to the Snowshoe Mine, and Lafe then moved it the remainder of the way during the winter through Crescent Meadows over the Coxey Creek Trail and then over to the ranch. He packed in doors and windows the same way.[361]

During the Coxs few precious years at the ranch they hired Jim Carpenter as a cook for their hunting parties and as a part-time caretaker. He also helped Lafe pack in modern conveniences such as a Montgomery Ward gas washing machine and modern woodstove.[362]

The main house at the property finished by Lafe Cox.

Ernest "Hardrock" Elliott's headstone at the ranch.

The remains of the Mile High Ranch in the early 1980s.

From Mile High, Cox ran a fairly successful outfitting and guiding service in the fall, hunting both the Big Creek and Chamberlain Basin areas. In the summer they guided fishing trips along the Middle Fork and in the off time put up over fifty tons of hay each year, and raised chickens, turkeys, and pack animals.

The Coxs were sad to leave Mile High after all of their hard work at the remote ranch, but wanted the opportunities provided by the family business. As a result Mile High was eventually sold in 1947 to William and Vera Williams of California.[363]

Williams, Three Airstrips, and a Wrecked Fairchild

Sometime between the Cox's departure and their sale of the ranch, an airstrip situated north-south was roughed in at the top of the property near the house. This runway saw some use mainly by local Johnson Flying Service pilots. To improve access to the ranch, Williams began constructing another airstrip on the lower ridge of the property parallel to Big Creek. After consulting with Johnson Flying Service in McCall about the airstrip's potential, the project was abandoned. No records exist as to whether or not an aircraft landed on this strip. After Johnson Flying Service's input, Williams focused effort on building the presently-used airstrip on the north side of the property near the east barn. The strip was built with a horse-drawn blade, which can still be seen at the top of the runway in the turnaround area. Originally the runway was built to a length of 1100'. The lower 350' of the airstrip was actually extended onto USFS land. The typical landing procedure used by most pilots was to land at the bottom near the barn and then give a blast of power to get to the top.

When Williams had nearly completed the runway, McCall-based Johnson pilot Warren Ellison decided one day while flying by that he would give it a try in one of the company's Travel Air 6000s. Ellison set it down at the bottom of the strip and powered up to the top. Telling the story fifty years after the fact he said it was one of the best landings of his career.

M. Dorris

The Elliott constructed hay barn on the east side of the property.

M. Dorris

The ruins of the main house in the 1980s.

IDFG

An early 1960s view of the third and final runway constructed on the ranch running east-west. The barn in the center (slightly right) of the photograph was the touchdown area when the field was actively used.

"Once I got comfortable landing at Mile High Ranch it was one of my favorite trips to make in the Idaho backcountry."[364]

Some time passed and Ellison was hired one morning to fly a group of men around the backcountry. As he worked his way down the Big Creek drainage, flying one of the Travel Air 6000s, the passenger in the right seat asked him if he had noticed that the oil temperature gauge was not working properly. Ellison commented that it had recently been acting up and a replacement was on its way from their shop in Missoula. He also added that the old Wright radial engine did not know what a hot temperature was. Curious, Ellison turned to the guy and said, "Sounds like you might know something about aviation." With a smile, the gentleman glanced over and responded, "I know some, I work for the CAA." It turned out that everyone on board was from the CAA Los Angeles District Office.[365]

Unfazed by the passengers' occupations, Ellison slowed the Travel Air down and started a descent. "You should have heard the howls from the men in the back when I turned down the canyon and came back up to land at Mile High Ranch." He had another good landing, but the group was not overly impressed with the trip until they landed safely back in McCall.[366]

Williams used a Fairchild 71 to access the ranch and not long after the airstrip was completed he crashed the airplane on a landing. After getting airborne from the ranch he realized he had forgotten to remove the rudder lock. He then decided to turn the craft around, land, and detach the lock. However, on the landing he lost control and badly damaged the aircraft. It was then hauled to the nearby barn where the skin was removed and used to cover the inside of the building's interior walls. Later the wallpaper was torn down after a passerby mentioned that the fabric from the plane contained nitrate dope, which is quite flammable.[367]

Salvaging the Fairchild

The Fairchild sat in pieces at Mile High for roughly thirty years until the late 1970s when Dean Wilson, who maintained and restored aircraft for Joe Terteling's private aircraft collection near Boise, obtained salvage rights to it.[369]

Wilson hired Idaho Helicopter of Boise to airlift the plane to the Big Creek landing field where it would then be trucked to Boise. After several months of planning, Wilson coordinated a date with the helicopter company and flew to Mile High to prepare the old Fairchild for the airlift. When he arrived the plane had already been removed. Apparently another fellow had caught wind of Wilson's plans and went behind his back, hiring another outfit to haul it out.[369]

Word passed through the Idaho aviation community about what had happened and eventually the owner was shamed into giving the Fairchild 71 wreckage to Wilson. The airplane sat for a number of years in the Terteling collection awaiting restoration (several incomplete Fairchild 71s were going to be combined to make one), however, the entire collection was auctioned off in 1986 before any headway was made on the project.[370]

The IDFG and Ford Tri-Motors

In 1949 Williams sold the 160 acre ranch to the IDFG, shortly after he had his airplane accident.[371] Around the same time the ranch exchanged hands, Johnson Flying Service pilots Penn Stohr Sr. and Bob Johnson were carrying loads of cargo to be dropped on a nearby fire with Ford Tri-Motors. After several passes over the drop zone it was determined that the winds were too high. One of them suggested that instead of returning to McCall they should wait the winds out at Mile High.[372]

Stohr and Johnson each landed the Fords and taxied up to the top of the airstrip. Soon after the landing Bob Fogg, also flying from McCall for Johnson in one of the company's Travel Airs, passed over Mile High. Flying over the strip some thirty years later in the early 1970s on a return trip to Missoula, Fogg recounted the story to Penn Stohr Jr. Fogg who

was receiving some recurrent training from the young Stohr, dipped the wing and commented that he was not necessarily amazed that two Fords had landed at the Mile High Ranch, but was more amazed that the two pilots were able to squeeze enough room out of the top of the airstrip to park the big birds. Fogg had later found out that the two pilots had quite a discussion, not only about the parking situation, but also about where to shutdown and start up again.[373]

Mile High Ranch Licensees

The runway was used little by aircraft as the property became a non-functioning ranch under the ownership of the IDFG. By the late 1950s the department began leasing their backcountry properties, mainly to outfitters and guides to help pay for annual costs. In 1960 outfitter Don Leeper of Caldwell, Idaho, leased the acreage, followed in 1961 by John Gillihan's G&S Guide Service. In 1963 after a year in which the property sat vacant, Rex Lanham of Cabin Creek's Flying W Ranch obtained the lease. An issue arose concerning overgrazing and the lease was not renewed again until 1966 when Dr. Maurice Hornocker secured it. Hornocker intended to use the property through the end of 1968 to keep stock that was being used for his cougar study. Neighbor John Vines helped manage the lease area (for more information see Taylor Ranch).[374] Once Hornocker persuaded the University of Idaho to purchase the Taylor Ranch in 1969, his need for the grazing ground was over.

In 1970 Lanham regained the lease and kept it through 1977. During this period Lanham was insistent with the department about the use and maintenance of the airstrip. Although it received some use during these years from small aircraft such as Piper Cubs, it was slowly deteriorating.[375] Lanham, evidently concerned, contacted acquaintance Governor Cecil Andrus. The governor responded stating, "What this all boils down to, Rex, is that - - yes - - the Mile High Ranch airstrip may be used, but it is certainly at the pilot's discretion and his own risk. Hopefully, this resolves the question you had in mind. Sincerely, Cese."[376]

In 1974 Lanham sold the Flying W Ranch to the USFS. Son-in-law Ronald Vaughn obtained the hunting area and eventually the lease to Mile High in

1978.[377] Vaughn, also a pilot, worked on maintaining the runway each season through 1980. Vaughn, who was primarily an agricultural pilot, was killed in August 2002 while spraying on a mosquito abatement project. His 182A (N4085D) collided with a series of high-tension lines north of Emmett.

Scott Farr, who had previously been working from the IDFG's Hotzel Ranch property in Chamberlain Basin under the name of Wilderness Outfitters, acquired Vaughn's hunting area in 1981 and obtained the Mile High lease. Farr concluded that the area had too much public access for quality hunting and sold out after the 1986 season to Jerry Jeppson. The IDFG began terminating all leases on the their backcountry properties in the early 1990s, adjusting to new management objectives. In 1993 the Mile High lease ended.[378]

The Current Airstrip

During the later years, the lower 540' portion of the once 1100' runway slowly eroded away and became too rough to use. This left only 560' of usable runway with a touchdown area slope of nearly twenty-two percent and an average runway slope of eighteen percent. Taking off from the shortened strip has its problems, as the majority of the runway is not visible even when lined up on the departure end. This makes knowing a few pertinent landmarks crucial for appropriate alignment before beginning the takeoff roll.

A few pilots, mainly commercial operators, learned the complexities of operating at Mile High. These pilots not only flew small planes such as Piper Cubs off the runway on a regular basis, but also moved freight during hunting season with Cessna 180s, 182s, 185s, and 206s. With the increase in use of the airstrip from professional operators, its popularity also grew within the Idaho aviation community. Many pilots saw it as place to prove themselves – the mentality that if you have not flown Mile High, you have not mastered the Idaho backcountry or as a must-do to put a notch in the belt. Others thought it was simply crazy. The hype generated around the old ranch has created a mystique over the years as well as a lot of accidents, some nearly fatal.

Landing at the Mile High Ranch.

The top of the current airstrip with Mike Dorris's Cessna 170 parked on the south side. Farm equipment such as this one in the foreground lingers at the ranch as a reminder of the past.

A Rescue

One unfortunate accident occurred in November 1990 when capable and well-respected pilot Gary Hubler was giving instruction to a friend from the rear seat of 180 horsepower Scout. Hubler had reviewed the proper practices at Mile High with the student prior to arriving at the airstrip. Sometime between short final and the touchdown, Hubler repeated several times to his friend to "go right." The student interpreted Hubler's instruction as "go-around." The pilot then jammed the power forward. With no time for Hubler to react, the airborne airplane cleared the ridge at the top of the strip, but did not have enough altitude to climb over the oncoming trees. Realizing that he was not going to make it, he caught sight of a gap between two large trees and cranked the aircraft ninety degrees in an effort to try and knife edge the plane through them. Seconds after the pilot's frantic control inputs the wings struck the trees, which quickly brought the airplane to a rest in a draw on the south side of the airstrip.[379]

Pat Dorris, heading to McCall with a load of hunting supplies from the Middle Fork in a Cessna 206 (N7216N), spotted the downed airplane while flying up Big Creek. He radioed his brother Mike who was flying another full load of hunting gear from the Middle Fork. Mike had flown some hunters out of

Pilot Pat Dorris with a Cessna 206.

Mile High earlier in the day and confirmed that the wreckage was new. With a short discussion on a plan of action it was decided that they would both land at Cabin Creek, unload Mike's 206 (N7520N), and head up to Mile High. It just happened that Pat's load of supplies was comprised of many things that could aid in a rescue, including a cot that could be turned into a stretcher. They threw in the few pertinent items and took off.[380]

During the short flight they were unable to make contact with the outfitter's camp on the northeast side of the Mile High Ranch buildings, but could see activity, as a man was leading a large black mule up the airstrip.[381]

A 1988 aerial of the Mile High airstrip showing the salt damage on the upper end of the runway.

The result of the illegal salting done over the winter of 1987–88, nearly rendering the airstrip unusable.

The Dorris bothers landed, secured the airplane, and unloaded the rescue equipment about the same time the man with the mule arrived at the parking area. The pilots right away recognized Hubler, although he was a little banged up. After a quick recounting of events they made their way down to the wreckage. Hubler informed the Dorrises that while at the outfitter's camp he was able to make contact with Life Flight in Boise and they were en route. The student, who was very overweight, was still alive, propped up next to a tree and in desperate need of medical attention. Hubler was able to pull his friend out of the wrecked airplane through the firewall, but could not get him any farther on his own.[382]

Due to the man's size the three rescuers had extreme difficulties moving him up the steep mountainside on the cot. However, they made headway inches at a time. In spite of his horrific injuries they decided to put him on the mule, as it was the only possible way to get him up to the airstrip. After reaching the runway they loaded him in the back of the 206, keeping him on the stretcher to provide comfort.

While waiting for Life Flight the three debated time and time again whether or not they should just fly to Boise or McCall to get medical help, but kept returning to the fact that Life Flight was already dispatched and in the air. Forty-five minutes later the helicopter was heard coming down Big Creek. However, the helicopter flew right over their location. In desperation, Mike made contact with the helicopter and directed the pilot to the airfield. A short time later the badly injured patient was in the air, headed for medical treatment. The Dorris brothers then departed and took Hubler out with them. Both men involved in the accident eventually made full recoveries.[383] Unfortunately, Hubler, who was an avid air racer in addition to a crop duster, was killed in a midair collision at the 2007 Reno Air Races.

The springhouse is the last standing building on the ranch.

The original runway located below the main house is difficult to see after years of neglect, but is running diagonally up the hill to the left.

Looking west-southwest down the unfinished second runway on the ranch with the Big Creek drainage to the left. The initial construction of a turn around area can be seen in the lower portion of the photograph.

More on the Airstrip and Ranch

In the 1980s the USFS attempted to close the runway due to its poor condition, wilderness designation, and the number of accidents that accumulated over the years when novice pilots tried to land. Many believed the agency did not have the authority, as the active portion of the runway is on state land. At about the same time as the controversial closure, extreme wilderness supporters targeted the airstrip as a site for eco-terrorism. In the winter of 1987–88 the strip fell victim to the intentional placement of granular salt sacks on the upper portion of the runway. Similar to other acts of salting found on airstrips in the Selway-Bitterroot Wilderness area during the same era, the objective of the activity was to attract winter game populations. The game tear up the salted ground, making large holes that eventually causes an accelerated case of erosion. The hope was to create enough rapid erosion to completely damage the runway beyond repair.

In the spring of 1988 the illegal attempt to destroy the airstrip at Mile High was discovered by Mike Dorris. Officials were contacted at the IDFG as well as people at Senator Jim McClure's office.[384] McClure sent an aide to McCall where he was flown to Mile High to photograph the damage. Dorris immediately removed the salt, which helped to prevent it from leaching into the soil and thus cause further damage.

IDFG Regional Supervisor Stacy Gebhards became very irritated by the vandalism to state land, particularly after the culprit(s) targeted the runway a second time in the spring of 1989. Gebhards contacted lease-holder Jerry Jeppson. The lease contained requirements that made him responsible for repairs to the property. In the letter to Jeppson, Gebhards noted, "These overt acts by persons unknown have (1) resulted in damage to state property; (2) interfered with public access and established long-term use of the landing site; (3) created a public hazard to aircraft utilizing the sites; (4) placed the department in a liability situation. If the salt were placed to attract big game animals for the purpose of hunting, this also is in violation of Fish and Game regulations."[385] Although Jeppson was not a suspect in the crime, he did repair the damage, as he used the airstrip in connection with his outfitting business.

Mike Dorris inspecting the leveling device used during the work on the second runway in the fall of 2010.

The IDFG continues to own the ranch property. In 2000 an unfortunate event occurred at Mile High when a large wildfire swept the Big Creek area burning many historic structures including all but one building at the Mile High Ranch. In addition to the one structure, two previously-constructed airfields remain visible. Through the mid-1980s pilots flying Super Cubs used the first landing strip near the main house. Parts of this runway are still in good shape, but since the wildfire of 2000, other portions are in rough condition. A sizable amount of work is still evident on the second airstrip to the south. It was constructed to considerably larger dimensions than the first and third strips, but is also steeper, with an estimated average slope of twenty-five percent. The original hand-built horse-drawn harrow used to construct the runway can still be seen halfway down the airstrip to the north. Many of the commercial operators who have used Mile High over the years have discussed using this larger abandoned airstrip. These same pilots believe it would accommodate a Cessna 206 on takeoff at gross weight. But the surface was never smoothed enough for use. The beginning stages of an aircraft turnaround are also unmistakably evident at the top of the runway.

"The Monument" on Monumental Creek where the drainage earned its name.

MONUMENTAL LANDING FIELD/ MCCOY RANCH

The Early History

In 1913 Richard A. Wallingford first occupied the property at the mouth of Holy Terror and Monumental creeks for one year. Rufe and Ora Hughes then took over the place. The Thunder Mountain Gold Rush apparently lured Hughes to the country. His main residence was the old schoolhouse from the town of Roosevelt that he had moved down to the property. Hughes left this acreage and relocated downstream to what is now referred to as Simonds, where he built the main cabin later occupied by the Taylors.

Roy Elliott then acquired the property and in 1928 received a homestead approval for 95 acres at the location. At the time of approval the ranch consisted of a house, barn, blacksmith shop, and cellar.[386] Elliott hoped to make a living by developing a fur farm. He, along with the help of his brothers, attempted to capture native pine marten by setting out box traps along the Mud Creek drainage. Evidence of their traps existed well into the 1950s.[387] With little success starting the fur farm, Elliott moved on.

The McCoy Years and Airplanes

In 1933 Gil McCoy bought the property and made many improvements. McCoy, who worked for the Idaho NF, began negotiating a sale with the agency in 1939. The USFS was interested in purchasing the property with the intention of building an airstrip for better access to the area. The ranch had a two-story log cabin, log barn, and several other

149

1 *The main house on the ranch photographed in the early 1950s.*
2 *The blacksmith shop on the ranch as it appeared in the early 1950s.*
3 *Gil McCoy seen here purchased the property in 1933 and later sold it to the USFS.*
4 *Roosevelt Lake in the 1920s with remnants of the former town still present.*

Roosevelt Lake in the early 1950s.

Looking up Monumental Creek at the lower end of the proposed runway in 1958.

small outbuildings along with 60 acres of hay. In fact by 1939 several planes had landed on the snow-covered hayfield.[388]

Although the USFS reported only ski-equipped planes as landing here, several wheel-equipped biplanes from Boise and McCall made successful landings in the mid-1930s. The Collord family, who owned mining claims in the Thunder Mountain area, had permission to use the place as an access point during certain parts of the year.[389]

The Collords chose the McCoy location as a secondary access point during the winter, as they originally intended to land ski-equipped aircraft on the frozen surface of Roosevelt Lake. In the fall of 1933 an effort was made to clear the lake of debris. The lake was the location of the gold-mining town of Roosevelt until May 1909 when a slide dammed Monumental Creek and flooded the settlement. Remaining in the body of water for many years were the remnants of several buildings and town rubble visible above the lake's surface. The McRae and Collord families poured diesel fuel on the buildings and burned them, clearing the lake's surface of obstacles that would hamper winter landings. The following winter of 1933–34 was extremely warm. Many lakes in the high country did not freeze, including Roosevelt Lake. This warming event rendered the lake landings useless and the McCoy Ranch the next best option.[390]

USFS Buys – Plans for an Improved Airfield

In August 1941 the USFS purchased the McCoy property.[391] The next year the agency surveyed and drafted plans for a formal airstrip under the title of

Looking up Monumental Creek at the former ranch location and runway.

The dilapidated ranch house in 1958 before it was burned roughly two years later.

McCoy Landing Field. The strip was to be approachable in both directions with the runway positioned roughly northeast-southwest. The landing field was to be 2400' long by 150' wide.[392]

Nothing happened for many years until 1955 when a prospector staked out a mining claim on the old homestead. The USFS responded with an inspection and decided once again that it was ideal for a landing area. The same year Alternate Big Creek District Ranger Ervin K. Bobo noted work was completed at the site, "The irrigation ditches are filled and the squirrel mounds leveled, the small trees cut and sagebrush cleared for a landing strip."[393] The mining claim was denied and the USFS withdrew the land for administrative purposes in September 1957, with plans to further develop the runway.[394] No other discussion of the old ranch becoming a serviceable airfield was documented again. In 1959 or 1960 the buildings were burned.[395]

However, a commercial operator from Lewiston used the old ranch into the 1960s, making several wheel landings. A client who was a professional photographer chartered the aircraft on flights from Lewiston to Monumental Creek in search of wildlife in the area.[396]

The airstrip in 1968.

MONUMENTAL RANCH

George Dovel

In the summer of 1959 George Dovel built the airstrip at the location of the present Monumental Ranch. Dovel, a native of Virginia, moved to Idaho based on a suggestion from some friends he met while flying in Korea and Japan for the military. Dovel came to the Big Creek country as a contract pilot with the USFS while operating his GEM Helicopter Service based in Boise. Shortly after the start of his flying business he was hired by Leon "Si" and Ursala Simonds on a charter flight to their place on Monumental Creek in one of his helicopters. Within a short time Dovel and the Simonds became friends. Through the Simonds he acquired two unpatented mining claims that make up the present ranch.[397]

A Mining Claim Becomes a Ranch

In 1959, shortly after acquiring the claim, Dovel was able to patent the ground. The same year he began work on an airstrip to access his property. Prior to this he was using the downstream Simonds airstrip. Dovel sold his flying business in 1959 but he retained a Cessna 180 that he used for many years in the backcountry, mainly to improve his property on Monumental Creek.[398]

The Cessna 180 was instrumental in flying a Farmall tractor to Simonds, which helped him build his landing field. The tractor was flown in piece by piece and then packed to the property over a small wagon trail that Simonds cleared with another small tractor. The Farmall was then reassembled and put to use. Referring to building the runway, Dovel said, "The place was a lodgepole jungle, over mature, and only growing a foot apart. It was a real mess, it was so thick not even a maintained USFS trail existed."[399] Dovel used the Farmall with a small choker cable to pull tree stumps and then leveled the field with a horse-drawn grader that he also flew in. Before snowfall the same year he made his first landing at the new airstrip.[400]

After the strip was finished he excavated a foundation and built a small residence. At this time Dovel began living at the place, with the exception of a few trips out in the winter months to spend time with his family. He carried this routine on for several years and named the mining claim Monumental Ranch. During his time on Monumental, Dovel worked as an outfitter and guide on lower Big Creek. For a few years he leased Jess Taylor's ranch and hunting area and then moved upstream for a year, leasing the Moore Ranch.[401] In 1969 Dovel started his own monthly newspaper called, *The Outdoorsman*. The publication focused on issues related to the Idaho backcountry, forestry, wilderness, and game management. Most of the articles were written by Dovel and voiced his distrust toward management by government agencies and their policies. The paper was short-lived, ending in 1973.

New Owners and a Flying Pickup

A year after the last copy of *The Outdoorsman* was printed, Dovel sold Monumental Ranch to Bill Gaechter and DeRay Lombardi.[402] Before selling the property, Dovel flew in a larger John Deere bulldozer that he purchased from Pistol Creek. Every piece of the dozer fit into the cabin of his Cessna 180 except for the dozer blade, which he fastened to the bottom of the fuselage. With the bigger piece of equipment he planned to extend the runway, however, he sold out before this happened.[403] In constant battle with USFS since his patenting of the property, he made one last parting shot to the federal employees by relocating the Monumental Creek Trail to the west of his ground with the new dozer.

Lombardi worked with the Donner Corporation based in the Reno and Lake Tahoe areas. The corporation was involved with the development of several condo projects around Sun Valley and it is most likely that he heard about the availability of the Monumental property during this time. Gaechter owned a large sporting goods store in Denver, Colorado. The two originally planned to build the ranch up and then sell it to the USFS with the condition of lifetime use.[404]

In 1978 the partners hired builder Ray Hamell of Hamell Contracting to construct a log lodge and generally improve the property. Planning to start construction the following year, Lombardi bought a new Cessna 206 and had it transported to Boise. The plane was going to be used for hauling supplies and crews to the ranch. Hamell, a pilot, agreed to fly the plane and went to Boise Air Service to take delivery. Excited to use the 206 in the backcountry, he was quickly disappointed as it was equipped for city flying. It was outfitted with standard tires, wheel skirts, and other features Hamell knew would quickly be torn off. He put a call into Lambardi and it was decided to have Boise Air Service make it backcountry ready.[405]

When the snow melted on Monumental Creek, Hamell began flying supplies and workers to the ranch with the 206. A base of operations was set up at the unoccupied Simonds cabin downstream. First on the list of improvements was to finish lengthening the runway, a project started by Dovel with the 1010 John Deere dozer. They were able to increase the airstrip

length from 800' to a little over 1200'. Hamell and his men then knocked down the existing residence, saving most of the foundation, in preparation for the new lodge.[406]

When the road opened to Stibnite all of the building materials unable to fit in the airplane, including precut logs, septic system, and various other items were trucked to the airstrip. Columbia Helicopters happened to be logging near Deadwood Reservoir, and they were hired to airlift the supplies from Stibnite with a Vertol helicopter. Wanting to be sure a crew was in place to help unload the material, Hamell and an employee flew to the ranch. In fact the first helicopter load was a three-quarter ton four-wheel-drive Chevy pickup. Strapped in the bed of the pickup were the parts for the septic system. Not knowing the area very well the pilot flew past Monumental Creek. It was not until he was over the Flying B Ranch on the Middle Fork that he realized he had gone too far. Hamell noted he was over due and got on the radio and helped direct him back to the proper landing location. The next helicopter loads went well.[407]

By the fall of 1979 most of the construction was completed, except for a hay barn that was later finished by caretakers. Lombardi was killed in a car accident before the year's end. The Gaechters used the ranch a few times, but quickly lost interest.[408]

The Professor Buys

The ranch was not on the real estate market long before being purchased in 1982 by Heinrich von Staden of Princeton, New Jersey.[409] Von Staden currently is a Professor emeritus of Classical Studies and History of Science at the Institute for Advanced Study in Princeton. At the time of buying the Monumental property he was a Professor of Classics and Comparative Literature at Yale University. He has authored numerous publications on ancient Greek and Roman medicine, biology, and intellectual culture.

Von Staden bought the ranch, sight unseen, late in the year, but he knew it was the remote place he had always dreamed of owning. With the snow falling in central Idaho he made a trip west to discuss his new purchase with Big Creek District Ranger Earl

Looking upstream at the Monumental Ranch runway.

Dodds. It became evident to Dodds throughout the conversation that the professor was a strong wilderness advocate. Dodds had never seen anyone so excited about buying a piece of property, and later delighted in having a wilderness supporter as an owner of a private in-holding on the district.[410]

Over the years von Staden made a real effort to remove most of the motorized equipment. From the beginning he and his family have exclusively flown with Ray Arnold and his pilots at Arnold Aviation.

Arnold noted in regards to cleaning the property that the pickup truck was neatly tucked away and has not moved in a long time, "About as mechanical as Henrich gets is maybe using a wheelbarrow. It is really a primitive outfit."[411] It took Arnold threatening not to use the airstrip anymore to get him to do some small tree removal and trimming along the sides for safety. Von Staden and his family continue to use the place extensively during the summers.

SIMONDS

The Early Years

Claude and Elsie Taylor at neighbor Wilbur Wiles's cabin downstream from their claim on Monumental Creek.

Rufe Hughes, who moved downstream from his ranch at Holy Terror Creek, first occupied the property. Hughes constructed a well-built log cabin at this location that was used by later occupants.

In the 1920s, after Hughes left the area, Claude and Elsie Taylor began mining gold at this location. Taylor's father came to the Salmon River Mountains at the time of the Thunder Mountain Gold Rush and his predominant occupation was selling game meat to area miners. For many years the couple processed a small amount of gold on the property with an on-site mill. The Taylors made several improvements to the site.[412]

During World War II Leon "Si" Simonds and Walter "Swede" Hanson began spending time in the area. Shortly after the war Simonds purchased the claim from the Taylors. Simonds and his wife Ursula lived on the property for about twenty years, from March to December, in the beautiful log cabin. In addition to the Simonds's log cabin, the Hansons also built a small residence even though they had their own claim nearby.[413]

Building an Airstrip

Over the course of about five years Simonds roughed in an airstrip for easier access. Amazingly, the whole strip was built with a little two-cylinder John Deere MC tractor that was walked down Monumental Creek by Del Davis. At the time, Davis was operating the Big Creek Lodge with his wife Thelma and son,

Buzz, for owner Carl Whitmore. Upon completion of the 500' strip, Simonds radioed George Dovel via Billie Oberbillig that it was ready. Although Simonds did not fly, he owned a Piper Super Cub that Dovel used for the first landing.[414]

Later Dovel helped Simonds extend the runway to include a dogleg on the upper end. This mainly required the removal of a few trees, burning stumps, and a little reshaping with Dovel's larger Farmall dozer.[415] The final overall length was about 900' feet, but it remained narrow, with tall trees off the south end across Monumental Creek. Also making the strip tricky to this day is the four percent slope of the runway toward the creek and the slight up and down grades on each end.

The End of an Era

In 1966 Simonds's mining patent application was denied when insufficient minerals were found in the samples. However, they were given a lifetime use of the property under the 1962 Church Johnson Act. The act provided a way for people who were not really mining anymore to continue living where they had lived for a long time on federal land. After the death of Si and Ursula Simonds in the early 1980s, their ashes were spread on the property above the

cabin. The USFS reclaimed Simonds's property along with Hanson's in the fall of 1985, and razed all the structures.[416]

In the 1980s, outfitter and guide Jerry Jeppson used a camp up Copper Creek above the old cabin site. Jeppson used the hunting area through the mid 2000s and hired Mike Dorris to shuttle clients and supplies via the airstrip. For many years Dorris used a Cessna 206 and then transitioned to a Cessna 170 for the job, hauling 350 to 400 pounds per trip between the Big Creek Ranger Station and the strip. In one day alone he made sixteen trips transporting hay for Jeppson's stock.

The USFS has threatened closure of the strip, but a small group of pilots continue to use it. To some aviators it is regarded as the most difficult airstrip in the Idaho backcountry. The small grave of the Taylor's first son, who died as a child, is located halfway down the length of the airfield to the east.

M. Dorris

Holm

Holm

Photos by Holm

1 The simple, but elegantly built cabin on the mining claim.
2 A Johnson Flying Service Piper PA-12 (N2577M) parked at the top of the airstrip in July 1975.
3 Mike Dorris (second from left) helps surveyors at the airstrip.
4 Looking upstream at the 900' Simonds runway in the 1980s.
5 Mike Dorris and his Cessna 170 (N4385B) at Simonds in the fall of 2010.
6 A view from the top of the runway looking upstream to the south in 2011.
7 Landing at Simonds.

Looking down Big Creek with the distinctive formation of Soldier Bar on the right.

SOLDIER BAR

A Significant Event

The Soldier Bar airfield sits on a naturally flat bluff above Big Creek. Given the distinctive level formation, the bar was used frequently by humans far before aircraft arrived. Shoshone Indians camped, hunted, and fished at the site. On August 19, 1879, soldiers in search of the Indians found a large camp on the east end of the high plateau. It contained ten wikiups (pole and brush structures),[417] which the soldiers burned.[418] One day later, while soldiers were leaving, they were taken by surprise. The Indians, who had retreated from the encampment several days earlier, had crept down the rock cliffs from above and attacked. During the skirmish Private Harry Eagan was shot through both thighs. A doctor came to the aid of the wounded private and put him under with chloroform to amputate his leg. He died during the operation.[419] Eagan was buried at the bar, thus creating the name Soldier Bar.

A Remote Monument

When Colonel W. C. Brown retired from the military he began recording many of his career's events. Included among his writings was the story of the Sheepeater Campaign of 1879. Although Eagan was not under his command during the campaign he thought a memorial should be established at the place to mark the location of the military engagement and the grave. In the early part of 1925 Brown made an inquiry with

The monument at Soldier Bar with a Cessna 206 in the background.

Clover Postmaster Joe Elliott who lived at the Mile High Ranch about the location of Eagan's grave. It is believed Elliott helped to establish a correspondence between Brown and lower Big Creek resident Dave Lewis, who was an Army packer during the campaign. Several letters and notes about the project ensued among the three men for several months.[420] In one of Lewis's letters to Brown he verified that he could show him the exact location of the gravesite. However, he expressed some doubt that Eagan's remains were still present by stating, "I always understood that in a year or so, his remains were taken up & sent to Boise, or elsewhere. It was 20 yrs. after the battle at Soldier Bar, before I came back into the Big Creek country . . . At any rate the grave was opened & shows it to this day."[421] Brown, apparently satisfied with Lewis's knowledge of the grave's locality, was able to persuade the United States Army to fund the Soldier Bar monument.[422]

Following the standard protocol set by the United States, an order was placed with the Vermont Marble Company of Proctor, Vermont, to make a headstone for Eagan. The military's World War I design was slightly modified at Brown's request to include extra lettering on the stone to give some explanation to the event surrounding Eagan's death. Due to the stone's proposed isolated location, the War Department's Construction Service designed the special conical base for the headstone.[423]

With arrangements made between Brown and Elliott the United States Army hired Elliott to transport the materials for the monument and to build it. On June 15, 1925 the stone was shipped from Proctor to Boston, Massachusetts, where it was placed on a steamship and taken to Portland, Oregon. From Portland it was delivered by rail to McCall on September 4. Elliot then hauled the 300-pound stone by wagon to Edwardsburg via Warren and then packed it the remainder of the way to Soldier Bar along with all the necessary construction supplies.[424]

On his way to Soldier Bar he stopped at the Lewis Ranch, where Lewis happened to be entertaining friend Harry Shellworth. The two offered to help in the building of the monument and by the end of October the project was completed. Some quibbling between Elliott and the United States Army occurred over the costs of transportation and construction, which totaled to $281.10. One Army individual wrote Elliott, "The request to do this work is not made so much on account of any small profit or pay which may be gotten for the work, but it is understood that you would undertake the work through patriotic interest." Elliot threw in his own jabs and made comments such as, "It all takes time in a country like this" and "I always try to be as patriotic as the next one."[425]

The Airfield

Work on building the airfield began in 1932 with the majority of the labor carried out the following year. USFS employees Bill Parks, John Cook, Tom Coski, and Dan LeVan did most of the work.[426] Cabin Creek resident Merl "Blackie" Wallace provided additional

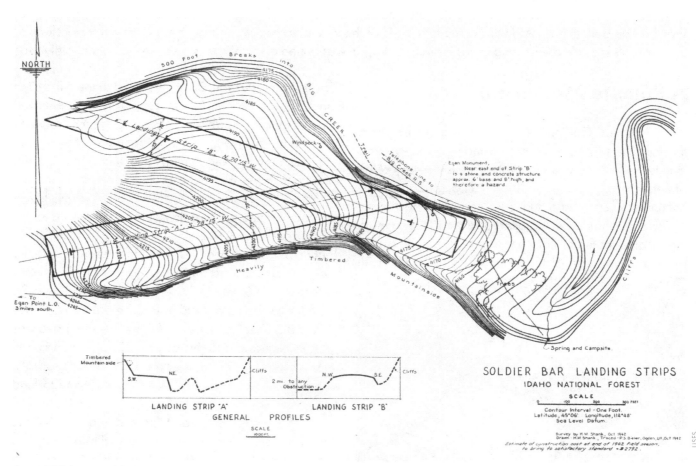

A 1942 USFS diagram of the Soldier Bar runways.

In 1933 Bob Johnson landed the first plane at Soldier Bar with Travel Air 6000 NC8879. The runway construction crew is photographed here on the special occasion (l to r): Bill Parks, John Cook, Tom Coski, Bob Johnson (pilot), and Dan LeVan Sr.

Johnson's Travel Air 6000 in 1933 with the monument on the far right.

Pilot Bob Fogg flying a Travel Air 6000 on final approach in September 1945. The short runway, which he is lined up to land on, did not receive the dogleg extension until the mid-1950s.

Soldier Bar as it appears today with the 500' dogleg extension on the upstream end.

help, packing supplies to the site.[427] In 1933 takeoffs had been made on both runways, which crossed at thirty-degree angles to each other. Bob Johnson of Johnson Flying Service was the first to land on the bar with Travel Air NC8879.[428] At this time the east-west runway measured 1500' and the northeast-southwest one measured 1150'.

After several landings had been successful, runway end markers made of rock were added to each end and measured 2' X 25'. Along with the rockwork the fields were further plowed with a horse-drawn log drag made on site to facilitate leveling. Included with the grading was the clearing of trees around the entire area, but primarily near the monument and to the southwest of the short runway.[429] In 1935 both runways were widened.[430]

By the end of the 1950s the shorter runway was moved slightly to the north and a 500' dogleg extension was added, bringing the field to its present length. This is the primary runway used at the facility today and the only one recognized by the FAA. However, the other portion of the longer field is still visible when on the ground. A few pilots occasionally use it to takeoff upstream, but generally tall grass makes it very difficult to see the actual surface.

A Johnson Flying Service Cessna 185 (N4022Y) parked at Soldier Bar in the late 1960s.

Holm collection

Wrecked Airplanes and Parts

In 1955 Big Creek District Ranger Bob Burkholder instructed summer employees Bill Little and Andy Finn to bury the remains of several airplanes that had wrecked at Soldier Bar. After digging one hole and making little progress, Burkholder selected two of five pits that he found in the talus slope as disposal locations. These pits were constructed by Indians, and most likely used to store caches. The two men hauled the material uphill, filled the holes, and then covered them with soil and rocks.[431]

However, long before these items were buried, Big Creek residents had scavenged the wrecks. Jess Taylor, of the upstream Taylor Ranch, packed the entire tail section of a Luscombe on a horse to his property. He then built a smoker by situating the tail vertically on a rock foundation and lined it with open racks. A small woodstove and pipe were then plumbed into the invention for a perfect fish smoker.

Other area inhabitants of the drainage packed off small souvenirs. Ross Geiling retrieved aluminum from an airplane that pilot Bill Woods wrecked at the bar in the early 1950s. As a gift he made dustpans for friends. One of these pans is still in use by an upper Big Creek resident. Other items carried off are also in use, including a Stinson flap handle.

In 1959 the USFS again buried more parts of wrecked airplanes. A crew comprised of Dub Horn, Liter Spence, Dave Stoops, and Ron White dug holes behind the trees along the south side of the airstrip and disposed of numerous parts. After they were done they smoothed out the airstrip surface and built new runway markers.[432]

A Sizeable Air Operation

In the summer of 1970 Soldier Bar became the location for one of the largest air operations to occur in the backcountry. What started as a slow fire season quickly changed on August 24, when the USFS contract aerial patrols first responded to a fire call reported to be near the mouth of Big Creek at the Middle Fork of the Salmon River. None of the fire lookouts in the area could see the base of the smoke, but everyone was reporting a large column.[433]

As it later turned out the fire had started as the result of an unattended campfire set by boaters camped near Porcupine Rapid on the Middle Fork just a couple of miles below Big Creek. Once started, it spread rapidly up the ridge between Wall Creek and Golden Creek.[434]

Intermountain Aviation Chief Pilot Bob Nicol dropped a load of smokejumpers from a Twin Otter on the ridge above the fire. The jumpers reached the ground, but were unable to stop the fire and had to evacuate the area. It became a project fire later the same day. Even though the fire was not on the Payette NF, most of the resources came from or through McCall and so they gained management of it.[435]

Transportation to the fireline primarily became a helicopter show. Fixed wing airplanes carried fire crews from various places to McCall. From McCall they were reloaded mainly into USFS DC-3s and then

A single engine de Havilland Otter departing Soldier Bar in the early 1970s.

Pilot Bob Nicol taking off from Soldier Bar in an Intermountain Twin Otter in late August 1970.

Jess Taylor salvaged the rear portion of an airplane fuselage from a wreck at Soldier Bar and with a little ingenuity created a smoker at his ranch.

flown to Chamberlain and Cold Meadows for further transportation to the Soldier Bar airstrip, where a base camp had been set up.[436]

Initially all flights to Soldier Bar were accomplished only by helicopter. The USFS DC-3s and Intermountain Twin Otters were used to drop supplies onto the Soldier Bar fire camp. The fire boss was Krassel District Ranger Ed Heikkenen. One morning about a week into the establishment of the fire camp, Nicol and his pilots showed up to fly some cargo drops. During the drops, Heikkenen asked Nicol over the radio if he could land at Soldier Bar. Since Nicol had landed the Otter at the strip on a checkout flight a year or two before, he told him sure. It ended up saving the USFS quite a bit of money in rigging, retrieving, and flight time, and that is how most of the cargo was delivered from then on.[437]

While the Twin Otters could operate fairly well in and out of Soldier Bar if the conditions were right, the weight had to be kept down, particularly for takeoff. The Twin Otters carried many fire crews to the airstrip, but not many out. Nicol recalled that the faces of the fire crews were much lighter in color after landing there, particularly the crews from Region 8 (Southern Region). When it came time to close the Soldier Bar camp, the crews were carried by helicopter to Chamberlain or Cold Meadows where DC-3s or Twin Otters flew them back to McCall or Boise.[438]

After the fire was out and all the crews were gone it became a smokejumper project to clean up the mess. Nicol and his pilots flew in rakes, garbage bags, etc. Nicol said, "It seemed like there was no end to it, but it actually took about two weeks. I stayed on contract until the end of September and my logbook shows my last flight to Soldier Bar was on September 20th."[439]

The result of the whole project was an estimated 200 takeoffs and landings made by Intermountain pilots in Twin Otters. The Otters mainly used for the Soldier Bar work were N7705 and N774M. During the peak workload two additional Otters (N790M and N7711) were also used mostly for passenger/freight flights into Chamberlain and Cold Meadows. The USFS had one or two DC-3s based in McCall during that time.[440]

Before and after the busy summer of 1970, outfitters and guides used the airfield regularly. The hunting area around Soldier Bar was originally permitted to the Taylor Ranch. Similar to the Indian habitation on the bar, outfitters utilized the spring on the east end. After 1982 the University of Idaho no longer accommodated outfitters at Taylor Ranch, and the field saw a little more use, as camps were often set up on Soldier Bar in the fall.

TAYLOR RANCH

Early Occupants, Dave Lewis, and a Homestead

A view from Eagan Point in the mid-1930s. The undeveloped site of the current Taylor Ranch airstrip can be seen in the center left of the photograph.

Starting sometime around 1900–03 a man with the name or nickname of "Bull" occupied the area at the mouth of Pioneer Creek and is believed to have prospected in the area.[441] John and May Conyers followed him in 1910, moving downstream from Cabin Creek. The Conyers built a decent sized cabin near the confluence of Pioneer and Big creeks.[442]

"Cougar Dave" Lewis was the next person to occupy the ranch. In 1921 Lewis took over the cabin built by Conyers and applied for a patent. Lewis first came to the Big Creek country as a packer for the military during the Sheepeater Indian Campaign of 1879. At the time his ranch was surveyed in 1924 he was living in a four-room log cabin. The property also contained a log bunkhouse and blacksmith shop. In 1928 he received homestead approval for 64.84 acres.[443]

Lewis made a modest living trapping, packing, and outfitting from this location. His reputation quickly grew and he eventually earned his nickname by claiming he had killed the largest number of cougars in the state. He outfitted for many influential figures in Idaho such as timberman Harry Shellworth and Governor H. C. Baldridge. It was around one of Lewis's fall campfires during a hunting trip that the idea of the Idaho Primitive Area was formulated.[444] Two of these men sat on the Governor's Committee on the Proposed Primitive Area in December 1930 along with members of the Idaho House and Senate. This group saw the issue through until it became official the following year.[445]

For his amazingly remote lifestyle, Lewis gained much attention in newspapers and magazines across the nation. Many of these media articles helped create a legend, but also leave behind many mysteries about whether his tales were fact or fiction. Several publications and books in the last few decades have tried to unmask this historical backcountry figure.

Jess and Dorothy Taylor - The Taylor Ranch

In 1934, prior to Lewis's death two years later at age eighty-one, he sold the property to Jess Taylor. Living in Boise and running a contracting business, Taylor had little time to spend at the ranch in his early years of ownership. In 1948 he married Dorothy and the two moved to the remote property with plans to build a guest ranch. The Taylors spent the first winter with few enhancements made to the place. Over the winter Taylor felled logs near Lobear Basin for a new house and a duplex for guests. Taylor then skidded the logs out over the ice with horses. When the ice went out in Big Creek he then floated them down to

1 Dave Lewis at his ranch with friend Harry Shellworth in the mid-1920s.

2 The house Jess Taylor completed in the early 1950s.

3 Robert "Bob" Diers Sr. in the cockpit during his World War II military service.

4 Jess and Dorothy Taylor with one of pilot Bill Woods's Staggerwing Beechs at Soldier Bar circa 1948.

5 Jess and Dorothy Taylor (right) circa 1955 standing at the end of their airstrip after receiving supplies from a Johnson Flying Service Travel Air 6000 (NC8112).

his property. At the ranch he stretched a cable at a forty-five degree angle from the horse crossing at the bottom of the hill upstream from Pioneer Creek. The logs naturally caught and angled into the bank, where he then hooked them to a team of horses and pulled the logs onto dry ground. By 1952 Taylor had completed both buildings.

One of the more modern conveniences brought to the place during their first year was a huge Monarch cook stove. Taylor hired Bill Woods of Boise to fly the 500-pound stove to Soldier Bar. Although it was more convenient than packing the heavy item all the way from the Big Creek Ranger Station, it was still a distance. Wanting direct air access Taylor began carving a strip parallel to Big Creek the same year.[446] All of the clearing and leveling was carried out with hand tools and horse-drawn equipment. Before the runway was finished that fall, Bob Diers Sr. made the first successful landing with a Stinson on only the upper portion.[447]

Diers, an impressive entrepreneur and pilot born and raised in Mackay, Idaho, opened Diers Flying Service after returning home from World War II. Enlisting in the Army Air Force at the beginning of the war, Diers soon found himself in China flying P-51 Mustangs. By the end of the long war he had earned the rank of Major, commanding the 528th Fighter Squadron. Diers wanted to continue to fly and bought several postwar aircraft, flying on the side when not running his hardware store or local Buick auto dealership. He frequently flew to the Taylor Ranch until he sold the flying business in the late 1950s.[448]

With everything in place, the Taylors operated the ranch for many years, running an outfitting business under the name Taylor Ranch Outfitting. The Taylors also maintained their construction business and a residence in the Boise area. While at the ranch they were often kept busy entertaining clientele, but were also visited by relatives. One niece, Lena Taylor, was a famous jazz singer who went by the stage name of Lee Morse. They also had two nephews. Ivan visited the property occasionally, and was at one point mayor of Mackay. The other was United States Senator Glen Taylor. This nephew was often seen around Idaho pitching campaign slogans as a country western singer with a backup band comprised of his wife and kids. He became more famous after his political career fell

apart for developing an early toupee known as the "Taylor Topper," which made him millions.[449]

Taylor Sells, Stan Potts, and the University of Idaho

Even though Taylor enjoyed outfitting, he was never overly interested in managing stock and packing. As a result he generally hired someone to help him with this end of the business. By the early 1960s he leased his hunting area to Larry and Mae Garner then to George Dovel. By the end of the decade Taylor and Dovel had a falling-out at which point he contacted Verl and Stan Potts who owned Chamberlain Basin Outfitters. Verl and Taylor were acquaintances from the Pahsimeroi Valley and he liked the Potts's reputation.[450]

The father-son team saw it as an opportunity

Chamberlain Basin Outfitters

FLY IN ONLY   **HUNTING ELK, DEER**

BASE CAMP TAYLOR RANCH IN AREA 26 Lower Big Creek

We are Not in the Volume Hunting Business . . . We Take from
30 to 50 Hunters Per Year on 9-Day Hunts
From 4 to 8 Hunters Only at Any One Time

HUNT NO. 1 — Special hunt for 1 to 8 persons. Use of entire area, including all spike camps, personnel, and equipment. $8,000.00 for 9 days.
HUNT NO. 2 — Individually Guided Hunts. $1,500.00 per person for 9 days.
HUNT NO. 3 — 2 to 3 Persons Per Guide. $1,000.00 per person for 9 days.

Also Winter Mountain Lion hunts. $1,500.00 per person. Bighorn Sheep and Goat hunts by Fish and Game Department drawings. Only by special arrangement.

Spring bear hunting. Summer pack trips to high lakes. Summer steelhead and salmon fishing trips.

For Information Telephone or Write Winter

STANLEY POTTS
Clover Valley   Wells, Nevada
Telephone 702-752-3697

MEMBER IDAHO OUTFITTERS AND GUIDES ASSOCIATION — LICENSED AND BONDED
MEMBER INTERNATIONAL PROFESSIONAL HUNTERS ASSOCATION

19 YEARS AS BIG GAME OUTFITTER   3% SALES TAX ON ALL HUNTS

IOGA

An advertisement for Chamberlain Basin Outfitters. Stan Potts and Jess Taylor are shown with trophies from the previous year's hunt.

M. Hornocker

Dr. Maurice Hornocker working in the Big Creek area during his cougar research project.

W. Rubey/Fogg collection

Taylor Ranch in the mid-1960s.

to expand their business, enabling them to take clients on sheep and goat hunts. They did retain their Chamberlain hunting area through 1972, when the whole operation was moved to Taylor Ranch. The Pottses leased from Taylor both the hunting area and the use of his ranch. About this time Taylor indicated that he wanted to sell the place. Potts wanted it, but did not have sufficient funds nor did anyone else that was interested. Dr. Maurice Hornocker, similar to Potts, really wanted it but for a different reason. Hornocker thought it would make an excellent base for research. Being creative he pitched the idea to the University of Idaho and they agreed. The University then signed a $5,000 one-year option on the property with Taylor.[451]

Hornocker, a graduate student at the University of British Columbia, came to the Idaho Primitive Area to conduct an extensive study on cougars. He hired expert outdoorsman Wilbur Wiles, a longtime Big

Creek area resident, to assist him. Also helping move supplies for the study was packer and outfitter Stan Potts. Hornocker first saw the Taylor Ranch in 1964 during the preliminary stages of the study and was enamored. In subsequent years he and Wiles used the ranch during the winter months while conducting the study.[452]

With the one-year option nearly up, Potts approached Taylor about the possibility of selling the place to him, but he had already given the University an extension on the option. In 1969 the deal was finalized and it officially became the University of Idaho Taylor Ranch Wilderness Field Station. When Taylor sold the ranch he built a new large home on the rim above Boise were he lived his remaining years.[453] The Taylors stayed actively involved in the ranch until their deaths in the early 1980s.

However, Taylor was a bit crafty and did not disclose in the sale that he maintained the ownership of the hunting area, which Potts continued to lease on five-year contracts. In an effort to make the University's new purchase viable they continued leasing the ranch to Potts, which he used for his business.[454]

Needing a full-time caretaker, Hornocker contacted Potts to see if he knew of anyone who would be interested. Potts recommended employee Arlow

In 1969 the University of Idaho purchased Taylor Ranch making it a field station for research.

Lewis. Because Hornocker had spent time around Potts and his crew in the primitive area, he was familiar with Lewis and hired him for the job. In addition to his duties for the University, he maintained his position with Potts during the hunting season. Lewis remained as the caretaker until he died of old age at the ranch in 1980.[455]

The 1970s at the Taylor Ranch were busy years. The University had scientists from multiple disciplines coming and going, and Potts was running his outfitting business. By the end of the decade Hornocker gained national and international recognition for his cougar research. In fact his study changed the tide for cougar management. Based on his findings the cougar became a big game animal and was no longer considered a bounty animal. A multitude of publications reported the study, putting Hornocker and the research facility on the map. Potts too was making a name for himself at the ranch, and several well-known people hired him for trips. He and his wife Joy were also featured in a 1972 edition of *Life Magazine.*

With the growing business Potts, needed more space for guests and contacted the University about building living quarters. They agreed and gave him a specific building site on the west side of Pioneer Creek. With their approval he constructed a large 12' X 48' bunkhouse. A few years later, after Cecil Andrus was appointed Secretary of the Interior, he made a trip to the station and for some reason felt the Potts building was an eyesore. He told the University that it needed to be moved. The school turned around and asked Potts to move it and he refused. They then spoke with Taylor, who was still frequenting the place, and

he agreed to do it. Amazingly, Taylor dropped two giant cottonwood trees and lined them up like a set of railroad tracks across Pioneer Creek. He then pulled the structure over the creek and set in down at the new location. The only damage done was one broken window.[456]

In the spring of 1976, Big Creek flooded beyond normal levels. During the event large deposits of thick sand were spread across the runway rendering it unusable. The crew at the station used a horse-drawn slip-scraper and moved tons of the material off to the sides. The low mounds along the runway are reminders of the event. Once the material was moved, the runway was re-leveled and seeded.[457]

In 1977 Potts renegotiated his lease with Taylor and sold his outfitting business to one of his guides, Con Hourihan. The Pottses helped their former employee the following year as part of the agreement. They continued outfitting on a smaller scale under the name Stanley Potts Outfitters in an area north of Taylor Ranch. Potts, a genuine Idaho backcountry personality and a fantastic storyteller, has published four autobiographical books covering many of his experiences. The books include: *The Potts' Factor Versus Murphy's Law, Look Down on the Stars, The Potts Factor's Return,* and *The Potts Factor's This Olde House.*

Hourihan operated his outfitting business from the ranch as had Potts, and then sold. At the time of the sale the University stopped leasing the facility. The new outfitter, Steve Zettle, moved his base camp farther up Big Creek.

Longtime Taylor Ranch manager Jim Akenson (right) in the early 1990s with a McCall Air Taxi Cessna 185.

Taylor Ranch in August 2011.

The Field Station

When the University ended the sixty-year tradition of outfitting and guiding at the ranch, a new era was born. The Taylor Ranch Wilderness Field Station focused on providing students and scientists opportunities to study and conduct wilderness research. Graduate and undergraduate students frequented the ranch, accomplishing a wide variety of studies. Hornocker continued his involvement at the station and in 1985 founded the Hornocker Wildlife Institute.

Ongoing work by several universities, scientists, professors, and students includes research on bobcats, ungulates (deer, elk, bighorn sheep), various mammals, birds, reptiles, stream ecology, fisheries, plant ecology, soils, and anthropology. The longest serving scientists to occupy the Taylor Ranch Field Station were wildlife biologists Jim and Holly Akenson. The couple became a fixture on Big Creek, conducting a wide variety of field studies in addition to preserving much of the area's history. At the ranch the Akenson's honed their knowledge and use of primitive equipment, which helped to guide a historically correct restoration of the Lewis Cabin. After more than twenty years of managing the station, they left in the spring of 2010 and took on new wildlife positions elsewhere.

With growing numbers of people at the station, several of the buildings were modified and others added. In 1990 when the USFS naturalized the Cabin Creek property, the Akensons arranged with the agency to airlift the motel unit built by former landowner Rex Lanham, which helped with the housing shortage. In 2000 the Diamond Point wildfire burned over the ranch. The cookhouse and bunkhouse were the only structures lost. A new log building was constructed in 2004 as a replacement. The logs were lifted to the station with a helicopter from Stan Potts's Colson Creek airstrip located at his home along the Main Salmon River. In 2005 the Akensons' experience during the fire was published in the book, *Forged In Fire: Essays By Idaho Writers.* Holly appropriately titled her piece "Jumping From the Frying Pan."

Writer Pat Cary Peek has also added to the sizable amount of literature related to the ranch. While Peek's husband, Dr. Jim Peek, conducted vegetation studies at the station, she became fascinated of the history at the ranch. Based on her interests she wrote an account of Dave Lewis's life entitled, *Cougar Dave: Mountain Man of Idaho.* She also wrote about living at the station in the book *One Winter In the Wilderness.* In the latter publication she included several stories of flying to and from the ranch with backcountry pilots.

Aircraft - A Tool To Wilderness Access and Research

Since Taylor built the roughly 1800' airstrip, aircraft have become an important link in the

1 *The restored interior of the Lewis Cabin.*

2 *The interior of the Lanham building relocated to the property from Cabin Creek.*

3 *Johnson Flying Service Travel Air 6000 (NC8112) on a downstream departure in the mid-1950s.*

4 *Stan Potts and employee Bill Kornell at Taylor Ranch with Kornell's de Havilland Otter.*

5 *Ranch manager Arlow Lewis (left) is visiting with (l to r) John Messick, Wilbur Wiles, and John Seidensticker, who were working on the Hornocker cougar study in the winter of 1971–72. The Johnson Flying Service 185 in the photograph was used for radio collar tracking.*

6 *Transporting bighorn sheep for testing at a IDFG lab in Boise with a McCall Air Taxi Cessna 206 (N7216N).*

B. Nicol

Pilot Bob Nicol delivering supplies to the ranch with an Intermountain Twin Otter in the early 1970s.

newer Cessna 180 (N9715G) that he purchased from friend Bob Stevens. He eventually sold this airplane and has since owned several others.[460]

George Dovel, prior to Potts, also used the airstrip in connection to the lease. In Taylor's time at the ranch Dovel was the only one to wreck an airplane on the strip. The Super Cub he was flying was actually owned by backcountry neighbor Si Simonds. He cracked it up on takeoff after some cargo was improperly tied down in the back; the loose items jammed into some of the controls. Instead of aborting the takeoff, Dovel attempted to get it airborne and "piled up the plane pretty good. His head was under water . . . but he got out ok."[461]

Outfitters were not the only ones to use the Taylor Ranch airstrip, as it has also been an integral part to the operation of the ranch. For Taylor it enabled him to bring guests, supplies, and material to and from the property. During his early years he mainly used the services of Diers, Woods, and Johnson Flying Service's branch in McCall.[458] Taylor was proud of his airstrip, but he also understood the implications for abuse in the future. His concern was illustrated during the sale of the property to the University, when he stipulated that the airstrip remain forever private. In a 1970 interview Taylor commented, "[I]ts a private field, and that's its status . . . and they [University of Idaho] just hadn't better step over the line either."[459]

Potts also used the strip frequently. When first involved at the ranch he flew a Cessna 180 (N2242C). He had one emergency landing at the ranch when a faulty oil filler cap popped off and blew out a majority of the engine oil. In 1974 the 180 was destroyed in a windstorm at their home in Nevada. Potts replaced the 180 with a Cessna 336 (N4633). He used this airplane for about one year, but from the beginning the plane caused him nothing but trouble and he unloaded it for a Cessna 206 (N8647Z). The 206 served as a real workhorse, but after he sold the outfitting business it was more airplane than he needed. Potts then downsized to a

research conducted from the site. Hornocker realized the importance of airplanes and obtained a private license from Johnson Flying Service pilot and friend Bill Dorris. After earning his license he purchased a Cessna 180 (N2418C) from backcountry pilot Bill Jeffs in the early 1970s. Hornocker used the plane mainly as transportation to and from the ranch, as well as for other research projects in Montana. He sold this airplane and in the early 1980s bought a Cessna 182 (N2889R). He flew for another ten years and then sold the airplane after having some problems with it.[462]

Besides Hornocker's personal use of aircraft, he also developed some pioneering aerial telemetry with airplanes while at Taylor Ranch.[463] The program's origin stemmed from the need to gather quantitative data on the movements and other activities of mountain lions and elk in the mountainous terrain of central Idaho. Helping Hornocker design the equipment and techniques was University of Idaho PhD. candidate John Seidensticker.[464] The main airplane used in these early studies was Johnson Flying Service's Cessna 185 N4546F, flown by Bill Dorris.

Following in Dorris's footsteps were his sons, who also became involved with aerial wildlife tracking.

The Dorrises transported several caged and sedated mountain lions for Hornocker's research via airplane to and from the ranch. In the early 1970s Bill Dorris flew Hornocker and one of his male cougars to Portland. Hornocker loaned it to the zoo for eighteen months until they obtained another for their exhibit. When the agreement ended the two returned to Portland and flew the cougar directly to the Taylor Ranch. The big cat was well sedated for both trips. While Gadwa attracts cliental from northern Idaho, Pete Nelson and his pilots at Middle Fork Aviation located in Challis fly many people from the eastern side of the state to the ranch. Hornocker noted, "The cougar quickly recovered when we landed at Taylor and followed me up to his enclosure up Pioneer Creek. He acted right at home."[465]

A current view of the 1800' Taylor Ranch runway.

In 1986 Mike Dorris flew three kittens that had been rehabilitated at the zoo in Boise to the Taylor Ranch. Abandoned at a young age, the kittens, two small females and a larger male, were deemed to be healthy enough for reintroduction to the wild. The Wildlife Research Institute under the direction of Howard Quigley became involved and the Taylor Ranch was suggested as the site to release the recovered cougars.[466]

Dorris picked the three sedated cougars up at the Boise airport in individual dog kennels. With the Cessna 185 N93039 stuffed to the roof he took off for the Big Creek drainage. En route weather obscured the normal flight path and a fair amount of time was spent working his way around low-lying clouds and squalls. Not planning on being in the air that long, Dorris found that the male lion began to slowly awake from the sedative. Fortunately he reached the ranch before it became too much of an issue, but Dorris will never forget the boisterous screams from the male lion, "It made the hair on my neck stand up and added a bit of stress to the flight." The cougars were unloaded and kept in outdoor enclosures for sometime before being released.[467] Dorris has flown many other animals connected to research at Taylor Ranch. Starting in 1988 he hauled out several live bighorn sheep for disease testing at a IDFG lab in Boise.

Many people associated with the University accessed the ranch via airplane from the Pullman-Moscow airport. Glenn Ottmar of Ottmar Aviation flew many of these people with a Cessna 182 (N92519). Palouse Aviation followed Ottmar in 1974 and picked up the University business. During these years Jack McGee piloted most of the flights to the ranch. In 1983 Inter-State Aviation owner Doug Gadwa then bought out Palouse. While Gadwa attracts cliental from northern Idaho, Pete Nelson and his pilots at Middle Fork Aviation located in Challis fly many people from the eastern side of the state to the ranch. Gadwa continues today flying University officials using a Cessna 182 and 206.[468] Since the 1980s Ray Arnold has also flown for the Taylor Ranch and its employees. He and his pilots have been mentioned in several publications dealing with the ranch over the years.

The airfield continues to offer great access to visitors, students, and scientists. The largest aircraft to operate in and out of Taylor Ranch were Intermountain Aviation Twin Otters in the late 1960s. Since Intermountain's use of the airplane at the location, the USFS has also used their Twin Otters here through the years.[469]

Bayok collection

A 1930s view of the Garden Ranch looking up Big Creek.

VINES RANCH

The Early Years

Wes Ritchey is the earliest known settler at the location now often called "Vines." By November 1898 Ritchey built the small log cabin on the south side of Big Creek later occupied by John Vines. Ritchey was a friend and business partner of the Caswell brothers, who lived on Cabin Creek.[470]

In March 1914 Arthur E. Garden and his wife, Viola, homesteaded 160 acres at the location. At this time the place was known as the Garden Ranch. For several years during their ownership Viola served as the area's postmistress for the Clover Post Office. The official post office was run from their home located on the north side of Big Creek. Also in the country were their nephews, known as the Elliott brothers. These brothers were associated with property on Monumental Creek and at the Mile High Ranch, where the Clover Post Office was eventually moved. In 1918 Arthur Garden became quite ill after getting caught in fall storms while moving stock from Old Meadows, Idaho, to Big Creek. He returned to Old Meadows for treatment, wet, and sick. While there he died in the hotel.

John Vines

After Garden's death his wife sold the property to E. I. and May Osborn, who sold it in October 1942 to Art and Margaret Francis. Nearly two years later in September 1944, John Vines purchased the land.[471] Vines, a veteran World War I pilot and later a test pilot for Lockheed Martin, was forced out of flying when he developed a heart condition. At the closing of his career in aviation he and his wife opened a string of successful restaurants called Top Hat Bar and Grill in San Francisco and Sacramento, California. Vines and his wife had a falling out and he then moved to Idaho, where he remained for roughly thirty years.[472]

He came to the property with very little and lived in the cabin once occupied by Ritchey on the south side of Big Creek. It had not been used for years and Vines did very little to improve it. It had a dirt floor, stove, bed, and a cramped sitting area. He did build all of his own furniture, and some of the pieces made of willow were quite unique.

During one of his early winters in the Big Creek country Vines needed to leave, so he hired upstream neighbor Dewey Moore to care for his horses. When he returned months later to trail his animals back down to his ranch he found that Moore had taken his money and nearly starved the horses. The two hardly ever saw eye to eye or rarely spoke again. Vines used to tell visitors, "Old Dewey tried to tell the truth once and nearly choked to death – he couldn't do it."[473]

Vines lived a modest life on Big Creek and

John Vines (left with hat) sitting at his cabin in the 1960s.

John Vines in 1967 relaxing in a handcrafted willow chair at his cabin sipping a glass of "Big Creek Low Ball" – straight whiskey.

Vines crossing Big Creek on his cable car to the north side of the river.

was adored by his backcountry neighbors (except Moore) and visitors. He always had an entertaining story to tell and if it was after five o'clock he insisted on pouring himself, along with his guests, a glass of "Big Creek Low Ball," which was mainly straight Granddad Whiskey, purchased by the case.

Beyond a good story and an evening cocktail, Vines had his regular daily and seasonal routines, hunting, fishing, walking, and chopping wood. He did not believe in keeping a woodpile, which seems odd considering he lived on the dark south side of the river, where even on a clear day in the dead of winter the sun did not shine. When people asked about this peculiarity he explained that it kept him healthy and gave him something to do every morning.[474] "Besides," Vines would explain, "A mans got to cut wood everyday in this country anyway and if he doesn't, he's going to die."[475]

Vines continually had interesting and hilarious stories to tell visitors as they passed through. One year he had a series of pesky bears who kept getting into his "dishwasher," which was nothing more than an old bathtub that he piped flowing water into from the nearby ditch. He seemed to think that storing the dishes in the running water kept them sanitary. One of the bears liked what remained on the dishes and continually made a mess, but Vines could never catch the critter in action. Vines became irritated and baited the bear in with meat attached to a contraption of cans. When the cans rattled he planned on shooting the bear. However, his scheme went awry when the bear sat down in front of his door to eat the meat and he could not get out.

The Airfield

Sometime in the early 1960s downstream neighbor Loren Hollenbeak bladed in the runway. It is believed the piece of heavy equipment was walked up Big Creek when it was frozen thick with ice during the winter. When the job was finished the D8 Caterpillar was walked back the same way to Cabin Creek.[476]

Johnson Flying Service's PA-12 delivering mail and supplies to the ranch.

M. Jager

Vines enjoyed the new airstrip as it gave him direct mail service instead of having to walk down to Cabin Creek. He also was able to bring in specialty items that he could not receive before. Vines began ordering fifty-five gallon wooden barrels of shelled peanuts. At certain times of the year the floor of his little log cabin was ankle deep in peanut shells.[477] At one point Vines lived off peanuts after he unfortunately leaned over the woodstove and his false teeth fell out and burned up. Unable to chew any tough foods, he ground up peanuts until he could get another set of teeth.[478]

Besides barrels of peanuts, Vines brought in other things via Johnson Flying Service. This included a small Sears tractor/lawnmower and matching trailer.[479] He used the piece of equipment originally to move supplies between the strip and various parts of his property, but later it was outfitted with a small four-foot blade to help maintain the rocky surface of the runway.[480]

When the plane could not land on his airstrip due to certain weather conditions, the mail was dropped off at Cabin Creek. Vines then had to cross the river using his homemade cable car and travel the river trail downstream. He would often use one of his horses, but if they were out grazing and not close by, he simply would walk, pushing a wheelbarrow that he kept on the trailside of the river. He could then return without having to carry anything.[481]

Deciding to Sell and a New Cabin

In the late 1960s as Vines became older and less mobile he began to think about selling the ranch. The higher-ups in the USFS wanted Big Creek District Ranger Earl Dodds, who had a good relationship Vines, to discuss a possible sale.

Dodds was not thrilled about the task, as the USFS wanted to pay Vines practically nothing. On a spring day Dodds rode on the mail route with Johnson Flying Service pilot, Bill Dorris. The two were greeted and invited inside for a chat. Along with his mail, Vines had placed his usual order of raw peanuts and Olympia beer. Dodds put the offer right out there, and was in many ways very apologetic. Vines understood his position, but could not accept such a low offer. As if nothing happened the three continued on in conversation eating peanuts, Dodds and Dorris drank coffee, and Vines opened a can of beer. He was someone they both admired and respected.[482]

About the same time offers for the property were coming in, he was busy trying to finish a new log

175

The unfinished Vines cabin located above the original Ritchey cabin on the south side of Big Creek.

cabin with a loft. The new place sat above the original cabin. It was rumored that during the project Vines and his hired hand got into a disagreement while nailing down shingles on the roof. The helper apparently threw a hammer at Vines and started yelling. Vines went down to his old cabin and returned with a gun, which sent the guy running – he never did come back.

A Buyer, Dorris, and McCall Air Taxi

In 1969 the property eventually sold to Idaho cattle operator Harry Bettis and partner Mike Jager. Jager, who lived in California, ended up using the property annually with his family. After several years of ownership he arrived in McCall trying to charter a flight with Johnson Flying Service but was told their business in the region would soon be winding down, and they no longer had the equipment or pilots to fly to the strip. Jager then asked what had happened to former Johnson pilot Bill Dorris, as he had flown them in many times. The person told Jager that Dorris had retired. Surprised by the information he looked Dorris up in the telephone book and gave him call. Dorris told Jager that he was far from retiring and was actually starting his own air taxi operation. Jager hired him. In fact Jager turned out to be a major backer for Dorris's

charter company, McCall Air Taxi.[483]

Dorris's newly-started company, which consisted of a Cessna 170, an old office trailer, and gas truck, quickly grew to have a new hangar, a new Cessna 185 and many leased aircraft. Dorris, a World War II Marine pilot from Roundup, Montana, loved aviation and in the spring of 1956 came to McCall to work for the IDFG. While working for the department he came up with the idea of using his personally owned Cessna 170 for work to save time and money when he needed to reach remote management areas. By 1965 he became a professional pilot again, working for Johnson Flying Service in McCall. When Johnson began the first of several failed buyouts, Dorris became uneasy and in 1976 started McCall Air Taxi.

Several years after establishing the company, thanks to his own skills and Jager's financial help, Dorris brought in several pilots, including Rod Nielsen, Bruce Minter, and Andy Anderson. Eventually three of his five sons joined the business, starting with Mike who established an arm of the operation in 1979 at the Stanley airport. Sons George and Pat soon followed. Mike bought Wilderness Aviation owned by the Combs family in Salmon and for a short time called the business McCall and Wilderness Air. As the business picked up steam, Bill slowly retired. He died in March 2000 after suffering from a stroke.

At the height of Mike's ownership and management he had seasonal highs of twenty-five employees and fifteen aircraft before selling it in 2002 to Dan and Laura Scott who renamed it McCall Aviation. Mike worked several years for the company and then like his father went out on his own when he bought Sawtooth Flying Service. As before, Mike brought in family to help during the busy parts of the year.

Harry Bettis packing to the Vines property in the summer of 1969.

Margie and Mike Jager at the Middle Fork Lodge in June 1977.

McCall Air Taxi founder and pilot Bill Dorris with his Cessna 170 (N4385B) in McCall.

A Wonderful Place

Usually Jager flew his family from California to McCall in his Beechcraft Bonanza (N5610S). While in McCall the Jagers planned a series of shuttles with the Dorrises from the Big Creek Ranger Station to the property, as they left the Bonanza at the station. Jager, an accomplished pilot in his own right, flew the same Bonanza around the world with his wife Margie and a friend.

Jager spent ten years enjoying the place and the surrounding wilderness area. When he and his family first started spending time on the property, Vines was still living in the small cabin and provided many memorable stories. During their ownership they made few changes, mainly enjoying it as a spectacular place to camp, hike, and fish. Jager's son Bill lived at the ranch one summer and took on several projects such as pouring a concrete floor in the newer cabin, reviving the old vegetable garden, and improving the water system. The upper log cabin was never finished and they used it as a place to sleep, while the lower Ritchey-built cabin was used more for storage.

The only improvements made to the airstrip were an occasional leveling using the Vines tractor. Jager commented, "The darn runway actually grew rocks. Every year with the freezing and thawing action we accumulated more and more rocks." Another issue with the runway during their years at the ranch was a rather tall tree off the downstream end of the field. Bill Dorris used to hint to Jager that it needed to be removed, but it was on USFS land. It only made the approach for takeoff and landings a little more technical. This tree along with a few others that were mighty tall later burned in a forest fire.

In the end the USFS purchased the property in 1979.[484] The Jagers have revisited their old place a handful of times and on occasion Mike and Margie have flown over it on their many travels. The remaining buildings burned in a 2000 wildfire. The airstrip is still used by some, and like others in the Big Creek drainage, has come under threat of closure.

1 An early advertisement for McCall Air Taxi.
2 Some of the Jager family with their Beechcraft Bonanza at the Big Creek airfield awaiting an airplane shuttle downstream to their property.
3 Looking downstream at the rocky surface of the airstrip with Horse Mountain in the background.
4 Flying the approach to the Vines airstrip.

M. Jager

Holm

Photos by Holm

A group of McCall Air Taxi airplanes parked at the top of the steep Willey Ranch airstrip.

CHAPTER 3

South Fork
of the
Salmon River

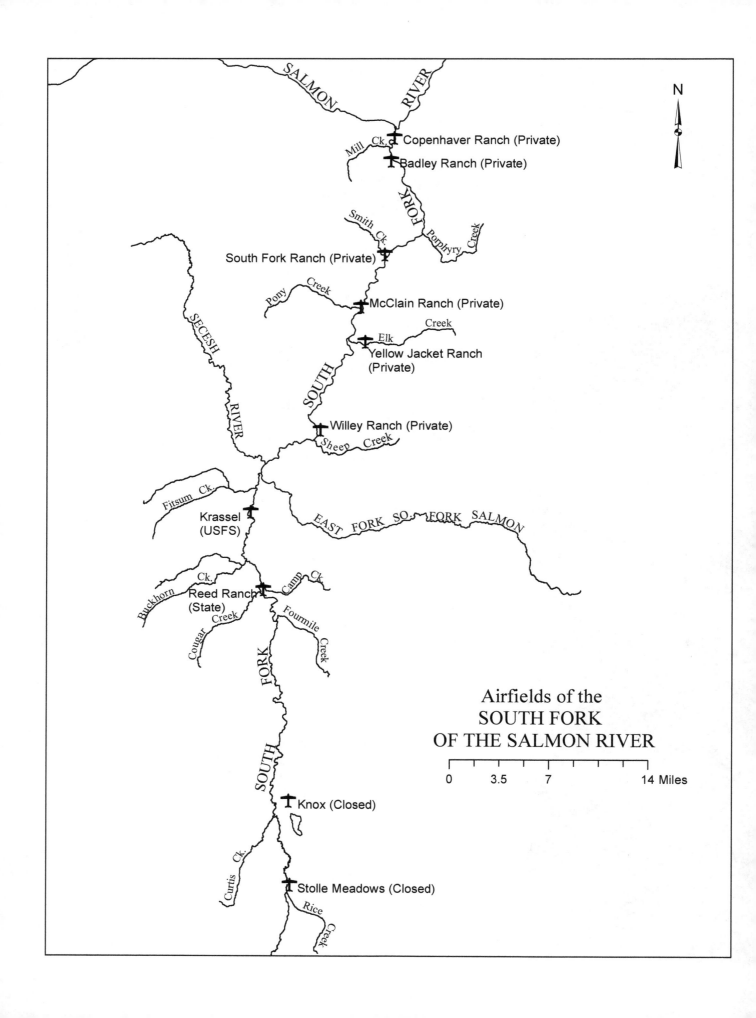

Airfields of the
**SOUTH FORK
OF THE SALMON RIVER**

Looking upstream at the Badley Ranch with Round Mountain to the left.

BADLEY RANCH
Early History

The Badley Ranch is currently comprised of two homesteads. James Rains first occupied the upper portion of the property located to the south. Rains and his brother William came to the South Fork area in the mid 1860s, acquiring mining claims as early as 1866. William eventually moved away and James married Mary Weber.[1]

In 1879 Rains was warned about the conflict between the United States government and the Sheepeater Indians. Taking precautions, he moved his family to Warren. On August 17 he and two friends were haying at the ranch while his brother-in-law, Albert Weber, was in the cabin. Gunfire broke out and the two friends took cover in a nearby creek. Figuring Weber was killed Rains made an effort to reach the cabin and was shot twice, but made it inside. The other two headed to Warren for help. Weber, unharmed, tried to help Rains but he died. Weber then escaped by exiting out a rear cabin window and also trekked to Warren. When volunteers from Warren returned to the ranch they found a smoldering cabin ruin and no signs of the Indians.[2] Rains's body was located and buried in the Warren Cemetery.

Mary Rains later remarried and in 1885 sold the ranch to Fred Burgdorf. In 1899 Freeman Nethkin settled land to the north of the Burgdorf property and eventually purchased Burgdorf's parcel for $1,000. Nethkin patented both tracts as one homestead in 1915.[3] Fred Badley and business partner Roy Stover purchased the ground in 1924.[4] Stover sold out two

years later. Badley and his wife Bessie lived on the South Fork for many years and raised four sons. After Badley died in 1954, Bessie retained the property.[5]

The second portion of the current Badley Ranch is farther down the South Fork and is often referred to as the "Old Homestead" or "Middle Homestead." Squatters first occupied this plot of land at the turn of the twentieth century. These early inhabitants built two log cabins that Adrian Carlson acquired in 1911. Carlson greatly enhanced the property and in October 1919 received homestead approval for 132 acres.[6] Andrew Nelson, an area cattle rancher, eventually acquired the parcel. Nelson had been involved as early as 1909 with the Burgdorf and Nethkin properties and under his ownership it became known as the Nelson Ranch.[7] In 1938 Fred Badley bought the land.[8]

Both original homesteads remain in the Badley family. The southern portion of the ranch contains the maintained 1250' runway and modern dwellings. The extensive historic structures associated with the Middle Homestead stood unoccupied but intact for many years until they were burned in a 2007 wildland fire.

An entrance sign to the ranch.

Al Tice and Airplanes Arrive

After Al Tice's first year of outfitting in Idaho on French Creek above Riggins he decided to increase his pack animal inventory. Word got out that he was looking for stock and he was put in contact with the Badleys on the South Fork. After inspecting the animals he made a deal, and in the same transaction he had the opportunity to lease the ranch from Bessie Badley. He took the chance and ran his business from the property starting in about 1954. At this time he and his stepson Dick remodeled an existing framed house at the Middle Homestead for their family and guests. During these years Bessie lived in another house with her sons and they split their time between the ranch and Grangeville.[9]

Tice had been a pilot since his initial days of outfitting near Sacramento, California, and incorporated the use of aircraft in the Idaho operation. In the early years at Badley Ranch he simply left his planes at Mackay Bar. However, wanting to make it more convenient, he approached Bessie about building a strip on the upper portion of the homestead and she had no objections.[10]

In 1957 Tice started construction on the runway. Dick and some of Tice's hired hands felled trees, blasted stumps, and moved brush. The crew then pulled homemade drags behind Jeeps to help level the field. In addition to the Jeeps the crew also used an old Farmall tractor owned by the Badleys. After the final touches, Tice gave the strip a try with one of his Piper Cubs with Dick as a passenger.[11]

The First Incident

A year or two after the airstrip was finished a newly checked-out Johnson Flying Service pilot overshot the runway with a Travel Air (N447W). The plane ran nose-first up into a grouping of rather tall saplings. Mowing down several of the trees the pilot shut the engine down and climbed out quite embarrassed. Al and Dick helped by pulling the plane out of the tangled trees and got it turned around pointing it back down the strip. The pilot still a little rattled, looked the plane over and could see no physical damage. He then opted to fly it back to McCall. The Tices just shook their heads.[12]

Not a week later another Johnson pilot, Dean Logan, was flying the same Travel Air from Chamberlain back to McCall. Logan came over the top of Horse Heaven Ridge and the plane started shaking so badly he thought the whole aircraft was going to fall apart. He pulled the power back and pitched for best glide speed. With few options for an emergency landing in the nearly vertical South Fork canyon he was able to nurse the plane down to the Hettinger Ranch (currently called South Fork Ranch). After a quick inspection of the aircraft he found several inches of a propeller blade had broken off.[13]

Holm

1 *A look at the airstrip from a lower hayfield.*
2 *Bill Dorris loading supplies and goats into a Johnson Flying Service Cessna 206 (N29024) in the mid-1970s.*
3 *A McCall Air Taxi Cessna 185 parked at the ranch in the early 1980s.*

M. Dorris

M. Dorris

185

COPENHAVER

The Early Years

A view to the south from homesteader Tom Copenhaver's cabin site. A small piece of equipment is all that remains of his time on the flat.

During the eighteenth and nineteenth centuries, this stretch of the South Fork and the confluence with the Main Salmon River were large wintering grounds for Northern Shoshone-speaking people. Archeological evidence of these activities still exists.

In 1918 William T. Copenhaver moved to the lower South Fork property now known as Copenhaver Flats. At the time of his arrival a 12' X 16' cabin was already there. Copenhaver further improved the property by building a woodshed, and a pole corral, and brought in a portable sawmill. By 1923 he had successfully established a garden and several fruit trees. He eked out a living on the flat, originally farming about twelve acres. To help with improvements he worked for the USFS as a fire lookout, and hunted cougar and coyote. In December 1924 his homestead application was approved for 92.85 acres.[14]

In 1930 the Fred Badley family purchased the property and used it along with their other in-holdings for farming and grazing. A few years after Badley died his wife Bessie leased the ground to Al Tice of Mackay Bar. Tice used it for grazing stock. In 1969 the parcel was then transferred to son Jack Badley and then in 1970 to son Orland. In 1985 Orland subdivided the land into twenty-four lots, and an additional 68 acres was created for a common area that is now maintained by the Copenhaver Ranch Subdivision Homeowners Association.[15] At the north end of the flat Orland had plans to build a large lodge where he could operate a hunting and guiding business, but neither ambition materialized.

An Airfield and Cabins

Wanting to have air access to the property, Orland consulted with Mike Dorris. Dorris flew Orland into the Badley Ranch airfield and they hiked down to Copenhaver and surveyed the property. It was decided to build one runway on the upper bench of the acreage to the west and a second shorter, but more accessible airfield paralleling the river and the homeowner lots. Although the upper strip would have allowed for aircraft with bigger loads, Orland opted to first build the lower airstrip along the river. The larger strip, although still platted, has not been built.[16]

In May 1985 Orland started construction on the lower runway with a small John Deere dozer. He radioed out to Dorris in the middle of the summer that the strip was roughed in, plenty long, and ready for a landing. From McCall Dorris flew Cessna 170 N4385B and circled the strip once for a good look. He then set up a downstream approach figuring the terrain was more forgiving if a go-around was needed. However, it was not necessary as the roughly 800' airstrip was adequate.

After the successful landing, little activity occurred at Copenhaver for several years. Eventually numerous people purchased and sold lots at the location, including Dorris, but by the early 1990s this

M. Dorris

1 *Summer 1985 – the first airplane to land at Copenhaver. Notice the fresh grading contours on each side of the runway.*
2 *Blasting and leveling an additional 400' of runway on the upstream end in the early 1990s.*
3 *Looking south from mid-field at Copenhaver.*
4 *A Cessna 182A landing at the property.*

B. Dodge

Holm

Holm

Landing upstream at Copenhaver.

little subdivision's property was almost completely sold and many cabins were built. Also during this time the homeowners built a boat tie-up area with a ramp to the airfield, along with a cable car system across the South Fork. These cabin owners not only have unique access by air, but also by jet boat. The residents are the only individuals, along with the Badley family, allowed to boat up the South Fork.

As other improvements were made during the 1990s the property owners also extended the runway to about 1200'. Copenhaver is a tight-knit group of individuals who enjoy their backcountry cabins for hunting, fishing, socializing, boating, and flying. Each spring they collectively try and get to together for a work weekend, bringing in family and friends to help.

Over the years several residents have operated their own aircraft at the strip. Included among them is a distinguishable blue and white Cessna 206 (N5119U) owned by Duane Smith, two 182As, one owned by Jerry Robinson (N6466A) and the other by Jerry McCauley (N9995B), and a Piper PA-12 (N2936M) owned by Brian Howard.

Aircraft and Pilots

On July 1, 1994 a recently-licensed nineteen-year-old pilot walked into a Nampa Fixed Base Operator (FBO) with a request to rent an airplane for the day. After further discussion, the pilot explained that he was headed to Mackay, Idaho, to show a friend a cabin he had helped build. Completing the necessary paperwork the young pilot and his friend loaded into a Piper Tomahawk (N24201). They did not fly in the direction of Mackay, but rather Mackay Bar. The pilot knew he would never have been able to rent the plane if he told the folks in Nampa where he was really going. As they flew over the confluence of the South Fork and Main Salmon Rivers the pilot pointed to Copenhaver, describing the cabin he had worked on.

With fifty total hours of flight time under his belt he held the yoke with a tight grip and set up for a final approach, landing upriver. For whatever reason as the pilot neared short final he rejected the landing. With unbelievable luck he was able to maneuver the plane back for another attempt at a landing.

On the second try he succeeded. The pilot and

The aftermath of attempting to takeoff on a hot summer day from Copenhaver with a Piper Tomahawk. The plane did not fly long before settling into the South Fork of the Salmon River.

The wreckage of John Harper's Cessna 170 at Copenhaver.

his friend scoped out the cabin and looked around. Well after lunch, the pilot decided they should get the plane back to Nampa. The temperature by this point in the day had risen to over a hundred degrees, but he reasoned with the plane configured for a short field takeoff they would make it. Sure enough the first stab at a departure failed, the plane barely moved.

On his second attempt he gave himself a little more room, hanging the tail off the end of the upstream runway as far as possible. Holding the brakes to full power he released them in hopes of better performance. This time the Tomahawk broke ground right at the end of the airstrip. Still in ground effect the plane's wings sunk as they hit the air over the South Fork and it simply quit flying. The airplane settled into the river and the two occupants scrambled out safely.

The Tomahawk was a complete loss. Two days later it was dismantled and hauled to Vinegar Creek by Heinz Sippel in a jet boat. From there it was trucked to Montana for salvage and the registration number reassigned to a Cessna 182.

Three years after the Tomahawk mishap, Copenhaver property owner John Harper of Kirkland, Washington, wrecked his Cessna 170 (N1487D) at the strip. Bob Dodge, another cabin owner was enjoying the Labor Day weekend with family and friends and heard the plane fly over as they were finishing dinner. Many in the group had come in on horses, while others flew in. Several of the horses were out grazing along the airstrip. With almost everyone watching the runway they noticed his approach was high and unusual for a landing at Copenhaver. Dodge concluded that he was going to land at Mackay Bar. Others sitting on the deck agreed and they decided not to worry about rounding up the horses.[17]

However, within a few moments they rushed to try and get the horses safely out of Harpers way when the plane was spotted coming up the South Fork on final approach. Worried he was going to hit the horses, Harper attempted a go-around. Trying to avoid several tall trees he crashed the Cessna 170 into some timber on the right side of the runway.[18]

Seeing and hearing the crash they all knew that he was in trouble. The Dodge crew rushed to help him out. Luckily Bob had grabbed a fire extinguisher and was able to dowse a small fire caused by dripping gas. They safely removed Harper from his plane and laid him down, not wanting to move him any farther.[19]

Dodge and his friends then contacted Mackay Bar who sent a call out to McCall Air Taxi. Owner Mike Dorris who was at home hurried to work and grabbed friend Dave Dewey, a Donnelly EMT and Copenhaver cabin owner. Dorris was suppose to fly McCall EMTs, but they were not at the airport and time was a factor with daylight waning and a man's life on the line. The two were en route when not ten minutes later the McCall EMTs wanted to know why the plane had left without them. Having to follow protocol, Dorris turned around, unloaded Dewey and flew the others in. By the time he reached Mackay Bar it was nearly dark, but he managed to land safely.[20]

Dorris and the EMTs hitched a ride to the cable car, crossed, and the EMTs went about their business. As they got Harper stabilized the whole crowd heard a helicopter in the distance. Life Flight from Boise had also been dispatched and showed up. Luckily the helicopter pilot was familiar with the area and was able to make a night landing. Harper was flown out and recovered.[21] He was later killed in another airplane accident.

In 2003, cabin owner Bill White planned to attend the annual work weekend scheduled at the end of April. He loaded his Cessna 182 (N5595B) full of supplies for the event including groceries and bags of cement. Departing Caldwell the weather was good and it looked like he could make it to Round Valley. As he approached Ola his flight path was obscured. He decided to climb above the cloud layer with the hope of finding a hole over the Main Salmon to drop into the ranch. He continually had to keep climbing to avoid going into instrument conditions. He hit a wall of nasty weather past McCall at 15,000' and the airplane could not out-climb the accumulating clouds. It then became too late to navigate out of the situation.[22]

The clouds full of freezing moisture instantly caked the airplane with ice. White became disoriented and the plane went into a spin. Catching up with his instruments he was able to make a recovery. At about the same time that he broke out of the zero visibility conditions at 9,000' he spotted a hole in the clouds where he could see an open space blanketed in snow. He pushed the nose of the plane over and was able to get beneath the layer and discovered it was a mountain lake. He flew around the perimeter of the shoreline looking for a way out, but he was trapped by low mountain obscuration and falling snow. White then decided to make an emergency landing. Landing with wheels in what turned out to be snow in depths of over ten feet, he flipped, tearing off both the left main and nose gears.[23]

For the next two days he remained in his upside down Cessna on the frozen snow-covered lake. Amazingly some area snowmobilers discovered the wreck over the weekend. Their curiosity got the best of them and as they approached, a door kicked open. Both parties were shocked. After a quick conversation it became evident that White did not know where he had crashed. The snowmobilers told him Box Lake. The group was thrilled that they were able to help and hauled him out to McCall where he obtained proper medical treatment. White fully recovered and a helicopter later retrieved the plane.[24]

Looking south at the Copenhaver Ranch Subdivision. The possibility of the upper airstrip along the bench to the right can be seen above the flat.

On another work weekend in 2009 the Copenhaver crowd experienced not snow, but persistent winds. Several homeowners jet-boated in, while others flew. Because of the wind, a few of the pilots landed at Mackay Bar and used the cable car to cross the South Fork. The following day one pilot offered to walk over and fly a friend's Cessna 182 back from Mackay Bar so it would be at their cabin when they wanted to leave. It all sounded good. The pilot retrieved the plane at Mackay Bar, made a routine takeoff and approach to land downstream at Copenhaver.

After the plane's wheels contacted the ground the pilot applied the brakes. The grass was wet, which caused the plane to skid and slide sideways. With plenty of runway left, the pilot firewalled the engine for a go-around, but due to a malfunctioning carburetor the plane sputtered and hesitated. The pilot then decided to maintain forward direction on the ground and reduced the power to idle. Fighting the runway conditions, he threw in brake and rudder inputs as necessary. He almost had it stopped when the left wing nailed a windsock pole.

Little damage occurred to the craft except a few dings on the wing and a bent strut. With half the cabin owners watching the event, the experienced pilot then received a ribbing from his friends. One even threatened to paint everything he owned "windsock orange." The owner of the damaged 182 also tossed a few jokes his way. The best came a few weeks later when the owner hung a full-sized red and white stop sign about halfway up the windsock pole. When his buddy who wrecked the plane saw it, he explained that he just wanted to make sure the pole was visible to other pilots.

The open area to the north (left center) of Warm Lake was the location of the Knox townsite and later the Knox Ranch.

KNOX

A Town, a Homestead, a Swindle, a Lodge, and Airplanes

In 1903 Arthur Cline and Charles C. Randall settled on the property. The location became a popular stopping place for people traveling to and from the Thunder Mountain mining area. As a result several stores, saloons, stables, and rooming houses sprang up and became known as Knox.[25] The name Knox was actually derived from prospector John Wesley Knox, who came through the area in 1894.[26]

In 1904 Randall established the Knox Post Office and even filed a homestead claim in July 1909, but it was never approved.[27] Randall's partner, Cline, died the following year on the property. Cline's grave can still be seen north of the junction of the Warm Lake Highway and the Stolle Meadows Road.

William and Molly Kesler moved to the area around this same time. Kesler built his wife a fine cabin. In about 1915 a fellow passed through claiming to own the old townsite, which was deserted. He indicated to the Keslers that he would sell it. Recently seeing an increase in the number of travelers and not knowing that they were being swindled, they thought it was a great opportunity. According to the thief they had become the proud new owners of nine buildings in the settlement, besides their own home. It all appeared legal until the following year when a surveyor appeared to look the land over for a claimant they had never heard of. The Keslers fought back, but knew it was a losing battle. At this time they moved about four miles to the east on Warm Lake where they legally purchased a large piece of land close to the lake. The Keslers built the Warm Lake Hotel, which

became well known in the area.[28]

Daniel Robnett was the person who forced the Keslers to move.[29] When the land was surveyed in May 1916, the surveyor noted a well-built 16′ X 20′ log cabin and a 24′ X 50′ log barn. He mentioned several other buildings, but understood that "they represent the remains of the old town of Knox, and did not belong to the entry man." He also indicated that a post office in the area was still active.[30]

Daniel G. Drake acquired the property from Robnett circa 1917 and his homestead entry was approved in March 1922 for 159.99 acres.[31] Drake made several changes to the property including the construction of a lodge for guests dubbed Drake's Lodge. Like other occupants of the site he moved on. After leaving he started a bar in Yellow Pine called Dan's Place.[32]

By 1929 Ben and Ruth Seaweard obtained the acreage. The Seaweards also owned a mining claim on the Middle Fork of the Salmon River. They used the Knox property as a headquarters for their outfitting and guiding operation. During their early ownership the lodge burned. In 1934–35 they built a

The remains of the lodge built in 1934–35 by Seaweard and Forbes.

new lodge with assistance from Frank Forbes.[33] This lodge became popular and was commonly referred-to as the Knox Lodge. One of the Seaweards biggest enhancements to the property was the leveling of the main hayfield, making it suitable for aircraft landings. The roughly 1000' airstrip was actively used with both wheel and ski-equipped airplanes into the 1940s.[34]

In 1946 the Seaweards sold the lodge. Charles and Constance Reineke then acquired the place. Their family continued to use the lodge for many years until 1976 when it was sold to Bud Hoff of Hoff Lumber Company. In March 1978 the old ranch was involved in a land trade with the USFS.[35] During the agency's ownership no maintenance was ever performed, although the lodge and associated buildings were listed on the National Register of Historic Places. In 2007 the lodge and a majority of the buildings were burned in an intense wildfire. The same year, helicopters used the landing field.

Knox Resident – Molly Kesler Saves an Airliner

Many years after being defrauded of their land at the old Knox townsite, the Kesler's Warm Lake Lodge was doing well. In the late 1930s and early 1940s Johnson Flying Service regularly delivered mail here with ski-equipped airplanes that landed on the snow-covered lake.[36]

In March 1935 Molly became a local hero when she was credited with saving the United Airline's Salt Lake to Portland flight. The Boeing 247 airliner became lost in the Warm Lake area en route.[37] Lying in bed Kesler heard the aircraft circle, leave, and return several times. It was snowing hard and Kesler walked outside of the lodge, but with the weather could not see the plane. She knew the aircraft was in trouble and contacted the Boise airport. The officials in Boise knew the plane was lost and were excited that someone could confirm its location.[38]

The weather miraculously lifted a little and she built fires on the lake leading the lost plane to Cascade. Kesler called her neighbors in the area and they also built fires, which dotted the landscape to the Cascade airport. Several townspeople drove their automobiles to the airport lighting the runway with headlights. A successful landing was made by the United pilots. As a thank you Boeing Aircraft Company gave her a model of the airplane and United Airlines sent her a lifetime pass to ride anywhere on their routes for free. It is believed that she never had any occasion to use the gift.[39]

Looking west down the Knox runway.

An aerial view to the east of the Knox homestead.

KRASSEL |

A 1940s photograph of George Krassel's cabin on the south side of Indian Creek looking west toward the South Fork of the Salmon River.

Shortly after the creation of the USFS, the agency found the area known as Dutchman's Bar to be an ideal location for operations. In 1909 they built a small log cabin that became known as the Indian Creek Ranger Station, named after the nearby creek that split the bar.[40]

Miner and homesteader George Krassel arrived on the South Fork a few years later and made a claim called Rhubarb Placer on the ground south of Indian Creek. He built a modest log cabin, mined, and often worked for the USFS. However, before settling here he wanted to lay claim to the property that became the Reed Ranch. William "Deadshot" Reed also wanted the area that now bears his name. In a confrontation between the two men, Krassel was shot and killed.[41]

The USFS continued to use the ranger station and named it after their former employee. Starting in the late 1930s the agency used CCC labor to construct a new Krassel Ranger Station complex. With a major focus on fire suppression an airfield was platted on the bench above the new facility. Clearing for the runway was started in 1936 and finished two years later. In 1939 the ranger's dwelling below the airfield along the South Fork was completed. Other buildings joined the lower complex into the late 1950s.[42]

The airstrip had 1300' of usable length in 1938, but additional work was carried out in 1939 with a D7 Caterpillar. It was reported that during the first year of use the runway had an "undulating grade thru the center line," which was improved with the dozer. Other modifications included extending the field another 200', along with the clearing of multiple large trees on a ridge across the river to the south for better approaches.[43]

The field saw regular seasonal use from the time of its inception through the late 1950s. It is interesting to note that the Idaho Department of Aeronautics' records indicate that the field was closed for a few years in the early 1960s to general air traffic and only available for emergency use. Whatever the problem was, it was cleared up and the department removed it from this status.[44]

About the same time the closure was lifted the airstrip became a USFS helicopter base. Mainly connected to fire suppression efforts, the helicopter activity developed into the creation of the Krassel Helitack program. With the expansion of helitack throughout the 1970s, a housing complex was built for crew and support staff. In 1976 a permanent office was constructed on the airfield and later a concrete helipad was poured.[45]

Even with the increase in helicopter traffic, fixed-wing aircraft continued to use the strip. On multiple occasions during Johnson Creek Fly-ins the field has often been confused with that of Johnson Creek, even though they are not in the same drainage.

Working one morning in the early 1980s near the airstrip, Krassel District Fire Management Officer Larry Swan watched a single-engine low winged plane come in and skid right up to the south end. Nearly over-running the runway, the pilot had the where-with-all to

The CCC built Krassel Ranger Station as it appeared in 1948.

Looking upstream at the 1500' Krassel runway.

A downstream view of the Krassel airstrip in September 1945.

make a 180-degree turn before sliding off the end. A fellow hopped out a little miffed that a couple of his friends had told him it was a long and fairly easy strip.[46]

After complaining about how his buddies had led him astray, he asked Swan where everyone was. Swan, puzzled about the whole conversation, had no idea what he was talking about. The guy then said, "Well I'm here for the Johnson Creek Fly-in. Where are all the planes and people?" Trying to remain expressionless, Swan broke the news to him that he was not at Johnson Creek, but rather at Krassel. Putting all the pieces together the pilot figured his friends had not lied to him after all. With a few directions from Swan the pilot was back in the air bound for the big fly-in.[47]

The main house on the property as it appeared when McClain purchased the ranch.

MᴄCʟᴀɪɴ Rᴀɴᴄʜ

Early Inhabitants

Starting in the 1870s a group of miners occupied the property now often referred-to as the McClain Ranch. Among the individuals was George Woodward, who settled on the acreage, and built several permanent structures. Woodward's partner, Amasa D. "Pony" Smead, then acquired the property.[48] Smead married a Native American woman named Molly and they had eight children together. Several times during the Sheepeater Indian Campaign of 1879, *The Idaho Tri-Weekly Statesman* noted Colonel Bernard and his troops stopping at the Smead Ranch.[49] Both Smead and his wife are buried here along with several others, near a large ponderosa pine known as the "Grave Tree." Pony Creek, which flows through the ranch, is named in their memory.

The Dustin Homestead

Bailey and Mary Dustin obtained the ranch from the Smead children and in February 1917 received a homestead patent for 157.3 acres. At the time of purchase the ranch had a house, barn, and hay shed.[50] Mary had several children from a previous marriage with the last name of Carrey.[51] A rough wagon road was in use by this time from Warren Summit to the South Fork Bridge and passed through the ranch.[52] The Dustins eventually moved to Cascade and son Brad Carrey ended up with the place. It then became known as the Carrey Ranch.[53]

A High Heeled Woman in the Backcountry

In 1946 Sylvia McClain purchased the ranch. She had stumbled upon the Idaho backcountry through her nephew, who was interested in buying a piece of property on the South Fork of the Salmon River. The nephew wanted McClain to take a look at the place as she was involved in California real estate. She agreed. It was late in the fall and snow already covered the high country, but arrangements were made for McClain to fly with Bob Fogg to Warren where a person would transport her down to the river.[54]

Several Warren residents were waiting at the Warren airstrip when Fogg landed and shut the plane down at the south end. McClain gently unlatched her door, stepped out, and shocked the town. She was wearing a black dress with matching fur coat, pillbox hat, lace veil, nylons, and high heels. The people of Warren all smiled and under their breaths said, "This

Sylvia McClain in 1953.

lady is not going to last long in this country."[55]

From Warren they headed to the river. As they drove the vehicle along the winding road to the South Fork, McClain vowed to herself that if she made it down the twisty mountain path and back up in one piece she would never return. The two reached the bottom of the canyon and looked at the nephew's real estate interest. However, McClain was also shown another piece property – the old Dustin/Carrey Ranch. The feeling that came over McClain that day when she stood on the property was something she had a hard time describing the rest of her life, other than to say that she knew it was home. Not long thereafter she bought the ranch. McClain proved herself and the town's people of Warren wrong as she spent most of her remaining life at the South Fork. The nephew that stirred her curiosity in the area lasted only one year.[56]

The McClain Years

In the early years McClain lived at the ranch nearly full-time, occupying the Dustin's former home, which she came to cherish. The four-room house was constructed of hand-hewn logs that measured over seventeen inches in diameter. The main room was 24' X 24' and adorned by a large river rock fireplace and

Sylvia McClain (right) at her South Fork ranch in 1948.

mantle. Off one end of the house was a breezeway connected to a huge stone cellar. Also on the property was the original barn, which stood until 1961. A fully-equipped blacksmith shop that was a roadhouse during the Thunder Mountain Gold Rush, was also at the site.[57]

When McClain was not at the ranch; she continued to sell real estate in McCall and also spent time at her house in Warren. For a few summers in Warren she served as the main cook for crews building roads in the area during the mid to late 1950s.

All four of McClain's children also enjoyed the ranch, some lived with her and others spent the summers. Her two sons Bill and Terry Barkell outfitted

197

and guided from the ranch for about five years starting in the mid-1950s. Under the name of Barkell Brothers Packers and Guides, the two took clients on fishing and hunting trips and also contracted with the USFS.[58]

Until the fall of 1964 McClain homeschooled her youngest daughter Julie at the ranch, but decided as the girl approached her teenage years that it would be better to winter in McCall. Her son Bill continued on at the ranch, but his stay was short-lived as embers from the fireplace landed in the cellar sawdust. The fire that ensued burned McClain's precious old home to the ground. McClain built another log house the following year as a replacement.[59]

Working in the McClain Ranch orchard in the fall of 1952.

J. Schwane

Trails End Subdivision and a Runway

The same year the house burned, McClain also platted the Trails End Subdivision. Previously she had deeded her kids a quarter of the ranch's property, but they only wanted the money and planned to sell. She then decided it would be better to subdivide the land herself and give them the money.[60]

In the late 1960s, Julie moved to the ranch and began raising her kids. During the winter of 1970-71 Julie's youngest came down with a bad case of pneumonia. Although the young girl overcame the condition, McClain did not want her kids or grandkids to be at risk again and devised a plan for an airstrip at the ranch.[61]

McClain initially hired a heavy equipment operator who laid out a strip in the fall of 1971 and began work the following year.[62] This runway when finished was only going to measure about 600' long. Even though it was short it had the benefit of allowing takeoffs and landings from either direction.[63]

With the runway half roughed in, McClain knew it was not quite right and called Bob Fogg of Johnson Flying Service in McCall for further consultation. He and Bill Dorris walked the area and pointed out that she was not taking advantage of all the possible runway length. With Fogg's suggestions the strip was relocated to its present location. In 1974 McClain hired Joe Edwards for the dozer work. In the end Fogg's ideas squeezed another 600' feet of length into the runway through the use of a contoured dogleg and small uphill section. The finished product was about 1200' of runway with a five to seven percent uphill slope.[64]

In April 1974 before the strip was completed, Ray Arnold made the first landing here flying Piper PA-12 N3729M. For the first few years of use, the runway was plagued by drainage problems, mainly due to soil type. However, as time wore on the problem lessened. Several small accidents have happened at this strip, mainly related to adverse tailwind conditions on landing, causing pilots to land long and skid off the upper end.

Out Of Gas

One of the more entertaining stories about this airfield occurred during a spring runoff when a couple of kayakers rented a Cessna 172 from SP Aircraft in Boise. Apparently the pilot and passengers were scouting the river for a possible trip down the South Fork. Near the McClain Ranch the plane ran out of gas. Not knowing the area the pilot made a forced landing in the largest open spot he could find. Amazingly the plane was put down on the strip without a scratch. The crew then unloaded from the airplane and looked for help.[65]

Tom Roberts, the grandson of McClain, heard a knock at his door and thought it was odd. He had not heard an airplane land and the road was still closed, not to mention he had already seen the neighbors for the

McClain's daughter, Julie at the ranch in 1957.

A McCall Air Taxi Cessna 206 (N7372Q) waiting out a fall snowstorm at the McClain Ranch.

Mike Dorris's Cessna 185 at the 1200' airstrip, while on the winter mail route.

Landing at the McClain Ranch.

heard an airplane land and the road was still closed, not to mention he had already seen the neighbors for the day. His curiosity got the better of him and he opened the door only to find a few young guys ill-equipped for the backcountry. They were all wearing short sleeve shirts, shorts, and sandals. With really no way out of the ranch he helped the best he could by placing a call to town. The group was eventually picked up by airplane and flown to Boise.[66]

Several days later Mike Dorris flew to the ranch with a friend and filled the 172 with gas and flew it out for SP Aircraft. When Dorris showed up to retrieve the plane he could see where the kid had locked the brakes and nearly skidded off the runway leaving huge ruts. Roberts, who was at the strip while Dorris fueled the plane, mentioned that the kid had not realized that he was on a designated airstrip. He thought he had just found a smooth pasture.[67]

More History...

Roberts is the last remaining relative of McClain to still own property on the old ranch. He has lived on the place since the age of twelve and as the years have passed he and his wife have purchased additional lots. Years after the subdivision was created, McClain again sold more of the ranch in five and ten acre parcels. McClain kept the ten acres of land where her home was located. Due to several family related issues she sold her home to Bill Turner in 1985. She died seven years later.[68]

The gravesite of the Reed family infant who died in May 1929 is adorned with iris and lilacs.

REED RANCH

Early Occupants and Homesteaders

In the 1890s John Reeves settled on the bar now known as Reed Ranch. In 1906 Paul Forester followed Reeves. Forester built a small cabin on the upper portion of the bar, but abandoned the site a year later and moved farther downriver. William C. Caldwell settled a year prior on the lower bar. Caldwell worked hard to prove up on the land, but his life was cut short when he was killed by a neighbor in 1913 over a trap line dispute.[69]

Earl Tucker and William "Deadshot" Reed both wanted the land, but Tucker won out eventually, homesteading 134.8 acres in 1919. Between Caldwell and Tucker a well-established ranch was built on the lower end of the property near the river. Meanwhile Reed and his wife Bessie moved their family to the cabin on the upper portion of the bar in August 1914. He slowly improved the ranch and homesteaded more acreage along with purchasing all of Tucker's land.[70] The name of the area at this time changed from Reeves Bar to the Reed Ranch. The Reeds moved to the property with two children and by the time they left the South Fork in 1929 they had

seven children. One other child was born, but died.[71] The child's grave is still visible at the property today.

As years passed a sizable operation was created, including a cabin, barn, hay shed, woodshed, chicken coop, cultivated land, irrigation, and a garden. Not only did the ranch grow during their years on the South Fork, but so did Reed's reputation. As he traveled about buying and selling livestock he often told stories. Reed became a legend, often associating himself with the Texas Rangers and other tall tales. Somewhere in the midst of all this he was dubbed "Deadshot" Reed. Although no one will ever know for sure what was truth or fiction, he was known

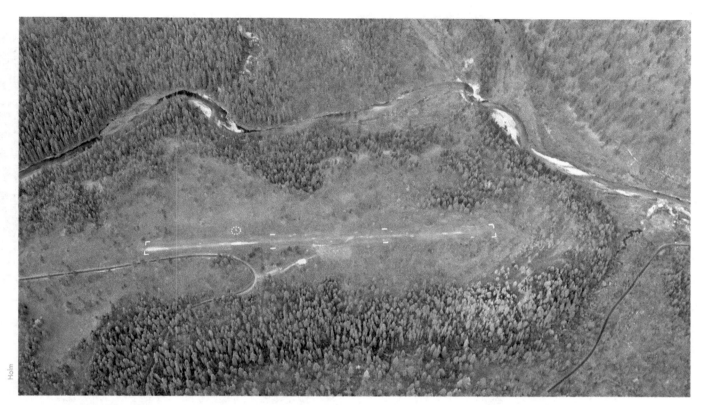

An aerial of the Reed Ranch property facing west. The Reed family buildings were located in the bottom left of the photograph, while the Caldwell/Tucker structures stood to the far right on the north side of Camp Creek.

to be an excellent marksman.

Reed was in constant conflict with his neighbor George Krassel. Krassel, who was a loyal German immigrant, often flaunted news concerning Germany during World War I when passing through the ranch. The German support did not sit well with Reed. Another conflict between the men was who was going to obtain the Tucker property after he died. Not to mention they also had disagreements over grazing rights. Local papers often reported on the feud and it all came to head on June 26, 1919. Krassel by this point had moved upriver to take care of Tucker's property as he had fallen ill. Irritated over Reed's cattle grazing on Tucker's land, Krassel arrived on Reed's property armed with a rifle. A conflict followed with Krassel firing a shot at Reed. Reed turned around and shot Krassel off his horse with a pistol.[72]

Reed notified officials in Cascade via telephone of the incident. The Valley County sheriff, prosecuting attorney, and coroner arrived the next day and it was declared self-defense. Krassel's body was buried at the ranch.[73]

There have been several accounts written about Reed and his family. Many are only glamorized accounts of his life, while others are quite factual. The most accurate and supported by his family was written by Kathy Deinhardt Hill entitled *For Better or Worse: The Legacy of William "Deadshot" Reed.*

Reed Sells and Brown Builds an Airstrip

Several factors led the Reeds to sell the property, the main one being the death of their youngest baby. The family sold the ranch to the South-Salmon Placer Mining Company of Nampa, Idaho, and moved to Emmett. The mining company found no gold on the property. While many of the roads were being developed in the area during the 1930s the CCC had a small camp on the south end of the property. These structures are believed to be associated with the large CCC facility once located north of the ranch on Camp Creek. Decades later, while under bankruptcy, the property was auctioned off to C. G. Halliday who in turn sold it to William Deinhard.[74] The new owner understood the value of the big ponderosa pine trees and in 1946 Brown's

201

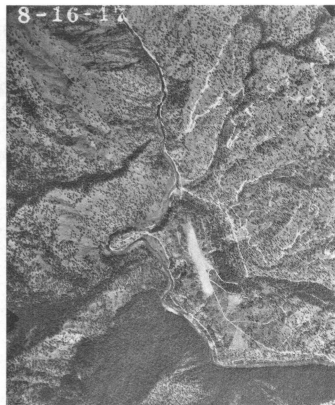

Before and after photographs of the Reed Ranch airstrip – the image on the left was taken in 1946 while the image on the right was taken in 1947.

Tie and Lumber Company of McCall began logging this portion of the South Fork. Just a few years later in 1951 the lumber company owner, Warren Brown, purchased the old ranch.

In 1947, several years prior to purchasing the property, Brown built a 2100' airstrip. Brown owned several backcountry properties that supplied timber for his mills, located in Riggins and McCall. Brown was a pilot and used this strip as an access point for business. The company took over the CCC Camp Creek buildings and turned them into a logging camp. Logging equipment was used to improve the runway and its surface. Most likely Brown was the first to land here.

One of Brown's logging employees, Ken Roth, picked up flying on the GI Bill after World War II. Roth, who was a former McCall smokejumper, enjoyed flying and purchased a sixty-five horsepower Piper Cub for $500 when he went to work for the lumber company. He was also an avid baseball player and used the Cub to commute back and forth between

McCall and the South Fork logging operations, playing in the weekly games for the Payette Lakes team. During the summer of 1951 Roth constructed a crude hangar out of poles and pine boughs to house the plane at the Reed Ranch airfield. Roth's love of flying ultimately caused him to leave Brown's Tie and Lumber. He went to work flying full-time for Johnson Flying Service, retiring in the mid-1970s.

Brown continued to use the strip on and off to access his various logging operations. By the time he purchased the place little remained of the early homesteader's hard work and he somewhat maintained the strip. However, his interest in the property dwindled for two reasons. First, he was able to purchase the old Parks Ranch on the Secesh River at Zena Creek a few miles upriver from its confluence with the South Fork. This became his base of operations in the area for several years. Secondly, his use of the Reed property was impacted by the moratorium placed on logging in the South Fork region in April 1965. Several severe storms, including one in December 1964, washed

Under the ownership of Brown the airstrip was consistently used as a safe place to set down during bad weather. Here a group of air taxi operators wait for a fall snowstorm to pass.

Ken Roth in a Johnson Flying Service Ford Tri-Motor.

out a large network of roads. Over four hundred mudslides occurred in the area. Similar events have plagued the drainage since. Evidence surfaced that these catastrophic events, probably caused by some of the road construction, were destroying the fragile fisheries in the river.

A New Era

As Brown's use of the runway waned, it primarily became a backup field mainly for commercial air taxi operators to land in times of bad weather or in an emergency. The only maintenance carried out during this time was an occasional grading by the county when they worked on the South Fork Road. The Brown's daughter Diane and her husband Judd DeBoer purchased Brown's Industries in 1980, which included the Reed Ranch property. Many years later the DeBoers, who also owned Brundage Mountain Ski Resort near McCall, began to negotiate with the USFS to exchange the property for land near the resort. The land exchange was finalized in 2006 and the Reed Ranch was transferred to the USFS.

Certain groups in the aviation community were concerned that the USFS would close the airstrip. Technically the runway was listed for only emergency use. The Idaho Division of Aeronautics, along with the Idaho Aviation Association became involved and worked out an agreement with the USFS to keep it open.

Looking upstream at the 2100' Reed Ranch runway.

SOUTH FORK RANCH

The Early Years

C. F. Smith's homestead cabin circa 1925.

In the 1870s C. F. "Frank" Smith settled at the mouth of Smith Creek, which is now commonly known as the South Fork Ranch. Smith, who was a distant relative of the well-known South Fork resident Sylvester "Three Finger" Smith, received his homestead patent in 1913 for 100.08 acres. He raised four children there and built a substantial ranch that included a log home, barn, and cultivated fields. There was also tragedy during their years at the ranch, which is evident by a small cemetery containing five graves located above the property. It is probable that at least three of the graves are Smiths. One is likely that of Smith's six-day-old daughter who was born prematurely in July 1879. Another could be of his first wife, Carrie who died June 15, 1894. A third might be of Smith's second wife, Marianne who died April 20, 1916.[75] Smith sold the ranch to Art Miller, who then sold it to Louis Coski, who sold it a short time later to Tom Carrey and his business partner John Kimbrough.[76]

Coming back from Chamberlain Basin on a hunting trip in 1928 Louis "Lou" Thompson made a deal with Kimbrough for the property. The transaction included the deed to Thompson's farm located in Indian Valley, near Cambridge, Idaho. Thompson, a widower with three children, had recently remarried and moved his whole family to the property, where they raised a small garden and ran cattle.[77] The kids, Glenn, Lavelle, and Doris attended school elsewhere in the winters and returned to the backcountry in the summers for many years. Both boys went on to have successful careers with the USFS. The Thompson's life on the South Fork was well documented by daughter Doris in her self-published book, *Tommy: The Autobiography of Doris "Tommy" Thompson.*

McDowell and the Incorporation of Airplanes

In 1943 Thompson sold the ranch to Wallace and Ruby McDowell. McDowell was a mining engineer who helped to develop the Golden Hand Mine. After the purchase, Thompson stayed on the ranch to help finish a new log house that remains on the property today. Warren Postmaster Otis Morris provided additional help in the construction along with building a Pelton wheel for electricity. When McDowell purchased the property the road ended at Hays Station, halfway between the ranch and Warren Summit. Thus, all of McDowell's equipment and supplies came to the property through the McClain Ranch and down the river trail on pack animals.[78]

In 1950 the first aircraft landed at the ranch; a helicopter that came in for a medical emergency to help Leland Waggoner, who had fallen off a horse while bear hunting. After seeing the aircraft's capabilities and wanting to obtain quicker access to the ranch, McDowell consulted with Johnson Flying Service in McCall about the possibility of an airstrip. With their suggestions, in 1951 McDowell roughed in a runway with horse-drawn equipment. The original strip was rolled, but not graded. It did have several culverts installed to help prevent erosion.[79]

Soon after construction, one of Johnson Flying Service's Ford Tri-Motors landed on the runway to

The South Fork Ranch in the early 1930s with Smith Creek flowing through the center of the property.

A headstone in the cemetery above the ranch.

deliver a Ford tractor. This is the largest airplane known to have landed on the strip. The event was captured in a photograph and sent to the Ford Motor Company. Ford used the picture in a 1952 tractor advertisement that appeared in *Readers Digest*.[80]

Baldwin and Hettinger

In 1952 McDowell sold the ranch to Toot Baldwin and silent partner Larry Hettinger. Hettinger became sole owner of the ranch a few years later. During his ownership it was known as the Hettinger Ranch. Hettinger was the owner of Boise-based Producer's Lumber Company and had plans to log portions of the South Fork River drainage. The idea was to float the logs down the river to a mill on the property, saw them into rough lumber, and haul them to Boise via truck for finishing.

To execute the first part of the plan Hettinger brought in a D8 Caterpillar to punch a road to the ranch from Hays Station. Cat skinner Henry Holt worked on the project for a little over a year.[81] Once the road was in place the same Cat was used in the summer of 1958 to further improve the runway to its current approximate length of 1000'.[82] Hettinger was a pilot and owned a Cessna 182A that he used to access the ranch.[83]

Prior to buying the 182, Hettinger owned a Piper Tri-Pacer. His wife Edna was also a pilot and a member of the Idaho Chapter of the Ninety-Nines. She obtained her pilot's license, using the Tri-Pacer and the help of Boise instructor John Peterson. After Hettinger purchased the 182, their son, Larry Jr., also learned to fly.[84]

With the road in place, equipment was hauled to the ranch to build the mill, which still stands on the bank of the river. After everything was assembled and ready for operation, logging permits were restricted and it became a losing venture. Hettinger hung onto

1 *Forester Lavelle Thompson was raised on the ranch. Here he stands on Two Point Peak in the Middle Fork country.*
2 *The 1000' South Fork Ranch runway in 1958.*
3 *The wigwam burner portion of Hettinger's sawmill still stands on the property.*
4 *The entrance to the South Fork Ranch.*
5 *A modern view of the ranch looking downriver.*
6 *Looking down the South Fork Ranch airstrip.*
7 *The current log residence at the property.*

the property for sometime, leasing it to various outfitters as a hunting camp. He also leased it to Mackay Bar owner Al Tice, who wintered stock at the ranch.

With the moratorium on logging, the Hettinger family sold the ranch circa 1967 to Robert Hansberger who was on his way to owning all of Mackay Bar.[85] In 1969 Hansberger achieved his goal by buying Tice out of Mackay Bar completely. He eventually incorporated the Hettinger Ranch along with several other pieces of property along the Main Salmon into Mackay Bar Corporation.

Hansberger – The South Fork Ranch

Under Hansberger's ownership the name of the property was changed to South Fork Ranch. For many years the corporation owned more hunting permits, along with river rafting permits, than anyone else in the backcountry. To support the outfitting business during hunting season the corporation had large numbers of pack animals, which were raised and wintered at the South Fork Ranch. Once the snow melted, many of these animals were then trailed to the Stonebraker Ranch in Chamberlain Basin, which Hansberger leased for many years for fall hunting.

Later Hansberger transferred the ranch ownership to Futura Corporation, a venture capital organization that he also owned. Hansberger really never spent any time at the place during his life and over the years had several caretakers. In 1989 he hired Tim and Judy Hull who had been caretaking at Sulphur Creek Ranch for ten years. Even after Hansberger's death the Hulls have continued to manage the property for Futura.

During their tenure they raised three daughters at the ranch and Judy wrote a cookbook entitled *Backcountry Cooking* published in 2007. The Hulls continue to raise and winter stock at the ranch in addition to outfitting and guiding in the fall.

Photos by Holm

Landing upstream at the ranch.

STOLLE MEADOWS |

A view up the South Fork of the Salmon River at Stolle Meadows.

The USFS built a rough north-south airfield here in the 1930s that measured about 1000' long. A slight outline of the landing area can still be seen on the west side of the road, south of the current Stolle Meadows Guard Station complex, parallel to the South Fork of the Salmon River.

Johnson Flying Service used the airstrip mainly with ski-equipped Piper Cubs, as a nearby site was designated as a snow survey location.[86] Small, capable wheel-equipped airplanes continue to land here on rare occasions.

As early as 1908 Stolle Meadows served as a USFS administrative site.[87] The name for the early post was derived from a packer who cut and sold hay from the meadow.[88] With the boom of the CCCs in the 1930s, a satellite or spike camp from the neighboring permanent Warm Lake Camp was established in the area near the present Vulcan Hot Springs Road. This camp was responsible for running a pole-treatment plant, the construction of many roads, and the building of the current structures at the guard station.[89] The station remains in use by the USFS as part of the Boise NF's recreational rental program.

A view of the Willey Ranch facing east.

WILLEY RANCH

The Early Homestead

In 1895 Simeon and Mary Willey began occupying the property now known as Willey Ranch. They built a large log cabin measuring 40' X 16' in addition to a bunkhouse, cellar, barn, blacksmith shop, hen house, spring house, and two hay sheds. In 1921 Willey was cultivating over 33 acres of land and had a sizable orchard that grew a wide variety of trees: 150 apple, 50 peach, 35 cherry, 20 pear, 25 prune, and 10 plum. He also kept up to forty head of cattle at the ranch. Willey and his wife raised eight children at the remote property.[90] Older son Ernest homesteaded a parcel adjacent and south of the ranch on lower Sheep Creek, and patented it in 1921. Two years later the original homestead was also approved and the 240 acres were operated together.[91]

The children were homeschooled, often being helped by their father, who was well educated and had an extensive library. His brother Norman was also scholarly and served as Idaho's second governor. The schoolhouse used by the Willey children was later turned into a bunkhouse and then a chicken coop before being burned.[92] In 1937 Willey died and his estate sold the property to Wallace McDowell three years later. McDowell sold the property a short time thereafter, relocating to the present day South Fork Ranch.[93]

The Rebillet's Long Ownership

Clarence and Reva Rebillet purchased the ranch in the early 1940s and moved into the original Willey residence. The Rebillets continued many of the same operations as the previous owners, even retaining the name of Willey Ranch. They raised two teenage children on the property, Louis and Bonnie. Louis spent a majority of his early life at the ranch helping his parents with the haying, watering, and harvest each fall. He also helped his parents bring in additional income by starting the Willey Ranch Outfitters. The ranch was used as a base camp for the operation, with Reva tending to the cooking and Clarence caring for the stock and related equipment. His hunting area not only consisted of the South Fork, but extended into the eastern edge of Chamberlain Basin.[94]

Beyond the regular annual maintenance the Rebillets made many changes. In the mid-1950s they built a road up the South Fork to the ranch. In 1962 the two Rebillet men started construction on a new house above the original homestead. Several years prior they had transported a portable sawmill in to utilize much of the property's surrounding timber. Before it was finished Clarence died. Louie continued on at the ranch and completed the house. When the structure was finished, Reva and Louis moved in and the original Willey homestead dwelling became more of a storage area.[95]

In 1967 Reva died and the following year

1 The Rebellets photographed at the ranch (l to r): Reva, Clarence, and daughter Bonnie.
2 Louis Rebellet at the ranch with a prize cougar.
3 The house built by Clarence and Louis in the early 1960s.
4 Bonnie with her daughter Joyce, riding on the South Fork in the 1950s.
5 Landing at the Willey Ranch airstrip.

her daughter Bonnie married Del Davis. Bonnie and her daughter Joyce also adored the ranch. That summer the Davises moved to the property as the two children had inherited equal shares from their mother. Eventually Louis sold his part of the ranch, along with the outfitting and guiding operation, to his sister. He became a long-haul truck driver and lived in Boise. A short time after his departure the USFS posted new trail signs in the area indicating it was the Davis Ranch, even though the family continued to call it by its original name.[96]

After obtaining sole ownership, Del and Bonnie made some changes to the property adding a waterwheel for electricity, a new Alaskan sawmill, hot water piped from a spring across Sheep Creek, and a small venture in gold mining. However, in the midst of Davis's work on the property he stopped watering the orchards along with other cultivated areas and they slowly died of stress. Davis did continue the operation of the Willey Ranch Outfitters, which ultimately became his main focus. Some years later his son Buzz joined the business.[97]

Davis and Arnold Build an Airstrip

In 1975 Davis wanted to further improve his outfitting venture and approached Ray Arnold of Cascade about designing a runway at the ranch. Arnold thought it was possible and went about seeing what approach would best work. Cruising around one day in PA-12 (N3729M) he was flying low looking at different approach angles and got himself into a jam. Trying to outmaneuver some climbing terrain at full power, one wing clipped a cottonwood tree. Arnold continued to fly the plane but the collision with the tree spun the Cub a 180 degrees slamming it to the ground. Arnold managed to climb out of the wreckage with only a few scratches. However, on impact the back of his calves got caught under the seat attachments and badly bruised them, making it difficult to walk. Looking back on it Arnold said, "I just fouled up. The terrain got ahead of me. I did only miss the top of the tree by five feet. I

still have the plane in pieces and will rebuild it one of these days. I became a little more conservative with my flying after losing two more airplanes to accidents. I also realized I could not afford to stay in business much longer if I kept it up."[98]

Even with the mishap Arnold figured out the correct approach and Davis took his advice and bladed the strip in with a RD6 Caterpillar. In 1976 Arnold flew a Cessna 180 (N4781U) to the airstrip to see how it worked. He continued to fly many of Davis's hunting and fishing clients for several years, making over 150 takeoffs and landings from the strip.[99]

All personal and business relationships have a breaking point and Davis and Arnold had a falling out. Arnold had the opinion that the old boy was a mean drunk but when he was sober could be a heck of a nice guy. Davis, according to some, thought a lot of Arnold too, but had a few issues with his business practices and flying. However, Arnold continued to fly his hunting clients to the ranch. On one trip Arnold caught a tailwind right as he was about to touchdown and it pushed him up to the end of the runway. In the processes he nicked the prop, forcing him to leave the airplane at the ranch. It then came to a head. While Arnold waited for a ride out he became involved in an argument with Davis. The two had some fierce words. Davis threatened to permanently commandeer the plane, while Arnold shared his own thoughts. Returning to retrieve the airplane Arnold had anticipated the worst and asked a friend, who also happened to be a local law enforcement officer, to join him. Davis acted calmly when Arnold and his friend arrived. They were

The RD6 Caterpillar that Del Davis used to build the airstrip remains at the ranch.

Del Davis (left) visits with Mike Dorris (right), while George Fritser (center) climbs into a McCall Air Taxi Cessna 206 (N7520N) at the top of the airstrip.

able to hang a new prop on without problems and ferry the plane back to Cascade.

Reactivation

For a few years the strip became unusable due to inactivity and poor maintenance.[100] This changed on a spring day in 1983 when Mike Dorris departed from the Yellow Jacket Ranch downriver and started a climb for McCall in a borrowed Piper Cub (N2473M). The engine began running roughly. Initially Dorris thought he could nurse the Cub back to McCall by making a few circles to gain altitude and continue upriver. This maneuver had the opposite effect and he lost altitude. With limited options Dorris was able to coax the plane to the Willey Ranch and ever since the place has been used fairly regularly.[101]

A few days later Bill Dorris flew Mike and the company mechanic to the Willey Ranch to try and repair the Cub and get it back to McCall. They gave the engine a good going over, putting it through its paces on the ground. The little motor performed just fine. Mike loaded up and took off with his dad following. Just as he made the turn upriver for McCall it started to act up again. To add insult to injury he then started to encounter less than favorable weather but made it back to McCall. After a more thorough inspection it was discovered that the engine had three cracked cylinders and two fouled spark plugs in one cylinder.[102]

Davis, Fritser, and a House Fire

Davis died in the fall of 1990 after living in a McCall retirement home for a while. Mike Dorris flew his body to the ranch in October with a Cessna 206 (N7216N). A small funeral was held and his remains were buried at the ranch southeast of the second home site. Bonnie continued to live at the ranch most of the year, often being visited by her daughter. Del's son Buzz continued general maintenance at the property along with some outfitting and guiding.[103]

For a number of years prior to Davis's death Bonnie took in veteran South Fork resident and downstream neighbor George Fritser in the winter.

Fritser grew up on the South Fork and was the last of his nuclear family to live on the original homestead. In his later years Fritser insisted on living at his remote house.[104] Many local people, particularly a group of young McCall pilots, frequently made airdrops and checked in on him. But he became too feeble for the cold winters to be alone at his isolated home and thus stayed with the Davis family.[105]

Fritser often suffered from sleepless nights and would get up and have a cigarette. In December 1991 after smoking he fell asleep in a chair on the main floor and his smoldering cigarette started a fire. Shortly thereafter the whole house became engulfed in flames. Buzz who was sleeping in the basement fought the flames, badly burning both hands at an attempt to rescue Fritser, but his injuries combined with the ever-growing fire made it impossible. Fritser perished in the fire.[106]

Dorris happened to spot the smoldering remains of the fire the next morning on his weekly mail run. Bonnie also happened to be in the Cessna 185 (N93039) with plans to be dropped off. As they turned the corner after departing from the McClain Ranch the smoke was visible. Dorris over flew the runway and saw Buzz waving at the top. He set up for an approach, but several issues raced through his mind and he aborted the landing. He decided they were not going to accomplish much without medical assistance. In a short time Dorris switched to a Cessna 206 (N7520N) and grabbed his mechanic Chris Benford who was an EMT. Buzz was waiting at the top of the runway when they returned and explained the whole story. Dorris made a few more trips that day hauling various people in and out.[107]

Family issues arose surrounding the future of the ranch and in the end Bonnie became the sole owner, while Buzz retained the nearby mining claim and outfitter's license. Bonnie continued to spend time at the ranch until her death in 2001 when her daughter Joyce Lukecart of McCall inherited it.[108]

The Ritlands

Since the mid-1980s Mike Dorris had continued to stay involved with the ranch as a pilot and helped Lukecart find a buyer for the place. He flew several perspective buyers to the ranch including Steve and Stan Ritland. The two brothers from Flagstaff, Arizona, purchased the property in the spring of 2006 and had high hopes of making many improvements. They had helicopters fly in new equipment and work started right away. One of the first projects tackled was the widening of the turnaround area at the top of the runway. The broadened area also allowed for more airplane parking. This runway is the steepest in the backcountry at an average slope of twenty-three percent over a mere length of roughly 600'. [109]

It was the Ritland's intent to save the original homestead cabin, but it became an overwhelming project. The old barn was beyond repair and it was removed along with the cabin. Two small cemeteries are located on the property, one containing the graves of several Willeys. The progress on rebuilding the old ranch was squelched with the tremendous wildfires of 2007. Since then work has slowly progressed each year.

Steve is a neurosurgeon in Flagstaff who enjoys flying his own collection of aircraft, some of which he uses at the ranch, including a de Havilland Beaver (N243A) and a Cessna 182 (N5793B). Other airplanes in his repertoire are a Grumman Albatross (N7025J), a Rockwell Turbo Aero Commander (N940AC), and a Cessna 195A (N450RE).

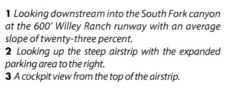

1 *Looking downstream into the South Fork canyon at the 600' Willey Ranch runway with an average slope of twenty-three percent.*
2 *Looking up the steep airstrip with the expanded parking area to the right.*
3 *A cockpit view from the top of the airstrip.*

The current Yellow Jacket lodge with the Anderson's headstones in the foreground.

YELLOW JACKET RANCH

The Early Homestead

Ed Anderson moved to the property now called the Yellow Jacket Ranch near the turn of the twentieth century and built a house, barn, and hay shed.[110] It is believed that a forest fire destroyed the first Anderson structures, but that they were later rebuilt at about the same location as the current lodge. In 1907 Anderson married Stella Severson.[111] A year later Anderson was away from the ranch and returned on his horse with a gunshot wound to the head. When he was conscious he could no longer speak English, but reverted back to his native tongue. His wife cared for him the best she could. It was never known whether the shot was self-inflicted or caused by an altercation. At the age of forty-two he was buried in front of his home overlooking the property. Stella continued on with the ranch and in January 1913 received homestead approval for 160 acres. Six years after her husband's death she died at age fifty and was buried next to him.

Flora Hackett's headstone located in the cemetery near the present access gate to the ranch.

Stella had two children, Harold and Flora Severson from a previous marriage. Flora married Jim Hackett in 1899 while living in Michigan. Hackett, a professional baseball player, pitched for the St. Louis Cardinals in the 1902 and 1903 seasons. The Hacketts moved to the South Fork a few years after Ed died and took over day-to-day operations; it then became known as the Hackett Ranch. The two built their own living quarters on the lower portion of the homestead near Elk Creek. Hackett not only ran the ranch, but he also took an interest in mining and became partners with Warren Smith who was the son of early South Fork homesteader Sylvester "Three Finger" Smith.[112]

Flora died in 1935 and was buried on the property near the present access gate. Her husband died in 1961 in Michigan. The property then changed hands several times among relatives.[113]

A New Owner and an Airplane

One of the first airplanes used on the place was in the spring of 1961 when Bob McBride decided to look at the ranch before purchasing it.[114] McBride, who was an Idaho state representative from Valley County, took an interest in the ranch when he noticed several tax liens on it. Wanting to see the property in a timely manner he hired Bob Fogg to fly him in. Fogg and several others landed at Yellow Jacket when conditions were good, just to the southeast of the small draw off the current runway. This informal landing area was used through the early 1980s, mainly by small aircraft, such as Piper Cubs.[115]

Yellow Jacket owners, Kathleen and Roger Cadwalder enjoying a picnic on the South Fork.

Cadwalder, Lodge, and an Airstrip

McBride made no improvements to the property. Under his ownership the only standing structure was a small uninhabitable-framed shack near Elk Creek that burned in the 1985 Savage Creek Fire. In December 1985 McBride's estate sold the property to Dr. Roger and Kathleen Cadwalder.[116] After this purchase the name Yellow Jacket, which had previously been given to the place, was reapplied.

Legend has it that during the Sheepeater Indian War of 1879 the soldiers camped on the lower section of the ranch. One of the soldiers was stung by a yellow jacket and thus the soldiers named the camp "Yellow Jacket."[117]

Cadwalder wanted to improve aircraft accessibility to the property by building a more formal runway and consulted with Mike Dorris for the best layout. After Dorris located the strip, Lonnie Owens of Warren roughed it in with a D8 Caterpillar that he walked from Warren late one fall. When finished, the Cat was then walked out over Elk Creek Summit, as Owens was afraid to ford the South Fork at high water levels. Later a grader pulled behind a crawler further shaped the field. The final length of the airstrip was roughly 1000' with a thirteen percent slope. On July 19, 1986 Dorris made the first landing on the new strip with a Cessna 170 (N4385B). With success, he returned later the same day in a Cessna 206 (N756WZ).[118]

At about the same time the airstrip was built, Cadwalder proceeded with other plans to build up the ranch. He bought logs and other materials from builder Kim Helmich. Helmich then constructed a driveway and main road up to the building site on the upper portion of the property near the location of the former Anderson dwellings. Helmich brought in brother-in-law Jay Hester to help build the house and shop. The house slowly evolved into a beautifully crafted lodge. Hester and his wife Floy essentially became full-time managers of the property, living at the ranch eight months a year, starting in the early 1990s. During their time on the ranch they raised their children and Jay slowly built a substantial complex of custom structures including a barn, caretaker's house, and several outbuildings.[119]

Having a soft spot for history the Hesters were involved with relocating two historic structures to the ranch. The first project was finishing the old Lum Turner cabin that was dismantled by Helmich and moved to the ranch from Huntz Gulch on the Main Salmon River, near the Wind River Pack Bridge. The cabin was restored and rebuilt behind the lodge as a guest cabin with the help of Raleigh Hamell. The second project was similar, but it entailed moving and rebuilding the 1925 South Fork Guard Station house to the ranch in 2010–12.[120]

1

Holm

2

M. Dorris

3

M. Dorris

4

M. Dorris

5

Hester

1 *The access gate to the ranch.*
2,3&4 *Jim Eldredge (on grader) and Raleigh Hamell (on dozer) grading the 1000' runway.*
5 *Longtime ranch managers Jay and Floy Hester.*

1 *Rebuilding the 1925 South Fork Guard Station at the ranch in the fall of 2011.*

2 *Pilot Jerry McCauley (left) and guest visit with Jay Hester at the top of the airstrip.*

3 *Jerry McCauley (left) and his Cessna 182A (N9995B) at the Yellow Jacket.*

4 *The Idaho "wild bore" shot by Cadwalder and proudly displayed in the lodge.*

5 *The current layout of the Yellow Jacket Ranch with the airstrip in the foreground, the main lodge (left), manager's house (center), and barn (right).*

Photos by Holm

Landing at the Yellow Jacket.

When the Hesters first undertook many of the Yellow Jacket projects, area roads were either closed due to regular seasonal conditions or washed out from slides. To solve the problem Cadwalder purchased a swept tail Cessna 182 with friend Bob Long and it was frequently used to haul passengers and supplies to the ranch. This partnership dissolved and Cadwalder bought a 182A (N722BS). Several McCall pilots flew the plane for the ranch including Jim Eldredge, Lyn Clark, Jim Larkin, and Jerry McCauley.[121]

Cadwalder, who lived in Texas operating rehabilitation clinics, visited the ranch several weeks a year, mainly during hunting season. He and his wife did live at the complex for one year before deciding it was a little too remote for their taste. Most of his hunting experiences were connected with upstream neighbor Del Davis. Heading up to see Davis one morning, Cadwalder spotted what he perceived to be a bear on the river near the Fritser Ranch. Excited to add a bear to his collection of mounts in the lodge he took aim and dropped it on the spot.[122]

Eager to claim his new trophy he managed his way across the South Fork, but the closer and closer he got to the big beast he soon realized it was not a bear. By this time he was darn irritated. He had shot one of Davis's domestic pigs that had gone wild years ago and roamed the river. The Idaho "wild bore" was stuffed and remains mounted in the lodge with a Texas counterpart.[123]

Cadwalder last visited the ranch in the summer of 2006. Suffering from multiple health issues he came down with pneumonia and died in November the same year. His family continues to use the ranch, visiting it as he did in the fall.

A 1930s view looking downstream at the original 1700' Bryant Ranch airstrip.

CHAPTER 4

EAST FORK OF
THE SOUTH FORK
OF THE
SALMON RIVER

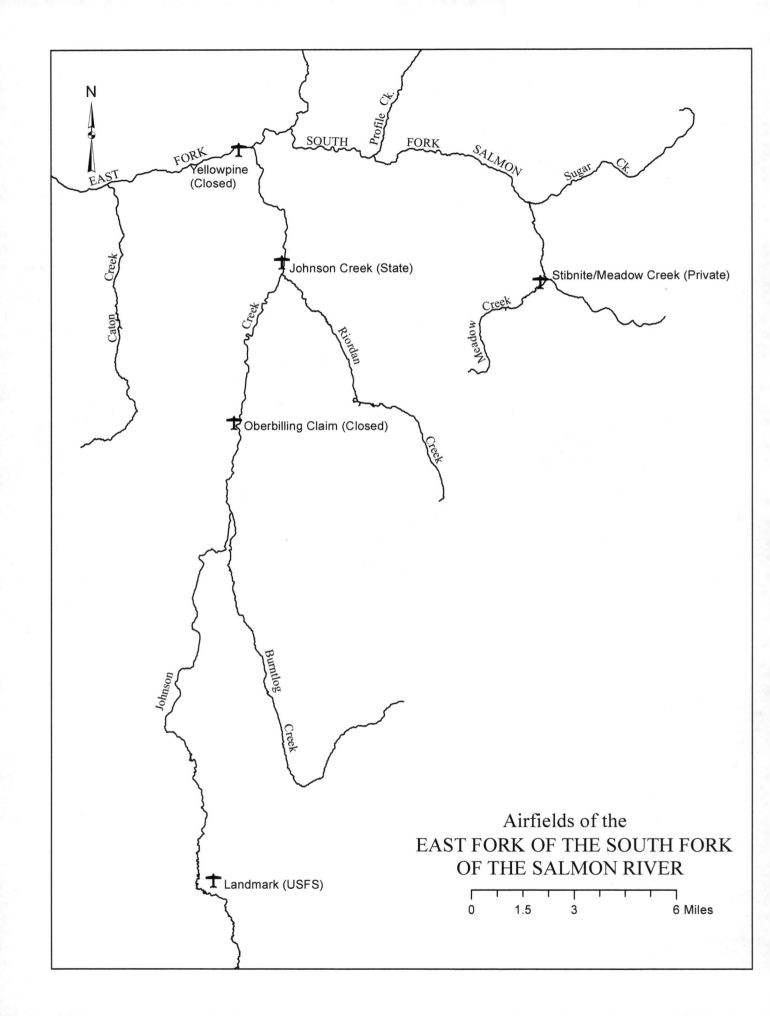

N

EAST FORK Yellowpine (Closed)

SOUTH FORK SALMON

Profile Ck.

Sugar Ck.

Caton Creek

Johnson Creek (State)

Creek

Riordan

Stibnite/Meadow Creek (Private)

Meadow Creek

Oberbilling Claim (Closed)

Creek

Johnson

Burntlog Creek

Landmark (USFS)

Airfields of the
**EAST FORK OF THE SOUTH FORK
OF THE SALMON RIVER**

0   1.5   3   6 Miles

Holm

The Bryant's 1923 three story "Cookhouse" still stands on the property. The third floor of the structure was called "The Watch Tower" as it afforded an excellent view of the fox farm, which was situated below it.

JOHNSON CREEK

Early Activities, Fox Farm, and a Lake House

Starting in roughly 1903, Al Hennessey occupied the area where most of the current Johnson Creek runway sits. In 1919 he received patent on 160 acres. Hennessey was involved in locating the original mining claims that eventually made up Stibnite. The Johnson Creek homestead property was later split into two sections.[1] H. H. Bryant, who owned several business ventures in Idaho, including a Ford dealership in Boise, ultimately purchased the southern portion. Having the Ford franchise was not a coincidence, as Bryant's sister Clara was married to Henry Ford.

Bryant was introduced to the country by his friend Lee Lisenby, who worked for the USFS. The two, along with Lisenby's brother-in-law Clement Hanson, spent a week hunting and fishing in the area and returned for several more years on summer vacations. By the late 1910s, after Bryant and Lisenby became acquainted with the Hennesseys, the three decided to go into the fur business together, calling it the Three Star Fox Farm. Hennessey furnished the land and the Bryants the foxes. At about the same time, the Bryants bought Hennessey out and built their beautiful three-story home on the property, finishing it in 1923. This structure was later dubbed "The Cookhouse." The following year a second home was added to the ranch, where the family visited regularly. To please Mrs. Bryant, who often felt out of place in the rough Idaho backcountry, the architecture of the building mimicked that of the Bryant's family vacation home on Lake Michigan.

Bryant's son Melvin managed several of the family businesses, and the fur enterprise was set up for Harry, another Bryant son, to run. However, several years into the endeavor it became a losing prospect and Melvin and his wife Emma took over the property and began using it solely as a second home. Due to the business failure and some family turmoil, Emma disliked the Fox Farm name often associated with the property and much preferred that it be called the Bryant Ranch.[2]

The first floor of the original house initially contained an icehouse, blacksmith and carpenter shops, and an area for processing the fox meat and furs. The second floor contained a large kitchen, living space, and bedrooms. The third floor was referred to as "The Watch Tower." From here the foxes were watched, especially during mating season. According to Emma, "[C]areful records had to be kept because so many days after mating the bitch was fed a live

1 *The Bryant Ranch's unique 1924 lake-style house.*
2 *The interior of the Bryant home on the ranch.*
3&4 *Early 1930s photographs of airplanes using the Bryant Ranch airfield.*
5 *The Bryant family with one of A. A. Bennett's Zenith biplanes (NC134) at the ranch in the 1930s.*

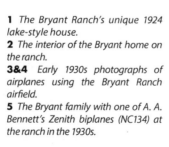

An Alexander Eaglerock biplane at the field in the early 1930s. Note the ranch house in the background.

chicken. They ate feathers and bones and the whole thing. If this was not done the fox ate her young at whelping time. The chicken provided something, which they got out in the wilds that the bitch needed."[3]

A New Tractor, an Airfield, and Neighbors

Even though the farm aspect of the ranch ended, the Bryants continued to improve the place. One item that became a staple at the ranch in the mid-1920s was a prototype Fordson tractor. The Tractor was given to the Bryants by Henry Ford and was used to help clear a rough airfield measuring 1700'. The Fordson was later donated to the Henry Ford Museum.[4]

A. A. Bennett was the first to land here with a biplane circa 1931.[5] Pilots used the airfield extensively well into the early 1950s with few changes. Most pilots during the first thirty years of use continued to refer to the place as the Fox Farm. The Bryants, along with many residents along Johnson Creek such as the neighboring Cox Dude Ranch, used the airstrip.

Lafe and Emma Cox moved permanently to the dude ranch in the spring of 1942 after spending a few years at Mile High Ranch on Big Creek.[6] The property was originally homesteaded by Alec Forstrum and sold to Lafe's parents Clark and Beulah. Lafe had a rich childhood growing up at the ranch and returned to take over the family business when his parents retired. Clark and Beulah moved to Riggins and spent their retirement years traveling.[7] Lafe and Emma continued

Cox Dude Ranch
YELLOW PINE, IDAHO

LAFE AND EMMA COX, Owners
Licensed and Bonded

This ranch has been operated by the same family
for 45 years as a sportsman's retreat.

We have many accommodations to offer the year around
MODERN Lodge and Housekeeping Cottages
5 semi-modern housekeeping cottages
TRAILER COURT with water and electricity
FISHING—Streams and lakes
HUNTING—Bear, Elk and Deer
TRAIL TRIPS or by-the-hour rides on guided tours
SQUARE DANCES—Featured yearly
SNOWMOBILING—Groups from January to May

Write for information via Cascade, Idaho 83611 or
call Boise, 344-0497 or Emmett 365-2396

An advertisement for the Cox Dude Ranch.

to operate the ranch until 1974, when they sold it and moved to another parcel along Johnson Creek that Clement and Ida Hanson had homesteaded in 1921. The Coxs renamed the acreage the V. O. Ranch and lived there until the mid-1990s. Eventually they moved full-time to Emmett. Lafe passed away in the early 2000s and Emma died in the spring of 2011. Emma

The 3400' Johnson Creek airstrip.

The Wapiti Meadow Ranch situated upstream from the Johnson Creek airstrip and previously owned by the Cox family.

published a wonderful book in 1997 about their life in the Idaho backcountry titled, *Idaho Mountains Our Home: The Life Story of Lafe and Emma Cox.*

Chet Moulton, an Easement, and an Expanded Runway

The Bryants, like the Coxs, experienced changes while living on Johnson Creek. In 1957 the Idaho Department of Aeronautics approached the Bryants about selling an easement for the use of their land to expand the existing runway for public access. Emma Bryant, recently widowed, saw it as an opportunity to ensure that she could afford to keep the ranch. An agreement was reached and the state began improving the strip in the same year. The state also obtained a special use permit from the Boise NF Cascade Ranger District to stretch the facility northward onto federal land.[8] Idaho Director of Aeronautics Chet Moulton awarded the job to Ray Nissula of Cascade. Two of Nissula's main dozer operators on the project were Jack Marshall and

Duane Peterson. Peterson noted that they cleared a lot of timber. A local person skidded these logs onto private land where he had a small sawmill. After the trees were cleared, Moulton visited frequently, landing on the old portion of the strip with the state-owned Piper Cub to inspect the work.[9] The following year, with the field completed to a length 3,400', the state held a dedication ceremony led by Moulton.[10]

In 1959, designated areas were developed at the airfield to include outdoor barbeques, outhouses, and a well for potable water. The state also built a tractor shed to house maintenance equipment.[11] Annual work parties regularly enhanced the site over the years.

A few years after enlisting a seasonal caretaker at the field in the early 1960s, Moulton introduced one of his legendary state courtesy cars to the facility. This unique program provided state-owned automobiles at various airports in Idaho for pilots to use. This is the only known backcountry airstrip to have one of the cars, and the state continues to provide these vehicles to the public.[12]

Since the 1970s this field has gained much attention and is the most-widely used airstrip covered in this book. Since the 1990s the Idaho Aviation Association and the Idaho Department of Aeronautics have made the facility their flagship airport and over the years have continued to add camping amenities.

Barry Bryant overlooks his family's legacy (the Johnson Creek airstrip) from the porch of the 1924 Bryant home.

The Bryants, Aviation, and a Visit From the Ford Family

Unlike the ever-evolving airstrip, the Bryant Ranch has remained in the family. It was put into a corporation in 1971 and equal shares were divided among the four Bryant children. After Emma died in 1980, another house was added to the ranch for the growing family.[13]

One of her grandchildren, Barry, continues to be involved with the family ranch, but also owns the former Cox Dude Ranch with wife Diana, now called Wapiti Meadow Ranch. Barry began spending summers at his grandmother's ranch starting in 1958. He obtained a job working for Moulton on a bridge replacement project that was part of the easement agreement with the Bryants. Moulton's passion for aviation quickly influenced Barry and in time Barry earned his commercial pilot license. He also worked several seasons for the state, maintaining various airport facilities. His brother William also spent a few summers working for Moulton. He too became a pilot and later went to work for Cessna in Wichita, Kansas. They were not the only ones in their family with an interest in aviation, as their father was also a pilot who flew F4U Corsairs and F6 Hellcats for the Navy during World War II. Prior to joining the Navy he worked for his uncle Henry Ford at the Willow Run aircraft manufacturing plant in Michigan.[14]

In 1999 Barry, with a Cessna 206 (N717CM), started an air taxi operation called Thunder Mountain Air. The small air carrier based at Johnson Creek in the summer, moved clients for Wapiti Meadows Ranch in addition to other work in the

Johnson Creek from the Bryant property.

backcountry before closing in 2007.[15]

A year before selling the air operation, Barry's wife received a telephone call from a group of easterners who were looking for a backcountry dude ranch experience to follow a Main Salmon River float trip. After hammering out the details she asked them for a name and it turned out to be none other than the Ford family. The complete happenstance reconnected the two families. Barry flew several trips along with another pilot, bringing Edsel Ford IV and his family and friends from Lewiston to Johnson Creek where they then stayed for a week at the ranch. Much of the conversation during their stay revolved around the family connection and the old days. At the end of their visit the Fords were flown to their vacation home in Sun Valley.[16]

The Oberbillig family, involved in the early mining development of the area, was also connected to the current property that makes up the Johnson Creek runway through several claims off the airstrip. In fact one of the Oberbillig cabins can still be seen on the northeast end of the runway. The Oberbilligs, were involved in large mining operations such as Stibnite and Mackay Bar, and also in hundreds of smaller claims located around the backcountry. The Oberbilligs, looking for investors, would reportedly enhance small claims with showy improvements such as nice work facilities and equipment to attract capital to keep other operations going. At one claim, about a mile south of the present Wapiti Meadow Ranch, they cleared a large acreage parallel to Johnson Creek and scraped in a 1500' airstrip to impress prospective shareholders. Although the airfield was never used, parts of it are still visible.

Looking north down Johnson Creek. The flat section of land south of Wapiti Meadow Ranch, once contained the cut of a 1500' airstrip built by the Oberbillig family.

| Landmark

A view to the north of the 4000' Landmark airstrip.

The first runway associated with the Landmark Ranger Station was built in the mid-1930s three miles to the south, an area now indicated on maps as Pen Basin. Situated north-south, the airstrip originally measured 1508' long. By 1942 the strip was expanded an additional 300' to the south and another 100' to the north, almost intersecting with the road to the ranger station.[17] However, prior to this expansion Johnson Flying Service successfully operated their largest Ford Tri-Motor NC435H here in 1937, hauling freight for the USFS.[18]

Looking south over the current Landmark airstrip (the south end of the active strip is on the left) at the original airfields south of Johnson Creek.

After World War II an 1800' northwest-southeast runway was added, crossing the existing field.[19] In spite of the dual airstrips, the facility was abandoned in 1956 when construction ended on the current 4000' north-south runway. The old airstrips were plagued with constant drainage issues and not usable during certain times of the year. Faint outlines of these runways are still visible from the air. The current airstrip to the north of the old facility was built on drier ground and also had the advantage of being closer to the USFS administrative site.[20]

Holm

1 *Looking west at the faint outlines of the two intersecting runways.*
2 *An early piece of equipment at the Landmark USFS administrative site, likely used to build the first runway.*
3 *Pilot Willy Beebe's Cessna 185 parked at Landmark.*

USFS

W. Beebe

230

The construction of the airfield in the fall of 1930.

R. McRae

STIBNITE/ MEADOW CREEK

Mining and Town Development

Gold and other valuable ore deposits were found in this area around the turn of the twentieth century. Antimony and stibnite dominated and are both used as steel hardeners. At the time of its discovery these ores were not in high demand. Interest slowly developed during the time of the world wars, leading to sizable mining operations in this remote area.

In 1919 Al Hennessey located claims and formed the Meadow Creek Silver Mines Company with partners J. L. Niday and John Oberbillig. A short time after its creation, their property was sold to United Mercury Mines Company headed by Oberbillig. The new company then acquired many other claims. Hennessey and Niday went on to locate claims on the East Fork of the South Fork and formed the Great Northern Mines Company. This firm later became the Yellow Pine Mine.[21]

By 1928 Oberbillig and his associates confirmed many favorable deposits and an option was signed for $1.5 million with F. W. Bradley. The Yellow Pine Company was then formed and controlled by Bradley with participation from other mining companies. By 1937 most of the financially extractable ore was mined out of the Meadow Creek deposit and the company moved to another claim originally located by Hennessey. The high operating costs of the gold mining operation severely cut into their profit. In the late 1930s F. W. Bradley died and the Yellow Pine Company was taken over by Bradley Mining Company of California.[22]

Under the new ownership, son Jack Bradley ran the mining interests in Idaho and eventually took over the whole company. Extending into the World War II era, the Bradley Mining Company and the company-owned town of Stibnite boomed. The floundering gold operation came into its own as the wartime demand for antimony increased. The company could barely keep up with the production demanded and was at first restricted by the available electricity provided by their generators. This was solved in 1944 when Idaho Power completed a hundred-mile transmission line. New equipment was brought in and they were milling up to 700 tons per day. The whole town was transformed. Within a year the population peaked at roughly 600 people. The company invested in over a hundred modern homes, a four-room schoolhouse, general store, a new hospital, service station, a recreation hall with bowling lanes, a restaurant, and an auditorium.[23]

By 1945 much of the tungsten ore was gone and the company expanded, buying options on the Sunnyside Mine and Dewey Mines in the Thunder Mountain area. Even with an optimistic outlook by the early 1950s, things slowed down. Miners encountered several operational problems and health hazards from arsenic fumes. Then in 1951 the antimony market collapsed. In 1955 the company liquidated its assets in Stibnite.[24] The structures were eventually purchased by Warren Campbell of McCall and trucked out. Many of these houses were then relocated to various Idaho communities including McCall, Cascade, Donnelly, Council, Cambridge, Payette, Emmett, and Bruneau.[25]

In the 1970s, Ranchers Exploration and Development Corporation of Albuquerque, New Mexico, acquired an option on the patented mining claims retained by the Bradley family. By the end of the decade the Ranchers firm began working with a mining company called Canadian Superior, a collaboration that lasted a number of years. A Canadian oil company that had a minerals division then bought out Canadian Superior. Mobil then acquired the oil business. Shortly after that acquisition, the site was declared a superfund site and Mobil spent several million dollars in cleanup efforts.[26]

In more recent years the Bradley family sold their patented claims in the area to Midas Gold of Spokane. A large amount of high-tech drilling and exploration has taken place and large gold deposits are believed to still exist in the area. In fact one of the large gold ore bodies may be right below the old runway.[27]

The Role of Aviation – 1930–45

Aviation played a major role in the operation and development of the mining efforts in the Stibnite area. The airfield built in the fall of 1930 was sometimes called Meadow Creek, named for the mining claim on which it was constructed. The first aircraft landed here on November 24, 1930 when George Stonebraker and pilot Ray Fisher brought in passengers and supplies in a six-place Bellanca.

One of A. A. Bennett's Zeniths (NC392) on skis at the upper end of the Stibnite airstrip in the early 1930s.

C. Walker/M. Dorris

Stonebraker had the mail contract from Cascade to Yellow Pine and Stibnite. He bought the plane to make the trip much faster in the winter months.[28]

In the winter of 1932 the airfield became important again as the mine lost all of its fuel supply when a pipeline buried deep beneath the snow ruptured. In order to keep the mill running, A. A. Bennett flew in petroleum. He flew it all in with two Zenith cabin biplanes, hauling five thirty-gallon drums of oil per trip. He also used an open cockpit Stearman that carried one ninety-gallon tank per trip. Within one month he and pilots Bob King and Chick Walker had brought in 12,000 gallons of fuel to keep things running.[29]

In these early years of operation the strip was only used by ski-equipped aircraft during the winter months, as the surface was too rough and unimproved for wheel operations. As time progressed the company developed it into a nice gravel runway measuring 2450' long. Even though a road was finally constructed from Yellow Pine to Stibnite by the early 1930s, it was not plowed during the winter until 1941. Even when it was kept open, it periodically closed because of slides and rapid snow accumulation. As a result, airplanes were widely used for transporting equipment, supplies, and residents.

The World War II tungsten boom at Stibnite equally affected the use of aviation in the operation.

Bennett Air Transport delivering supplies to the snowbound town in the 1930s with a Zenith (NC134W).

Penn Stohr Sr. (center) stands with James Bradley (left) and Jack Bradley (right) in front of a Johnson Flying Service Travel Air 6000 in the early 1940s.

A Ryan B-1 (NC4561) at Stibnite in the late 1930s.

Bradley mainly contracted with Johnson Flying Service during those years. Penn Stohr Sr. handled the majority of the flying from Johnson's operation in Cascade along with Dick Johnson, leaving brother Bob to run the Missoula end of the business. The war years for Stohr and D. Johnson were very busy, particularly flying for Bradleys and their mail contract. The two pilots used multiple company aircraft for these flights, including several different Travel Airs.

Stohr lived full time in Cascade and for national defense reasons the pilots were deputized as law-enforcement officers. Going along on many of these trips was Stohr's oldest son Dan. The young Stohr saw a lot of exciting events and interesting cargo in connection to the mining operations. On several occasions he sat in the back while hauling cases of liquor. His job was to prevent them from smashing together in the rough air. One return flight Stohr never forgot was when they had to bring out the body of a dead miner who been killed in a accident. With the

cold winter conditions and the contraction of muscles at the time of death, his body was in a very odd position. Several men, including the dead miner's brother were at the airfield trying to help Stohr maneuver the body through the small back door of the Travel Air. Watching the scene unfold was young wide-eyed Dan. He had never seen a dead person before and then the brother of the guy started cussing and mumbling under his breath, "You always were a no good S.O.B. . . you never did want to cooperate . . . get on in here."[30]

Warren Ellison – Springfield Equipment Drop

Johnson Flying Service continued to fly for the Bradleys after the war. In 1946 Johnson pilot Warren Ellison was flying a Ford Tri-Motor for the company. Bradley wanted to rush some equipment to a new prospect at the head of Springfield Creek, which flows into Little Pistol Creek and then the Middle Fork. The plan was for Ellison to make several trips from the Stibnite airfield, drop the supplies with chutes and then return until the several tons of equipment including pumps, pipe, drill rods, bailed hay, and gas engines were all delivered. With two trips under his belt, Ellison returned to the spot with his third load. While cargo kickers began unloading the supplies the right outboard engine lost all power.[31]

In 1943 the Bradley Mining Company constructed this hangar. Parked in front to the left is a Fairchild 24 (NC50801) and to the right is a Curtiss Robin model J-1 (NC527N).

A Johnson Flying Service Travel Air 6000 (NC8112) departing Stibnite on skis in the 1940s.

Ellison knew with the aircraft near gross weight he could not maintain sufficient altitude to return to Stibnite. He gave the cargo kickers instructions to start throwing the remaining supplies out the door to lighten the plane. With the orders given to his crewmembers he focused on flying. Knowing the terrain fell away toward the Middle Fork he pointed the Ford in that direction. He navigated his way down Little Pistol Creek and was able to make a safe landing at Thomas Creek.[32]

When he figured he had the runway made he pulled the power back and noticed the right outboard engine was idling just fine. After shutdown Ellison determined that the throttle rod connection had come loose and caused the engine to go to idle. The manufacturer had put in place an automatic spring-loaded device that in such an event was to throw the engine to half power. However, the backup device failed. Once the problem was discovered, Ellison and his crew fixed it and within the day returned to Stibnite for another load and finished the job.[33]

Aircraft Service Company and Bradley Field

Johnson Flying Service continued to fly their bigger aircraft for Bradley, but less frequently because in 1943 Jack Bradley started his own aviation division. The same year a large permanent hangar was constructed in Stibnite. In 1946 Bradley expanded the business to include an airport facility in Boise (Garden City) called Bradley Field. Prior to this he did have a smaller flight operation located at College Field in Boise.[34] At the old location he predominantly used a Curtiss Robin and a Stinson Voyager.[35] The company eventually purchased a Travel Air 6000 (NC8865) and slowly incorporated several Navions.

Bradley Field was dedicated in memory of Jack's father. This airport became known nationally for its innovative design and features such as a motel for guests right off the tie down area. Fitting for the modern futuristic postwar America, the facility was often advertised as a "sky port for wilderness flyers" or as a "skytel."

Other than attractive guest accommodations and supplying the mining operations, which also expanded during these years to other locations in the state, it was a full service FBO. The flight department of the mining company was officially called Aircraft Service Company, which consisted of fuel sales, a maintenance shop, flight training, and an air-taxi service. Various general managers ran the operation and several full time pilots came and went over the

Bradley Mining Company's Travel Air 6000 (NC8865) taking off from Stibnite in the late 1940s.

years. These included: Les Randolph, Glenn "Ike" Eichelberger, Ray Crowder, Jim Cutler, Glenn Higby, Larry Fisher, Harold Dougal, and occasionally Bob Clarkson.[36] In the early years of the Bradley Field operation, flying lessons were offered at highly discounted prices to mining employees. About a dozen people in management positions took advantage of the offer.[37]

The aircraft division reached its apex in the early 1950s. They had added several Navions, a Ford Tri-Motor (NC8407), a Cessna 195, and leased a Cessna 190 from local pilot Joe Terteling. In November 1959 Jack Bradley, his wife, Jane, and his brother Worthen were killed in a car accident in San Francisco. Not only did the family struggle through the following years, but the mining operations did as well. By the mid-1950s the flight department became less important, as it was primarily a function of the mines. In 1957 through 1958 the other parts of the Aircraft Service Company, such as the charter business, could not justify their operation and the assets were liquidated.[38] Over the years Bradley Field had other flight services come and go, but the airport was permanently closed in 1973.

Postwar Activity

Aircraft access had clearly become a part of life in Stibnite. The subject was regularly covered in the town's local newspaper, *The Stibnite Miner*, and even made national publications. For example the *Saturday Evening Post* covered the subject in the December 8, 1951 edition under the article, "Want to Get Away From it All" by Neil Clark.

In February 1949 the town made local newspaper headlines when the road from Warm Lake to the town was closed by nearly forty slides. Unable to re-open the roads when one storm followed another, the town was completely cut off. The Bradley employees were unable to plow out most of the slides because some were thirty feet deep and full of heavy rock debris. Each slide had to be carefully dynamited, and then heavy equipment cleared out the road.[39]

The Boise area papers caught wind of the event and several politicians decided that they were going to save the starving town. In reality the community had enough to survive, but the Air National Guard based in Boise became involved. The Guard made several cargo drops with their Douglas C-47s, buzzing low right over the runway. As the town stood watching they thought they were getting bombed. Food such as potatoes exploded into a thousand pieces as it hit the hard-packed runway. It turned out about only half the cargo chutes opened. Other goods lost in the cause were hams, bread, and produce. Although some of the food was usable, the overall outcome was a major loss of resources. The local dogs had a field day. A few days after the emergency drop the roads were opened. [40]

Few aircraft crashed at the airfield. One of the earliest known accidents occurred in September

The Aircraft Service Company Navion piloted by Jim Cutler.

1942 when a single-engine plane stalled after takeoff and went into the tailings dyke behind the assay office near the airfield. [41] A couple of years later in 1948 the company's Travel Air 6000 was ground-looped on takeoff, causing wing damage.[42]

Another accident happened in November 1953 when one of the company's Navions piloted by Jim Cutler was carrying out two game wardens. Trying to beat a snow squall coming down the valley Cutler got in a hurry and it is believed that he did not remove some ice that had formed on the airplane's surfaces. The plane stalled shortly after clearing the end of the runway on takeoff. It hit the ground square on the tail and flipped over. The occupants were injured, but after a few days of treatment at the Stibnite Hospital were given a good bill of health. Cutler went on to have a career with West Coast Airlines.[43]

More Aviation Activity

Many of the subsequent mining companies in the area also used the airstrip for quick access. In the 1970s Ray Arnold of Arnold Aviation, located in Cascade, contracted with several of these companies. Arnold used a wide variety of aircraft ranging from a Piper Super Cub to a Cessna 210. Over a thirty-year time frame Arnold himself hauled parts that ranged

from those that would fit in his shirt pocket, such as a few o-rings, to cargos at gross weight, full of inch-and-a-half steel cable. The cables were needed to haul out a mining truck that had gone off the road. When they brought them back up to the airstrip the clevises on the ends of the cables had been pulled straight.[44]

The majority of the flights were not hauling parts, but rather shuttling personnel and gold between Stibnite and Spokane. A guard often accompanied the gold in the early years, but this was later changed. Many friends joked with Arnold about disappearing with the gold. He said it never really crossed his mind. Although with a million dollars worth of gold on board, he knew that if he ever had to make an emergency landing, someone would want to find him.[45]

Flying similar flights was Pioneer Aviation based in McCall and owned by Kirk Braun. Braun and his pilots flew comparable planes for Hecla Mining Company, located in Coeur d'Alene. Pioneer transported employees to and from Stibnite to their Coeur d'Alene headquarters and flew gold to Salt Lake.[46]

With the rise in gold prices in the early 2010s the area again boomed. Arnold once more became involved with the transportation aspect of the operation, along with G&S Aviation owned by George Dorris.

Holm

Looking east with the town of Yellow Pine in the background – the old runway is visible in the center of the photograph.

| YELLOW PINE

The town of Yellow Pine was originally referred to as Yellow Pine Basin. Albert Behne was the first person to settle here in 1902. About three years later Behne brought a post office to the small settlement. Several others followed Behne, including Theodore Van Meter, who started a general store. Behne lived there until his death in 1945.[47]

The small settlement never evolved into anything more than a popular stopping point for people headed to the various mining areas. It served as a good place to grab a bite to eat, buy a few groceries, and maybe some gas. However, it has always been known as a good town for local watering holes. In more recent years the town has capitalized on its rustic appearance and holds an annual harmonica festival that attracts hundreds of people for one weekend each summer.

In the late 1930s the USFS built an east-west landing field west of town on the opposite side of the river. A small road and bridge were built across the East Fork of the South Fork to access the strip. The finished runway measured 2300' long and 100' wide.

The field was to provide quick access to the area for personnel and fire suppression efforts. However, most of the recorded use of this field was by area mines that used it for freight transportation.[48]

At certain times in the history of Stibnite their airfield could not be used, particularly for big loads during wet springs. Still in need of material Stibnite would plow to Yellow Pine, and haul by truck the material that was delivered to the lower Yellow Pine airstrip.[49] Johnson Flying Service of Cascade hauled a lot of freight to the Yellow Pine strip during these periods, especially in the spring of 1942 and 1943. Dick Johnson and Penn Stohr Sr. flew most of the freight. In April and May of 1943 Johnson alone flew to the strip from McCall for thirty days straight using

A 1950s view of Yellow Pine.

B. Dustman

Johnson Flying Service Ford Tri-Motor NC7861 parked at the Yellow Pine airfield circa 1942.

R. McRae

238

Looking west at Yellow Pine with the cut of the abandoned airstrip paralleling the East Fork, opposite the road.

company Travel Airs and Ford Tri-Motors. There were multiple days when several trips were made per day; the most impressive being four freight flights on both May 27 and 30 of 1943 with Ford NC8400.[50]

It was no surprise that with the operation of the larger aircraft at the field that the maximum amount of space possible was desired. The topic arose in May 1942. The Idaho NF had discussed clearing a few large trees along the southwest half of the landing field. Stohr was consulted and helped the USFS mark forty-nine trees for removal.[51]

The field received little use after World War II and over the years trees slowly encroached. The outline of the runway is still visible. The bridge from the main road was removed and later replaced by a cable car.

The last attempted landing on the strip occurred in the 1980s when a student pilot was signed off for a solo cross-country to Johnson Creek. Upon arriving in the vicinity the pilot confused the Yellow Pine strip for Johnson Creek. She set up for a landing even though she knew it was not right. Mowing down small trees, the plane was destroyed but the pilot escaped with minor injuries.

B. Newbrough/USFS

A 1953 north facing view of Chamberlain, showing the unfinished east-west runway.

CHAPTER 5

CHAMBERLAIN BASIN

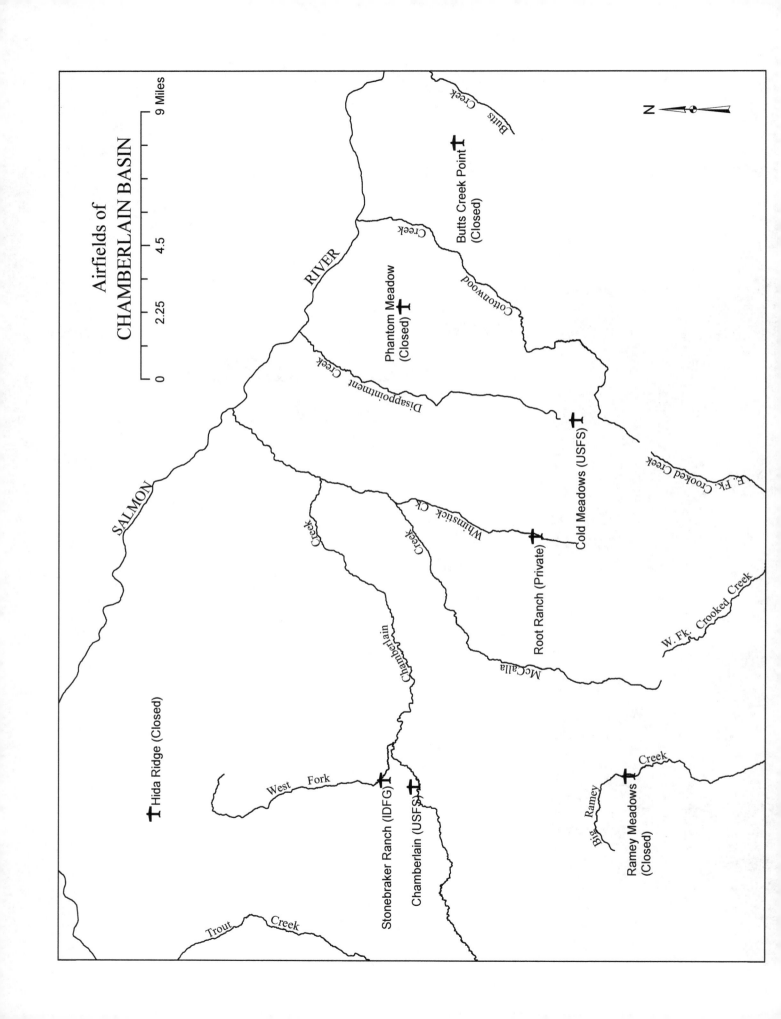

Airfields of
CHAMBERLAIN BASIN

0   2.25   4.5   9 Miles

N

SALMON

RIVER

Butts Creek

Butts Creek Point
(Closed)

Creek

Cottonwood

Phantom Meadow
(Closed)

Disappointment Creek

E. Fk. Crooked Creek

Cold Meadows (USFS)

Creek

Whimstick Ck.

Root Ranch (Private)

W. Fk. Crooked Creek

Creek

McCalla

Chamberlain

Hida Ridge (Closed)

West   Fork

Stonebraker Ranch (IDFG)

Chamberlain (USFS)

Big   Ramey

Creek

Ramey Meadows
(Closed)

Trout   Creek

Looking north toward the Main Salmon River – the outline of the overgrown Butts Creek airfield is visible. At the end of the long ridge sits the Butts Creek Point Fire Lookout.

BUTTS CREEK POINT

The Butts airfield is aligned northeast-southwest on a ridge south of the Butts Creek Point Lookout at an average elevation of 8050'. CCC crews constructed the roughly 2500' runway in the late 1930s and used a rock rake to smooth the surface. The gathered rocks were then used to create runway markings. By 1943 the airfield was listed on state aeronautic maps. Landings could have been made here into the 1970s, but not much is known about the airstrip's use. The runway is still visible, but heavily covered in lodgepole pine.

Facing south, the runway outline begins at the end of the burn in this 2010 photograph. Two distinct lines running lengthwise can be seen in the trees on either side of the airstrip.

CHAMBERLAIN

Trappers and Homesteaders

A view to the west of the Chamberlain administrative site in the mid-1930s.

It is believed that the earliest Caucasians to have discovered the lush Chamberlain meadows were from the Rocky Mountain Fur Company in the 1830s. The origin of the area's name came from 1880s era trapper John Chamberlain. The location's unique topography attracted many people looking to settle. As a result the open countryside contained several different approved and unapproved homesteads.

The first successful homestead was that of W. A. Stonebraker at the turn of the twentieth century (see Stonebraker Ranch). His homestead, still clearly evident and now owned by the IDFG, is about one mile to the northeast of the USFS complex along the West Fork of Chamberlain Creek. In 1906 Louis (also spelled Lewis) Stephenson attempted to homestead on Flossie Creek near the west end of the present long runway. Stephenson's 140 acre parcel contained a log cabin and fencing. After Stephenson abandoned the site, Albert L. Nixon moved onto the land in 1916. He then attempted to patent 153.87 acres of ground,

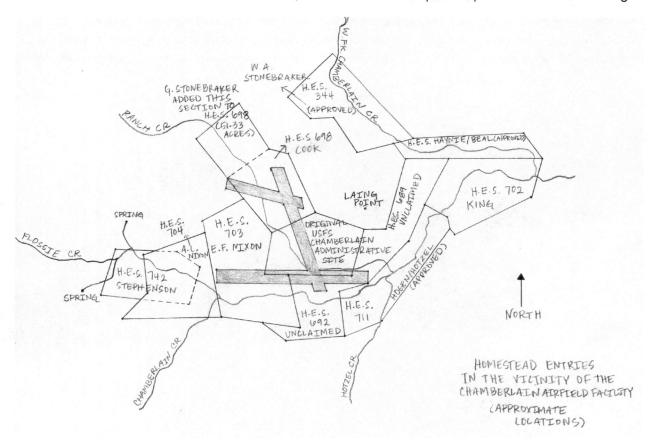

A layout of all the approved and unapproved homesteads in the vicinity of the Chamberlain airfields.

One of the pre-1937 Chamberlain Ranger Station buildings.

some of which overlapped with that of Stephenson's. A year later Nixon's relative, Ezra Fred Nixon also took a crack at homesteading a similar-size parcel adjoining Albert's to the east. However, both tracts were revoked in 1929 and the properties reverted to the USFS.[1]

Just to the east end of the long runway, another early homestead was established known as the Hotzel Ranch (see below for more information). Not far from this place was the Beal Ranch, which was first claimed by John Haynie in 1907. Several succeeded Haynie, but due to lack of improvements failed to prove up on the claims. Phillip G. Beal then acquired the land, built a small log cabin, and patented 90.17 acres in 1929. He then sold it to Clarence Paulsen, and moved to Acorn Creek on Big Creek. Sandwiched between this property and the Hotzel Ranch was a 151.07 acre section claimed by John W. King, but like many others it was revoked in 1929.[2]

Warren Cook attempted to settle another homestead in the area that now makes up the majority of the north end of the short runway. However, he let the 158 acre spread go about a year later. In 1916 W. A. Stonebraker's brother, George, then claimed the property and built a log cabin and barn. Three years later another brother, Sumner, laid claim to the parcel but made few changes and in 1925 it was revoked. Following Sumner, Susan E. Jefferies took a stab at applying for the land, but by then the USFS had development plans for the acreage.

The same year the agency withdrew the land from public entry and added it to their administrative site. Out of the nearly twenty individuals who attempted to homestead in the immediate vicinity of the present airfield complex, only three were approved, while the rest of the land remained with the USFS.[3]

A Remote USFS Outpost

In 1906, just one year after the creation of the USFS, the agency sent David Laing to the remote area to establish a management outpost. By the fall he had constructed a small log cabin on a flat east of the present north-south runway. The highest point on the ridge separating the Stonebraker Ranch and the USFS airfield was named Laing Point in 1907.[4]

This early building was abandoned in 1916 when W. A. Stonebraker, under contract with the government, built a two-room log cabin southeast of the current USFS buildings. About the same time a log barn and woodshed were also added.[5]

In 1936 timber was felled for a new ranger's house and allowed to cure over the winter. By the next fall a new two-story log cabin was finished. The following year a log commissary was added to the complex and is still in use along with the ranger's dwelling. When the newer buildings were finished,

A 1953 photograph of the 1937 Chamberlain Ranger Station dwelling that is still in use. Later an addition was added over the front porch.

245

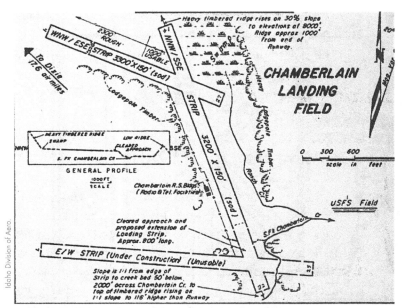

A 1950 Idaho Division of Aeronautics diagram of the Chamberlain airstrips.

the 1916 era structures were razed and the north-south airfield was extended. Escaping destruction was the original Laing cabin that was moved directly behind the new ranger's quarters to the west. This structure was later turned into a washhouse but burned in 1960 and was replaced by the current woodshed.[6]

Another building that was relocated to the 1930s era administrative site was the Stephenson homestead cabin built near Flossie Creek. In 1954 this structure was skidded into place north of the other buildings and turned into a tack shed. It remains in use today and is one of the oldest structures in the River of No Return Wilderness.[7]

In 1958 the Chamberlain and Big Creek Ranger Districts were consolidated and the site became designated as a guard station. In the 1960s and 1970s the station saw heavy use and expansion was necessary. Items added to the grounds over the years included: a washhouse, fuel storage facility, fenced garden, helipad, corrals, sauna, irrigation system, large directional sign map, cellar, and three log bunkhouses. In the early 1990s many of the features from this era were removed. In 2004 the property was listed on the National Register of Historic Places. Making the listing unique is the inclusion of the north-south runway as a contributing element to the historic property.

The Beginning of Aircraft

Circa 1931 the meadow adjacent to the present day guard station was first used as an airplane landing area. To make landings possible, the USFS cleared timber on the north end for an approach and leveled the meadow.[8] Bob King is believed to be the first pilot to land here, either using a Curtiss Robin or Fairchild monoplane in the summer of 1931.[9] The new landing area became valuable for transporting men and equipment into the Idaho Primitive Area during the Salmon River Breaks Fire. However, the Stonebraker landing field was also used at this time. Joining the north-south airfield was also a northwest-southeast strip that crossed at the north end. This runway measured 3300' long, but was extremely rough. During its time of use, pilots estimated that it only had 1000' of usable length.[10]

In the summer of 1933 Idaho NF Supervisor S. O. Scribner flew with pilot A. A. Bennett to examine many of the backcountry airstrips. In regard to his inspection of Chamberlain he noted, "We still need to do some work at Chamberlain to put this field in proper shape to take off in the 4 directions originally contemplated. The cross-runway is still altogether too short for a loaded plane. Ranger Dan LeVan plans to make further improvements on this field this season."[11]

A current aerial of the Chamberlain facility showing the faint outline of the older north-crossing runway.

Johnson Flying Service Travel Air 6000 NC8112 on the north-south airstrip.

The plans for this cross-runway were never completed. Oddly, USFS publications of the period did not depict the airfield, while the state of Idaho circulated information about it through 1950.

The current east-west cross-runway was not built until much later. However, the original runway provided the USFS excellent access to the remote region for several years. With an increase in trail building, fire lookout construction, and aerial fire patrols, the new landing area proved essential to annual activities.

Along with the other airstrips in the area, the Chamberlain landing field was enhanced in many ways, including end markers, a windsock, rock clearing, and some leveling throughout the decade. By 1938 the north-south airfield measured 3000'.[12]

In 1940 many modifications were made to the north-south runway, including better leveling and drainage. Much of this work can be credited to the small Clark Air tractor that was walked in by Glenn Thompson under then "Primitive Area Regulations." The same year, Thompson, along with Johnson Flying Service pilots Bob Johnson and Penn Stohr Sr., located and laid out plans for further development of the north-south runway and a large east-west strip to the south. With the beginning of World War II these plans were put on hold.[13]

Expansion and a War Hero Visits

In 1949 Thompson's expansion plans began with labor from the McCall smokejumpers. The jumpers felled and burned large amounts of timber and used the Clark Air tractor for stump removal and leveling. The cable-driven blade on the tractor caused more of a rollercoaster effect than a leveled surface and a D7 Caterpillar later improved the surface in the 1952 through 1954 field seasons.[14]

The D7 was walked in on a similar path as the Clark Air tractor. It was first hauled to the Big Creek Ranger Station where it was then readied for the long trip to Chamberlain Basin. The D7 was operated by Payette NF cat skinner Hank Crowman, and was first walked to the Werdenhoff Mine, then to Pueblo Summit, and on to the Golden Hand Mine. From this point it became more difficult and Crowman relied on a crew to help him guide the machine on a path of least resistance, with an effort to follow trails when they could. Staying on designated trails was not always possible and crewmembers such as Bill Cluff rode ahead on horses to scout the best route. Often it took falling trees on a path the width of the machine to get it over obstacles. From the Golden Hand, the Cat went to Mosquito Springs, through the Cow Corrals, and then followed the South Fork of Chamberlain Creek to the airfield.[15]

It was not until October 1954 that the new east-west runway was open for use. The field's completion was rushed, as the Payette NF was selected to take an important government employee, General Matthew B. Ridgway, on an elk-hunting trip. Ridgway was a common media figure of the time and earned his fame for the creation of the legendary 82nd Airborne, the introduction of paratroopers into the United States military, and his leadership of the predawn raid on Normandy, which lead to the success of D-Day. He is also credited with turning the tide of the Korean Conflict in favor of the United States.

Johnson Flying Service Ford Tri-Motor NC9642 parked along the west side of the north-south runway. Notice the man on the left with the cranking rod to windup the inertia flywheel for starting the left outboard engine.

General Ridgway's 1954 Chamberlain Basin elk hunting trip (l to r): Val Simpson, Lavelle Thompson, Ridgway, Tom Coski, Tackie Patton, Ted Koskella, and Boyd Rasmussen.

The preparation for the Ridgway elk hunt took months of planning and was completely bankrolled by the government. For hosting the hunt, the Payette NF received all new camping, packing, and stock equipment for the occasion. Wanting to impress the General not only with the finest equipment, the Payette NF appointed their top employees as guides for the trip.

Even with a priority placed on finishing the new runway, Payette NF officials could not guarantee completion prior to Ridgway's arrival. To ensure that the General could make it to Chamberlain, Mountain Home Air Force Base sent a C-47 with its best pilots to shoot several approaches and landings on the original north-south strip.

The practice from the Air Force turned out to be unnecessary, as Ridgway, his wife, and staff were able to land in fine style on the new runway. Ted Koskella led the Ridgway hunting party (the General, his wife, and assistant Lloyd "Larry" Lehrbas) with the help of Val Simpson, Lavelle Thompson, Tom Coski, Tackie Patton, and Boyd Rasmussen.[16] Meeting the C-47 at Chamberlain with the USFS employees and additional supplies for the trip were Johnson Flying Service pilots Bob Fogg and Ken Roth. The two hauled the equipment in with a company Ford Tri-Motor.[17] In the bright fall sunlight many photographs were taken of the party. Roth even captured the event on film with a handheld 8 mm camera.[18]

The USFS crew set up a first-class camp several miles north of the airfield at Dillinger Meadows. The party spent four nights hunting from the remote location, but saw only small, distant herds of cow elk. Despite the lack of game, everyone had an enjoyable time, telling stories around the campfire in the evenings and taking in the amazing autumn scenery during the day. With no luck the party returned to the Chamberlain airfield.[19]

The following morning, with time to waste before the airplane arrived to take them back to civilization, Koskella took the General on one last short hunt. The two spotted some fresh tracks in the snow and honed in on the herd. Koskella recalled the account by writing, "Tying up our horses, we followed the tracks on foot and after about three miles we topped a small ridge and right across the draw was the herd. I could see the big bull partially hidden in the trees with about six cows milling around nearby. I tried to point out the bull to the General, but with all the cows, he was unable to see the animal that was so well hidden in the shade of the trees. I told him to shoot as soon as he could locate the bull, but somehow the herd got wind of us and they thundered off. After the animals disappeared the General said, 'He was as big as a freight train and WHAT A RACK!' Disappointed, we headed back to the station, as there was no chance we could do any good following the herd, as they were spooked."[20]

After the Ridgway hunt the USFS focused on refining the airstrip and further developing the administrative site. Improvements included: construction of a large lodgepole fence bordering both runways, burial of the original Clark Air tractor near Ranch Creek northwest of the big runway, and walking of the D7 over to Cold Meadows. After the official opening of the large east-west runway, the short northwest-southeast runway was officially closed. This older abandoned strip is still visible.

The burial site of the Clark Air tractor near Ranch Creek.

The airplane camping sites were one of many 1960s developments welcoming the public to the Chamberlain facility.

The Cold War – Radioactive Material

With the onslaught of the Cold War it seemed that every prospector placed a priority on obtaining a Geiger counter. While out searching for other minerals they would often pull out the radioactive detector and take a look around just in case. One of the best prospectors in the entire Idaho Primitive Area, Wilbur Wiles, was also looking for radioactive materials on occasion. Wiles had a reputation for finding rich deposits of rare minerals but he often feared damage to the land and thus did not pursue everything he located.

An old ranger in the Chamberlain area told Wiles that the Bureau of Mines had found radioactive material near the Chamberlain Ranger Station in the 1930s. Wiles prospected a majority of the Chamberlain Basin in 1953 and 1955 while searching for gem-quality beryllium, he searched on the side for the radioactive material. He found no beryllium, but did find several deposits of monazite, a radioactive material, including some near the airfield. However, the majority was located north of the field at Wet Meadows.[21] Although Wiles did actively run an opal mine in the Idaho Primitive Area, he did not act on his Chamberlain Basin discoveries.

The 1960s and the Flossie Fire

In the 1960s the agency focused on meeting public demand for an increase in outdoor recreation in the postwar economy. The airstrip became a popular destination for camping by recreational pilots, and airplane campgrounds were developed in 1961 along the south side of the east-west runway.[22] In addition to providing camping, the area became a popular jumping-off point for hikers, and in the fall offered an entrance to world-class big-game hunting for both outfitters and private parties. To help orient visitors to the area, a large hand-carved sign was erected outside the ranger's house. One side of the sign featured a map with a depiction of local trails and the other side gave a brief history of the basin.

In September 1966 the airfield and vicinity became a hub of activity, as it was the main fire camp for the Flossie Fire. Within the first thirty-six hours strong southwest winds fanned the lightning-caused fire to 5,500 acres. Several hotshot crews from the Southwest and Montana were flown in. The Idaho National Guard also came in to maintain the camp. Thousands of pounds of gear and over 400 people were flown to the airfield. The Guard's main job was to cook and they set up a large cooking area on the west side of the north-south runway near the corrals.[23] During the Flossie Fire the airstrip was used by the

This large wooden map was erected in 1961 along the north-south runway to help visitors navigate around the relatively high, but flat basin.

Intermountain Aviation's de Havilland Caribou hauling equipment in and out of the area for quick repairs in the 1960s.

largest airplane to ever make a landing in the basin; a USFS C-46. All types of aircraft were involved with the effort, including single engine Cessnas, DC-3s, and a variety of helicopters with the largest being a Sikorsky S-58.[24]

After two weeks the fire was almost under control when a large storm cell moved in, bringing moisture. This might have been good for control of the fire, but with warm temperatures it caused an inversion blanketing the area around the airfield in fog. For several days the strip was socked in. In order to get supplies delivered to the camp, a large helium weather balloon was tethered to a 600' rope at the center of the airfield. The balloon served as a target for paracargo drops containing supplies for crews that were relying on air support.[25]

After one cargo-dropping run, pilot Jim Larkin

and a group of McCall jumpers in a USFS DC-3 had a complete engine failure. Larkin was able to feather the left engine and shut it down without any issues. He nursed the plane and crew back to McCall with no problems.[26]

Developing a Water System and an Air Rescue

By the late 1960s the USFS placed new requirements on drinking water standards and sources. Similar to other government activities, the water had to meet a certain criteria and code. The water systems at most of the remote locations did not meet the guidelines, especially the configurations at Chamberlain and Cold Meadows. The Chamberlain system was a shallow well located behind the main house. This was essentially no better than surface water, which was prohibited for use.

The first attempt to solve the issue was to bring a drilling rig into the station. This was brought in with a USFS DC-3. The engineers crunched some depth calculations and started drilling. After some work a well was drilled on the west side of the short runway, southeast of the main station building. Proud of the accomplishment a couple of them grabbed a cupful of water and took a sip. That was all they needed before spitting it out. It was absolutely foul tasting water. One fellow figured they had drilled into a peat bog.

The rigging device was flown out the same way it came in, and the engineers then developed the idea of creating a gravity feed water system from a spring located above Ranch Creek. The system was designed fairly simply. A main feed from the spring was routed to a large water cistern that built additional head pressure, plus storage. From the cistern a pipeline was hand-dug the length of the north-south meadow, to deliver water to the station.

The problem with the system came about when building the cistern box. Claude Avery, the forest carpenter and jack-of-all-trades, designed a concrete 10' X 10' X 10' cistern. Due to the remote location and availability of equipment, he had to build it in several separate pours. When it was all finished Avery noticed it leaked. It was then decided to coat the inside with a special fiberglass resin.

By this point in the project it was late October and the days were becoming short, with high humidity readings, cold temperatures, and rain. These conditions were not conducive for drying the resin. Avery and Chamberlain worker Jack Higby then decided to set a propane heater on the inside overnight to hasten the drying time. The two returned the next morning. Lowering a ladder down into the box, the two noticed it smelled and found the heater had gone out due to the lack of oxygen. They both climbed in and Avery began handing items up to Higby standing on the ladder. Avery then started inspecting the lower portion of the cistern to see if the resin had dried. He could not see well and lit a match near his face and it caused a massive explosion. Most of the blast was forced up through the small opening at the top where Higby was standing. It was so extreme that it blew the four concrete walls apart.

The explosion was heard for miles around and the nearby crew digging the water line immediately dropped their tools and ran up the small incline. They found the two men badly burned and in extreme pain. A radio call was made from the station to the forest dispatcher for an airplane. However, the weather was so bad that they could not get a flight. Over the course of the crisis that was being broadcast on the backcountry radio, Al Tice of Mackay Bar happened to be in the air on the Main Salmon River. Tice heard the desperation and radioed back commenting that he would try to squeeze into Chamberlain and pick the men up. It is unknown to this day how he fought the nasty late fall weather back to McCall, but he got the men to the hospital. Higby and Avery had scars for the rest of their lives.

After the destruction of Avery's efforts, a new bunch went in to build a second cistern. The new project foreman was Bruce Yergenson and helping him were several McCall smokejumpers. Yergenson's major change was to create the cistern in one pour. This almost did not work as the gas-powered cement mixer blew a head gasket part way through the pour.

One of the jumpers saved the day and made a new gasket out of aluminum foil. To everyone's surprise it worked. This water cistern is still in use and can be seen off the north end of the runway above the trail junction to Flossie Lake and the Stonebraker Ranch.

August Hotzel's homestead cabin as it appeared in the mid-1970s. At some point the log structure's exterior was covered with shingles.

Hotzel Ranch – Outfitters and Guides

One of many early twentieth century homesteads near the Chamberlain airfield is the Hotzel Ranch located to the east of the large runway. Mike Hogan first claimed the 157.42 acre property in the fall of 1906 and abandoned it with no development by 1913.[27]

In 1915 German born August Hotzel settled on the place. Hotzel who immigrated to the United States in 1907 after serving in the German army, began work as a gold miner near Stevens, Washington. He made his way to the Salmon River country and eight years after settling on his Chamberlain Basin ranch received official ownership of the property. During his early years on the place he built a three-room log house, hay barn, chicken coop, and storage building. Hotzel used a unique European-style log craftsmanship with

1 *A 1975 image of the approach to the long east-west runway. The Hotzel Ranch located on the north bank of Chamberlain Creek can be seen to the right.*
2 *The main house at the Hotzel ranch constructed in 1966–68 by Stan Potts.*
3 *Hotzel Ranch outfitter Stan Potts was not shy about advertising on the side of his Cessna 180 (N2242C).*
4 *Outfitter Scott Farr with his Cessna 206 at Thomas Creek.*
5 *Hotzel's homestead cabin (right) along with the guest cabins (left) built by Farr.*
6 *The Hotzel Ranch building complex in 1996.*

the incorporation of dovetail corners.[28]

By 1923 Hotzel ran several horses and over twenty head of cattle on the ranch. Regarding early ranchers in the Idaho Primitive Area, longtime USFS employee Glenn Thompson commented, "The spirit backing these early livestock settlers is represented in an account of August Hotzel . . . after being informed he could own land by merely working it, he shed tears of joy and blessed America as God's land. Although not an exceptionally strong man, he performed the tasks of five men in building his property and caring for his cattle."[29]

Another early forest inspector had made similar observations of Hotzel and in a 1915 homestead report wrote, "[A]pparently he knows nothing but work. Part of his claim is wet and he is working upon a system of drain ditches to get rid of the surplus moisture. The day I visited the claim he was clearing brush and cutting wild hay with a scythe. The hay he packed to his proposed building site on his back."[30]

By the mid-1920s Hotzel's health began to fail. He liquidated much of his livestock and eventually moved in with his friends the Thompsons at their ranch on the South Fork of the Salmon River (now named South Fork Ranch). Hotzel lived here a short time and died in 1929.[31]

After Hotzel's death the property sold to neighbor Phillip Beal. In 1932 Beal sold this acreage and his property abutting the Stonebraker Ranch to Clarence Paulsen. The latter then sold both homesteads to W. T. McGill in 1947.[32] Two years later the IDFG bought the Hotzel property for $12,200.[33]

After acquiring the parcel, the IDFG leased it to various outfitters. One of the earliest was Courtland "Slim" Horn followed by Louis Bicandi in 1963. Bicandi had worked with Horn as a packer in 1940 and heard his operation was for sale. After operating for one year he and his wife had big plans for the old ranch, including the construction of a large log lodge to accommodate guests. Post hunting season, Bicandi ran afoul of the bank and the law, but through a series of pleas to the IDFG was able to renew his lease.[34] However, things did not work out and he sold his equipment and eighteen head of stock to Stan Potts.[35]

Potts stumbled upon the opportunity in 1964 when his father Verl, who was managing and operating

the stock at the Cape Horn (Boy) Scout Reservation, heard of the prospect. His father called him at his ranch in Wells, Nevada, and asked him if he would be interested in being partners in the venture. The two agreed that it sounded good and shortly thereafter on August 4 Potts flew the Wells Flying Club's ninety-horse Piper Cub (N7296D) to Homedale, Idaho, and picked up Bicandi. The two proceeded to the Chamberlain airstrip to look at the property.[36]

Looking back years later Potts laughed, "I had never even been to Chamberlain Basin. Here I was a fledgling pilot flying a ninety-horse Cub, in search of a deal." Potts received a full tour and liked what he saw. The stipulations to sealing the transaction were the inclusion of eighteen mules and horses, and that Bicandi had to stick around for the first season to show the Pottses the hunting areas. He agreed and the Pottses started Chamberlain Basin Outfitters.[37]

After the first night with the opening hunting party, Bicandi was gone with the money and never seen again. The father-son team quickly learned, and were lucky to have Stan's wife Joy, who ran the base camp.[38]

Before Potts bought his own airplane he either flew ones owned by the Wells Flying Club, which he helped start, or he borrowed aircraft from friends flying everything from small Cessnas to Piper Colts. He frequently flew a Cessna 150 (N7107X). One morning after dropping his father and some gear off at Cabin Creek in the 150, Stan pushed the throttle wide open and noticed the airplane struggling to get airborne. Already committed to the takeoff, he pushed the nose over and figured he was in for quite a ride. "At one point Cabin Creek itself started looking just as large as Big Creek, but I made it out." He limped the airplane around the backcountry for the remainder of the fall and eventually flew it back to Wells. A mechanic took a look at it and found that the plane was only running on three of four cylinders. The best cylinder was only pushing forty pounds of pressure.[39]

Over the years the Pottses built a viable outfitting business at Hotzel, serving on an average thirty to thirty-five clients per season. The Potts family constructed a second building at the ranch between 1966 and 1968, as the original log house built by Hotzel was all that remained in 1964. The Pottses also poured a concrete floor over the dirt in the original house, which was only really used as a storage area. Looking for windows to fit the new building, Verl approached Big Creek Ranger Earl Dodds about the possibility of salvaging windows from the Rocky Point Lookout near their Hot Springs Meadow spike camp. Dodds had no issue, so the windows were salvaged and reused.[40]

Stan eventually bought his own airplane, a Cessna 180 (N2242C), to accommodate the demands of the growing business. With several years under their belts Verl and Stan were contacted by Jess Taylor of the Taylor Ranch to see if they were interested in leasing his place on lower Big Creek. Taylor and Verl were acquaintances from the Pahsimeroi Valley. Eager to learn more about sheep and goat hunting, Stan thought it was a good opportunity. The first season Taylor and Verl worked together outfitting in the Big Creek area, while Stan and Joy ran the operation from Hotzel. Verl and Taylor did not see eye to eye on the operation and the following years they switched personnel, with Stan and Joy running the Taylor Ranch solely on their own.

In the early 1970s the Potts family moved their entire operation to the Taylor Ranch, selling the Chamberlain portion of the business to Scott and Shelda Farr in 1972. The Farrs named their company Wilderness Outfitters. Similar to how Potts purchased the business, their first sight of the area was from the air. Potts picked the husband and wife up in Salmon and flew them to the ranch in his Cessna 180 (for more information on Stan Potts see Taylor Ranch).

Scott Farr was not new to the outfitting business as he started his career as a guide for George Matteson in 1963 at Running Creek on the Selway River. The

Most of the Hotzel Ranch burned in a 2000 wildland fire – the few things that did survive were removed.

A view of the Hotzel Ranch after the IDFG cleaned up the property.

following year he partnered with Newt Killpatrick on the Middle Fork and Main Salmon Rivers under the name of Quarter Circle A Outfitters. After a tour in Vietnam, Farr returned to the Selway country, leasing the Selway Lodge for his base of operations. He sold the Quarter Circle A Outfitters to Rick Hussey. While looking for a new area to hunt he came across the Hotzel Ranch lease.[41]

The Farrs set out to enhance the old ranch by first adding running water and an indoor bathroom to the Potts building. Within the first few years of the operation the Farrs began homeschooling their three children and lived at the ranch from spring until the snow became too deep in December. Wanting more space for family and clients, Farr built two framed cabins and a tack shed. In need of more windows in the remote country, he followed Verl Potts's idea and packed the remaining windows from the Rocky Point Lookout.[42]

Wanting to build all three structures out of native material he approached Ranger Dodds about the possibility of falling dead lodgepole across the meadow to the south toward Lodgpole Point. However, Dodds denied the proposal due to the risk of tearing up the fragile meadow. Farr decided it was perfectly legal to fall full thirty-two foot sections of dead standing trees for "firewood." So, he and his wife cut what they needed, then walked two of their best mules over and tied each log between the mules and packed them over to the ranch as not to damage the meadow. Farr humbly commented, "The first log went across the meadow a little faster than we wanted to go, but it somehow worked out." With the logs already cured he was able to go to work right away.[43]

In 1975 Farr decided tying an airplane to the business would be greatly beneficial. An opportunity arose to trade carpentry work at the Big Creek Hotel for flying lessons and a part ownership of a Cessna 180 (N4688U). He jumped at the chance and eventually bought sole ownership of a Cessna 175. Determining the 175 was a little underpowered for backcountry flying, Farr upgraded to a Cessna 182 (N3158Y). In an effort to make the airplane more affordable he leased it to Jim Searles of Air Unlimited, based in Challis. The plane crashed in July of 1979, while on a IDFG sheep count in Fox Creek near the East Fork of the Salmon River. Farr replaced the aircraft with another 182 (N3128Q), which was later traded for a 206 (N9469G).[44]

About the same time Farr bought the 206 he had his eye on moving his outfitting operations to Cabin Creek on Big Creek. For several years he had reminded owner Rex Lanham that he was interested in obtaining his hunting area if it ever became available. When Lanham sold the Cabin Creek property to the USFS, Farr missed the opportunity, as Lanham's son-in-law Ronald Vaughn acquired it. However, Vaughn's ownership was short-lived and Farr took over the area in 1980, leaving the Hotzel Ranch. It was a bittersweet departure, Farr remarked, "I loved the place, but I did not always enjoy trophy hunting in the lodgepole, it

was really thick in those days."[45]

The Farrs remained at Cabin Creek for six years, then moved their business to Canada. They returned to the Idaho backcountry, settling permanently in 1995 after buying a business connected to the Middle Fork country.[46]

With Farr's departure Ed and Peggy McCallum took over the Hotzel lease in 1981 and held it through 1995. During the McCallum's years at the property they battled with the USFS and the IDFG on water rights, trail rights-of-way, grazing, noise, aircraft, and several other issues. Many of their concerns were valid.[47]

One particular issue related to aircraft occurred in 1985 when the International 180-185 Club had a fly-in at Chamberlain with an estimated seventy airplanes. Peggy McCallum summarized her dissatisfaction of the event in a letter to Krassel Ranger Earl Kimball, "In one day, there were more landings than we have ever seen in the entire first week of hunting. The people who came by Hotzel Ranch looking for Stonebraker Ranch had no concept of this being a Wilderness area. They were all dressed for a social event and expressed dismay that they would have to walk at least a mile for their barbecue. One fellow asked me in amazement, 'And how do you get in here? Do you have a car?' I wonder how it is possible for a person to fly from Boise to Chamberlain Basin and not notice where the roads end. Another man seemed very upset when informed he would have to fly out his beer cans; that there wasn't a dumpster handy. I realize we can't discriminate in who is allowed to use the Wilderness, but neither should a convention like this be encouraged."[48]

In spite of the few upsets, the McCallums had wonderful years at the old Hotzel Ranch. After the 1995 season the McCallums left their outfitting area, with part of it going to Tony Kreckeler and part to the Flying B Ranch's operation. The IDFG never renewed a lease on the property as they had preliminary plans to exchange land with the USFS.[49]

In the 2000 wildfire that ravaged Chamberlain Basin, fire crews did not protect the Hotzel buildings and they were allowed to burn. In 2001 with almost everything at the site scorched, the IDFG hired a helicopter to bring in equipment and buried everything not claimed by the fire.[50]

Ed Allen grading the north-south Chamberlain airstrip with mules in July 1974.

The 1970s and the Move to Wilderness

The 1970s were golden years at the Chamberlain Guard Station for both aviation enthusiasts and USFS employees. But it was also a time of finding balance. Although Chamberlain had been managed as a primitive area since the creation of the Idaho Primitive Area in 1931, the Wilderness Act of 1964 eventually led to profound changes at the Chamberlain facility. The Payette NF made an effort to return their portion of the Idaho Primitive Area completely back to primitive methods and ways. When this portion became a study area for wilderness, forest officials decided it had a better chance of gaining the designation if it was managed as such. As a result, the Big Creek District took the ideas and goals of wilderness to heart. Out went the gas-powered machines and in came the crosscuts, hand axes, and horse-drawn equipment.

Through the late 1960s and early 1970s the Payette NF made an effort to balance the new ideals of "primitive," while maintaining public access. Ed Allen ran the station for the majority of the decade starting in 1972. During Allen's tenure the runways were cut regularly with horse-drawn equipment and camping areas further developed.

About the same time Allen took on the new position, flying magazines promoted the location, touting the recreational opportunities the remote strip offered. A 1971 article from *The AOPA Pilot* entitled, "Chamberlain: Heart of Idaho's Primitive Area" by

John C. Gosling is just one of several dozens from the era encouraging the sport of flying to Chamberlain and the backcountry.

In the article Gosling wrote, "I have always heard Idaho referred to as an outdoorsman's paradise, but I had come to believe there was really a much better definition. I had come to believe that it was a *flying* outdoorsman's paradise. Why? Because, with the exception of the light plane, Idaho's enormous primitive and wilderness areas are relatively inaccessible to the average outdoorsman. Yet, within these areas are all the things an outdoorsman's dreams are made of."[51]

In addition to endorsements and advertising in flying magazines, local and national flying clubs also took notice. These clubs and associations started using some of the bigger more improved backcountry airstrips such as Chamberlain for fly-in events. Not only did the private sector of the flying community become more interested in taking advantage of these remote areas, but non-flyers did as well, leading to an increase in commercial charters.

Looking back at the use of aircraft at Chamberlain during this period, Allen commented, "In those days the pilots always brought their clients to the Forest Service station to drop them off. The real benefit of this was that it brought almost all visitors to the Forest Service's doorstep. We met a lot of nice visitors because of the way we were set up and in those days we felt somehow that it was part of our job. We served a lot of cups of coffee during those days. All the pilots knew that if they came in early in the morning they would be offered a cup, and sometimes a roll to go with it. It was a two-way street then, as the pilots all liked us and would go out of their way to accommodate us if needed, and we did the same for them."[52]

Ray Arnold, who started his air taxi business, Arnold Aviation, during this era, occasionally spent his days off at the station in the summer. "Ed [Allen] had the place really nice. I'd take my family in and the kids all played together. They would ride horses from the Hotzel Ranch and we all played a few games of volleyball. It was a different place in those years, far from what it is now. We all had a lot of fun."[53]

Ted Trueblood and Chamberlain Basin

Ted Trueblood, one of the most noteworthy outdoor writers and conservationists of the twentieth century, spent a good deal of time in the Idaho backcountry. He and his wife Ellen honeymooned in 1936 at Sulphur Creek. But, of all the special places he came to know and write about, Chamberlain Basin undoubtedly ranked among one of his favorites.[54]

Working first as a freelance writer in Boise he eventually became an editor in 1941 for *Field & Stream*, and wrote for the magazine until his death in 1982. Beyond working as the magazine's editor he authored hundreds of other articles appearing in countless periodicals, and wrote seven books.[55] Unlike most writers who are paid to take trips and write about the happenings, Trueblood went places he wanted to go fish, hunt, hike, or boat. He then based his writings on his life's adventures. After gaining fame, Trueblood traveled far and wide, but from the 1940s through the 1970s he spent time fishing and hunting the drainages of Chamberlain Basin almost annually. He considered the place home.[56]

Truebloods final book *The Ted Trueblood Hunting Treasury*, a compilation of his favorite articles, revealed his passion for the Chamberlain country, particularly in chapters: "The Old and the New," "Reward for Virtue," and "Spell of the High Country." In these few samples he described some of his favorite hunting areas, including Pup, Queen, and Deer creeks, all within reach from the Chamberlain airstrip.[57]

Trueblood believed strongly in aircraft access. He commonly chartered aircraft with Bill Woods of Floating Feather or Johnson Flying Service in McCall. Once in Chamberlain he often camped at the intersection of the two runways and occasionally used his connections with the IDFG to stay at the Stonebraker Ranch. Friend and outfitter Slim Horn packed for him on elk and deer trips. In the 1950s Trueblood used spike camps at both Quaking Aspen and Arctic Point.[58]

The importance of the Idaho backcountry to Trueblood and the need to protect it caused him to create the River of No Return Wilderness Council in 1973. The goal of the council was to gain wilderness status for both the Idaho Primitive Area and the Salmon River Breaks Primitive Area. The small grassroots group caught the eye of wilderness proponent Idaho Senator Frank Church. Over the course of five years Church worked with Trueblood and his group and their goal was met in 1978 with the creation of the River of No Return Wilderness. Church credited Trueblood with the achievement of the wilderness designation.

Trueblood used his notoriety as an outdoor journalist, writing countless articles about Idaho's wilderness debate. These appeared in a variety of national magazines. Article titles were telling of his position on the issue: "To Pay A Debt," *Outdoor America*; "Save Our Public Land, Inc.," *Outdoor America*; "What Price Wilderness?: Money cannot buy the essence of wilderness," *Idaho Heritage*; "Struggle on the Salmon: Will Congress provide proper wilderness protection or be swayed by Boise Cascade and other interests?," *The Living Wilderness*; "Help! A Chunk Of Your Wilderness Is Up For Grabs," *True's Hunting Yearbook*; and "How They're Won," *Field & Stream*.

Trueblood also penned countless letters to congressman, senators, and other government officials. In addition to these letters he wrote many updates to council members of their progress. In an August 1, 1975 letter, Trueblood wrote, "To Members and Friends: I recently flew home from Chamberlain Basin after two days of steady rain which, added to heavy snow runoff, had Chamberlain Creek, just south of the airstrip, out of its banks. Yet its water was as clear as gin! It was the only clear water I saw that day. Every other stream we flew over on the way to Boise

Ted Trueblood taking in the scenery of his favorite place in the backcountry – Chamberlain Basin.

A group of air taxi aircraft parked at Chamberlain in the 1980s.

was muddy, some of them almost chocolate colored. Chamberlain Creek has no roads or logging on its watershed; all the others do. The effect of this 'multiple use' was so obvious that it doubled my determination to help preserve the River of No Return Wilderness – – no matter how long the struggle may last."[59]

Living a modest life style, Trueblood turned to many friends such as the members of the wilderness council to support his nonprofit efforts. One person helping out when he could was Nick Long, a professional photographer who had recently returned from a Vietnam helicopter assignment. Long had grown up in Nampa with Trueblood's kids and looked up to this rugged outdoorsman as another father. Utilizing both of his skills as photographer and camp grunt, he flew to Chamberlain with Trueblood to shoot publicity photographs of wildlife and scenery for the council's use.[60]

The following morning Trueblood set out to document flora and fauna on Dog and Pup creeks and Long hiked toward Red Top Meadows to do the same. They both agreed they would meet up the next morning at base camp. In perfect Trueblood style the expert outdoorsman left with only the quintessential survival items: a handful of teabags, a small tin pot, a tarp, and five of his wife's oatmeal raisin cookies that he called

"Strength Cookies."[61]

The next day Trueblood arrived back at camp first and discovered Long, who was the last one out of the tent the day before, had forgotten to tie the tent flap closed. A typical afternoon rain shower had engulfed the area and filled the tent with water, completely soaking their sleeping bags. When Long appeared back in camp Trueblood casually commented, "I sure chose a poor camp partner." The rest of the trip Trueblood gave him a hard time. Trueblood then wrote about the incident in one of his published stories. It was something the two laughed about for some time.[62]

The mid-1970s trip with Long turned out to be Trueblood's last time in Chamberlain Basin. In early 1982 he was diagnosed with terminal bone cancer. Upon hearing of his condition Senator Church wrote him on June 25,1982 giving his sympathy and gratitude for all he had done for the wilderness movement, "Actually, whatever I may have done in the Senate for Idaho in creating the wilderness and national recreation areas, was largely due to your inspiration. Your love of the outdoors, the many articles you wrote about camping, fishing and hunting, and the following you built throughout the state made it possible to secure the dedicated citizen support without which no legislation could have been passed. So it is my belief, Ted, that the River of No Return Wilderness, the crowning achievement, is a natural monument to the kind of life you led and the leadership you gave to the cause of conservation. Many contributed, to be sure, but you stood above all others. This is my view, as to which I'm sure no knowledgeable person would take exception."[63]

With the pain and knowledge of what was going to happen, Trueblood took his own life with a self-inflicted gunshot wound on September 12, 1982.

The first USFS administrative quarters at Cold Meadows circa 1924.

COLD MEADOWS

Cold Meadows was originally named Upper Cottonwood Meadows and was supposedly renamed because of the persistent "cold" temperatures the area experiences throughout the year.[64] By 1924 the USFS established a permanent ranger station on the southeast end of the meadow. To the main dwelling over the next several years were added a commissary, bunkhouse, and fly shed. In 1955 a washhouse was built.[65] The remote outpost functioned as the main headquarters for the original Cold Meadows Ranger District, which was later combined with the Chamberlain District, then the Big Creek District, and eventually the Krassel District.

In 1932 the airfield stretched north of the ranger station, and measured 1800'. However, the width was inconstant and at certain spots narrowed to an almost unusable size for planes with long wingspans. This problem was fixed the same year along with relocating a telephone line that extended from the ranger station to Roots Knob Lookout across the south end of the meadow. Drainage pipe was buried to prevent washouts and soft areas. Stones larger than a man's fist were removed and the field was leveled with a log drag powered by two horses. In addition to the leveling and drainage changes, a windsock was added to the site, along with runway end markers built of rock.[66]

In 1955 the D7 Caterpillar that built the large Chamberlain airfield was walked over to Cold Meadows. During the summer of 1955 the north portion of the runway was extended by 1400'.[67] In August, Bob Fogg of Johnson Flying Service flew to Cold Meadows to consult with the USFS engineers on additional improvements. From this meeting it was decided that the field clearance width on both sides of the runway needed to be at a distance suitable for Johnson Ford Tri-Motors, and this was accomplished.[68] In fact the wing clearance of the field was widened enough that Johnson Flying Service pilots Bob Johnson and Warren Ellison were able to land the first DC-3 on the strip.[69]

Through the field seasons of 1956 and early 1957 more work was completed on the runway with the dozer. In addition, a large lodgepole fence was built along its perimeter and many upgrades were completed at the guard station complex. Overall the strip was expanded to its current length of 4550' and the south end parking and taxi areas were carved out.[70] After runway completion, the Cat was walked down Crooked Creek and back to the Big Creek Ranger Station, where it had started from several years before.[71]

In the early years the Cold Meadows runway was crucial for early forest patrol planes. It also allowed the USFS to have easy access for firefighters, equipment, and personnel at this remote location. Later it became a great point of entry for hunters, fisherman, and other recreationists.

Despite the field's fairly long length, the 7030' elevation has caused many pilots and aircraft havoc. After several accidents the USFS created a large wooden sign near the parking area showing the safest departure procedure to the south and out Cottonwood Creek. With the wilderness movement the sign along with the lodgepole fence around the airfield were torn down. The airstrip continues to have active use from the public and the USFS. In 1994 the historic guard station was listed on the National Register of Historic Places. The airfield was also added to the register in 2010 and is one of three listed in the Idaho backcountry.

1 *Cold Meadows before the development of the airfield circa 1924.*
2 *The Cold Meadows Ranger Station under construction in the summer of 1924.*
3 *Pilot Bill Gowen with an early fire patrol plane at Cold Meadows in the early 1930s.*
4 *The Cold Meadows building complex in the early 1950s.*
5 *An August 1957 field meeting with USFS personnel and pilot Bob Fogg concerning the runway renovation project at Cold Meadows. The D7 Caterpillar is parked alongside Johnson Flying Service's Travel Air 6000 NC9038.*

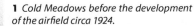

260

6 Looking south from the top of the airstrip during the mid-1950s airstrip expansion.

7 Bob Nicol (left) of Intermountain Aviation picking up smokejumpers with a Twin Otter in 1969. Observe the large wooden sign behind the airplane that cautioned pilots to depart down Cottonwood Creek.

8 Installing the proper runway drainage in August 1955.

9 A McCall Air Taxi Cessna 185 stopped to help a Cessna 206 that had a bad day while trying to takeoff in too deep of snow on wheels.

10 Looking north at the 4550' Cold Meadows runway situated at 7030'.

Looking north at the progress of the Hida airstrip during the summer of 1938 – trees are cleared and the stumps are ready to be pulled.

W. Johnson/Zaunmiller

HIDA RIDGE |

In 1936 the Hida Ridge airfield was approved for construction. The field, located approximately one-hour flight time from McCall, was built to provide quick and efficient access for fire suppression.[72] By 1938 the runway, situated northeast-southwest was constructed to roughly 1800'.[73] Nearby Salmon River resident Joe Zaunmiller, who lived at Campbell's Ferry, was contracted as the project foreman. Zaunmiller frequently worked for the USFS during this period, usually as a packer.[74] Large drainage ditches were constructed on each side of the runway and lined with rock that was removed from the field's surface. Most of the rock was moved with the help of a horse-drawn rock boat. A few years later the runway was lengthened to nearly 2000'.[75]

The USFS stressed that "only light single or two place ships" land or takeoff at this location. Recommended takeoff was to the northeast and approach for landing was to the southwest. Located about a half-mile up the trail toward Highline Ridge was a convenient camp with water.[76] Two miles to the northeast along the same ridge as the airfield was the Hida Point Lookout. The lookout saw only a few years of use in the late 1930s and early 1940s, primarily during times of high fire danger.[77] Johnson Flying Service used this strip occasionally throughout the 1940s.[78]

Jim Larkin often told a story related to the Hida airfield. Sometime in the early 1950s while working at the Johnson Flying Service hangar in McCall, a small beat-up old Stinson taxied up. The pilot clambered out in a terrible mood and wanted gas. Larkin tried to start up a conversation while fueling the plane and asked him where he had come from. The man grumbled that he had just been at the Chamberlain airstrip, which a friend of his told him had a good runway. The pilot then explained that it was the worst runway he had ever seen and that it nearly tore up his airplane on landing and takeoff. The pilot went on to describe the strip and that he had maneuvered the airplane over the Salmon River. Larkin concluded that the pilot had been off-course and even though he thought he was at Chamberlain, had instead landed at Hida.[79]

Pilots with ski-equipped Piper Cubs used the strip into the 1970s. Even at that time the runway had grown in with small trees and was no longer usable for wheeled airplanes.[80] Today large lodgepoles cover the runway, but it remains somewhat visible from the air.

1 The Hida Ridge construction crew led by foreman Joe Zaunmiller (center with hat) of Campbell's Ferry in 1938.

2 Joe Zaunmiller (foreground) with his crew and horses pulling stumps to clear the runway surface.

3 Looking north at the Hida airstrip with the stumps completely pulled and the field leveled. The rocks on the surface were later removed and piled along each side.

4 A 1947 view of the airfield – notice the smoothed runway surface and the small trees beginning to grow.

5 A 2010 view to the north of the grown-in airfield from the south end – all that remains open is a USFS trail.

6 Rocks gathered during the runway's construction continue to outline the abandoned airfield.

7 A view to the north of the Hida Ridge airstrip with the Salmon River canyon in the background.

8 A 2009 view of the airfield looking south.

PHANTOM MEADOW

A July 1952 view to the south of the unfinished Phantom Meadow airstrip.

In 1936 this airfield was designed and named Hungry Creek Landing Field, which was later changed to Phantom Meadow. The airfield was to provide an access point for getting men into the isolated area quickly for fire suppression. The USFS could have a crew in the area within one hour's flight time from McCall. It already had a nearby telephone system and had several maintained trails in the vicinity.[81]

Construction on the strip started in 1942 with labor provided by the CCC. It is interesting that the crew cleared 2100' of runway with a width of 50', but aligned the runway north-south. Revisions intended for the 1943 field season were to change the runway heading ten degrees to the northeast and clear 2500' of runway with a width of 100', combined with 100' clearings along each side. The recommended takeoff and landing was to be made to the north. However, no aircraft were known to have landed here, as World War II interrupted the construction indefinitely.[82]

The meadow received its name in the mid-1920s from then Cold Meadows Ranger Merl "Blackie" Wallace. Ranger Wallace located the meadow and related the story to Idaho NF Assistant Supervisor William McCormick, who wanted to be taken there. Later Wallace went on a trip with McCormick to show him the site but was unable to relocate it and it thus became known as the "Phantom Meadow." Frustrated, Wallace returned later to search for the mysterious meadow, and did in fact find it.[83]

A 2009 view to the north of the uncompleted Phantom Meadow airfield. The runway cut can be seen to the left of Phantom Meadow with the Salmon River canyon in the background.

Cold Meadows District Ranger Merl "Blackie" Wallace (right) taking a break on a fire during the mid-1920s. Wallace was responsible for the naming of Phantom Meadow.

A 2012 aerial of Lower Ramey Meadows. The cut of the unfinished airstrip is visible north of the meadow.

RAMEY MEADOWS

Similar to the Phantom Meadow airfield, work on the Ramey Meadows airstrip began during the summer of 1942. At this location, clearing and burning was started to create a landing strip nearly 2,000' in length.[84] The remaining work for the following year was to pull stumps and move 1,500 cubic yards of borrow material to create the proper grade. None of this work was carried out and the project was abandoned.[85]

Looking south at Lower Ramey Meadows – the uncompleted runway (center) has nearly grown-in.

While maps of the era simply named the locality Ramey Meadows, the site is actually located in Lower Ramey Meadows. The unfinished airstrip was platted to sit mainly east-west, providing landing approaches to the west and departures to the east. Even with the recommend landing procedure it was suggested to use extreme caution because of the curving approach that was needed to get an aircraft low enough for landing.[86] However, most likely due to an unreliable topographic survey, the airstrip was built farther to the south and oriented more north-south. An area of 800' X 75' was approximately cleared. It has since filled in with a stand of young lodgepole pine.

A southern view of the partially built airstrip in 2009.

ROOT RANCH

The Homestead

Jess Root (left) with a group of friends most likely from Warren.

In 1911 Jess Root, who grew up in the Chamberlain Basin area, first began occupying the property now known as the Root Ranch. Root grew hay, ran cattle, trapped, and worked some for the USFS. He received homestead approval for 157.65 acres in 1919 and developed the property, building a log cabin, two barns, and several other outbuildings.[87] Around 1920 Root moved to Warren where he ran a saloon and served as the local postmaster. In 1935 he drowned on the Salmon River near the Whitewater Ranch.[88]

The entrance gate welcoming guests to the ranch.

A Famous Actor, Airplanes, and an Airfield

With Root's death the property taxes went unpaid and in 1936 R. L. Campbell acquired the ranch on back taxes. He in turn sold it the following year to well-known actor Wallace Beery.[89] The famous Hollywood resident had been on several big-game hunts in the area with guides Blackie Wallace and John Routson and planned on using the ranch exclusively for hunting and fishing.[90] On more than one hunt in the 1930s he visited the Routson family on Big Creek. In fact Routson gave Beery a hide from a bear that he shot at the Werdenhoff Mine. It was to be a trophy for Beery's Hollywood den.[91]

The same year Beery purchased the ranch the USFS approached him about obtaining an easement for the construction and use of an airfield.[92] Beery, a pilot and huge aviation buff, gladly worked out a deal. It is not known if Beery piloted any of his own aircraft to the Root Ranch, but there are accounts of him at Idaho airports with some of his high-end planes. Between 1927 and 1939 Beery owned nine different airplanes.

Combining his two hobbies of flying and fishing, he often sent a specially-equipped station wagon to a lake, river, or stream and he would fly to the nearest airport and meet up with the outfit. The automobile had a special transmission, cooling system, oversized gas tanks, and was replete with camping gear. In an article written about Beery, author May Mann commented, "Whenever he can get away for a trip . . . he sends this station wagon on ahead, then makes the jump in his plane. But that's only one aspect of angling, – in the course of a season he may visit the High Sierras of California and Nevada, the Snake River in Idaho (where Wally has a ranch near McCall), the Henshaw Dam in California, the Klamath River in Oregon, and numerous other lakes and streams."[93]

Actor Wallace Beery owned the Root Ranch from 1937 to 1943. Here he poses cheerfully with hunting trophies.

WALLACE BEERY AND HIS FAVOURITE 'PLANE

Beery leased an easement to the USFS for the construction of the ranch's airstrip. This small 1930s promotional postcard shows his interest in flying.

Looking south at the Root Ranch airstrip built by the USFS.

Even during the Great Depression Beery bought some of the most expensive planes on the market including a 1928 Travel Air 6000. This particular plane, serial number 816 and registered as NC9015, was the most costly Travel Air the company ever built, with a final price tag of $20,000. The large bill was due to all the extra items Beery ordered including larger wings to handle long-range tanks that could carry a total of 130 gallons. The extra fuel was needed as the plane was fitted with a hefty 420-horse power Pratt & Whitney radial engine. All of the interior seats were upholstered in plush velour, and there was a custom-designed couch where he liked to take naps during long flights. He also had it equipped with hot and cold running water for the rear lavatory, as well as a built-in collapsible card table.[94]

Beery often flew the 6000 as he held a transport pilot license. It is interesting to note that this model of airplane was frequently used in the Idaho backcountry. His 6000 most likely never made it to Idaho as it crashed in San Gabriel, California, on March 25, 1930 with one of his experienced pilots, George "Slim" Maves, at the helm, and two other passengers aboard.

The airstrip at the Root Ranch was finished by 1939–40 and originally measured 1900'. It was later extended to 2100'. The USFS mainly used the airstrip as an entry point for fire suppression activities.

267

The original Root built barn among some of the corrugated structures constructed during Ruth Vernon's ownership.

Landing to the north at the Root Ranch.

A Tough Sale

In 1943 Beery sold the ranch to Howard Elkins.[95] Elkins operated it for a number of years, but the place was for sale during most of his ownership. In 1952 Bill Guth Sr. was interested in the property and arranged a date to meet with Elkins. Although Guth was a horseman and disliked flying he chartered a flight with Bill Woods in a Travel Air 6000. Woods flew to Stanley from his base of operations at Floating Feather near Boise and picked up Guth and his two boys, Norman and Bill Jr. For young Bill it was his first airplane ride. The group arrived at the Root Ranch but could not find Elkins. Guth looked the ranch over and was willing to pay $9,000. As they took off Woods pointed out the window, motioning to Guth, "Take a look over there on the ridge, I bet Elkins is there somewhere. Every time I fly a prospective buyer in here he disappears, I'm not so sure he ever wants to sell it." Guth lost no sleep on the matter and became a backcountry landowner at Middle Fork Lodge.[96]

Shortly after the flight with the Guths, Woods flew in prospective buyer Ruth Vernon, who already owned the Flying B Ranch on the Middle Fork. Woods was her main pilot, operating several airplanes that she owned or leased. Her trip was a repeat of Guths, as Elkins was nowhere to be found when they arrived to look at the property. Vernon who was a no-nonsense businesswoman devised a plan to just show up one day and put Elkins on the spot, which she did. Vernon and Woods flew in and caught him at the ranch. The two unannounced visitors were invited in for a cup of coffee. Sitting at the table in the log cabin, Vernon looked Elkins square in the eyes and said, "What is it going to take?" At the same instance she began laying out thousand dollar bills one at a time. Bill after bill went down on the table. It was a fairly silent event Woods told people later on, who just watched, while drinking a cup of coffee. As the twenty-third bill hit the table, Elkins seemed happy and Vernon finally had what she wanted.[97]

At the time of her acquisition the ranch had the original homestead cabin and one log barn. She added several corrugated structures including five bunkhouses and a dining hall along with other sheds. The ranch was primarily operated in conjunction with her Flying B property.[98] Johnson Flying Service flew in many of the supplies for the ranch's improvements from McCall. Ken Roth with Ford Tri-Motor NC8419 carried in several loads along with additional trips made by Bob Fogg in Travel Air NC9038.[99]

landed at the Root Ranch. The air was rough and he experienced some uncomfortable winds on approach. The passengers slid out of the airplane and walked around as he and some of the ranch help unloaded the freight. Not liking the conditions, Woods decided they should wait awhile, hoping the wind might die off. Time passed and the Texans started pressuring him to go, worried about missing their commercial flight in Boise.[102]

Again not wanting to disappoint Vernon or lose her business, he gave in. They all loaded up, but Woods still had his doubts about making the attempt with the adverse conditions. As he closed the door on the plane he told the ranch manager if there was any trouble to have Billie Oberbillig (backcountry radio operator) get a hold of Jim Larkin in McCall to come in and rescue them.[103]

An Error in Judgment

In 1954 Vernon had purchased a new de Havilland Beaver and Woods was racking up the hours on it. On a hot summer day Woods dropped a few guests off at the Flying B. Vernon was there waiting with four more clients that needed to be taken back to Boise so they could catch a commercial flight to Texas later in the evening. Woods expected the additional passengers, but explained that he had a half load of supplies for the

The result of Bill Woods's de Havilland Beaver accident at the ranch.

Root Ranch also needing delivery. He said he would make a quick run up to the Root and be back for the four Texans. Woods did not want a heavy load on takeoff coming out of the Root Ranch with the day's high temperatures.[100]

Vernon became pushy and firmly told Woods she had promised the four men a scenic flight and he would have to take them. With the hot weather and rough air Woods knew better than to cave, but he was also under pressure from the owner of the airplane to make the flight.[101]

Woods cranked the Beaver up and they wound their way out of the Middle Fork, up Big Creek, and

Trying to get all he could out of the conditions he lined up at an angle in a corner at the north end of the runway. He then waited for a blast of wind to come across the strip and ruffle the grassy surface before he firewalled the throttle. The plane leaped into the air about halfway down the runway. He made a small course correction and continued trying to horse the bird into the air. His concern regarding the conditions were affirmed when they hit a series of downdrafts right off the end of the airstrip - struggling to remain airborne - he stayed with the lumbering airplane. By this point he knew the only way he was going to save himself, the passengers, and the aircraft was to attempt a turn and head back to the airstrip. Woods executed a turn and sustained a pitch for best rate of climb. Meantime he continued to catch down air and nothing played out to his favor. He had the plane lined up with the runway at full power, but he could not out climb or avoid the trees. The plane's landing gear hit the treetops and the plane smashed to the ground.[104]

No one was horribly injured – one broken leg, a few cracked ribs, scrapes, and bruises. The new airplane was a total loss. Larkin was contacted as requested and rescued the bunch.[105]

Pilot Mike Loening (right) visits with his employees Arch Marsing and Red Hill.

Flying Resort Ranches manager Bill Guth Jr. with one of his Cessna 206s at the ranch in 2001.

New Owners, Outfitting, and a Parked Airplane

In 1955 Vernon lost the Root Ranch to the Idaho First National Bank.[106] During the bank's ownership the acreage was leased to Mike Loening for his outfitting and guiding business from roughly 1960 through 1963. Loening hired Arch Marsing and Frank Hussey to run the operations at the ranch, while he mainly took care of the flying.[107]

The bank finally sold the property circa 1964 to Flying Resort Ranches Inc. who then owned the Flying B Ranch. Loening worked out a deal with the corporation to manage an outfitting business from the ranch. The arrangement lasted nearly through the end of the decade. Roughly five years into the Resort's ownership the USFS officially released their easement for use of the runway.

When Loening left the property as manager, others took over. One was Bill Kornell, who operated Acme Air Taxi based in Salmon. While flying rafters from Mackay Bar in the summer of 1975 in his de Havilland DHC-3 Otter (N521BK), he noticed he was extremely low on oil after landing at Mackay Bar and determined it was a bad prop seal. Not wanting to carry out a heavy load with the malfunction he contacted Carol Jarvis of Salmon Air Taxi to have a pair of Cessna 206s fly in and pick up the gear and passengers. Kornell assessed the plane, added oil and figured he could safely ferry it back home. However, a mix-up occurred and only one 206 arrived, leaving four passengers without a ride. Kornell figured it was not enough weight to matter.[108]

Riding in the front of the plane was outfitter and river guide Bill Bernt. Bernt remembers the trip well, commenting, "Bill's notion was to land at Cold Meadows and re-oil. The idea was that even with higher elevation, it would be cooler, and a late morning landing would be OK. As he lined up on final at Cold Meadows, he grabbed a big wad of paper towels, reached out the side window, and wiped oil off the windshield as he landed. We re-oiled and Bill was feeling pretty good about things, hadn't lost as much oil as he had expected. We took off again, me in the right seat watching the oil pressure. Over Black Lake it went to zero. Back to Cold Meadows, paper towels on the windshield. We got on the USFS radio, and Jarvis came back and got us."[109]

Kornell later returned to Cold Meadows and hopped the Otter over to the Root Ranch to make the

The remodeled interior of one of the two lodges.

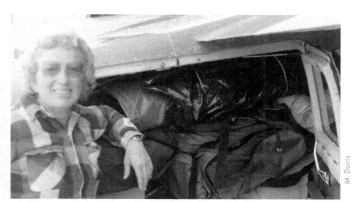

Mountain pilot Lyn Clark with a Cessna 206 in the late 1980s.

The present building complex at the Root Ranch.

repairs. However, in the process he discovered the engine was destroyed. Incapable of replacing the motor immediately, the project was delayed, but then winter storms made it impossible to fly the Otter out – so there it sat. But it was not that easy, as Kornell had actually sold the airplane in August to a fellow in California. The new owner allowed him to use the aircraft during the remainder of the season, but then wanted delivery. Needless to say the new owner was very displeased. [110]

When the Root Ranch field firmed up enough for landing the following spring, Kornell flew in mechanic Lloyd Cool, who owned Lloyd's Aero Repair in Salmon. Cool had quite a reputation with airplanes, as he was Loening's mechanic on his P-51 during the Reno Air Races. Kornell had hired him to help overhaul the Otter when he had purchased it for a song about a year earlier. It turned out this airplane had flown for two years with the Army's 54th Aviation Company in Vietnam. Kornell had purchased it from a wholesaler as a re-built airplane. However, when it arrived it needed everything. At the Root Ranch Cool and Kornell pulled the Otter's engine, using a homebuilt hoist made from cut lodgepole. They then hung a new motor and eventually transported the plane to the new owner. [111]

Updates

Flying Resort Ranches updated the facility by building a new lodge in the late 1970s. However, the new construction project nearly caused them to lose both backcountry properties in the spring of 1979, when for a brief period they were unable to pay taxes. [112] The group recovered and as the years passed they continued to maintain the place. In the early 1980s the original homestead cabin, generally occupied by the property manager, received new sill logs and the old barn was repaired. In the 1990s, under the management of Bill Guth Jr., several buildings were remodeled and a second lodge was built with dining and kitchen facilities. Also in the early 2000s a log one-airplane hangar was constructed near the parking area and an additional log cabin for guests was built. [113]

A Tragic Accident

In July 1997, well-respected McCall pilot Lyn Clark was giving duel instruction on mountain flying in a Cessna 182 (N3134S) owned by the student. The two flew from McCall to the Flying B and then Clark agreed on the return flight to do an informal airdrop of a plastic bag containing cookies and a birthday card for someone staying at the Root Ranch. [114]

After they made a steady descent over the strip from the south, the package was dropped out the left window. With the aircraft owner at the controls, full power was added to climb above oncoming trees. As the plane began to climb it veered to the left and likely stalled. The swerve to the west forced the plane into a tall stand of timber, bringing the craft to the ground about 1400' north of the strip. Both pilots were killed instantly. [115] In 2001 Clark was inducted into the Idaho Aviation Hall of Fame.

STONEBRAKER RANCH

An Early Homestead and the Stonebrakers

Homesteader W. A. Stonebraker (left) with his brother Sumner (right).

In 1907 George W. Otterson of Dixie was the first to file a homestead application on the majority of this in-holding now known as the Stonebraker Ranch. Otterson started the homesteading process the previous year, but his 160 acre claim was rejected on the grounds that only 100.5 acres was suitable for agricultural development. Otterson wrangled with the land office regularly through 1909, but for unknown reasons his interest waned.[116] In 1914 he relocated to the north side of the Main Salmon River near the confluence of Cougar Creek, where he built a log 18' X 16' cabin and cultivated ten acres of land, on which he received homestead approval in 1923.[117]

In August 1911 William Allen Stonebraker took notice of the unimproved Chamberlain Basin property, and the next year, after a further more detailed examination of the parcel, filed a homestead application. By 1914 he had his family established themselves on the place by building a house, barn, and cellar. The following fall the Stonebrakers added a blacksmith shop, storehouse, chicken coop, and corrals.[118]

In the summer of 1915 Assistant District Forester A. C. McCain inspected the Chamberlain Basin homesteads and stayed with the Stonebraker family at their newly-built ranch. In his report about the trip he noted, "Stonebraker seems to be trying to make this claim a success. I judge he is not a practical farmer; however, he is making headway and now has

The Stonebraker Ranch in early 1950 looking west-northwest with the West Fork of Chamberlain Creek in the center of the photograph.

The homestead cabin built by Stonebraker as it appeared in 1950.

The Stonebraker Ranch in 2008 – the large barn is one of the original homestead structures.

a fair stand of timothy, red clover and alfalfa. Hardy vegetables seem to thrive; the greatest menace being the deer. The night I stayed there, deer visited the garden and topped the beets . . . The claimant formerly had a few head of stock cattle, but has disposed of them and is now running a small bunch of mares."[119]

Stonebraker received homestead approval for 159.9 acres five years after McCain visited the ranch.[120] Stonebraker came to the Salmon River Mountain country, operating a packstring in connection with William Campbell of Campbell's Ferry on the Main Salmon River. Stonebraker packed supplies along the route of the Three Blaze Trail that ran from Dixie south to the Thunder Mountain mining area. He and Campbell built the trail.

Stonebraker's wife, Golda, and stepson, Adolph "Bill," helped construct several buildings at the ranch, including the barn and the well-built two-story house (both still standing). His relatives also helped from time to time at the ranch. He had three brothers: Jude (L. E.), Sumner, and George Jr., as well as two sisters Myrtle and Leeta.

When the gold rush at Thunder Mountain ended they found other avenues of income. Stonebraker began running the mail with a dog sled team to various residents in the backcountry and started an early dude ranch, promoting the best big game hunting in the area.

Historic Events – The First Airplanes

Airplanes were seen more frequently after World War I. Airplanes based in Spokane with the National Guard's 116th Observation Squadron were used for aerial work in the region. One of the main pilots with the squadron was Nick Mamer who also operated his own aircraft on the side. Mamer and Stonebraker became partners, Mamer as an aviator, and Stonebraker as an outfitter and guide. Together they created the first fly-in dude ranch in the area and made the first backcountry airstrip and landing.

Mamer made the first landing in the hayfield in the early 1920s and by the fall of 1925 was advertising in the *Lewiston Morning Tribune* and Grangeville's *Idaho County Free Press* to promote airplane trips for big game hunting. In both papers the advertisement read, "Big Game Hunters – Will place you in deer and elk hunting grounds [Chamberlain Basin] in one hour from Grangeville by airplane. Phone Nick Mamer."[121] It is not known if the site of the current Stonebraker airstrip is the location Mamer was actually using. The other possible site was his brothers' property, occupied a short time by George and Sumner between 1916 and 1925 (for more information see Chamberlain Airfield section).

Within the next several years, Mamer was flying people to the ranch from all over the country, and Stonebraker was guiding them to places where game was plentiful. Many happy customers wrote Stonebraker with words of praise.

Mr. Jay Stewart from Brooklyn, New York, was a very satisfied client. In his thank-you to the Stonebrakers he referred to Allen as "Stoney" and wrote, "Our trip seems almost like a dream. We had been planning it for six months, ever since last Christmas and now that it is over and we have had the wonderful experiences that we did, although it's a real factor and reality, still it seems to me that some things we did could hardly be true. We saw some wonderful sights and experienced some tremendous thrills, but, Stoney, after all, as I view the trip in retrospect, I am certain that the outstanding thing about it all was the personalities and the characters we came into intimate touch with . . . among them all is Stoney and his family. God Bless you."[122] Another satisfied customer, Paul Patton of Kansas City, Missouri, came out West on the recommendation of another friend and was elated with Stonebraker's operation.[123]

Also about the same time Mamer taught Stonebraker's brother George Jr. to fly, and the latter started his own commercial operation based in Cascade.[124] Stonebraker bought a brand new 1930 Bellanca.[125] This plane crashed on West Mountain, southwest of McCall in January 1931, while looking for lost cattle. Stonebraker's hired pilot, Ray Fisher, was killed. The other four passengers on the aircraft survived.[126]

George Stonebraker's life was also cut short. He and his wife Thelma started their own ranch north of Cascade. The two were known to have frequent domestic fights and in April 1945 Thelma shot him twice during one of their squabbles. She was eventually acquitted of a first-degree murder charge and released.[127] Little remains of this ranch except a barn and a street that bears the family name.

Through Nick Mamer's business relationship and friendship with Stonebraker, he too became involved with Chamberlain Basin property in 1932. Spokane friend Clarence I. Paulsen,[128] nicknamed "Cip" or "Cippy," was Mamer's financial backer.[129] He purchased the Beal and Hotzel Ranches adjacent to the Stonebraker's property. One might guess that they had plans to build a lodge to serve as a major hunting and fishing destination accessible only by airplane, but this never happened. In 1947 he sold both homesteads to W. T. McGill.[130]

Nick Mamer in the late 1920s (sitting in the homebuilt aircraft with pilot hat and goggles). Among the crowd standing between the two airplanes is student and friend Penn Stohr Sr. (far left).

Nicholas Bernard Mamer

Known as the "Grandfather of Backcountry Aviation," Mamer was born in 1898 in Hastings, Minnesota. To fulfill his dream of becoming a pilot he ran away from home at age sixteen to join the Army. Lying about his age, it is believed that he was one of Minnesota's first military pilot recruits. Apparently he had become enamored with aviation after performing parachute jumps at local county fairs.[131]

Soon after joining the Army he earned his wings and became a lieutenant at Kelly Field, Texas, before being attached to the 187th Aero Squadron. From July through the beginning of December 1918 he was stationed in France where he was credited with shooting down three enemy aircraft. Several days before the war ended, Mamer was shot down by three German Fokker airplanes in the Meuse-Argonne Offensive, but survived with minor injuries.

Mamer (center) stands in front of a Swallow aircraft with two of his best students, Bob Johnson (left) and Penn Stohr Sr. (right).

Most historians consider this battle the bloodiest single battle in United States history. For his heroic efforts he was awarded the French Croix de Guerre with Palms, in addition to three citations of valor.[132]

Returning to the States he moved to Spokane to work for the United States Aircraft Corporation and remained active in the National Guard's 116th Observation Squadron. While in Spokane he carved out a niche for himself working with forester Howard Flint. Beyond making some of the first landings in the backcountry, other "firsts" included the first aerial seeding project in the Inland Empire, and the first to fly an airplane over Glacier National Park.

As his National Guard obligations lessened he started Mamer Air Transport and Mamer Flying Service Inc. at Felts Field, and bought two brand new Ford Tri-Motors (NC9612 and NC8403). With the success of these two undertakings Mamer expanded and opened International Air Transport Company with Paulsen. He also became a dealer at various times of Swallow, Travel Air, Curtiss Wright, Stearman, and Buhl aircraft. With one Buhl Sedan named the Spokane Sun God, he and associate Art Walker set a record in 1929 by making the first transcontinental refueling flight and the world's longest non-stop

Mamer's military headstone at the Evergreen-Washelli Cemetery in Seattle.

mileage for an aircraft in flight (7200 miles continuous without landing for five days and five nights).

Throughout his years at Felts Field he broke barriers in aviation and trained some of the best early mountain pilots in Idaho and Montana, including the likes of Bob Johnson and Penn Stohr Sr. Although a smart and frugal businessman, he had invested a majority of his earnings in the stock market and lost almost everything in the 1929 crash. He faced the setback with tenacity and in less than ten years accumulated an estate worth more than $80,000.[133] This was a huge feat, considering the struggles associated with aviation business, and the hard times of the Great Depression.

Mamer left his business in 1934 when he failed to obtain a government contract. At this time he moved his wife and daughter to Seattle and went to work for Northwest Airlines. He continued behind the scenes at his flying school in Spokane, which was eventually bought by friend and former student Roy Shreck. Mamer's name remained with the new owner as Mamer-Shreck Air Transport. Near the time of his move to Seattle the *Seattle Post-Intelligencer* noted Mamer's success by stating, "[T]oday recognized as having more mountain flying experience than any other pilot in the world."[134]

On January 10, 1938 Mamer sadly met an untimely death at age thirty-nine. His Lockhead Zephyr (NC17388) fell from the sky, while flying over the rugged Bridger Mountains near Bozeman, Montana. Investigations revealed that the craft had a poor tail design that failed due to a vibration. The malfunction eventually led to future modifications of the aircraft. The accident killed copilot Fred West and eight others aboard the plane.[135] It is rumored that Mamer was so cool and collected that he described the airplane's reactions to his control inputs over the radio. He apparently knew there was little he could do, but wanted people to understand what was happening with the aircraft.

Mamer is buried in the veteran's section of the Evergreen-Washelli Cemetery in north Seattle. A large four-sided concrete art deco style clock that stands to this day was constructed and dedicated to Nick Mamer in May 1939 at Felts Field to memorialize his life. Spokane residents donated $5,324 for the project, believing that he was "one of the 15 greatest aviators of his day."[136]

In 1936 two years before his death, Mamer passed the million-mile mark in flying. At this milestone he commented, "The pilot of a decade ago was a colorful, if sometimes irresponsible individual, concerned chiefly in keeping the airplane in the novelty field. The pilots of that era deserve much credit. They were the stopgap between the war and the Lindbergh flight to Paris, the real beginning of the present flying era. Today, airline pilots are highly skilled, self-disciplined, the world's finest airmen. As to the future, the sky is boundless and we have just begun to explore it."[137] Most mountain pilots of the Idaho

Pilot Bob Fogg leased the ranch from the IDFG in the early 1950s with partner Slim Horn. Fogg (second from right) and his partner's brother Dub (far right), stand with a group on the porch of the Stonebraker cabin.

backcountry can trace some sliver of knowledge or instruction back to Mamer. For his pioneering efforts in aviation he has been inducted into the Pathfinder Award honorees and the Idaho Aviation Hall of Fame.

Tough Times

The Stonebraker Ranch was doing well for itself, particularly in the middle of the Great Depression. Stonebraker was an avid photographer and documented many of his activities in the backcountry. These wonderful photographs can be seen in Special Collections at the University of Idaho. In the summer of 1931 the Salmon River Breaks Fire broke out and the ranch became a vital access point for the USFS. Johnson Flying Service and Mamer Air Transport were the main air carriers bringing in firefighters and supplies.

With the ranch finances in the black, the Stonebrakers' hard work had paid off. However, in September 1932 a huge loss occurred in the family when Stonebraker died of a heart attack at age fifty-three. On his way out for supplies for the ranch he was breaking camp in the morning, twelve miles from the Werdenhoff Mine. He sat down to enjoy his tobacco pipe, when he experienced heart pains and fell over. His stepson, Bill, rode to the Chicken Peak Fire Lookout to get word out that he had died.

Outfitter Al Tice poses for a photograph with one of his Cessna 206s at the Stonebraker Ranch in 1965.

Mackay Bar's **STONEBRAKER RANCH**

in the Chamberlain Basin Primitive Area

Business Office: P.O. Box 1099
Boise, Idaho 83701

Comfortable accommodations in roomy tent cabins. Excellent food, relaxation at the ranch house. Lake fishing within two hours of the Ranch; stream fishing within 10 minutes. Accessible by plane or pack train. Great for the whole family. A terrific backpacking headquarters.

Phone (208) 344-1881

A 1975 advertisement for the Stonebraker Ranch.

The IDFG and Outfitters

Unable to continue operating the ranch, Golda looked for a buyer and contacted family friend Harry Shellworth, an executive with the Boise Payette Lumber Company. Shellworth was also a promoter of the Idaho Primitive Area and often came through the ranch on his elaborate annual pack trips with prominent friends. Shellworth looked for an interested party but recognized the Depression would make the sale difficult. In an October 1932 letter to an associate who had stayed at the ranch during a trip, he commented, "I shall assist where I can in 'Stony's' interest, but the purchase of a backcountry ranch under conditions existing here at present, will be very difficult to make. The Forest Service may be able to buy his mules and horses but their value is very low now."[138]

Incapable of paying the property taxes Golda and Bill sold the ranch five years later to John Rothchild of Boise for $3,000. A few years into the ownership Rothchild brought in partners Walter Altman and George R. "Blondie" McGill. McGill lived at the ranch, running cattle and outfitting. By 1947 Wallace McGill acquired full possession of the ranch and two years later sold it to the IDFG. At the same time the department also bought McGill's adjoining property downstream on the West Fork of Chamberlain Creek,

His body was packed back to the ranch and flown to Lewiston (where he was buried) by Bob King and Stonebraker's brother George Jr.

formally known as the Beal Ranch.[139]

The two ranches were then leased together to commercial outfitters. One of the first to obtain the lease was Courtland "Slim" Horn and partner Bob Fogg who flew for Johnson Flying Service.[140] The two called the Stonebraker-based business Fogg-Horn Outfitters.[141] Circa 1958 Al Tice picked up the lease. He used the Stonebraker Ranch as a place to guide fishing trips in the summer and elk hunting in the fall, as a satellite operation to his main camp located at the Badley Ranch, and later permanently at Mackay Bar. However, he had begun operating in the Chamberlain area as early as 1955 when he set up a tent camp on the south side of the Chamberlain Ranger Station airstrip at the junction of the north-south and east-west runways.[142]

Once established at Stonebraker he utilized the airfield, house, barn, and a bunkhouse for his operation. Dick Tice did a lot of the early repair work at the site, building corrals, fences, and adding a few tent frames for guests. Although a large amount of stock was kept at Stonebraker during the summer, the place was mainly used for elk hunting parties. Tice obtained many of the hunting permits around the area and had spike camps located throughout the western portion of the basin.[143]

With a good reputation behind his outfitting business, along with prime hunting grounds, the

277

D. Hardy/IDFG

Pilot Ray Arnold (right) visits with some IDFG employees at the ranch in the early 1990s.

Stonebraker end of the operation flourished. Tice attracted many big names. In the early 1960s Adam West, star of the *Batman* television series hunted from Telephone Camp north of Stonebraker near Harlan Meadows. In fact West even brought his own cameraman to film the event. The television star had a successful hunt after he shot a nice bull elk off the north end of the old Hida Ridge airstrip.[144]

Harmon Killebrew, a major league baseball player who played for the Washington Senators and who was originally from Payette, Idaho, hunted from the ranch. He was taken on a trip through Haypress and Ramey Meadows and also had a successful hunt. Dick did a lot of the guiding during his trip and said, "The guy nearly ran my legs off."[145]

Others taken on hunting trips include Cal Worthington, a big shot Dodge dealer, Howard McNear (Doc) and Ken Curtis (Festus) both from the *Gunsmoke* television series, and Judge Will Cummings, a personal friend of President John F. Kennedys. The judge was a tough old Tennessean that was eighty-one years old when he was on the hunting trip and sported a wooden leg.[146]

When Tice sold Mackay Bar to Robert Hansberger in 1969, the latter also acquired the lease of the Stonebraker and Beal Ranch properties. The lease was used in much the same fashion. Several updates were made to the property under their lease agreement, including many renovations to the original homestead structure, a bathroom facility, and construction of additional outbuildings.[147]

The IDFG Regains Control

In the summer of 1991 problems arose with non-fenced pack animals grazing in riparian zones and on USFS land. Exacerbating the situation were a few IDFG violations issued to past employees. Unable to resolve the problems, the department terminated the lease in December of the same year.[148]

A new issue then came about between the USFS and the IDFG over the use of wagon trails between the Chamberlain airstrip and the properties at Stonebraker and Hotzel. In 1993 the Payette NF banned the state agency from using the wagon trails, since it was viewed as being non-compliant with wilderness. Being cut off was a real threat, as in the 1970s the IDFG deemed the Stonebraker airstrip unsafe for aircraft with passengers. Their restriction required individuals and freight to come and go through the neighboring USFS strip, which was accessed with horse-drawn wagons. Not being able to move large loads of freight became a burden. However, the Payette NF did issue a special use permit allowing the IDFG to use the wagon trails. It was rarely exercised and has since expired.[149]

In 1995 the IDFG no longer wanted to be reliant on a use permit, and opted to improve the Stonebraker airstrip. A small Kabota tractor was broken down and flown in by SP Aircraft in two Cessna 206s from Boise. The 800' strip was extended to a total length of 1000' by removing a fence and moving material on the upper end near the original cabin. When work ended, the Kabota was flown out the same way it came in.[150]

The improved runway allowed the department to bring in cargo and supplies needed for preservation work on the homestead. In the early 2000s, Britten-Norman Islanders were used to haul in material for new roofs. Sill logs on the historic homestead building were replaced and the kitchen remodeled. Under the department's ownership the ranch has been used for some aquatic studies and occasionally provides housing for summer employees.[151]

1 *Reassembling the tractor at the Stonebraker ranch in 1995 for the runway expansion project.*
2 *Looking west at the Stonebraker Ranch airstrip.*
3 *Looking east down the 1000' Stonebraker Ranch runway.*
4&5 *The Stonebraker Ranch in 2010.*

D. Hardy/IDFG

Holm

Holm

Photos by Holm

Two Close Calls

In March 1950 Johnson Flying Service pilot Jim Larkin flew a roof-shoveling crew to the Stonebraker Ranch with Travel Air 6000 NC9038 on skis. He had no problems landing and since it was a sunny day he kicked around enjoying the weather while the group worked. Late in the afternoon they loaded up and Larkin prepared for a takeoff. He gave the aircraft normal takeoff power and began getting the airplane up to speed. However, he did not account for a thick icy crust that had formed over the runway due to the day's high temperature. Larkin commented, "Before I knew it I was skating down the runway looking out the windscreen at a row of lodgepoles the hard way. . . last second I jammed full throttle and full rudder. She switched ends, still going thirty miles an hour, but backwards! It ended up alright and not damaging anything, but it was the only Travel Air I've ever known to have reverse thrust."[152]

In the early 1970s pilot Harold Dougal also had an interesting experience on a takeoff at the Stonebraker Ranch, flying an empty Cessna 206 (N4928F). During the takeoff roll Dougal noted the heavy grass was slowing him down, but he felt he had a reasonable airspeed to add more backpressure on the controls to get the bird in the air. Just as the airplane's wheels broke ground he heard a loud bang in the back of the craft. This was more than the usual sound of rocks hitting the tail surfaces, but the strip was already behind him and he figured an inspection at his next stop (Mackay Bar) would be sufficient.[153]

The 206 performed nicely and after clearing the large trees, Dougal pushed on the controls to lower the nose and make a turn. The controls would not move. He then began pushing with all of his might to shove the yoke toward the instrument panel, but no amount of effort sufficed. With an extremely nose high attitude and nearing a stall alarmingly close to the ground and trees, he pulled some throttle back. The nose then lowered and he was able to maintain altitude, but the controls were completely jammed. With the plane somewhat stabilized, Dougal went through a few checks and discovered he could only control the 206 with the rudder, ailerons, and throttle. The elevator was locked in the up position. Looking out the window at the aft portion of the plane he spotted a five-foot long tree limb, about the size of a large "walking stick" had lodged between the elevator and the horizontal stabilizer.[154]

Realizing that he had to get the airplane back on the ground, he carefully maneuvered the plane for a landing at the Chamberlain USFS strip. A successful touchdown ensued and Dougal was able to take several deep breaths. He then removed the limb and carried on with his flying. The "walking stick" was saved as a souvenir.[155]

The original Mackay Bar airstrip in 1935.

CHAPTER 6

Main
Salmon River

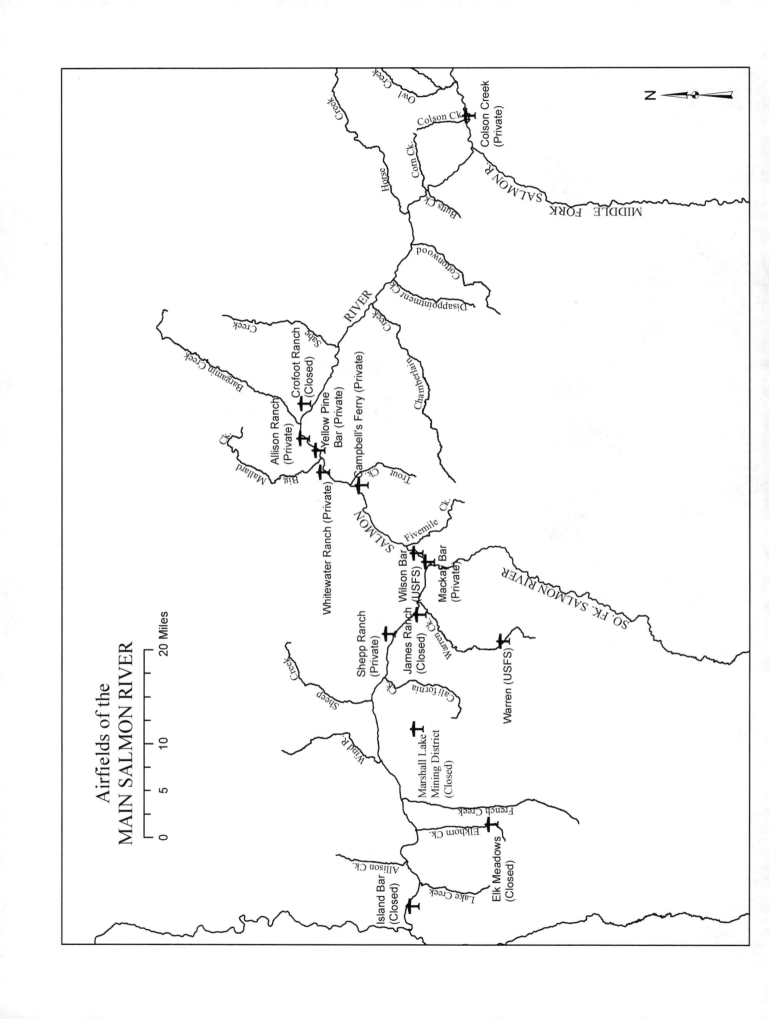

Airfields of the
MAIN SALMON RIVER

0   5   10   20 Miles

Colson Creek (Private)

Colson Ck.

Owl Creek

Corn Ck.

Horse Creek

Buts Ck.

MIDDLE FORK SALMON R.

Cottonwood

Disappointment Ck.

Chamberlain

Crofoot Ranch (Closed)

Yellow Pine Bar (Private)

Allison Ranch (Private)

Sabe Creek

Bargamin Creek

Mallard Ck.

Big Ck.

RIVER

Campbell's Ferry (Private)

Creek

Whitewater Ranch (Private)

Trout Ck.

SALMON

Fivemile Ck.

Wilson Bar (USFS)

Mackay Bar (Private)

SO. FK. SALMON RIVER

Shepp Ranch (Private)

James Ranch (Closed)

Warren Ck.

Warren (USFS)

California Ck.

Sheep Creek

Wind R.

Marshall Lake Mining District (Closed)

French Creek

Elkhorn Ck.

Elk Meadows (Closed)

Allison Ck.

Lake Creek

Island Bar (Closed)

N

The original homestead barn built by Sam Myers.

ALLISON RANCH

The Early Years

Sam Myers is the first known Euro-American to occupy the now Allison Ranch. Myers was a veteran of the Civil War and served under General Sherman. He moved to Idaho after the war and lived on the Salmon River for forty years.[1] By 1913 Myers had constructed a log 14' X 20' residence, an 18' X 14' storehouse, a 30' X 50' barn, and had ten acres of ground under cultivation. In 1916 he received homestead approval for 61.45 acres.[2] Myers died in 1923 and was buried in Dixie.[3] In the spring of 1924 Elmer C. Allison purchased the place from Myers's estate.[4]

The property became known as the Allison Ranch in 1924 after Elmer C. Allison purchased it.

The mid-1940s cabin constructed by Allison with a few additions.

The property from this point on became known as the Allison Ranch. Allison removed the original cabin and constructed his own. In 1929 Allison persuaded Joe Zaunmiller and his first wife Emma to join him at the ranch and build a cattle business together. As a result the Zaunmillers were granted a half interest in the ranch. By 1931 the Zaunmillers left for other pursuits.[5]

Allison remained at the property, making a modest living. In 1943 hard luck hit when his house burned. With little income he was forced to sell the ranch to survive. However, he found a group of California investors who wanted to buy the place as a hunting destination. Allison and the new owners came to an agreement that he would become the manager of the ranch and construct a new lodge with the help of neighbor George Wolfe.[6]

Excited for the opportunity, he purchased all the necessary supplies in Salmon and nailed them together as a raft that he floated down the river. Soon the place was up and running again. He then added a lower cabin mimicking the lodge's construction as

The lodge Allison built for the California investors in the late 1940s.

living quarters for the new owners. By 1950 Allison had moved to Lewiston.[7] The property continued under the ownership of the California group until January 1961, when John and June Cook acquired it.[8]

The Cook Years and an Airfield

While recovering from a heart attack, Cook decided it was time to retire. Cook's father, Warren, was one of the Idaho NF's earliest district rangers and had attempted to homestead various properties in the backcountry. Growing up, Warren instilled a passion for the area in his kids and John knew it was where he wanted to spend the remainder of his life. Prior to purchasing the Allison Ranch he was a partner with Warren Brown on a large cattle ranch located near Whitebird. He sold his share when he moved to the river.

Due to Cook's fragile heart condition he needed to see a doctor every few weeks. During the summer he rode a horse downriver to Whitewater where he kept a car and could travel to town. However, in the winter travel was more restricted and he decided an airplane would be the most efficient means to reach his doctor appointments. With a resolution in mind he set out to build an airstrip at the ranch. His son, Dave, along with backcountry neighbor Avon Hill, and others along the river, helped.

In 1963 tree clearing and rock removal was started for the runway. They had a large portion of it cleared when numerous sizeable boulders were encountered. Several attempts were made at blasting with dynamite, but were ineffective. Frustrated with

The interior of Allison's main cabin.

the runway project, Cook contacted friend Bob Fogg of Johnson Flying Service in McCall for advice. Fogg came in and surveyed the ranch property and pointed out that even if the large boulders could be eliminated the strip was going to be too short and unnecessarily steep. Fogg encouraged Cook to move the entire strip slightly downriver and more perpendicular. The main hurdle to jump would be the removal of four huge trees to clear an approach from the river to the runway.

With Fogg's input, Cook contacted the USFS about removing the four trees located on federal land between his property and the river. The agency told him they would not allow the trees to be cut. Undeterred, Cook devised a plan. His son Dave who was in the military at Fort Hood, obtained 1,500 rounds of .30-06 ammunition. Cook found a great spot with a perfect angle and distance to the trees. He then shot hundreds of rounds in a straight line across the four trunks, weakening them. As expected the tops

Allison Ranch owner John Cook.

A mid-1960s aerial of the Allison Ranch. The cut from the first attempted airfield can be seen running parallel and to the right of the current airstrip, which is perpendicular to the river at the far left along the tree line.

of the confers broke during the next major windstorm. It worked out perfectly, as the cutting looked natural.

In the spring of 1964, with the approach problem solved, work on the realigned airstrip began. Again, Avon Hill, who owned the Cook Ranch (unrelated) at the head of Big Mallard Creek, was helping. Hill used a sixty-five horsepower Piper Cub that he owned to go back and forth for supplies. One day in May he flew to Grangeville and on his way back to his ranch he hit the side of a mountain in bad weather near the Red River Ranger Station at the head of Trapper Creek and was killed (see Cook Ranch for more information).[9]

Despite the accident, work continued on the airstrip and was finished the same year. The completed "S" shaped runway was short, rough, and full of rocks, but serviceable for Cook's use. Fogg using a Piper Super Cruiser (N2577M) was the first person to land at the ranch. The cut of the abandoned

airstrip remains visible.[10]

Cook used the runway for a few years, generally being flown by Fogg or Warren Brown. He then decided to move closer to Riggins and bought 160 acres at Elkhorn Creek, about fifteen miles upriver from town. In 1966 the Allison Ranch sold to Robert Hansberger of Boise.[11] Hansberger had Al Tice work extensively on the airstrip. During his ownership, Tice started flying Super Cubs on the strip but eventually moved up to Cessna 206s as changes were made.[12]

A New Owner and an Improved Airstrip

The ranch sold several more times, until February 1973 when Harold Thomas, a co-founder of the Trus Joist Corporation, bought the place. At the time of his purchase the property contained the original barn and storehouse, along with the Allison built lodge and guesthouse. Over the years Thomas and his wife Phyllis added a cabin for themselves, a cabin for friend Tom Close, and a caretaker's house. Phyllis maintains a small museum of artifacts and photographs highlighting the river's history.[13]

In the early years of owning the ranch, Thomas used his Cessna 180 on Tice's improved airstrip, which was slightly shorter than 900'. In the mid-1970s he flew in a Fresno that he pulled behind a Ford 8N tractor. Moving some soil, along with more clearing, he modified the strip's touchdown area and eliminated a side-hill issue that made landing difficult.[14]

The major overhaul to the airstrip came as

1 *Phyllis and Harold Thomas at the ranch in 2003 with one of their Piper Cubs.*
2 *The cabin the Thomas's built for friend Tom Close.*
3 *The unique Yellow Pine carved staircase in the Close cabin.*
4 *Looking down the current 1100' Allison runway.*
5 *A 1974 advertisement for the Allison Ranch.*

Landing at the Allison Ranch.

a result of a rainy day incident in 1990. After a routine approach and landing, Thomas applied the usual heavy braking on his Cessna 206 (N9922Z). However, the wet grass instantly caused the airplane to slide. Unable to regain directional control to make the "S" turn, the plane slid into some nearby rocks causing substantial damage including a prop strike. After smashing up one of his favorite airplanes, Thomas vowed to fix the runway, which he did by creating the current up-sloping 1100' airstrip.[15]

For many years Thomas operated a hunting and guiding business from the ranch, and early in the morning would often fly his clients upriver to the Crofoot Ranch. With guides, the group would then work their way back downriver to Allison.[16]

Thomas and His Airplanes

Thomas, a successful businessman, has had a lifetime interest in aviation and has recently written about many of his experiences in his autobiography, *A Pilot With A Purpose*. He first came to the Idaho backcountry flying a Cessna 180 (N699HR). He then bought a Super Cub (N4248M), which he kicked around in for fun, while the 180 was more of a workhorse. He then traded the Cessna 180 for a Cessna 185 (N4579F). Over the years, like other backcountry pilots, he was always after his next best aircraft suited for the demands of mountain flying. In an effort to gain extra performance he bought a Cessna 206 and had it outfitted with a Soloy Aviation Solution 450 horsepower turbine conversion. Thomas was impressed with the airplane's performance but never quite trusted it in the Idaho backcountry. He then leased the aircraft to an operator in Florida, where it was ultimately sold.[17]

Going back to the more traditional backcountry roots, he then purchased several Cessna 206s, including N7372Q and his favorite N9922Z, which he operated at the ranch for over eighteen years. Currently his son Rick, who is also a pilot, flies an early model Cessna 182A (N5011D) to and from the ranch. Thomas's other son Marvin also enjoys the backcountry and can often be found at his Mackay Bar cabin.

Rick Thomas (right), with his two sons Tyler and Nick, and a Cessna 180 (N52095) at the ranch in 1988.

The prototype KODIAK parked at the Allison Ranch with two MAF Cessna 206s in 2008.

Rick Thomas's Cessna 182A at the ranch.

Thomas and Mission Aviation Fellowship (MAF)

In 1986 Thomas and his wife Phyllis transferred the property to the Allison Ranch Ministries. For over thirty-five years the Thomases have welcomed the Mission Aviation Fellowship (MAF) based in Nampa to stay at their ranch. The fellowship's mission is to raise ministry support for the privilege of serving God and helping people in need in countries throughout Africa, Asia, Eurasia, and many other places. They meet their goals through aviation and technology, which helps them get much-needed supplies to isolated areas of the world. MAF groups generally come to the Allison Ranch three times a year, in April, June, and October.[18]

While MAF is at Allison Ranch, flight instruction on mountain flying is given to new participating pilots. At the ranch the pilots have the best training ground in the lower forty-eight states. Pilots practice mountain approaches, takeoffs, and landings on various strips mainly along the Salmon River with permission from area residents. MAF primarily uses red and white turbocharged 206s, but in more recent years has moved toward the Quest Aircraft Company's KODIAK, designed exclusively for their type of work.[19]

The MAF has purchased several of the KODIAKs from Quest. They have proved to be good ships with their modern STOL design, rugged construction, high useful load capability, and reliable turbine power. Thomas serves as a Quest board member. In 2008 the prototype KODIAK (N491QK) was flown to the Allison Ranch and it performed as the pilots and company had hoped it would. This KODIAK along with a few locally flown Britten-Norman Islanders are the largest aircraft to land at the ranch.[20]

R. McRae

CAMPBELL'S FERRY

The Early Years

Early Campbell's Ferry occupant Warren Cook photographed circa 1905.

Circa 1897 William Campbell settled on the property known today as Campbell's Ferry.[21] Campbell created a self-sufficient ranch and sold goods to people who were coming and going from the Buffalo Hump area to Thunder Mountain. In 1901 Campbell along with friend W. A. Stonebraker built the Three Blaze Trail that connected these two regions. A major river ford was necessary at Campbell's ranch so he capitalized on those passing through by building a ferry. He charged $.50 per person and $1.00 per head of stock to cross. Campbell disappeared a few years later; most suspected he drowned in the river while trying to cross an ice dam.[22]

Holm

Today many of the historic structures remain in use at Campbell's Ferry including the hastily built Cook cabin (far right).

Warren and Rose Cook then occupied the property. In 1905 a cabin built by Campbell burned. With winter near, a replacement cabin was quickly thrown together by Cook and his two brother-in-laws Oscar and Joe Aiken. This is the cabin that is located at the ranch today. Another tragedy occurred about the same time when Rose died during childbirth along with her baby. They are both buried on the property.[23]

With Cook's great loss he moved on, and Ernest F. Sillge acquired the place. Sillge added several log buildings to the property and in March 1918 filed homestead papers for 88.70 acres.[24] Before Sillge received approval on the ranch, he, like Campbell, died in an accident along the river and his

J. Hockaday/USFS

Joe and Frances Zaunmiller at their ranch in 1952.

body was never found. Robert A. Hilands then moved to the ranch and in July 1927 received homestead approval for 85.19 acres.[25] Hilands later sold an interest in the ranch to Joe Zaunmiller, who had been living at what is now the Cook Ranch at the head of Big Mallard Creek. Zaunmiller eventually became the sole owner of the ranch, making a living working the land in addition to running an outfitting business. He also packed occasionally for the USFS. During the Zaunmiller years most of the present buildings were improved or added.[26]

A New Face, a Bridge, and an Airstrip

In 1940 Zaunmiller met Lydia Frances Coyle, who was working at the Stonebraker Ranch. He was in need of a cook for his outfitting business and she agreed to the job, moving to the property the same year. Two years later they were married and Frances stayed at Campbell's Ferry for the rest of her life.[27]

Originally from Texas she remained in contact with her relatives, mainly through frequent letter writing. When her brother Tom was stationed in Assum, India, during World War II, he would often share her letters with his friends. They all came to enjoy the events at Campbell's Ferry deep in the Idaho Primitive Area – a world far away from the horror and tedium of war. A friend of Tom's knew the daughter of an editor for the *Idaho County Free Press* in Grangeville and suggested Frances contact him. This connection led Frances to have a regular column in the paper where she wrote about her observations and experiences

living at the isolated ranch.[28] In 1986 friend Donna L. Henderson compiled many of her columns in the book, *My Mountains: Where the River Still Runs Downhill.*

It was through these columns that she gained political support for the Campbell's Ferry Bridge. She wrote multiple stories about the need of a bridge to connect the north and south side of the Salmon River in this remote area. In 1955 her writings sparked people's interest and construction on the bridge was started. Most of the building materials were floated down on rafts from the Mallard Creek Road. The project was completed the following year.[29]

At about the same time the bridge was started, Bob Fogg of Johnson Flying Service in McCall helped design an airstrip. Fogg hiked to the Ferry and looked things over. The original purpose of the airstrip was to allow aircraft to bring in additional supplies to the bridge construction crew. Zaunmiller, with the help of the USFS, filled in some holes and did a little leveling on the hayfield and called it an airstrip. Fogg was most likely the first to land on the roughly 800' strip with an average slope of thirteen percent. The airfield became an important link to the outside for the Zaunmillers.

Changing Times

In 1958 the Zaunmillers decided to sell their property. Neither one of them wanted to, but Joe was starting to slow down and money was tight. Two years before, Frances had been diagnosed with throat cancer. She had beaten the disease, but treatment was expensive. Luck came their way when a prospective buyer from California became interested.[30]

John Crowe of Redding, California, had recently been on an elk-hunting trip with Loren Hollenbeak at Hollenbeak's Cabin Creek Ranch on Big Creek. In fact a whole crowd of Redding people owned backcountry property including Hollenbeak, Frank Santos at Crofoot, Sid Hinkle at Selway Lodge, and later Bryant Roberts at James Ranch. Crowe had caught wind of the Ferry acreage after running into college friend Warren Brown at the McCall airport. Brown had recently purchased Yellow Pine Bar and knew the Zaunmiller's situation. Crowe was familiar with Zaunmiller as the two had met in the backcountry

1 *A mid-1960s photograph of the Campbell's Ferry airstrip.*
2 *Final approach at Campbell's Ferry.*
3 *Looking down the roughly 800' runway.*
4 *Mary Crowe at Campbell's Ferry in the early 1960s.*
5 *Ranch owner John Crowe at the Ferry in the early 1960s.*
6 *Frances and Vern Wisner (right) with a pilot (left) at the Ferry in the mid-1960s.*

while he was on an elk hunt.[31]

Soon after running into Brown, Crowe and friend Rex Kettlewell arranged to see the property. After viewing the place the two made a deal. Part of the sale agreement was that the Zaunmillers had lifetime use of the ranch and could remain living in their cabin. Kettlewell only stayed involved for a few years and sold his interest to Crowe. The Zaunmillers and Crowes became close friends, as the Crowes spent vacations at the ranch when time permitted. In 1960 they eventually built a small one-room framed cabin near the runway.[32]

The Crowes owned a large cattle business in California known as the Crowe Hereford Ranch and had recently bought a new tractor for the operation. In 1960 the old tractor, a Farmall, was dismantled and trucked to McCall. From McCall, Fogg flew it to the ranch in a Travel Air 6000. Zaunmiller, who had put hay up with horses his whole life, loved the little machine and named it Lucille. For the next two years he ran the heck out of the tractor. He even cut out a flat turnaround area for airplanes at the top of the airstrip.[33] At age seventy-one Zaunmiller died of a heart attack at the ranch.[34]

At the time of Zaunmiller's death Vern Wisner was renting the Crowe's cabin. He had been hired by the Crowes to help keep the place up. He and Frances slowly became well acquainted and married in 1963.[35] The two lived happily at the ranch until he died in March 1974 at the age of eighty-one.[36]

Frances...

In December 1985, after a long and fruitful life at the Ferry, Frances was forced to leave. Her cancer had returned and she was physically unable to get around. Many friends along the river had looked after her the best they could. She no longer greeted Ray Arnold of Arnold Aviation, who had been delivering her mail for nearly a decade. Instead, on mail days he walked the mail down to the cabin and checked on her. The time had come. Frances was flown to Grangeville for medical assistance. She knew she was dying and wanted to do so at her beloved place on the Salmon River. She became very ill and the return trip to the Ferry never materialized. On

Campbell's Ferry owners Phyllis and Doug Tims at the property in 2004.

January 7, 1986 she died, eighteen days after leaving the river.[37] The book, *Haven in the Wilderness: The Story of Frances Zaunmiller Wisner of Campbell's Ferry* written by Carol Furey-Werhan was published ten years later. The account gives a look at her life on the river.

The following spring her friend and executrix, Linda Karki, held a memorial/wake party at the Ferry for Frances. People from all over the backcountry attended. An auction of her personal belongings was combined with the celebration of her life, and the proceeds were used to help pay outstanding medical bills.

A New Era

Following Frances's death John and Mary

Holm

Doug Tims greets pilot Mike Dorris and visitors at the Ferry.

Crowe also realized they too were not getting any younger. Their years at the Ferry had been wonderful, but they felt it was time to move on. The Crowes sold the property in July 1988 to Trust For Public Lands.[38] At the time of the sale they hired Mike Dorris to fly their belongings out of the ranch. Using a Cessna 206 (N7216N) Dorris even flew the Farmall tractor out making eleven shuttle loads all in one day to the Whitewater Ranch.[39]

Roughly one year later the organization sold the scenic easements to the USFS and then planned to put the property on the market. However, it never hit any real estate listings. Appraiser Brad Janoush was working with Trust For Public Lands, performing appraisals at the Polly Bemis Ranch, when he caught wind of the Ferry property. The place piqued his curiosity. He and a friend went upriver and camped for one night to see what it was like. The following night Janoush met up with another friend, Doug Tims, for dinner. Tims had recently sold his Middle Fork rafting business and was directing his attention to building his Maravia boat line and Selway rafting company. Even though Tims was busy and had never seen Campbell's Ferry, Janoush's description of the property intrigued him. He said, "Hell, lets buy it."[40]

In 1990 the two bought the historic homestead and made a rafting trip down the river to stay at their new property. Tims, seeing the place for the first time, was pleased even though it needed a lot of work. Recalling his first encounter with the homestead Tims

reminisced, "I realized how powerful childhood smells and memories were linked . . . I walked in the cabin and the smell took me back to my dad's hunting camps along the Mississippi and Arkansas Rivers when I was boy. It is an incredible place. I'm just glad we were able to pull it off. Never have regretted it."[41]

Log building expert Bruce Dreher started the restoration on the cabin the same year. Janoush and Tims donated $10,000 to the Idaho Historic Trust with the agreement that half would go to supplying materials for the project and to pay Dreher. It was a starting point as the property had literally sat idle for years. During the time between Frances and the new owners, little maintenance had been done.[42]

Since Tims and Janoush bought the ranch many of the original furnishings have been returned and many repairs made. In the beginning they relied on volunteer caretakers, but as their lives have become less hectic, Tims and his wife Phyllis have taken over the job, staying from early spring through late fall at the property. To keep up momentum, funds, and enthusiasm, the two owners sold interests in the place to friends over the years. Currently all six owners are from the small town of Cleveland, Mississippi. The group includes: Doug and Phyllis Tims, Brad and Patricia Janoush, Sam and Annie Langston, John and Beverly Janoush, Rex and Kelly Lyon, and Leland Speakes III.[43] The Timses co-authored the book *Merciless Eden*, an excellent historical look at the property from the early years of the Ferry through the twenty-first century.

Close Calls and Airlifts

When Crowe purchased the ranch he owned a Cessna 182A. He had previously owned a Piper PA-14 that he operated from his private ranch strip in Redding. The Piper was too slow to commute back

1&2 *John Crowe's final accident at the Ferry that destroyed his Cessna 182A.*

3 *Airlifting the Crowe's 182 out of the Ferry to the Chamberlain airstrip.*

4 *A Johnson Flying Service Cessna 180 awaits an airlift in 1963 after it was damaged on a landing.*

5 *The wings of the wrecked Cessna 180 mounted on pilot Mel Guerrera's Bell helicopter. The awkward load required one wing to be tied on after he was in the helicopter. The reverse then had to be done with a crew awaiting his arrival at the Chamberlain airfield.*

6&7 *The damage caused to the unpiloted Cessna 180 that slid backwards down the Campbell's Ferry airstrip.*

8&9 *Airlifting the Cessna 180 from the Ferry to the end of the road at North Fork.*

10&11 *A Johnson Flying Service Travel Air 6000 (NC8112) landing and taking off at the Ferry during the 1956 bridge construction project.*

W. Johnson/Zaunmiller

1 *A Johnson Flying Service Piper PA-12 delivering mail to the Ferry in early March 1972.*
2 *Crop-duster Bob Edling of The Dalles, Oregon, who flew seasonally for Frank Hill led the group for many years.*
3 *The Jim Moore Place in 2010.*

W. Johnson/Zaunmiller

Holm

and forth between Idaho and California, so he traded it in on the Cessna.[44]

In the summer of 1960 Crowe left McCall in the 182 with his wife and two children headed for the Ferry. Everything looked and felt good until they came over the river on final approach and encountered huge down air. With full power, Crowe could not arrest the descent. He was unable to push the nose over to pick up additional airspeed because of the terrain, and the aircraft smashed into the ground. The impact was so severe that it did not just fold the nose gear back, but actually collapsed it with the wheel forward. There was also damage to the propeller, main gear, cowling, and fuselage. Johnson Flying Service of McCall flew in with mechanics and patched the airplane together so that it could be flown to McCall for major repairs.[45]

In June 1961 Crowe had another bad experience with the 182 at the ranch after arriving over the airstrip early one morning. He checked it out as usual and made the final approach turn. Just as he lined up to the runway the sun peeked over the ridge and shone directly down the airstrip. Crowe could not see but realized he had to land. Looking through the side window he tried to orient himself to the shiny roof of his upper cabin. Considering the situation, he did fairly well but overshot and flew into some large yellow pine trees at the top of the runway. Fortunately he was not hurt too badly. The plane was a complete loss. A few pieces of the front cowling can still be found around the ranch. Crowe suffered from poor eyesight due to cataract surgery he had as a young man. After the last accident he decided to hang up his wings.[46]

A few years later, in 1963, Fogg had a hard landing in a company Cessna 180 (N2816A). After he initially set the plane on the ground, it bounced back into the air and for a quick second Fogg saw the left wheel of the airplane shoot ahead. Doing a double take out the window, he saw that the wheel was in fact gone. At that moment he knew he was going to wreck. He tried to slow the plane down as much as he could before the spring gear caught and looped the plane. His quick reaction saved him but caused damage to the aircraft.[47]

Then Fogg's wrecked airplane joined Crowe's Cessna off the edge of the runway. Missoula-based Johnson Flying Service pilot Mel Guerrera flew a Bell 47 G3B1 (N73224) to the Ferry along with mechanic

Dale Gyles to airlift the wreckages out. Meeting them there were Fogg and McCall-based mechanic Wilbur Burkhardt. The crew disassembled the two airplanes and between October 17 and 19, 1963 Guerrera lifted them both out in several loads to the Chamberlain Guard Station. The trickiest loads were the two sets of wings. Each pair had to be loaded on the side of the helicopter. In order for Guerrera to get into the cockpit they had to tie one wing on after he was seated. For him to get out, the crew at Chamberlain had to remove it. The method of wing transport also caused problems with visibility, as he could only see straight ahead, nothing to the sides. Surprisingly the helicopter handled fairly well with the two wings, but he was glad that he encountered no winds during the flights. The last pieces of the airplanes to be airlifted out were the fuselages, which were slung below the helicopter.[48]

With all the parts at Chamberlain, Ken Roth and Cookie Calloway flew Johnson DC-3 N49466 from Missoula to Chamberlain. The wreckages were then loaded into the cargo area and flown back to Missoula. The Crowe 182 was parted out and the 180 was repaired and put back on the flight line.[49]

Another airlift by Johnson Flying Service occurred about a decade later. Johnson pilot Phil Remaklus flew a load of supplies to the Ferry in a ski-equipped Cessna 180 (N2418C) that was leased from McCall pilot Bill Jeffs. Remaklus landed and parked in the normal side area. Frances met him at the plane as usual with her sled that was used to pull supplies down to the cabin. The two transferred the freight to her cabin and returned to the airplane. He and Frances then attempted to reposition the plane for departure. Fighting the awkwardness of the snow and skis, the plane quickly ended up in a compromising position. They had moved the plane to a point of no return. Using all of his strength Remaklus could not prevent the plane from sliding and the Cessna 180 skated backwards down the runway. Moving at a good clip the tail struck the lower ditch and bounced the plane into the air. In the process it bent the skis, damaged the left wing tip, and smashed the empennage.[50]

Dispatched to haul the wreckage out was Missoula pilot Bill Wiles, flying a Johnson helicopter along with mechanics Don Micknak and Gary Markham. When they arrived no one could believe the damage. The whole empennage was a loss and Micknak had to chisel it off. It took the crew two days of work and Frances would not allow them to stay at the ranch. It was a bit of an inconvenience but the parts were transported to the end of the road near Corn Creek, and it was easy to spend two nights in North Fork, Idaho. The parts were loaded onto the old Federal truck that had fetched lots of Johnson mishaps over the years, and driven back to Missoula by Micknak.[51] The plane was repaired and delivered back to Jeffs.

Jim Moore Place – Another Airstrip Considered

The land across the river from the Zaumiller's property was settled by Jim Moore in 1900 after he came to the Salmon River country two years earlier from Kentucky. Within a fifteen-year period Moore built nine log structures, created a substantial orchard and garden with irrigation, raised cattle, and dabbled in placer mining. Living a full life Moore died in 1942 at about age seventy. [52] Taking care of him during his last days was good friend and neighbor Frances. After his death in the Zaunmiller cabin, Moore was buried above his house on the north side of the river.

The mining claim was left to Frances and she sold it to Bert Rhodes. Sub Woods bought the claim in 1943, only owning it a short time before selling it to Jack Wenzel. Wenzel and his wife, Zip, had a primary residence in Dixie, but made a few improvements to the Moore property. In October 1951 he attempted to file a homestead entry on the land but in 1953 was instead issued a special use permit from the USFS. Five years later Wenzel's use permit was terminated. Months before his permit ended the USFS withdrew the land from public use as it was to be used as an administrative site.[53]

The spark in administrative interest stemmed from an airplane ride taken by Dixie District Ranger Howard Higgins. In 1957 Higgins was flown to Campbell's Ferry by pilot Bob Fogg. During the flight Fogg pointed out the possibility of putting an airstrip on the property situated northeast-southwest. Higgins thought it was a great idea as the USFS was only allowed restricted use of Zaunmiller's strip to

collect smokejumpers and fire gear. Also, Zaunmiller packed fire equipment for the USFS frequently to the current Whitewater Ranch where it was then trucked to Dixie.[54] Forest Supervisor A. W. Blackerby agreed, "An airfield at this proposed site would be strategically located from the standpoint of fire control work on the Nezperce and Payette Forests. Fortunately, too, it seems to have about the best approaches and terrain for an airfield of any site in this portion of the Salmon River Canyon."[55]

After the site was withdrawn for administrative purposes, Fogg and engineers, were consulted. It was figured a 2100' runway was possible at the location. The Nez Perce NF received strong support for the new field's construction from the regional office and the neighboring Payette NF. Some on the forest even had plans for a proposed guard station to join the runway. However nothing materialized, possibly because the two people spearheading the project, Higgins and Blackerby, were not there to see it through. Ranger Higgins retired the same year the project was approved and Blackerby sadly lost his life a year later in an airplane accident at Moose Creek Ranger Station.

In addition, USFS policy changed, which forced them to meet the demands of the Wild and Scenic Rivers Act and the proposed wilderness designation for the nearby Salmon River Breaks Primitive Area. In 1971 the administrative withdrawal was reversed and the historic significance of the place was recognized. Red River District Ranger Ernest Andersen noted in a letter to the Forest Supervisor, "Because of changes in the philosophy of management of wilderness (and primitive) areas since 1962, the original reason for withdrawing the Jim Moore place is no longer germane."[56]

In 1976 the property was listed on the National Register of Historic Places. In the early 1980s many of the buildings were stabilized by the USFS to help preserve them for the future.[57] In 2007 the place almost burned, but fire crews created an effective barrier and were able to save the historic structures.

B. Ehrstrom

Colson Creek owners Bill and Sherrie Ehrstrom in the 1990s.

COLSON CREEK

The Early Years and an Airstrip

In November 1916, Arthur W. Pope homesteaded the 61 acre ranch at the location of the current Colson Creek airstrip.[58] Across the Salmon River, Walter J. Smith homesteaded another smaller 13.35 acre parcel.[59] The Pope property was eventually subdivided into small lots. Very few of the lots sold before environmental restrictions were put in place, requiring larger individual parcels for septic approvals.[60]

William Ehrstrom of Pocatello obtained the property in 1985 from area resident Rodney Tibbetts. At the time of his purchase the property contained a rough airstrip paralleling the river. It had been built in the late 1950s and resembled a two-track wagon trail. Ehrstrom, a pilot, enhanced the strip considerably by clearing and grading what was already in place. With the improved 1000' long runway, Ehrstrom flew in and out of the property with a Helio Courier (N700AA) and a Cessna 182 (N2070X). He also added a nice cabin to the property and sold a few of the adjacent lots.[61]

The Potts Years and Planes

Stan and Joy Potts, successful outfitters and guides bought an acre parcel in the late 1980s and in time constructed a permanent home and moved from Hailey. Potts, a man of many talents, helped Ehrstrom sell his cabin and he then purchased the remaining acreage. Potts subdivided the property into large parcels and also planted a tree farm.[62]

Potts, like Ehrstrom, is a pilot and has flown a number of aircraft from the property. When he first

Final approach to Colson Creek as seen from the cockpit of Ehrstrom's Helio Courier in 1993.

Ehrstrom's Helio Courier and Cessna 182 parked at Colson Creek.

moved to the place he flew a M4 Maule (N2058U). In 1998 the plane nosed over on a landing when it broke through some hard snow at Colson Creek. To cover the repair costs, Potts was forced to sell the plane. Potts replaced it with a Kitfox Model 5 (N1392SP) that he built. He flew the Kitfox until March 2002, when he had an engine failure shortly after takeoff from Colson Creek. The airplane came to a rest right side up in the river and Potts was able to get out relatively unharmed.[63]

Owl Creek Neighbor – Fred Porter

In 1960 Fred Porter was traveling through North Fork and became interested in real estate in the area. He purchased a place at Owl Creek, upstream from Colson Creek. Porter was no stranger to aviation, having flown two tours during World War II in Spitfires and P-51 Mustangs. After the war he remained in the Air Force, flying various jets. With his

Ehrstrom's Cessna 182 departing Colson Creek.

Colson Creek owners Joy and Stan Potts.

Potts's Maule at Colson Creek.

interest in aviation he soon began flying seasonally for Mike Loening and often based one of Loening's planes at Colson Creek overnight for early flights the following morning. By the mid-1960s Porter went to work for Johnson Flying Service in Missoula mainly flying TBMs during the fire season. He also had short stints flying for Hillcrest Aviation in Lewiston, and Reeder in Twin Falls.[64]

Porter and another neighbor, Bob Smith, who was most known for his river running, bought a Cessna 180 that they kept for the most part at Colson Creek.

The plane mainly functioned as a support vehicle to fly supplies for Smith's commercial boating parties along the Middle Fork and Main Salmon Rivers. Over the years Porter grew more and more interested in boating and retirement. As a result he had Smith build him a custom jet boat and as payment traded his share of the Cessna 180. Although Porter no longer flies, he continues to live at Owl Creek and enjoys the river.[65]

CROFOOT RANCH

Early Owners

Frank Santos (center) with his in-laws, Wally and Viola Belden, in the converted barn used for living quarters.

In 1910 Bruce Crofoot came to the Salmon River, and eleven years later homesteaded 50.41 acres at the location now known as the Crofoot Ranch. By 1914 Crofoot had three acres under cultivation and had constructed a 12' X 18' log residence along with a 10' X 10' log barn.[66] Later, a blacksmith shop, cellar, and orchard were added to the place. He mainly made a living by trapping and worked enough land at the ranch for his subsistence. Crofoot trapped some with nearby neighbors Ed Harbison and Vic Bargamin for whom Bargamin Creek is named. In 1926 word reached him that his sister was ill and he went out to see her. He never returned.[67]

In the interim, Joe and Emma Zaunmiller, along with Emma's sister, Addie and her husband Thomas Newsome, cared for the property, living in Crofoot's dwellings. Thomas Newsome died of blood poisoning while at the ranch. His grave is located near the top of the runway to the west. Addie and the Zaunmillers went on to occupy other Salmon River properties. Next came George and Reho Wolfe. Their family lived at the location for one year, starting in 1942, before relocating to Allison Ranch and later to a place across from Lemhi Bar.

A Few More Owners, Frank Santos, and the Airfield

The property was then sold in 1951 to Thomas Dale and James Smith. The partners owned it for a short time and in 1954 sold it to Walter and Mary Elaine. In 1959 the ranch traded hands again and was sold to Frank and Bessie Santos.[68] Santos, from Redding, California, had discovered the property through several Redding friends who had places in the Idaho backcountry. He bought the property after seeing it from the air.[69]

When the Santos family obtained the acreage they began spending summers at the ranch. During their first season, Crofoot's cabin, which stood in the center of the upper meadow, was removed as part of the preliminary construction of the runway. The old barn located farther down the property on a smaller flat toward the river was modified. The two-story structure was built into the hillside, making it easy to load hay directly from the back into the top of the barn. Santos continued to use the back part of the barn during his early ownership. The bottom portion of the barn, designed for animals, was remodeled to include a kitchen, dining area, and sleeping quarters. Outside the barn several tent platforms were built to house the three Santos daughters, friends, and hired help. Another tent platform was built on the knoll above the large flat for Bessie's parents, Wally and Viola Belden, who helped immensely with ranch projects.[70]

Santos, who owned Santos Brothers Logging, a large operation in Redding, had access to many resources to make considerable improvements to the property. He floated in a sawmill, a D2 Caterpillar,

Frank Santos looks onward toward the barn after a day of haying.

A look at the 950′ Crofoot runway shortly after it was completed circa 1961.

An aerial of the Crofoot Ranch in the mid-1960s showing the road, airstrip, and lodge (center right).

The Crofoot Ranch lodge and outbuildings built by the Santos family.

and a Jeep to the site. The equipment boated down the river by friend Bob Smith, allowed him to build the airstrip and a good-sized lodge.[71]

The bulldozer, once unloaded off the boat, was used to carve a road from the river up to the ranch. After the road was complete Santos was able to construct a roughly 950′ runway with an average slope of fifteen percent. He could then bring in guests and supplies to the ranch both by river and air.

The USFS was not pleased about the road crossing federal land from the river to the Crofoot property. The Nez Perce NF dispatched neighboring Magruder District Ranger Dale Thacker to investigate the situation. A Johnson Flying Service helicopter stationed nearby and piloted by Rod Snider flew Thacker to the Crofoot Ranch. As Thacker departed the aircraft he mumbled, "Keep the engine running,

there could be trouble here." Thacker disappeared for some time and came back with not much to say. Snider never really knew what became of the issue, but the road remained in use by Santos.[72]

With equipment and living quarters established at the property, Santos constructed a main lodge, several guest cabins, a shower facility, generator house, a meat room, and several other outbuildings. By 1961 Santos believed he could make a living at the ranch by outfitting hunting and fishing trips. As a result he moved his wife and three daughters from Redding to McCall, where they purchased a home and enrolled them in school. The family considered the Crofoot Ranch home and spent as much time as they could there. Santos enjoyed tinkering with things and the ranch was never believed to be completely finished. The family nickname for the ranch was "The Project." When the main lodge and associated structures were finished the original barn that they had occupied in the beginning was burned.[73]

To travel back and forth from the ranch Santos

305

A 1960s Crofoot Ranch brochure with Santos's Cessna 182.

An Intermountain Aviation PC-6 Pilatus Porter departing the Crofoot Ranch in the late 1960s.

procured a jet boat and with the help of Bob Smith learned to navigate the river. Santos also knew how to fly and sold his Piper Cub that he purely used for business travel. He replaced the Cub with a 1956 Cessna 182A (N5549B), which allowed him to haul supplies for the ranch. Although Santos had been flying for several years, he never carried any passengers, as he did not have a private license – he had only soloed.[74] McCall pilot Bill Dorris helped him with his backcountry flying. Dorris gave Santos and Bessie both a few flying lessons in the 182, but they never completed their licenses.[75] Santos continued to fly in and out of the ranch for many years by himself.[76] If people needed air transportation, Dorris did the flying with their airplane or flights were chartered with Johnson Flying Service.[77]

The Later Years and the USFS

For many years Santos ran an outfitting business from the property, but it did not create enough revenue. He then moved back to Redding where he more closely managed his logging company,

Santos family

The Santos family in their jet boat at the Crofoot boat ramp.

Holm

The overgrown Crofoot runway.

M. Dorris

The airstrip in the late 1980s with small tree seedlings beginning to grow.

Holm

A 2009 view to the north of the Crofoot property – the road and runway remain visible.

although he continued to spend as much time as he could at his beloved Salmon River property. Over the years he leased the ranch to several outfitters and had numerous caretakers. Even though the ranch was his favorite place in the world, it not only became a financial burden, but he was meticulous and it became too much for him to maintain. Wanting to keep a place in the Idaho backcountry he developed a more manageable residence downstream at China Bar that he kept well into the 1980s. This property was linked with another cabin owned in Riggins, where Santos stayed often after retiring in 1970.[78]

By the mid-1970s Santos had refused several offers from the USFS. He knew if he sold the Crofoot to the agency that all of his hard work and care would be destroyed. Santos actively sought a private buyer for several years and had multiple interested parties, but all the deals fell through.[79] By 1978 Santos began to run out of options and as a last resort sold the ranch to the USFS.[80] The following year the USFS placed two white "X" markings on the runway and received closure approval from the FAA office in Spokane.[81] However, local pilots continued to use the airstrip well into the 1990s.

After the USFS purchased the ranch they dismantled all of the buildings and then put items up for auction. Zeke West of the Whitewater Ranch placed a low bid on all the wood siding, but then decided by the time he hauled it down the road to the river and transported it back to his property it would not be worth the effort.[82] Most items on the old ranch were burned or buried. A large dump is still evident with the hull of a jet boat visible. Also noticeable is the airstrip being reclaimed by trees, as well as the small road winding down to the Main Salmon.

In 2005 Frank Santos died in Redding at the age of ninety. Knowing that the Crofoot was one of his life's biggest passions, Bessie and his daughters contacted family friend Doran Bricker to make one last trip up the Main Salmon River to the Crofoot. After the jet boat ride and hike to the top of the old ranch, Santo's ashes were spread over the property.[83]

ELK MEADOWS |

Looking north at Elk Meadows in the fall of 2011. The airstrip is faintly visible along the east side of the meadow between the tree line and the creek.

The USFS started work on the Elk Meadows airstrip in 1936 and completed it in 1937.[84] The runway, 2040' long and situated nearly north-south along Elkhorn Creek, had several amenities. The airstrip was positioned near the junction of several USFS trails and had a small Rocky Mountain style log cabin built the same year the runway was finished. The location also had a serviceable telephone.[85]

In 1942 further clearing was accomplished and more was to be done the following year to improve the approaches at each end.[86] It is unclear if much maintenance was provided after the facility was finished, but through the early 1950s the Elk Meadows airstrip did have annual airplane activity. The USFS closed the field in 1957 and abandoned the cabin around the same time. Sheep companies that held grazing permits in the Elkhorn/French Creek Grazing Allotment then used the cabin. However, the area and cabin were burned in the 1994 Corral Creek Fire, putting a final end to much activity at the location.[87]

In the late 1960s and early 1970s the need for the airstrip diminished even more when the USFS built roads into the meadow and surrounding area for timber harvest. Despite the closure and the construction of the roads, pilots continued to use the airfield into the early 1980s for recreational purposes. The field is rough, but some believe it could still be used as a viable emergency landing location.

M. Dorris

Looking upstream at the freshly bladed Island Bar airstrip in the early 1980s.

| ISLAND BAR

Pilots occasionally use this rock bar as a place to land in poor weather. In the early 1980s Mike Dorris worked with then landowner Ken Walters to develop Island Bar as an actual landing area. He hoped to target river rafters wanting a quick trip back to civilization after float trips. Dorris even had friend and fellow pilot Jerry Robinson bring in a piece of heavy equipment from his logging shop in Riggins to rough in a 1400' runway parallel to the river. The idea never fully materialized, as the strip was never long enough to fly out heavy loads on hot summer days. A second landing area was selected, but interest in the project faded.[88] In 1992 Walters traded the land to the BLM.[89]

Walters recalled his first airplane ride from the airstrip was memorable. Dorris called him on the telephone and invited him for a ride around the airfield's traffic pattern. Shortly after takeoff Dorris gained a little altitude and swooped around Walters's house explaining how a second airstrip could be constructed in the hayfield near his home. Before Walters could

say anything, the Piper Cub (N2473M) was bouncing along the hayfield. Without commenting, Dorris pushed the plane to full power, negotiated a tight steep turn at the top of the field and took off the opposite way he had landed. Walters was flabbergasted.[90]

Prior to settling on the location of Island Bar for a runway, Dorris and Riggins resident Ray Hamell looked at several other places upstream from Riggins. Unlike Dorris, who was interested in finding a place from which he could haul river rafters, Hamell's goal was to find a potential landing area to bring tourism to Riggins. He saw it as an opportunity to improve the economy that was devastated in 1982 by the accidental burning of the sawmill owned by Brown's Tie and Lumber Company. Hamell made one successful landing on a hayfield paralleling Elkhorn Creek at the Howard Ranch. However, he abandoned this location for Shorts Bar, situated closer to Riggins.[91]

Hamell pushed for Shorts Bar, a site that was owned by Walters and the BLM. Brown's Tie and Lumber Company had previously used the locale for log holding ponds and to store equipment. Funding was in place for the project and initially several in town supported the endeavor. In fact the road was realigned to accommodate the runway and the possible future development of a destination resort that was to include a golf course, lodge, and a beachfront area. Soon after the road was relocated to its present position the project was shut down due to lack of public support. Other areas considered for the fly-in resort included the old Riggins airstrip across the Salmon River from town, and the former Riggins Rodeo Grounds, where successful landings were also made.[92]

A downstream view of the James Ranch in the late 1960s from the rear door of a PC-6 Pilatus Porter.

JAMES RANCH

The Homestead and Owners

In the late 1800s Chinese placer mined the property now known as the James Ranch. In 1901 Orson James, for whom the place is named, arrived and stayed for twenty years. James, like other Euro-American settlers, built a small log cabin and planted an orchard and a garden. In 1920 James received a homestead patent for 67.97 acres and then in time sold it to Norman Church.[93]

After Church's ownership the ranch sold several times and was then bought by Clayton Watson. It was around the mid-1950s when Watson used a team of horses to carve out an airstrip. It is believed pilot Jim Larkin was the first to land here.

In 1963 Bryant Roberts, a retired millionaire, acquired the ranch. He had the intention of running an outfitting business at the location and hired Joe Bayok to build a small lodge. Roberts also owned the Romine Ranch located several miles up Warren Creek from the Main Salmon, along with the Indian Creek Ranch on the north side of the river.

In late 1969 Roberts sold all three properties that he held under The James Ranch Corporation to Dr. Howard Adkins of Boise. Adkins only owned the James property for a short time, running a small fishing operation that was managed by Steve Jordan. It became a losing business and Adkins focused his efforts on developing the Indian Creek Ranch into a first-class backcountry getaway.[94]

Richard Mott purchased the James Ranch with other partners, but then bought them out. During his ownership Norm and Joyce Close, along with their two daughters Donna and Heather, managed the place. The Close family eventually retired from the managerial position when they purchased their own property on Cow Creek near Riggins. Mott then sold to Stanley Wolosyn, who subdivided the ranch into several lots big enough for individual cabins.

Airstrip Troubles

Over time high water has slowly washed out the downstream end of the runway. As a reference, the water can regularly reach the lower section of logs on the old James Cabin.[95] However, two major

310

Jim Larkin's Cunningham-Hall at the James Ranch. The plane was used to fly in supplies for the Roberts built lodge.

natural events took their toll on the airstrip. In 1974 when the river peaked at its highest recorded flow of 130,000 cubic feet per second, the cutbank grew deeper and shortened the airstrip considerably. The other big incident occurred in mid June 2001 when heavy rains caused a massive slide to come down on the ranch airstrip. The deluge of material skirted around a float group who happened to be camping at the property. Amazingly the debris formed around them in a V-shape and managed to miss the campers entirely.[96] As a result of these events the already short 900' strip was trimmed down to 700'. Wolosyn gathered friends to help clear and smooth the runway back out, but additional smaller slides continued. After each disaster he worked to clear it off.

Ray Arnold nixed the location from his mail route after the 2001 landslide. Previously he had landed frequently with Cessna 206s. Regarding the use of the strip Arnold stated, "You don't land an airplane there; you have to plant it on, immediately get on the brakes and try and get the sand to push up in front of the tires. It is a really tricky place to land in the winter; a person absolutely has to use wheels and no matter the time of year getting the plane turned around can be just as hard as landing."[97]

Mail Days

Since the 1970s no one has continuously lived at the James Ranch. However, starting in 1988 caretakers Greg Metz and Sue Anderson from the Indian Creek Ranch on the opposite side of the river walked or rode horses down for their mail. In the summer they kept a small raft and would paddle across. But retrieving the mail was much trickier in the winter when the river froze between Indian Creek and the James Ranch. Also adding to the complexity of the winter mail runs was the lack of daylight hours. It took all day for Metz and Anderson to hike the six-plus mile roundtrip. On top of these difficulties they did not always know if Arnold was going to make it into the canyon due to weather conditions. To cross the river they developed simple methods of testing the safety of the ice bridge. One was to "thump" the ice sheet with a walking stick or send their faithful twenty-five pound dog out a short distance. If either test went well they tiptoed across.[98]

At that time mail day was only twice a month (the first and third Wednesday), so it made for a bi-monthly adventure to gather and send mail. Many years they opened Christmas presents around Valentines Day or Easter, as some packages were left downriver at Shepp Ranch until the spring thaw. On the days Metz and Anderson successfully crossed the river they then had the task of helping Arnold get his plane turned around. As the years wore on, Arnold became worried that they were going to get killed trying to cross the river, so in 2000 he began doing airdrops for free in the meadow at the Indian Creek Ranch. Metz and Anderson left Indian Creek after nineteen years of managing the place for Dr. Adkins. They moved upriver for another management position at Yellow Pine Bar.[99]

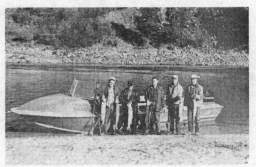

B. Nicol

1 *An Intermountain PC-6 Pilatus Porter departing the James Ranch in the late 1960s.*
2 *A 1970 advertisement for the James Ranch.*
3 *Looking downriver at the James Ranch in 2012.*

Holm

B. Zimmerly Jr.

The Zimmerly's Zenith parked on the south end of the Mackay Bar runway in the mid-1930's. Although difficult to see in this image the airplane's main wheels are wrapped with automotive chains to help with the snowy conditions.

Mackay Bar

The Early Years, Homestead, and an Airstrip

On both sides of this stretch of the Main Salmon River there is evidence of habitation by Indian people. The bars and banks are covered with shallow depressions, indicating the presence of pit houses that may have been used seasonally over thousands of years.

In the early 1890s, William Mackay moved to the location currently known as Mackay Bar. Mackay and his partner W. S. Howenstine built a considerable complex of buildings, including a 14' X 14' log home, a 16' X 16' barn, a 14' X 14' woodshed, a 10' X 12' blacksmith shop, a 16' X 16' hay shed, and a 10' X 10' cellar. The men also cultivated about fifteen acres of land, and had a two acre orchard and a nearby gold placer claim. Prior to the land being surveyed in September 1920 Howenstine died and was buried on a northern corner of the property, north of Mackay Creek. In December 1920, soon after the survey took place Mackay died and he was also buried in the same area. Both of the graves are still visible today. In May 1922 the 61 acre homestead was approved.[100] Mackay had understood that approval would be transferable, and he left all of his property to his friend Perry Nethkin.

In 1923 Mackay's estate was settled and Nethkin did in fact obtain the acreage.[101] Nethkin tried to make a living on the bar but he mainly leased it to cattle operators and miners. In 1933 a crude area on the bar was cleared for a landing field. The first person to land here was Roy Dickson from Lewiston with a Ryan airplane.[102] Supposedly the field was cleared by area miner "Dynamite" Henry Moore. Moore had nearly killed himself in a small cabin when nitroglycerine exploded after he started a fire in the stove. Spending four days in sheer pain before being given medical attention, he vowed that if he ever recovered he would build a landing area for quicker emergency access to the outside. Most likely Moore had heard of the landing fields in other parts of the Salmon River Mountains. Badly crippled from his injuries he cleared the first airstrip at Mackay Bar by himself.[103]

Mining, Air Activity, and a Rescue

The following year Lee Herman leased John R. Painter's Surprise Mine upriver from Mackay Bar with the option to buy. Herman poured money and labor into the project, but wanted better access. He hired the Zimmerly brothers from Lewiston to do the majority of the freight hauling. Fred Zimmerly flew frequently to Mackay Bar's airstrip. The supplies were then hauled and packed the additional few miles to the mine. Trying to make the operation more efficient,

313

Herman hired Zimmerly in May 1934 to fly in and walk up to the mining property to see if a landing field could be constructed at the immediate site of the Painter homestead and mine.[104]

Zimmerly surveyed the property and concluded it was indeed feasible, but estimated that twenty fruit trees and fifteen acres of farmland would need to be cleared for the runway. Herman decided the costs would outweigh the benefits, as he would then have to ship in a considerable amount of food for his crews.

In October 1935 the National Geographic Society and USGS utilized the Mackay Bar strip for emergency purposes. The group was surveying the Salmon River country by boat, starting at the headwaters of the Middle Fork at the beginning of the month and ending weeks later in Lewiston at the confluence of the Snake and Clearwater Rivers. On the trip were several important figures of both the Salmon River Mountains and government agencies. One key character credited with the success and use of aircraft in the Idaho and Montana backcountry was USFS employee Howard Flint. Flint, a regional forest inspector at the time, had advocated for the construction of the Moose Creek and Chamberlain airfields. He was also directly involved in the use of aircraft for fire patrol and the first aerial mapping of Idaho's forests.

Due to his reputation and innovative ideas he was asked to join the expedition down the Salmon River. He provided the group with many of his aerial photographs, in addition to expert knowledge on plants, animals, and access to air support along the route with cooperating Washington National Guard pilots Clare Hartnett and E. C. French.[105]

Unfortunately Flint fell ill on the trip, contracting a bad cold that was further exacerbated by a sinus infection. Knowing Flint was in trouble, one of the men in the crew walked ahead from their camp on the Main Salmon below Barth Hot Springs and made contact with the outside.[106]

A rescue was arranged with Flint's friends Bob and Dick Johnson of Missoula. With the weather cooperating, on October 13 Dick Johnson took off from Missoula in NC928V, an open cockpit New Standard powered by a Wright J5 radial. The plane was suited for the job but could not carry enough gas for a round trip flight. The drawback was a common problem in the early years of Johnson Flying Service's operation in the backcountry and as a result a cache of gasoline was kept at the Chamberlain airstrip. With a quick diversion for fuel at Chamberlain, Johnson headed to Mackay Bar as quickly as he could.[107]

When Johnson landed at the bar he found the crew waiting with Flint bundled in blankets and a sleeping bag. They helped load Flint into the New Standard and Johnson flew back to Missoula. Once in Missoula, Flint was taken to the hospital but did not live long. The original cause of illness was thought to be pneumonia, but it was later determined to be a case of acute encephalitis. Johnson wrote in his pilot logbook for the day, "Misla, Chamberlain, Mackay Bar & Ret – USFS& USGS – Howard Flint." The total flight time of the rescue mission was five hours and five minutes.[108]

An article about the entire trip, rescue efforts, and Howard Flint was written by two of the crewmembers and published the following year in the July 1936 edition of *The National Geographic Magazine* under the title, "Down Idaho's River of No Return." Flint's wife, Elizabeth C. Flint, in her 1943 book, *The Pine Tree Shield: A Novel Based on the Life of a Forester*, further immortalized Flint's life through the fictionalized character Hugh Kent. She wrote the book based on a combination of their experiences together and his personal papers, which are now archived with the Forest History Society.

The Oberbillig Mining Operation

In 1937 John J. Oberbillig purchased the bar and founded the Salmon River Placer Company. The company had big plans to develop the area around Mackay Bar into a large mining operation. The Zimmerlys and Johnson Flying Service flew much of the equipment and men to the bar during these years. Johnson even used a few of his early Ford Tri-Motors for transporting some of the larger pieces of equipment to the property. Oberbillig financed the road on the

1 *Pilot Fred Zimmerly (second from right) delivering miners and supplies to Mackay Bar with a Zenith in the mid-1930s.*
2 *Fred Zimmerly (far right) with the "Gordon Prentiss Party" of miners at Mackay Bar in early 1937. Airstrip builder Henry "Dynamite" Moore (far left) is standing next to Clyde Painter and Mr. Rice.*
3 *Johnson Flying Service's Dick Johnson in his pilot uniform.*
4 *Rescue pilot Dick Johnson is standing on the tire of the New Standard at Mackay Bar, while USGS men load the sick Howard Flint into the rear cockpit.*

315

north side of the river from Dixie to the bar. It was used later for getting the larger pieces of equipment into the remote area.

One of the biggest undertakings by the company was dynamiting the tunnel on the north side of the river below Mackay Bar at the confluence with the South Fork. The idea was to have a tunnel that would divert enough water flow to turn a large turbine for power. The project never materialized but the blasting is still evident. Despite the amount of money and time spent on trying to get the Salmon River Placer Company up and running at this location, it never came to fruition as World War II required most of the nation's labor force.

Pilot Penn Stohr Sr. and a Full-time Manager

In the early 1930s Bob Johnson looked to Idaho as an avenue for expanding his business. He successfully bid on several United States Postal Service contracts over the years and set up satellite operations, first at Boise's College Field, and then later moved the branch to Cascade, and then to McCall after World War II. While Johnson held down the Montana end of the business he appointed Penn Stohr Sr. as pilot and manager to head up the Idaho business. Stohr's skills as a pilot quickly earned him a reputation in the backcountry and along the way he made many good friends. One such person was Mackay Bar owner John Oberbillig.

The Oberbillig family had long been involved with mining interests in the area and when he started building the Salmon River Placer Company he was looking for a full-time manager at Mackay Bar. Stohr connected him with his father, Willis Wood Stohr of Plains, Montana. Willis had recently lost his farming operation to the bank and was looking for work. The two hit it off and Willis worked for Oberbillig from 1937 through 1940 at Mackay Bar. During one summer he hired grandson Dan Stohr to help with chores.[109]

Throughout Willis's years at the bar his son frequently visited. When operations ended at the start of World War II, Willis moved to Cascade and worked part time for Johnson Flying Service. Additionally, he

Backcountry pilot Penn Stohr Sr. in the cockpit of a Travel Air 6000.

served as a security guard at the Cascade airport, which was a wartime requirement at airports where air carriers held government contracts.[110]

Penn Stohr Sr. remained with Johnson Flying Service until he died on June 19, 1957 at age fifty-five in a Ford Tri Motor (NC9642) accident near Townsend, Montana. He had learned to fly from Nick Mamer and became the first pilot and aircraft owner in his hometown of Plains. Stohr and the Johnson brothers developed a close relationship and struggled through the Great Depression together trying to make a living as professional pilots. At times they were even known to have illegally transported alcohol from Canada to Idaho and Montana to make ends meet. Through his thirty-five year career as a pilot he accomplished many things, including daring rescue attempts, the pioneering of ski use for Johnson-equipped aircraft, and the dropping of the first Region 4 smokejumpers. Stohr's passion for flying lived on in both of his sons, Dan and Penn Jr., who became pilots, as well as in a few of his grandchildren. Two halls of fame have recognized Stohr's pioneering efforts and the Plains airport is named in his honor as Penn Stohr Field.

Al Tice standing at Mackay Bar with a Cessna 206 in the 1960s.

The Beginning of the Tice Years and More Airplanes

The postwar years ushered in outfitter and guides Al and Mary Tice. The couple came to the Main Salmon River country to run their first business at French Creek. Tice then leased the Badley Ranch for a few years but had his eye on obtaining Mackay Bar. Circa 1960, after John Oberbillig died, the Tice family was able to purchase Mackay Bar, giving them a more permanent location to run their outfitting business. Tice's plan was to turn the property into a first-class operation.

At the time of acquisition the property had only an equipment shed/barn and old framed miner's bunkhouse measuring roughly 70' X 40'. Tice and his stepson Dick spruced up the barn and remodeled the vacant bunkhouse into living quarters with a great room. They gave it the feeling of a hunting lodge by finishing the interior in knotty pine and adding a large stone fireplace. Soon after the renovation was completed an accidental fire burned it down.[111]

Undeterred by the setback, Tice rebuilt the lodge in roughly the same location. He included all of the modern conveniences. Aiding Tice in the lodge reconstruction was client and friend Frank Johnson from California's Long Beach area. Johnson was a paint contractor by trade and quite handy. Looking for a way to make his backcountry operation solvent, Tice subdivided a portion of the bar into twenty-two lots and sold them mainly to his hunting and fishing clientele. He also served as the general contactor

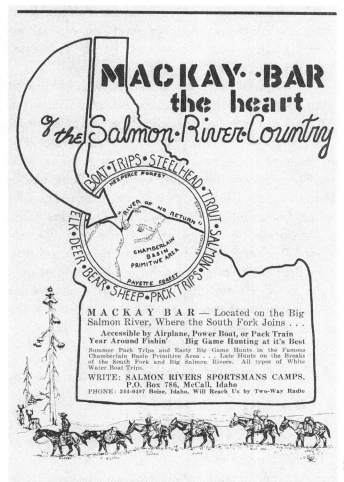

A 1964 advertisement for Tice's Mackay Bar.

for the building of cabins on the parcels. Materials were brought in by jet boat from Vinegar Creek and oversized items were trucked in via the Dixie Road. Early lot and cabin owners included Jack Simplot, John Edwards, Frank Johnson, and Bill Humphreys.[112]

Humphreys was from Boise and, like Johnson, helped Tice with construction projects at the property. Humphreys flew back and forth to Boise with a Staggerwing Beech, often hauling subcontractors for various jobs. He had a small accident with the plane shortly after departing Mackay Bar, trying to outfly the weather near Warren.[113] The plane was later repaired in Warren and flown back to Boise.[114]

Several years prior to Humphrey's mishap, he wrote a humorous story about flying his Beech from Boise to Mackay Bar in April 1962 with a load of supplies and cement for the construction of his cabin. His story was published along with several photographs of the Idaho backcountry in the August

317

1969 edition of *Private Pilot* under the title "Bad Bear: Finding a place to put down amid that vertical real estate is tough enough, but then to find a . . . big bad bear on the runway!"[115]

A fatal accident occurred with contractor Edgar A. Tuttle who also commuted by airplane from Mackay Bar to Boise using his yellow and blue Stinson L-5 Sentinel (N58995). Tuttle, in a desperate effort to return to Boise, tried to find a hole in the weather by flying up Warren Creek, but the weather quickly deteriorated. He attempted to turn back down the creek, but unfortunately hit the side of a ridge a few miles above the confluence with the Main Salmon River. The crash killed both Tuttle and his passenger John Brock. Tice discovered the plane days later while flying along the drainage. McCall smokejumpers and a helicopter were used to retrieve the bodies.[116] A few pieces of the wreckage still remain.[117]

An Improved Airfield and Tice's Experiences

In 1964 Tice hired equipment operator Norm Close of Riggins to help with several projects at the ranch. The original airfield was very crude and by the time he employed Close he had transported enough equipment to the bar to re-align and improve the runway. Close used an International TD-9 and a 1010 Caterpillar backhoe to move the runway out toward the river. In addition he pulled down the side of the mountain on the upstream end of the runway, making for a wider and longer approach. He used the extra material to fill in a large depression at the same end of the airfield, giving it considerably more length. He also expanded the downstream end of the runway and created a broad turnaround and aircraft parking area. Close's work led to the current 1900' runway.[118]

Aircraft were very important to the success of Tice's business as he often flew in family, guests, employees, and supplies. He also used air transportation to commute back and forth from Mackay Bar to the Stonebraker Ranch in Chamberlain Basin, which he started leasing circa 1958 from the IDFG. The lease allowed him to take clients on fishing trips in the high country during the summer months and opened up vast opportunities for high-quality elk hunts in the fall.

During Tice's years of operating in the backcountry he had several different airplanes, including a few Piper Super Cubs, a Super Cruiser, a Family Cruiser, Cessna 206s, a Stinson, a Cessna 185, and a Cessna Skymaster. During his countless hours in the backcountry he had several accidents related to engine failures.[119]

An early accident occurred soon after takeoff from Chamberlain when the engine in his Piper PA-12 (N5104H) quit over Red Top Meadows. With not enough altitude to make it back to the ranger station strip he opted for an emergency landing. With an effort to utilize the longest length of the meadow he glided in over some trees but came up a little short, and clipped the wings between two trees. He then tried to avoid the meandering creek through the meadow but was unable to do so. The main wheels collided with the streambed and collapsed the landing gear. Despite the damage to the aircraft, Tice got out unhurt. He then walked all the way to the Stonebraker Ranch.[120]

The airplane was then airlifted by helicopter to the Stonebraker property where Tice began the necessary repairs on the plane. The wings were hauled out and rebuilt by Johnson Flying Service in McCall and a new engine was ordered. All the replacement parts were brought into Stonebraker and assembled. Shortly thereafter Tice flew the airplane out with no trouble. When the mechanic tore the Lycoming 150 down he found that the impulse on one magneto had flown off and jammed into the magneto drive on the other side, stripping the gear teeth. The mechanic told Tice he had never seen anything like it, nor had the manufacturer. Needless to say, it was the last Lycoming engine Tice ever owned.[121]

Another engine failed on Tice while flying his Family Cruiser from Mackay Bar to McCall in the winter. He was hauling a cylinder head for a jet boat motor and had it strapped into the backseat. Just after he crowned Secesh Summit the engine began sputtering. Knowing he would not make McCall, Tice opted to set the little plane down on Upper Payette Lake and take his chance of flipping over. He had departed Mackay Bar on wheels with the knowledge that McCall's runway had recently been rolled. Sure

1 *A 1964 view of Mackay Bar showing several of Tice's improvements, including the runway extension (hill excavated on far end), several customer cabins, and the new lodge (right).*

2 *Looking upstream at the Mackay Bar runway built by Norm Close.*

3 *An Intermountain Aviation Twin Otter landing upstream at Mackay Bar.*

4 *Tice's Piper PA-12 after a forced landing at Red Top Meadows in the early 1960s.*

5 *Two of Tice's Cessna 206s parked at Mackay Bar in the late 1960s.*

6 *Tice's Cessna 206 (N3958G) east of the Stonebraker Ranch following an engine failure on takeoff.*

enough, as he gently set the aircraft down the main wheels caught and the plane nosed over. On impact, the heavy engine head launched out of the backseat, came over his head, broke through the front windscreen, and landed in the snow, missing the back of Tice's skull by inches.[122]

Tice stumbled out of the downed plane unscathed. The airplane was equipped with a long trailing antenna that stretched out during flight. He manually pulled it out and switched on his radio to the backcountry frequency. Through his efforts he was able to reach Johnson Flying Service in McCall. Johnson pilot Dave Schas hopped in one of

Al Tice (center) with his kids (l to r): Pat, Bob, Dick, (Al), Mary Jane, and Sissy.

the company's ski-equipped planes, headed north and landed on the frozen lake just as it was getting dark. Schas transported Tice and the engine head back to McCall and the next day they made arrangements to retrieve the plane. The engine problem was later determined to be a fuel supply issue.[123]

Beyond these two accounts of engine failures, Tice had several others. They included one in California, one south of McCall in a Piper PA-12 where he was able to set the plane down on Highway 55, and another one on takeoff in a 206 (N3958G) from the Stonebraker Ranch, where he was able to land in a meadow east of the airstrip.

A Family Operation

Al and Mary Tice raised five kids at Mackay Bar: Dick, Mary Jane, Bob, Sissy, and Pat. The whole family thoroughly enjoyed growing up in the backcountry. For three years some of the kids were homeschooled. The Tices hired Mrs. Bridge, a retired schoolteacher from Meridian, to instruct the children. When the Tices sold the operation in 1969 the children attended school in Notus, Idaho.[124]

While the kids lived at the remote home year-round they found wholesome avenues of entertainment. The majority of the kids inherited their parent's passion for horses. Tice bred most of his packhorses at Mackay Bar and his wife Mary raised Appaloosas. Mary Jane particularly took an interest in horses and became an avid barrel racer and competitor in rodeos all over

the Northwest. During her younger years she ordered horse ribbons from catalogs and held her own shows at the ranch with her siblings. To show one of the family's prized horses, an Arabian purebred named Arab, at the annual Riggins rodeo, her father loaded the animal onto one of his jet boats and motored it to town.[125]

Dick enjoyed horses too, but also like his stepfather took up flying after buying an eighty-five horsepower Piper Cub (N21881) at the Strawberry Glenn Airport. The plane had been wrecked and repaired but not paid for, so Dick purchased it for the $1,200 outstanding bill. Next the Tices worked a deal with local Fish & Game pilot, Bill Dorris, to pasture his personal horse named Blaze in exchange for Dick's flying lessons. It was a great trade for Dorris as he was able to fly his Cessna 170 from McCall to Mackay Bar and have his horse on the river for business.

Dick's Cub was also used to haul feed. The little plane was later left out over the winter at Mackay Bar and mice got into the fabric on the lower portion of the fuselage and ate the cloth away from the ribbing. One of Tice's friends, Grid Rowles of McCall who often worked and flew for him, took the plane to McCall one spring day. During the early stages of flight Rowles could not figure out why it was flying so slow. About the time he reached Secesh Meadows he figured out the problem with the fabric but it was too late to do much about it and he just kept flying to McCall. After that flight, Tice sold the airplane to Jack Pickell of Warren.[126]

Longtime Mackay Bar owner Bob Hansberger (center) delivering a gift to neighbor Buckskin Bill (left) of Five Mile Bar.

Hansberger's private residence at Mackay Bar dubbed "The Ram House."

The Hansberger Years

In 1969 Robert "Bob" Hansberger bought Mackay Bar, and the Tices continued to manage the operation for the Mackay Bar Corporation. Hansberger originally hailed from the Midwest and graduated from Harvard Business School. Early in his career he worked for Chicago-based Container Corporation of America, headed by Walter Paepcke, who was involved in building postwar Aspen, Colorado, as well as establishing the Aspen Institute. It was through this connection that Hansberger got a taste for the mountains. He then took a job in Portland were he developed his forte of revamping small sawmills to make a raw material for producing paper products. He moved to Idaho after being hired as president of Boise Payette Lumber Company in 1956. Traveling all over the western United States for the company, he perfected his ability to merge sawmills, which eventually led to the formation of Boise Cascade Corporation.[127]

Starting in the late 1950s, Hansberger and his friends began annual hunting trips with Tice.[128] Hansberger approached Tice several times about purchasing Mackay Bar but Tice was unwilling to make a deal. In need of financial backing around the same time the bar was subdivided, Tice turned to Hansberger, making him a minor owner in the operation. As the years progressed Tice slowly sold more and more land to Hansberger in an effort to fend off debt. However, in the end Mary wanted out of the operation and a final sale was arranged with Hansberger.[129]

Part of Hansberger's original investment in Mackay Bar included a lot and the construction of a cabin. As for other cabins, Tice acted as the general contractor and hired Jack Vincent and his brother, both from Boise, to build the place as a hunting lodge. Vincent, who was a pilot, started construction on the house in 1962 and finished during the summer of 1964.[130] The lodge still serves as a prominent landmark on the river. Hansberger named the place "The Ram House," which was derived from Ram Golf, a then small golf company owned by him and his brothers.[131]

Hansberger became infatuated with the Idaho backcountry and through the course of his life owned large sections of property along the Salmon River's canyons including Allison Ranch, Painter Mine, Ludwig, and the South Fork Ranch. For Hansberger the area was a way to truly relax. At his various properties he was able to tinker with things such as equipment, horses, and fences.[132]

Part of the enjoyment for Hansberger was getting to his properties, as he had a fascination with flying. Prior to the military diagnosing him with a heart murmur, he had spent a short time during World War II as a pilot before being reassigned as a torpedo engineer. Always wanting to justify his hobbies, he often connected them to his venture capital business, Futura Corporation. The business enterprise at one time linked his backcountry properties and the associated leases together. At the height of his operations Hansberger held several outfitting and guiding licenses, running floating businesses down the

1 *Looking upriver from "The Ram House."*
2 *Bob Hansberger and wife Klara (right) visiting at Mackay Bar circa 1970.*
3 *Hansberger often used Mackay Bar as a place to entertain friends and business associates. Congressman Orval Hansen (left) and Senator Len Jordan visit in "The Ram House" on a June 1971 trip.*
4 *Klara Hansberger at their Mackay Bar home in the early 1970s.*
5 *A 1976 advertisement for Mackay Bar.*
6 *Longtime backcountry packer Shorty Derrick (right) with his wife, working at the bar during the hunting season of 1976.*
7 *An advertisement for Hansberger's Mountain Air Charter.*
8 *Looking south from the Dixie Road at Mackay Bar – notice the bighorn ram in the bottom right of the photograph.*
9 *A 2011 view of Mackay Bar.*

MACKAY BAR LODGE

On the "River of No Return"—the Big Salmon River

and the *STONEBRAKER RANCH*

Located in the very center of Idaho's Primitive Area of Chamberlain Basin

● **BIG GAME HUNTING** — Chamberlain Basin areas 19, 20, and 20A. Elk, deer, bear, sheep, goat.

● **FISHING** — Steelhead, Cutthroat, Dolly Varden, in river, lake and stream.

● **FLOAT TRIPS** — Middle Fork and Main Salmon River.

● **JET BOAT TRIPS** — On the River of No Return. A trip to remember for a lifetime.

● **PACK TRIPS** — Into Idaho's high country . . . fishing, camping, and riding.

● **FAMILY FUN** — At Chamberlain Basin or Mackay Bar. Guest rooms and roomy tent cabins hearty meals and good fellowship.

● Licensed, Bonded, Experienced Guides

● Transportation by Boat or Air Charter.

BUSINESS OFFICE: Mackay Bar Lodge
Drawer F, Suite 1010
One Capital Center
Boise, Idaho 83702
Phone: (208) 344-1881

Member of The Idaho Outfitters and Guides Association   Payette National Forest

322

8

Main Salmon River and the Middle Fork of the Salmon River, and offering hunting services along the Salmon River Breaks and half of Chamberlain Basin.[133]

In the mid-1970s Hansberger started his own air taxi, called Mountain Air Charter, to access the many properties. The small outfit owned two Cessna 206s (N27MB andN47MB) and was supplemented by Boise Air Service, which at the time operated fourteen planes. When Boise Air Service dissolved in 1981, SP Aviation, also based in Boise, took over until Mountain Air Charter was disbanded in the early 1990s.[134]

More Recent History

Over the years Hansberger made an effort to purchase subdivided lots at Mackay Bar as they hit the market. After he died his sizable in-holdings were divided and traded among his family and business. In 2007 the main tract of land at Mackay Bar was sold to Kenneth Cameron. Making the Mackay Bar lodge and surrounding property more salable, a majority of the Painter Mine property was traded to the USFS in exchange for the land where the Mackay Bar lodge sat, since the southern portion of the building was illegally constructed on USFS ground.[135]

Cameron and his family operated the lodge in the same fashion as Hansberger; however, they did open the airstrip to the public and encouraged fly-in breakfasts. In the fall of 2010 Cameron sold Mackay Bar to Don and Andrea Betzold. Betzold, a pilot, purchased a Cessna 182 (N3434R) to access the place. In January 2013, Buck and Joni Dewey of Grangeville acquired the acreage. It was a natural fit for Buck, who is a jack-of-all-trades in the backcountry, and grew up spending time at a family cabin located at nearby Copenhaver. Additionally his parents, Chris and Dave, have been longtime caretakers at Pistol Creek Ranch on the Middle Fork of the Salmon River.

MARSHALL LAKE MINING DISTRICT

A 1947 north facing aerial of the Marshall Lake Mining District. The outline of the airstrip is in the lower center of the photograph.

In May 1901 gold was discovered in the current Marshall Lake Mining District. The locale was named for area miner and trapper James Marshall, who also operated a halfway house between the towns of Warren and Florence. After the finding of rich minerals, a multitude of claims were staked out on several of the drainages flowing into the Main Salmon River including Bear, California, Carey, White, and Maxewell creeks.[136]

By the 1920s numerous permanent mines were established with the help of investors. A number of operations came and went. The longest lasting names associated with the district are the Sherman Howe, Golden Anchor, Leadville, and Kimberly. Hydroelectric power provided electricity for the mining machinery and permanent structures were erected to house crews year-round. James Harris, the owner of Burgdorf, sold goods and distributed mail to the encampments.[137] The Postal Service later routed mail to the mines through an office established at French Creek that was open all year.[138]

In 1936 a rough airstrip was constructed to more easily obtain goods and services, as well as to send out ore samples.[139] The miners situated the runway west-east in a saddle directly west of the Kimberly Mine (slightly west of the current USFS road 318). While a wide swath of trees was cut down, 2000' in length and 200' wide, the runway surface was never cleared of stumps and thus not used by wheel-equipped airplanes. It is believed the airstrip was used a few times during the winter with airplanes mounted on skis.[140] The airstrip located on BLM land has since grown-in and is difficult to recognize.

Until the start of World War II, the Marshall Lake Mining District was actively worked. Some mining resumed during the postwar era, but tapered off into the 1950s.[141] Small resurgences of mineral exploration have continued since then.

A view of Shepp Ranch in the mid-1960s looking north up Crooked Creek.

W. Rubey/Fogg collection

SHEPP RANCH

A Brief History – Shepp, Klinkhammer, and Filer

The earliest Euro-Americans on the property date to the turn of the twentieth century. The first ones who stayed any length of time were Charlie Shepp and Peter Klinkhammer. The two met in the Buffalo Hump mining area and became fast friends. Shepp found his way down Crooked Creek while prospecting and later filed a claim called the Blue Jay. For a small buy-in price Shepp cut Klinkhammer in on the claim and they built a cabin together.[142]

The partners had some rough times in the beginning but made a go of the place, running stock and growing a wide variety of fruits and vegetables. On the side they worked in various mines, trapped, and did odd jobs. In September 1922 Shepp received homestead approval for 135.81 acres.[143] The two became well liked on the river and had many friends. The partners took good care of well-known backcountry figure Polly Bemis after she became widowed. Under the condition that she would leave them the property, they built her a new house so she could return to the river after her first home burned. When she died in 1933 they took over the place and eventually received homestead approval and operated it along with their original parcel. In 1936 Shepp died and left everything to his partner.[144] He was buried at the ranch and his grave can be seen behind the lodge along with the graves of Charles A. Bemis and Alex Blaine.

Klinkhammer left during World War II to work in the defense industry at the Kaiser Shipyards near Portland, Oregon.[145] After the war he returned to the ranch and continued working the property. He died in

1970 and was buried in Grangeville.[146]

In the mid-1930s Klinkhammer became well acquainted with Paul and Marybelle Filer, who first operated a general store in Orogrande and then later in Elk City. The friendship grew over the years as Klinkhammer bought most of his supplies from them. The Filers eventually went into the cattle business with Klinkhammer in 1950 and constantly reminded him that if he ever wanted to sell the Shepp Ranch they were very interested. A deal slowly evolved and was finalized with the caveat that Klinkhammer could have lifetime use of the place.[147]

Most of what exists at the ranch today is the result of the Filer's tremendous hard work. Filer became a well-known boatman on the river and even improved many of the routes used to maneuver equipment up the river with outboard-powered boats. One example was when he and others dynamited Dried Meat Rapid below the ranch. Many items were floated down to the place on large rafts. Over the years Filer built a sawmill, a flume, a power plant, a duplex, two guest cabins, and modified the original Shepp-Klinkhammer cabin into a lodge.[148]

1

2

3

4

5

6

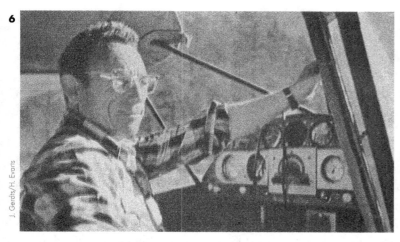

7

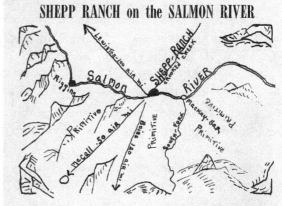

8

9

1 *The main lodge at the ranch built by Klinkhammer and Shepp that was later modified by Paul Filer.*

2&3 *Interior views of the Shepp Ranch lodge.*

4 *The grave marker of Charlie Shepp.*

5 *A The Oliver HG dozer used by Filer to carve out the airstrip in 1950.*

6 *Paul Filer sitting in the cockpit of his Piper Family Cruiser at the ranch.*

7 *A 1963 advertisement for the Shepp Ranch.*

8 *A sign along the path from the airfield to the lodge welcoming guests to the ranch.*

9 *A group of Salmon River residents at the Shepp Ranch in the mid-1960s (l to r): Paul Filer, Peter Klinkhammer, Marybelle Filer, Mary Tice, Al Tice, and unknown.*

Filer added an airstrip, which paralleled the west side of Crooked Creek. The strip was one of the first projects he took on when he became involved with the ranch. He built the runway with a small Oliver HG bulldozer and blade that were first driven down the Dixie Road to the Mackay Bar Bridge. The equipment was then floated down to the ranch. By December 1950 he had scraped out the south section of the strip as far up as Strawberry Creek. The leveling of the ground was not the only challenge, as he had to remove several large ponderosa pine trees, a grove of cottonwoods, and many enormous boulders. The following year he added a culvert, piping Strawberry Creek water to Crooked Creek. The routing allowed Filer to extend the airstrip upstream to its present length of about 1900'.[149]

Although he had a finished airstrip at the ranch he did not own an airplane or know how to fly. Always wanting to tackle a new challenge, Filer contacted acquaintance George Foster in Grangeville who owned and operated Grangeville Air Service. He took a few lessons but the two did not interact well in the cockpit. Frustrated, Filer nearly gave up until he discussed his problems with friend Ivan Gustin who owned Hillcrest Aviation in Lewiston. Gustin was the first to tell Filer that he needed to learn to fly if he wanted to keep the ranch solvent because he could not afford to pay a commercial operator. Agreeing that his friend was right, he gave it another shot and earned his private pilot license within a month. Soon after his check ride, he and Marybelle took a flying trip to San Diego, California, for a vacation. With a pilot's license in his pocket and a checkout on the airstrip, he purchased a Piper Family Cruiser that he used for many years at the ranch. He even built a small hangar on the lower southwest side of the airfield to keep the plane out of the weather. Filer eventually upgraded to a Piper Super Cruiser before selling the ranch and hanging up his wings. In the fall of 1970 the Filers moved to Riggins where they both lived their remaining years.[150]

The First Accident

In September 1966 a group of twenty men booked an elk-hunting trip with Filer. Several of the people in the party were prominent easterners tied to the Kennedy family, including Mrs. Robert Kennedy's brother, George Skakel Jr. Flying part of the group to the ranch from Boise was Donald Adams, an Air Force Master Sergeant stationed at Mountain Home Air Force Base. How the group came to hire Adams is unknown but he divided his clientele into two separate flights. Johnson Flying Service pilot Bill Dorris flew in a third group of the hunters and their gear with a Cessna 185 (N4022Y). Dorris had unloaded his plane and was standing off to the side of the runway visiting with Filer when they noticed Adams overhead coming in with his second load in a Cessna 185 (N1590F). Adams was familiar with the strip but made an unusually high approach.[151]

As he came around on final approach over the river, Dorris and Filer noted that he was a bit high but thought that he could make the necessary adjustments for the landing to work out. The 185's wheels hit the ground about halfway down the runway. Although it would have been tight, Adams had adequate room to stop but instead he panicked and configured the plane for a go-around into the steep terrain of Crooked Creek. Dorris and Filer stood in awe. Not seeing the plane come back they knew Adams was in trouble.

The two men immediately got in Dorris's plane and located the wreckage of Adams's aircraft about five miles up the creek. Unable to determine from the air if there were any survivors they returned to the ranch as quickly as they could. Filer promptly saddled two horses and they rode up to the accident scene and found that no one had survived. It was the first accident at the ranch.

The aircraft wreckage later became a destination for guests on horseback rides and hikes. Often the guides on these short trips were boatmen who were not all that fond of stock and dust and preferred to be on the river. The joke among these guides became looking up at every plane passing overhead in the forlorn hope that it might crash closer to the ranch and thus shorten the day-rides.[152] In the early 1990s the USFS decided that the wreckage needed to be removed and hired Shepp Ranch employees for assistance. The remnants were packed to the ranch on mules and then loaded on a jet boat and taken out.[153]

New Owners

The Filers had sold the property to a group comprised of ten individuals under the name of Shepp Ranch Inc. The original Polly Bemis property was sold

Jim Campbell's 1973 IOGA advertisements.

to another party. In 1973 James Campbell, a nuclear physicist with the Idaho National Laboratory (INL) in southern Idaho, acquired complete ownership of the ranch and ran it for several years with his wife Anita Douglas.[154]

Campbell merged several facets of the outfitting business together by offering float trips down the Main and Middle Fork of the Salmon River. At Shepp Ranch he also offered fishing, hunting, pack trips, and boat tours from the property. Frank Hill of Grangeville supplied the ranch by air in the early years of Campbell's ownership. However, Campbell, like Filer, quickly realized that paying a commercial air taxi operator to supply the ranch was too costly. Ultimately he and Phil Remaklus purchased a Cessna 206 (N8428Q) together. Not being a pilot he hired Remaklus, a former World War II pilot who flew many years with Johnson Flying Service's branch in McCall, to fly the aircraft for the ranch. Campbell also became a skilled jet boat operator and even trained his wife to do the same, which made her the first woman to become certified on the river.[155]

While the Campbells ran the base of operations at the ranch, they hired river guide and writer Cort Conley to manage the rafting side of the business, called Wild Rivers Idaho. At the height of their venture the company moved more than six hundred people down Idaho rivers each year, often gaining national attention in publications such as the *LA Times* and *New York Times*. Big newspapers were not the only ones writing about the famed Idaho backcountry.[156] While working for Campbell, Conley began collecting and writing the history of the Main and Middle Fork of the Salmon Rivers and wrote two comprehensive books with longtime river friend Johnny Carrey. Conley continues to author books, primarily on Idaho and the West.

Like other functioning backcountry ranches, Campbell struggled with cash flow in spite of his hard work. He originally banked on the hope of selling a scenic easement to the USFS. Budget issues arose by the time the agency reached his section of the river and the sale did not materialize. As a result he brought in a business partner that he knew from his days at INL to

W. Garret/C. Conley

Shepp Ranch employee Cort Conley displays his steelhead catch from the Main Salmon circa 1974.

help financially. Within a few years the partner wanted out. In 1979 Campbell then sold interests to Paul Resnick and his family. In 1982, still in need of more money, he sectioned off a large parcel of the ranch on the upstream side of Crooked Creek and sold it to Allison Ranch owner Harold Thomas. This section of the ranch was never developed. In the late 1990s Thomas sold it to the USFS.[157]

Able to hold the Shepp Ranch together through the assorted sales, Campbell ventured across the river and bought the Polly Bemis property with three partners. They subdivided it and sold shares. Original shares included the right to use the Shepp Ranch airstrip as an access point where they could then boat across the river. Campbell's dream of living permanently on the Main Salmon faded and he was forced to sell his interests in both properties.[158]

The Resnicks became the sole owners of the Shepp Ranch and built a large private home on the property. The Resnicks enjoyed the remote place for many years until 2002 when it was sold to Tim Turnbull. Turnbull, a pilot, often accesses the property with a Cessna 185 (N520YH). Although he spends a fair amount of time at the ranch, it continues to function as a working guest operation run by longtime caretakers Mike and Lynn Demerse.

Holm

Landing at the Shepp Ranch.

330

Downtown Warren in July 1946.

WARREN

A Mining Town

In July 1862 James Warren discovered gold in the area now known as Warren. Soon hundreds flooded into the area hoping to strike it rich. The small town of Washington (later changed to Warren) sprang up, offering goods and services to miners. When the surface claims were exhausted, the population of the town slowly dwindled. The townsite had never been platted and in 1931 the General Land Office subdivided it and began auctioning lots.[159] Between 1932 and 1942 three dredging companies purchased many of these land tracts.[160] Dredges were brought into obtain the deeper placer gold deposits, which sparked new growth in the mountain community.

The Airfields, Pilots, and Planes

During this new era the first Warren airfield was located, roughly where the present runway is today. The landing area was built in 1931 based on suggestions from pilot A. A. Bennett of Bennett Air Transport Company in Boise.[161] Within the first year of its construction, Bill Gowen wrecked a Curtiss Wright Travel Air on takeoff. No one was injured but the Travel Air was considered completely destroyed.[162] It is believed a person from Warren hauled the remaining part of the fuselage to his home and turned it into a shed (Gowen Field in Boise was named for Gowen's brother Paul, who was also a pilot and lost his life in 1938 while on a military flight near Panama City).[163]

Starting in 1934 and through 1936 the location of the first airstrip was dredged by the Warren Creek Dredging Company.[164] The company, along with the USFS and people of Warren, still needed air access, so a new field was created about two miles to the north along the east side of Warren Creek below its confluence with Guard Creek.[165]

In 1935 the north-south runway measured 1500' long and was in serviceable condition. The USFS noted that it was being used almost every day during the summer. Because of its frequent use and location within the dredge area the agency wrote, "The landing field will be moved as dredging progresses."[166]

Beginning in 1937 and continuing through 1938 construction of the current airfield was started. The Warren Creek Dredging Company, in cooperation with the USFS, built the field.[167] In October 1938 the state of Idaho offered to provide state funding to assist in the runway construction, which would allow for better public access. The USFS declined the offer, fearing that if state funds were used they might lose full control of the field.[168]

The northwest-southeast runway was leveled with a D8 Caterpillar. By the end of the 1938 season the strip was only 1300' long. The USFS did report that it would be open and smoothed for the use of ski-equipped aircraft that winter. The following year the strip was extended to 1995' in length.[169] In the early years this runway had a reputation of being really rough. In 1943 USFS engineer Francis Woods noted,

Johnson Flying Service Travel Air 6000 N9038 at Warren in February 1959 waiting out a snowstorm.

Landing south at the Warren airfield in the winter.

"This strip was constructed from gravel deposit . . . the result being a field which looks usable but which in reality is far too rough for use by ships of the five-place type. In fact pilot Penn Stohr told me he would not put his ship down on this field except when it was covered with snow as the field is so rough that it literally shakes the ship apart."[170]

By the early 1950s additional fill had been added to the airstrip, making it smoother, and by the end of the decade the runway was lengthened. Warren residents, including Robert Newcomb and Jack Pickell, assisted in pushing tailing material into two old dredge ponds off the west end for extra distance, bringing it to a total length of 2400'. Many town people of Warren have helped improve the runway over the years through general maintenance. They also expanded the turnaround and the parking area to the east on Bill Harris's land. In the late 1970s Valley County re-built the road to Warren. The location of the road was altered slightly, which impacted the airfield. The parking area actually became narrower on the southeast end where the road bends through town today. The present Warren runway measures 2765' in length.[171]

Starting in the late 1950s Jack Pickell was the first to keep an airplane at the Warren airstrip. Pickell was raised in the area and spent most of his youth working his family's claims in Pony and Keystone Meadows. He and his brother both served in World War II in artillery units. When they returned to the states, their parents had followed mining jobs to Stibnite. Pickell also moved to Stibnite and about this time learned to fly. His first plane was a Waco. After Stibnite closed he moved back to Warren and bought a 1938 Piper Cub (N21881). Wanting to keep it out of the weather he obtained a special use permit circa 1963 from the USFS and built a small log hangar. Pickell flew regularly through the mid-1980s until he sold the Cub to Jim Newcomb, who eventually sold it to Mike Dorris. When he parted with the airplane the USFS revoked the use permit and tore the hangar down.[172]

Starting in 1973, another Piper Cub (N2473M) owned by Newcomb was also kept at Warren. Newcomb along with his brother Russ grew up in the town. He was first introduced to flying by riding on several Johnson Flying Service planes, but was strongly encouraged by Pickell to take it up. When his father, who was the local mailman, died, Jim Newcomb eventually took over the position, running the route from McCall to Warren, then to the South Fork of the Salmon River with the Cub. Newcomb later sold the route to Dorris and became a career military pilot, retiring in 2010.[173]

Longtime Warren resident and backcountry pilot Jack Pickell at the airstrip on mail day with Johnson Flying Service PA-12 N2577M.

McCauley's Stearman crash near Slaughter Creek.

Warren cabin owner Steve Burak of Emmett landing at Warren with his Cessna 180 in December 2010.

An Early Accident

Newcomb was not the first pilot in his family to catch the flying bug. His uncle, Joseph Russell "Ding" McCauley, became a pilot in 1928 when he joined the Navy. Discharged in 1935 he returned to Warren where his family was involved with mining. He quickly went to work as a pilot, flying for various operators around the general area. McCauley often dropped in by airplane for family visits.[174]

In August of 1936 while using the temporary field he was flying a Stearman C-3-B Special (NC5500) with friend Don Goodman. The plane was owned by Tom McCall's flight operation, located in the town of McCall under the name of Intermountain Air Transport.[175] The two came in above Warren in the Stearman and made a banking turn over the flat east and slightly north of town. While in the turn the plane encountered a severe downdraft. McCauley was at the controls and was unable to recover, forcing the plane into timber near Slaughter Creek. Several people working on the Mickey Mouse dredge near town saw the plane in a dive and dashed to the scene to help. The two pilots walked away, but the plane was a complete loss.[176]

Goodman was also a pilot and his family is credited with building the McCall airport in 1929. He went on to be a career pilot and was killed in the 1970s while flying a Douglas A-26 Invader converted for retardant work.[177] McCauley also continued on as a professional pilot flying DC-3s for American Airlines. In 1945 at the age of thirty-four he was killed while attempting to land at Palmdale, California, after being rerouted from Burbank, California, due to poor visibility and fog.[178] He is paid tribute with others who lost their lives as pilots in the airline business in Ernest Gann's *Fate Is The Hunter*.

More Recent History

The airfield has had its fair share of small incidents and accidents over the years. However, it continues to be a safe, well-maintained facility. Since the 1980s many vacation cabins have been built in the general area and several of these line the southwest side of the runway. A few of these residents are pilots and frequently use the airfield throughout the year.

WHITEWATER RANCH

Early Occupants

A view of the Whitewater Ranch airstrip in the mid-1960s.

In 1879 C. Eugene Churchill settled on the bar. In 1915 Churchill drowned and was buried at the location where his body was found near Richardson Bar. Several years later his wife Ella married C. H. Prescott and the two stayed on the property. Bad luck struck again when Prescott was killed in an accidental hunting incident. In February 1922 Ella obtained homestead approval at the location for 120.22 acres. The same year she became ill and died.[179] Her grave remains visible on the ranch near the barn and present hydropower plant.

In 1924 Ella's sister Bertie Hoover and her husband Joe took over ownership of the ranch. Bertie suffered from psychological issues and was admitted to the mental hospital in Orofino, Idaho, where she later died. Hoover then sold the ranch in 1930 to Floyd and Goldie Dale.[180]

A Remote Winding Road

During the Dale ownership a significant change occurred to the property when the USFS decided to punch a road in from Red River down to the ranch to access the Main Salmon. Construction of the road (currently 421) began in 1935 by the Red River CCC Camp F-192. By 1936 or 1937 the road extended as far as the Salmon River Breaks, but their efforts were interrupted when the camp was moved to Montana. The USFS resumed work on the road and completed it in 1938.[181]

The Wildts, an Airstrip, Dynamite, and a Mad Hermit

The property exchanged hands one more time before being purchased in 1944 by Lewis and Katherine Wildt.[182] By the mid-1950s the Wildts moved to Riggins and leased the property to several people. Two leaseholders at the end of the decade were Marvin Hornback of Pistol Creek Ranch and Al Tice of Mackay Bar. The men leased the property with the option to buy and planned on developing it into a

Old advertising at the ranch.

backcountry destination such as they both had done at their own places. Hornback named the property the Whitewater Ranch and remained involved with it into the mid-1960s.

At first Hornback and Tice cleared an area big enough to land their Piper Cubs. In 1959 Hornback moved summer employee Glen Baxter from Pistol Creek over to the new operation. Baxter's main job was clearing and removing the remaining stumps around the airstrip for a better approach and a larger landing area.[183]

Baxter encountered one large stump at the top of the runway. He used the last of the dynamite, figuring all of it would be necessary. The dynamite was hauled around in an old Jeep pickup; it was protocol to have the vehicle pointed downhill for safety. It turned out that using all of the dynamite was overkill. As Baxter set the charge he ran for the pickup, got inside, and the darn thing would not start. He knew the dynamite was about to explode so he pushed the clutch in and with one leg kicking out the door he had the old heap rolling down the runway. It was good

he was in the vehicle as it became engulfed in flying stump debris.[184]

With the runway expanded, Tice and Hornback were able to bring in supplies via air. The two also piloted early jet boats on the Main Salmon to haul supplies and guests to the property. Hank "the Hermit" Kemnitzer, who lived across the river from the ranch, grew to dislike Hornback, as he did not enjoy the airplanes flying low over his little house built in the ground.[185]

Baxter wintered at Whitewater in 1959-60. Over the long winter he and his wife befriended Kemnitzer and often took him cake and cookies. No matter how many sweets they gave Kemnitzer, it did not affect his dislike of Hornback and his noisy airplanes. Baxter felt wary about staying too long at Kemnitzer's home when the stove was lit, as he kept nitroglycerine near it.[186]

Periodically Hornback would bring supplies to the couple, but Baxter also kept his own eighty-five horsepower Piper Cub on wheels at the property. In fact the first accident on the airstrip was the result of a cracked landing gear on this aircraft. The crack gave way and the gear collapsed on a hard landing causing the nose of the airplane to dig in, hitting the prop. Hornback helped Baxter get the plane repaired and then checked him out on skis with the same airplane.[187] The development of the property by Hornback and Tice did not work out and they relinquished the lease. However, the name the partners assigned to the parcel lived on.

Robertson, West, Bowen, and Shotwell

In 1966 Edward Robertson of Nampa bought the property from Wildt, who died in 1968 and was buried in the Riggins cemetery. Robertson owned and operated Robertson Wholesale, one of the largest plumbing wholesalers in the Northwest. Robertson made many improvements to the property, including a new lodge and several other smaller buildings. Joe Bayok of McCall completed many of these projects. Robertson also traded some lodging in exchange for some runway work with hunter Bob Zolber.[188] The final runway measured 900' long with a ten percent

Looking down the 900' Whitewater Ranch airstrip.

The May 1967 burning of Hank Kemnitzer's home on the Salmon River, across and upriver from the Whitewater Ranch.

A Johnson Flying Service Cessna 206 (N29024) delivering mail at the ranch.

average slope.

In 1968 Zeke and Marlene West began leasing the property for their outfitting business in addition to managing the ranch from time to time. Eventually West built a cabin on a two acre parcel that he bought from Robertson.[189]

In 1993 Dr. Thomas and Patricia Bowen of Moscow, Idaho, bought the Whitewater Ranch from Robertson. In December of the same year Tom Bowen was killed in an accident while traveling to the ranch when a dead standing lodgepole fell and struck him. The blow knocked him off his all-terrain vehicle and in the end cost him his life. As a memorial to Bowen, Dr. Carlos Arnaldo Schwantes, a good friend and history professor at the University of Idaho, dedicated a book in his name titled, *The Pacific Northwest: An Interpretive History.*

Even with the loss of Bowen, the family kept the ranch and improved it by upgrading several cabins built by the Robertsons and restoring the late 1800s hydro plant. This incredible hydro machine was first used in rural Pennsylvania and then sold as surplus in the 1930s when electrification reached many remote parts of the United States. Several of these machines were then shipped overseas. The Whitewater's plant was destined for Taiwan but was waylaid on a shipping dock in San Francisco due to customs issues. Robertson somehow obtained the piece of equipment and hauled it to the ranch.[190]

The massive hydro plant fascinated the Bowens and they had it completely restored as a working piece of equipment that provides power to all of the buildings. Housing the extraordinary machine is a beautifully-crafted log building that was actually constructed by a group of high school students in California as an industrial arts project and reassembled at the ranch. The whole setup continues to be a main attraction for ranch visitors.

Thirteen years after the Bowens bought the place it was sold to the Shotwell family of Filer, Idaho, under the name of Whitewater Ranch LLC. Dick Shotwell and his son Steve, along with their respective families, use the property regularly. Similar to other owners they have rebuilt many of the structures, including the original Churchill homestead cabin.[191]

Dick Shotwell at the top of the runway in September 2011.

The late 1800s hydropower plant.

The restored Churchill homestead cabin.

WILSON BAR

The Early Years

A view down the 1500' Wilson Bar runway in the spring of 2012.

The location was originally known as Jackson Bar named after miner Bill Jackson. In 1936 Howard "Haywire" Wilson moved his wife and twelve children to the bar from Seattle. Wilson was hit hard by the Depression and could no longer put food on the table for his family. With few choices left, he knew a man in the scrap metal business who had property in Idaho. Wilson decided to buy a claim on the land, sight unseen, which is now Wilson Bar.[192]

Wilson built a modest home, grew a large garden, and farmed ten acres on the river, providing enough food to raise his family. In 1946 Wilson was killed in a car accident. His wife and the younger children remained on the bar until 1950, then moved to Grangeville.[193]

Schemes, Dreams, and a Crude Airfield

In the late 1950s Harry Eaton of Boise, who was an acquaintance of outfitter Al Tice, made an effort to claim the bar. Eaton owned a decent-sized dairy farm located between Boise and Nampa and became involved with Tice in the jet boat business on the Salmon River. He and Tice were inspired by the possibilities of using modern jet boats after reading an article in *Sports Illustrated* about their use on rivers in New Zealand. After some research the two established some contacts and became dealers of Buehler Turbocraft boats.[194]

The business partners then decided they would build a landing field at Wilson Bar. In late spring 1958 an International TD-22 was hauled on a truck from Boise through Grangeville to Dixie. Beyond Dixie the road became impassible with deep snow, causing a delay for a few weeks until the snow receded enough to proceed down to Wilson Bar. With the TD-22 Tice and his stepson Dick scraped in a rough runway,

mainly moving rocks, brush, and a few trees. "It was not much of a runway when it was built," said Dick, "but it worked well enough to land an airplane on it. We never really used it, nor did anyone else when I was back there."[195]

Once the strip was constructed, Tice was the first to land on it with one of his Super Cubs. Eaton was also a pilot and occasionally flew in the backcountry.[196] In fact for a short time Eaton owned a Travel Air 10D (N518N) as well as Travel Air 6000 (N9084). Eaton approached Boise-based pilot Harold Dougal about going into the flying business together, since Dougal had been flying Eaton's two airplanes under contract with the previous owner. Nothing ever materialized, other than Dougal transporting him around the backcountry a handful of times.[197] After a year or two the business connection between Tice and Eaton dissolved. Fading with the boat sales and aviation interests was Eaton's ambition to gain control over the old Wilson mining claim.[198] Circa 1965 the USFS burned the Wilson home and other improvements.[199]

Pilot Frank Hill and a Cessna 180.

An Icon of Public Access

From the 1960s through the mid-1970s the Wilson Bar airstrip was used very little. Most commercial air taxi operators of the time used the runway at Mackay Bar. During these years Mackay Bar accommodated air taxi services, as they brought customers to their front door. However, Mackay Bar Corporation ventured into the aviation business for several years and realized they could limit the private airstrip's use and thus eliminate competition.

With no other public airstrip between the town of Salmon and Slate Creek, pilots turned to improving the nearly abandoned Wilson Bar airstrip. Only a handful of people really used it, the most frequent being longtime backcountry pilot Frank Hill of Grangeville. Hill owned property at Five Mile Bar, and the Wilson airstrip served as his primary means of access.

Debate over the strip came and went and by the early 1990s conflict ensued again. In 1992 the USFS placed a closure on the runway claiming it was adverse to wilderness, had little record of usage, and was beyond repair. The Idaho aviation community responded in an uproar. Much of the effort to reopen the airstrip can be credited to two events.

Hill sparked the first event when he decided to act alone and perform some very needed runway maintenance. He flew in and sawed down several huge trees and did some other clearing. After discovering the cuts, the USFS launched an investigation and was able to verify that Hill was the culprit. Infuriated, the agency issued multiple citations to Hill for his illegal activities. Hill kept the event very quiet and other backcountry aviators having the same concern instigated another clearing just weeks later. This group mainly made up of air taxi operators came together with the idea of seeking forgiveness, not permission. The crowd flew in armed with chainsaws and cleaned up the remaining encroaching vegetation and removed several large hazard trees. As they were about to finish, a river patrol boat pulled up on the bank of the bar. All of the pilots scattered to the airplanes and left before the government employees reached the top of the airstrip.

The second event that helped lift the Wilson Bar closure occurred when Partners Afloat decided to address the controversial airstrip as part of their annual float trip down the Main Salmon River. Started in 1987, Partners Afloat aimed to bring together various agencies involved with management along the Main Salmon River corridor. These included the BLM and USFS, as well as stakeholders like the IOGA. Partners Afloat asked air taxi owner Mike Dorris to join the

Landing at Wilson Bar.

group and address the history of aircraft at Wilson Bar. Assuming the group was open-minded about hearing the aviator's perspective he joined them. After hearing the agenda he told the spokesperson over the telephone that he would meet the group at Wilson Bar via airplane. The reply was – absolutely not, the airstrip is closed to all aircraft. Being a good sport, Dorris had his brother Pat drop him off at Campbell's Ferry where he met the group and boated down to Wilson Bar.

The crowd stopped for the night at the campground upriver from Wilson Bar and the following morning Dorris held a discussion about aircraft usage at the location. Very few were receptive. In fact several in the group strongly believed he was lying, stating that no airplanes had ever landed at Wilson Bar. Recognizing that certain individuals were not going to be open to anything but their own jaded agenda, he shrugged it off. However, not one hour later the momentous second event occurred when a black, yellow, and white Cessna 182A circled the strip and positioned for a landing at the bar. The chatter among the group was entertaining at best. Several of the aviators, including Dorris, knew who was piloting the airplane and were a bit surprised as the individual was supposed to be on the Partners Afloat trip, but did not show at the last instant. Within a few minutes the plane neatly touched down on the airstrip and rolled up to the end near the road.

Those folks that did not believe airplanes could land at Wilson Bar simply looked at the ground. The conversation among the USFS employees was hilarious. In paraphrase the federal workers were splitting hairs – Are we going to give a citation?, Who wants to deal with this one?, How are we going to approach this one in front of all these people?, and on and on it went. In the end the pilot was not reprimanded.

The landing at the Partners Afloat trip, combined with Hills efforts, forced the USFS and others opposed to the airstrip to deal with the closure publicly. As before, the USFS had simply closed it with no public discussion. For the aviation community it proved that the airstrip was usable, had some history of continued use, and was suitably maintained. In 1995 the USFS officially reopened the runway. In the end the agency also dropped the charges issued to Hill.

Looking upstream at the first airstrip built at Yellow Pine Bar before owner Warren Brown improved it.

YELLOW PINE BAR

Early Homesteaders

Yellow Pine Bar had a few early occupants and in 1922 Truman G. Thomas received a homestead patent for 36.54 acres at the location. By this time he had constructed a 40' X 20' log residence, 25' X 20' barn, and 24' X 12' cellar.[200] Thomas lived here until he died in 1927 at age eighty-three. Thomas was buried at the bar northeast of the original cabin. In 1931 his wife Celeste sold the property to Charlie Ayers.[201]

Ayers and his wife Sarah moved to the property with their kids and built a new log cabin, since the Truman place had burned. Several years later he improved the property on the other side of the river at Richardson Bar and constructed a second cabin. After Sarah's death Charlie split his major assets among his three boys. The Yellow Pine Bar property was given to his son Gene who then sold it in 1947 to Tracey Watson. In 1949 Ayer died at the age of seventy-two and was buried in Elk City.[202]

In 1948 Tracey and his wife Doris had their son-in-law Earl Eidemiller build a new cabin on the property. The same year a group of river residents constructed a one-room schoolhouse at the bar, where Doris taught eight children. The school was short-lived as enrollment declined and most went to larger communities for their education. The schoolhouse was later removed along with the home constructed by the Ayers family.[203]

Warren Brown

The Watsons sold Yellow Pine Bar in 1951 when Tracy developed health problems. Harry Owen purchased the property and then sold it two years later to Brown's Tie and Lumber Company, owned by Warren and Jayne Brown of McCall.[204] Brown bought the property sight unseen for $4,000 with the understanding that it had an overgrown runway and a rundown cabin. He was not even sure where it was located other than that it was twenty miles upriver from Mackay Bar, but it sounded like a heck of buy and he could not resist. Warren commented later, "Actually I hurried to write him a check before he changed his mind – I couldn't move fast enough. He went home and in a couple of days he sent the deed to the property."[205]

The Browns were busy during the late 1950s and did not get to the property for four or five years.

Warren Brown (right) stands with his Super Cub and grandkids at Yellow Pine Bar.

Brown landing his Cub at the property prior to many of the runway enhancements.

A view down the runway in June 2011.

After the first trip in by boat, Brown hired an old equipment operator from Dixie to come in and repair the airstrip enough so he could land his Piper Cub. In the early 1960s, Brown was the first to land on the roughly 800' runway in many years.[206]

Brown began flying in the fall of 1945 and took his first instruction from Johnson Flying Service pilot Jack Hughes in McCall.[207] The following year he finished his license with Bob Fogg and eventually purchased a 125 horsepower Piper Cub. Brown mainly used the plane for business trips and timber surveys. In 1953, Brown's son Frank also learned to fly from Fogg using the family Cub. In 1965 the 125 horsepower model was sold and Brown upgraded to a 150 horsepower Super Cub (N7153Z).[208]

By the mid-1970s Brown became fearful that the federal government was going to force the sale of deeded lands with no improvements that were located within the river corridor. At this point the Browns decided that they would build a new home there.[209]

Airstrip Work, a New House, and Rainbow Falls

Being a pilot, Brown went to work on designing a larger airstrip. In 1976 he hired Charles "Matt" Wallace who was an excavator from McCall along with his brother, Leonard Wallace, to do the work. Brown had a connection with a helicopter logging company and had them fly a Bobcat loader to the property. The little loader was first used to build a boat ramp and then a road from the river to the airstrip. The road project took the Wallace brothers seven days to complete.[210]

At this time Brown had a jet boat haul in a Jeep so he could move building material from the boat ramp

The Brown's home at the bar.

Rainbow Falls located across the river from Yellow Pine Bar.

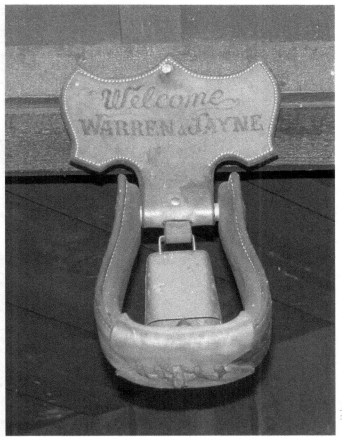

A sign welcoming guests at the main house.

to the construction site. As items were being brought to the property the Wallaces worked on building a wider, smoother, and longer runway. In the end they extended the runway 200' and cleared an amazing amount of trees and brush. Brown paid the Wallaces for their efforts with a one acre parcel of land on the bar.[211]

While the runway work was being carried out, the new house was also under construction. The Browns hired builder Joe Bayok of McCall, who came to the Salmon River country with the CCC in the early 1930s and later worked for the USFS, specializing in construction with logs. He eventually started his own construction company. Bayok, his wife Marcella, and his crew finished the Brown's cabin within two years. Some of the interior wood was hauled from an old mine at Thunder Mountain that the Browns owned in

partnership with Jim and Marge Collord. Bayok, a skilled craftsman, created a special gift for the Browns, which was a beautifully laid granite rock entry with a rather large hand-carved stone in the outline of the state of Idaho. Bayok etched out the Salmon River drainage and labeled the location of Yellow Pine Bar. At the same time the new home was being built, the old Watson cabin was renovated as a place for caretakers to stay.

When the house was completed the Browns held a big party. During the evening's activities, a discussion came up concerning a spring on the other side of the river. Wondering about the source of the dripping water, a group of them boated over to investigate. The idea then arose that if all of the water were channeled into one direction it would then go straight over some rocks and form a waterfall into the river. A few people boated back to the cabin, fetched some picks and shovels, and returned. The scheme worked and Jayne Brown named it Rainbow Falls.[212]

The Wallace's cabin located at the bar.

A memorial plaque placed near the Wallace cabin remembering Matt Wallace and his friends.

The Wallaces Build

After the work for the Browns was completed the Wallaces built a cabin on their one acre lot that the family still owns. Matt Wallace was a pilot and often flew a Cessna 182 to access the property. He later upgraded to a Cessna 206 (N35699), which he shared with Duane Smith also of McCall.

On November 17, 1984, Wallace was hunting from the family cabin with a group of friends. It was common to fly the friends farther upriver, so they could hunt on their way back to Yellow Pine Bar. This particular morning Wallace made a routine takeoff with his 206 loaded with three hunters and gear. However, once he cleared the treetops on the downstream end of the runway he attempted to make a sharp left upriver turn. The plane, which was being watched by other hunters on the ground, disappeared and then they heard it crash. Everyone aboard was killed.[213]

Another Bad Accident

In September 1997 the Brown's son Frank flew to Yellow Pine Bar with good friend Bert Armstrong in the family's Super Cub. The two were flying along with another Super Cub (N5753Z) piloted by Rod Nielson. The friends were out enjoying a morning in the backcountry and planned on grabbing a cup of coffee in Dixie. Nielson took off first and once clear of the area heard Brown over the radio say that he was rolling. Not hearing any further transmissions or having a visual of the departing plane, Nielson

turned around and spotted the red and white aircraft in some trees. It appeared that as the aircraft became airborne during takeoff it drifted to the right and struck some trees about half way down the runway. Nielson quickly made a landing and pulled up to the downed aircraft where he did all he could to help Brown. However, Nielson was puzzled as he could not figure out what had happened to Armstrong. He then pieced together that Armstrong had escaped uninjured and ran back to the cabin to get help for Brown who was badly hurt. A helicopter came in and airlifted him to a Boise hospital. He has since made a recovery.

Yellow Pine Bar Managers

The Brown's daughter Diane and her husband Judd DeBoer purchased Brown's Industries in 1980, which included the Yellow Pine Bar property. However, the Browns continued to enjoy the place after the sale. Warren died in 2000 and Jayne in 2006.

Starting in the late 1970s the Browns hired Terry and Donna Beeler of Elk City to maintain the place. The Beelers took on the project of cleaning the property and shoring up the 1948 Eidemiller log cabin. In addition to their work at the bar Terry worked as a packer for the USFS and Donna staffed Oregon Butte Lookout for many years.[214]

Following the Beelers in the early 1980s were Newt and Sharon Haigh. The Haighs also made some major changes to the place with the construction of a large garden, modest swimming pool, and a remodel to the caretaker cabin that included a second floor and larger living room. When not working on the place or the garden, the Haighs ran a woodworking business

The beautiful garden kept at Yellow Pine Bar.

A McCall Aviation/Salmon Air Taxi Cessna 206 (N376ME) parked at the top of the airstrip.

Landing at Yellow Pine Bar.

on the side, which they marketed to river travelers who stopped in during the summer. Haigh, an exceptional craftsman, built custom wood products from area yellow pines in a woodshop located behind their living quarters. He constructed items such as intricate toys, kitchen gadgets, and yard ornaments. [215]

In 2007, after many wonderful years at the property, the Haighs retired to Idaho's Treasure Valley. Greg Metz and Sue Anderson, who had been managing the Indian Creek Ranch on the north side of the Salmon River, moved in the same year as the new caretakers. The two continue to take impeccable care of the place. Anderson keeps an immaculate garden and Metz turns out beautifully handcrafted metal tools and knives from a vintage blacksmith shop situated on the property. They also have developed a unique Salmon River history room connected to the shop area. It is filled with interesting photographs and artifacts related to the canyon, and is often open for river travelers to view. [216]

Johnson Flying Service Ford Tri-Motor (NC8400) landing north at the Dixie Ranger Station in 1942.

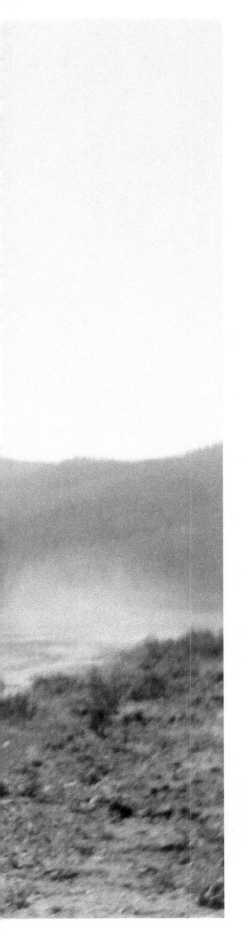

CHAPTER 7

CLEARWATER MOUNTAINS AND VICINITY

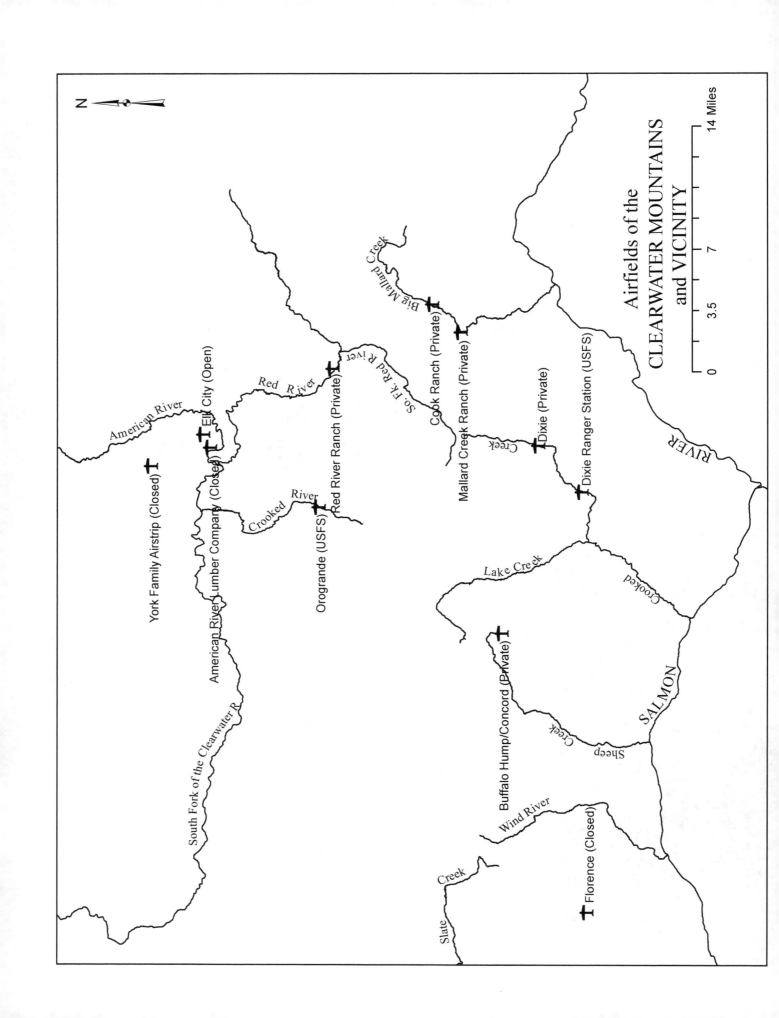

Airfields of the
CLEARWATER MOUNTAINS
and VICINITY

0   3.5   7   14 Miles

N

York Family Airstrip (Closed)

Elk City (Open)

American River Lumber Company (Closed)

American River

Red River

Red River Ranch (Private)

So. Fk. Red River

Crooked River

Orogrande (USFS)

Cook Ranch (Private)

Big Mallard Creek

Mallard Creek Ranch (Private)

Dixie (Private)

Creek

Dixie Ranger Station (USFS)

Lake Creek

Crooked

South Fork of the Clearwater R.

Buffalo Hump/Concord (Private)

Sheep Creek

SALMON

RIVER

Wind River

Florence (Closed)

Slate Creek

Looking north at Walt Remer's property in the early 1950s prior to the construction of the airstrip with Buffalo Hump in the background.

BUFFALO HUMP/ CONCORD

Remer, Gustin, and the Airstrip

Walter Remer bought the Buffalo Hump property prior to World War II and over the course of his life owned several mining claims in the area. Remer and his wife Mary lived most of the year in Lewiston, where he later worked for what became Twin City Foods. In the mid-1950s Remer had friend Ivan Gustin help him build the roughly 1400' airstrip. Gustin was a commercial pilot who started Hillcrest Aviation based in Lewiston. A native of the north Idaho town, Gustin learned to fly from the Zimmerly brothers and then became an instructor for their company while they operated a CPTP during the war. Gustin brought in fellow pilot Gerry Wilson as a partner in 1959, and he ultimately purchased the operation by the late 1960s. Wilson's son continues to run Hillcrest as a helicopter-only business. Gustin's son Ron also took an interest in aviation and in 1968 when his father retired started his own aircraft maintenance shop in Lewiston under the name of Gustin Aviation.[1]

Ivan Gustin (left) and Walt Remer in the 1950s at the Buffalo Hump property.

Gustin and Remer used a large grader to put the final touches on the strip. Gustin, who also owned land in the nearby mining district, was the first to land an airplane here and used the airstrip occasionally. Remer had relied on aircraft for many years at the location. Originally he hired the Zimmerly brothers to make airdrops. By the early 1950s Gustin incorporated a few helicopters that were used in the open area near the main cabin.[2] With an average field surface elevation of 7648' Concord remains the highest used airstrip covered in this book. The only airstrip higher was Hoodoo Meadows near the Bighorn Crags. It closed in 1974.

Showalter and Restrictions

After Remer died, his wife Mary sold the property to Gary Showalter of Vancouver, Washington. Showalter also owns another private airstrip on the South Fork of the Clearwater River. Showalter generally accessed the Concord property with a Cessna 180 (N224H). Since purchasing the parcel he has cleaned the place up and preserved the old mining cabin along the west side of the runway. Since his ownership, a series of aircraft accidents and mishaps have occurred on the airstrip involving individuals who did not have permission to land. With these issues he has placed very strict terms of use on the runway.

Although Showalter is a supporter of backcountry aviation, too many people took advantage of his airfield. The event that almost forced him to close the airstrip happened during the summer of 1994. A property owner in the vicinity of the airstrip contacted Showalter about using the strip to haul in supplies. He approved it since he knew the owner and the pilots of McCall Air Taxi who were doing the flying.

With the order in place, George Dorris departed McCall with a load of water and sewer pipe in a Cessna 207 (N6385H). Jack McGee followed in a Cessna 206 with similar cargo. McGee participated in the usual backcountry radio chatter on the way in and as he was landing a fellow in a Cessna 182 contacted him.[3] The 182 pilot had heard the planes and wanted to confirm the best landing approach procedure at Concord. He had not landed there before, but had arranged an appointment with Showalter in advance.

Killing a little time, McGee relayed a quick version of how to land at the strip. He mainly emphasized that if you are not on the ground by the little cabin a go-around is possible. Thinking nothing more of it, he landed. McGee and Dorris unloaded the airplanes and took some time to visit with Showalter, who was there with his family on vacation. Dorris had parked his plane at the south end of the strip and McGee parked his 206 off to the side as far as he could. The strip is not big enough for an airplane to take off and have one parked along the runway, so careful positioning has to be accounted for, which they did.[4]

Just as Dorris was getting ready to crank up his airplane he glanced up and caught sight of the 182 on a high approach to the airstrip from the north. McGee had mentioned nothing of talking with the 182 pilot. To add more confusion to the event, it was later determined on the way in that Dorris's 207 radios were malfunctioning. Thus Dorris did not even know McGee had talked to the pilot.[5]

What unfolded next happened very quickly. With the 182 in sight, Dorris thought, "What in the hell is this guy doing buzzing the airstrip?" He promptly realized that the pilot of the 182 intended to land, and that the plane was going too fast and was too high to stop in time before the end of the runway. Dorris saw the plane at about five feet above the ground whip by the house where a pilot's best option would have been to attempt a go-around. Seeing the 182 barreling straight for him and the parked 207, he sprinted for cover in the timber. As he left his plane the 182's propeller spun across the wingtip of the 207 and the wings collided.[6]

Everything then became quiet. When the dust settled, Dorris met McGee running up the strip. He also had watched the whole thing in disbelief. The pilot of the 182 got out of his plane safely and then the group exchanged some fierce words.[7] Surprisingly the 182 sat just short of a thick bed of six-foot wide boulders and a small drop off. The plane was amazingly damaged very little considering the circumstances.[8]

Happening to be in the area returning to McCall from a fish-planting mission was Steve Passmore, another McCall Air Taxi pilot. Passmore noted the activity on the ground and decided he should stop. At the time he was not only a pilot for the company, but also the maintenance director. He took an assessment of the 207's damages and returned a few days later with mechanic Chris Benford after obtaining a ferry permit. The plane was patched together and flown out for further repairs. Surprisingly the 182 pilot decided his plane was flyable and flew it out the same day the accident occurred.[9]

1 *Remer's friend Sid Hinkle with his Cessna 185 (N9808X) at the airstrip in the early 1960s with over eleven feet of snow on the runway. The two-story building is nearly covered and the windsock on the far right is barely visible.*
2 *A close-up of the windsock with over eleven feet of snow at the airstrip in the early 1960s.*
3 *Property owners Walt and Mary Remer in the early 1980s.*
4 *Pilot Frank Hill (left) and property owner Gary Showalter (right) in the early 1990s.*
5 *The cabins on the west side of the airstrip that are maintained by the Showalters.*
6 *Looking south at the 1400' Buffalo Hump/Concord runway.*
7 *Looking north at the Buffalo Hump/Concord airstrip.*

Cook Ranch |

Cook Ranch owner (1973–88) Harold Thomas in April 1968 with his Cessna 180 (N699HR) at Cold Meadows.

R. Thomas

Located at the head of Big Mallard Creek, the Cook Ranch was first occupied by Pete Mallard, an area prospector. In the 1910s Vic Bargamin and Edwin C. Harbison followed Mallard to the property. The two trapped and hunted from the location, eking out a humble living.

By 1914 the two had patented land next to each other. On the western portion of their spread was a residence, chicken coop, barn, and milk house, while the eastern parcel contained a separate residence and barn.[10]

It is believed that during the Bargamin and Harbison partnership that Bargamin inhabited the eastern buildings, while Harbison, more the farmer, used the other larger complex. Apparently Bargamin's home contained living quarters on the second floor, while the main level served as a crude general store for people passing through. Bargamin also had a packstring, which he used to distribute Harbison's farm goods to area residents.[11]

In 1930 Harbison sold both properties to Marcus Cook and it became known as the Cook Ranch. In 1952 Harvey Avon Hill bought the place.[12] Hill modified the meadow into an airstrip and used it frequently to access the property with a Piper Cub (N40912). The airstrip remains largely unchanged since its construction. It is more or less an unimproved meadow. Hill retained the Cook Ranch name and headquartered his outfitting business at the property,

living the remainder of the year in Nampa.

In May 1964 Hill took off from the Grangeville airport headed for the Allison Ranch on the Main Salmon River, where he was helping John Cook with the building of a runway (no relation to Marcus Cook). Hill encountered poor weather and was unable to land at area airstrips due to fog. With the designated landing areas socked in and his destination unreachable, he opted to make an emergency landing on the Dixie Road. His attempt was unsuccessful and he crashed off the road into tall trees on Jack Mountain. The blue and white plane was spotted two days later by an Elk City resident and Hill was found dead.[13]

In 1970, Hill's widow Dorothy sold the ranch to Maurice "Bud" Painter and partner Del Holbza of Nampa. Harold Thomas purchased the ranch three years later. Thomas first flew to the ranch in his Cessna 180 (N699HR) with Sid Hinkle, who showed him how to follow a foot trail into the ranch as a good landing approach to the runway. After his first landing Thomas used a mower to define the usable portion of the meadow. During the winter he accessed the ranch with a Piper Super Cub (N4248M) on skis.[14]

The roughly 2000' Cook Ranch airstrip situated parallel to Big Mallard Creek. The ranch's building complex (right) is located to the north of the airstrip.

When Thomas bought the ranch very little had been done to the property and all the original homestead structures were intact, but very run down. Deciding the original buildings were beyond repair, he hired Ralph Gormley of Elk City to manage the property and construct a new lodge. Gormley and his brother did a beautiful job salvaging many of the logs from the historic Harbison barn. Since the lodge completion, several other buildings have been added.[15]

In the mid-1980s Thomas wanted to concentrate on improving his Allison Ranch property and sold the Cook Ranch to a group of investors. However, he got it back rather quickly for lack of payment. In 1988 he was able to make a final sale.[16] The property then exchanged hands a few more times until Don and Ann Eberle purchased it in the early 2000s. Eberle, a retired United Airlines captain, accesses the ranch with a Cessna 185 (N3370S).[17]

The Eberles cleaned the place up after years of neglect by past owners, and focused on improving the airstrip. They brought in a few pieces of equipment at the time of their purchase. Eberle has since widened and lengthened the runway to approximately 2000'.[18]

Looking north at the USFS Dixie airfield. In the upper center of the photograph the town of Dixie is visible.

DIXIE RANGER STATION

This site was first used by the USFS for administrative purposes in 1922 and was known as the Dixie Meadows Ranger Station. Two years later, construction of a log ranger's house and tack shed was begun. Since the initial buildings were erected, the USFS added an office building (1926), commissary (1926), cookhouse (1931), barn (1931), root cellar (1934), cabin (1934), oil house (1936), and pump house (1940). The original 1924 structures were removed at some point and in the 1950s several more buildings were added to the site. In 1968 the Dixie and Red River Ranger Districts were consolidated and the Dixie Ranger Station became a firefighting base and summer work center.

Airstrip construction at the station was started in 1930 and finished the following year. It was one of the first runways completed in Region 1. The original north-south strip first measured 2400' long. To improve fire suppression efforts and the efficiency of transporting freight to the facility, the field was extended in 1942 to a total length of 3200'. The same summer, Johnson Flying Service flew two Ford Tri-Motors to the strip. They were the first planes to land on the new field. In the fall of 1955 the USFS further improved the runway by realigning and extending it to 4500' in length.

The Dixie Ranger Station in 1935.

B. Wilson

Holm

1 *The first Ford Tri-Motors to land at the airstrip in 1942.*
2 *In 1968 the station became a guard facility for firefighters and summer work crews.*
3 *Looking south at the 4500' Dixie USFS airstrip.*

Holm

Looking north up Crooked Creek at the town of Dixie. The runway is to the right on the east side of the creek.

DIXIE TOWN

In August of 1862 two Euro-Americans first discovered gold at the current location of Dixie. One of the men was Frank Benedict and the other remains nameless. The gold rush in the area followed soon after. There are two stories on how Dixie earned its name. The first version is that the two prospectors were southern sympathizers and so named it. The second version is that the hometown of one of the prospectors was Dixie, Georgia.[19] Whatever version one believes the town formed north and south along Crooked Creek, with development spilling over to the west as well.

The town grew and shrank over the years, but a few people always remained. Jack and Zip Wenzel, who owned the Sportsman Club tavern, purchased the original townsite in 1954. The area totaled about 153 acres and the couple began selling lots for $25 apiece. In the beginning nobody would buy, but by the time the Wenzels retired in 1980 the investment had paid off.[20]

In 1965 Wenzel decided to make the lots and surrounding area more attractive to prospective buyers by creating air access directly in town. Helping Wenzel was local pilot Sid Hinkle. Wenzel and Hinkle determined the old Burrows and Beller placer part of the town would be a well-suited location for an airstrip. The location also had good material, which was flattened to a hard runway surface.[21] With the ball rolling, Wenzel hired local cat skinner Harold

"Pete" Peterson to work the ground, moving the old dredge material.[22]

In the process of building the south end of the strip toward the ranger station, Peterson started pushing and leveling material that was not a part of Wenzel's property. The USFS showed up and put a halt to it; hence the still visible incline on the end of the runway.

In 1966 when the airstrip was finished, Hinkle was the first to land at the site with his Cessna 185 (N9808X). Wenzel and Hinkle bought a road grader that was also used on local roads, and used it to smooth the surface. The final length of the runway was 3000'.

In 1992 Jack Wenzel died at the age of seventy-nine. Zip then sold the airstrip in 2002 to Jerry McCullough of Ellensburg, Washington, who

Both photographs show downtown Dixie circa 1937 – these original buildings no longer exist.

Jack Wenzel at the Dixie Town airstrip in the early 1960s with Sid Hinkle's Cessna 185 (N9808X).

Sid Hinkle visits with Jack Wenzel in Dixie.

has a second home in Dixie. McCullough did not really want to have his own airstrip, but as a pilot he heard a rumor of another person buying the land with plans to develop a portion of the runway.

During the big fire year of 2007 when most of the town was wrapped in fireproof material, USFS fire crews came into do additional pre-suppression activity, removing hundreds of dead trees and other fuel loads. The USFS could not get the fuel removed fast enough and needed a staging area to store it and run it though chipping machines. Based on a handshake with the USFS, McCullough gave them permission to use the runway with the requirement that they were responsible to repair any damage.[23]

As McCullough predicted, substantial harm was inflicted to the runway surface. However, it turned out to be one of the best handshakes he ever

made as the USFS re-leveled and graded the whole airstrip. No work had been done since the late 1960s and it ended up being better than when he purchased it. In more recent years the strip has seen a decline in use and McCullough is the only resident in Dixie who actively uses it to access the town. As did Sid Hinkle, McCullough flies a Cessna 185 (N93943).[24]

357

Jerry McCullough and his Cessna 185 at Dixie in 2005.

Looking down Crooked Creek at the 3000' Dixie runway.

Facing north at the Dixie airstrip.

Holm

Looking south down the current 2600' Elk City airstrip on a foggy day.

ELK CITY
The Original Airstrip

The first landing site for airplanes in Elk City was a field located two miles north of town below and parallel to Ericson Ridge.[25] The field, measuring 2100' long, was in use circa 1930. The York family used this field privately for many years.[26]

Elk Valley Community Club Airstrip

In 1911 O. P. Langton settled the land where the airfield is currently located. The property changed hands several times before being purchased by H. W. McFarland in 1923. In 1930 Allen Manes bought the acreage and then Warren Bullock and James Dyer eventually acquired it.[27]

In 1947 several community leaders collaborated on the idea of building a town airstrip. The leaders formed the Elk Valley Community Club, a group focused on runway creation. Included in the group were Paul Filer, Ole Johnson, Dave Schwarz, Con Nitz, Jack Fisher, Bill Bullock, and Marlin Galbraith. The two owners agreed to sell the land at a discounted price of $5 an acre to the club.[28]

By the fall of 1948 the group was able to purchase most of the land and found companies to donate equipment and time to help with construction. In the spring of 1949 the Warren Creek Dredging Company provided several pieces of equipment and many locals provided the labor to start the clearing process.[29]

The group ran into several drawbacks and was only able to create a 1400' long runway instead

of the intended 2500'. By the fall of 1949 several successful landings had been made.[30] In 1971 government money was funneled to the community to help improve the airstrip facility. By the end of the year the runway was extended to its current length of 2600'.[31]

On August 13, 1956, Johnson Flying Service pilot Frank Small, who was flying Travel Air 6000 NC447W, used the Elk City field. After dropping two Missoula smokejumpers on a fire near Running Creek, Small was returning to Grangeville with spotter Mike Malone riding in the right seat. As they neared Elk City, Small told Malone that he felt faint and ill. They quickly figured out Small was experiencing a heart attack. Malone was not a pilot, but remained in the airplane instead of jumping with his chute. Small spotted the Elk City airfield and managed to land the airplane. As he opened the door and his feet touched the ground he stumbled and then collapsed.[32]

Malone notified the authorities and Frank Hill from Grangeville flew in Dr. D. J. Soltman, but it was too late. At the age of fifty Small had already died at the airstrip. The same day Johnson Flying Service sent an airplane down from Missoula, and pilot Penn Stohr Sr. retrieved the Travel Air and Small's body for funeral services in Missoula.[33]

Johnson Flying Service Ford Tri-Motor N7861 parked at the American River Lumber Company airstrip after the forced landing. The man is pointing to where a portion of the propeller blade shot through the side of the aircraft. Also notice the punctured tire caused by the engine-tilting forward.

The broken piece of the propeller blade blew a hole in the side of the fuselage where the man is holding his hardhat. The projectile then shot through the bottom of the left wing and out the top.

Pilot Frank Borgeson (left) examines the engine he lost from the Ford.

American River Lumber Company Airstrip

In the 1950s an additional airstrip owned by the American River Lumber Company was built west of Elk City, paralleling the current main road. This field was used in connection with their business and occasionally used by others with permission.

In early September 1963 a fire call came into the Grangeville smokejumpers requesting a jump near the Trilby Lakes area over fifty miles to the southeast. Johnson Flying Service of Missoula assigned Frank Borgeson with Ford Tri-Motor N7861 to fulfill the Grangeville jumper contract that year. When the call came in, seven jumpers on the callboard readied their gear and loaded up. Borgeson cranked up the three radials and they headed for the fire. Acting as spotter in the right seat was Ted Nyquest.[34]

Enjoying the cool September air over the Idaho mountains, the old Ford and its crew cruised along nicely until reaching Elk City. As the plane approached the little mining town, twenty odd miles short of their destination a huge explosion shook the aircraft, followed by a violent vibration. Borgeson and Nyquest turned their attention to the right outboard engine. The big radial was tilted forward and the cowling was seconds from shaking off. Trailing behind the crippled engine were sparks and raw gas streaming out of a broken fuel line. Borgeson instantly shut the fuel off to the engine. Then the engine slanted forward even more and the propeller sliced into the right main tire, whacking off a big chuck of rubber, without puncturing the inner tube. Next the whole engine broke away from the mounts, severing all the actuating cables as it plunged to the earth.[35]

It was later discovered that the engine landed in a muddy area close to the log deck at the American River Lumber Company. Parts of the engine were also located along the nearby road.

Borgeson focused on keeping the Ford airborne while Nyquest turned to the back to inform the jumpers to bailout, but most were already out of the door. After all the jumpers exited the airplane, Nyquest rearranged the cargo upon Borgeson's request so he could better control the airplane. Next Nyquest got on the radio and made a mayday call.[36]

By this time Borgeson had set up to make an emergency landing at the American River Lumber Company airstrip. He nursed the Ford down to the runway almost coming up short, but not quite. As the right wheel hit the dirt the exposed tire tube blew, sending the plane into a full 360-degree ground loop. However, it stayed upright.[37]

After the dust settled Borgeson and Nyquest began to inspect the airplane and noticed holes in both sides of the fuselage behind the bulkhead. It became clear that several inches of one propeller blade broke off, causing the engine vibration. Additional holes were located where the propeller tip had shot through the bottom of the left wing and exited out the top after being hurled through the fuselage. Moments before the incident occurred smokejumper Bill Locklear, who had been sitting behind the bulkhead, moved to the back of the airplane after growing tired of sitting on a chainsaw box. Had Locklear remained in the same location, the prop tip would have struck him.[38]

Dispatched to help repair the wounded aircraft were Johnson mechanics Gene Ball and Ed Lonnevik. The only replacement engine they had on hand was a Pratt & Whitney R-985; a very different engine from the other two mounted on N7861, which were Wright R-975s. The mechanics had little choice and loaded additional welding materials in the company pickup to fabricate the necessary modifications for the dissimilar engine. It did not take long for the field repairs to be made. After a thorough ground check days later, Borgeson flew the Ford back to Missoula where the other two engines were updated to matching R-985s.

FLORENCE/ IDAHO MINING AND MILLING INC.

A 2011 close-up of the overgrown runway.

In the early 1860s the Florence area was part of a large mining boom. Gold was first discovered in the basin in August 1861. News about the findings leaked and a town quickly grew. Among one of the first residents was Dr. Ferber who named the town Florence in honor of his adopted daughter.[39] The town rapidly went bust and many moved on to other mining districts, such as Warren and Idaho City. A second smaller boom occurred ten years later. By the 1930s a few dozen people continued living and prospecting in the area.[40] Not much remains of this mining development except for a unique cemetery.

In the late 1950s, Philip Jungert, owner and operator of Idaho Mining and Milling, Inc., began an effort to develop Jungert Mine, located a mile north of the old Florence townsite. The company believed a large of amount of gold remained along Meadow Creek. In 1959 the outfit constructed a sawmill, office, lodge, and equipment shed. The following year a large dredge from Warren was relocated to the site.[41]

Active dredging occurred from 1961 through 1962. After the machine moved material in 1961, a dozer leveled tailings and created an airstrip. The runway was used by the Lewiston-based mining company through the mid-1960s. At the same time the runway was roughed in, operations were shut down because of conflicts with the Idaho Dredge Mining Protective Act.[42]

Threatened with closures and in need of money, Idaho Mining and Milling came up with a desperate scheme. Starting in July 1964 the business advertised 500 ten-acre mining claims for sale in the *Wall Street Journal*. In the July 22 edition of the paper a small spread appeared with photographs painting a flowery vision of owning a place in the "fresh Idaho mountains." The article even fully disclosed the conflict with the dredging act, but asserted that there was no problem with a small miner working his or her own claim. "It is the opinion of the company that small claim holders will not encounter difficulties mining on

Looking north at the Idaho Mining and Milling, Inc. Florence airstrip (center).

a small scale as the Idaho Dredge Mining Protective Act only applies to operations that have equipment capable of moving 500 cubic yards of earth material per day. The act does not apply to the small miner." The write-up also touts the ability to reach the claims with easy access by airplane, but stated, "The airport has been used but needs more work to put it in a safe, serviceable condition. The company will improve the airport and make it safe and serviceable after 100 ten-acre mining claims have been sold."[43]

Although creative, the scheme was not successful. More mineral testing was carried out, but the site was left undeveloped. In 1984, due to inactivity, the USFS requested that the claim owners remove all of the buildings. With no response from the mining company, the agency tore all the structures down in 1985–86. Cultural resource surveys conducted around the same time found evidence of earlier mining operations, mostly destroyed by the activity of the large dredge.[44] The relatively unfinished airfield has since grown in with trees.

Sid Hinkle in the cockpit of his Cessna 185 (N9808X) in the early 1960s.

MALLARD CREEK RANCH

George M. Annable first settled the property now known as the Mallard Creek Ranch. In February 1922 he received homestead approval for 159.68 acres. At the time of authorization Annable had built a main residence, cabin, and barn.[45] A story told about Annable is that at some point while on the ranch, he obtained a mail-order bride. She eventually arrived, but with a teenage daughter in tow. After some time the teenage daughter became pregnant. People connected the dots and the local authorities hauled Annable to the Idaho County Jail. While in jail he came to the conclusion that if he castrated himself that he might be let off. His jail surgery did not go well and he had to be taken to the local hospital after nearly bleeding to death.

In 1931 after Annable's issues the property was sold to L. Balanski. During his four-year ownership he built a beautiful lodge measuring roughly 25' X 40' on the northern portion of the property. The lodge had concrete footings combined with stone floors and on one end it had a huge fireplace.

In 1937 Floyd and Goldie Dale purchased the place. While the Dales owned the ranch, an agreement was made with the government to put a road through the property. In 1944 Chester Haight bought the acreage and sold it by the mid-1950s to Clement Zelinski. During Zelinski's ownership he raised cattle and farmed the old homestead living at the place year-round. He even held an annual rodeo on the property in July that was mainly attended by residents of Elk City. To supplement his income he was an outfitter and guide for a few years. It is rumored that some of his guests became cold and cut out a few beams in the lodge for firewood, not knowing they were major support beams. The place eventually collapsed under heavy winter snows.

At some point a caretaker's cabin was also

Holm

The structure near the south end of the airstrip that was once occupied by Jack Eagle.

added to the property near the south end of the airstrip. Around the time of Zelinski's ownership a bachelor named Jack Eagle from Mount Idaho began occupying the cabin. The front room contained a circular fireplace with a large metal hood that funneled toward the ceiling eventually forming the chimney. Eagle was so lazy that he just threw his garbage out the window on one side of the building. The trash, mainly whiskey and beer bottles, reached such a height that it nearly came back in the window when it was opened.

In 1962 Sid Hinkle purchased the property. He and Bob Black came in and cleaned the place up. The big pile of alcohol bottles was buried with a D6 Caterpillar borrowed from Clyde Baker. At the same time an informal runway was roughed in, measuring 1200' long. Hinkle later extended the north end of the strip, bringing it to a total length of 2500'.

After constructing the initial airstrip, Hinkle leased the property to Herman Konrad of Stites, Idaho. Konrad and his two brothers operated an outfitting and guiding business at the location from 1964 through 1985. Often Hinkle would fly in toward the end of hunting season and haul out all the deer and elk hides. The return on the hides was not much, but he would donate the money to a local charity in Grangeville.[46]

Hinkle's original plan for the property was to create a backcountry fly-in destination. Fulfilling this goal, he subdivided the ranch into several-acre lots. The first sales started in the mid-1970s and steadily continued through the early 1990s.

At about the same time as Hinkle's development another 106.12 acre homestead to the north also became subdivided. In 1922 William M. Logan patented this parcel.[47] The two parcels currently appear as a single development.

Several owners have come and gone since Hinkle created the subdivision. Harvey Blake of Montana lived here full-time for a few years. Dr. Bob Olsen of Lewiston has maintained a second home for several decades and spends much of the summer at his Mallard Creek property. Even though the area has had continual interest, very few of the lot owners have used it as a fly-in development.[48]

Jim Babb of Grangeville was one of the few owners to access the property by air. Babb and his wife first bought at Mallard Creek in the late 1970s with another family. Babb flew regularly to the property using Piper Super Cub N3761Z and Cessna 182 N3063F. Eventually he acquired another lot, but about the same time a dispute arose among cabin owners concerning the function and safety of the airfield. Babb later sold due to the issue. However, others interested in the aviation aspect of the place remained. Dr. Robert Iacono of Southern California, who also owned the Running Creek Ranch had property here and would stop occasionally in his Cessna 180 (see Running Creek for more information). Also adding to the aircraft list were partners from Utah that flew to Mallard Creek in a Cessna 210.[49]

Looking south down the 2500' Mallard Creek runway.

A view to the north up the Mallard Creek airfield.

Looking north-northeast at the 2800' Orogrande runway.

OROGRANDE

The town of Orogrande originated in the mid-1860s along with other mining booms in the region. The area had several well-developed mines that processed mainly gold, but also silver. Various types of mining occurred, including placer, hydraulic, dredge, and cyanide leaching. Some production continued into the 1940s.[50]

The Jerry Walker Cabin in 2004.

Jerry Walker (left) donated his cabin in the 1980s to the USFS. In this 1964 photograph Walker stands with Grangeville pilots Bob Black Sr. and Jr. with their Cessna 170 (N2423D).

In 1959, roughly three miles north of the townsite, the USFS built an airstrip on an unpatented mining claim worked by Vernon and Clair Finch of Spokane. The runway was scraped in with heavy equipment, using old mine tailings. The 2800' long strip had little use and went off the radar for many aviation enthusiasts. In the 1990s interest in the field was re-kindled by the Idaho Department of Transportation Division of Aeronautics. With the cooperation of the USFS, the runway was reactivated.[51]

Off the north end of the strip, the IDFG operates a fish hatchery. The historic Jerry Walker Cabin stands southwest on the other side of the road that parallels the runway.

In about 1930 Shorty McMillian built the Walker Cabin. McMillian used the place as a residence while working on the Washington Water Power Dam located on the South Fork of the Clearwater River. In 1963 the dam was removed with dynamite.[52]

After the dam was finished, McMillian occupied the cabin during summers until he sold the lease circa 1960 to Jerry Walker of Grangeville. By the early 1980s the Nez Perce NF refused to renew recreational leases. Fearing that the historic cabin would be destroyed, Walker decided to donate it to the USFS. Embracing the idea, the agency continued maintenance and made the structure available to the public through their recreational rental program.[53]

The 2500' Red River Ranch runway (center) situated parallel to Red River and the main road.

RED RIVER |

The USFS tried for several years to locate a suitable site for an airfield near the Red River Ranger Station. Most of the locales found to be suitable for the project were on private ground. The idea for the project was sparked when Nez Perce NF Supervisor A. N. Cochrell came across a memo revealing how Air Force personnel from Geiger Field during World War II had built airstrips as part of their training program. Three airfields were constructed in Region 1 under this program, two on the Coeur d' Alene NF and one on the Kaniksu NF. What really caught his interest was the aspect of free labor.[54]

Starting in 1945 Cochrell began writing the regional office about the possibility of getting a similar project arranged for the Nez Perce NF. The regional office agreed that an airfield in the vicinity of Red River and Elk City would greatly aid in fire suppression efforts. A trail of correspondence concerning the matter continued into the late 1950s, even though the Air Force showed no interest in the project from the beginning.[55]

In 1945 and 1946 the USFS narrowed the scope of possible airfield locations down to three. The main determining factors on the sites were the willingness of the private owner to sell, the cost, and the amount of money it would take to build on the site since most of the three had wet meadow areas.[56]

One location contemplated was southwest of Red River Hot Springs near Shissler Creek. This site was dismissed because of the amount of fill it was going to take to make it usable, and the approach

to the northwest was crowded.[57] The second area considered was located along Red River at Galena Creek.[58] This was the USFS's most-favored location. The third site surveyed was along Red River northwest of the ranger station near Bronco Creek. Concerning this location the USFS noted, "The ground appears to be dry. Construction costs will be light. The approaches are crowded on both ends . . . Prevailing wind is from northwest. In general, it is not a desirable site for a landing field."[59]

Ironically out of all the sites looked at, the latter is where the only airfield was built, but not by the USFS. The agency could never come to an agreement with any of the property owners or find the proper funding.

In the early 1960s Douglas Mullins constructed the 2500' airstrip built near Red River. Mullins and his wife Edith had a primary residence in Florida and in 1955 began spending summers in Idaho. In 1959 the

The Red River Ranch owned by the Mullins family.

Looking west-northwest at the Red River Ranch airstrip built by Douglas Mullins in the early 1960s.

two bought a cabin on the Nitz Ranch along Red River north of the runway.

Originally the property was three separate homesteads. In 1917 George Hill homesteaded one of the properties. The same year John Woods purchased the land from Hill and in 1923 received approval on another adjoining parcel of land. The following year Ernest Saunders combined these two properties with another early homestead. He sold the whole property to Donald Eason who in turn sold it in 1950 Jim and Ethel Lightfoot.[60] During their ownership the place became simply known as the Lightfoot Ranch. The Mullins then purchased the property from the Lightfoots and renamed it the Red River Ranch.[61]

Since the Mullins bought the place, they rebuilt one of the original homestead cabins and turned it into a guesthouse. The main house and associated structures built by the Saunders have been well maintained and updated over the years.[62]

Douglas Mullins owned and operated a large contracting and lumber business in Florida. With his background the building of a private airstrip was an easy task. Through many of their Idaho friends he was able to locate a few pieces of equipment. He then hired a USFS engineer to help him determine the grade, slope, and necessary drainage.

Mullins started flying after World War II, taking advantage of inexpensive lessons offered through the GI Bill. Over the years he owned several Cessnas and flew them to Idaho from Florida. Mullins became good friends with many local aviators, including Frank Hill and Sid Hinkle. In fact Mullins helped build the strip at Hinkle's Mallard Creek property.[63]

In 1977 Mullins purchased a new Cessna 182 registered as N182DM. Sadly he and Edith took off from the ranch one day and the plane crashed shortly thereafter. Their family who had seen them depart was aware that something went wrong. They gathered help and got to the plane as quickly as they could, but Douglas had died. Edith was in rough condition, but recovered from injuries. After the accident the strip was closed to fixed-winged aircraft. However, Edith continued to allow the occasional helicopter to land, under specific circumstances. In spite of the event, the Mullins family continues to enjoy the Red River Ranch each summer.

A late 1950s aerial looking down Moose Creek. Several of the drainage's private in-holdings and airstrips can be seen in the photograph. Both airstrips at Moose Creek Ranches are visible in the foreground. Farther downstream the clearing on the left is Jim Renshaw's Bitterroot Ranch, followed by the Seminole Ranch (right), and the cross-runways at the Moose Creek Ranger Station (left).

D. Hess

CHAPTER 8

SELWAY–
BITTERROOT
WILDERNESS

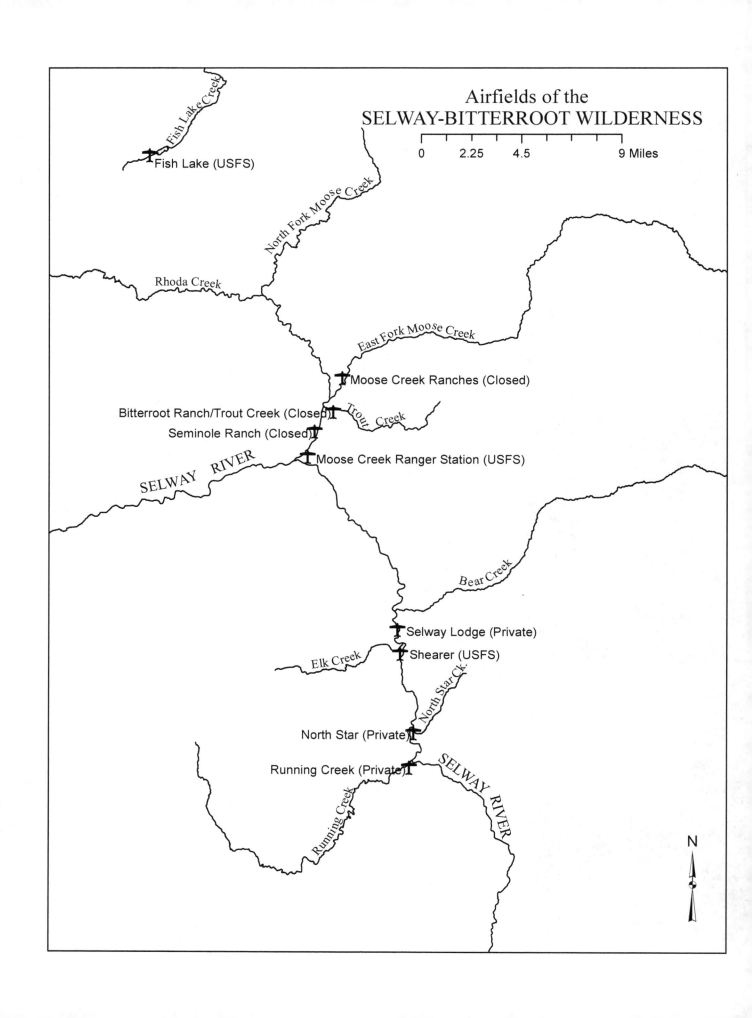

Airfields of the
SELWAY-BITTERROOT WILDERNESS

SELWAY-BITTERROOT WILDERNESS

SELWAY RIVER

NORTH STAR RANCH

The Early Years

Looking down North Star's primary airstrip in the spring of 1964.

In August 1924 William Reap homesteaded 113.98 acres at the confluence of North Star Creek and the Selway River.[1] Portions of this parcel were sold at various times from the 1930s through the 1940s to J. P. Harriman, M. F. Stewart, and R. E. Starb. This group came to form what Selway residents referred to as the "California Corporation." In 1935 Sid Poppe bought separate pieces of property at this location as well. Poppe's parents grew up on a ranch in Montana that was often visited by famous artist Charles Russell. Poppe worked for the USFS and frequently leased the North Star in-holdings to a variety of people. One family to lease the ranch was Archie and Midge Baldwin. The Baldwins attempted to buy the property while operating it as a dude ranch, but could not make ends meet.[2]

Wolfinbargers and an Airstrip

In the 1940s Richard "Ole" Wolfinbarger was hired as the caretaker of the California Corporation's part of North Star. Wolfinbarger first came to the Selway country when he worked odd jobs for the Renshaw family. At North Star the corporation allowed him in his spare time to do some guiding and cattle ranching. By the decade's end Wolfinbarger was joined by his nephew, Kenneth "Punk" Wolfinbarger.[3] Beginning in 1949 Ole was able to start buying portions of the ranch. Punk remained at North Star,

ultimately purchasing the property in 1966 from his uncle. In 1949 Punk had married Caroline Knapp and she lived with him at North Star until her death in 1982. In 1976 he sold a section of river frontage to the government and in 1992 another portion to Trust For Public Lands. After living most of his life at the property he moved to Victor, Montana, and in 1998 sold the ranch.[4] Punk died in June 2010 at the age of ninety while living in Victor.

In about 1958 Punk and Loren Newman, of Running Creek, walked a D2 Caterpillar in from the Paradise Guard Station to the ranch. They used the dozer to construct the main more east-west, roughly

1 *Kenneth "Punk" Wolfinbarger circa 1960.*
2 *The main lodge at the ranch in the early 1960s.*
3 *Buildings at North Star with guest cabins on the right.*
4 *An early 1960s aerial of the property showing the ranch complex along North Star Creek and the two runways to the right.*
5 *Jim Mitchell with his Cessna 185.*
6 *Sid Hinkle (left) and his Cessna 185 with Punk Wolfinbarger (center) and friend Fred Boynton at the ranch.*

900' airstrip. Newman and Wolfinbarger shared the D2 between North Star and Running Creek Ranches. Initially while at North Star it was used to upgrade the 1400' unimproved landing area situated in the lower hayfield that paralleled the river. Several trees were also cleared on the north end of the airstrip. This field was generally utilized only when wind conditions did not favor the formal runway. This Cat currently remains at the Running Creek property.[5]

Another D2 Dozer and Damaged Aircraft

When Moose Creek Ranches sold to the USFS, Wolfinbarger bought their old D2 Caterpillar. Once it was broken down into several pieces, neighbor Sid Hinkle flew it to North Star in his Cessna 185. In order to fit the blade into the airplane the two men cut it in half. The weld marks where it was put back together are still evident.[6]

Before the pair of Cat tracks was delivered to North Star, Hinkle flew them one trip at a time to Grangeville to have them rebuilt by Brown's Motors, the local Caterpillar dealer. Hinkle then transported the tracks one at a time to North Star, using his 185. On the first trip in he had the track sitting on a wooden plank. He figured the sheer weight would prevent it from moving if he got into any turbulence. His calculation went awry when he encountered some really bumpy air prior to his descent into the Selway River drainage near Wylies Peak. By the time he landed at North Star the headliner in the rear of the plane was torn and he had three fist-sized holes in the top of the fuselage from the track banging against it.[7]

Wolfinbarger used the D2 to keep his airstrips smooth, in addition to maintaining odds and ends around the ranch. Eventually Wolfinbarger started flying and bought a Piper Cub for which he built a little hangar on the upper end of the strip. Later on Wolfinbarger had a rough landing at the ranch and damaged the plane fairly badly. He and friend Dick Walker were able to move it to the hangar with the D2, where eventually the proper repairs were made. Not long after that Wolfinbarger purchased a Scout with a 180 horsepower engine.[8]

A Cessna With Bounce

Another interesting event at the ranch occurred when Jim Mitchell of Green Acres Flight Service came in to land on the short runway, flying a Cessna 185. On short final Mitchell noted he was coming in way too fast. At about the same time he was trying to correct his airspeed, he hit some terrible air, only worsening the already bad situation. Looking straight ahead, right through Wolfinbarger's living room window, he panicked and feared he might overrun the strip and crash into the house. Next he committed one of the biggest backcountry flying errors by firewalling the airplane for a go-around. The plane wallowed back into the air right in the face of the towering terrain. With the help of the engine and propeller torque, he quickly turned the airplane to the left toward North Star Creek. In the midst of the turn the Cessna's main wheels impacted the face of the smooth hillside, loading the spring gear and ricocheting the plane back into the air toward the river. With little time to ponder how in the world he was still in the air, Mitchell regained control of the airplane, caught his breath, and went around again and landed. Wolfinbarger stood outside his house with his jaw on the ground watching the whole event unfold.[9]

More Recent Years

In 1998 Donald "Gus" Denton and several members of the Athens family from Tulsa, Oklahoma, purchased North Star. Denton and his family own and operate the Lochsa Lodge in north central Idaho along Highway 12. For several hunting seasons after the group acquired North Star they leased it to outfitters and guides. However, in more recent years it is only used privately.[10]

A 2012 view of North Star.

RUNNING CREEK RANCH

The Early Years

Looking downstream at the Running Creek Ranch circa 1960.

Thomas Running is the first known Euro-American to occupy the now Running Creek Ranch.[11] Circa 1910 Martin R. Moe followed Running and attempted to homestead the property but was unsuccessful. Francis "Frank" Horrace then moved onto the parcel and filed a homestead application for 107.72 acres. When the land was surveyed in 1916, Horrace was living in a 12' X 14' log cabin and had three acres under cultivation. In March 1927 Horrace received his homestead approval for only 67.23 acres.[12] By the early 1920s Horrace was joined by his brother Bill. The two improved the ranch, building several structures, clearing fields for growing hay, and ran some cattle. Due to the Horrace brothers' failing health, Fred Kottbey purchased the ranch in 1948 and later sold it in 1951 to Art E. Wilcox.[13]

A few years passed and Wilcox sold the parcel to Ace J. Hewitt of Elk City and Joe McCarthy, a sawmill owner from Orofino. In 1957 Loren "Lynn" Newman then purchased Hewitt's half of the property. A little over a year later Newman was able to buy McCarthy's half, wanting to have complete control of the ranch. According to Newman he worked McCarthy a little, "Mr. McCarthy was afraid of rattlesnakes so every time I saw him I buttered him up with a dandy rattlesnake tale, which seemed to help the negotiations immensely."[14]

Loren Newman, an Airstrip, and the Mattesons

Newman bought the Running Creek property after living twelve years in Alaska, where he was a heavy equipment operator in the summer and trapped the Sheenjek River country in the winter. Newman grew up in northern Wisconsin and dreamed of the mountains. At the age of sixteen he moved to Wyoming, working as a ranch hand and outfitting in the fall. Eager to get back to his reason for moving west he wanted to start outfitting and guiding again.[15]

Newman worked with the Wolfinbargers of the North Star Ranch, running an outfitting business. In about 1958 the partners bought a D2 Caterpillar and hauled it to the Paradise Guard Station. From Paradise the two men walked it up the mountain, down Bad Luck Creek, around and over Gardner Peak, then down the ridge to the North Star Ranch. The whole trip went without problems except for throwing a track off on Bad Luck Creek, which cost them a day in repairs. For Newman and Wolfinbarger it only reinforced the name of the creek.[16]

The two business partners walked the Cat back and forth between Running Creek and North Star across the Selway River by loosening the fan belt and putting a plastic bag over the oil filler tube. Newman stated, "When the little dozer got into deep water it made like a submarine and worked great."[17]

Shortly after walking the D2 in, Newman built the runway at Running Creek, making the first landing here with his personally-owned Piper PA-18. Newman operated this same airplane regularly from North

Newman and Wolfinbargers' business card for their outfitting service.

Loren "Lynn" Newman at the Running Creek Ranch.

Star's hayfield until his strip was finished. Soon after completing the Running Creek airstrip he extended the lower portion in September 1960, which brought the field to its present length of 2000'.[18]

In addition to the construction of the runway, Newman did some fencing and built two sheds for maintaining his stock. In 1962 with talk of the Selway area becoming a designated wilderness, Newman was worried about having his grazing rights cut off. With the chance of losing the grazing for his horses, he sold the ranch to George M. Matteson. Newman then moved full-time to a nice spread near Culdesac, Idaho, where he eventually retired.[19]

Matteson and wife Doreen "Dody" were from Los Angeles, California, where he retired from his career as a test pilot for North American Aviation (Rockwell). Over the course of his ownership he had three different Cessna 185s. He was very proficient with instruments and even devised his own instrument

approach into the ranch.[20] He kept the place for several years until selling half the property in 1975 to Edward Houghton. A few years later Houghton bought the remaining portion of the ranch, while other sections were sold to the USFS.[21] Houghton then built a log home about a half-mile up Running Creek above the main complex of buildings.

Hornocker Wildlife Institute

In 1988 Houghton split the ranch in half and gifted one portion to the Hornocker Wildlife Institute headed by Dr. Maurice Hornocker. During the institutes tenure many wilderness research projects were conducted, ranging from invasive plant species to animal population studies. Most notably the ranch served as a holding area for problem wolves during the initial 1990s reintroduction. Another noteworthy project conducted by the institute at Running Creek was the study of wilderness vegetation changes in relation to the decline of elk populations.[22]

The institute was eventually forced to sell, as the Houghtons wanted out of the other portion of the ranch. Dr. Hornocker went ahead with the purchase of the remaining piece, which helped him stall for time in his efforts to find matching funds. To his dismay, the funds were not located and he was forced to put the entire ranch on the market.[23]

The Iacono Years

In the spring of 1998 Dr. Robert "Bob" Iacono purchased the ranch from the Institute.[24] He spent a few short years visiting Running Creek, piloting a Cessna 180 (N4569B) to access the property. Several area residents and pilots witnessed his wild and crazy flying in the backcountry. Rumors circulated that several reports were filed with the FAA for his antics.

Jim Eldredge of McCall, a logger, contractor, and backcountry pilot became acquainted with Iacono when he first arrived in Idaho looking for property. In fact Eldredge introduced the Running Creek acreage to him and in the end worked on several projects at the ranch, freighting material with his own Cessna 180 (N2984C).[25]

One of the major undertakings at the property involved building an irrigation system to water the runway and surrounding areas. Eldredge was hired to help on the endeavor. Upon arrival he found that Iacono had already hauled in several twenty-foot lengths of four-inch aluminum irrigation pipe. Eldredge asked him how he had managed to transport the large pieces to the ranch. Iacono explained that he had flown them in from Hamilton and was headed back for more. Eldredge remained confused, as there was no possible way that twenty-foot sections of pipe would fit in a Cessna 180. Iacono further clarified that he did not fit them inside the 180 but was strapping three sections on each side of the airplane to the strut and the horizontal stabilizer. Since the aircraft's doors would not open with this configuration he crawled through the left side window. In disbelief Eldredge made an effort to explain just how dangerous it was to secure things to the outside of the plane, particularly heavy objects far aft of the aircraft's center of gravity, let alone on the horizontal stabilizer.[26]

Iacono shrugged it off and said he was headed back for more. Throughout the course of the day he brought in enough twenty-foot sections to run the length of the 2000' runway. On the last load Iacono stacked seven sections of pipe on each side and admitted to Eldredge that he barely made the landing at the ranch, nearly stalling the plane several times. While owning the property Iacono hauled in other oversized items to the property tied to the outside of the airplane and it somehow always worked out.[27]

Another incident involving Iacono occurred in April 2005 when Eldredge received a call requesting his help. Iacono and his family had landed at the closed Seminole Ranch airstrip on lower Moose Creek. While taxiing for takeoff at the top of the steep runway, he abruptly hit the brakes while turning the airplane downhill. The plane nosed over damaging one propeller blade and a wing tip. The weather was poor and he had no survival gear with him. In need of help he hiked downstream to the Moose Creek Ranger Station and was able to get ahold of Eldredge in McCall. The weather was terrible and Eldredge called several other operators in other towns to see if they could provide any assistance, but weather was also an issue for them. Looking for any kind of relief, Eldredge eventually made contact with the Selway Lodge and described the situation. They assured Eldredge that Iacono was fine as they had just seen his 180 fly by the lodge headed for Running Creek.[28]

Soon after the incident Iacono explained to Eldredge that he had fixed the airplane enough to fly it back to his ranch. Eldredge shaking his head wondered how someone could justify taking the risk of flying an airplane with a bent propeller and a bad wingtip with passengers. Iacono reasoned that he had straightened the blade out enough by bending it with the aid of a fence post. He had to confess the plane shook and vibrated horribly, but got them home to the ranch.[29]

On June 16, 2007 a different kind flying claimed his life at age fifty-five. While en route from Los Angeles to Mississippi he crashed his twin-engine Beechcraft Baron (N6750R) into the western side of a mountain in New Mexico's Sandia Mountains.[30]

Iacono was a successful neurosurgeon who created a national reputation for himself during the early 1990s while practicing and researching at Loma Linda University Medical Center. He was best known for performing a controversial surgical procedure called pallidotomy on patients with Parkinson's Disease. At the time of his death he was adding the finishing touches to his book, *Reversing Parkinson's Stress and Aging* that discussed his surgical procedures and medical findings.[31] Iacono left the ranch to his children after his death. It has since been leased to various groups and is maintained by caretakers.

1 *Newman's Piper PA-18 parked about halfway down the Running Creek airstrip.*
2 *A view upstream at the Running Creek Ranch and the 2000' runway.*
3 *The Running Creek airstrip from the cockpit of Newman's Piper PA-18.*
4 *George Matteson and Punk Wolfinbarger with Matteson's Cessna 185 N8723Z.*
5 *The Running Creek barn.*

379

SELWAY LODGE

The Early Years

The Alvin Renshaw family at the 51 Ranch in 1935 (l to r): Billie, Alvin, Jim, Jean, and Elna.

In 1898 William Wylie first occupied the property now known as Selway Lodge. He and Frank Harsh built a cabin and, similar to others in the area, ran a cattle operation. Henry Pettibone, who was also in the cattle business, eventually acquired the place and in 1919 received homestead approval for 91.02 acres. His partnership in the cattle operation with his relative George Shissler dissolved after the severe winter of 1916–17. Pettibone's brother Rufus moved in with him and they made many enhancements to the property.[32]

In 1931 at age seventy-three Pettibone decided to sell his ranch to Alvin Renshaw, as he was beginning to have health problems. In the fall of 1931 Pettibone set out to leave the Selway country by way of an airplane from the newly constructed Moose Creek Ranger Station airstrip.[33] However, he never quite made it to Moose Creek, as he died October 21 of a heart attack at the Bear Creek Ranger Station. Pettibone was buried at the top of his homestead overlooking the land he had worked for many years.[34]

Alvin Renshaw's 51 Ranch

In the spring of 1932 Alvin Renshaw packed his family up the Selway River Trail and moved into what was referred-to then as the Pettibone Ranch. Renshaw renamed the property 51 Ranch after buying two packstrings from the Decker brothers who were going out of business. Included in the purchase was their brand name "51." Although Renshaw never registered the brand, he found the name fitting for his ranch and outfitting business.

Renshaw and his family had many fruitful and difficult years at the ranch. By about 1937 Renshaw finished a new home and had modified several of the existing Wylie and Pettibone structures.[35] The 51 Ranch became a destination hunting and fishing location.

The entire family worked hard to attain success, and the nearby Shearer airfield was a great asset. When the field was finished in 1934, customers could fly to one of the most remote parts of the United States with relative ease. Then when they arrived they were greeted with great accommodations and world-class fishing and hunting. In reference to the 51 Ranch, backcountry pilot and author Charles Duus wrote in his book *Soaring with Eagles*, "It became one of the best-known wilderness lodges in Idaho . . . A guest could fly his trophy elk out of the wilderness in a matter of hours. Very few hunters went home empty-handed."[36]

While the Renshaws used the Shearer airfield for business, it was also used for emergencies. One of the more heartbreaking family experiences at the ranch occurred in June 1939 when their youngest Bobby became ill. The Renshaws chartered a plane to take Bobby to Kooskia for medical attention. Sadly, no diagnosis could be determined and at one year of age he died and was buried in the Kooskia cemetery.[37]

The Renshaw built lodge circa 1940. Construction on the place started in 1934 and was finished in the fall of 1937.

An early 1940s view looking upstream at the ranch where the current runway is now situated.

Building the thriving ranch required outside help. During the Depression, Renshaw often put a roof over a young man's head and food on the table as payment for a hard days work. Many came and went in this fashion. Harry Nielson was one such man. In fact he even built a small cabin on the ranch below the present day airfield. The building was later moved during World War II to an upper part of the property. In 1940 Nielson, along with the Renshaws, played an important part in a rescue mission in the Selway-Bitterroot area. On July 15, 1940 Johnson Flying Service Travel Air NC450N piloted by Robert Maricich was dropping supplies on a fire near White Cap Creek.[38] After two passes over the drop zone and coordinating with cargo kicker Del Claybaugh, it was determined from the drift chutes that in order to get an accurate drop the plane would have to be maneuvered to a lower altitude.

Maricich positioned the Travel Air accordingly for a third and final pass, which proved disastrous. The plane hit a pocket of turbulent air followed by a huge downdraft that pushed the aircraft into an unmanageable sink. Trying to counteract the problem, Maricich shoved the throttle wide open, but it was too late. The plane struck some treetops and cartwheeled into a shallow pond. Maricich was killed instantly and Claybaugh was knocked unconscious.

Harry Nielson was manning nearby Cub Point Lookout and reported the accident to the Moose Creek Ranger Station over the telephone. Nielson wanting to help the occupants of the aircraft asked permission from the district ranger to leave his post. His request was denied. Risking his job with the USFS and in outrage, Nielson told the ranger he quit and headed to the scene of the accident to help.

At about the same time Nielson arrived and was giving first aid to Claybaugh, a Johnson Flying Service plane piloted by Earl Vance was circling above. Shortly thereafter, smokejumper Chet Derry parachuted down to help. This was the first rescue jump preformed by a smokejumper. After Derry was safely on the ground the plane dropped more supplies, including a radio, which enabled the two men to communicate that Maricich was dead.

Word reached 51 Ranch and the USFS requested Alvin Renshaw to retrieve the men and the body from the small pond roughly two miles southeast of Cub Point Lookout. Renshaw readied his packstring to rescue the men.[39] Meantime Dr. Ohlmacher was flown to Shearer so he could meet the rescue crew returning with the injured Claybaugh. It was treacherous terrain from the end of the trail down to the crash site, but Renshaw and the others were successful in their efforts and made it back to the ranch where everyone involved was flown out from the Shearer airfield.[40]

Alvin and his wife Elna reared five children at the remote ranch, ran a successful business, and enjoyed the lifestyle. In 1948 Alvin developed back problems and Elna became quite ill with tuberculosis. Looking for a way to move closer to town Alvin and Elna offered to sell the ranch and business to their sixteen-year-old son Jim. Although Jim enjoyed their way of life, he was too young to know what he wanted and could not see a future in the ownership at the time.[41]

1 *The Renshaw kids enjoying life on the Selway (l to r): Jean, Jim, Bobby, and Billie.*

2 *Some of the Renshaw family at the ranch circa 1944 (l to r): Elna, Jean, Allen, Billie, unknown, and Alvin.*

3 *The wreckage of Johnson Flying Service Travel Air NC450N in a pond about two miles east of Cub Point that claimed the life of pilot Robert Maricich.*

4 *Looking down on the Maricich crash site in 1959.*

5 *After Jim Renshaw's parents sold the property in 1948 he returned several different times working as an outfitter from the place.*

6 *Jim Renshaw and his wife Darlene (right) met at Selway Lodge while Jim worked for her parents who were leasing the property. Here the couple is photographed in 1958 at the Moose Creek Ranches with their three children (l to r): Sunnie, Gail, and Gary.*

The Start of the Selway Lodge and the Renshaws Move On

Several perspective buyers quickly became interested in the property. The first person meeting the asking price was Carl Coons who purchased the ranch and renamed it Selway Lodge.[42]

The Renshaw family relocated to a large acreage off the Middle Fork of the Clearwater on Suttler Creek north of Kooskia, Idaho. In 1949 Alvin was accidently shot on a hunting trip and died as a result of his injuries. His kids carried on his passion for the outdoors. Daughter Jean wrote of many of these family experiences in her memoir *I Never Felt Poor Except In Town: Selway Saga 1932-1948*. Son Jim followed closely in his father's footsteps as a professional outfitter, retiring from the business in 1998. He operated in much of the same country as his dad, often based at Fish Lake and his Bitterroot Ranch property on lower Moose Creek.[43]

Early in Jim Renshaw's career he went to work for Coons as an outfitter and guide. Shortly after purchasing the lodge, Coons lost the property in a divorce to Irene Shields. Shields continued to use the Selway Lodge and leased it to various outfitters. In the fall of 1952 Frank and Minnie Wilson leased the lodge and hired Renshaw to help outfit. By August the next year Renshaw married their daughter, Darlene.[44]

Jim's younger brother Allen came and went through the Selway country as well. For several years he worked for the USFS as an aerial observer and occasionally worked for Jim's outfitting business. Exposed to aviation at a young age while growing up on the Selway, Allen earned his private pilot license at Hillcrest Aviation when he was nineteen and flew on and off for several years.[45]

Sid Hinkle, an Airstrip, Airplanes, and Pilots

In early 1958 Shields sold the lodge to Sid Hinkle of Redding, California. He brought in silent partner Gil Warden, also of Redding, for a very brief period before buying him out. He also took in business partner Alma Hinds of Redding for a few years, but eventually bought her share. Hinkle had come to the Idaho backcountry twice on hunting trips with friend Loren Hollenbeak who owned property at Cabin Creek on lower Big Creek. Hinkle was taken by the Idaho backcountry and learned of the Selway property from Hollenbeak.[46]

Hinkle, like Hollenbeak, was involved in the logging business in California, but his main line of work was his family's oil distributorship, E. B. Hinkle and Son. The company owned several gas stations, bulk plants, and a trucking operation. He sold the business and moved to Idaho, residing mainly in Grangeville where he and his wife Mae owned and operated the Elkhorn Motel.[47]

Hinkle learned to fly later in life from a former truck driver employee, Frank Wolfe, who was a retired Air Force colonel. Having to fly in and out of the lodge was an aspect of the job that he enjoyed. His short-term partner Hinds also relished flying. She served as a Women Air Force Service Pilot (WASP) and a Ferry Command pilot during World War II. In these programs she piloted B-17s, B-24s, and C-47s. After the war she returned and purchased the Benton Field Airport in Redding and started H&H Flying Service. In her spare time she flew powder puff derbies around the country. At the time the two shared the lodge together they co-owned a Cessna 180.[48]

During Hinkle's ownership he had a D2 Caterpillar flown to Shearer. En route from Shearer to the lodge, the D2 was used to repair the old wagon road, making it more serviceable. Hinkle then used the Cat to build a 1400' runway in the lodge's hayfield.[49] By late 1958 Hinkle, who also owned a Cessna 182A, was using the airplane on the new airstrip.[50] However, Charles "Frenny" Frensdorf made the first known landing at the lodge in the late 1940s or early 1950s while on a winter game count with a ski-equipped Piper Cub.[51]

In 1961 Hinkle purchased a new Cessna 185 (N9808X). In addition to this airplane, he and Hinds bought an early Cessna 210 that they planned to use for quicker travel between Idaho and Redding. Hinkle only flew it to the Selway area one time before selling it. The maroon and white 185 became his favorite backcountry airplane and he had it fully outfitted with all the latest equipment, including the best retractable skis money could buy. Many in the Selway country believed that Hinkle was a great pilot, although he operated the 185 more like an old pickup truck than an airplane.

Fly in and Hunt
the Selway Primitive Area
90 per cent Hunter Success for the 1962 Season

We Have an Abundance of Deer and Elk
HUNTING SEASON SEPTEMBER 15 - NOVEMBER 30
Reservation and Deposit Required
To Assure Hunter's Choice of Hunting Dates
Licensed and Bonded Outfitters and Guides
Family Accommodations and Modern Facilities

For Further Information Write
SID HINKLE, BOX 166, Grangeville, Idaho
— or —
Contact by Phone, 344-0497, Boise, Idaho

SELWAY LODGE

7

J. Renshaw

8

J. Hinkle/B. Block

9

D. Waite

10

W. Beebe

1 *Sid Hinkle (third from left) at Shearer in 1958 with a Cessna 182.*

2 *Alma Hinds and Annette Graves (far left) stand with a group of people at the lodge in 1960. Outfitter Erv Malnarich and caretaker/guide Gene Alford are standing on the far right.*

3 *The Selway Lodge as it appeared in 1960 under the ownership of the Hinkles.*

4 *A 1963 advertisement for the Selway Lodge.*

5 *Cutting ice out of the Selway below the bridge – the lodge's barn can be seen in the background.*

6 *Jerry Hinkle (right) with his father in the cockpit of the Cessna 185.*

7 *Jim Mitchell's Green Acres Flight Service at Orofino.*

8 *The tractor and wagon used to transport guests and supplies between the Selway Lodge and the Shearer airstrip.*

9 *Sid Hinkle's Cessna 185 (N9808X) parked along with Dick Waite's Cessna 185 (N9822X) at North Star. Waite was one of the original shareholders in the Selway Wilderness Ranch.*

10 *A McCall Aviation Britten-Norman Islander (N634MA) landing at the Selway Lodge.*

One of the first things Hinkle hauled to the lodge with his 185 was a CJ5 Jeep that he drove from Redding to Grangeville. He then disassembled the vehicle and flew it in pieces to the lodge. Some of the parts had to be cut with a torch and welded back together.[52]

Hinkle hired several outfitters to take clients on trips during his ownership. Reservations and arrangements for the lodge's services were made through the Elkhorn Motel, where they also had a backcountry radio.[53] One of the better-known guides to work for Hinkle was Gene Alford, also of Redding. While living at the lodge in 1961 he killed a cougar that was one of the largest ever taken. Many years later on a 1988 hunt in the Selway area he beat his record by taking the second largest cougar to date recorded with the Boone and Crockett Club.

Hinkle or Hinds flew the clientele to the lodge generally from Grangeville. However, Hinkle became involved with friend Clyde Baker, who partially-owned Green Acres Flight Service. Baker's partner Jim Mitchell served as the primary pilot, as well as an occasional guide at the lodge. While originally based at Baker's private airstrip near Mount Idaho, outside of Grangeville, Hinkle used their company when things were busy. By 1965 Mitchell moved the Green Acres operation to Orofino. A few years later he was killed while crop dusting.

Also helping Hinkle with some of the flying from Grangeville to the property was his future son-in-law Bob Black. Black's father, Bob Sr., the auto parts storeowner in Grangeville kept a Cessna 170 (N2423D) at the airport. Black occasionally used the 170, particularly during hunting season.[54]

On one trip in the 185, with Hinkle flying and Black in the right seat, they took a big nick out of a prop blade while landing at the lodge. The nick was bad enough that the whole plane shook, even when taxiing. When this happened the two pilots looked at each other and Hinkle shut the plane down. Black turned to him and said, "Well what do you want to do?" Hinkle grinning, jumped out and commented, "I have an idea." He disappeared for a while and came back with a hacksaw in hand. Before Black could say anything, Hinkle was cutting away on the bad blade just above the imperfection. The two men then took a measurement of what was cut and then did the same on the good blade. This arrested the vibration and they returned safely to Grangeville. Soon after flying with Hinkle, Black piloted helicopters in Vietnam. Later

he returned to Idaho and flew in the backcountry for several years.[55]

In 1964 Hinkle sold the lodge. He acquired property at several other backcountry locations, including Mallard Creek and Dixie, and spent considerable efforts improving these places. By 1967 Hinkle and his wife Mae built a nice home in Dixie and spent the majority of their retirement at the location. Hinkle eventually sold his Cessna 185 and replaced it with a Piper Super Cub. The two lived in Dixie until they were no longer able to get around. Hinkle died in 1995 and within the following year Mae also died. Bob Black and Frank Hill spread their ashes over the Dixie town airstrip from a Super Cub.[56]

The Selway Wilderness Ranch Inc.

Hinkle had sold the lodge to a group of people, including Rolla Briggs, Robert Hall, Dick Waite, and Bill Guth Sr.[57] The group then offered shares of the lodge for sale under the name Selway Wilderness Ranch Inc. Hinkle remained loosely involved as he kept two small parcels of land near Ditch Creek. Briggs and his wife Artist served as the managers, living at the place year round for about three years. The couple also ran the outfitting and guiding portion of the business in the fall.[58]

The group felt that the runway's design limited the type of aircraft they could operate at the lodge and often used the Shearer airstrip. However, the USFS put pressure on them to stop using the wagon road to Shearer. In 1965, wanting to bring in larger aircraft, Briggs and Waite went to work expanding the airfield. Using the D2, they moved one building off toward the river and cut an uphill dogleg to the south near Pettibone's burial site.[59] Alvin Renshaw dubbed this portion of the property Mount Mariah, after Masonic stories that told a tale of a mountain with a grave.[60]

The approximate 640' dogleg extension allowed airplanes to carryout heavier loads. Their work brought the runway to its present total length of about 2000'. However, the complete dogleg portion is often not usable, as the pilot still has to be at a suitable speed to negotiate the turn onto the main portion of the runway.

Waite and Briggs were both pilots. Waite mainly flew a Cessna 185 (N9822X) and Briggs a Cessna

182A. Briggs had a close call one day in the plane while flying from the lodge to Hamilton. As he flew over the top of the ridge at the head of Rock Creek on the west side of the Bitterroots, the plane ran out of gas. With very few options for an emergency landing in the extremely steep tree-covered terrain, he picked a small rockslide area in a draw where a snowslide had occurred. Coming down fast he stalled the plane within a few feet from the ground right into the deep snowslide.[61]

One observer who flew over the accident site said, "He perfectly mushed it in like a bird landing in a nest." It was a lucky forced landing considering the topography and that he had to flare into oncoming terrain that was at an angle of more than forty-five degrees. Briggs walked away essentially unhurt. The plane was later lifted out with a helicopter. Many pilots who saw the 182 when it was hauled in were amazed at the aircraft's good condition. Damage to the crankshaft was not even questioned since the prop had not been turning at the time of impact.[62]

Not only did Selway Wilderness Ranch Inc. improve the field, they also updated many of the buildings by adding water, propane, and other amenities. The overall master plan was to divide part of the property into forty one-quarter acre cabin sites for resale. The land was platted, but the plan was not executed because the owners could not carry the operating costs. Hall, the group's main financial backer, died during heart surgery. After several years of enjoyment and some personal setbacks they decided to sell. [63]

The Peirce and Millington Years

Selway Wilderness Ranch Inc. sold in 1971 to Everett Peirce of Colorado. However, Hinkle held onto his small parcels even after Peirce's acquisition.[64] Included in the sale was Guth's Cessna 180 (N3150D), which Peirce flew for several years. The Peirces added many new structures to the lodge property. Peirce was wilderness-oriented and made an effort to dispose of items he felt not fitting. For example he dug a large hole with the D2 and buried many items deemed non-wilderness, including two operating sawmills located off the north end of the airstrip. Peirce also struck up a deal with an area pilot from Conner, Montana, to fly the Cat out. The agreement was basically a trade. The pilot would haul supplies to

the lodge at little to no cost in return for the D2. Over time the pilot flew supplies in and took bits and pieces of the D2 out until he had assembled a complete machine in Conner.[65]

Several smaller pieces of the original homestead had been sold over time, and Peirce made an effort to purchase and rejoin these other properties. In 1976, the same year he acquired Hinkle's last parcel, he sold roughly half of the lodge's land to the USFS.[66]

Throughout Peirce's ownership he restricted the use of the airfield. Area pilots including those that flew for outfitters leasing the lodge generally always gained permission before landing. Why? Peirce usually laced the lower end of the strip with unmarked logs or wire strung across the width of the field as a message to deter unwanted aviators. When he did permit people to use the runway it was an unwritten rule not to use the uphill dogleg, as it was kept as a well-manicured lawn.[67]

In 1990 the Selway Lodge sold to Patricia Millington of Picabo, Idaho. Don and Virginia Rhinehart were caretakers for Millington. In the winter of 1992 the Rhineharts decided to winter at the lodge. In the middle of their stay it became extremely cold and they realized the wood supply was running low. Don decided to cut a few trees on the edge of the property bordering USFS land.[68]

Not thinking much about it, the two wintered well. On March 30, Virginia's birthday, she heard two helicopters overhead. She went to the radio and asked the ships to identify themselves. After repeated attempts and no response the helicopters landed on the lodge's airstrip. Before Virginia could get outside she heard a knock. She opened the door to find a fully-armed federal marshal. Virginia recognized the fellow and told him that she would not be willing to help until he disarmed himself, which he did.[69]

It turned out that they wanted to talk with Don about the tree removal. Don was more than willing to help them "investigate" the so-called "situation." The agents became very irked, as the Rhineharts found the whole event amusing and poked fun at the men taking samples of the illegally chainsaw-cut firewood. After a few hours of the conversation going in circles, Don looked at the head marshal and said, "What's it going to cost me." In the end the total fine was $150. The Rhineharts figured that was cheap for thirteen cords of wood.[70]

During the Rhinehart's years caretaking for Millington larger airplanes began to land at the lodge, starting when McCall Air Taxi pilot Rod Nielson landed an Islander (N555JA) with a load of oversized lumber.[71]

The Renshaw built lodge in 2011.

Pilot Dick Williams with Wilderness Aviation owner Richard Combs in the 1980s.

To this date Islanders operate regularly in out of the lodge. It is interesting to note that many experienced pilots consider the Islander easier to operate at the airstrip, due to its lower approach speeds, than some other aircrafts.

A Hunting Season Tragedy

The Combs family, of Salmon, Idaho, who owned and operated Wilderness Aviation, flew regularly for Millington during her ownership. The Combs also flew supplies and guests for Rick Hussey, an outfitter and guide that leased the lodge for fall hunting, starting in the late 1960s.

The Combs entrance into the commercial flying community was unique. Richard Combs, the son of Glenn and Marge grew up in Salmon wanting to be a pilot. He and his father earned their private pilot ratings from Carol Jarvis of Salmon Air Taxi. Richard dreamed of flying the backcountry commercially and after high school graduation attended a flight school. Acquiring a majority of his ratings, he returned to Salmon looking for a job. Salmon Air Taxi pilot Dick Williams told him

he did not have enough flight hours to be hired on and encouraged him to build time and learn the backcountry, which he did.

Combs purchased a Cessna 172 and started building time instructing and flying for fun. He then brought his father up to speed and was able to get him through his commercial ratings. In 1984 the family obtained a 135 Air Taxi Certificate from Ken Linn and started Wilderness Aviation. Not capable of fulfilling many FAA requirements, the Combs hired Williams as the company's chief pilot. Incapable of attracting many clients with only a 172, they purchased a Cessna 206 and Williams bought a third share of a Cessna 207 (N6257H) with them. Once the company was underway Williams moved on to other flying jobs based in Boise and sold his portion of the airplane to them.

Five years after achieving his life goals, cancer claimed Richard's life. Following the family's loss the business continued, but ended badly on November 19, 1992. At the end of the hunting season the Husseys prepared to leave Selway Lodge and chartered two airplanes from Wilderness Aviation. The planes arrived at the lodge mid morning after battling weather.

Once loaded, the planes headed back to Salmon. Pilot Mike Walton flew the Cessna 206 (N7372Q) while Glenn Combs piloted the 207 with Hussey's wife Helen and son Skily aboard. The two planes encountered poor weather again on the way out, with low ceilings, mountain obscuration, rain, and falling snow. Combs tried picking his way through a low drainage, but soon found himself trapped. Unable to outmaneuver the tight topography, he smashed into the mountainside, killing all three aboard. Walton had been in constant radio contact with Combs and when he could no longer reach him, he knew what had happened. At that point Walton realized he was not going to be able to endure the weather beneath the low ceilings. He then climbed out on instruments back to Salmon

A McCall Aviation Islander delivering supplies in May 2008.

and reported the horrific news. The plane was located and the bodies were recovered. Even after the tragedy, Hussey continued to operate an outfitting business in the Selway region and two of Richard Combs's sons went on to become commercial aviators.

New Owners and More Airplanes

Millington sold the lodge to Bob Greenhill in the mid-1990s. Under the new ownership Mark Tabor and Marge Kuehn-Tabor became the caretakers in 2006. The following year the two went to the lodge to do some final cleanup work before closing for the winter. A malfunctioning propane water heater caused a fire in one of the main houses built by former owner Peirce and the fire burned the structure to the ground.

Using the old footprint the owners built a new structure starting in the spring of 2008. While supplies were being flown in, Greenhill took the opportunity to continue restoration on the other cabins. Most material was brought in by helicopter from Darby, Montana, while McCall Aviation flew in additional loads and workers.[72]

McCall Aviation often had pilots Rod Nielson and Jerry McCauley Sr. in two Islanders and Walt Smith in a Cessna 206, each flying five full loads of supplies per day, either from McCall or Hamilton. On one trip in April the year before, Nielson had the left engine's starter engage on climb out from Hamilton in an Islander (N634MA). With a full load and one engine failed, Nielson pitched for an open meadow. However, the plane struggled to stay airborne, forcing Nielson to forgo his originally chosen emergency landing location. The aircraft was a complete loss, but he survived with minor injuries.

Landing at the Selway Lodge.

Not only has the lodge seen high aircraft activity for construction and property improvements, but also for a wide variety of visitors from family to scientists who conduct wilderness field studies. In recent years hummingbird studies have been seasonally carried out at the lodge. The large Islanders and Cessna 206s continue to operate in and out of the property's challenging runway, helping to keep the lodge up and running.

SHEARER

The Early Years and an Airstrip

Selway homesteader Phil Shearer.

Phil Shearer moved to the Selway area to work seasonally for the USFS and to visit his relatives, the Shisslers, after serving in the United States Navy. He liked the country and decided to make it home.[73] In 1924 he officially homesteaded the property where he ran cattle, grew a large garden for commercial use, and brewed spirits during prohibition.[74]

In 1932 the USFS approached Shearer about building an airstrip in his hayfield to allow them better access into the upper Selway area. He agreed as he too thought air travel would be a nice feature to have for such a remote place. Construction on the runway was started in 1933 and finished in 1934.[75] Nick Mamer was the first to land an aircraft on the strip the same year. Shearer enjoyed having the amenities the airstrip offered.[76]

Even though the runway was completed, pilots operating large or heavily loaded aircraft would not use it. One of Mamer's good friends, Bob Johnson, refused to land his larger ships at the field. After complaining to the USFS, Johnson offered many suggestions for improvements that would allow the use of bigger planes. By the fall of 1935 the agency took heed of Johnson's advice. Ultimately trees were slashed and cleared on both ends of the runway, the windsock was moved and raised, the gravel material located along the east side was re-leveled, and additional drainage was added on the north end.[77]

Air Access Becomes Popular

Shearer and the USFS were not the only parties who benefited from the strip. It enabled Alvin Renshaw of 51 Ranch (now Selway Lodge) to bring in clients to

Pilot Fred Zimmerly (right) with fishermen at Shearer (the catch is on the Zenith's propeller blades) in the mid-1930s.

his downstream homestead for hunting and fishing.[78] In 1943 access between Shearer and Renshaw's 51 Ranch was improved even further. In the summer of 1943 a crew of Italian prisoners of war was flown to Shearer and stationed at the Bear Creek Ranger Station. By happenstance the Italians were in an American port when the United States declared war on Italy. The prisoner's main function was to provide cheap labor for building several new bridges across Bear Creek and the Selway River. Supplies were brought in using Johnson Flying Service Ford Tri-Motors to Moose Creek and Shearer airstrips. To move supplies down the Selway the prisoners built a wagon road from Shearer to Renshaw's ranch. Taking advantage of the road,

A Travel Air 6000 delivering supplies to the USFS's first administrative site at the upper southwest corner of the airfield.

Renshaw used an iron wheeled wagon to carry supplies, family, and guests between Shearer and his ranch.[79] The subsequent owners of Selway Lodge followed suit until their hayfield was developed into a runway.

In roughly 1942 legendary backcountry pilot Abe Bowler flew an open cockpit Ryan to Shearer for a day of angling. Bowler fished his way down the Selway to the 51 Ranch. With his creel full he wondered up to the Renshaw's lodge in hopes of finding a person to help him start the plane, so he could return home. To his dismay the men of the ranch were gone and the only individual Bowler saw fit to help him was ten-year-old Jim Renshaw. The youngster jumped at the opportunity not fully realizing what the favor entailed. After arriving at the plane on the upper end of the Shearer field, Bowler hoisted Jim into the cockpit. The pilot then described to Jim how to crank the magneto handle while he went to the front of the aircraft to hand prop the engine. The youthful Jim was no longer so enthusiastic, "There I was just a kid by myself in the plane . . . I thought what if the darn thing took off." However, he wanted to show Bowler he was tough and did as he was told. On the first pull of the prop the radial engine roared to life. Startled, Jim sprang up from the pilot's seat and fell out of the idling airplane to the ground. Bowler, un-phased by Jim's reaction, extended his gratitude as he helped him up. Bowler then leisurely climbed into his machine and flew off. [80]

Shearer and the USFS

The USFS only held a lease on the airfield into the late 1930s, and was using it to supply their Bear Creek facility. Flying hay in for the USFS stock became

The Hinkles picking up guests with their Jeep at Shearer to transport them back to Selway Lodge in 1961.

expensive. As a result the agency struck a deal with Shearer and he sold nearly twenty acres of his homestead for haying purposes. The USFS also developed an administrative site by constructing a decent-sized log structure at the top southwest corner of the runway. A hay shed was built on the opposite side of the airstrip at the same time. In the 1950s the administrative building was relocated below the north end of the runway and turned into a commissary. When this structure was remodeled the USFS hay shed was burned along with Shearer's original hay shed on the riverside of the runway. Later the commissary was also completely removed.[81]

Shortly after Shearer sold the acreage to the USFS his health began to fail and he leased the remainder of the property to them, keeping a small portion around his home and outbuildings for living purposes. Even with his declining health a new barn was built to match the newer house he had constructed in the 1930s. In 1944 soon after the new agreement, Shearer died. His estate was settled ten years later and the USFS acquired the whole parcel.

Big Planes, a Longer Runway, and Buildings

The first large airplane to land on the Shearer strip was a Boeing 247D (NC13352) piloted by Bert Zimmerly Sr. and Don Wolfe. Zimmerly was using the 247Ds as part of Zimmerly Airlines. He had booked a large hunting party that required two airplane loads. Instead of using two aircraft for the job he opted to fly the larger airplane to see if it could be done. It was the only time Zimmerly used the 247D in the backcountry.[82] Later Johnson Flying Service set a new record when they began operating a DC-2 at the strip starting in the late 1950s. The first pilot to fly a DC-2 to the airstrip was Cookie Calloway in N4867V.[83]

The USFS continued to use the airstrip into the early 1950s and continually upgraded it, including lengthening the runway from its original 1400' to its current 2000'. At the same time, the agency saw the need to update the administrative site. The USFS determined that the buildings were "nearing the end of their useful life." It was also decided that the original homestead structures located off the north end of the runway were hazardous in the event of an engine failure on takeoff.[84]

By the end of the decade the USFS had burned Shearer's first home and other buildings, and replaced them with two structures they moved from the Bear Creek Guard Station. In 1955 Moose Creek District Ranger Jack Parsell oversaw a group of smokejumpers that used a tractor and cart to move the two buildings the mile and a half upriver. These structures, originally built in 1923 and 1930, make up the present-day Shearer Guard Station.[85]

Stuck Ford Tri-Motors

In April 1956 Gerry Wilson was hired by the Selway Lodge to fly in a newly purchased Ford tractor from Orofino to Shearer. Wilson and co-pilot Arnie Brandt disassembled the tractor and squeezed it into the Ford Tri-Motor. The plane was loaded in such a way that they both had to climb in from the front.[86]

The flight went as usual, including the normal procedure for overflying the field and the approach.

As Wilson piloted the heavy ship onto the ground, he began to apply the brakes with no reaction. Realizing the problem was a wet field, he grabbed for full brakes and the old Ford skidded its way up to the end. The two pilots then felt the plane starting to sink. Wilson's instant reaction was to pour full power to all three engines, but it was too late.[87]

Wanting to prevent a prop strike, the engines were immediately shutdown and the two pilots looked at each other as the plane continued to sink, finally coming to a rest with the bottom of the fuselage mired in the mud.[88] This drainage problem at Shearer was nothing new to pilots, as a year or two before, Johnson Flying Service pilot Warren Ellison had sunk Ford Tri-Motor NC9642 in a similar fashion.[89]

Wilson and Brandt climbed out of the side windows, as the tractor was blocking the rear door. At first assessment Wilson looked at Brandt laughing, "It could not have worked out any better, she'll [the Ford tractor] be easy to unload this way." The two unloaded the dismantled tractor. Then they dug the plane out of the mud and were back in the air.[90]

More Recent History

By the late 1970s the field suffered from lack of maintenance and continued to be plagued with drainage problems. The USFS, however, kept it open even with opposition from strong wilderness advocates.

In the spring of 1983 several salt blocks were intentionally placed in the middle of the airfield. The salt attracted large groups of deer and elk causing enough damage that the strip had to be closed at times. The salted areas were excavated with the hope that the animals would not return. However, salt was placed on the airfield continually through 1986.[91]

In the spring of 1987 Moose Creek District Ranger Dennis Dailey received reports that severe damage had been done again to the airfield, including the use of salt. Upon investigation it was found that twenty-one large holes were dug with posthole diggers in a strategic pattern on the runway with the intention that time and weather would deteriorate the field beyond use.[92] Senator Jim McClure and many aviation enthusiasts fought for the use, repair, and reopening of the airstrip. Since this incident the field has been refurbished and remains active.

1 *Phil Shearer's remaining buildings in 1958.*

2 *Phil Shearer's second house.*

3 *Looking downstream at the Shearer airstrip in the late 1950s. Shearer's homestead structures, which were later burned, can be seen in the background.*

4 *A Johnson Flying Service Cessna 180 dropping off Selway resident Punk Wolfinbarger at the upper end of Shearer.*

5 *A view down the Selway River at the Shearer and Selway Lodge airstrips circa 1960.*

6 *The Shearer runway has been consistently plagued with drainage issues. Here Johnson Flying Service pilot Warren Ellison is attempting to dig out a stuck Ford Tri-Motor.*

7 *A McCall Aviation Cessna 206 (N9374Z) landing at Shearer.*

SELWAY-BITTERROOT WILDERNESS

MOOSE CREEK

BITTERROOT RANCH/ TROUT CREEK

The Bitterroot Ranch cabin built by Jim Renshaw in the late 1950s. Renshaw is hanging meat, while his kids Gail and Gary are standing above.

In April 1924 John Carothers homesteaded 50.76 acres near the confluence of Trout and Moose creeks.[93] The Carothers family lost the land to the bank during the Depression.[94]

Glen Davidson, a railroad station manager in Stites, Idaho, bought the old Carothers place for back taxes in the early 1930s for investment purposes only. The few improvements on the homestead were left unmaintained and he even sold off some of the equipment, including a water-powered sawmill. The little mill was purchased by Alvin Renshaw and transported up to the now Selway Lodge. With the intention of turning a dollar on the property, he sold the acreage in 1956 to Alvin Renshaw's son Jim.[95]

Jim Renshaw named the place the Bitterroot Ranch and used it to run his outfitting business. In 1958, while working for the contractor building the long runway at the Moose Creek Ranger Station, Renshaw and distant relative Ralph Dawson, walked a TD-9 bulldozer to the property and cleared much of the ranch's overgrown timber. Over the next two years he constructed a two-story log cabin built over the footprint of the original homestead dwelling. In addition to the cabin, the ranch had a barn and two sheds, one of which was also renovated from an early homestead structure.[96]

In 1972 Renshaw sold the ranch to Gene Nichols. Nichols was not satisfied with the Ford tractor that came with the sale. He walked a D2 Caterpillar, which he had flown to the Moose Creek Ranger Station strip, to the property. The small and capable D2 Cat was used to rough out a 1200' runway in much of the same area Renshaw had already cleared. The airstrip sat perpendicular to Moose Creek and only received one or two landings.[97]

Shortly after the aircraft landings, circa 1976 the USFS bought the property and closed the runway. The agency torched the buildings and allowed the property to grow in. However, Nichols had accidentally burned the main cabin down prior to the sale when attempting to dry out some saddle blankets next to the stove.[98]

1 Renshaw kneeling on the porch of one of the original Carothers homestead buildings.

2 Working one of Vanderwall's dozers at the ranch in 1958.

3 Larry Dutcher (left) on the tractor and the Jim Renshaw family in the wagon at the ranch for a Thanksgiving celebration in 1963.

4 An aerial of the Bitterroot Ranch before the airstrip was constructed.

5 A 2011 view of the 1200' Bitterroot Ranch airstrip built by Gene Nichols.

MOOSE CREEK RANCHES

The Early Years and the Ranches

A 1965 view of the large flat at the confluence of North and East Moose creeks originally called Three Forks and later Moose Creek Ranches. Both the upper and lower airstrips are visible.

This area at the confluence of North and East Moose creeks was originally referred to by the USFS as Three Forks. Early USFS personnel used a cabin near the confluence called "The Scurvy Cabin."[99] The cabin earned its name after the ill-fated builders experienced troubling events during the winter of 1894–95. Three trappers, Will Blair (aka Jack Craig), John Shean, and E. A. Wheeler, set out from Hamilton to the forks of Moose Creek to trap for the winter. After the cabin was built the men had several good weeks of hunting, trapping, and fishing.[100]

As the winter progressed, everything fell apart. By May 1895 Craig left the Moose Creek area for Hamilton after burying his two partners, who had died of scurvy. Other losses were two dogs and eleven horses.[101] Foul play was suspected and authorities returned with Craig to investigate the deaths. Upon examination of the bodies, the authorities exonerated Craig. The graves near the cabin were re-sealed and marked. The area became known for a time as "Dead Man's Flat."[102] These graves are still visible.

This large flat area at the forks of Moose Creek eventually became divided into five private homesteads owned by Jay Randall, John Van Horn, Mary Ellen Dodds, Charley Halford, and George Case. Various people throughout the years owned these properties. In 1944 Bert Zimmerly Sr. of Lewiston bought the Dodds place and created Moose Creek Ranches Inc. During 1944–45 friends of Zimmerly also became interested and purchased surrounding homesteads. One friend, Joe Rozenkranz, acquired both the Randall and Van Horn parcels from Paul Bloom, and Tom Kiiskila obtained the Halford homestead.[103]

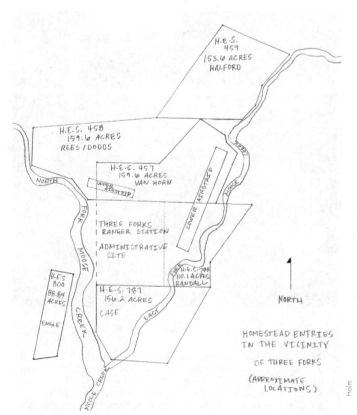

The approximate locations of the original homestead entries at the forks of Moose Creek.

A 1945 view to the east of the upper airstrip built by Paul Bloom.

Brothers Bert and Fred Zimmerly with a Cessna Airmaster in the early 1940s.

Under Zimmerly's name of Moose Creek Ranches Inc. the group operated the four separate properties as one commercial venture. Later owner Paul Christman combined all these properties, along with the old Case homestead, into one 745 acre private in-holding.[104]

Before Zimmerly started the Moose Creek Ranches Inc., brother Fred Zimmerly made the first landing on the upper bench of the property in 1937 with a Piper J-2 Cub. Hard labor and hand tools were used to clear the landing area. After Zimmerly affirmed the possibility of aircraft use at the location, a formal 1400' airstrip was roughed in. Most pilots dubbed the runway "The Upper Strip."[105] The original runway was carved out by then owner Paul Bloom. In addition to the airfield, Bloom remodeled the original Randall cabin into a lodge and constructed several outbuildings.

Bert Zimmerly Jr. (right) at Moose Creek Ranches in the mid-1950s preparing to load a Stinson SM7-A (N216W) with elk meat. Ranch employee John George is standing on the left.

Zimmerly Brothers

Fred Zimmerly began flying in 1928 and a few years later he was barnstorming the Northwest. In 1934 brother Bert had also earned his necessary licenses and the two formed Zimmerly Brothers Air Transport Service. The brothers saw market potential in north and central Idaho and established a base of operations in Lewiston. The two purchased a distinctive Zenith biplane (NC935Y) for large loads and many additional airplanes including Travel Air 6000s. Soon the business became a staple of the backcountry, serving customers in the Selway-Bitterroot area and as far south as the Middle Fork of the Salmon River.[106]

The two were not rich, but became well established and respected operators in the state. In 1938 Bert took over flight operations and Fred went to work for Northwest Airlines. By 1942 Bert moved the business to neighboring Clarkston, Washington. From the new location he capitalized on the opportunities provided by World War II and started a CPTP.[107]

Bert also focused on establishing air routes connecting major cities in Idaho as well as Spokane. For these flights he bought several Cessna Airmasters.

The hydro dam located on North Moose Creek.

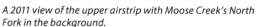

A 2011 view of the upper airstrip with Moose Creek's North Fork in the background.

When the war ended he shifted his business efforts toward developing scheduled air service. By 1946 he earned approval from the Civil Aeronautics Board (CAB) and created Zimmerly Airlines, which was later renamed Empire Airlines.[108]

On February 17, 1949, Bert was returning from a business trip in Spokane, flying a company Cessna Airmaster (NC19496). The weather deteriorated and he tried pushing his way back to Lewiston in low visibility and flew the plane into some high terrain south of Pullman, Washington. In spite of the loss of Bert, his brother continued flying the remainder of his life, becoming a chief pilot for Northwest Airlines. Fred died in May 2004 at age ninety-four. Bert's son, Bert Jr., also took up flying. Early in his career he flew the backcountry like his father and uncle for various Idaho operators and eventually went on to fly corporate jets.[109]

More Changes

Once the Ranches were combined, the owners devised a plan to improve their business venture by creating a first-class hunting and guiding destination. They brought in a T-20 International crawler to the Moose Creek Ranger Station with plans to walk it up Moose Creek to the ranch to smooth out the airfield. Prior to

moving it to their properties the USFS leased the T-20 for $50. It was used to haul sand and gravel for the building of bridge piers below the ranger station airfield.[110]

When the crawler was done smoothing the runway, the group of owners hauled in a green Willeys Jeep in a Travel Air 6000. The Jeep's body had to be cut in half and other parts disassembled. Once all the parts were at the ranch the Jeep was reassembled. The body was tied back together using strap iron and bolts, making it a real rattle trap and a little precarious to drive, but it worked. The hulk of this old machine remains buried at the ranch.[111]

In the summer of 1948 the owners decided to build a hydroelectric dam across North Moose Creek to bring more modern convinces to what was becoming the finest hunting and fishing destination in the Idaho backcountry. Zimmerly offered the services of his company if the Ranches were willing to pay for the time on the aircraft. Everyone agreed and Zimmerly along with Stan Hepler flew in most of the supplies for the ranch renovations, in addition to those needed for the dam project. Hepler alone flew 200 sacks of cement for the dam. The majority of the flying was carried out in Zimmerly Travel Air 6000s and Cessna Airmasters.[112]

The Disappearance of Rozenkranz

Similar to the summer, the hunting season of 1948 was busy at Moose Creek Ranches. Guests came and went frequently by airplane. On Saturday October 24 Bert Zimmerly Sr. took off in a Stinson with a full load of elk meat, headed for Lewiston. It was nearly dark and weather was becoming an issue with low ceilings and obscured mountains. Zimmerly kept the Stinson fairly low following the Selway River out, eventually snaking his way into Lewiston. Zimmerly unloaded the plane and headed home for some rest.[113]

Zimmerly's friend and a shareholder in the new airline, Joe Rozenkranz, who held a private pilot license, had taken off from Moose Creek Ranches about forty-five minutes after Zimmerly in his personally-owned Stinson 108 (NC6404) loaded with gear and passenger W. J. "Bud" Bolick. The two men were also headed for Lewiston but faced worse conditions than Zimmerly had fought on his way out. Bolick was an electrician from Lewiston who was hired to wire the new hydroelectric dam.[114]

The next morning, pilot Dick Wagner flew a load of hunters to the ranch. In a casual conversation with others at the lodge, they asked what time Rozenkranz made it back to Lewiston. Wagner assured the folks that he never arrived. Within hours a search was launched for the two missing men and the maroon Stinson 108.[115]

The USFS, Civilian Air Patrol (CAP), Idaho Aeronautics Department, several private individuals, along with Zimmerly and his employees conducted the search. Zimmerly flew several barrels of gas to the Moose Creek Ranger Station to create a base of operations for the search. This was done as several hunting camps in the vicinity had seen or heard the airplane attempting to maneuver around the weather. Zimmerly flew a Stinson 108 on the search and one of his employee's, Stan Hepler, flew the company's new green and silver Cessna 170 (NC3919V). The two pilots combed the areas below the confluence of Moose Creek and the Selway in hopes of seeing a fire or any scrap of the Rozenkranz Stinson.[116] During this period 150 landings were made by search planes at the Moose Creek Ranger Station to support the efforts.[117]

Hepler noted that those who were involved searched diligently, but several problems plagued the operation. Cooperation between the agencies was cumbersome, search teams were going off hearsay from hunters, and the area where he and Zimmerly thought the dark painted airplane might be was full of dense timber. In addition to these problems several pilots from southern Idaho who had political connections with Rozenkranz took charge only to burn up the majority of the state provided gasoline, as they did not know the area well.[118]

Meanwhile, Rozenkranz, who at the time was running as a Democratic candidate for Idaho state representative from Nez Perce County, was declared the winner of the election. Search parties continued to get tips from hunters, including one group claiming to have found broken treetops along a ridge. Every lead was investigated and rewards were offered. After weeks of searching and winter weather moving in, the hunt for the men and airplane was called off. The following spring a few additional searches were made, but nothing turned up.

Newspapers and gossip about the crash created lore and legend. Since Moose Creek Ranches was known for its good time – heavy drinking and high stakes gambling, many believed large amounts of cash to be aboard the aircraft. Some people thought someone could have found the plane, taken the money and never reported it for fear of being caught with all the loot. Every rumor imaginable was drummed up concerning the disappearance of the two men. Throughout the late 1950s and early 1960s local newspapers ran updates with people claiming that they had found various parts of the airplane along the Selway River. Although no bodies or wreckage of the maroon Stinson 108 could be produced as evidence.

The mystery went unsolved until early April 1987 when a former Nez Perce NF employee, Jay Jones was antler hunting and found the airplane. The crash site was discovered on the Glover Creek drainage off the north side of the Selway River. Jones, not knowing what he had found, removed the aircraft identification tag and reported the wreckage to the Idaho County sheriff.[119]

Idaho County officials returned to the crash site and the remains of the two men were found scattered about the wreckage and were positively identified as Rozenkranz and Bolick. It was determined that they were both killed on impact. In the wreckage the decayed leftovers of two wallets were also recovered. The remnants of the aircraft were hanging near a large rock, which explains why it was difficult to see from the air with its dark maroon paint scheme.[120] The wreckage of the plane with only fifty total hours on the airframe and engine remains at the site today.

1 *The well-developed structures at the Moose Creek Ranches.*

2 *A large garden area at the Ranches.*

3 *Moose Creek Ranches at dusk with a skiff of snow. Owner Paul Christman used this photo for a Christmas card.*

4 *Leaving the Moose Creek Ranger Station for the Ranches with the new Jeep (left) and deep freezer. The other Jeep belonged to the owners of what later became the Seminole Ranch.*

5 *Looking west at Moose Creek Ranches in 1956.*

6 *The natural salt lick near the Ranches was popular with guests.*

7 *A 1963 advertisement promoting the services offered at Moose Creek Ranches.*

8 *Moose Creek Ranches in the fall of 1966 after it was burned.*

9 *Johnson Flying Service pilots Cookie Calloway and Penn Stohr Jr. at the controls of a DC-2 (N4867V), while hauling generators and other miscellaneous items from the Ranches.*

10 *A 1964 photograph of Larry Dutcher's Cessna 185 at Moose Creek Ranches (l to r): Larry Dutchter, Jim Renshaw, Dave Christensen , and Gary Dutcher.*

7

8

J. Hinkle/B. Black

9

P. Stohr Jr.

10

J. Renshaw

401

The 1950s

Even though cataclysmic events overtook Moose Creek Ranches in the late 1940s, the decade of the 1950s ushered in a new pinnacle for the operation. Many of the same owners continued using the facilities, and numerous outfitters came and went.

For three years in the early 1950s Bob Johnson treated his employees at Johnson Flying Service to a company picnic at the Ranches in the spring. Johnson, who was not much of fisherman, was most likely persuaded to do this by his two main mechanics, Art and John Pritzl, who were avid sportsmen. Johnson flew the group to the annual event using company Ford Tri-Motors.[121]

On one of the yearly picnics he damaged the tail section of a Ford on landing. It was important on the old upper strip to set the plane down right on the approach end to ensure plenty of stopping room, especially when heavily loaded. As Johnson brought the Ford in on short final he slowed the airplane to set up for a nice three-point landing. However, he flared a little too early and dragged the tail through some small saplings off the end of the runway. Needless to say he was embarrassed with his bad landing in front of his employees, particularly since most of them were pilots whom he would have lambasted for the same incident.[122] It was also well known that while Johnson was an excellent mountain pilot and had mastered all of his airplanes, he required the use of eyeglasses. However, he complained that when he wore his glasses and opened the pilot's side window on the Ford they were generally torn off his face. Tired of buying replacement glasses all the time he preferred to keep them in his shirt pocket.

In 1956 Paul Christman from California purchased a portion of the operation after coming to the Ranches as a guest for several consecutive years on hunting trips.[123] In 1960 Christman bought out additional owners.[124] After Christman's initial purchase he began pouring money into the Ranches, making it one of the most revered fly-in backcountry locations in the state. One of his first purchases was a D2 Caterpillar that was flown to the Moose Creek Ranger Station strip in a Johnson Flying Service DC-3 and walked up to his property.[125] The little piece of equipment allowed him to carve out a 3,200' north-south strip near the lodge. At this time the original east-west strip on the upper bench was abandoned and the larger strip became known as "The Lower Strip."[126] The newer runway was able to accommodate Johnson Flying Service DC-3s.

Prior to the completion of the longer runway, Johnson Flying Service also flew in a big load of supplies in a DC-3 to the ranger station airstrip, which included a new red Jeep and a huge walk-in deep freezer to store client's game meat. These two items were brought to the Ranches by downstream neighbor Jim Renshaw, who owned Bitterroot Ranch at Trout Creek. Christman met him at the Fae Smith property across from Seminole. Renshaw hauled the deep freezer on a horse-drawn wagon and Christman drove the Jeep up at the same time. Worried that the Jeep would not make it through the deep water of Trout Creek, they stopped and got the wagon through first. Afterwards they went back for the Jeep, which was turned off and shifted to neutral. They then connected the horses to the front bumper of the Jeep and hauled it across.[127]

In addition to bringing in new equipment, Christman modified the already existing hydroelectric system. He also moved two existing buildings located down on East Moose Creek and added them to the rest of the complex. He turned one into a meat house and the other into a pack room for horse equipment. Christman then built an additional bunkhouse and improved the laundry facilities.[128] At times during his ownership he had five to six employees living at the ranch year round. This number increased to about twelve in the fall.[129]

The Closing

In the early 1960s Ken Christensen, an executive of Northrup-King Seed Company, bought the Ranches for $130,000 from Rex Kimberling of Orofino, who only owned it a short time after purchasing from Paul Christman for $125,000. Christensen's son Dave acted as general manager and lived at the location most of the time during their ownership.

In June 1966 Christensen sold the large parcel and all of the structures for $209,000 to the USFS.[130] The Ranches property was liquidated of all salable merchandise. Jeeps, dozers, generators, and anything else imaginable was sold and flown out. Johnson Flying Service flew several loads of hay in for Dave Christensen, who continued to outfit from the location, and flew out heavy equipment. All of these flights were made with two DC-3s (N49466 and N24320) and one DC-2 (N4867V). Pilots on the project included Penn Stohr Jr., Bob Christensen, Ken Roth, Chet Dolan, and Milton "Cookie" Calloway.[131]

On Friday night August 26 USFS crews applied the first torches to the world class hunting facility. The following Saturday the remainder of the buildings were burnt to the ground.[132] Area pilot Sid Hinkle flew his Cessna 185 to the Ranches the same morning to pick up the few remaining items he purchased from the liquidation sale. While there he took several pictures of the buildings going up in flames. Aggravated, he sent his photographs to Grangeville's *Idaho County Free Press*, where they were published on the front page of the paper. The edition caused quite a stir among its readers.

Cleanup at the Ranches continued into early October. USFS crews reseeded areas and used air-hammers to break up the remaining concrete building foundations. Crews also removed all stone-lined paths, roads, and markers for the airstrips. What was not flown out or burnt was buried.[133] After the cleanup was completed both airstrips at the location were permanently closed.

P. Stohr Jr.

A cockpit view of landing at Moose Creek Ranches in 1966 from Johnson's DC-2.

P. Stohr Jr.

Johnson's DC-2 at the Ranches. Notice the burned areas in the foreground and the generators sitting to the right.

1 *Loading a generator into a Johnson DC-3.*
2 *A Johnson DC-2 and DC-3 preparing for takeoff.*
3 *A Johnson Flying Service DC-3 landing downstream at the Moose Creek Ranches.*
4 *A 2011 view looking down Moose Creek's East Fork at the lower runway covered with trees.*

G. Turner/USFS

The Moose Creek Ranger Station circa 1933.

MOOSE CREEK RANGER STATION

The Early Years – A Remote Location

In the spring of 1909 Adolph Weholt first ventured into the Selway area as a relatively new ranger for the USFS. He initially established administrative facilities for the Moose Creek area, then known as Three Forks, located at the confluence of East Moose and North Moose creeks. He and his men took up residence at an existing cabin. This site later became incorporated into the Moose Creek Ranches.[134]

The Three Forks Ranger Station was in use until 1921 when Ranger Jack Parsell moved the headquarters to its present location. Parsell became the first ranger of the newly created Moose Creek District the previous year. He set up his office in a tent and lived there with his new bride, while he and several other USFS men built the ranger station. The large, beautifully-built structure became known as "The Honeymoon Cabin."[135]

After Parsell left, the position was filled by several rangers including Bert Kauffman (1922–24), Fred Shaner (1925–31), George Case (1932–43), and A. B. Gunderson in 1944. During these rangers' tenures the complex expanded. A barn and corral were first added in the 1920s to help maintain district stock. In the early 1930s an additional log residence was added, a woodshed was constructed that also served as a cookhouse, and a storage shed was built. By the middle of the decade an official ranger's house was constructed along with a well-equipped bunkhouse. Many other buildings were later added to the site.[136]

An Airfield, Smokejumpers, and a Close Call

By 1930, after much urging from forester Howard Flint, plans for an airstrip to access the Moose Creek administrative site were underway. In the preliminary stages of the project several people in the USFS examined the possibility of constructing the strip at the old site of the Three Forks Ranger Station. The older location was favored because of the more open terrain. Selway NF Supervisor Wolfe was an ardent supporter of the airstrip at the Moose Creek Ranger Station. In a June 1930 letter to the regional forester he argued, "A landing field immediately tributary to the ranger station would be more valuable than one located five miles above the ranger station. The landing field clearing could be used for pasture purposes and pasture is very badly needed at this point. Construction work could go ahead without undue inconvenience since the camp would be established at the ranger station. The prevailing

Progress on the Moose Creek airstrip in the fall of 1930.

A 1936 view of the Moose Creek administrative site and runway looking downstream.

winds at Moose Creek seem to come from the south and southwest and it is very probable that they could be relied on to a greater extent than those at Three Forks".[137]

Wolfe and his supporters won the dispute and clearing for the northeast-southwest 1700' airstrip was well under way by the spring of 1931, using horse-drawn equipment and hand tools. Moose Creek Ranger, George Case, directed crews through the end of June, at which time the field was deemed suitable for landing. Nick Mamer was the first to land on July 1 with passenger E. J. Jost, a USFS observer. Jost noted $8,000 had been spent and recommended another $1,200 was needed to properly finish the project.[138]

According to Jost, Mamer thoroughly inspected the field and determined one of his Ford Tri-Motor "transports" could land on the runway even in its unfinished condition. Mamer returned with a Ford five days later and made the first Tri-Motor landing in the Selway-Bitterroot. With Mamer's success Bob Johnson also agreed that he would be more than willing to use the field with his Travel Air 6000 carrying up to five firefighters or 1,000 pounds of freight.[139]

The following spring, remaining brush piles and logs were burned. In addition to this general cleanup work, the strip was extensively rolled and leveled. By 1936 more work on the runway was completed and it was extended to the current 2300'. The airfield became hugely popular and was used by many early operators to move not only USFS officials, but also outdoor enthusiasts.

Some of the post 1931 improvements were the result of the large Selway Fires of 1934. That year marked the first time that the USFS had air access to the remote area to increase fire suppression efforts. Bob Johnson was hauling a majority of the freight for the government and consistently had problems with winds. The air moving up Moose Creek, combined with the heavy loads, led him to favor landing over the ranger station dwellings, downhill. However, tall timber above the structures caused slight damage to his aircraft on two occasions. Johnson urged the removal of these trees in addition to the removal of the remaining trees on the opposite end of the runway, noting their potential hazard to an airplane during low visibility conditions, such as forest fire smoke.[140]

In the summer of 1940 the airfield provided another unique opportunity as it served as a great location to base Region 1's newly created smokejumping program. A parachute loft was constructed of poles and shakes at the top southeast corner of the runway. This was the first USFS-constructed loft in the United States.[141]

In 1940 all seven Region 1 smokejumpers were station at Moose Creek. They had gone through extensive training at a facility in Seeley Lake, Montana.[142] On July 12, 1940 a fire call requested the new program to act on a fire located in Martin Creek on the Nez Perce NF. Bob Johnson's brother Dick was dispatched to Moose Creek in Travel Air NC8112 to pick up the jumpers.[143]

After arriving, Rufus Robinson and Earl Cooley loaded into the plane with their gear. Fellow jumper

A group of Grangeville sportsmen at Moose Creek with pilot Fred Zimmerly (second from right) and his Zenith during the 1930s.

The clearing that was made after the 1934 Selway Fires. The cut allowed airplanes to land in both directions.

The International TD-9s that were used to construct the large runway at Moose Creek were brought in and hauled out with Johnson Flying Service DC-3s.

Merle Lundigan hopped aboard as cargo kicker and spotter. Shortly after takeoff they were over Martin Creek. Robinson jumped first and overshot the landing, but indicated to Cooley that he was safe. Then Cooley jumped.[144]

This first fire jump almost ended the program as quickly as it had started. Two of the three jumpers involved, later revealed that they were practically killed. When Lundigan kicked the last load out the door of the Travel Air he caught his foot in the cargo rope and almost fell out of the plane. At the last second he somehow managed to jam his legs open to catch himself in the door. Head first out of the airplane he then grabbed the steps with his hands and pushed himself back in. When Cooley jumped, his chute did not open immediately and became entangled within the risers. It eventually opened, but it was a close call. Many safety procedures were ultimately developed to prevent these mishaps. The two made it safely and went to work on the fire. The following day, after it was contained, a trail crew met them and they worked their way back to the station.[145]

Johnson noted in his logbook that he made several trips back and forth from the airstrip to the jump site to ensure the safety of the men. Capping the landmark day, Johnson wrote, "First Smoke Jump on a fire – Rock Pillar Fire – on Martin Creek Ruffus Robinson + Earl Cooley."[146]

Johnson Flying Service became a mainstay in the smokejumper program. Moose Creek continued to be used as a jump base through the 1943 season when it was moved to Nine Mile outside of Missoula, where it remained for ten years.[147] By the early 1950s the crude parachute loft was removed.[148]

The Large Runway

With increased usage of the airfield into the 1950s the USFS decided in 1956 to carryout the proper engineering and surveying to build a larger cross-airstrip. The idea was not new as H. G. Strictch started the discussion about a location for a larger runway at Moose Creek in 1936, followed by surveys in the late 1940s.[149]

In August 1957 contractor Henry "Hank" Vanderwall and crew started work on the larger 4100' north-south airstrip. Johnson Flying Service flew two disassembled International TD-9s and additional equipment for the crew to Moose Creek in a DC-3 piloted by Ken Roth. As the project progressed, Johnson brought in more equipment in DC-3s, including 8,000 gallons of diesel fuel in fifty-five gallon drums, 1,000 gallons of gasoline in fifty-five gallon drums, 1,595'

1 Contractor Henry Vanderwall's dozer working on building the large airstrip.

2 Adding some finishing touches to the runway in the spring of 1958.

3 Pilot Floyd Devlin hauled in additional fuel for the runway construction project in 1958 with Travel Air 6000 N9842.

4 Seeding the new runway.

5 Moose Creek employee Ed Collins poses with the freshly grown runway grass in 1960 before it was cut.

6 A Johnson Flying Service DC-3 (N49466) at the Moose Creek Ranger Station in the late 1950s.

Looking up the Selway River at the USFS Moose Creek airstrips circa 1958.

of drain pipe, 7,000' of wire, and steel fence posts.[150] During the first week of December, work on the runway was discontinued for the year.

In April 1958 Vanderwall brought in some of the same crew along with new faces to finish the project. Included in the final crew were Ralph Dawson, Vance Baker, Rex Maynard, and Jim Renshaw. Hired as a cook to feed the group was Renshaw's wife, Darlene. Before the field was completed additional diesel fuel had to be hauled in for the dozers. Pilot Floyd Devlin, who worked for Tom's Flying Service, flew it in using a Travel Air 6000 (NC9842) leased from Hillcrest Aviation.[151] On July 30, 1958, the new field was completed and inspected. In the end Vanderwall's crew removed twenty-four acres of timber, stumps, and brush. Near the close of the project the empty fuel drums were painted orange and used as runway markers.[152]

Since its opening, the new field has rarely been utilized by pilots, even with larger aircraft such as the DC-3. The advantage of the extra runway length on landing approaches off either end is not really usable because of the terrain. Beyond the non-usable runway, the field suffered from drainage problems, which continues as an issue today. The USFS generally closes the larger north-south runway in the fall because it tends to develop soft spots.

A United States Air Force C-47 training at Moose Creek in the late 1950s.

R. Snider

The aftermath of Bob Culver's August 4, 1959 Ford Tri-Motor accident at Moose Creek that claimed the lives of three passengers.

A Dreadful Accident and Ford Tri-Motors

The summer of 1959 was a busy fire season for the USFS. On August 4 the agency dispatched Johnson Flying Service pilot Bob Culver to drop two Grangeville-based smokejumpers to a fire on Pettibone Ridge. Also on the passenger manifest were spotter Roland M. Stoleson and Nez Perce NF Supervisor Alva Blackerby who joined the trip to observe the operation. The previous day, Culver flew the Ford Tri-Motor (N8419) requested for the mission from Grangeville to Missoula for routine maintenance.

On his return to Grangeville early in the morning on August 4 he dropped freight off at the Moose Creek Ranger Station.[153]

In addition to carrying the smokejumpers, the plane also contained a second load of freight for Moose Creek. Aspiring to deliver the goods bound for the station in the cool morning air Culver opted to make the landing prior to dropping the jumpers. With the thought of landing first, Blackerby decided to ride in the cockpit's right seat with Culver, a position normally occupied by the spotter. As a result Stoleson sat in the back with John A. Rolf and Gary G. Williams.[154]

At about eleven o'clock Culver made a routine pass over the airstrip and made a gentle turn down the Selway for an upstream landing on the short field. Fifty years after the event Stoleson explains, "We dropped down on final approach and after reaching the near end of the strip, I thought we were slow in putting down. I thought we were having a tailwind and were being pushed ahead. Bob put it down and yelled back to us that we were going to hit. We did and there was a momentary silence when I thought we had made it. But then there was a 'whoosh' of flames back through the fuselage searing my face and I dove out the open door on my immediate left (John and I were facing aft) and found myself crawling through the burning needles of a tree that had been knocked down by the crash. I swatted at the sparks on my clothing and rolled on the ground after clearing the tree. Bob came running toward me from the front right of the burning aircraft. The others were on the opposite side of the wreckage and I never saw them before ending up on a cot in the back of the ranger station."[155]

Hours after the crash Stoleson recalls, "A doctor was flown in and I remember him giving me a shot to relieve the pain. Until he came, a very kind lady who kept my burns covered with a damp cloth tended to me. A friend and ex-jumper turned helicopter pilot for Johnson named Rod Snider also came in and talked to me. Williams died on the site. Rolf died in the Grangeville Hospital that afternoon and Blackerby several days later. Culver was taken to a Missoula hospital and Dean Logan flew a Travel Air 6000 with Smokejumper Foreman Hugh Fowler aboard to Moose Creek from Missoula and transported me to the Grangeville Hospital."[156]

A memorial to those who lost their lives in the crash was placed at the Moose Creek Ranger Station in 1989 at the prompting of retired Region 1 Chief Smokejumper Foreman Fred Brauer and the Nez Perce NF Supervisor Tom Kovalicky.[157] In September the same year, a small dedication ceremony was held at the station. Stoleson, then supervisor of the Sawtooth NF and the only survivor of the heartrending accident, attended the somber event with his wife.[158] Pieces of the Ford Tri-Motor remain buried near Moose Creek, not far from where the plane came to rest at the top of the runway in 1959.

Thinking back about the tragic crash, former Johnson Flying Service pilot, Penn Stohr Jr. noted, "There was not a Ford Tri-Motor crash at Johnson Flying Service that did not have some strange consequences or circumstances surrounding it. It created a horrible aura for a great airplane."[159]

Stohr was the last to land a Ford Tri-Motor in the Idaho backcountry on June 27, 1994, almost sixty-three years to the day after Mamer landed with the first Ford. Stohr as pilot and Ken Roth as co-pilot flew Evergreen Aviation's Ford (NC9645) with a load of former Johnson employees and family to Moose Creek Ranger Station. Running up the strip after they landed was a Moose Creek USFS employee who thought he was hallucinating. Out on trail work he was making his way across the bridge below the airstrip when the plane roared overhead. The young man was absolutely astonished.[160]

Both large 5-AT and small 4-AT model Fords operated for decades in and out of Moose Creek. Standing around the Ford that day in 1994 the group all had their own personal stories. Roth remembered ferrying loads of lumber in a Ford from Moose Creek to Shearer for a USFS bridge project. He noted that as the morning progressed the wind picked up and he returned from Shearer to Moose Creek for another load with a wicked wind blowing straight up the Selway River canyon. With ease, Roth circled and set up an approach flying downriver right over the trees above the ranger station, landing downstream on the short strip.[161]

Stohr recalled making a trip as a copilot on Ford

Pieces of Ford Tri-Motor N8419 were later buried near Moose Creek and can still be found. Here two sections of the wings can be seen including part of a dropdown baggage compartment.

N7861 in July 1964 with Frank Borgeson. The two had freighted some material from Gates Park located in the Bob Marshall Wilderness that needed to be relocated to Moose Creek. They reached the ranger station and unloaded the goods.[162]

The next task was to haul out an old horse-drawn hayrake. After much maneuvering and cussing, Borgeson and Stohr determined the rake was not going to fit. To solve the problem they simply put the large part of the rake in the back of the airplane with the tongue portion hanging out the back door. To secure the rake to the aircraft they found some rope and lashed it to the strut between the wheel and the right outboard motor. The

1 The last Ford Tri-Motor (NC9645) to land in the Idaho backcountry.

2 One of Nick Mamer's original Ford Tri-Motors (NC9612) seen here at Moose Creek in the mid-1950s piloted by Abe Bowler.

3 Johnson Flying Service Ford Tri-Motor N7861 at Moose Creek in the late 1950s.

4 Jack Hughes and Bob Johnson in one of the company's first helicopters.

5 Pilot Abe Bowler and a Ford Tri-Motor.

6 Building helipads in the early 1960s.

flight back to Missoula was a success.[163]

Dick Hughes, who was a smokejumper based in Grangeville in 1965, and son of Johnson Flying Service Chief Pilot Jack Hughes, also spent a lot of time around the Fords as a kid and later a jumper. Hughes remembered the opportunity that arose one late afternoon hanging around the Grangeville airport. Borgeson was detailed to the Grangeville jumpers from Missoula with Ford N7861. When he was in Grangeville he was often out of the watchful eye of Johnson higher-ups and tended to bend the rules a bit. Earlier in the day he had been approached by a couple of guys shooting advertisements for Hamm's Beer asking him to haul them, cargo, and canoes to Moose Creek. Borgeson agreed to a little under the table deal as long as they donated to his "coffee can fund" to pay for the fuel. He then needed someone to go along with him to help load and unload. Hughes agreed to tag along, riding in the front seat.[164]

The two had the main area so full of gear for the Hamm's Beer group that one canoe was strapped onto the right strut of the Ford. Borgeson returned for one more load and Hughes gave his seat up to another jumper. The Hamm's folks really wanted to capture Selway Falls, but apparently floated down the Selway snapping photographs and running film footage for their ads along the way.[165]

Years later Hughes mentioned the event to his father. Jack Hughes was not surprised, as rumors ran thick at the company concerning Borgeson's larks and the running of his "coffee can fund."[166]

Abe Bowler from Orofino also operated a Ford Tri-Motor (NC9612) often at Moose Creek during the late 1940s and 1950s, carrying supplies for the USFS, generally from Grangeville. In addition he flew hay and supplies to the strip for nearby private landowners. Bowler sold his Ford to Johnson Flying Service in 1957 and subsequently went to work for them.

Prior to his brief years at Johnson many stories of Bowler and Fords floated around the country. One event related to the USFS and Bowler was when he flew a sick employee and some gear from Moose Creek to Grangeville with his Ford. When he landed at the Grangeville airport it was dark and the USFS personnel waiting for him noted his landing lights were not on. When questioning Bowler about the safety concern, he responded by saying landing lights were overrated and not needed. "With a good moon a person can see fine. To miss mountains and know your location you just use the lights in the various fire lookout houses, it brings you right from the ranger station to Grangeville."[167]

The fellow, aghast at Bowler's response, made a comment to the affect that he should have the light replaced. Bowler, adding humor to the situation, mumbled something about installing an old fashion candle instead of a new light bulb.[168]

Helicopters and Higgins Ridge

In 1949 Region 1 first explored the use of helicopters in connection to forestry and fire management in the Moose Creek area. Jack Hughes of Johnson Flying Service, who was the first licensed helicopter pilot in Montana, served as the operator. Using a Bell 47D helicopter (NC177B) he mainly picked up fire crews from remote locations and flew them back to the ranger station. It was during these experiments that Hughes was dispatched to the devastating Mann Gulch Fire on the Helena NF near the Missouri River. Hughes flew out the bodies of thirteen Missoula-based smokejumpers who lost their lives in the fire. Returning to Moose Creek, experiments were carried out the remainder of the season, but opinions differed on the machine's effectiveness.[169]

In the fire season of 1953 helicopters demonstrated their worth on the Moose Creek District. It saved the USFS large amounts of money and proved to be an effective and efficient way to suppress remote fires in the Selway-Bitterroot country.[170] In succeeding years Region I continued to explore the use of helicopters for aerial patrols, fire lookout support, and overall quicker transportation for fire related-activities.

Contracting exclusively with Johnson Flying Service, pilots such as Jack Hughes, Elwood "Swede" Nelson, and Fred Gerlach were used in the early helicopter fire suppression attempts. Learning from these great pilots was Rod Snider.

Starting in the summer of 1959 Snider

received his final checkout from Gerlach. He could then fly helicopters in the Idaho backcountry and took over the project of building helicopter landing locations in the country surrounding Moose Creek Ranger Station, where the seasonal helicopter base was located.[171]

By 1961 Johnson Flying Service had helped to establish helipads at Pettibone Ridge, Wylies Peak, Boxcar Mountain, Trout Peak, and Higgins Ridge, among many others. To be within reach of these remote locations, Johnson kept a helicopter and pilot on standby at Moose Creek.[172]

In 1961 the USFS contract was filled with Snider and a turbo-powered Bell G-3 (N8409E).[173] On the morning of August 4 Alternate Ranger Deane Hess and Snider departed the ranger station in search of a fire reported to the northeast. Once the fire was spotted near Higgins Ridge, fire management dispatched two Stearmans based in Grangeville for a retardant drop. Many in Grangeville and in the USFS dubbed the group of Stearmans, "The Chinese Air Force." Hess, who had been dropped off by Snider, joined another crew bound for the fire. Hess, watching the retardant drop, radioed back that it was ineffective. Next Johnson sent a couple of TBMs from Missoula.[174]

By this time Snider had returned to a nearby ridge with Moose Creek District Ranger William Magnuson. The two could see little impact from the air tankers and the decision was made to have Hess's crew return to the ranger station.[175] At this point, eight Grangeville-based smokejumpers were called to the fire, followed by twelve Missoula jumpers.[176]

At about four or five o'clock in the afternoon Magnuson and Snider headed back out on patrol to see if the smokejumpers had made any progress on the fire. Maneuvering the Bell around the blaze, Snider and Magnuson could not see a single jumper. The two started searching and Snider sighted a handful of the men on the ground wearing orange shirts. He immediately scanned the terrain to see if he could find a way out of the flames for the jumpers. On the east side of Higgins Ridge a rockslide appeared to be the solution.[177]

Snider and Magnuson then noticed that several of the smokejumpers had made their way to the Higgins Ridge helipad previously built by the USFS. With no radio contact between the helicopter and the men on the ground, Snider wanted to land and get the message about the rocky area to Fred "Fritz" Wolfrum, the group's squad leader. As Snider fought his way through the smoke with nearly zero visibility the air became extremely turbulent.[178]

Snider noted that he was fighting a west wind, which was then tumbling over the ridge and creating a tailwind, exacerbating the situation. In his first attempt to land he came directly from the west, but a tailwind moving up the east slope, made it unworkable. Snider then attempted a sideway landing from the south, followed by an attempt to back the aircraft into the landing area. With the situation growing worse for the men on the ground he got aggressive and nosed the helicopter into the wall of smoke straight toward the helipad.[179]

Fighting growing flames, thick smoke, giant airborne embers, intense heat, and a wind of over sixty miles per hour, the helicopter was lowered into the inferno. Snider hoped that the severe downdraft he was fighting would be stopped by ground effect when they reached the bottom, right before hitting the ground. However, ground effect was not there that day. As the helicopter broke through the smoke they gained better visibility of the ground and more orange shirts appeared directly below the aircraft.[180]

Wanting to arrest the descent, Snider exercised the engine well beyond the maximum manifold pressure of thirty-six inches to an amazing seventy-two inches. He ended up with a safe landing. The helicopter was maxed out beyond its limits.[181]

Snider stayed in the copter while Magnuson went over to discuss the escape route. Now on the ground, Snider was able to take a better look at what was going on and noticed empty water containers that were beginning to burn, and one of the jumper's pants on fire, which another guy help to extinguish.[182] The original plan was to tell the jumpers how they could get out. But Wolfrum voiced opposition toward the plan feeling it was far too risky. The flames became dangerously close on all four sides, entrapping them on top of Higgins Ridge.[183]

At that moment Snider told two jumpers to load up and he took off leaving Magnuson and eighteen others behind. Taking off in zero-zero visibility, trying to avoid trees he could barely see, he

N8418E

1 A group of Stearmans stationed at Moose Creek in the summer of 1961.
2 Johnson Flying Service's Bell G-3 (N8409E) piloted by Rod Snider idles, while USFS personnel (right) decided how to handle the beginnings of the Higgins Ridge Fire in August 1961.
3 The burned-out landing area on Higgins Ridge that Snider used to rescue the group of smokejumpers.
4 A Johnson Flying Service TBM attempting to put the Higgins Ridge Fire out.
5 Johnson Flying Service pilot Rod Snider.
6 A painting given to Johnson Flying Service depicting Snider's Higgins Ridge rescue.

ferried the men south to a meadow below Freeman Peak where the smoke had not yet reached. Over and over again Snider landed on the burning ridge, carrying jumpers four at a time, until the final trip when he moved out Wolfrum and Magnuson. Each time was a real scramble getting in and out. He wanted to land at the helipad like a helicopter is suppose to – straight in, but it was never possible. Every time in and out he also had to over boost the Bell's engine to forty-five inches of manifold pressure, but it held together.[184]

Talking about the rescue forty years later Snider commented, "Anyone would have done it. When you are faced with a situation like that you do not even think." To this day he does not see himself as doing anything heroic.[185]

Snider credits the success of the Higgins Ridge rescue to several factors. First he acknowledged Wolfrum for keeping his men together in such a difficult and stressful situation. He also admired Wolfrum and Magnuson as they voluntarily stayed behind, wanting to get the others off the ridge first. His final praise for the rescue being a success was the aircraft. The Bell G-3 did not fail under the extremely demanding conditions.[186]

Snider and the Bell G-3 (N8409E) used at Higgins Ridge had an amazing history together going back to the day the aircraft left the factory. He flew it from the factory to Missoula for Johnson Flying Service. While en route it began burning almost more oil than gas. Snider called the Bell factory and they sent a mechanic out to Colorado to fly the rest of the way with him to Missoula. When the new helicopter arrived at Johnson Flying Service it was outfitted with a new engine.[187]

Soon after the motor was replaced Snider experienced a problem with the throttle setup while landing on a mountaintop near the Red Ives Ranger Station in northern Idaho. The crash nearly cost him his life and the helicopter, which caught fire, was nearly a complete loss. However, mechanic John Pritzl rebuilt it the following winter. The landing skids were painted red and the helicopter became nicknamed "Red Legs." It was the first turbo-supercharged helicopter that Johnson Flying Service owned. Compared to other equipment available at the time it was one of the only helicopters capable of the task demanded of it that August day in 1961.[188]

Following the Higgins Ridge rescue, Snider was awarded the North American Fire Service Medal for his outstanding heroism, and the Stanley-Hiller Jr. Pilot of the Year Award. Furthermore Johnson Flying Service received a black and white painting of the event as a gift from Bell. The painting hung in Johnson's office until Snider left for other flying opportunities. When he moved on, Jack Hughes gave him the piece. It now hangs in Snider's workshop. Over the years he has also received many thank-yous and kind words of admiration for his efforts and skills as a pilot and a person.

One thank-you occurred at a smokejumper reunion decades after the Higgins Ridge event when a grown man came up and introduced himself as Tom Kovalicky. Kovalicky mentioned that he was one of the young smokejumpers rescued at Higgins Ridge. Snider remembered him. Kovalicky, who retired from a successful career as forest supervisor on the very forest he was nearly killed on, thanked Snider for saving his life. During the conversation Kovalicky showed him a burn scar he had from the incident, explaining he had grabbed onto the hot exhaust pipe when climbing aboard the helicopter.[189]

Several bad accidents have occurred over the years at Moose Creek. Here USFS employee Steve Roberts studies the accident that claimed the life of pilot Charlie McNeil and McNeil's eleven-year-old son on the bank of Moose Creek in August 1958.

Incidents and Accidents

Moose Creek felt the impact of the postwar economic boom of light aircraft sales. People used the remote airstrip to access backcountry camping, fishing, and hunting. In a nine-year period from 1947 to 1955 the number of aircraft landings increased by thirty percent at Moose Creek.[190] However, many incompetent pilots and aircraft have been easily

B. Zimmerly Jr

Fairchild 71 N9708 at Orofino, when Bowler owned it.

D. Hess

The wreckage of Fairchild 71 N9708 in 1960 at Moose Creek.

deceived by the airfield's relatively low elevation and somewhat forgiving terrain. In an attempt to improve safety and access to the area the USFS constructed the larger airstrip. However, this runway did not really reduce the number of aircraft accidents by private, and in some rare cases, commercial pilots.

Fairchild Loses Rudder

On the Moose Creek side of the long runway toward the north end, the remains of a Fairchild 71 (N9708) sit in the trees. Not much is left anymore, other than the airframe and some scraps of fabric. This airplane was based in southeastern Idaho until it was purchased by Abe Bowler and brought to Orofino.

Holm

The wreckage of Fairchild 71 N9708 still remains at Moose Creek.

Bowler operated the aircraft for several years until it was sold to Tom Kiiskila of Tom's Flying Service, also based in Orofino.[191] While under ownership of both Orofino operators the plane was called, "Dumbo."

The plane crashed during the summer of 1960 while being piloted by Jessie Lee Atkins, who was carrying hay and several barrels of fuel for Moose Creek Ranches, and food for Jim Renshaw's fishing party at Fish Lake. Atkins was nearly to his first destination, flying a common direct route. As he flew over Rhoda Creek into the North Moose Creek drainage for a descent to the Ranches, all but six inches of the rudder broke off. Struggling to control the aircraft he continued his descent thinking he could make the Ranches without any trouble. By the time he was over the strip, he had not lost enough altitude and was unable to make much of a turn with only the ailerons.[192]

Foregoing his first landing opportunity he pointed the ship down Moose Creek with the idea he could land south on the long ranger station runway. His plan was to get the aircraft over the end of the airstrip and reduce the power. However, he panicked at the last minute, fearing he was going to overshoot, and pulled the power back to idle. The power reduction caused a slight yaw to the west, toward the trees along the edge of the runway. With no rudder he was unable to correct the drift with just the ailerons. Focused on trying to avoid the trees, his airspeed diminished and he stalled the plane over the top of the very trees he was attempting to avoid.

The trees cushioned the aircraft and he got out unhurt but stunned. The plane was destroyed coming down nose first, pretty much as it sits today. With gas dripping from various points on the airplane, ranger station employees found Atkins sitting near the plane smoking a cigarette.[193] Many pieces of the plane have been hauled off over the years as souvenirs and the registration number has since been assigned to a restored Fairchild 71.

George Foster, the founder of Grangeville Air Service.

Frank Hill and a Cessna 180 at Moose Creek.

Grangeville Air Service

Growing up in American Falls, Idaho, Frank Hill developed a zeal for flying. Starting in high school he began taking lessons and earned his license before joining the Navy in the early 1940s. In World War II he flew DC-4s in the Pacific Theater. Returning home he pursued a career in aviation and flew for five years based in Enterprise, Oregon, before moving to Grangeville. In 1952 he went to work for George Foster, owner of Grangeville Air Service. Foster had established a respectable business that offered agricultural spraying and backcountry charters.

A decade later Hill and his wife Joanne bought Foster's company. Many people in the area learned to fly from Hill, including Joanne. Over the years Hill built an excellent reputation and in 1992 retired from his air charter business. Hill died November 7, 2006. Hill's son Greg followed in his footsteps, earning a private pilot license at the age of sixteen. Greg served seven years in the United States Navy and returned to Grangeville in 1980, joining the family business.[194] Similar to his father, he became a well-respected mountain pilot.

On November 20, 1986, Frank and Greg were busy finishing flights for hunting clients. Working together with two airplanes they were hauling loads of hay to Moose Creek and shuttling hunting gear piled at the station back to Grangeville. Squeezing in another trip before lunch, Frank departed Moose Creek with a full load. Greg took off immediately behind him in Cessna a 206 (N7311Q).[195]

Frank gained sufficient altitude and tried to contact his son for a position report, since they were to be in close proximity to one another. Unable to raise him he continued his flight until he heard the squeal of an ELT signal in his headset. The signal was in fact being emitted from the company's 206 about a half mile down river from the Moose Creek airstrip.[196]

A medical rescue helicopter located in Orofino was promptly dispatched and arrived on the scene. Also arriving at the accident at the same time was Frank along with two Idaho County Sheriff officers, and USFS employee Penny Keck. The contents of the demolished plane were strewn about. Greg did not survive the impact. However, passenger and friend Pete Schoo did, but was badly burned.[197]

Schoo later noted that they both heard a terrible noise immediately after takeoff. In an attempt to return to Moose Creek, Hill made a tight turn in the canyon. In the middle of the turn the engine lost all power and the plane struck some trees.[198] The cause of the terrible accident remains unknown. An inspection of the engine revealed everything in proper working order.

A Creative Field Repair

In the 1960s Frank Hill hired friends to help him out when business picked up in the summer months. Travis Wadly was one of these friends. Working one morning in the Selway area he ground-looped one of Hill's Cessna 180s at Moose Creek, damaging a wing.[199]

Hill and friend Bob Edling, another pilot, flew to Moose Creek to repair the airplane enough to ferry

Frank and Greg Hill unloading hunters at Moose Creek in the early 1980s.

The Johnson Flying Service Lockheed Electra L-188 (N7137C) that performed a missed approach at Moose Creek in 1974.

it out. Edling had his own operation called Wyeast Flying Service located at The Dalles, Oregon. He was known around the aviation community for landing his Super Cubs on various glaciers located on Oregon's Mount Hood and Mount Adams.[200] Hill and Edling assessed the damage and it was decided to fall a small green lodgepole tree. The wing of the plane was pulled off and the limber tree was stuffed into the leading edge to act as a spar. The stump end of the tree was then cut to the right length and the wing re-hung.[201]

Edling then ferried the plane to Rex Kimberling's shop in Kamiah, as he was the closest mechanic. To ensure he made it, Hill followed in the other airplane. Kimberling took one look at the homemade wing spar and shook his head in disbelief. Unimpressed with their work, he made the proper repairs.[202]

A Practice Approach With an L-188 Electra

In the early 1970s Johnson Flying Service of Missoula, which also had an airline division, purchased two Lockheed Electra L-188 turboprop airliners. On July 19, 1974, Johnson check airman, Penn Stohr Jr., was giving pilot Ken Roth a six-month instrument proficiency check in an Electra (N7137C).[203]

After completing the necessary instrument approaches, Stohr instructed Roth to leave the Missoula airspace and climb to 16,000' on a southwestern heading. While Roth maneuvered the airplane under simulated instrument conditions, performing the necessary air work such as steep turns, stalls, and a few emergency scenarios, Stohr caught sight of the ground below. He noticed the Moose Creek airstrip and mentioned it to Roth, who by this time was becoming a bit irritable in spite of his expert flying skills. To add a little humor to the tense situation, Stohr, half joking, told Roth that they should shoot an approach with the Electra into Moose Creek. Roth gently pulled the power back to start a descent toward the Selway while asking Stohr if he was serious. "Why not Kenny?"[204]

Like kids in a candy store the two became excited at giving it a try. After all they both had flown DC-3s in and out of Moose Creek hundreds of times and the ninety-nine foot wingspan of the Electra was only four feet wider. Plus with nearly 16,000 horsepower of instant turboprop thrust, hardly any gas, and only two of them on board it would put the performance of any DC-3 to shame. Next thing they knew, Roth was winging the big four-propped, hundred plus foot-long Electra down the Selway River at a 140 knots. With the gear down and the landing checklist completed, a tight turn to final was made back up the Selway below Divide Creek. Roth then slowed the airplane down a little more as the plane came over the confluence of Moose Creek and the Selway. About three feet before the main wheels hit the turf of the short runway, Roth shoved the throttle levers forward and the Electra shot nearly vertically into the air up Moose Creek. On the flight back to Missoula the two pilots were laughing hysterically at the stunt they had pulled.[205]

The laughter did not last long as Chief Pilot Jack Hughes was waiting for them when they landed.

419

It turned out that the Moose Creek employees called Region 1 Fire Control Officer, Chuck Kern, in Missoula when the big plane circled the airfield. The employees thought the airliner was crashing. With a quick description of the aircraft, Kern quickly realized it was a Johnson plane. The employees were scared out of their minds when they then looked up from the ranger complex and saw the big machine barreling right at them. Terrified they took cover in the thick timber.[206]

Hughes chewed Roth and Stohr up one side and down the other, using about every swear word in the book. Both the pilots pointed the finger at the other claiming not to be the pilot in command. Hughes stared Stohr down and told him that he was the check airman on the aircraft and therefore he was the pilot in command. As a result Stohr had the privilege of calling Kern to get yelled at a second time.[207]

Misfortune On the Selway

On the morning of June 6, 1979, Dick Thompson, a Nez Perce NF dispatcher, called the Payette NF in McCall and requested a USFS DC-3 to fly a group of seasonal employees from Grangeville to the Moose Creek Ranger Station on June 11. Pilot Marvin "Whitey" Hachmeister and copilot John Slingerland flew DC-3 148Z to Grangeville and arrived on time. The two pilots loaded the cargo, briefed the ten passengers, and had the plane back in the air promptly.[208]

About twenty minutes after takeoff Hachmeister noticed abnormal engine gauge indications on the left engine. The pilots decided to turn around and return to Grangeville. Slingerland informed the passengers of the situation, while Hachmeister feathered and secured the left engine, followed by the correct procedure to maintain altitude, which required a large increase of power on the right engine.[209]

Seconds after Hachmeister poured the coals to the right engine and initiated a gentle turn back to Grangeville; the number eight cylinder on the running engine separated and was hurled through the cowling. A fire ensued from the blown cylinder, shrouding the right engine in flames. Within no time the fire began sweeping across the wing. Both fuel valves were then pulled to off and when the situation could not

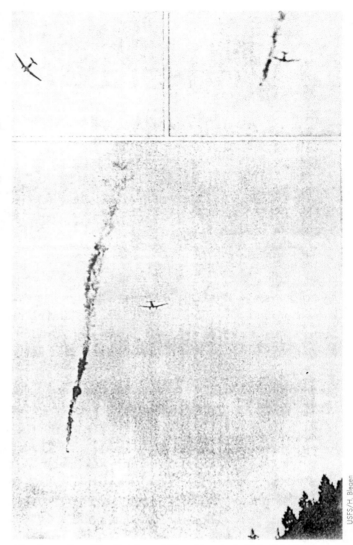

USFS/H. Blegen

A few frames from hiker Hal Blegen's film of the crippled DC-3 (N148Z) over the Selway River. The larger image clearly shows the outline of the airplane with smoke trailing from the falling right engine.

get any worse the right engine twisted off its mounts and plummeted toward the earth. As the engine tore away from the wing, the right landing gear dropped. With no options remaining and in a fight for their lives, the pilots struggled to maintain a flight attitude that would take them toward the Selway River.[210]

On the ground at the same time was a group of young men hiking up the Selway above Selway Falls. One of the men was Hal Blegen, a photographer and employee of *The Spokesman-Review* newspaper based in Spokane. Not sure what they were seeing, Blegen dropped his backpack from his shoulders and managed to dig out his camera. It had the wrong lens, but he snapped as many shots of the crippled airplane as he could before it disappeared.[211]

Recovering a portion of the DC-3's fuselage from the Selway River.

The memorial plaque at the Moose Creek Ranger Station remembering those who lost their lives in the June 1979 crash. The other plaque is in memory of the USFS employees who died in the 1959 Ford Tri-Motor accident.

Upriver and in the air from Blegen, Hachmeister and Slingerland were amazingly combating every aerodynamic impossibility, maneuvering the wounded aircraft through the walls of the Selway canyon. As the plane lost altitude the left wing struck a tree about 200' above the river, causing Hachmeister to lose all control.[212]

Believing the plane was in serious trouble Blegen and his friends stepped up their pace. As they continued up the trail, the group noticed debris coming down the river indicating that the plane had crashed. The hikers pulled what they could to the banks.[213]

Hearing aircraft, the hikers knew rescue crews were searching for the downed airplane. A helicopter working the search landed on a large river bar and met the hikers. The group shared what they could and Blegen handed his film to the pilot requesting it be delivered to *The Spokesman-Review*.[214]

The next day on the front page of the June 12, 1979 *Spokesman*, Blegen's amazing and tragic photograph revealed the outline of the DC-3 and a smoke trail coming off the tumbling right engine. Looking back at the photograph some thirty years later Blegen softly commented, "I wish the photograph which has brought me the most recognition, would not have been that one. The whole thing was really too bad."[215]

In the end it was determined that both pilots were killed on impact along with passengers Catherine Hodgin, Thomas Terkeurst, Ronald Hagan, Don Easthouse, Robert Cook, Philip Leber, and Pat McGreevy. Three passengers and a dog were able to escape from the wreckage. Robert A. Taylor made it out, but later died from his injuries. Charles Dietz survived after being treated in the Lewiston hospital. Survivor Bryant Stringham and his dog struggled out of the wreckage and river, then hiked ten miles to the Moose Creek Ranger Station for help.[216]

A memorial stands at the Moose Creek Ranger Station today remembering those people on the flight of 148Z on the dreadful day in 1979. In addition, Moose Creek District Ranger Art Seamans and professor Dr. Jim Fazio put in place a memorial fund at the University of Idaho, commemorating the crash victims and in memory of Fazio's student Philip "Kevin" Leber.[217]

By the end of June 1979 both Pratt and Whitney R-1830 radial engines were recovered from the Selway River for examination.[218] During the review process many concerns about aircraft maintenance surfaced. The final accident report noted that maintenance records for 148Z were incomplete for the aircraft and particularly for the left engine. The spherical dry-powder fire extinguisher bottles had been removed for hydrostatic testing and were not in the airplane at the time of the crash. Had these been present it could have helped retard the fire on the right wing.[219]

Morrison-Knudsen Aviation Center in Boise, completed the 100-hour inspection on the airframe and right engine only, as the left engine was nearly timed out. After more use, 148Z was brought back to Morrison-Knudsen to hang a new left engine and complete a "preseason inspection." On May 25, 1979 the airplane was test-flown and released to the USFS.

Other details in the accident report indicated issues with the left engine. Apparently the remanufacturer (Morrison-Knudsen) had used uninspected replacement parts. It was also found during the teardown that the crankshaft to propeller shaft oil-transfer pipe was left out upon assembly of the engine and nose case. This caused the overheating problem. This conclusion was further supported by the discoloration of gears and metallic analysis.[220] Total actual time since rebuild on the left engine was only eight and one half hours.[221]

On the right engine both bronze and steel washers were found on the number eight cylinder hold-down studs, when they all should have been bronze or aluminum. The studs were broken and nuts were loose or missing. The number eight cylinder "parted at lower skirt in a preexisting crack."[222] The right engine had 29.1 hours of time since the 100-hour inspection with a total time of 1,078.1 hours.[223]

Overall the accident report stated, "The coincidence of the 2 engines failing within less than one minute in flight is extraordinary; probably greater than 1 million to 1."[224] The reality behind this whole accident and careless loss of lives is that it could have been prevented if the responsible parties had put in place a proper maintenance policy.

At the time of this accident the USFS maintained all of their airplanes as defined by the FAA under "public aircraft," meaning aircraft owned and operated by the United States government were exempt from maintenance deemed appropriate by the acting agency (USFS). It is interesting to note that contractors for the USFS in 1979, operating identical DC-3s with Pratt and Whitney R-1830 radials were held to higher maintenance standards than those of 148Z. For example, at the preseason inspection, the contractor's R-1830 engines could not have been over the 1,000-hour mark to operate for the USFS.

It is also interesting to note that the USFS was able to operate aircraft for less money than a contractor of any size, because of the leniency provided under the FAA's "public aircraft" policy. This is one reason they decided to create their own fleet of aircraft. The use of "public aircraft" for USFS airplanes was reformed in the beginning of the twenty-first century when several air tankers crashed while operating under these exemptions. The public took notice and asked questions. For the crew and passengers of DC-3 148Z, the policy that ultimately caused their unfortunate fate is now corrected.

Penny and Emil Keck at Moose Creek with one of Frank Hill's Cessna 180s.

The Kecks – Longtime Employees

Emil and Penny Keck became Moose Creek icons during their combined twenty-four year stint of working at the ranger station. Most pilots and visitors passing through the Moose Creek area while they occupied the station, have a story about one or the other.

Emil first came to the district in 1963 after many years of logging. Proving to be a jack-of-all-trades, Emil shared his skills of working with primitive tools. He prided himself in not using power equipment, often completing tasks thought impossible, while being in compliance with wilderness standards. Besides building bridges, repairing structures, packing, and working trails, he was also in charge of hiring district summer employees. In 1967 he hired Penny Kummrow, the district's first female employee, as the lookout on Shissler Peak.

A current view down the 2300' Moose Creek runway.

Looking upstream at the short runway in 2011.

In 1990 the Moose Creek Ranger Station was listed on the National Register of Historic Places.

Penny turned out to be every bit as tough and knowledgeable about the outdoors as Emil, and the two were married in 1968. Due to USFS regulations of the era, husbands and wives were unable to be employed together. Penny solved the problem by simply volunteering for her husband on the district. In 1979 Emil was forced to stop working and they switched positions. In 1988 the couple left Moose Creek and Emil retired, while Penny continued to work for the USFS at Fenn Ranger Station. Emil died two years later at the age of seventy-seven.

Current Happenings

Although Moose Creek is not one of the more challenging backcountry airstrips, it is arguably one of the most beautiful public strips in the entire Idaho backcountry. In 1990 the Moose Creek Ranger Station complex was listed on the National Register of Historic Places. At the time of the listing both runways were included as important contributing elements to the historic property.

About twenty years later the airplane camping facilities were updated and many were relocated to the "Island" area near the Selway River between the two runways. When the renovation occurred, several fire rings and picnic tables were removed to be more in keeping with wilderness.

A few years before the picnic tables were removed, they were the subject of a dispute involving Hollywood actor Harrison Ford and a Moose Creek USFS employee. For many years Ford and his pilot friends have trekked to the Idaho backcountry on what they call a "Backcountry Safari." Ford owns several of his own aircraft including a two-tone green and yellow de Havilland Beaver (N28S) that he pilots on these trips. His entourage generally flies around in a pack of Huskies.

Apparently Ford and his friends set up camp on the lower end of the short runway and once settled in, gathered all the picnic tables not in use and pushed them together at their spot. A USFS employee happened by and was not too pleased when she discovered what they had done. After a bit of a wilderness lecture the tables were returned to the appropriate locations.

Believing everyone was on the same page, the employee retired to the station only to be interrupted again when the group ran out of potable water. Instead of making the nice leisurely walk up to the ranger station where water is available to the public, Ford cranked up his Beaver, taxied up the runway to the station, filled his containers, and then taxied back. Ford's actions did not sit well with the USFS employee and she returned to the camping area and gave him a piece of her mind. In the end Ford apologized for not respecting the unwritten wilderness rules. A few days later he even sent the Moose Creek employee flowers with an apologetic card attached. She remained unimpressed.

SEMINOLE RANCH

Early Occupants

Omar Richardson who owned the ranch from 1952–55.

In October 1921 Frank Freeman received homesteaded approval for 122.6 acres at the location now known as Seminole Ranch. Freeman worked for the USFS starting in 1909, and established the nearby lookout that now bears his name.[225] It is believed that before Freeman lived on the land it was used by his relative, George Shissler for his cattle operation, which extended up North Moose Creek. Freeman built a small cabin, root cellar, and garden, eking out a living here for many years. Freeman sold the place in 1925 to Alson Johnstone. One year later Fred Shaner, who served as the Moose Creek ranger from 1925 through 1931, acquired the parcel.[226]

In 1952 Omar Richardson, a part owner and operator of Orofino Building Supply, purchased the Freeman homestead from Shaner. He named the property Selway River Ranch. Richardson took to the place right away. To work on the ranch he bought a Farmall Cub tractor from the USFS (used at Moose Creek Ranger Station) for $5. He made many improvements to the large acreage, including the construction of several buildings. For the few years that he owned the property he accessed it with his own Piper Cub that he tied down at the Moose Creek Ranger Station strip.[227]

While Richardson really enjoyed the isolation of the area, his wife did not. He told many people in regards to the property that it was similar to an addiction, "You plan to go in for a week, but end up staying for a month, and you just never want to leave."[228]

The Orofino Owners

After leasing the place in 1954 to outfitter Ray West, in 1955 Omar Richardson sold the property for $18,000 to Gwen Maynard and Joe Richardson (not related) also of Orofino. These two partners went to great effort to enhance the place, which they called Moose Creek Ranch. Although the ranch already had the existing log buildings, the two men constructed a large lodge and barn. To help them make the upgrades, a portable sawmill was brought in, along with a Willys Jeep.[229]

Most of the materials and equipment for the new buildings were flown to the airstrip at Moose Creek Ranger Station and hauled across a newly-built bridge over Moose Creek. Johnson Flying Service brought in the oversized loads including the Jeep with DC-3s.[230] Tom's Flying Service, based in Orofino, hauled in the remainder of the supplies. Pilot Arnie Brandt, who flew for Tom's Flying Service, remembered flying load after load for the new lodge and barn. Included in the material he flew from Orofino were several loads of stone that had been transported from the Midwest.[231]

In the summer of 1961, Maynard, the more involved partner of the ranch, died leaving Richardson as the sole owner. Richardson decided to sell as it was not his primary interest.[232]

The structures built by Omar Richardson.

The bridge and main house constructed by Maynard and J. Richardson.

Unloading the Maynard/Richardson Jeep from a Johnson Flying Service DC-3 (N49466) at the Moose Creek Ranger Station.

The Griffiths Years

In July 1964 the ranch sold to Robert "Bud" and Alice Griffiths of San Jose, California.[233] Griffiths was an entrepreneur and was involved with multiple companies over the course of his career, ranging from slot machines to lumberyards. His final enterprise, Century Concrete, primarily provided ready-mix concrete.[234]

Griffiths first came to the Selway country on a hunting trip at Moose Creek Ranches in the early 1960s. On a day trip from the Ranches the outfitter trailed the group by the old Freeman homestead, and the place intrigued him. Following further inquiry Griffiths found out that the parcel was for sale. Soon after purchasing, he named it the Seminole Ranch in honor of close family friends, the Augusts, who were part Seminole Indian.[235]

While not an avid hunter, Griffiths enjoyed the camaraderie of the sport and through the fall of 1968 had outfitters and guides at the ranch.[236] Family, friends, and clientele were commonly flown to the Moose Creek Ranger Station airstrip and then driven by Jeep to the Seminole footbridge. Similar to previous owners Griffiths brought in updated equipment, including

a new Jeep and a D2 Caterpillar; both machines were delivered to the ranger station airfield with DC-3s. At the time the new Jeep came in, the old one originally transported in by Richardson and Maynard was hauled out.[237]

After several years of accessing the ranch by airplane and Jeep from the ranger station Griffiths decided he needed direct entry to the property. Grangeville pilot Frank Hill helped to design the general layout and approach for the roughly 1200' airstrip with 900' usable.[238] In 1967 a cat skinner from Missoula used the D2 to begin clearing large trees, brush, and stumps. The construction of the runway was a huge undertaking and was finished the following year.[239] The project required a massive amount of fill and material to be moved during the leveling process. In fact most of the large trees that were cut during the endeavor were used as fill for the runway's base. Years later as the trees decayed it caused erosion holes to form in the airstrip's surface, which required constant repair. It is believed that Hill was the first pilot to land a plane on the field.[240]

Years later Hill urged Griffiths to consider building a second longer airstrip situated north of the first runway and parallel to Moose Creek. Some initial tree clearing was done for this strip, but nothing more was completed.[241] The majority of this preliminary cut can still be seen.

Throughout Griffiths's ownership he visited the ranch about four times per year in two-week increments. On his vacations he found some pleasure fishing and hunting, but most of all he liked the solitude of the area and the work involved in keeping the place going. Griffiths preferred not to hire outside help for ranch

Bud Griffiths relaxing on the porch of the Seminole Ranch in June 1975.

maintenance; therefore, he took projects on by himself or invited friends to vacation with him in exchange for labor. One of the bigger upgrades he added to the Seminole was the instillation of the hydroelectric system.[242]

The Griffiths children, Bob and Judith, also delighted in visiting the remote location. When Bob and his wife Robin were married they honeymooned at the ranch in 1972. As the Griffiths family grew, grandkids also came to love the place during their summer vacations. In the late 1980s Griffiths was diagnosed with the early stages of Alzheimer's disease. Around this period his family arranged for him to visit the Seminole Ranch one last time. They also agreed to make estate planning decisions and the ranch was divided into three shares between Alice and the two kids. Bud died in March 1996 and Alice approximately five years later. Although Bob and his family adored the Seminole, the upkeep and financial strain became too much to handle. Once the choice was made to part with the ranch The Conservation Fund became the primary prospective buyer.[243]

The Closing

In 2001 the Griffiths family decided to sell the property to The Conservation Fund. The non-profit organization then searched for volunteers to help manage the newly acquired asset. Joe Rimensberger and his wife, along with another couple volunteered for the position from May 2003 though the fall of 2006. Rimensberger now a retired captain from SkyWest Airlines started Osprey Aviation, a Hamilton-based 135 Air Taxi operation, in 1999. When working for the airline

Pilot Frank Hill lining up for takeoff from the ranch in the fall of 1978.

he adjusted his summer schedule to allow for flying the backcountry and volunteering at the Seminole.[244]

Rimensberger and his friends mainly flew back and forth between Hamilton and the ranch, which required the runway to be maintained. The crew revived an old tractor and mowing machine to cut the airstrip's grass and continually filled holes. During these years Rimensberger flew his Cessna 185 (N104DE). He later lost this airplane to a landing accident at the North Star Ranch caused by a cracked landing gear.[245]

The volunteers lived at the Seminole about five to six days a week, spring through fall. In 2005 The Conservation Fund sold the Seminole Ranch to the USFS. Initially the sale only included the land, giving The Conservation Fund volunteers more time to remove valuable contents before the federal agency took complete ownership. In April 2005 Rimensberger made the last legal landing at the ranch with his Cessna 185 before the airfield was permanently closed.[246]

One of the main items the Griffiths wanted from the ranch was the Jeep, as it had provided many

B. Griffiths

Bob Griffiths and his son Scott at work.

good memories for their family. Rimensberger spent sometime getting the vehicle running, so it could be moved out of the barn to a location suitable to be airlifted out by helicopter.[247] In 2006, Bob hired Salmon River Helicopters of Riggins for the job. The company successfully slung the Jeep from the property and flew it to Riggins, where Bob met them with a trailer. It was then hauled to California.[248] Later the D2 dozer was also airlifted out. After the USFS finalized the content portion of the sale, the ranch sat idle for several years until 2010 when the dismantling process started. With the Seminole airstrip closed, discarded materials from the property were shuttled to the Moose Creek Ranger Station airstrip and flown out.

In regards to the ultimate fate and sale of the Seminole Ranch Bob commented, "My hope was that The Conservation Fund would place some restrictions on the property and put it back in private hands. However, we were warned that it might end up as government property. But at the time we financially had no choice...the final outcome was very disappointing to me."[249]

J. Rimensberger

Joe Rimensberger and his dog Cessna at the Seminole Ranch.

B. Griffiths

Bob Griffiths mowing the runway in the 1980s.

The Fae Smith Place

Directly across from Seminole was another smaller 33 acre in-holding homesteaded in 1925 by Fae Smith.[250] It was commonly known as "The Fae Smith Place." Smith turned down multiple offers from the USFS, which wanted to purchase the parcel. In 1963 Robert Fletsher obtained the property. He then sold the old homestead in 1968 to the USFS, and shortly thereafter everything was removed.[251]

1 *A 2011 aerial of the Seminole Ranch. Notice the irrigation pond has been rendered unusable and the bridge and cable car have been removed. The end of the runway is visible in the upper right corner.*

2 *The main lodge at the Seminole Ranch.*

3 *A 1966 advertisement for the Seminole Ranch.*

4 *The Seminole Ranch's large barn above the lodge.*

5 *The view from the top of the 1300' airfield in 1995.*

6 *Looking up the Seminole Ranch airstrip.*

7 *The Fae Smith cabin in the late 1950s.*

SELWAY-BITTERROOT WILDERNESS
AN ADDITIONAL AIRSTRIP

FISH LAKE
The Early Years

The current Fish Lake cabin in the late 1930s.

The airfield was started in 1933 and finished the following summer. On August 11, 1934 Roy Shreck with the Spokane Air National Guard was the first to land at the airstrip with one of his squadron's patrol planes (NC1598). Also on board the aircraft was USFS employee Howard Flint.[252]

The Zimmerly's Zenith at Fish Lake in the 1930s.

Prior to the building of the airstrip, Lew Fitting, an early trapper in the Lochsa area, built a small log cabin across the creek from the upper end of the landing strip opposite the current cabin. In 1921 Ranger Elmer Walde headquartered the Fish Lake Ranger District at Fitting's cabin. Two other cabins near the lakeshore were also believed to have existed, but little is known about them. The Fitting structure was burned when Ranger Ralph Hand had a crew build a new larger log cabin west of the upper end of the airstrip.[253]

The structure built under Hand existed only for a short time before it was abandoned for the present cabin, erected in 1933 on the extreme west end of the runway. In 1935 this cabin, constructed under the Selway NF, was transferred to the Clearwater NF. The USFS regularly staffed the cabin through the early 1950s. A storage shed was added to the site in 1944 to house horse-drawn equipment used to maintain the airfield.[254] This small shed no longer exists, as it collapsed under heavy winter snows.

The revamped Fish Lake airfield as it appeared after being reopened in 1955—notice the muddy conditions.

A 1960 advertisement for longtime Fish Lake outfitter Jim Renshaw.

The Runway Renovation

In 1952 the USFS hired Johnson Flying Service to fly a small Farmall tractor to Fish Lake in a DC-3. The hope was that they could better service the runway with the mechanized equipment. A storage shed was erected thirty feet from the cabin to house the new machine. The ends of the shed were later covered in wood to help prevent porcupines from eating the rubber tires on the tractor.[255]

The next year Johnson flew in a small mower attachment for the Farmall to help with runway upkeep. While equipment was being flown to Fish Lake, Missoula smokejumpers were also brought in. The jumper's main contribution was cutting a large stand of massive spruce trees on the approach end of the runway.[256]

In the fall of 1953 USFS crews began the task of completely reworking the runway. The main goal was to create a smoother surface and improve drainage. USFS crewmember Jim Renshaw noted that they wanted to form a slight crown in the runway. To accomplish this the little Farmall was used to bring soil in from the edges to the center. The strip was then leveled using the tractor, which pulled a small grader. Before winter set in the crew had half the strip plowed lengthwise and the other portion remained in sod.[257]

In 1954 when the snow melted, the USFS placed a closure on the airfield to complete the remaining work. By the end of the field season the new runway surface was completed and reseeded. Fish Lake opened again in 1955, but should have stayed closed, as the field was exceptionally muddy from the previous two years of work. This caused problems for several pilots and their aircraft.[258]

Renshaw, who by trade was an outfitter and guide, operated a hunting camp from Fish Lake from 1953 through 1972. His main camp was located a half-mile up the old trail from the cabin toward Fish Lake Saddle. After 1972 he moved his hunting operation farther north to the Lochsa area, but continued to guide fishing trips from Fish Lake until 1998 when he retired from commercial outfitting. Over the years he was associated with many events that occurred at Fish Lake.[259]

In the mid-1950s when the field was still muddy, two student pilots from Pullman landed a sixty-five horsepower Piper Cub. The boys got out, took a look around and decided that they would try and takeoff again, regardless of the density altitude. Hearing the little engine windup, Renshaw turned his attention to the airfield. About halfway down the runway the student pilot chopped the power, realizing he was not going to get airborne. The plane taxied back and shut down at the west end of the strip.[260]

Renshaw walked over, saying little to the boys. They insisted that they were going to try it again. Realizing he could not stop these two kids from trying to attempt suicide, he thought he could at least give them more of a fighting chance. He disassembled part of the fence located between the cabin and the end of the airstrip giving them 300' more of runway.

Two of Tom Kiiskila's airplanes mounted on skis at the airstrip hauling out hunters late in the year.

Ken Roth on a snow survey job with a Johnson Flying Service Cessna 180 (N2816A).

Renshaw again voiced his doubts, but the two did not listen. Nervously watching, Renshaw saw the plane barely leave the ground at the far end of the strip. The Cub along with the two novice pilots should not have made it, but somehow the aircraft found some magic air and squeaked out.[261]

Years later the USFS reported that they had extended the runway to its present length of 2650', but in actuality they only removed the same fence Renshaw had moved for the two student pilots. At that time Renshaw had permission to use the cabin for storage, and loading and unloading aircraft was easier if the planes could taxi up to the porch. Depending on how careful the pilot was or was not when turning around in this area, a blast of power could fill the little cabin full of dust.

A Snow Survey Tail

Snow surveys were conducted annually at Fish Lake for many years as part of a larger study to collect snowpack data. Johnson Flying Service generally flew to Fish Lake to collect the samples during the spring. In 1956 Penn Stohr Sr. and Dean Logan flew to the lake from Johnson's base in Missoula with a Cessna 180 equipped with hydraulic Federal skis. Stohr much preferred the old style straight skis with no hydraulics, but the newer ones were easier to use. If the plane they were using was not equipped with retractable skis, the company flew to a small meadow up Rattlesnake Canyon that was generally right above

the snowline. Here the snow was hard enough to land with wheels and they would then switch to skis.[262]

Stohr and Logan arrived at Fish Lake with no problem until they went to turn around in front of the cabin and one ski broke through the wet snow. With the idea they could pack enough snow under the sunken ski to lift it to the surface, Stohr hoisted himself up on the end of the opposite wing, while Logan shoved snow into the hole. The men tried this a few times until Stohr became so exhausted that he slipped off the wing landing on his midsection. It was later determined that he had dislocated several ribs. Recognizing that they were going to be stuck for the night and that Johnson would dispatch another plane to look for them in the morning, they started a fire in the cabin and settled in.[263]

The next day they awoke to the sound of an airplane. Logan stepped out and could tell it was one of Johnson's PA-11s. The small Piper piloted by Ken Roth landed and taxied up to the crippled airplane. Lady Luck was not on their side, as Roth also got stuck. He and Logan worked the remainder of the day trying to get Roth's plane moved, but to no avail.[264]

Stohr often traveled with a jug of sprits and plenty of extra cigars for just this type of event, and had Roth fetch the items from under the rear seat of the Cessna 180. The three had a nice evening shooting the bull in the Fish Lake cabin. The next day another Johnson plane flew into help. With the additional manpower and colder temperatures all three airplanes were able to get back to Missoula with no problems.[265]

431

Airplanes That Never Left

Throughout the years that the airport has been in use it has had a number of bad accidents. As a result, the USFS put a sign up warning aviators to use extreme caution. The sign indicates that there have been six wrecks and eight fatalities over the years. Since the sign was posted other accidents have occurred.[266]

The first major plane wreck at Fish Lake was an Ercoupe that crashed circa 1948. After an enormously long takeoff roll the Ercoupe barely became airborne and the pilot was not able to get the aircraft out of ground effect. The plane crossed the lake and crashed about 350' below the lake in a clearing that is now covered in timber. On impact the plane caught fire. Renshaw's in-laws, Frank and Minnie Wilson who were outfitting in the area, heard the plane attempt to takeoff and then crash. The two arrived at the scene as quickly as they could, but they were only able to help one of the two men out of the wreckage. The other man was already dead. Remains of this aircraft can still be found in the area.[267]

Roughly two years after the Ercoupe accident a Cessna 140 operated by two military men was out flying around. They were unfamiliar with the hazards of the airstrip. Similar to the previous wreck these men were unable to get the little Cessna horsed into the air before they crashed into the center of the lake. The USFS had the tough task of pulling the bodies out of the wreckage, and the airplane out of the lake. To dispose of the wreckage the USFS built a small raft and floated it out in the middle of the lake and blew it to pieces with dynamite. This is the only airplane at the bottom of Fish Lake.[268]

Several accidents occurred in the mid-1950s, starting with a Piper Cub. The Cub's pilot could not quite keep the craft in the air after leaving the strip and put it into the shallow area on the left side of the lake. The pilot and his passenger walked away unhurt. The airframe was a total loss, but some of the parts, including the engine, were salvaged. For years the trashed prop hung on a tree in Renshaw's hunting camp and the seats were also put to use. The one undamaged wing was stored in the tractor shed until 1964 when it was buried with the remains of other airplanes.[269]

Following the Piper Cub an Aeronca Sedan

Larry Dutcher's Cessna 185 in the fall of 1963 at Fish Lake with Renshaw employees (l to r): Howard and Carol Weise and Charlie Breeden.

crashed into the center of the lake. All the occupants of the aircraft were uninjured, but the airplane was totaled. The USFS hauled this wreckage out and buried it in the timber near the lower end of the lake.[270]

Before the end of the decade a Stinson Flying Station Wagon also crashed in the lake after takeoff. The pilot of this airplane spent the day fishing with a friend knowing he had to wait for the afternoon heat to dissipate. Anxious to get back home they only waited until early evening, which was not long enough. Renshaw heard the crash from his camp and came down on a horse as quickly as possible. He could tell it was too late to help the men, whom he knew.[271]

The authorities were notified and the county sheriff came into recover the bodies. Renshaw helped and they rigged up a dragging device with four sturgeon hooks and were able to recover one body fairly quickly, but the pilot's body was not found until sometime later. It was discovered that both men had gotten out of the wreckage but could not swim.[272]

The first body was packed up to the airfield by Renshaw and flown out by a pilot flying a Cessna 175. He was in the area at the time and was willing to help. Due to poor weather no other planes were able to reach Fish Lake. The pilot of the 175 offered to take the body and the sheriff back to Grangeville in spite of the bad weather. Once in the air it became evident that Grangeville or any other landing location in that direction was not an option and the storm chased them all the way to Kellogg, where they stayed the night.[273]

Abe Bowler later flew a Ford Tri-Motor in and retrieved the pilot's body. It was rumored that the pilot had an interest in the Ford with Bowler and owed him money. Bowler apparently sent the family a bill for the flight. The Stinson was pulled to the edge of the lake and

Pilot Larry Dutcher and his Cessna 185 (N1687Z) at Fish Lake in 1964. He was killed in the airplane near this exact location just a few months after the photo was taken.

resided there for several years until it too was buried.[274]

Years earlier Bowler himself had a close call at Fish Lake in a Cessna 195 while ferrying supplies from Lewiston for a hunting party. Bowler was committed to the takeoff when a USFS horse came running along his right side and cut in. The horse struck the landing gear, resulting in a dead horse and a completely torn off gear.[275]

In the fall of 1964 one of the most deadly and tragic accidents of all happened at the lake, killing pilot Larry Dutcher. Dutcher operated Selway Flying Service in Kamiah and was a good friend of Renshaw's. He not only flew regularly for Renshaw hauling supplies and clients for his business, but the two spent a lot of time kicking around the Selway-Bitterroot area. Dutcher would often land a ski-equipped plane at Renshaw's ranch on the Middle Fork of the Clearwater at Suttler Creek.[276]

Renshaw and Dutcher had prearranged several flights for the hunting season between his Bitterroot Ranch on Moose Creek and Fish Lake, where he held permits. In the middle of October Dutcher was to fly one group in and another out. However, things did not go as planned and one group of hunters showed up early and persuaded Dutcher to fly them in ahead of schedule to Fish Lake.[277]

When Dutcher landed with the new crowd in his Cessna 185 (N1687Z) he was greeted by two of Renshaw's hired hands that were holding down the main camp with the cook. Renshaw was at a spike camp on Wounded Doe Creek near the salt licks with the first group of hunters. Dutcher assured the hired hands that he would help entertain the new hunters

for one night at Fish Lake, while they waited for the others from Wounded Doe. Everyone agreed to the plan and they began unloading the plane and packing the gear to camp.[278]

The next morning, October 16, Dutcher and the men in his camp awoke to a cold frosty day. After breakfast one of the hunters in the group became pushy. He wanted the guides to contact Renshaw to find out the day's arrangements. It was in the years of CB radios and they did not work well in the rugged terrain. Due to Renshaw's location he could not be reached. The hunter who was a flatlander pilot then started pressuring Dutcher to fly over the camp with the radio to find out the agenda. Dutcher eventually caved in.

Several of the men walked from camp down to the airstrip with Dutcher and found the 185 had a thick layer of frost and ice. They started removing some of the ice, but it was determined that their efforts were ineffective. Dutcher then decided if he taxied down the runway and back up that the movement would flex the wings enough to break the ice and make it easier to chip off. There is debate to this day on what really occurred next, as eyewitnesses reports vary. Some at the lake noted that Dutcher only taxied down to the far end of the strip near the lake and then took off, while others stated that he taxied up and then returned to the far end. One fact that is not disputed is Dutcher never stepped out of the airplane again to finish clearing the ice.[279]

It is assumed Dutcher thought he had broken enough ice off the wings by taxiing on the strip for a safe takeoff. He then executed a takeoff from the northeast end of the runway with no favoring wind. The empty 185 leaped off the ground and as he climbed about 200' west of the cabin and several hundred feet in the air, he was forced to make a slow, low altitude turn to avoid oncoming terrain and heavy timber. When he entered the turn the plane dropped out of the sky. In one of the most critical stages of flight, with no altitude for possible recovery the 185 barreled straight into the ground on the south edge of the runway roughly 300' from the cabin.[280]

Sid Hinkle, making a slight detour en route to

433

the Selway Lodge, spotted the wreckage. He made radio contact with the men on the ground and found out the story. During the discussion Renshaw was able to hear Hinkles's transmissions and could talk directly to Hinkle as he flew over. It was the first Renshaw had even heard that these men had showed up early. Hinkle then flew to Selway Lodge, picked up the manager's wife, Artist Briggs, and flew to Kamiah where he broke the news to Dutcher's wife.[281]

It was not long before people began pillaging the highly equipped and relatively new 185. Ski apparatuses were stolen and other items such as rotating beacons were removed for souvenirs. The USFS eventually dug a large hole and buried the airplane along with the previously wrecked Stinson and lingering Cub parts.[282]

More wrecks piled up at Fish Lake after Dutcher's demise. In the early 1980s a military man flying a Piper Cub with a passenger crashed on approach before even coming over the lake. The accident killed both occupants. Following this accident outfitter Tim Craig hired a helicopter to help him look for missing stock in the area. The helicopter had a bad landing when the pilot set it down in some soft snow and tipped the aircraft over on its side. Fortunately no one was injured.[283]

Recent Years

In more recent years the USFS has opened a volunteer position to staff the cabin. The airstrip continues to be a popular destination for backcountry aviation enthusiasts. Although the fishing at the lake can be excellent, many believe that Moose Creek should be renamed Fish Creek and Fish Lake should be called Moose Lake. The reason for the name switch is that Fish Lake is historically known for having large populations of moose. Over the years pilots have seen several head of moose swimming in the lake at one time.

When Renshaw started outfitting and guiding from Fish Lake he recalled days that he would see two-dozen moose in one day. Early on it was an oddity not to see at least one per day. The area at one time had about six moose permits available per year. The number of permits has since dropped as the moose population has decreased. Even today with the

An aerial of the 2650' Fish Lake runway looking west in 2007.

reduction of moose in the area it is still a good place to see one of the enormous creatures.

With consistent air traffic into the twenty-first century a group of volunteers approached the USFS about improving some of the camping facilities, including a new outhouse. The USFS agreed to provide the pre-manufactured unit and to fly it in, as long as volunteers assembled it. When the project was finished volunteers found an old pipe with hooks attached to it in the shed. The odd looking device appeared to have no use, so they mounted it on the inside wall of the new latrine as a deluxe coat and hat rack.

Renshaw happened to arrive on a camping trip at Fish Lake the summer the volunteers finished the outhouse. Proud of their work they showed the new structure to the area veteran. Renshaw checked it out, and said the job was well done. However, he did have to tell them that the fancy coat-and-hat rack was the drag device used to pull a deceased pilot from the bottom of the lake. Not knowing what to say, the volunteers made light of the situation.

1 Jim Mitchell leaning against the strut of his Cessna 206 (N4884F) with the L. J. Little family in the mid-1960s.
2 A Cessna 185 (N3424Y) at Fish Lake in the late 1960s owned by Kamiah commercial operators Linda Cummings and Roy Ebert.
3 A Cessna 206 at Fish Lake in the late 1960s commercially operated by Linda Cummings and Roy Ebert of Kamiah.
4 Packing the runway at Fish Lake in the late 1960s.
5 Green Acres Flight Service's Cessna 185 (N9951X) with owner Jim Mitchell at the controls in October 1965.

435

Pilot Frank Hill circling Wylies Peak – one of Idaho's most iconic fire lookouts located in the Selway-Bitterroot Wilderness.

CHAPTER 9

MORE ON
BACKCOUNTRY
AVIATION

EVOLUTION OF SMOKEJUMPER AIRCRAFT

A Johnson Flying Service Travel Air 6000 picking up jumpers and gear at Sulphur Creek.

Complete books have covered the subject and history of smokejumping. This brief section provides a glimpse at the development of aircraft used in the USFS Region 1 and 4 programs.

Starting in the late 1920s various USFS regions began their own experimental cargo-dropping tests by hiring local pilots. The majority of these early drops did not use cargo chutes. By the mid-1930s the USFS became more serious about developing an aerial program and purchased a five-place Stinson Reliant (NC2166) based in California. Officials in the state were told it was underpowered for the demanding work and it was transferred to Region 6's Chelan NF in Washington.

In 1939, David Godwin, who was the assistant chief of fire control in the Washington D.C. office of the USFS and the head of the new Aerial Fire Control Experimental Project, began exercising the Stinson. Several different experiments were carried out related to fire suppression. By October the same year the preliminary smokejumping experiments began with Captain Harold King at the controls of the plane. The Eagle Parachute Company successfully won the bid to design the chute that turned the smokechaser into a smokejumper.

With some success, experiments began as soon as possible the following year, not only in Washington but also in Region 1. Johnson Flying Service of Missoula successfully won the contract to fly the smokejumpers and in the end became a critical part of the program's development. The first activity for Johnson started in June at Winthrop, Washington, using a Travel Air 6000 (NC450N). After training in Winthrop ended, the company began flying the new Region 1 jumpers at Seeley Lake, Montana, in the same airplane. By the first part of the summer a crude operation was established for the Region 1 smokejumpers at the Moose Creek Ranger Station. On July 12, the first jump on a wildland fire was made from the Moose Creek base, nearly a full month before one was made in Region 6. The pilot on the drop was Dick Johnson, flying Travel Air 6000 NC8112. The same year Johnson used two 4-AT model Ford Tri-Motors in the program, NC7861 and NC9642.

In 1941 many improvements were undertaken to advance the program. The most notable was the development of the static line deployment, which pulled the ripcord when the jumper left the aircraft. The previous year this was done manually by the jumper. The static line system also helped immensely in cargo dropping operations. The same year a more permanent smokejumper base was established at Nine Mile Ranger Station west of Missoula, which was used through 1943. The base had its own airstrip and utilized the facilities of the former Stoney Creek CCC Camp. In 1944 a more permanent camp was built about a mile below the Nine Mile operation and used through 1953.

In 1943 the smokejumper program expanded by establishing a base in McCall. These jumpers were trained at the Nine Mile facility the first year until their base was completed. Johnson Flying Service's Idaho operation flew the jumpers and pilot Penn Stohr Sr. made the first drop in the region, flying Travel Air 6000 NC655H.

Keeping an eye on the smokejumper program

Pilot Bob Fogg (second from right) talks with Region 4 officials in Ogden after a demonstration jump was performed with Johnson Ford Tri-Motor NC9642.

from its inception was the United States military. Major William Carey Lee, who became known as "The Father of the United States Army Airborne," visited Region 1 and later incorporated many of the USFS techniques into the first paratroop training facility at Fort Benning, Georgia. The military made one significant change, which was the utilization of the more modern Douglas C-47.

Johnson took note and after the war purchased a pair of military surplus C-47s (NC24320 and NC49466). Johnson then modified them to meet the requirements of a civilian type certification to carry passengers, which technically changed them to DC-3s but retained the larger military rear cargo doors. In addition to these aircraft the company also utilized a Douglas DC-2. Although these planes were initially used extensively in the Region 1 program, they were not used in Region 4 until 1949 when one was flown from Missoula to help during the demanding fire season.

In 1948 the McCall operation expanded to Idaho City and the USFS bought a government surplus Noorduyn Norseman as the jump plane. Region 4 Chief Pilot Clare Hartnett mainly piloted the Norseman

until his retirement in 1953. Karl Bryning was hired as Hartnett's replacement. Bryning was unimpressed by the performance of the Norseman and felt the Idaho City program would be better served with a surplus C-45 Twin Beechcraft, which was purchased in 1955. A similar situation arose in Region 1 after the war when their Chief Pilot Floyd Bowman also purchased a C-45 that was occasionally used to drop jumpers. This plane was affectionately known as "Bowman's Bomber."

Although the USFS acquired a few aircraft, Johnson Flying Service carried out the majority of the work on a "general contract" basis. Over the years the company added a wide variety of aircraft to their fleet, including Twin Beechcraft C-45s and Twin Beechcraft AT-11s. By the late 1950s the AT-11s were phased out due to airworthiness directives concerning the strength of the center section. Instantly two of the four planes failed inspections. As a result they were merely salvaged for parts. Twin Beechcraft E-18s replaced these airplanes, which were their postwar commercial counterparts.

Following the Idaho City expansion, Region 1 utilized several satellite smokejumper bases and

Ford Tri-Motor N7861 at Moose Creek in 1962.

One of Johnson's first DC-3s after it was delivered to Missoula.

in 1951 established a base in Grangeville. Once fire season was underway, Johnson Flying Service generally stationed a Ford Tri-Motor and pilots to serve this end of their contract.

By the early 1960s new sleeker aircraft hit the Idaho backcountry scene and Johnson Flying Service was slow to accept the change. In Region 4, Johnson phased out the Travel Air 6000s and Ford Tri-Motors. The USFS integrated a few more in-house aircraft for point-to-point work, moving personnel and fire crews. In Idaho City they also brought in other contractors. For a short time Jim Larkin operated on his own, flying jumpers with a Cunningham-Hall PT-6F (N444). In 1963 Loening Air of Boise took over the Idaho City contract, flying a Twin Beech and Cessna 206s. At the end of 1965 Johnson Flying Service lost the Region 4 smokejumper contract in McCall. Even though it was already being somewhat supplemented, it was a loss to the company. Reeder Flying Service of Twin Falls filled the region's needs for the 1966 season, flying a Beechcraft E-18 and a PC-6 Pilatus Porter (N13201) equipped with a Pratt & Whitney PT-6 turbine engine.

Intermountain Aviation of Marana, Arizona, outbid Reeder for the 1967 season and gradually took over the region's needs from McCall. Intermountain was a highly solvent company that held large government contracts with the United States government. Their primary revenue came from providing air operations around the world in places such as Vietnam. They also worked as the exclusive carrier for the Central Intelligence Agency (CIA). As a result of their lofty earnings the company incorporated the newest high-tech equipment into the smokejumper program.

In 1967 Intermountain put online two PC-6

Johnson Flying Service's DC-3 N24320.

Pilatus Porters powered by Garrett TPE-331 engines. In July 1967 pilot Dave Schas experienced a fuel controller failure on takeoff from McCall while flying jumpers. The plane was a complete loss, but quickly replaced. In 1968 Intermountain Aviation introduced the smokejumpers to the de Havilland Twin Otter. Several different Twin Otters were used, including N7705, which was actually a pre-production model leased from de Havilland. Although it was an early 100 series version compared to the later 200 and 300 series, it had a higher horsepower to weight ratio than other early models, as it was stripped of all frills. The McCall jumpers lovingly nicknamed it "The Spoiler."

Immediately the smokejumper program was impressed with the Twin Otter's capabilities. For several years thereafter their fleet of blue and white Twin Otters became a mainstay in the Idaho backcountry. They even moved into Region 1, flying occasionally from Grangeville. Johnson Flying Service then began leasing Twin Otters to remain in compliance with their

A practice jump out of Johnson DC-3 N49466.

Looking out the door of a DC-3 on a drop run.

While contractors moved toward the modern turbine-powered airplanes, Region 4 began adding to their own fleet of aircraft. In 1963 the USFS purchased its first DC-3. Johnson Flying Service remained the lead contractor for the jumpers in Region 1 until Evergreen Helicopters acquired the company in 1975. It happened to be the same year the contract was rebid and the Evergreen higher-ups overbid, believing the company's history with the jumpers would outweigh anything else. When Evergreen failed, former Johnson employees were dismayed. Winning the bid for the 1975 season was Christler Flying Service of Thermopolis, Wyoming.

Eventually the smokejumper contracts were cancelled and both Regions transitioned to an in-house-only operation. Several DC-3s, Twin Otters, and Sherpas were acquired. In 1970 the Idaho City base was consolidated with Boise, which had been started in 1964. Ten years after the merger the group was moved to McCall. In 1991 the first USFS-owned DC-3 was updated with turbine engines. It was initially based in McCall and flew its first turbine mission on the Bear Creek Fire located within the Payette NF.

Until the 2011 fire season the smokejumper programs tied to Idaho were ruled by the versatile capabilities provided by the Twin Otter and DC-3. However, the USFS's aviation managers decided, because the DC-3 was "too old," to pull them off the flight line. In spite of the millions of dollars poured into renovations and inspections, and the uproar from pilots, the famous jumper airplane was grounded.

Region 1 general contract. Starting in 1966 the Fords and Travel Airs were written out of the contracts in Region 1. The two planes that once symbolized the smokejumper program were deemed outdated and dangerous. However, because of the demanding 1967 fire season the two airplanes were listed on an emergency rental agreement ("call when needed basis"), which was again repeated during the 1968 season. As a result, a few more missions for each aircraft were flown before Johnson liquidated the remaining inventory of these planes.

1 A Region 4 Noorduyn Norseman in 1949 at Idaho City.

2 A pair of Johnson Flying Service Twin Beechcraft E-18s at the Region 1 base in Missoula.

3 Jim Larkin (second from left) and smokejumpers at Idaho City with Larkin's Cunningham-Hall PT-6F (N444).

4 A pair of Intermountain Aviation PC-6 Pilatus Porters at McCall.

5 The old and the new at Grangeville in 1968. This photo was taken after the completion of the Ford's last smokejumping mission.

6 An early USFS owned DC-3.

7 A turbine powered USFS DC-3 at Chamberlain in 2007.

Backcountry radio operator Lesley "Billie" Oberbillig at her home office.

THE DEVELOPMENT OF BACKCOUNTRY COMMUNICATION

Following the establishment of many mining communities in the 1860s, the first reliable communication brought to the backcountry was United States post offices. Next was the creation of the single line telephone. The somewhat simple systems were developed by the USFS to connect remote ranger stations and fire lookouts, generally to aid in the war against wildland fire. Early single-line systems were established on most backcountry forests circa 1910 using #9 galvanized wire attached to glass and porcelain insulators. Main lines were first strung down major river drainages and then spur lines were developed as time permitted. Since many of the lines were along drainages, they passed through homesteads and thus the USFS allowed backcountry residents to tap into the network. Switchboard operators controlled the system and each telephone had a specific identification, created by a series of short and long rings.

Although the telephone system was effective, it was costly to maintain as limbs, trees, and weather caused frequent damage. After World War II the USFS transitioned more and more to radio technology, abandoning the telephone system. Seeing an opportunity for a radio-based communication business, Don and Lesley "Billie" Oberbillig of Boise created a backcountry service to the remote residents. The Oberbillig family had been connected to the backcountry through mining in the Yellow Pine area since the turn of the twentieth century.

Don ran the technical side of the business while Billie served as the operator, becoming a well-recognized voice to all in the backcountry. Billie was originally born in Boise and moved to Tillamook, Oregon, at a young age. After graduating from high school she attended the College of Idaho in Caldwell, where she met Don. In 1934 the two married and eventually had five children.[1]

The Oberbillig's radio license was held under the name of Mountain Messages, which was also the name of the business. Most of the communication equipment was situated on Shaffer Butte north of Boise and the office was located at their home. The company provided services to backcountry ranches, pilots, mining operations, and several flying services. They also operated a two-way car radio service in the Treasure Valley area. In 1964 Don died of cancer and Billie continued to run the business for several more years. In 1971 Billie sold the company and moved to Waldport, Oregon, where she became a realtor. She remarried and ultimately retired first in Depoe Bay and later Salem, Oregon. Billie died August 3, 2009 at the age of ninety-six.[2]

Billie sold Mountain Messages and all of the communication equipment to Sherrill and Joyce Benham of Challis. Similar to the Oberbilligs, the Benhams had ties to the backcountry, as Joyce's father was Rex Lanham who once owned Cabin Creek. The two also owned and operated Valley Flying Service. The communication venture was relocated to Challis where they served customers mainly on the eastern side of the backcountry.[3]

In the early 1970s Arnold Aviation of Cascade

VALLEY FLYING SERVICE

GATEWAY TO
IDAHO'S PRIMITIVE AREA

Sherrill and Joyce Benham
Owners • Operators

Hunting and Fishing
Reservations

Passenger Pick-up
at Boise, Pocatello,
and Idaho Falls
Airline Terminals

Back Country
Radio-Telephone
Communications

Experienced, Qualified,
Idaho Bush Pilots

FULLY LICENSED AND INSURED

Challis Municipal Airport
Box 156, Challis, Idaho
(208) 879-2462

Salmon Municipal Airport
Box 387, Salmon, Idaho
(208) 756-2150

Sherrill and Joyce Benham advertising their backcountry radio and flying operations in 1972.

Carol and Ray Arnold (right) with their son Mike (left) in Cascade.

also began to provide services to the backcountry, but from the west side. Ray Arnold moved to the Valley County area in the early 1960s and began taking flying lessons at Johnson Flying Service in McCall under the tutelage of Bill Dorris and Bob Fogg. Arnold and his wife Carol were both high school teachers who left the profession in 1975 to run their air taxi business full-time.[4]

The Arnolds realized that they needed a communications link with their customers and approached the Benhams about working together to set up operations for the western portion of the backcountry. When the Benhams were unwilling, Carol contacted Ernie Oberbillig, Don's brother, a mining engineer who was also savvy about the communication world. Ernie helped them with the necessary paperwork, which led to the procurement of their license and a frequency. While the Arnolds were not allowed to charge customers for the service, people paid a cooperative fee, and it brought the

Arnold's freight and passenger business. Since Ernie was well connected to area mining operations, he also influenced several companies to use their transportation services.[5]

For a struggling new business the communication aspect helped bring in a more stable income when in the late 1970s it was utilized as part of a medical grant. Local physician Dr. Moser obtained a three-year grant to provide medical care to backcountry residents, as well as to provide emergency care for them. Moser dubbed the program Idaho Wilderness Medical Service, and used a portion of the money to train EMTs, pay for standby time, and fund the Arnolds for the communication and flying. While Moser's service had good intentions, it did not work out.[6]

By the early 1980s the Arnolds were well established. Even the USFS at times has used the Arnold's equipment for emergency situations. The Benhams sold their communication company to Wilderness Aviation of Salmon, owned by the Combs family. Marge Combs ran the radio end of the business until 1993 when Mike Dorris bought the company, renaming it McCall and Wilderness Air. He continued the communication service at the Salmon office through 2003 when he sold to McCall Aviation. The services were eventually relocated to the McCall office under the new ownership and have slowly been phased out.

The Arnold's communication business remains and for more than thirty-five years Carol has been the friendly person that many in the backcountry have come to rely on for assistance. Over the years the

A 1979 advertisement for Arnold Aviation.

business has served people in Oregon and as far north as the Selway River. She has many warm memories of discussing grocery lists, recipes, gardening, wildlife sightings, and weather while running her station. She has also helped countless times in emergency situations involving downed aircraft, mining cave-ins, and injured recreationists. One of her favorite traditions on the radio is the singing of Christmas songs on Christmas Eve with her customers and friends.[7]

At the turn of the twenty-first century several backcountry ranches began to work with the StarBand Company to receive satellite broadband services. Although the Arnold's business has decreased with satellite telephones and Internet, they continue to have a strong customer base.[8]

Spruce Budworm Control Project

A spray operation based at Cascade in 1956.

In 1949 a widespread Spruce Budworm epidemic swept the Northern Rocky Mountains. The worm, viewed as a problem, eats the new growth of coniferous tree needles, killing the tips of the branches. The worm attacks all ages of conifers and in severe cases can make them susceptible to bark beetles, which in the end kill the trees. Foresters of the 1940s and 1950s who were managing public lands for economic production of lumber panicked. Reacting to the outbreaks, insecticides were applied to more than six million acres in the Northern Rockies between 1952 and 1966.[9]

In the Idaho backcountry aerial spraying accounted for much of the application, but there were also small ground crews stationed across national forests. The common concoction contained DDT mixed in fuel oil. The fuel oil served as a carrier for the DDT and unlike water carriers prevented the application from drifting or evaporating into the atmosphere. Forest entomologists were on hand at all times during each individual project. These specialists pinpointed nearly to the day when the tender little green worms were to emerge from the larvae. This stage in the worm's life is the most critical factor when applying the insecticide.[10]

A wide variety of aircraft were used in the chemical application, including Travel Air 6000s, Ford Tri-Motors, DC-3s, A-20s, B-18s, TBMs, Fairchilds, Stearmans, Fokkers, and a DC-2. In the early years of the program many of the planes, such as the Ford Tri-Motors, were equipped with spray pumps powered by miniature propeller-driven engines mounted to the aircraft's struts. The spray pumps then pumped the toxic liquid out of the interior tanks and into the spray booms. These little propeller engines were engaged and disengaged with a lever, mounted in the cockpit, that ran a brake on the motors, similar to automotive brakes. This system was later discarded for internally mounted gas-powered pumps commonly installed in the back of the aircraft. Most of these setups were manually operated and required a person to start and stop the motor at the engine instead of with cockpit controls.

Johnson Flying Service Ford Tri-Motor NC7861 spraying timber.

A view from the cockpit of a Johnson Ford Tri-Motor on a spray run.

Spraying timber in the Selway-Bitterroot area with a Johnson Flying Service TBM.

Aerial Salt Distribution

Pilot Bert Zimmerly Sr. (center) preparing for a salt drop.

In Idaho, the distribution of salt to big game animals started in 1921 when State Game Warden Otto Jones had his men put out 1,000 pounds of the mineral in the Selway and Lochsa areas. It was believed that the supplemental salt was not only good for animal dietary purposes, but also helped reduce travel to natural licks, supplemented winter feeding, and reduced mange and tick infestations. The salting program grew quickly, and by the late 1920s sulphurized salt was provided and considered a "cure-all" by game managers. A few years later plain white salt again became the standard. In 1926, packstrings were used to haul the salt to the Selway area where it was generally distributed next to natural salt licks.[11]

By 1930 a few managers began to rethink the salt program, believing that elk and deer had probably evolved over thousands of years with naturally occurring salt, and that the supplements were not needed. However, they also realized that the supplemented salt could be used to lure the animals off the winter ranges in the spring, allowing for more plant growth to sustain them over the following winter. The problem then was that many of the summer ranges were inaccessible to large packstrings, which carried the heavy salt.[12]

In 1938 the Idaho Fish & Game Commission (now Department) was established. The same year Charlie Gallaher helped pioneer the first aerial salt distribution with airplanes, in cooperation with the USFS. The aerial application enabled managers to place the salt strategically on the summer range. Originally drops were done with bagged rock salt, which was later changed to block salt. It was not until 1943 that more aerial drops were made. Over two tons of salt were distributed in the Selway area alone. While the packstrings continued to perform some of the work, they were removed from the salt program by the end of the decade. Early on several airplanes were found to be suitable for the aerial delivery of salt, but the IDFG considered the Ford Tri-Motor the most efficient.[13]

Throughout the 1940s and early 1950s the IDFG agonized over the restoration of big game winter ranges. Several factors during the first half of the twentieth century caused massive population increases in big game animals. For example the IDFG estimated the elk population for the state in 1926 to be 6,000 head. In 1954 population count estimates had grown to 60,000 head.[14] The winter ranges simply could not sustain the population growth and the agency explored ideas to combat the issue, including an increase in the amount of aerial salt droppings. In 1946 the salt program peaked, distributing 235 tons. In 1954 the amount of salt dispersed decreased to 129 tons. Even with the reduction, Idaho led the country with Montana following in a distant second with seventy-five tons.[15] By the early 1960s the IDFG and the USFS determined after several studies that the program was ineffective and it was discontinued.[16] The pits created where the big game populations "licked" the salt year after year can still be seen in the Idaho backcountry.

AERIAL BEAVER RELOCATION

In 1928 state game managers began relocating "troublesome" beaver to remote streams and rivers.[17] Nearly ten years later in 1939 the IDFG recognized the animal for its role in habitat creation instead of for its fur as a source of income. For several years beavers were relocated to high elevation streams by truck and packstring.[18]

In 1948 Conservation Officer Elmo Heater of McCall developed a wooden ventilated box to transport beavers. However, his design was not for packing purposes, but rather to be dropped out of an airplane attached to a cargo chute. The container was equipped with an automatic release device that popped the box open on impact with the ground. These crates were used extensively during 1949 and were generally dropped by Johnson Flying Service Travel Air 6000s. The aerial delivery method allowed the IDFG to efficiently relocate beavers to remote areas of the backcountry.[19]

The relocation efforts were part of the IDFG's Caretaker Program. The beaver portion of the operation ended in 1957 when open season on the animal was re-established. However, interest in beaver pelts dropped dramatically by the early 1960s. Complaint beavers in the state eventually became part of the conservation officer's job, but the aerial relocation method has not been used since the mid-1950s.[20]

FISH PLANTING

Looking back after a drop—note the small spattering of fish on the lake's surface below the horizontal stabilizer.

When the last Ice Age retreated about 10,000 years ago from the landscape that now comprises central Idaho, the valleys, rivers, drainages, lakes, mountains, and basins of the area were formed. Over 2,000 lakes can be classified as high elevation or alpine.[21] A few of these lakes had outlets that allowed fish to enter the body of water from a connecting stream, but the majority of the small lakes had no fish until stocked by an interested party.

Originally individuals or the USFS initiated stocking programs, transplanting small fingerlings in canvas packs or in milk cans filled with water, and strapped to pack animals. Both methods yielded poor survival rates because of the lack of oxygen, undesirable water temperatures, and rough trails. Also the correct species were not often selected for the environment.[22]

To overcome the heavy fish losses during the transportation process, the idea of aerial planting was tried in the 1920s from a World War I surplus Jenny. Several experiments were carried out into the late 1930s with mixed results. A few attempts were even made by pouring milk cans full of fish out the backdoor of a Ford Tri-Motor.

It was not until 1938, when the IDFG was established, that more refined experiments of aerial fish dropping were carried out. The pilots hired for the job were Lionel Dean and Gus Kelker, both from southern Idaho. Based on the results, Dean and the agency designed a metal tank with a water pump and fan to aerate the water, which helped to decrease the mortality rate of the fish. In the summer of 1941 the IDFG trucked fingerlings to the Stanley Basin. From there the fish were loaded into the tank, which sat in an open cockpit biplane. Dean, along with pilot Lamoine Stevens, planted 80,000 fingerlings in thirty-eight different Sawtooth area lakes.[23]

The aerial planting of fish did not resume until after World War II. In 1947 with the anticipation of the postwar boom in outdoor recreation, the IDFG began experimenting more with the concept, but did most of the stocking by truck and other ground methods. According to fisheries biologist Forrest Hauck, "In 1947, an intensive high-mountain lake stocking program was initiated. As a result, 146 lakes, inaccessible by car, were planted with trout. For some 51 of these it was the first stocking they had received. The department will attempt to keep them stocked by enlarging on pack and plane-planting operations."[24]

The following year Hauck's goals were met and pilot Edward "Joe" Monaghan was hired by the IDFG to help on the project.[25] In 1949 the IDFG developed a new fish-dropping tank that was partitioned, allowing two lakes to be stocked in one flight. It also allowed the department to stock the lakes with different fish species in one flight, if desired.[26] Each of the tank's compartments was fitted with a hose routed to an outside air scoop on the aircraft to circulate oxygen into the water, further assisting in fish survival. Also large levers were mounted on the metal tank for releasing the fish through two separate pipes run through the aircraft's inspection panels. By 1951 it was determined that the optimal height from which to drop the fish was between 200' and 300' above the lake's surface.[27]

While the aerial dropping of fish became a permanent part of the stocking program, the IDFG also incorporated scientific management. In the early years of the program no records were kept as to the lakes stocked, when they were stocked, the species, or the estimated annual harvest. In 1950 data were collected on a few specific lakes to help create a baseline.[28] By 1954 the IDFG determined that ninety percent of the early stockings consisted of eastern brook trout. This species can reproduce in tough conditions where other trout species cannot. However, it was determined that if the lakes were not regularly fished it tended to result in an overpopulation problem with stunted fish. The department began trying to find a balance between populating lakes with known successful species and those that would grow well, while making an effort to plant more desirable fish. As a result, rainbow and cutthroat trout, a more preferred species, were incorporated more and more into the

program, but because of the harsh lake environments they had a difficult time reaching sizes beyond nine inches. Other species planted in alpine lakes, starting in the mid-1950s, were golden trout and grayling, but at the time these were thought to be novelty fish.[29]

Beyond adding new species to the lakes, the IDFG began experimenting with the use of helicopters for fish "delivery" rather than "dropping." In 1958 trials were conducted in northern Idaho from the Sandpoint Fish Hatchery with the help of United States Air Force personnel and a helicopter. Fish were delivered to the lakes from a height of five to twenty-five feet above the water surface. The helicopters were able to carry small portable oxygen cylinders and aerating apparatuses to oxygenate the five-gallon fish containers during the transportation.[30]

While the success rate was estimated to be higher with the use of helicopters, it was determined to be too costly. By the early 1960s the IDFG no longer had access to an in-house pilot or airplane and began using commercial operators within the various regions of the agency. For the Salmon and Magic Valley Regions the department hired Hailey pilot Lawrence Johnson and for the Clearwater and Southwest Regions they hired Johnson Flying Service's McCall branch.

In 1962 fisheries biologist Stacy Gebhards began experimenting with new transportation methods for fingerlings to high elevation lakes. His goal was to come up with something that was lightweight and easy to carry without increasing fish mortality. Despite the failure of several containers, he discovered one element that changed the program, which was the addition of oxygen under pressure to fill the remaining space within the containers.[31] It was not until 1964 that Gebhards discovered a strong enough plastic bag that he could fill with three quarts of water, fish, and then inflate with oxygen. If kept at the right temperature the fish could live for as long as twelve hours. It was the answer to aerial dropping as each bag could hold thousands of fish, without the weight of the water cutting heavily into the aircraft's useful load. With this method most airplanes enlisted for the job were able to carry on average twenty-five bags, meaning about the same number of lakes could be stocked in one morning's flight.[32]

Gebhards's 1964 discovery of the plastic

Holm

1 *Lawrence Johnson's Staggerwing Beech and fish hopper in 1964.*
2 *The Dorris fish hopper design installed in a Cessna 185 with bags of fish waiting to be dropped.*
3 *Fingerlings ready for a short fall to their new high mountain lake home.*
4 *Loading Sawtooth Flying Service's Cessna 185 in Mackay for a morning mission. The fish bags are transported in coolers from the hatchery.*
5 *Mike Dorris navigating between lakes.*
6&7 *The Passmore fish hopper design mounted in a McCall Aviation Cessna 206 with bags of fish.*
8 *Pilot Steve Passmore positioning for a drop.*
9,10,11,12&13 *Views from the cockpit while planting fish in the Idaho backcountry.*

Holm

inflated oxygen bags required that he develop a new drop tank. Working with pilot Lawrence Johnson, he fitted together basic parts from a local hardware store. A four gallon metal bucket was fitted to a short wooden stand with a large hole drilled in the bottom. A short length of pipe was attached and sealed to the underside of the outlet. An inexpensive large removable rubber stopper was then used to plug the opening. The little apparatus cost about $10 and could be used in a variety of aircrafts as the bottom end of the pipe was simply routed through airplane floor inspection panels.[33]

The delivery bucket and pipe, that was eventually dubbed a "Fish Hopper," was first installed in L. Johnson's D-17S Staggerwing Beechcraft (N18V). On the initial test run Gebhards sat in the back of the plane next to the fish hopper, cut the designated plastic bag for the lake, filled the hopper, and on the final pass pulled the plug at the pilot's command. It worked beautifully. The fingerlings were literally sucked out of the fish hopper in seconds, from sheer gravity and the airplane's slipstream. They all landed within a 150' to 200' spread across the lake's surface.[34]

In 1965 McCall-based Johnson Flying Service pilot Bill Dorris adapted Gebhards's fish hopper design and made a more refined version. Dorris, who had worked several years with the IDFG, called a friend and obtained an old department milk can stamped "Idaho Fish and Game Department." He took the can and cut it down, leaving the stamp in the top, and welded on a funnel device with a reducer pipe. Dorris then used Gebhards's plug idea, but fitted it with a T-handle so it was easier to pull and insert back into the opening after the drop. Johnson Flying Service exclusively used Cessna 185s (N4546F and N4022Y), which were more maneuverable and could fly at slower speeds compared to L. Johnson's Staggerwing. The Cessna 185 with the Dorris fish hopper proved to be a great setup and was used until Johnson Flying Service/Evergreen closed in 1976.[35]

When the company sold, Bill Dorris started McCall Air Taxi and was able to obtain a rental agreement with the IDFG for fish planting. Using the same fish hopper he built for Johnson Flying Service, he installed it in his 1977 Cessna 185 (N93039). Son Mike eventually acquired the business and over the years this airplane and fish hopper setup, which

is still being used, has planted more fish in the Idaho backcountry than any other aircraft. In the early 1990s the FAA began to question the legality of the fish hopper attached to the airplane. Approval was eventually given but required that a rubber ring be placed around the top of the hopper, a safety cord had to be attached to the rubber plug, the hopper had to be better fastened to the floor, and a sign had to be hung in a window indicating that the plane was temporarily a restricted category aircraft. To the handful of mountain pilots experienced enough to fly the plantings, the added safety requirements were laughable.[36]

In the late 1980s and early 1990s the IDFG occasionally returned to fish planting via helicopter. Plagued with cost issues, the department only found it feasible when the USFS donated flight time that had not been used during the fire season. By 1992 all regions of the IDFG flew exclusively with McCall Air Taxi.[37] To handle the extra flights, Steve Passmore, pilot and maintenance director, built a second identical fish hopper and mounted it in a Cessna 170 (N4385B). With two planes running during the planting season the company dropped fish in lakes from one end of the state to the other.[38]

The IDFG biologists were pleased with the transition to only fixed-wing aircraft in the program, as they believed that the helicopters did not offer any great advantage. Based on biologists' observations it is believed that no fish are lost to impact mortality. However, it has been determined that there is a ten percent loss within the first twenty-four hours after the fish are planted. Most of the mortality is attributed to the larger fish in the lake eating the fingerlings before the young fish have time to find hiding places. In addition to the initial fatalities another ten percent are lost to natural causes every year. Accounting for the mortality rates, the department began a target of stocking 440 mountain lakes throughout the state on a three-year rotation.[39]

In 2002, Assistant McCall Fish Hatchery Manager Steve Kammeyer introduced the use of handheld GPS units programmed with the state's lakes. While pilots such as Dorris and Passmore had the terrain and locations well memorized, the GPS often helped with the process of elimination that sometimes required an extra circle or two around a cluster of lakes. At times the technology saved about a half hour of flight time per flight.[40]

In 2008 the program's flights became split between McCall Aviation and Dorris's Sawtooth Flying Service, both based in McCall. At the time of the changeover, Passmore constructed a taller all-plastic fish hopper with an external handle for dumping the fish. The Passmore design created a tighter and shorter spread of fish during the drop, but otherwise functioned the same as the Dorris design. The other difference in the setup was Passmore enlisted the use of a non-turbocharged Cessna 206 (N206KL), which had not previously been attempted. While he had his reservations in the beginning, the 206 has established itself as good airplane for the job.[41]

Due to the demands placed on the pilot and the aircraft, fish planting is considered one of the most hazardous and difficult mountain flying operations by most professional backcountry pilots. In order to get the airplane situated within the mountain cirques and less than a hundred feet above lake surfaces, it requires rapid descents to altitudes below treetop level. After the pilot says, "Pull," to the hopper operator, the airplane is shoved to full power, sometimes initiating a near vertical climb to outmaneuver oncoming trees or rocks. It is not uncommon for the aircraft to pull one to two g-forces coming out of a lake. Because of the on-again off-again power settings, turbocharged aircraft have not been used in the program, as there is not enough time for properly cooling the turbocharger.

As the fish planting program became more established after the 1960s, the only people allowed on the aircraft were individuals who were deemed as part of the required crew. This generally meant that only IDFG employees went along with the pilot, or on occasion a person associated with the specific aviation company. While drops can only be made early in the mornings when wind conditions are less than fifteen knots aloft, the air can occasionally be rough.

Many of the IDFG employees that went along to pull the plug on the fish hopper were unaccustomed to flying in light airplanes. The required tight turning, up, down, over, and around g-force flying did not add to their comfort. To help prevent passengers from unloading their upset stomachs willy-nilly in the plane's cabin, they were instructed to relieve their stomachs

into the fish hopper, which is then released on the next drop.

In mid-season 2010 the IDFG put a halt to all personnel riding on the fish planting flights. The suspension was extended, and now the two companies use their own employees to help. While no accident or incident has ever occurred in the fish planting program, the moratorium stemmed from two helicopter accidents in 2010 involving the IDFG, one of which caused three fatalities.[42]

Over the years the low flying over alpine lakes has created a few good stories involving unprepared spectators in the wilds of Idaho. On one occasion at the beginning of hunting season Dorris made a high circle over a lake to determine his exit after the drop. He noted a grouping of tents at the far end of the lake where he planned his departure down the drainage. It was not until he was right over the far end of the lake with the hunter's tents directly in his field of vision that he noted the camp was full of horses. Unable to do anything about his flight path he pushed the 185 to full power, to make it out. He felt terrible. While over the camp he skidded the airplane a little so he could see out his left side windows. Sure enough the horses had caused all hell to break loose at the camp.[43]

Another time during the fall a hunter tracked Dorris down at the McCall airport late in the day and accused him of scaring off a bull elk that he was about to shoot. Dorris apologized, assuring him that it was not intentional. He explained that he had been fish planting. The distraught hunter had never heard of such thing, accused him of lying, and then left in a huff. Within the hour Dorris received a call from the local authorities wanting an explanation. The issue was eventually resolved.[44]

Many campers and fishermen on the other hand have looked up with their jaws dropped in amazement as the Cessnas skim by spraying fish. However, the people working in fire lookouts in the Nez Perce NF have consistently found the activity anything but amusing. For several years in a row Passmore's fish drops have caused several complaints directed toward the IDFG. The way some of the lookout observers reported the incidents, it was as if an invasion had taken place directly on their mountain. Many of them demanded to at least be notified when the activity was going to take place in the future.[45]

GAME MANAGEMENT

Goats on Suicide Rock in the River of No Return Wilderness.

Almost since its inception, the IDFG has utilized aircraft as a tool for game management. One of the first documented uses of airplanes for aerial surveys took place in 1941 when the department was trying to gain a better understanding of the Pahsimeroi Valley antelope population numbers.[46] The study was considered a success and the concept quickly spread with the cooperation of the USFS to help manage other species, particularly deer and elk. While biologists realized they could not make a complete count of a population, statistical models were developed. Starting in the winter of 1942–43, overpopulation or "problem areas" in the state connected to large deer and elk herds were studied even further by air. Two of the most noteworthy areas in the state's backcountry were the Selway and Middle Fork of the Salmon River. The department widely supported the advancement of remote airstrips, not only for better management access, but also for improved hunting access. With the increased ability of the general public to reach these remote regions, the IDFG believed that they could help bring deer and elk populations to carrying capacity.[47]

The IDFG estimated that after World War I big game hunting in Idaho doubled and the department expected an increase of at least thirty to fifty percent after World War II. In 1944 the department stated in an annual report, "Under present favorable conditions and with proper game management, Idaho will have sufficient big game to provide much needed recreation for the boys returning from overseas."[48] They also reported that the use of airplanes and hunting had increased in 1942–43 and expected the upward trend to continue. To be proactive about the change in hunting, the department noted, "From a game management standpoint, the use of airplanes for travel to and from the hunting grounds is not objectionable. Road and pack string hunting tend to limit hunting to the perimeter of an isolated herd . . . With increased airplane use by hunters, game department officials will have to become more air-minded, and . . . will have to take to the air for patrol and management studies in isolated areas."[49]

After the war the IDFG's predictions came true and they reported that the hunting season of 1945 had the largest game kill in Idaho up until that time. However, the 1946 season surpassed it by approximately twenty percent. Regarding airplane use in the backcountry related to hunting, the department still believed it was desirable from a management standpoint, but new problems developed. "In 1946 we suddenly experienced a large increase in plane use. Especially was this true of private planes. Planes fly to remote areas from out of state, obtain game and fly out without ever stopping in Idaho except to land and hunt in those areas. Local planes fly in and out with little likelihood of being checked by game department personnel. It is desired that we have regulations protecting game from this uncontrolled hunting."[50] As a solution to these problems the IDFG again vowed to "[B]ecome air-minded and secure planes for patrol."[51]

The program did intensify aircraft use well into the 1950s, especially for deer and elk management. Annual counts in the "problem areas" became routine. In 1948 the first helicopters were used in the studies. While aerial counts had been toyed-with for other game species such a bighorn sheep and mountain goats, the latter two animals were not fully studied by air until radio tracking collars were utilized in the 1970s. Use of radio collars and aerial counts continue today for all types of research. Over the years IDFG has enlisted the use of aircraft for fish surveys, big game surveys, waterfowl surveys, animal relocation, herding, and law enforcement.

A mail drop from a Johnson Flying Service Travel Air 6000 (NC9038).

| MAIL ROUTES

When small mining communities came to life in the backcountry with the discovery of gold in the 1860s the United States Postal Service followed closely behind. Generally local people were contracted by the federal agency to deliver mail from a major town or city to a smaller more remote location where a permanent post office was established. These offices where generally run out of the home of the postmaster or postmistress. Little post offices were scattered all over the backcountry through the 1940s. Individuals then bid on separate contracts to haul the mail between the minor locations.

During winters in the 1930s, contracts were bid for aerial delivery, cutting transportation time from a several-day journey by horse, dog sled, or snowshoes to just a few hours. Two primary air carriers of the early years were A. A. Bennett of Bennett Air Transport Company and Bob Johnson of Johnson Flying Service. These companies had regular stops at a wide variety of locations including Warren, Yellow Pine, Mackay Bar, Stibnite, Knox, Krassel, Big Creek, Flying W Ranch, Sulphur Creek, Deadwood, Hood Ranch, Johnson Creek, and Warm Lake. Aerial drops to various mining camps were then mixed among these delivery points.[52]

After World War II the number of people living in the backcountry began to decline. With the customer base and quantity of mail reduced, the Postal Service determined that aerial delivery was most efficient and abandoned many of the offshoot spur routes contracted by on-the-ground carriers. By the 1950s, three primary factors led to the creation of what eventually became three separate aerial mail routes. The first developed when isolated ranches began constructing their own airstrips, which made direct delivery possible. The second factor was that people such as USFS employees did not necessarily inhabit dwellings year round, so when the stations were occupied it was an easy added stop on the route. Lastly it became more cost effective to contract with one person or company in a vast area, instead of with several individuals.

The first major postwar route established was from Johnson Flying Service's McCall branch and called the Cabin Creek Route. The route was considered a Star Route, meaning mail was to be carried for delivery to people's mailboxes and not just shuttled between post offices. Originally the company bid on the delivery of mail along Cabin Creek, replacing one of the last known horseback routes. However, in 1958 Main Salmon River residents Frances Zaunmiller, Paul Filer, and Al Tice urged the Postal Service to expand Johnson's run to include stops along their drainage. At the height of the route, which unofficially became known as the Salmon River Star Route, the company delivered mail to roughly fifteen private airstrips, depending on the season, and three USFS fields from late spring to fall. A wonderful article about this mail route appeared in the August 1975 edition of *Flying* entitled, "The Salmon River Run" by George C. Larson. The large fourteen-page spread featured Johnson Flying Service, along with their airplanes and pilots.

The second air route to develop after the war

Frances Zaunmiller and her dog Gretchen waiting for the mail plane (final approach center) at Campbell's Ferry.

Bob Fogg delivering mail at the Whitewater Ranch.

Bill Scherer delivering mail to Morgan Ranch caretaker John Peterson.

distributed mail along the Middle Fork of the Salmon River. This route, based from Boise, delivered mail to five private, three USFS, and two state-owned airstrips. In about 1960 Lynn Roberts of Roberts Flying Service first held the route. Roberts sold his fixed-wing business in 1963 to Mike Loening and moved to Arizona, specializing in helicopters. Loening ran the mail route with various Cessna airplanes since he was a Cessna dealer. In 1964 Loening pilot Bill Scherer and the route were featured in Cessna's magazine *The Cessna Pennant* under the title, "Post Office With Wings." Scherer flew a new Cessna 336 for the article. In 1969 Loening let the contract go when he sold the company to Boise Air Service, which held the contract until 1975.[53]

The third mail route was originally flown from McCall to Warren and then carried on the ground over the hill in various ways to the South Fork of the Salmon River. It was never actually designated as an air route, but slowly evolved into one during the winter months, and became a separate contract by the 1950s held by Bob Fogg. Once the roads closed for the winter he leased Johnson Flying Service equipment to run the mail by air. Born in southern Idaho, Fogg and his family moved to Cascade in the early 1930s, and the family ran a restaurant. After finishing high school in 1937, Fogg secured a job at the local sawmill and spent his extra money on flying lessons with instructor Dick Johnson at the Cascade airport. To earn enough cash to complete his various licenses he worked several jobs in Alaska and then moved to Missoula where Bob Johnson took him under his wing. During World War II Fogg instructed with Johnson Flying Service's CPTP. In 1944 he and his wife, Margaret, moved back to Valley County where Fogg ultimately became the manager of Johnson Flying Service's Idaho operation for nearly twenty years. In the postwar era Fogg evolved into the figurehead of the McCall airport, which he also managed on the side, along with serving a term in the Idaho House of Representatives. In 1976 Fogg retired from flying and died two years later.

Jim Newcomb of Warren inherited the South Fork portion of the mail route in 1974 and shortly thereafter obtained Fogg's route. He then combined the routes, flying them with a Piper PA-12 in the winter from Warren. Once the mail was picked up in McCall he made a stop at two private airstrips (South Fork and McClain Ranches) and an airdrop at the Fritser Ranch along the South Fork and then returned to Warren. The downside to his operation was that he only had straight skis, so he often had to make two separate flights on mail days, one with skis and one with wheels due to the lack of snow regularly found in the bottom of the South Fork canyon.[54] Newcomb sold his business, known as McCall Flying Service,

Fogg collection

Johnson Flying Service pilot Bob Fogg.

Holm

Mike Dorris dropping mail at Burgdorf.

in 1981 to Mike Dorris of McCall. Along with the sale Dorris acquired the mail route and currently still holds it. Dorris typically delivers mail to Warren using either a Cessna 170 or 185 with retractable skis and to several select South Fork airstrips, depending upon who is in residence.[55]

Ray Arnold acquired the other two air routes. In 1975 Evergreen Aviation successfully bought Johnson Flying Service, a company that had prevailed over the Idaho backcountry commercially since the early 1930s. People in Idaho knew that Evergreen was not long for the area. Arnold, fresh on the scene of commercial aviation, recognized that he had a viable chance at obtaining the mail contract, which would help put his recently established business on the map. As expected, Evergreen overbid and the new

kid on the block won out. At the same time Arnold also successfully bid on the Middle Fork mail route. To date he still holds both routes as one contract. He generally flies a Cessna 206 in the summer months and a Cessna 185 with retractable skis in the winter.

Over the years Arnold's business on the mail route has expanded and contracted. Along the way he acquired the ground mail contract that delivers mail from Cascade to Yellow Pine. For about a ten-year period from the late 1970s through the 1980s Arnold flew the mail to Johnson Creek because of winter road closures. Different from other official mail carriers he has also broken into the business of flying mail to ranches in the Selway River region on separate contracts during certain parts of the year.[56] The Selway, unlike the other major remote backcountry drainages, has never had an official contract. For several decades starting in the 1930s individual commercial air operators would irregularly carry mail along with other freight to clientele along the river. Pilot Larry Dutcher of Kamiah tried to make a scheduled circuit in the early 1960s delivering freight and mail to residences on the Selway, but it was short lived, as he could not make it pay.[57]

In 2009 Arnold nearly lost his aerial mail contracts with the Postal Service when budgets were cut due to the economic crises. However, backcountry residents rallied to his support and the contract was renewed. Arnold's backcountry mail route remains as the last official aerial delivery in the lower forty-eight states. He and his route have been featured in countless local newspapers and television programs, in addition to national news programs and media ranging from the *Wall Street Journal* to *Time Magazine*.

TALL TIMBER PILOTS – THE ICONIC BOOK OF THE BACKCOUNTRY

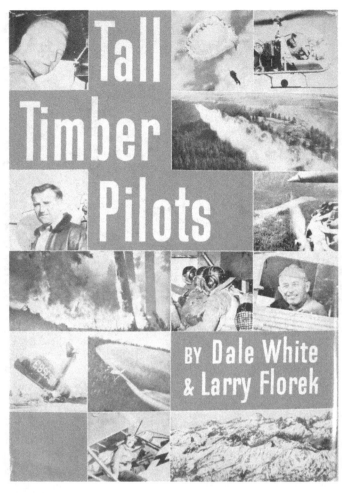

Viking Press

The book *Tall Timber Pilots* authored by Dale White and Larry Florek was published in 1953 by the Viking Press and became an instant regional and national success. The basic storyline reveals the lives of Bob and Dick Johnson and how they build their backcountry flying business through a fictionalized, but attempted realistic dialog. All of the characters throughout the novel are actual people. Although the book was to be read as fact, the truth is stretched in several places trying to create a triumph and tragedy adventure story.

While the book is a bit overworked it was influential to many future pilots and aviation enthusiasts. Several individuals were so taken by the book at a young age that they later sought work at Johnson Flying Service. Others who grew up in the communities Johnson served also came to adore the story. Several infatuated youngsters, now adults, still tell stories involving arguments among peers over how much better *Tall Timber Pilots* was than the Alaska counterpart, *The Flying North*, written a few years earlier by Jean Potter.

Many Johnson employees over the years claimed that the quiet Bob Johnson was not displeased or pleased with the book. However, most believed that Johnson never even read it, even though copies were sold at the Johnson Flying Service front counter through

the early 1960s, and kept around the pilot's lounge area for decades. On occasion, Bob could even be enticed by a tourist or passenger to sign his picture in the book. The second generation of Johnson pilots, many of them children of the first, found it ridiculously amusing. In the early 1960s, Gene Crosby, who was based in McCall, made a comment regarding the book 's prose to pilot Elwood "Swede" Nelson. In the conversation Crosby compared the writing to the popular *Dick and Jane* series of childrens' books. The two laughed about it and mimicked the dialog, "'I just wrecked the Ford,' said Dick. 'Ha ha,' said Bob."[58]

Nelson, a cantankerous prankster among his peers at Johnson Flying Service, started making jokes based on Crosby's interpretations of *Tall Timber Pilots*.

Johnson Flying Service's Missoula headquarters in the early 1960s.

One day while flying over Deadwood Reservoir in a DC-3, Nelson unbuckled his seatbelt, stood up, with head bowed, and crossed his arm over his chest. The copilot turned to him and said, "What in the hell are you doing?" Nelson, deadpan cracked "This is where the Mae Gerard [Travel Air] went down, I'm paying my respects." He then added a modified quote from the book, "Doggone it, for Bob it was like losing one of the family." The copilot did not quite get the joke, but laughed anyway.[59]

Nelson's humorous stabs at the book caught on, particularly with Bob Christensen and Penn Stohr Jr. To pass time while hanging around the office they read the book, soaking up quotes that could later be sprung on one another, especially if given the right lead-in while in-flight over the radio. One of the standard cues was pilot Chet Dolan's voice on the radio as someone would generally chime in quoting chapter eleven's title, "So Long, Chet." Another favorite quote to recite when discussing navigation was, "The plane carried no instruments other than a altimeter, airspeed indicator, bank and turn indicator, and motor gauges. No compass was needed for the man [Bob] who flew by instinct and memory of landmarks." And above all one of the greatest lines used when a person was thought to be telling a tall tale was to interject with a condescending lead-in, followed by, "[T]hose pine boughs spelled out to him that Idaho's wilderness had at last claimed a high price for invasion of its privacy."[60]

Johnson pilot Larry Florek of Hamilton, Montana, wrote the first draft of the book as a factual account of the company's history and publishers rejected it. Not being a writer, his only goal was to record the uniqueness of the company. Unwilling to waste his efforts Florek teamed up with Marian Templeton Place. Place was a teacher and librarian who authored books that focused on the American West. Over her career she published more than forty books, and earned multiple literary awards. She often wrote under the pen names of Dale White, R. D. Whitinger, and Wallace Blue. It is believed she completely re-wrote Florek's original manuscript, creating the storyline and dialog. In a 1990 interview Place said that she considered the book one of her three most important works.[61] Place died in Arizona in 2006 at the age of ninety-five.

Bill Woods and the History of "If I Could Write"

Pilot Bill Woods in his Idaho backcountry office.

Bill Woods's heartfelt essay, "If I Could Write," is undoubtedly the paramount piece of literature written about flying the Idaho backcountry. Above all other attempts thus far, Woods has come the closest to capturing the essence of flying in the remote region. Despite the title, Woods could clearly write well and his prose noticeably came from thousands of hours and decades of experience. Woods was a man of many talents and writing was a hobby he enjoyed throughout his life. At one point he even attended courses at Boise Junior College to further hone his skills in the art.

When not writing he worked extremely hard running several businesses in Boise. A native of Nebraska, he moved west to Crescent City, California, where he worked in a lumber mill. After seeing a barnstormer as a child, he finally fulfilled his life's dream of becoming a pilot at age nineteen.[62] By the 1930s he worked his way to Idaho and in 1938 purchased land northwest of Boise where he started his own airport by scraping in a rough dirt runway. Woods opened a small flying business that he first called Boise Valley Flying Service. In about 1946 it was simply changed to Bill Woods' Flying Service. His main area of expertise quickly became flying the Idaho backcountry. He officially named his facility the Floating Feather Airport.[63] In a 1969 interview Woods was asked how he came up with the name. His witty answer, "I often made poor landings and floated down the runway like a feather."[64]

On June 29, 1944, roughly six years after starting the airport, an Army Air Force B-24J (41-100019) stationed at Gowen Field attempted to make an emergency landing at the airfield. The plane had an outboard engine fire and the pilot ordered the crew to abandon the aircraft. Three of the eight crewmembers bailed out before the accident but the others perished in the wreck. The B-24 exploded on impact a few hundred feet from Woods's hangar, and a large fire spread over 1,000 acres into the surrounding grass.[65] While many airplanes parked at the airport were moved to safety a handful were lost. The fire eventually destroyed Woods's hangar and he lost a substantial amount of his parts inventory and cash. However, after the incident he was able to gather enough money and rebuild the facility.[66]

Over the years Woods operated a wide variety of aircraft from the Floating Feather including several different D-17S Staggerwing Beechcrafts (NC114H and NC50959), Piper Cubs, a Travel Air 6000, a Stinson Tri-Motor SM 6000B, a Zenith biplane, and a Bellanca Pacemaker, among many others. During World War II he operated a CPTP from the airfield, training cadets in Stearman Primary Trainers.[67] By August 1945 he had taught over 500 students in the program.[68] After the war he continued instructing, in addition to his regular flying schedule, and by the closing stages of his career had given duel instruction to 489 private students.[69]

In 1945 Woods married his wife Janet, whom he had met while he was instructing at Floating Feather. The couple had two children, Dana and Randy, who spent a good portion of their childhood growing up at

Woods at his Floating Feather Airport with a Staggerwing Beech and one of his Wirehaired Terriers.

One of the more well-known writings by Woods was his "Do's and Don'ts of Mountain Flying" published originally in 1950 on the backside of a state aeronautical map. The department and many other people have published these tips for decades. He also wrote several articles related to flying that were published in national magazines. However, his most famous piece, "If I Could Write" was written later in his life and self-published in a book among his other writings. The small inconspicuous book filled with wonderful works was primarily intended only for family posterity.

After 29,000 hours of flying, Woods was unable to pass a flight physical, although he did hang on to one Super Cub after liquidating much of his aviation inventory circa 1972. Woods died on March 16, 1974 at the age of seventy-three. "If I Could Write" was formally printed in the June 1974 edition of *Rudder Flutter*, the newsletter of the Idaho Division of Aeronautics, after his death.[74] When his son was asked why Woods might have written the poetic essay, he commented, "He [Woods] had a love affair with the backcountry. When I was younger I can remember my mother trying to get him to go to church with us on Sundays. He would say I go to church everyday."[75] Affirming his view on the backcountry was an inscription found on a black and white panoramic photograph in his scrapbook. The scene taken from the cockpit of an airplane showed a solid view of snowcapped Idaho mountains and was labeled by Woods as "The Land I Love – God's backyard – My front yard."[76]

Understanding how much Woods adored the backcountry his family felt it was only proper to spread his ashes there. Longtime friend and pilot Jim Larkin offered to take Woods for one last flight. On a beautiful morning over the Middle Fork of the Salmon River, daughter Dana opened the side window of Larkin's airplane and attempted to disperse the ashes. Instead of the serene moment she had anticipated, the wind blew a good portion of the ashes back into the aircraft. Dana was a bit startled, but Larkin just grinned and laughed, "Well, Bill and I flew a lot together. I can't think of a better friend to continue to ride in the cockpit with me."[77]

the airport and flying with their dad in the backcountry.[70] One of their most memorable recollections about flying with him was their inability to ride in the front seat, as his faithful Wirehaired Terrier, Rags, would boot them out. Woods always had a pair of the Terriers as flying companions and the others were named Tags and Toddy. During the summers the kids also spent time with their family friends, the McCalls, who lived where the Middle Fork Lodge is today.[71]

When not busy flying, Woods kept up with his other two businesses, Automatic Amusement House and Idaho Vending, which he ran from a shop located on the corner of Chinden Boulevard and 36th Street. Through these companies he sold tobacco products, sold and repaired slot machines, sold and leased jukeboxes, and installed background music systems.[72]

Woods was older than most of his fellow pilots and when his hair began to turn gray he took the maturity in stride and gave himself the nickname, "Old Man of the Mountains." During the postwar boom in aviation he developed a close friendship with Idaho Director of Aeronautics Chet Moulton and used his writing skills to help with some of the state's publications. He often wrote ideas and thoughts to Moulton, which later become printed. Many of his stories sent to Moulton were based on his backcountry flying adventures.[73] Woods is credited to this day with walking away from more major aircraft accidents in the backcountry than any other pilot. Estimates range from seventeen to twenty-three wrecks.

If I Could Write

By Bill Woods

If I could write I'd write of summertime and early morning flight, of pink-tinged mountain peaks with their green fir robes topped with caps of ermine white, of silver rivers far below winding thru multi-colored canyons, of the soft gray stratus clouds dissolving before the sun's first bright rays. I would try to tell of the pilot's highway, as the world itself, of the peace and eternal solitude and the deep sense of a adventure while gliding thru shadowy corridors among the ever changing cumulus clouds, and of the sweet, sweet song of a motor's roar, breathing the cold clean air high above the earth-bound dust and smoke as the remote earth, so very far below, slowly breaks into a million sunlit and shadowy patterns.

If I could write I'd try to tell you of midday flight when the sun's hot breath has awakened every devilish air current, of a plane being tossed around like a loose leaf before winter's early winds. I would describe that awful feeling of aloneness – – the chill terror – – and how mere seconds creep by like old and worn out years, as those wind devils slam your plane toward bleak canyon walls, your controls as dead as yesterday's dreams. I'd write of the quick panic you try to hold away as you wait for that life saving cushion of air that you can only hope is trapped beside the canyon wall. I guess I'd even try to make you feel the deep inside hurting of the clatter of an over-worked, over-heated motor fighting for precious altitude while those demanding downdrafts are pulling you down, down, down. I might even tell you how little and insignificant you felt when a thousand crazy air currents have grabbed your plane and are shaking it much like a hungry cur shakes a meatless bone, of broken tiedown ropes and a heavy load of loose freight floating up tight against the ceiling as the plane itself falls faster than the pull of gravity, and of the chaotic thoughts within your mind while you wait for the solid air and wonder if man-made wings of wood and fabric can take the shock.

If I could write of flights when the deep white snows have hidden and locked away every meadow and glade where-in a plane could find a haven, of black storms chasing one another at mile a minute speeds, of sullen clouds pregnant with snow, dragging their bloated bellies along the ground, hiding every familiar landmark, and of flying in blizzards when the visibility is less than a hundred feet and a hundred miles an hours seems like a million.

I'd write of the dull, clumsy, dead weight of a plane loading up with ice and of the anguished gasp of a radial motor breathing only wet and freezing air. I might even try to tell you of how it feels to be boxed in by the storms, of the helplessness that permeates your whole being while you are using all of the skill, cunning and knowledge that you have accumulated in a lifetime of flying just to hold death away a little longer. I'd write of how you will look at your hands on the controls and marvel at the wonderful pieces of flesh and blood mechanism that they are and wonder just how much longer they will obey the commands of your brain.

I would also tell of how your heart swells to almost a breaking point when you finally get thru and of how good the cold clean ground feels beneath your feet, ground that only moments before you had thought that you would never again feel and walk on.

If I could write, why most of all I would write of how good human companionship is after one of these flights, of how a baby's cry, a child's laughter, a woman's smile or friendly touch is worth more than the tinkle of golden coins in a blind beggar's cup. But what I could never hope to write about is that inconceivable pull, that ever constant compulsion, stronger and more demanding than steel cables that persists in taking you back and back, as though your soul were a veritable fragment of the air you breathe and fly in. Of that I could never write for I do not have the humble understanding, that belongs to God alone.

Bayok collection

Joe Bayok painting an aerial number on the Cold Mountain Lookout in the summer of 1936.

FIRE LOOKOUTS AND AIRPLANES

One of the more fascinating aspects about the region's more recent fire history is the development and implementation of the fire lookout system. Over 1,000 fire lookout locations dot Idaho's rugged landscape, more than in any other state. Many of these sites were developed with well-built buildings to house observers during the fire season and to protect them from the weather.

As aviation became prevalent in the remote parts of the state these structures became excellent landmarks for pilots to use as navigational reference points. Recognizing their importance, the United States Bureau of Aeronautics worked with the USFS to develop a numbering system that could be painted on fire lookout roofs, which then was referenced to aerial maps. The numbering system was enlisted on Idaho fire lookouts starting in the mid-1930s, but detailed information about the program is scarce.

After World War II the fire lookout aerial numbering system was taken over by individual states. By 1950 Idaho Director of Aeronautics Chet Moulton worked with the USFS to develop a statewide numbering program. The lowest number (1) was assigned to Little Snowy Top Lookout on the Kaniksu NF. In general the numbers increased in a southerly direction with the highest number (615) given to Hells Half Acre Lookout on the Bitterroot NF. For reasons unknown the numbers were not all consecutive. One

speculation is that the spaces might have allowed for the addition of lookouts or the numbering of more existing lookouts. The numbers were painted on the south side of the roofs, as the sun helped melt the snow, keeping them more visible throughout the year. It was originally proposed that an arrow with the distance to the nearest airfield be painted on the roof, along with the aerial number, but it is doubtful that this ever occurred. The system was popular among pilots and forest officials, but was slowly phased out by the end of the 1980s.

Although the aerial numbering system is no longer used, the remaining fire lookouts in the backcountry continue to be common reference points for aviators. Most pilots who have flown the backcountry for any length of time have at least one fond story or recollection of a fire lookout. It is not unusual to hear something about buzzing a roof, dropping food, newspaper deliveries, or radio chatter to a lonely observer.

Idaho Fire Lookout Aerial Numbers

No.	Name	No.	Name	No.	Name	No.	Name
1	Little Snowy Top	150	Surveyors Ridge	325	Salmon Mountain	382	Bear Creek
4	Port Hall	152	Clarkia Peak	330	Oregon Butte	383	Middle Fork Peak
6	Hall Mountain	153	Anthony Peak	333	Cold Springs	384	Rush Creek Point
10	Red Top	160	Priscilla Peak	334	Black Butte	385	Meadow Creek
11	Hughes Ridge	164	Black Mountain	335	Jersey Mountain	386	Martin Mountain
12	Caribou Hill	165	Baldy Mountain	336	Rock Rabbit	387	Gold Fork
14	Deer Ridge	171	Moscow Mountain	337	Chair Point	388	Thunderbolt
15	Gold Peak	172	Potato Hill	338	Dry Diggins	389	Big Baldy
17	Russell Mountain	178	Eagle Point	339	Elkhorn	390	Mahoney Mountain
18	Horton Ridge	180	Osier Ridge	340	Smith Knob	391	Little Soldier
22	Round Mountain	190	Patricks Knob	342	Hershey Point	392	Loon Creek Point
24	Black Mountain	194	Junction Mountain	343	Lick Creek Point	393	Fly Creek Point
26	Sundance Mountain	195	Scurvy Mountain	344	Oreana	394	Sturgill Peak
27	Binarch	204	Clarke Mountain	345	Heavens Gate	395	Indian Mountain
29	White Mountain	218	Horseshoe Lake	346	Butts Creek Point	396	Morehead
34	Lunch Peak	219	Rocky Point	347	Carey Dome	397	Big Soldier
35	Gisborne Mountain	220	Beaver Ridge	348	Sheepeater	398	Pinyon
36	Bald Mountain	225	Round Top	349	Arctic Point	399	Twin Peaks
37	Stone Johnny	231	Hemlock Butte	350	Grass Mountain	400	Grouse
39	Antelope Mountain	232	Weitas Butte	351	West Horse	401	Big Springs
40	Little Blacktail	234	Jerry Johnson	352	Ulysses	402	Tripod
43	Beaver Peak	236	Jay Point	354	Granite Mountain	403	Silver Creek
44	Bernard Peak	238	Castle Butte	355	Beartrap	404	Bear Valley Mountain
52	Spy Glass	240	Bear Mountain	356	Long Tom	405	Ruffneck
54	Spades Mountain	245	Brown Creek Ridge	357	Stormy Peak	406	Custer Peak
56	Little Guard Peak	247	Austin Ridge	358	Nelson Peak	407	Bishop Mountain
60	Mica Peak	248	Fish Butte	359	Jackley Mountain	408	Scott Mountain
64	Bumblebee	250	Frenchman	360	Pollock Mountain	409	White Hawk
68	Mount Coeur d' Alene	254	Diablo Mountain	361	Hard Butte	410	Red Mountain
75	Sunset Peak	256	Bailey Mountain	362	Bear Pete	411	Lookout Mountain
81	Frost Peak	258	Frisco Peak	363	War Eagle	412	Potaman
82	Polaris Peak	260	Woodrat Mountain	364A	Steamboat	413	Warm River
85	Eagle Peak	261	Walde	364	Chicken Peak	414	Hawley Mountain
88	Lemonade Peak	264	Coolwater	364	Pilot Peak	415	Jackson Peak
90	Dam Ridge	265	Shissler Peak	365	Acorn Butte	416	Deadwood
91	Wonderful Peak	266	Fog Mountain	365	Pilot Peak	417	Pilot Peak
93	St. Joe Baldy	267	Bearwallow	366	Cold Mountain	418	Swanholm
96	Mastodon Mountain	272	Lookout Butte	367	Stoddard Creek Point	419	Horton Peak
97	Arid Peak	273	Shearer	368	Sagebrush	420	Wildhorse
99	Hill 36	274	O'Hara	369	Hot Springs	421	Shaffer Butte
100	Dunn Peak	282	Indain Hill	370	Jureano Mountain	422	Thorn Creek Butte
102	Quaries Peak	284	Corral Hill	371	Horse Mountain (West)	423	Bald Mountain
103	Linstrom Peak	290	Pilot Knob	372	Smith Mountain	424	Trinity
110	Huckleberry Mountain	296	Anderson Butte	373	Granite Mountain	425	Iron Mountain
113	Siwash Peak	300	Bad Luck	374	Brundage Mountain	426	Danskin
117	Middle Sister	302	Fall Creek Point	374	Split Creek	427	House Mountain
123	Conrad Peak	305	Green Mountain	375	Williams Peak	450	East Mountain
126	Roundtop Mountain	309	Sourdough	376	Lookout Mountain	454	Packer John
129	Mineral Mountain	314	Burnt Knob	377	Short Creek	500	Sloans Point
132	Crystal Peak	315	Hells Half Acre	378	Lake Mountain	551	Mount Harrison
134	Lookout Mountain	316	Sawyer Ridge	379	Peck Mountain	575	Artillery Dome
138	Simmons Peak	318	Grave Point	380	Boulder Mountain	615	Hells Half Acre
139	Baldy Mountain	320	Slate Creek	380	No Business		
143	Snow Peak	322	Columbia Ridge	381	Missouri Ridge		
148	East Gold Hill	324	Sheep Hill	381	Miners Peak		

A list of Idaho fire lookout aerial numbers compiled from 1950–86.

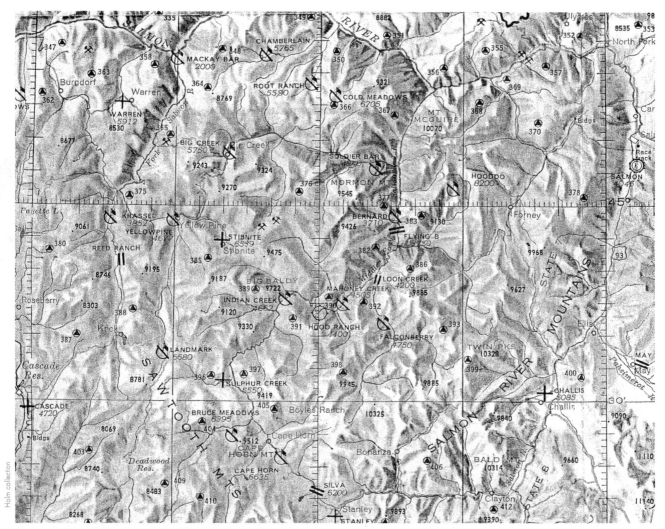

A portion of a 1954 Idaho Aeronautical Chart. Each circled triangle represents a fire lookout along with the associated state aerial number to assist pilots with navigation.

An example of the postwar aerial number painted on the Payette NF's Lookout Mountain.

467

Project Skyfire

R. Snider

Pilot Jim Ford and the Cessna 180 equipped with Project Skyfire's silver iodide burners.

Project Skyfire originated with the hypotheses that cloud seeding could be used to reduce lightning-caused fires in western forests by increasing rainfall or modifying lightning production in thunderstorms. The vehicle to alter the weather was the release of silver iodide nuclei from propane-driven burners. The overall goal was to minimize firefighting costs by lowering the potential of fire-causing weather conditions.[78]

Experiments carried out by the USFS began in the early 1950s, primarily using large ground-based generators. By the late 1950s and early 1960s several variations of aircraft mounted burners were designed for aerial applications.[79] Government contracts were issued to several air carriers for the studies. Johnson Flying Service obtained a contract and fulfilled it by using Cessna 180s with burners fixed to both of the airplane's struts.[80]

Covering areas of Idaho and western Montana, Johnson flew from Missoula with a researcher aboard when large thunderstorms loomed. Two temporary switches installed in the cockpit ignited the burners. Once the plane was close to the storm, the burners were lit. The pilot then skirted the storm, normally until the tanks were emptied. Pilots Jim Ford and Bob Sanderson were the primary pilots during the contract.[81]

Experiments associated with Skyfire lasted into the 1970s. The overall effectiveness of the project was somewhat inconclusive. However, researchers established that "[T]he cause of lightning fire ignitions was the continuing current in the lightning flash. Evidence was gathered that cloud seeding, if done properly, could reduce the numbers of cloud-to-ground discharges and the incidence and duration of continuing current discharges from a given storm."[82]

An example of one of the provisional certificates posted at the airfields.

FAA CONFUSION WITH BACKCOUNTRY AIRFIELDS

At the same time the debate over wilderness designations occurred in the Idaho backcountry, another more obscure conflict surrounded the airstrips. In 1974 the FAA sent word to Missoula's Johnson Flying Service, the longest and largest commercial operator in the Idaho backcountry, that they would no longer be able to use the remote airfields. The decision stemmed from the latest issued policy requiring Part 121 Air Carriers to operate only from certified airports, which were detailed in the newly created – Part 139 Airport Certification. In the most basic sense it outlined safety requirements for airports with air carriers operating aircraft with more than thirty seats; circumstances not found at even one of the Idaho backcountry airstrips.[83]

While Johnson Flying Service held a Part 121 Supplemental Air Carrier Certificate (currently a Scheduled Air Carrier Certificate) for larger operations (aircraft over 12,500 pounds), they also had a provisional letter allowing them to fly, on demand, charter and backcountry operations with aircraft below 12,500 pounds using Part 135 Air Taxi regulations. Because the company did not actually hold a Part 135 Air Taxi Certificate and were not allowed to apply for one, they were found to be non-compliant.

However, a large portion of their business was flying to the remote backcountry airstrips. Johnson Flying Service, in opposition to the restriction, pled their case to the FAA. After much verbal wrangling,

a loophole was figured out and a person was sent from the Seattle Flight Standards office to McCall to issue provisional Part 139 certificates for all of the backcountry airstrips Johnson was using at the time. When the man arrived, Bob Fogg flew him to the various places. At each location the two men posted provisional 139 certificates. It was required by the agency to properly display the classification. Following strict orders, Fogg and the government employee stapled and nailed the official looking pieces of paper to logs, trees, and fence posts.[84] In 1976 these certificates were withdrawn after Johnson Flying Service was sold to Evergreen Helicopters. Under later regulations it was determined to be only a technical matter.[85]

VISITOR USE SURVEY

Peter Mourtsen at the Little Ramey Creek Trailhead in the early 1970s.

Have you ever wondered why USFS employees or volunteers at several backcountry airfields record aircraft registration numbers? The data obtained are part of an ongoing study called Vistor Use Survey. In 1974, former Big Creek District employee Peter Mourtsen initiated it for the Payette NF's section of the Idaho Primitive Area. When the Idaho Primitive Area was considered for possible inclusion into the wilderness system, people were concerned about the amount of public use. Also, managers for the various districts received recreation money as part of their annual budget, based on the number of recreational users. To ensure a continued flow of money they generally estimated a ten percent increase each year to help justify more money for their district.[86]

By the early 1970s the numbers had clearly become embellished. Having no actual records for comparison, it was hard to verify the real statistics. At a 1974 annual budget meeting Mourtsen noted that he had spent twenty-nine days in the Payette NF's portion of the Idaho Primitive Area and only saw six other individuals (not counting his work crew) and two of them were USFS employees. He pointed out that the major river corridors carried the highest number of recreational users. He did concede that usage in these drainages could be increasing. However, he argued that there was little influx, year to year, of public usage in the high country locations. Discussion ensued at the meeting and others encouraged Mourtsen to design a study that would help prove his observations and establish a baseline of wilderness users.[87]

The result was the Visitor Use Survey initiated in 1974 on the Big Creek District. While other forests had previously established data collection on airstrip activity at places such as Indian Creek and Moose Creek, the Payette had only attempted to do so for two inconsecutive years at Chamberlain. With some information to go on, the Payette NF monitored the Chamberlain airfield; the only one the first year. Generally, USFS employees recorded the survey data in person. A statistical model was developed and the data were plugged-in at the end of the year. In 1975, improvements were made to the survey, and it was also expanded to include sampling at Big Creek and Cold Meadows.[88]

Within the first few years of the survey, experiments were made with different data collection devices. One of the first trial pieces of equipment was a recording device that was activated by the noise decibels of an airplane taking off. The recordings were then played back and counted. The USFS also tried using photograph counters that were checked every two weeks. This idea had great potential as it provided information about the various users – backpackers, hikers, hunters, etc. In the end it was determined that the most effective avenue for conducting the survey was to sample on randomized days in person.[89] The program still continues on the Payette NF and includes Big Creek, Chamberlain, Cold Meadows, and Cabin Creek.

Visitor Use Survey Data

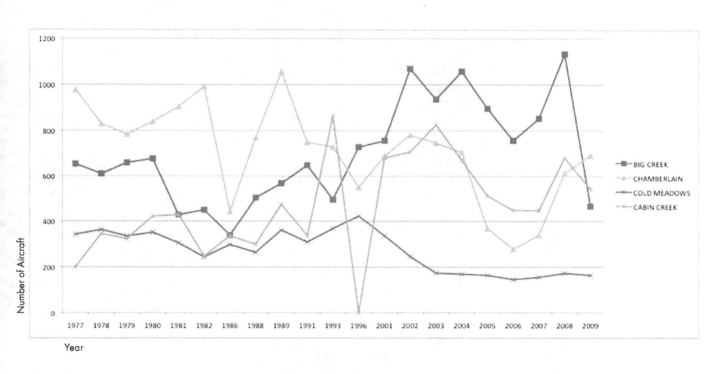

The graph is based on data collected by the Payette NF's Visitor Use Survey. For years where data was absent the number of aircraft was interpolated using the previous and following years where data was available. The major influx in usage varies and for the most part can be explained. For example the explanation for the sudden drop in use at Cabin Creek in 1996 was the runway closure caused by the washout. Another example is the reduction of usage seen in 2007, which was caused by the poor visibility from wildland fire smoke across the region. The final example is the dramatic drop of use at Big Creek from 2008 to 2009, which can be attributed to the absence of the hotel/lodge that accidently burned in the fall of 2008.

*The Twin Otter parked at Campbell's Ferry during the filming of **Total Air Support for Remote Operations**.*

CHAPTER 10

A Glimpse at Backcountry Flying in Film

THE FOREST RANGER (1942) – PARAMOUNT PICTURES

Actor Regis Toomey at the controls of a studio airplane mockup. Toomey filled the role of Frank Hatfield, the film's backcountry pilot and villain.

In the opening scene of this film a suspicious fire starts in Picayune Canyon, a typical western United States setting. Ranger Don Stuart, played by Fred MacMurray, dispatches USFS fire crews and gains help from local lumberjacks through friend and sawmill owner Tana Mason, played by Susan Hayward. While fighting the fire Ranger Stuart suspects an arsonist started the fire with matches and firecrackers.

On a mission to track down clues about a possible arsonist, he meets and eventually elopes with socialite Celia Huston, played by Paulette Goddard. The plot thickens when Ms. Mason, who is affectionately called "Butch" by all the men, also vies for the ranger's attention. Throughout the film the USFS receives assistance from regional pilot Frank Hatfield, who by the end of the film is discovered to be the villain.

None other than Bob and Dick Johnson of Johnson Flying Service fill the shoes of Hatfield's off-screen character. The Paramount producers traveled to Montana and Idaho in the summer and fall of 1941 to shoot footage, including several takeoffs and landings at the Moose Creek Ranger Station. Much of the film's final cut incorporates a mockup of a combination Travel Air 6000 and Curtiss Air Sedan airplane, which were both flown for the film by the Johnsons. However, one real clip that made the final cut showed a Travel Air departing Moose Creek. Another snippet of actual footage also made the cut, capturing a Johnson Flying Service Ford Tri-Motor (NC9642). For the movie the planes were painted in water-based red and yellow schemes and advertised a fictitious operator's name on the side. When the filming was done the paint was simply washed off.

While only short clips of actual flying were used in the film, a look at Dick Johnson's logbook from the middle of September through the end of October 1941 reveals nearly fifty hours of flying billed to Paramount, mainly using Travel Air NC447W along with two Ford Tri-Motors NC7861 and NC9642. Most of the smokejumper footage was filmed at the USFS's Six Mile training facility in Montana using the Fords. Two days were spent filming at Moose Creek with Travel Air NC447W. Other stops in Idaho with the Johnsons included Cascade and Orofino along with destinations in Oregon such as Lakeview and Eugene.[1] Apparently Lakeview was used because it was the nearest area where cameramen could obtain shots of real forest fires.[2]

Local newspapers in the towns where Johnson Flying Service operated were excited that the pilots were working with Hollywood. *The Payette Lakes Star* reported, "Director and cameramen were astounded at the feats performed by the two pilots and assured them that all future picture-flying work, outside the studio, would go to them."[3]

D. Richards.

David Richards during his years as a pilot.

David Richards – Johnson Flying Service Films (1950s)

In 1946 pilot David Richard Brechbill (he later changed his name to David Richards) began working at Johnson Flying Service as a flight instructor. Richards originally took an interest in flying when all of his friends joined the various branches of the armed forces during World War II. He was unable to join as he had a kidney removed as a child. He decided he needed to prove himself and dreamed of becoming an airline pilot. A native of Darby, Montana, he commuted to the Hamilton airport and earned his various pilot ratings from pilot Larry Florek. Florek later worked for Johnson and became locally famous for co-authoring the book *Tall Timber Pilots*. Richards then attended the Spartan School of Aeronautics in Tulsa, Oklahoma, where he earned a degree in airport management.[4]

When he arrived at Johnson in the spring of 1946 he was amazed by their operation and soon started to tag along as much as he could, helping in various ways. More than flying, Richards was fascinated with photography and film. Owning a 16 mm Bolex motion picture camera, he shot footage of people and airplanes while working. Richards proposed the idea to Bob Johnson of making films to document Johnson Flying Service's operation.[5]

With the green light from Johnson, he purchased a 16 mm Cine-Kodak Special camera and often followed agricultural spray work, smokejumping operations, and the spruce budworm projects. He hauled his equipment in a company Stinson 108 or Curtiss Air Sedan. The outcome was the production of two short films. The first entitled *Fire Call*, traces Johnson Flying Service from the time the USFS made a call requesting smokejumpers through the initial stages of fighting the fire. Richards persuaded fellow co-workers, such as boss Bob Johnson, assorted pilots, and secretaries, to act out their real life roles. Studying from as many movies as he could, he even mocked-up sets. One example worked into the film was the outside view of smokejumpers exiting a Ford Tri-Motor. To make the shot work he jacked up the tail of a Ford to mimic level flight, and had jumpers pretend to bail out while on the ground.[6]

The second film produced for Johnson, *Spruce Budworm Control*, highlighted capabilities of their pilots and aircraft in combating the spruce budworm, which was ravaging forests in Idaho, Montana, Oregon, and Washington. Often hanging out of the windows of DC-3s and Ford Tri-Motors with his camera, Richards documented this unique type of backcountry flying. To gain different camera angles he often flew along in a smaller airplane, capturing the spray planes laying down the toxic DDT mixed in fuel oil.[7]

Although much of this footage is still in existence, some of it was never put into official productions, as Richards quit his commercial aviation career. Near the end of 1953 Richards realized he could not qualify for a first class medical, which was required for airline pilots. Being rejected for the second time in his life for only having one kidney he decided to pursue his real passion, film.[8]

In 1954 he moved to Hollywood, where he joined the Screen Writers Guild of American West. After carving out a successful career in the film industry, working on shows such as *Lassie, Wagon Train, Big Valley*, and many others, he returned to his home state of Montana in 1965. Living in Missoula, Richards worked for over thirty years as an architect. He retired in the late 1990s and spent his winters in Palm Springs, California.[9] Richards died in December 2011 at the age of eighty-five.

DELBERT "DEL" ROBY FILMS – *ADVENTURE ON THE SELWAY* (1950s)

Film producer Del Roby (right) at a campfire.

Del Roby, of Kamiah worked most of his life in the timber industry. Frequently unemployed during the winter, he occupied his time with various odd jobs. Among his many occupations was outfitting and guiding fishing trips. In the early 1950s one of his clients suggested he document his adventures by investing in a 8 mm movie camera. He liked the idea and was able to scrounge together enough money to buy a better quality 16 mm camera.

Over the next several years Roby compiled footage and then headed to Hollywood with the hope of assembling it into a finished film. After the long trip to California the major companies rejected him. However, Roby did gain some knowledge about the business and figured out how to edit and add music. Undefeated, he then marketed his adventure films to communities around the Northwest. He made an annual circuit, showing them in places such as town halls and community centers.

Although several of his films highlight areas of the Idaho backcountry, *Adventure on the Selway* was the only one to include mountain flying. The film features one of the first boating/fishing trips down the Selway River. Transporting the crew, gear, and boats to the river was Tom's Flying Service, based in Orofino and owned by Tom Kiiskila. The planes shown in the production are a Cessna 180 (N2882A) and a Fairchild 71 (N9708). Captured in the film are the planes en route to the Selway region, and operations at the Moose Creek Ranger Station. The exact Fairchild used in the film was later wrecked at Moose Creek and the airframe still remains not far from the station (see Moose Creek for more information).

George Oliver Smith at work.

GEORGE OLIVER SMITH FILMS (1940s–50s)

Born into a rural Idaho farm family, George Oliver Smith always had a passion for Idaho. After graduating from Weiser High School he attended the College of Idaho and later the University of Southern California, where he majored in motion picture production. While in school he worked part time for 20th Century Fox. During World War II he served in the United States Army and sometimes worked as a cinematographer on training films. After the war he and his wife, Helen Stanfield, founded Film Originals, a Boise-based motion picture production firm.[10] When he began producing films, Idaho naturally became the focus of his subject matter. Over the course of his lifetime Smith produced about forty different projects involving the state.[11]

In the late 1940s Smith and his wife received their first big break when Idaho Director of Aeronautics Chet Moulton approached them about creating films to promote aviation in the state. Moulton felt there was a tremendous stigma about aviation and he wanted to show people how useful airplanes could be.[12]

The first production entitled *The Air Age* highlighted the airplane's utility uses in the state, ranging from the flying rancher to the person flying commercially. The film has wonderful examples of the airplane's uses in the backcountry, including images of Jim Larkin dropping smokejumpers with a Ford Tri-Motor (NC9642), freight being hauled to Stibnite by Glenn "Ike" Eichelberger in a Travel Air 6000 (NC8865), and Bill Woods moving freight to the backcountry with a red Zenith.

With the success of *The Air Age*, Smith's next production, *Telephone Creek*, was done not only for Moulton, but also in cooperation with the USFS. The 1950s fire prevention film follows the duties of the McCall smokejumpers and includes a few nice shots of a Johnson Flying Service Ford Tri-Motor piloted by Bob Fogg.

Another film that featured backcountry flying was *Airplanes Make Markets*. The primary purpose of the production was to promote the benefits a local airport could bring to any community in the state. The film spotlights the Stanley Basin and used actual residents as characters to create a basic plot. Airstrips shown in the film include Floyd Silva's ranch strip, Cape Horn, and the actual building of the runway in Stanley. It also shows several Idaho pilots such as Chet Moulton at the controls of the state's Cessna 195 (N3898V), and accomplished aviator Kenneth Arnold of Boise, flying a CallAir (N2912V). Additional shots of pilots include Bob Johnson and Bill Woods. One impressive shot captured Arnold landing on the road in Stanley, delivering orders from his Great Western Fire Control Supply business. In 1947 Arnold became a minor national celebrity after claiming to have spotted a series of "saucer like" objects moving through the air in a chain during a flight near Mount Rainer, Washington. The press came to call them "flying saucers." He is still credited as being one of the first in the United States to report an unidentified flying object (UFO).

Smith's films were well received throughout the state. Moulton was continually pleased with Smith's work and over the years they cooperated to create several more aviation related productions including: *Folks Around Here Fly, Mountain Flying, Agriculture Aviation, The White Clouds,* and *The Flight Decision.* Smith died in May 2005.

A Fire Called Jeremiah (1961) – Disney

Bob Schellinger and a Johnson Bell G-3 in the early 1960s.

The hour-long movie *A Fire Called Jeremiah* was one of many produced by *The Wonderful World of Disney*, a popular series that ran for twenty-nine years (1954–83). The film featured a simple western-themed plot set in the forests of Idaho and Montana near Missoula. Through the power of story, Disney explained to viewers the basics of firefighting and fire prevention by featuring the functions of fire lookouts, aerial patrols, smokejumpers, and how they all worked together.

The program's opening scene illustrates dramatic landscapes of the western forests and describes how one careless move could destroy the natural beauty. Transitioning from the mountain scenery the camera follows a USFS Cessna 180 (N112Z) flying the rugged wildlands outside of Missoula. With low music in the background, narrator Lawrence Dobbin seriously explains the role of the pilot and ranger in the Cessna 180, "The ranger's vigil is constant, one often carried out from the skies. From this vantage point, which he shares with the eagle and the hawk, he has a complete panoramic view of this seemingly endless domain. He scans the deep canyons below, the inaccessible pockets, and the windswept summits – his eye constantly sweeping from horizon to horizon. Always on guard, always on the lookout for the forest's arch enemy – fire. An air patrol is a passing view, a momentary glance. For around the clock scanning, the lookout tower is best. These are the permanent eyes of the Forest Service."

Moving from the airplane to the subject of fire lookouts, the camera focuses in on a lookout as the yellow and black Cessna 180 passes over the tower's summit. Introduction to the main character, Cliff Blake, whom the audience never hears speak, is brief. A quick rundown of his duties at the lookout station is speedy and the audience is told that he recently caught a big break in his career and was accepted as a Missoula-based smokejumper. Carole Stockner steps in as his replacement at the lookout.

Through Blake's new position the viewers get a full understanding of the smokejumper program and how to fight wildland fire. What makes the relatively slow, 1950s–60s heavy promotion of fire suppression interesting is the great footage of Johnson Flying Service aircraft. Disney exclusively contracted with Johnson and spent several weeks flying with them from Missoula.

Former Johnson pilot Rod Snider remembered cameramen asking the impossible, but he entertained their requests. On one occasion while filming the jumpers streaming out of both Johnson's DC-3s (N24320 and N49466) and DC-2 (N4867V), they asked Snider, who was following in a Bell G-3 helicopter, if he could chase one of the men down to the ground. Snider, chuckling, explained that he could, but the camera equipment would be unable to get any good footage due to the aircraft vibration. The cameraman insisted. Sure enough, it did not work and the maneuver scared the heck out of the passenger.[13] Not only does the film

Floyd Bowman and his Cessna 180 shown in the film.

show quality air-to-air footage of the airplanes, but also includes some good shots filmed from the ground.

Snider became a household name around the region the same year the show aired, but it was not for his behind-the-scenes involvement with Disney; rather it was his rescue on Higgins Ridge in the Selway-Bitterroots (see Moose Creek Section for the complete story). Snider's friend and fellow Johnson helicopter pilot Bob "Crash" Schellinger also flew in the film. In fact he is visible in several of the scenes, flying a yellow Bell G-3 (N2806B).

After the big thunder and lightning storm in the movie that showered Idaho's Nez Perce NF causing the big fire crises for the cast, Schellinger rescues an injured jumper. In addition he saves the fire observer moments before her fire lookout tower burns to the ground. After the rescues are completed the remainder of the film rushes through fire cleanup.

Schellinger's two cameos somewhat mirrored his real flying career. In spite of the nickname given by his friends when he was learning to fly at Johnson Flying Service and "crashed" an automobile, he was an exceptional pilot. More than once Schellinger risked his own life during remote mountain rescues. In the spring of 1981 he was killed in a helicopter accident in western Montana near Trout Creek. He attempted to rescue two surveyors in steep terrain. Realizing he could not land he tried having the men climb aboard his Sikorsky while he hovered next to sheer rock walls. It is believed that a mix-up occurred with one of the men who was supposed to be watching the distance between the helicopter's rotor and the rocks. Before either surveyor could get aboard, the rotor nicked the rock wall sending the helicopter off kilter.[14]

Knowing he was in trouble, Schellinger had the option of landing straight ahead into the hillside, a maneuver that would have saved his own life but killed the surveyors. Instead, he used his little remaining directional control to push the crippled aircraft away from the two men. The tactic cost Schellinger his life. Schellinger's wife Bonnie stated, "He wouldn't have wanted to live if those two guys were dead."[15]

Although Johnson Flying Service did most of the aerial work from Missoula, some other clips of scenery and aircraft are from California. To depict the mop-up and containment stage of firefighting they added several shots of TBMs and PBYs dropping retardant on fires, most likely in California. However, in the series of clips that showed retardant airplanes, a rare glimpse of Johnson Flying Service's yellow and orange Grumman F7F can be seen dumping water (probably filmed while on a test drop).

While Johnson Flying Service airplanes and pilots drew the most notoriety in the film, Floyd Bowman, a Region 1 USFS pilot, can also be seen flying the agency's yellow and black Cessna 180. Bowman, who was affectionately nicknamed "Flobo," was a regular fixture at the Missoula airport from about 1948 until his death in 1967.

TOTAL AIR SUPPORT FOR REMOTE OPERATIONS (1970)

An Intermountain Aviation PC-6 Pilatus Porter on takeoff from Campbell's Ferry.

Intermountain Aviation of Mirana, Arizona, had this nearly thirty-minute promotional film produced by Sound and Scene owner J. Douglas Allen. The film touts the many versatile aspects of their crews and aircraft in remote areas around the United States. To illustrate this, the program highlights their flying on Alaska's North Slope with a Douglas C-46, work in Arizona's Senora Desert with a Cessna 206 pulling a magnetometer, flying the Colorado Rockies with a Jet Bell Ranger for a military gravity study, and their work in the rough Idaho backcountry with de Havilland Twin Otters.

Without a doubt this is by far the most impressive footage in existence from this era in the Idaho backcountry, particularly with the then cutting-edge technology the company owned. They utilized various airstrips in the backcountry to show the capability of the Twin Otter, including Campbell's Ferry, Bernard, and Taylor Ranch. The opening of the Idaho section shows a 300 series Twin Otter, piloted by Bob Nicol, leap off the ground at Campbell's Ferry and climb out downstream, essentially straight over the ridge on the north side of the river. The landing is equally impressive and demonstrates the plane's short field capabilities. As the camera follows the Twin Otter into the Ferry, the narrator comments, "Along Idaho's Salmon River Intermountain's STOL de Havilland Twin Otters are making history. The STOL – short takeoff and landing aircraft is the bridge between conventional airplanes and the helicopter. It carries more useful load over a greater distance at less cost than helicopters and can operate out of strips that conventional aircraft cannot possibly use."

To show the large items that can fit through the Twin Otter's doors they show a group of USFS men hauling out a large kitchen counter unit at the Chamberlain Guard Station. In additional pitch on how great the airplane is for the backcountry, the film takes the viewer on a fire drop along the Main Salmon River with a group of McCall-based smokejumpers.

Most of the film footage was collected during the summers of 1968 and 1969 with additional clips added from the 1970 season, before the final cut was produced. Allen and his company Sound and Scene went on to create several more promotional films for Intermountain, but they featured very little of their Idaho work.[16]

A FIRE ON KELLY MOUNTAIN (1973) – DISNEY

Similar to *A Fire Called Jeremiah, The Wonderful World of Disney* again focused on the western theme of firefighting. The script was based loosely on Phil Pomeroy's book, *The Mallory Burn.* Pomeroy fictionalized the life of a young fire lookout observer. He wrote the book based on his own experiences of spending a summer on Kelly Mountain Lookout located on the north side of the Main Salmon River on the Nez Perce NF.

The book and movie both retain some recognizable names associated with the actual surroundings of Kelly Mountain such as Chair Point, Vinegar Creek, and the Salmon River. The movie keeps the same basic plot as the book, which follows a bored teenage fire lookout, Pete Mallory, played by Larry Wilcox, who is waiting for some action and adventure.

His wish eventually comes true when a lightning strike occurs nearby and he is given the go ahead to suppress it. Firefighting quickly loses its appeal and he discovers that it is hard work. In the beginning he is able to contain the fire, but a smoldering snag hit by wind nearby spreads embers into surrounding dry fuel causing a fire too big for one person to put out. The smokejumpers are called to help and all ends well. To illustrate the part of the jumpers, Disney borrowed footage from *A Fire Called Jeremiah*, showing quick snippets of a Johnson Flying Service DC-3.

FLYING IDAHO – IDAHO BUREAU OF AERONAUTICS (1992)

The short, roughly fifteen-minute, program hosted by John Maakestad and Dick Williams was created to promote flying safety in the Idaho backcountry. Maakestad at the time was the chief pilot for the Idaho Bureau of Aeronautics and Williams was a respected mountain flying instructor and pilot for Harrah's Middle Fork Charters. Williams first learned to fly the Idaho backcountry in the Selway area from instructor and friend Bob Black of Grangeville. After becoming familiar with the Selway region he ventured to other areas and began flying for Salmon Air Taxi. While living in Salmon he started Mountains to Canyons Flying School, the first formal public training for mountain flying. Williams created lesson plans and in 1981 wrote a book entitled *The Mountains to Canyons Flying Manual.*[17]

In 1987 Williams joined forces with several experienced mountain pilots to help the FAA put on the first River of No Return Mountain Flying Seminar in Challis. Instructors for the course included Bill Dorris, Gridley Rowles, and Frank Giles. As an instructional aid, Williams began to produce videos to help students visualize approaches and airstrip layouts.[18]

The film features flying by Maakestad with instructional advice from Williams, mainly in the department's Cessna Skylane. However, Williams demonstrates a high-performance takeoff with the Middle Fork Charters Twin Otter (N3H) at Indian Creek. Beyond the basics of flying the Idaho backcountry with helpful tips, the two also give a quick tour of several larger airstrips such as Chamberlain, Indian Creek, and Johnson Creek.

R. Williams

Williams and his Piper Cub.

MOUNTAIN FLYING WITH DICK WILLIAMS (1996)

During the production of *Flying Idaho*, which was created for the Idaho Bureau of Aeronautics, Dick Williams and producer Dave Tuttle became friends. A few years after finishing the department's film, Tuttle and Williams had the idea of creating and selling a series of instructional videos on mountain flying for retail. Only the first in the series was completed, which is *Mountain Flying With Dick Williams* produced by their company Inside Track Productions.[19] The nearly forty-minute film provided practical and safe information for flying the Idaho backcountry. Williams in his Super Cub (N8480H) and a Cessna 182 (N9085X) did most of the flying. Part of the instructional outline includes a nice overview of takeoffs and landings at some of the major public airstrips such as Chamberlain, Cold Meadows, Krassel, and Moose Creek. A unique aspect of the production is the mix of stories and recommendations from former Johnson Flying Service pilots Jim Larkin and Warren Ellison. Williams eventually retired from mountain flying instruction and went to work flying for Middle Fork Charters, in addition to managing the Middle Fork Lodge, before becoming a chief pilot on a Learjet 45.

The location of where the B-23 came to a stop on January 29, 1943 near the shore of Loon Lake.

CHAPTER 11

WORLD WAR
II MILITARY
AIRPLANE
CRASHES
IN THE
BACKCOUNTRY

The largest air war in world history took place during the United States' involvement in World War II. Surprisingly the Army Air Force (AAF) actually lost more aircraft to training and transportation accidents within the United States than they lost in combat against the Japanese army and naval air forces in the war.[1] The result of some these accidents can still be seen in Idaho, since nearly 300 of the 7,100 AAF airplanes lost between December 1941 and August 1945 were within the state.[2] Included in the area covered in this book, two significant AAF crashes happened in the winter of 1943, just two months apart. Both stories involve heroism, survival, triumph, and tragedy on the part of the AAF airmen and local citizens.

THE CRASH OF THE LOON LAKE DOUGLAS B-23

The Flight and Crash

The destroyed bombardier's compartment of the B-23. The access door into the cockpit (center) is visible.

In December 1942 the 4th AAF's 42nd Group, 390th Bombardment Squadron, based at Tacoma, Washington's McChord Field was ordered to Tonopah, Nevada, for tactical maneuvers.[3] The 390th had been flying submarine patrols along Washington's coast using North American B-25 Mitchells, a twin-engine medium bomber introduced in 1940.[4] The aircrews flew the squadron's bombers to Nevada, while ground crews traveled via troop train.[5]

While in Tonopah the B-25s were engaged in practice skip bombing and shadow firing on a bombing range. After three weeks of exercises the 390th prepared to return to McChord. On the morning of January 28 the planes and aircrews left in the squadron's B-25s while the support ground crews took a troop train back to Washington. The squadron had one Douglas B-23 Dragon that was used for transport purposes. This particular B-23 had been used to deliver personnel to Tonopah on its way to Sacramento, California, where an engine replacement was to take place. The twin-engine bomber built in 1939 was surpassed by other designs and became used more as a training and transport plane. However, not enough time was allowed for the engine change before orders were sent requesting the aircraft be delivered back to Tonopah for return to McChord. It was then arranged for the new engine to be available back at its home base.[6]

Assigned to B-23 39052 were a group of men who were previously unacquainted with one another, except for two individuals. Although the plane only required a crew of six, two additional men, Cpl. Earl Beaudry of Technical Supply and Paul G. Loewen of the Armament Department were assigned to the

aircraft for transportation back to McChord. The officer in charge of the group was 1st Lt. Robert "Bob" Orr as pilot. Acting as copilot was 2nd Lt. Adgate B. Schermerhorn, the navigator was 2nd Lt. James V. Kelly, and the radio operator was S/Sgt. Edward M. Freeborg. S/Sgt. Ralph Pruitt along with S/Sgt. Forest S. Hoover filled the positions of flight engineer.[7]

On the afternoon of January 28 the plane departed Tonopah with a clearance for an instrument flight route via Pendleton, Oregon. During climb out Orr noted high oil temperature indications on the right engine and decided to forgo the flight. Ground crews worked on the plane overnight to repair the malfunction. Late in the morning on January 29 the crew was able to leave and was cleared for an instrument route via North Dallas, Oregon. Mild weather was predicted for the flight, thus Boise and Pocatello, Idaho, were selected as alternate landing locations if weather prevented them from getting into the Tacoma area.[8]

At an hour and fifteen minutes into the flight Orr requested the altitude of 12,500' to stay above the cloud layer. At about the same time Seattle Control advised him the weather at McChord was poor and re-routed 39052 to Pendleton, Oregon. Forty-five minutes after making the navigation change, Orr requested a higher altitude again to avoid instrument conditions that he felt might contain ice. The cloud layers merged along the flight path, but he thought he could maneuver the plane to 18,000' and get on top of the layer. His prediction came true and by the time he reached 18,000' he had flown through severe icing conditions and the plane could not maintain altitude.[9] While the airplane iced up, radio operator Edward "Ed" Freeborg lost all communications. Then the navigational equipment stopped working.[10]

Panicked, Orr with only 332.25 total hours of flight time, abandoned his cleared route when he spotted a hole in the clouds that he thought he could get through.[11] Descending at a rapid rate while trying to stay out of the surrounding clouds the plane broke out of the layer at about 1,000' above the ground. One of the crew then spotted a set of railroad tracks and Orr began to follow them as it was snowing and he wanted to land the plane. Miraculously the tracks led them to a town, which they determined to be Burns, Oregon. Before the crew could find an airfield the snowstorm intensified reducing all forward visibility. While they were searching for an airport the Boise navigational radio beam was tuned in and worked. In stressful and limiting circumstances Orr made the quick decision to intercept the Boise Beam with the intent to land at Boise's Gowen Field.[12]

Orr then configured the plane for a quick

Looking north toward Loon Lake at the tail of the B-23 and the swath of trees that were mowed down.

ascent while on the radio beam. Climbing through the snow the plane began icing, and they lost the navigational beam. Orr felt the only way out of the situation was to maintain a northeast heading and get on top of the layer, which he did at 19,600'. Similar to the situation before the plane became laden with ice and he could not maintain the altitude, thus a slow descent was started. By this time Orr began to worry about their fuel supply. He ran a prompt calculation and figured only about one hour remained. Feeling

487

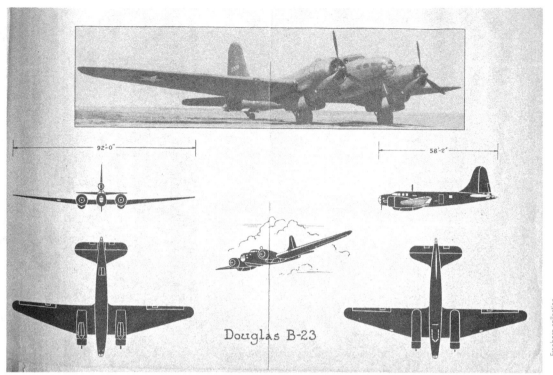

The Douglas B-23 Dragon.

helpless, he told the crew to put on parachutes and prepare to abandon the aircraft. He planned on staying with the plane, and the others who were ready to bail out started having second thoughts. While descending through 13,000′ the visibility increased and one of the crew spotted a small open hole to the north.[13]

Figuring he had nothing to lose, Orr cranked the airplane into the hole and as more visibility was gained he could tell they were in rough mountainous terrain. Orr then told the men that he did not want people separated and ordered them to remain with the ship. While speaking, the large white clearing of frozen Loon Lake was spotted and he told the crew to prepare for a crash landing.[14]

Trying to the slow the airplane down as much as possible he circled the lake. Orr's goal was to land south on the lake's surface with the wheels retracted, as he feared flipping the aircraft over on touchdown in the deep snow. Being restricted by the storm-enshrouded mountains he made his first effort at landing even though he could not get the flaps to work. On this attempt he came in too high and fast and made a go-around. When he shoved the power forward to initiate a climb the right engine backfired and it became engulfed with flames.[15] The second

approach was better, but the aircraft was still too high and on a collision course with a stand of trees on the edge of the lake. Committed to landing, Orr cut all power and yanked back on the controls stalling it into the trees. The plane overshot the lake by at least fifty yards and smashed through the timber. A deluge of snow, tree branches, and metal burst into the air as the bomber pushed its way through the obstructions. On impact both wings sheared off outside of the engine nacelles and the bombardier compartment was demolished.[i]

Once the plane came to a rest the crew scrambled out fearing the aircraft might explode. Orr crawled out of his emergency door on the left side of the cockpit, while others escaped out the rear door. A small fire did start but quickly burned itself out.[16] Orr promptly made a head count and noted someone was missing. The men rushed to the front of the plane and found Hoover slumped over hanging by his seatbelt in the copilot's seat. His face was down with his arms stretched out. Apparently moments prior to the crash Schermerhorn had been sitting in the copilot's seat, but got up and braced himself behind a bulkhead

---

[i] *While the accident reports indicate the fire was on the right engine, evidence at the crash site suggests the fire was actually on the number one engine on the left (port) side.*

with some others for the impact. Hoover hastily grabbed the seat and had just enough time to get buckled in prior to the crash.[17]

Recalling the scene years later, Loewen wrote, "No one spoke as we stood viewing his mangled body and then we heard a moan and we knew he was still alive. As we relieved him of his seatbelt, he regained consciousness and spoke to us. He was then carried away from the wreckage and laid out on the snow. How that man ever survived, I'll never know, and not once would he ever allow anyone to give him a shot of morphine which we had available from a survival kit. He looked very bad to us at the time but it was not until later that we discovered the very seriousness of his condition. The entire right side of his body had been scraped by a tree. His face was bleeding, the right arm and wrist broken, compound fracture of the thighbone and the right foot shattered and literally pushed up almost half way to the knee. We managed to remove his boot and sprinkled the wound with sulfanilamide powder, wrapping it up with parachute silk. The sulfa powder seemed to control the bleeding so it was used, right or wrong, for it was all we had."[18]

Beyond Hoover's injuries, Lt. Orr had badly cut his hand from hitting the instrument panel on impact, but was feeling fine. Others in the group had minor scrapes and bruises, but were okay.[19] As the men stood in disbelief of the day's events, the snowstorm they had been battling most of the afternoon moved in and they could barely see the lake. It had been four and a half hours since leaving Tonopah and the afternoon light faded in the falling snow.

Life at Loon Lake

Some of the men ransacked the aircraft for supplies, rations, and useful equipment, while others gathered material to build a shelter and a fire. Wanting to comfort Hoover the best they could, a life raft was inflated and he was situated in it with his leg elevated. Standing around the fire they recapped

The airmen's shelter and camp area.

Brown collection

the day's events. Several position reports had been transmitted even though the radio equipment was malfunctioning, including a mayday call before the emergency landing. However, it was questionable whether or not they were received. To stay warm, the crew adopted three-hour shifts to keep the fire stoked.

For the next two days the crew explored the area around the lake. Some tried to fashion snowshoes from pieces of the aircraft, but were unsuccessful. Walking around the area was difficult due to the deep snow. The reconnaissance affirmed their suspicion of being in a very remote area. However, the USFS's old Loon Lake Ranger Station built in the 1920s and seldom used by the early 1940s was located on the northeast side of the lake. It was debated if they should relocate to the cabin, but it was felt they should stay close to the aircraft since it was easier to spot from the air.[20] Also there was no way to stay warm in the cabin as some of the men had tried to build a small fire on the dirt floor, but it smoked them out.[21] Several useful items were retrieved from the cabin and brought to the camp including a frying pan and a dull axe.[22]

While some investigated the area others were given the task of hunting to supplement their small supply of vitamin rations. The aircraft was fully armed with three .30 caliber machine guns and one .50 caliber machine gun. Also aboard for emergency situations were a few 12-gauge shotguns and a Colt .45 pistol. All of the guns had the associated ammunition except for the Colt. Several birds and squirrels were obtained using the shotguns and cooked in the frying pan.[23]

On the third day, February 1, Freeborg spent hours patching the radio equipment together after discovering the batteries still had power. He tried sending several messages using Morse Code on various frequencies stating, "B-23, 39052, ALL CREW INTACT, 5000 FEET, SOUTH END LAKE, NEED FOOD CLOTHING AXE." Being unable to receive anything, he was not sure his efforts worked. The battery power then completely died.[24]

With continued snowstorms and foul weather the airplane became encased in snow and the men began to lose hope of being found. On the fourth night, February 2, Pruitt called a meeting a good distance from the shelter, so Hoover could not overhear them.[25] Pruitt and Hoover had become close friends after attending aviation mechanics school together. He instilled in the group that Hoover was going to die of gangrene if help was not found. Pruitt told the crew that he was walking out and would like someone else to go. Schermerhorn and Freeborg volunteered to join him.[26]

On the morning of February 3, the three fittest fliers gathered rations, survival equipment, a shotgun, and left camp. Staying behind with Hoover were Orr, Kelly, Loewen, and Beaudry.[27]

Rescue Efforts

While the B-23 crew clung to life on the frozen shore of Loon Lake, a huge search and rescue effort was launched. Unbeknownst to the crew, the B-23 had been spotted by several people when they had circled the town of Burns. Also at three different radiolocations the AAF received the transmission, "CALLING BURNS RADIO, B-23, 39052, RCR OUT, NO OXYGEN, 7000 FEET, PICKING UP ICE, ABANDONING SHIP."[28]

Believing 39052 had gone down approximately twenty-five miles southeast of Burns; a rescue operation was established at Pendleton Field.

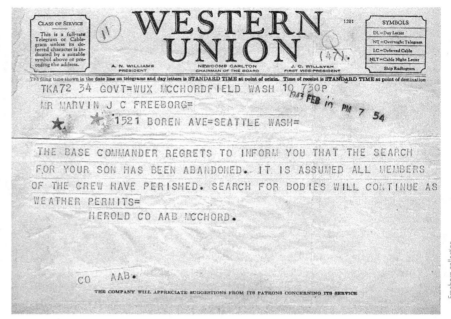

A telegram that was sent to the Freeborg family regarding the search.

Several airplanes and ground crews searched for three days, but found nothing. At about the time they were going to cancel the search a radio base in Victoria, British Columbia, Canada, picked up Freeborg's Morse Code message. Knowing the people from the missing aircraft were still alive the search was expanded. But the AAF was still puzzled as to the location of the lake referenced in the message.[29]

Over the next five days, when the weather cooperated, the military sent out twenty-four airplanes on the search. During the last few days of the hunt seventy-three airplanes were used. While the Civilian Air Patrol assisted greatly with small aircraft, the military used a wide assortment of planes including C-43s, C-78s, L-3Cs, L-4s, B-23s, B-24s, and B-17s. Many of the four engine bombers were equipped with aerial camera gear and over 400 photographs were taken and inspected for clues. On the morning of February 10, with the approval of Pendleton Air Base Commander Col. Lyman L. Phillips, and the 4th AAF's Lt. Col. Darrow, the search was discontinued. The families of the men aboard 39052 were then notified of the decision.[30]

B-23 Discovered at Loon Lake

As search and rescue efforts were carried out during the first several days of February, the five airmen at Loon Lake wondered if they were going to make it out of the situation alive. Orr later reported that they had heard several airplanes in the area.[31] With their hopes high they dismounted the .50 cal machine gun and brought it out near the edge of the lake and strapped it to a stump. The ammunition belts used in this gun were alternated with tracer bullets, which allowed the gunner to follow the trail to a target. The crew figured these tracers could be used in place of flares if another aircraft returned.[32] The crew at the lake spotted several other aircraft including two AAF planes. At the time they saw the AAF ships they "vainly" unloaded flares into the air, but they were not seen.[33]

Life at the camp became very gloom and doom. The crew began to hear things as if they were going crazy. Loewen wrote of the tension, "After being silent for hours, especially early morning hours, some would say, 'Listen.' We would ask what did you hear, and he would explain, 'I heard an airplane, or I heard a rooster crow or there is a truck on a nearby highway.' This happened to all of us, not just one person . . . One afternoon, Lt. Orr sat by the fire with his face buried in his hands, not moving or saying a word for a long period of time. Suddenly he jumped up and shouted, 'Why in the hell did it have to be me, why did I have to be the one to fly that son of a bitch and get you all in this predicament?' After we all expressed our feelings of faith in him and if that it had not been for his skill and ability to bring the plane in as he did, none of us would be alive. He sat back down and sobbed as though his heart would break. He held the responsibility and blame in himself almost to the breaking point."

On February 13, Johnson Flying Service pilot Penn Stohr Sr. was returning to Cascade from Warren in a Travel Air 6000 (NC623H) after delivering mail.[34] Stohr had been aware of the missing AAF aircraft and had looked for it while flying to various destinations around the backcountry. To his surprise as he approached Loon Lake he spotted the downed airplane and a few men milling about.[35] To let the men on the ground know he had found them he circled at treetop level and wagged the Travel Air's wings while waving out his side window. Loewen recalling the site of Stohr noted, "We absolutely went nuts. We were laughing and crying all at the same time. Even

Hoover managed to crawl out of the dugout alone and join us in our jubilation."[36] Stohr then flew on to Cascade and reported his findings to Gowen Field. He later revealed to friends that he was disappointed in himself that he had not spotted it earlier as he had been flying in the general vicinity several other times since it had crashed.[37]

Gowen Field was elated to hear word that the missing B-23 had been found. After Stohr gave them more details and the location, he offered to provide his help. However, the AAF warned him not to become involved and wanted to know if he, "was qualified to fly over this territory." Dismissing Stohr's skills as a pilot and his knowledge of the area, Gowen Field proceeded by sending out eight airplanes. The aircraft flew right over the crash site but could not locate it. Upon returning from the failed mission the AAF placed a call back to Stohr. With Stohr's help, an AAF plane was able to parachute supplies (mainly food), to the men at the lake by nightfall.[38]

The following day the AAF contacted Stohr and asked if he would be able to land on Loon Lake and retrieve the men. He figured the usable portion of the frozen lake surface to be a minimum of 2000' in length. Stohr humbly told the AAF that he had operated ski-equipped Travel Airs in worse conditions. The AAF told him that he was hired.[39]

That morning Stohr departed for the rescue mission flying the same Travel Air.[40] After landing on the lake he taxied the plane over to the south end and parked. When he arrived the airmen had just finished hauling in the supplies that had been dropped the night before. Loewen recalled, "When he [Stohr] got out of the plane we damn near hugged him to death. I remember him asking who was that fool on the machine gun who damn near shot me down? It was me, I didn't think I got near him, but I do know I must have about melted the barrel on that .50 cal."[41] In a brief conversation, Stohr was filled in on the events and was informed of the three men who had left for help. He told them that he would get a search party pulled together. In the meantime Stohr divided the fliers into two groups to ensure he would be able to get airborne.[42] In the first load he flew out Hoover and Kelly.[43]

On the second trip to the lake Stohr brought in Idaho NF Assistant Supervisor Gene Powers and

Region 4 Smokejumper Foreman Lloyd Johnson to search for the three fliers who had left the bomber eleven days earlier. The remaining three airmen greeted the airplane and again thanked him for all of his help. Overwhelmed and wanting to show their gratitude the fliers told Stohr and the rescuers they could have whatever they wanted.[44]

Stohr rushed Orr, Loewen, and Beaurdy into the plane as the afternoon temperatures and sun had caused the lake to become mushy and he was afraid the surfaces of the skis were going to freeze. A wind had also kicked up. To help pack down the takeoff run and compensate for the additional takeoff drag caused by the wet snow he taxied to the north end of the lake for a departure to the south. In order to get turned around he had the men get out of the plane and pull on one wing strut with a rope. When pointed in the right direction Loewen noted, "At first the plane seemed to be stuck but he succeeded in getting it moving and we sorta hopped along on the snow until he finally got airborne. Once again, Cpl. Beaudry and I were looking straight into the trees we had crashed into. Mr. Stohr used up the space on the lake in order to get airborne and we were still below treetops. He banked the plane and on wing tips we circled the outside circumference of the lake until he gained enough altitude to clear the trees. During our flight out, flying down the canyons, Mr. Stohr would dip the plane on its side to point out landmarks and directions we could have used as a route to shelter and the comfort of cabins equipped with food, firewood, and bedding."[45]

As the Travel Air departed, Lloyd Johnson and Powers started across the northeast side of lake toward the outlet creek. They picked up three sets of tracks headed down Loon Creek and followed them all the way to the Secesh River until they located the airmen's first overnight camp. Johnson and Powers who were carrying a handheld radio and telephone contacted the USFS in McCall to let them know the situation.[46]

A plan was quickly devised to have more men and supplies brought in so they could better track the fliers. The next day two Johnson Flying Service pilots flew to Loon Lake and met Powers and Lloyd Johnson. Stohr was flying Travel Air NC623H and Dick Johnson (unrelated to Lloyd) was flying Travel Air NC655H. Joining the rescue efforts were Ted Hardwood, Glenn Thompson, and Warren Brown. The group of five then set out on snowshoes in pursuit of the lost airman.[47] After the rescuers left, Stohr and Dick Johnson investigated the B-23 and the camp that the fliers had been living in. The two had their eyes on a few souvenirs. With a couple of items picked out they returned to the lake lugging their keepsakes to the empty Travel Airs.[48]

Dick Johnson and Stohr also aided in the search by flying over the terrain between McCall and the Secesh River looking for any signs of the missing men.[49] The ground crew trailed the three flier's tracks to Slick Rock Brown's Cabin where they found evidence that the airmen had been there a few days before. On the third day of the search they received word that the three fliers had made contact with people in McCall. The searchers then hiked out to the Krassel Ranger Station where Dick Johnson retrieved them in a Travel Air.[50]

When Stohr had left the lake on February 14 with the remaining airman he had flown them directly to Cascade. From Cascade ambulances transported the five men to the Gowen Field Hospital for medical treatment.[51] Back in Cascade Stohr's friend Gordon Squires, who owned all three of Valley County's newspapers (*The Payette Lakes Star, The Cascade News, and The Stibnite Miner*), dubbed him the "Miracle Pilot." Stohr figured it was just another day's work, and shrugged off the unwarranted publicity.[52] Although Stohr was close with the Johnsons his rescue escapade was rumored to have darn right irritated them. Apparently Dick placed a new sign on the Cascade hangar door, commenting to an employee, "Maybe this will remind people just who's flying service this really is."[53]

Walking Out and a Warm Reception

The men selected to walk out for help were Schermerhorn, Freeborg, and Pruitt. Schermerhorn was chosen as the leader as he had spent time in New York's Adirondack Mountains growing up. Apparently on the morning of February 3, before following Loon Creek to the Secesh, the three men hiked to the top of a nearby ridge to figure out the easiest route.

1 *Earl Beaudry, Paul Loewen, Robert Orr, and rescue pilot Penn Stohr Sr. at Loon Lake on February 14, 1943 with Travel Air 6000 NC623H.*
2 *Bombardier James Kelly.*
3 *Loewen and Forest Hoover at the Gowen Field Hospital.*
4 *Johnson Flying Service Travel Airs parked at Loon Lake during the search efforts for the three missing airmen who hiked out for help.*
5 *Don Goodman, a young family friend of the Stohrs, created this drawing as a gift to Penn shortly after the Loon Lake rescue.*

Freeborg collection

Freeborg collection

Brown collection

Stohr family

WHEN THE GOING GETS TOUGH. ——— TAKE A BUSH FLYER

Freeborg later wrote, "Believe me, that was the most disappointing sight I had ever hoped to see. Hills, hills and more hills in every direction. Believe me, I firmly believed that we looked in the face of death."[54]

With no snowshoes and meager winter equipment the three men trudged through the snow. At many points along the route it was impossible to walk. Rather they had to crawl, switching off with one another on breaking trail. Through several areas they became extremely exhausted as with each step they sunk up to their waists. Regarding their efforts Schermerhorn noted, "The first day we walked for 20 hours . . . It seemed like we traveled miles and miles, but the map in the ranger cabin here shows we couldn't have made more than 2 miles, after that we walked only eight hours a day. The second day we walked through snow up to our hips . . . The third day we came to a stream and since there is an old saying that to find civilization always walk downstream, so we did just that. I think it was eight days later we found an abandoned cabin."[55]

At this cabin, commonly known then as "Slick Rock Browns," they found food and a map of the Idaho NF (now Payette NF). The map proved to be a pivotal tool, as they were able to figure out for the first time where they actually were. The airmen spent three days resting and eating pancakes in the cabin. They then headed over Lick Creek Summit and down the other side. Crossing over Lick Creek was extremely difficult, as they had to traverse several avalanches. To avoid sleeping out in the open terrain they dug nine-foot deep holes at night to stay warm. The road that is now present on the east side of the summit was not completed until after the war, and they had a very difficult time locating the USFS trail indicated on the map. After reaching the top of the pass the going was easier as they came onto the road. On February 14, while making their way down the west side of the summit, they found the CCC camp at Black Lee Creek. The fliers broke a window in the camp's cookhouse/mess hall and built a fire and gorged themselves on canned foods, butter, tea, and coffee. They also found some sleeping bags and were able to get some good rest.[56]

Unfortunately when they awoke Pruitt could hardly walk because of a twisted knee and frost bitten-feet. Schermerhorn's feet were also in bad shape and

they decided to spend an extra day resting with the realization that they were getting close to the Lake Fork Ranger Station. On the morning of February 16 they decided to leave Pruitt behind at the CCC camp and press on.[57]

Schermerhorn and Freeborg followed the telephone lines along the road and after forty some miles and nearly two weeks since leaving the airplane they located the Lake Fork Ranger Station. The two built a fire and managed to find some food and a telephone. Schermerhorn picked up the receiver and to his astonishment heard a hum. He waited some time and finally an operator came on the line. The operator was Leona Hoff Park who had acted on pure curiosity as she thought that there was a short in the switchboard – the line had not illuminated since the previous fall. Schermerhorn and Hoff were both surprised. After hanging up, Hoff contacted her husband Don, who worked for the USFS and put together a search party that consisted of Yale Mitchell, Leonard Lietzke, John Wick, Bill Garrett, and Gil McCoy. During the rest of the afternoon and early evening the telephone at the station rang off the hook. Eventually the two fliers refused to answer it and fell asleep.[58]

The next morning Park and the rescuers arrived. Freeborg wrote, "About 7 o'clock the first rangers came and stayed for about an hour before going on up after Pruitt. Then some more came up at about 11 with a big toboggan for Pruitt and we sent them on up to the CCC camp, and went to sleep . . . The next morning they cooked us the biggest breakfast I have ever had."[59] Within the next day the airman were brought to McCall riding on the back of a sled pulled by a tractor. The whole town closed down, including the school to greet them. The rescued airmen were given free rooms at the Hotel McCall. The following day the three men were transported to the Gowen Field Hospital where they were reunited with the rest of the crew.[60]

Return To McChord and Another 390th Crash

When the men returned to McChord their high spirits were dampened by the news that two people in their squadron had been killed in an aircraft accident

494

the same day they had crashed at Loon Lake. One of the men, Captain L. T. "Buzz" Wagner, was a good friend to many of the airmen who survived Loon Lake. According to Loewen the crew at Loon Lake thought it would be Wagner who would find them, commenting, "While sitting around the fire at the crash site, we often reminisced that it would be Capt. Buzz Wagner that would be the one who would come flying down the canyon on wing tips and find us. It was very sad . . . to learn of his death."[61]

In an odd set of circumstances Wagner and his B-25 had accompanied the squadron's B-23 (39052) to Tonopah and then to Sacramento. When the B-23 was requested to transport men back to McChord, Wagner flew his B-25 to Hammer Field in Fresno, California. The next day, January 29, Wagner and his crew of six were cleared to Medford, Oregon, with a final destination of McChord. Similar to the Loon Lake crowd the B-25 encountered the same bad weather and could not make it. After turning around to return to Hammer Field they flew into severe icing conditions and the pilots struggled with the plane for sometime before Wagner ordered the crew to bail out. Five of the seven airmen made it safely to the ground, but Wagner and the radio operator, Robert Morris, did not make it out of the aircraft. Eyewitnesses saw the airplane break out of the low overcast in an inverted dive and then explode when it hit the ground in a hayfield five miles north of Placerville, California.[62]

More Happenings and More Trips to Loon Lake

A week after the eight airmen were rescued from the wilds of Idaho, the AAF arranged salvage efforts with the Idaho NF to retrieve "the most important and valuable" components from the B-23 wreckage. The crew from the local USFS included Tom Coski, Glenn Thompson, Walter Howard, and John Wick. Melvin Brock, a warrant officer from Gowen Field, joined these men on the mission.[63]

With recovery efforts expected to take at least a week, Dick Johnson flew one load of supplies to Loon Lake on February 21. The next day he transported the salvagers to "Jack Fernan's Place," an open area located on the west side of the road in Secesh Meadows.[64] Fernan's was only used by ski-equipped airplanes and was occasionally utilized to deliver mail if people were in residence. From the meadow the crew trekked to Loon Lake and began work. By March 2, using pack boards and a toboggan the men had transported out 1,200 pounds of parts to Fernans. The next day Stohr flew the men and aircraft parts out to McCall in two evenly divided loads.[65]

Many citizens from the area communities questioned what was on the airplane? Rumors spread about bombsights, guns, bombs, and high-tech equipment. Some suggested that the AAF wanted access to the crash scene to recover one of World War II's most top-secret developments – the Norden Bombsight. However, it is doubtful that B-23 39052 had a Norden, for two reasons. First, the autopilot system installed on the plane from the Douglas factory was not sophisticated enough to be incorporated into the Norden without major modifications. Secondly most Nordens were not integrated into mass-produced military aircraft until late 1942, which would not have given enough time to have one aboard the B-23 at Loon Lake.[66]

It would be interesting to know if the AAF asked any questions about the missing items transported out by Dick Johnson and Stohr, which are known to have consisted of shotguns, one Browning .50 caliber machine gun, boxes of ammunition, and tools. Although the items were considered "gifts," beginning in 1934 it became unlawful for any civilian to possess a fully automatic weapon (machine gun) in the United States. Stohr kept the gun well hidden and before leaving Cascade in 1945 got together with a few friends to try it out. They chained it down to concrete filled barrels and cranked a couple of rounds through it at the airport. However, the tracer bullets started a grass fire along the runway. They quickly hid the gun before the fire department arrived. The machine gun was later transported to Missoula and stored at Johnson Flying Service. It was occasionally set up for big events, such as the Fourth of July, and people took turns shooting it.[67]

By the early 1950s word spread about the illegal gun and that it was stolen. Whoever swiped the piece of equipment did not remain quiet and the Federal Bureau of Investigation (FBI) began to ask questions. Although the FBI interrogated people

Adgate Schermerhorn at the Lake Fork Ranger Station.

Edward Freeborg on the steps of the Hotel McCall after he was rescued.

around the Missoula airport, everyone denied having any knowledge of the machine gun.[68]

The Crew of B-23 39052

Robert Orr – A native of Iowa, Orr graduated from Iowa State and by September 1941 had earned his wings at Kelly Field, Texas. He was later transferred to Hammer Field, where he met and married his wife Billie. After his assignment at McChord he was stationed in Alaska before being deployed to the South Pacific, flying as a captain on B-24s.[69]

On November 19, 1944, Orr was returning to the Island of Nanomea (Ellice Island Group) from a mission where his group bombed Makin Island (Gilbert Island Group). It was a tough assignment full of bad weather and flak.[70] On final approach to Nanomea, Orr fought a fierce crosswind and decided to go-around for another try. When he shoved the power forward and executed the turn, the plane's right wing dipped, stalled, and crashed into the dense trees skirting the runway. The plane burst into flames killing the twenty-five year old Orr and five others. Four additional crewmembers of the B-24 were injured, but survived.[71]

Adgate Schermerhorn – A resident of Ausable Chasm, New York, Schermerhorn enlisted in the AAF in December 1941. After earning his pilot's wings he was transferred to McChord. He then spent the remainder of World War II flying in Alaska and

the Aleutian Islands. With an honorable discharge he returned to New York and obtained a master's degree from St. Lawrence University. Schermerhorn made a career of teaching and as a hobby bred horses and spent time in the Adirondack Mountains. After retiring he moved to Tucson, Arizona. He died in January 1999 at the age of eighty.[72]

James Kelly – Kelly was from Warren, Kansas, and was trained as a bombardier.[73]

Paul Loewen – Loewen was from Inola, Oklahoma, and was trained in armament and gunnery. His mother wrote Penn Stohr Sr. a postcard thanking him for his rescue, "I praise god for your faith and belief in the spoken word. Your greatest reward will be through the glory of our Lord and Savior. May you never lack for gas. Yours Truly."[74] He served the remainder of the war with the hope of being sent

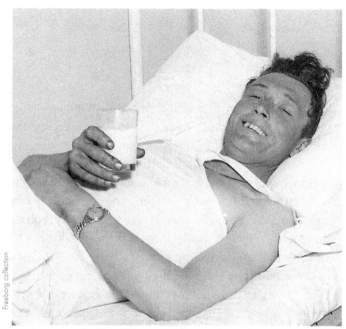

Ralph Pruitt recovering in the Gowen Field Hospital.

into combat, but his assignments kept him stateside as an instructor. After World War II Loewen became a manager for a Ford dealership in Greeley, Colorado, while living in nearby Ault.[75]

In August 1969 he returned to McCall and hiked to the site of the wreckage with his wife.[76] While there he recovered two souvenirs including the placard from the instrument panel detailing the use of the window defroster and the metal tag from the bomb bay area as that is where he sat to brace himself during the crash. In 1988 he wrote a story he had hoped to some day publish about the epic event at Loon Lake, but it never materialized. One lasting comment he wrote in reflection about the crash was, "As a child I could never accept my father's concept of fate but after that experience I have become a firm believer. God did not intend for us to die that day. He rode with us and delivered us from an inevitable fate to live the rest of our lives until He determined the time and day we should give up our mortal bodies here on earth.[77] Loewen died in Wichita, Kansas, on November 28, 2000 at the age of seventy-eight.[78]

Edward Freeborg – Originally from Spokane, Washington, Freeborg graduated from high school while living in Wallace, Idaho. He then joined the AAF and attended radio school at Scotts Field located in Illinois. When his training was completed he was stationed at McChord. After the Loon Lake

accident he spent time with his parents in Seattle. During this occasion he wrote his account of the accident, titled *Crash In the Hills*.[79]

When his active duty resumed he was deployed to India where he served as a radio operator on C-47s flying supplies over the Himalayan Mountains to China, a route commonly known as "The Hump." After the war he earned a degree in architecture from the University of Washington and eventually started his own company in Portland, Oregon.[80]

During his retirement years he hoped to revisit McCall with his wife Gloria and was eager to see what remained at the crash site. In 1991 they made the trip and hired McCall Air Taxi to fly them over Loon Lake. The following year Max Black of Boise contacted Freeborg after taking a group of Boy Scouts to Loon Lake. A friendship evolved and an arrangement was made for Freeborg to re-visit the site.[81] In a reflection about his 1992 visit, Freeborg wrote, "Once I got there, I had an eerie feeling, of déjà-vu – It was quite a surprise to see the results of almost 50 years of vandalism – Engines stripped, propellers gone, all the instruments gone and hundreds of bullet holes shot into and out of the main body – Almost all of the carryable items are gone . . . I suppose the parts should last a few more years for souvenirs. Nostalgia makes for interesting conjectures . . . the most memorable feeling to me was the difference in the seasons and how pleasant and beautiful it is in the summer. My memory of the scene in January 1943 was of the remoteness and isolation we all felt at the time and praying that we would find our way out to civilization."[82] Three years after visiting the wreckage Freeborg died at age seventy-two while playing golf with his wife.[83]

Forest Hoover – Hoover was from Missouri and enlisted in April 1941. Due to injuries incurred from the accident he had to have his foot amputated and was given a prosthetic. Shortly after recovering Hoover was honorably discharged from the AAF.[84]

Ralph Pruitt – Pruitt was from Wichita, Kansas. Prior to the war he lived in Kellogg, Idaho, where he worked for the Sunshine Mining Company.[85]

Earl Beaudry – Beaudry was from Portland, Oregon, and enlisted in February 1942.[86]

The Wreckage

Only thirty-eight Douglas B-23 Dragons were built before production ended in 1939. The plane, based on the company's successful DC-2 and DC-3 designs, was the first AAF aircraft to have incorporated a rear tail gunner position. The B-23 was equipped with Wright R-2600-3 engines that developed 1,600 horsepower each. The aircraft was far superior to other early twin-engine bombers, but was quickly surpassed by other designs before the start of World War II. After the war most of the B-23s were purchased as surplus and converted into executive transports.

In the late 1970s and early 1980s when the aviation industry began to recognize World War II era aircraft as collectable, it was noticed that no record copy of a military equipped B-23 existed. When the aircraft were modified during the postwar years the military features such as the bomb bay doors, bombardier's compartment, and tail gunner's clamshell were removed. While already a very rare airplane because of low production numbers, the Loon Lake B-23 became the most complete military example to have survived.

As aviation collectors began funding trips around the world to salvage World War II vintage aircraft, several had their sights on the Loon Lake wreckage. While it was debated by many as to what model of twin-engine airplane it actually was, they still wanted it. Starting in May 1981 the Payette NF began getting inquires about acquiring salvage rights to the wreckage. One salvage operator offered to pay the USFS $1 for the airplane and planned to have it lifted out by a helicopter. He argued that it was a detriment to the lake's water quality and it needed to be removed. The USFS gave the simple response of "No."[87] Other more legitimate inquires came from the curators at the McChord AFB Museum, the Travis AFB Museum, and the Confederate Air Force. While the queries trickled in, the USFS debated the ownership of the aircraft and its eligibility to be listed on the National Register of Historic Places.[88]

At about the same time the USFS determined that the wreckage did not meet the criteria of National Register eligibility, Terry Aitken, the senior curator from the Wright-Patterson AFB Museum, became interested. Aitken wanted several pieces from the airplane for the restoration of a B-23 that the Air Force was rebuilding to serve as the "military record copy." In the fall of 1998 Aitken arranged to have a Wright-Patterson crew survey the Loon Lake wreckage. The Idaho National Guard flew the survey personnel to Loon Lake in a Black Hawk helicopter. Based on the recon a Wright-Patterson salvage crew returned to the crash site during the summer of 1999 and removed various unique military components. The items were then airlifted out by helicopter.[89] While some of the parts will be reused, most will serve as templates. In the winter of 2001–02 the fuselage collapsed due to the removal of the major structural components of the airplane such as the rear floor and the two bulkheads.

Although the integrity of the Loon Lake B-23 was compromised, it still serves as the most intact World War II aircraft wreckage in the Continental United States. Since the fall of 2000 when the Payette NF built a bridge across the Secesh River from the Chinook Campground, access to Loon Lake has been greatly increased. The Payette NF also erected several interpretive signs to help tourists find the crash site. These two events have caused a huge rise in the popularity of the wreckage as a hiking and outdoor destination.

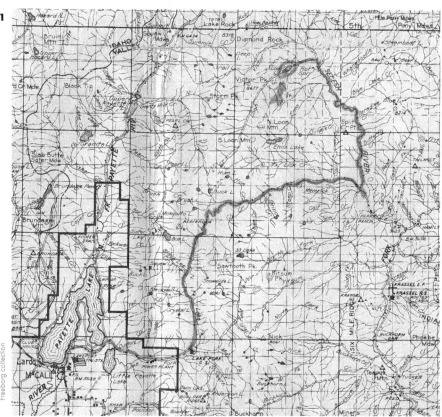

1 Freeborg drew the roughly forty-mile route the men walked on this 1940 edition of the Idaho NF map.

2 In 1992 Freeborg revisited the crash site. Freeborg is standing at the radio operator's station inside the aircraft, where he sat during the plane's ill-fated flight.

3 The location of the wreckage can be seen relative to the shoreline of Loon Lake.

4 The Loon Lake B-23 as it looked in the mid-1980s.

5 The rare clamshell doors that housed the Browning .50 caliber machine gun were one of many military features salvagers were after in the 1980s and 1990s.

6 The Wright-Patterson AFB salvage-crew examining the B-23 in the fall of 1998.

THE CRASH OF THE MIDDLE FORK BOEING B-17F

The Flight

A Boeing B-17F.

On March 30, 1943, the crew flying B-17F 42-29514 returned to their home base at Walla Walla, Washington, after about two hours of an instrument calibration mission. The airmen were part of the 2nd AAF's 88th Group of the 316th Bombardment Squadron. Helping the crew with the equipment was Lt. Bigelow, a navigational instructor. Without shutting the engines down the instructor climbed out of the B-17 and the crew took off for another local training flight at about 3:30 p.m. to practice instrument flying.[90]

Flying the airplane was 2nd Lt. Joseph Brensinger along with copilot F/O Harold Thompson. Other officers on the plane were navigator 2nd Lt. Austin Finley and bombardier George Smith. The enlisted men on the aircraft included Henry Van Slager, Howard Pope, Morris Becker, Harvey Wiegand, and Erwin Grundman.[91] Absent from the assigned crew on March 30 was Peter Durante, who had recently been hospitalized.[92]

Shortly after takeoff Brensinger flew several instrument exercises south of the base. After two hours of flying the plane was navigated back toward the base's gunnery range. On the new course the pilots flew into a thin veil of rain hanging down from the overcast. Thinking they would quickly break out of the moisture, they continued practicing on instruments. After several minutes with no forward visibility regained they started a descent, but gained nothing. Afraid of impacting area terrain Brensinger picked up the Walla Walla Beam and climbed to 8,000' to start an instrument approach. However, a few minutes after intercepting the signal the pilots could not hear the beam due to radio static.[93]

With the main means of navigation not working, the pilots turned to flying the compass needle, but decided it was giving erroneous information. They then asked Finley to shoot some fixes to help them figure out the plane's location in relation to the base.[94] When he was unable to do so, Brensinger ordered Morris, the radio operator, to notify the ground operation that they were lost. Meantime the power was pulled back to slow the airplane down. After a half hour of communication with the ground they were given an instrument clearance to fly to Boise's Gowen Field. Further orders would be sent the following day once the weather cleared.[ii]

With the new instrument clearance Thompson ran a few calculations and figured the plane had enough gas to make it to Salt Lake City, Utah, in a worse case scenario. He then asked one of the engineers to transfer gas from the bomb bay tank to the number two wing tank. After the pump ran for several minutes, Thompson could see no change on the fuel gauge associated with the tank. A series of cross checks ensued and Thompson concluded that instead of having 700 gallons of gas, they really only had 300 gallons of gas. A conversation followed about how much fuel they initially departed with, and they determined that the form the ground crew had filled out

---

[ii] *A few months prior the crew of ten had been assembled at Gowen Field.*

was incorrect. To conserve on the precious petrol the engines were pulled back to twenty-four inches of manifold pressure and 1500 RPM, propelling them at 130 MPH at 14,000'.

At about seven o'clock in the evening the plane and crew had been in the air for nearly four hours and their confidence was renewed when the clouds began to lift with an overcast layer at 16,000' and a broken layer at 2,000'. They confirmed their position with Walla Walla and gave a weather report. However, they had no idea the worst was yet to come. Twenty minutes after reporting everything was fine they became enshrouded in weather. For several minutes they continued on the Boise Beam toward Gowen, but then they lost all signal. In addition to the navigation loss they started picking up ice on the wings and props.

Fear overcame Brensinger and Thompson and it was decided to descend to a lower altitude with the hope they might breakout of the layer. As the altimeter needle passed through 10,000' a mountain abruptly came into view staring straight at them. Brensinger instantly heaved back on the controls and some how missed the oncoming terrain. He then climbed to 14,000' and leveled off. Shaking, he turned to Thompson and asked how much gas was left. Thompson estimated only about fifteen minutes of fuel remained. The two pilots donned their parachutes and Brensinger announced to the crew that they were going to abandon ship. The autopilot was switch to on and as the gyros warmed up, Van Slager checked the crews' harnesses and chutes. With the heavy bomber flying on its own, Brensinger rang the bailout signal just after eight o'clock in the evening. Exiting out the backdoor first was Pope, followed by Wiegand, Grundman, Becker, Van Slager, and Finley.[95]

Meantime Smith had to fulfill his bombardier duties, one of which was to destroy the Norden Bombsight. He located an emergency rifle stowed in the bombardier's compartment, but because of the cold temperatures the bolt was frozen. In a hurry he flipped the gun over and used it as a club to destroy the top-secret bombsight. With his responsibilities completed he crawled up to the flight deck and opened the front escape hatch.[96] Smith jumped, followed by Thompson and Brensinger.[97] Unknown to the men at the time, they had bailed out almost in a direct line dotting the Middle Fork of the Salmon River from roughly Soldier Creek to

AAF/USAF

The crash site of Boeing B-17F 42-29514 twenty miles southeast of Challis in Crane Basin. One of the large main tires can be seen in the foreground along with parts of the tail assembly.

Marble Creek.

The un-manned B-17, placed at a reduced power setting, continued flying northeasterly. Several Middle Fork residents spotted the plane as it flew onward. The plane made several swerves and turns and was also observed by people at the Blackbird Mine and the town of Forney.[98] The plane then lumbered along toward the community of Challis where it maneuvered itself into a slow thirty-degree bank, making several wide circles. Numerous citizens of Challis spotted the brightly lit bomber and around ten o'clock noted a heavy glow coming from one of the airplane's engines before it drifted off toward the Pahsimeroi Valley. About ten minutes later the plane crashed and burned in Crane Basin, twenty miles southeast of Challis. The aircraft amazingly had flown well over an hour after the men had bailed out.[99]

Search Efforts

A search team was launched from Challis to cover the Pahsimeroi area. By the afternoon of March 31 the team had found the wreckage of the B-17 still smoldering. With no indications of human remains, it was determined that the airmen had bailed out. Based on eyewitness reports, areas outside of Challis were hunted for signs of the bomber's crew.[100] Over the next two days an aerial search began by the military, Civil Air Patrol (CAP), and other willing pilots.

Charley Langer alongside the Stanley Ranger Station.

The Langer Monument on the Vanity Summit Road. Since Langer's heartbreaking death his descendants have returned to the area for the last seventy years in remembrance. Standing in this photograph are his children, Mary and Charley Jr.

In charge of the CAP planes was veteran mountain pilot A. A. Bennett. Other experienced backcountry pilots included Lionel Dean, Penn Stohr Sr., and Charles Reeder.

On April 3, CAP pilot Clell McDowell crashed a Curtiss monoplane two miles north of the B-17 wreckage. McDowell and his passenger survived without injuries. The men walked to a nearby highway and got a ride to Challis.[101] The plane was later recovered.

Bad weather was a continual issue that plagued the search efforts. On April 5 several military airplanes hunted the eastern portion of the current River of No Return Wilderness and adjacent areas. At the end of the day a UC-43 single engine Staggerwing Beechcraft did not return. The plane had been in radio contact late in the afternoon with other aircraft and it had also been seen from the ground near the Cape Horn Lodge. The military had little concern because it knew that it had enough fuel to fly until dusk. When the plane did not show up at any area airports, it was too dark for a search to be started, so they had to wait until the following morning.[102]

For the next two days a separate set of airplanes were assigned to look for the missing UC-43, while the others continued to search for the missing airmen. Starting on April 9, a large storm swept central Idaho and search planes were unable to fly until two days later. All hope of finding the occupants of the UC-43 alive were given up. Flying the UC-43 was Captain William Kelly with copilot Lt. Arthur Crofts, and Stanley District Ranger Charley Langer as observer. On April 13, a CAP plane found the wreckage of the UC-43 east of the Ruffneck Peak Lookout. By the following morning

rescuers arrived by ground and found all three men had been killed on impact.[103]

It was determined the cause of the crash was an engine failure. Evidence at the crash site found the fuel selector positioned for the center tank, which was empty. One of the plane's wing tanks was full, while the other contained several gallons. It was estimated that Kelly was flying low above the trees climbing up the drainage at about 9,000' when the engine quit. With little altitude to spare he did not have time to select another tank to re-start the motor.[104]

A large stone memorial indicated on maps as Langer Monument stands several miles from the crash site. Imbedded in the monument is a plaque honoring the heroic efforts of the three men. In addition to this site, a nearby peak and lake were named in memory of Langer.

While a great effort was placed on looking for the downed UC-43, the search of the lost airmen persisted and was successful. Through the combination of aerial surveillance and USFS ground crews the first group of airmen were found alive and relatively unharmed on April 5. In the succeeding days, three other survivors were found along the Middle Fork, leaving Van Slager as the only person not located. On April 18 the search was called off and Van Slager was presumed dead. His body was never recovered. Overall it was an incredible search and rescue effort, probably one of the largest ever-conducted in central Idaho. At one time over twenty airplanes participating in the search operation were based at Challis alone and well over a hundred men and women volunteered from surrounding areas.

The Initial Group of Five Airmen Rescued

Wiegand was the second person to leave the B-17. He landed near Sheepeater Hot Springs unharmed and began walking downstream looking for a flat sheltered area where he could wait until daylight. About a half hour after lying down he heard voices and yelled back. It was Grundman and Becker. Grundman was fortunate enough to have salvaged his parachute and the three wrapped in it to keep warm for the night.[105]

The next day the group stuck off downstream and spotted a small cabin on the other side of the river at the mouth of Greyhound Creek. They waded across the river and started a fire in the cabin's fireplace. The only food they found was musty flour, baking powder, a little grease, and sugar. Wiegand mixed the ingredients together and made a small batch of edible pancakes. Overnight the group dried their clothes the best they could. The next morning a hammer, axe, nails, and two saws were located in the cabin and they came up with the idea of building a raft to float down the river on. The three of them spent four hours constructing the raft, but it would only float one person. The scheme was abandoned and the raft was set adrift. With no food the men continued downstream until nightfall when they built a fire near a cliff overlooking the river. The following day, April 2, the three airmen trudged along through the deep snow until late afternoon when they heard someone yelling, "Hello, Hello." After focusing on the voice they spotted Finley and Thompson on the other side of the river.[106]

They all joined together and Finley led them to the Middle Fork Ranger Station (located near present day Pistol Creek Ranch and later moved to Indian Creek) where they had found warmth and a good supply of food. They all swapped their own stories about the event. Apparently Finley had landed on the side of a mountain in four feet of snow. Because the snow was so thick he opted to stay in his landing spot, where he dug a hole and spent the night. The next morning he worked his way down the slope to the river, but he grew tired of trying to push his way through the

The first five airmen rescued. Front row (l to r): Harold Thompson and Harvey Wiegand. Back row (l to r): Erwin Grundman, Austin Finley, and Morris Becker.

heavy snow and instead waded through the edge of the river. As darkness started to overtake the canyon he found Thompson, who was coming down the other side of the river. The two joined up and pressed on. To their surprise they came across a cabin and took shelter. On the morning of April 1 they set out again and located another cabin, which they stayed in until the following day when Finley discovered the Middle Fork Ranger Station.[107]

Resting and eating, the five men debated on what they should do next. Several had tried the wall-mounted telephone, but could not make it work. On the evening of Monday April 5, the sixth day since bailing out of the bomber, Finley found a box outside mounted to a pole. Inside was a switch that he flipped back and forth and left in the locked position. Not knowing it Finley had reconnected the telephone. A few hours later the telephone rang. Everyone in the cabin was ecstatic. Wiegand picked up the receiver and interrupted the conversation between Milt Hood of the Hood Ranch (near the Thomas Creek airstrip) and Fern Larsen, the caretaker at the McCall Ranch.[108] The two had heard of the downed airplane and were overjoyed that they were alive. Several calls were placed to the USFS who relayed the information to the AAF.[109]

The following day, April 6, Johnson Flying Service Pilots Penn Stohr Sr. and Dick Johnson were dispatched to the Indian Creek airfield to retrieve the five airmen.[110] The pilots were flying two nearly identically Travel Air 6000s (NC623H and NC655H).[111] Stohr took off with three of the men and Johnson followed carrying two. Both Travel Airs flew up the Middle Fork to Cascade where AAF personal from Gowen Field met them. The airmen were then transported to the Gowen Hospital for medical treatment.[112]

The Last Three Men Found

On March 30, Pope was the first person to float to the ground in the dark. He landed the farthest up the Middle Fork on the east side of the river near Soldier Creek. Not long after hitting the ground he discovered a small cabin that was well stocked with rations. When Stohr and Johnson flew five of the crew out from Indian Creek on April 6 they spotted tracks at the cabin on Soldier Creek.[113] Word was sent out to the search operation and a CAP plane piloted by Glen Notle flew over the cabin. Upon hearing the Johnson Flying Service Travel Airs, Pope using pine boughs had spelled out a message. Bob Speer, the son-in-law of Milt Hood, was dispatched from the Hood Ranch to rescue Pope.[114]

Hiking up the Middle Fork, Speer occasionally shouted, "Hello," and to his surprise he heard a reply. Not sure if it was his own echo, he fired his gun into the air. He then noted a faint, "I'm over here." Moving his way up the trail he followed the direction of the voice and discovered a gaunt, frail looking airman sitting near a tree. Speer thought he had found Pope and asked him why he had left the cabin. The airman said, "What cabin?" It was in that instant Speer realized he had located another one of the missing airmen. Smith introduced himself and Speer did the same, explaining that he was en route to retrieve Pope.[115]

After the brief formalities Speer began to help Smith. While Speer built a fire and laid out a ground signal requesting food and help, Smith filled him in on his story. When he pulled his chute open after exiting the airplane, it had snapped him upwards and yanked both of his boots off. With the darkness and falling snow he could see nothing. Next thing he knew he was breaking through tree branches and pine needles, and then his chute caught. He was stuck in a huge tree on a mountainside near the Greyhound Creek drainage. He decided that instead of injuring himself he would wait until daylight, which he did. With the light of dawn he discovered that he was at least ten feet off the ground and a good distance from

the tree's trunk. He eventually untangled himself and dropped into the waist deep snow that cushioned his fall. Immediately he ripped off the lower sections of his pant legs and wrapped his feet. He then climbed up a nearby a ridge to get a better view of the country. Smith later wrote, "As it got brighter, I could see for the first time where I was. The snowing had let up some and what I saw was the most desolate landscape I had ever seen: snow, mountains, trees, and the silence . . . For as far as the eye could see were more mountains – range after range of them – more snow and more trees."[116]

The next day, April 1, Smith climbed another ridge and spotted a river (the Middle Fork). On the second day of hiking he reached the river and started to follow it downstream. Every step was painful as the snow and shrubs cut his tender feet. He would occasionally stop to wring out the wrappings. He had no food and to survive he drank from the river and ate snow pretending it was solid food. By April 3 Smith's feet were so badly damaged that he gave up on walking and settled in, hoping to be found. He had no means to make a fire. On the eighth day of being alone and near death Speers had found him.[117]

Near sundown as Speer sat next to the fire bandaging Smith's feet and giving him some rations, a Curtiss Robin flew over, piloted by Lionel Dean. Dean read the message and was able to overfly the cabin at Soldier Creek and drop a note to Pope, letting him know people would be there to rescue him. In the interim Dean flew back to the Hood Ranch and picked up a flour sack full of food. With it nearly dark Dean used Speer's fire as a target to drop the food. He then returned to the ranch. Speer made Smith the first meal he had in over a week, which consisted of a bacon sandwich, pork and beans, and coffee.[118]

The next morning, April 7, ten men arrived with a stretcher and packed Smith eight miles to the Middle Fork Ranger Station. They did not arrive at the station until after midnight. Awaiting their arrival was AAF Dr. Alexander R. MacKay who was requested to give medical treatment to Smith. Charles Reeder had flown MacKay to Indian Creek and the two hiked upriver. Reeder later admitted that he had to make the landing at night and the only way he could identify the airstrip was the reflection of the snow between the trees.[119]

On April 9, the men carried Smith down to the Indian Creek airstrip where they were met by Lionel Dean and his airplane. The weather was very poor and Dean could not find a hole in the snowstorm to get out of the canyon. With no where to go he opted to land at Thomas Creek where they stayed for the next two days at the Hood Ranch. Dr. MacKay grew very worried about the condition of Smith's feet and was up nights over the issue. He revealed to Milt Hood that if he had the correct instruments that he would amputate the feet to save Smith's life. However, this was not a possibility and Smith kept his feet.[120]

As Dean, Dr. MacKay, and Smith waited for the weather to clear, Pope was brought to the ranch by his rescuers. He was in good shape and was able to help the others continue the search for Van Slager. Once the weather cleared, Pope and Smith were flown out to Challis. From there they were transferred to a plane piloted by A. A. Bennett and flown to the Pocatello Army Air Base (AAB) Hospital.[121]

Beating both Pope and Smith out of the Middle Fork country was their pilot, Joe Brensinger, who had been found the same day as Smith about three miles from the Hood Ranch. Originally Brensinger had landed in the vicinity of Marble Creek. He was in bad condition when he was rescued. At some point he had taken off his boots in an effort to dry them out. However, his feet were so swollen that he could not get them back on. Unable to walk he attempted to crawl around, but ultimately gave up and dug a hole in a snowdrift where he waited for two days trying to stay warm. He had nearly given up all hope of surviving, when he was recovered. Brensinger was transported to Thomas Creek and flown out to Challis by CAP pilot Alvar Swanson. From there Challis pilot Captain Keith Kelly flew him to the Pocatello AAB Hospital for treatment.[122]

The Final Outcome

Was the Boeing B-17 really out of gas? Should the men have bailed out? Many speculations can be made about the ill-fated flight, but based on the AAF's investigation it was all fairly simple. The AAF went back through the fuel orders for the aircraft and discovered that the plane had an ample amount of fuel to have made it to Boise, possibly even farther to a second alternate landing site. The crew of the B-17 reported years later that the crew chief that signed off on the fuel orders was court marshaled and held accountable.[123] While it may have given some of the crew reassurance that they made the right decision, it was confirmed by the AAF officials that Senior Crew Chief Private George Farrell completed his work accurately.[124] This was reaffirmed by the fact that the aircraft flew for well over an hour un-manned before it crashed.

The summary of the accident placed all the responsibility on pilot Brensinger. The final report by Lt. Col. Covington stated, "Due to the fact there was sufficient gasoline for the mission, there was an additional three to four hours fuel supply, and that the radio was working O.K. until they ran into bad static conditions; and in that the pilot did not execute a 180-degree turn after encountering instrument conditions that he could not cope with, it is deemed that the responsibility rests 100% with the pilot." Covington concluded that the specific cause of the accident was a, "Momentary lack of mental sufficiency and general lack of alertness." As for recommendations and actions for Brensinger, Covington entered, "None."[125]

Pilot Joseph Brensinger.

Bombardier George Smith.

A Near Repeat

Almost seven months later a nearly identical accident took place with the same model airplane (B-17F), in the same general vicinity (Challis and Salmon), and with the same outcome – an un-manned airplane with airmen scattered about the countryside. The heavy bomber was flying from Oklahoma City, Oklahoma, back to the crew's base at Pendleton Field. In a very similar series of malfunctions the two pilots along with a navigator, radioman, and engineer became extremely lost. They circled over central Idaho for a few hours above cloud layers before letting down near Salmon. With their fuel supply exhausted the pilot placed the B-17 on autopilot and the crew of five bailed out. These men were slightly luckier, as they parachuted out not over rugged remote mountains, but in the Lemhi Valley. The airplane was destroyed on impact, but all of the crew made it to the ground without injuries. A search ensued by many of the same civilian and CAP pilots, but most of the men were able to walk to nearby roads or farms near the town of Leadore, Idaho.[126] To top off the list of similarities pilot

Dick Johnson flew the crew from Salmon to Pocatello AAB in a Travel Air 6000 (NC8112).[127]

The Crew of B-17F 42-29514

Joseph R. Brensinger – After the accident Brensinger was first appointed to the 8th AAF's 301st Group of the 32nd Bombardment Squadron. Sometime later he was reassigned to B-24s and stationed in Italy. He and his crew took part in some of the raids on the Ploesti Oil Fields located in Romania. In 1945 Brensinger was honorably discharged with the rank of captain. He died in the early 1980s.[128]

Harold E. Thompson – It is believed Thompson was assigned to a B-17 crew as a copilot and was based in England.

Austin Finley – After the crash on the Middle

J. Smith

Harvey Wiegand in the early 1990s.

Fork, Finley was attached to the 8th AAF's 94th Group stationed at Bury St. Edmunds, England. He was assigned to a B-17 crew as a replacement navigator. Finley survived twenty-five missions, incurring only minor injuries.[129] He was honorably discharged with the rank of captain at the end of the war.

George W. Smith – After leaving the Pocatello AAB Hospital in June 1943, Smith was sent back to Walla Walla where he was to rejoin his crew for further training in Kansas. However, the medical staff at Walla Walla was not satisfied with the condition of his feet and he was operated on. Smith spent the remainder of the war in and out of various military hospitals. In 1945 he was honorably discharged based on the physical disabilities associated with his feet.[130] Smith returned to California and eventually retired with his wife Jeraldine in Carlsbad.[131]

Smith had longed to return to the Middle Fork country during the summer to retrace the events he endured in 1943. In 1993 after many years of talking about it he took action and made arrangements for himself and his wife to visit the town of Challis and several places along the Middle Fork. While in Challis

a fiftieth reunion of the crash event was organized and was attended by Wiegand and several of the rescuers.[132]

When Wiegand returned to Florida several days after the reunion, Smith and Jeraldine chartered a flight with SP Aircraft of Boise to Pistol Creek Ranch. The couple had prearranged a visit at the invitation of Chet and Sally Lancaster, who owned a cabin at the ranch. Lancaster, a pilot and history buff, heard of Smith's inquires and the two connected. SP Aircraft pilot Bill Scherer flew them to the Middle Fork in a Cessna 206. What amazed Smith the most was how the area had remained primitive and remote. During his stay on the river he saw sites that had historic meaning to him, including the location of the old Middle Fork Ranger Station, the Indian Creek airstrip, and the Middle Fork Lodge. On the final day of their Idaho vacation they were picked up by pilot Ray Arnold at the end of his mail route and transported back to Boise. On the flight out, Arnold made a couple of extra circles over the Greyhound Creek drainage – an area Smith had waited fifty years to see again. Smith later wrote, "I could see where I had landed and the route I had taken to get to the Middle Fork River. Even in the summertime it looked like real wild and rugged country and I was very impressed."[133] Smith died a few years later.

Henry C. Van Slager – No sign of Van Slager's parachute, clothing, or remains have been found. It is believed that he either drowned or his chute did not open. Based on the exit order from the B-17 and the drop pattern of the other men, it was estimated that he should have landed in the area of Artillery Rapid.

Harvey T. Wiegand – By July, 1943, Wiegand was assigned to the 8th AAF's 384th Group, 545th Bombardment Squadron stationed in Grafton Underwood, England. He was appointed to the crew of a B-17F (42-3230) named the "Yankee Powerhouse II." On August 17, 1943, Wiegand's crew and airplane were among 230 heavy bombers assigned to destroy a ball-bearing factory in Schweinfurt, Germany. His bomber was shot down and he bailed out behind enemy lines. Wiegand was captured and became a prisoner of war (POW) detained at Stalag 17, a POW camp situated several miles north of Krems, Austria, in Germany. As fate would have it, former crewmember

Grundman was on the same mission in another B-17 that was also shot down. In a double twist of fate they were both interned at Stalag 17. Months later Pope joined them, yet another crewmember from the Middle Fork accident.[134]

In April 1945 the Nazis evacuated the camp, forcing the prisoners to march about 280 miles across Austria to a wooded area north of Braunau, Austria. For days the POWs awaited death in the unpopulated region but were liberated by an American tank division. Wiegand and his Middle Fork crewmates survived and returned home.

Besides attending the fiftieth reunion in Challis with George Smith, he and his wife revisited the sites along the Middle Fork in the summer of 1987. From Boise the couple chartered a flight to Pistol Creek with SP Aircraft and were flown in by pilot Harold Dougal. Dougal took an interest in Wiegand's story and tried his best to show him the country he had crossed in April 1943. Dougal remembered very clearly the instant he pointed out the location of the old Middle Fork Ranger Station to Wiegand, "Suddenly Harvey stopped and just looked ahead as we entered the very same clearing. Nothing was said. I looked at him. He said, 'Harold, I'm sorry I'm little overcome right now.' As I looked into his face I could see his eyes filled with tears that were beginning to trickle down his cheeks ... There were no sounds, but if one listened closely, one might hear the water of the river in the distance or maybe the little breeze passing through the trees ... The front step and rock foundation were all that remained ... I watched him walk to where the cabin once stood. I stayed behind and remained silent as Harvey relived the moments that happened over forty-years ago." Dougal next took them to Indian Creek and then as they flew back to Boise he made a circle over Sheepeater Hot Spring where Wiegand had landed.[135] It was a wonderful visit. In June, 2000, Wiegand died in Florida.

Erwin R. Grundman – Grundman was attached to the 8th AAF's 305th Group, 365th Bombardment Squadron stationed in Chelveston, England. He became the tail gunner on a B-17 (41-24564) dubbed "Patches" and flew several missions. On August 17, 1943 his crew was one of 188 bombers to make it to the target over Schweinfurt, Germany, but on the return flight over enemy territory a burst of flak disabled two engines. The pilot, 2nd Lt. Douglas Mutschler was able to limp the crippled bomber along until a German Fw 190 shot the airplane down. With the entire left wing on fire the plane went into a spin and Mutschler ordered everyone to bailout. Of the ten men aboard only six made it out of the bomber before it crashed.

Grundman along with another gunner made it to the ground alive, but were badly wounded. They were then captured and taken to a hospital located in Brussels, Belgium. Once semi-recovered, the two were placed in Stalag 17. Grundman managed to survive and at the war's end returned to the United States.

Howard A. Pope – Pope was deployed and attached to the 8th AAF's 381st Group, 553rd Bombardment Squadron stationed in Ridgewell, England. He served as an engineer on a B-17. On January 11, 1944 his crew was shot down along with five other B-17s from the same squadron returning from a bombing run over Oschersieben, Germany. Pope successfully bailed out and made it to the ground, but was captured. As a POW he was placed in the Dulag 12 camp located in present day Poland. He was later imprisoned at Stalag 17. After the war he returned to the United States and died in December 1976 of a heart attack.

Morris Becker – Nothing is known.

A Zimmerly owned Travel Air 6000 being prepared for flight at McCall in 1937.

CHAPTER 12

TRAVEL AIR 6000S OF THE IDAHO BACKCOUNTRY

An Informal List and History of the Known Travel Air 6000s Flown in the Idaho Backcountry by Operator

Without a doubt the Travel Air Model 6000 became an icon of the Idaho backcountry to many residents, fishermen, hunters, smokejumpers, and foresters. What is often misunderstood by those who rode in these wonderful airplanes, or historians who look back on their activity in this isolated area of Idaho, is the actual number of them that operated. Most people believe there were only two or three Travel Airs used in the whole region. In fact logbooks, photographs, and various records show that at least sixteen different Travel Air 6000s were flown in the Idaho backcountry.

In 1929 Bob Johnson brought the first Travel Air 6000 (NC8879) to the country after buying it new from the factory. Lionel Kay of Boise, followed closely behind Johnson, purchasing his first 6000 in 1934. A year later Intermountain Air Transport Company, owned by Tom McCall of McCall and Boise, joined these two operators. These high performance airplanes were rugged and could carry large loads in and out of short, rough-surface airfields with little trouble. However, most small air carriers could not afford such airplanes. Built as the luxury liner of the day, most of the Travel Air 6000s that worked in the backcountry came in after a long career in the airlines or the executive world. Several companies and individuals other than those already mentioned flew the Travel Air 6000, such as Bill Woods, A. A. Bennett, and the Zimmerlys. No other operator owned as many as Johnson Flying Service of Missoula.

Over the years Johnson proved the aircraft was a perfect fit for the type of mountain flying found in Idaho and Montana, but the number he owned was not entirely due to his success with the machine. Out of the eleven he possessed five were lost, thus the high number reflects the fact he had to replace several. Generally he was forced into the replacement situation in order to fulfill various government contracts, which required a certain number of Travel Air 6000s.

The first Travel Air 6000 flew in the spring of 1928 after schematics were drawn for president Walter Beech, who urged the company to design a sedan-styled monoplane. With several successful test flights and well-received public reviews, production models were available by the end of the year. Throughout the plane's 150-unit production run, the model number changed. In general the numerical adjustment simply reflected power plant upgrades and associated aero-design modifications. About fifteen of the early 6000s were built with the 220 horsepower Wright J-5 Whirlwind, and designated as a straight 6000. This motor installation was not enough power for the airplane. The factory then hung 300 horsepower Wright J-6-9 motors on the next production lot, dubbing them as a 6000B. It is believed most of the early 6000 models were eventually upgraded to become 6000Bs.[1]

Travel Air also offered a very exclusive 420 horsepower Pratt & Whitney Wasp option that could be specially ordered. These planes were designated as A6000As. Due to the much higher power the wingspan was six feet longer, which enabled it to carry seven seats. It also allowed the plane's gross weight to become certified for an additional 1,000 pounds.[2] Tom McCall's NC615K is the only one of these believed to have operated in the Idaho backcountry.

In August 1929 Travel Air became a division of Curtiss-Wright and the popular 6000B was re-numbered as the 6B, and the rare A6000A became the A6A. These models are most recognizable by their "bird cage" style windscreens and slightly different tail. After World War II the 440 horsepower Wright R-975 became the engine of choice and many Travel Airs were retrofitted. When these postwar engine upgrades were made, predominantly on 6000Bs, it was necessary to graft on a Curtiss-Wright 6B tail. This included a jackscrew trim system, slightly larger tail feathers, provisions for a seventh seat, and an increase in gross weight. The characteristic Travel Air "notch" between the rudder balance horn and the vertical stabilizer was redesigned.[3] When many of these changes were made the aircraft often became re-designated as a different model. Because of the confusing numbering system and the engine changes that most Travel Airs underwent during their flying careers, the majority of people simply refer to them as "Travel Air 6000s."

The 1964 wreck of N9038 on the North Fork of the Payette River.

Hank Galpin with NC9038 in Plains, Montana, at the Penn Stohr Field dedication ceremony – October 2006.

Johnson Flying Service

NC9038
Model – 6000
Serial Number – 839
Manufactured – November 27, 1928

Bought new by Dixie Davis Flying Field, Inc. of Cincinnati, Ohio, December 1928. Sold to Earl Vollmer of Castle Farm/Cincinnati, Ohio, December 1930. Bought by Hugh Watson of Blue Ash, Ohio, March 1931. Sold to Curtiss-Wright Airplane Company of Wichita, Kansas, April 1931. Bought by The D. C. Warren Company of Alameda, California, January 1932. Sold to H. M. Dorris of Alameda, California, December 1932. Bought by Wildman Investment Company (aka Willamette Flying Service) of Portland, Oregon, October 1934. Sold to Vern St. John c/o Commercial Aircraft Company of Portland, Oregon, March 1941. Bought by Vern St. John of Yakima, Washington, November 1941. Sold to Johnson Flying Service of Missoula, Montana, November 1944, as a wrecked aircraft. The plane crashed in Portland in April 1940, which destroyed the right main and entire brake assembly. The right wing was also broken off completely, with considerable damage done to the left wing. In addition to these problems the engine was deemed a total loss.

Johnson repaired the airplane using parts from several other wrecked Travel Airs, including a wing from Travel Air NC623H. The company replaced the trashed 220 horsepower engine with a Wright R-975 and made the necessary updates making it a model 6B. The plane mainly operated from Johnson's base in McCall. On a flight in the summer of 1964 pilot Gene Crosby attempted an emergency landing along the North Fork of the Payette River just above Big Payette Lake after an accessory gear came loose and caused a complete engine failure. Crosby was headed to the Chamberlain Basin Guard Station with a load of gasoline, fertilizer, and wooden trail signs. He was able to set the plane down on Warren Wagon Road, which had recently been graded. The road narrowed due to terrain and one of the main wheels caught in a tire track left by the grader, which caused the plane to flip over into the river. Crosby survived and was back flying the next day. The plane sat in Johnson's McCall hangar for eight years. William J. and Barbara M. deCreeft of Homer, Alaska, bought the wreckage in November 1972. Hank Galpin of Kalispell, Montana, acquired the remains in November 1992. Galpin spent ten years and approximately 10,000 hours of work bringing it back to life as one of the best 6000s in existence.

NC9084

Model – 6000
Serial Number – 865
Manufactured – January 8, 1929

Bought new by Phillips Petroleum Company of Bartlesville, Oklahoma, January 1929. Sold to Travel Air Company of Wichita, Kansas, July 1929. The factory updated it to 300 horsepower and re-designated it as a B6000 (same as 6000B). Bought by Wichita Air Service & Provision Company of Wichita, Kansas, September 1929. Sold to Charles H. Lander of Wichita, Kansas, August 1930. Bought by Century Petroleum Company of Oklahoma City, Oklahoma, September 1930. Sold to Ted Colbert of Oklahoma City, Oklahoma, April 1930. Bought by William Monte Keenan of Pampa, Texas, March 1936. At the time of Keenan's purchase the aircraft was updated to a R-975 and the plane was completely overhauled and finished in June 1936. Sold to Duck Air Services (William R. Duck) of Oakland, California, December 1936. Inherited by Dawn Mercedes Duck (Duck Air Services) of Oakland, California, July 1939. Sold to Almer A. Bennett of Idaho Falls, Idaho, October 1940. Bought by Bennett Flying Service (A. A. & H. L. Bennett) of Pocatello, Idaho, January 1945. In 1946 Bennett had Zimmerly Air Transport hang a military surplus Wright R-975 rated at 420 horsepower. Sold to Eugene O. Frank of Gooding, Idaho, April 1948. Bought by Smith Stoddard (Salmon River Flying Service) of Salmon, Idaho, June 1948. Inherited by Neva Stoddard of Salmon, Idaho, January 1954. Sold to Elmer N. Darch of Boise, Idaho, January 1954. Bought by Harry Eaton of Boise, Idaho, September 1955. Sold to Johnson Flying Service of Missoula, Montana, June 1956. The plane was completely overhauled by Johnson before they used it. Most of the time under their ownership it was operated from Missoula. Sold to Kachemak Air Service (William J. and Barbara M. de Creeft) of Homer, Alaska, August 1969. The de Dreefts used it as a working aircraft for their business and had it on Edo Floats, operating it regularly in the freshwater of Beluga Lake near Homer. During their ownership the airplane was rebuilt twice. After the last restoration the plane sold to N81057 LLC (Howard Wright III) of Seattle, Washington, June 2008. Alaskan author Jim Rearden published an entire book in 2004 dedicated to this Travel Air titled, *Travel Air NC9084*.

NC8112 circa 1950 at McCall decorated as a wedding getaway vehicle.

NC8112

Model – 6000B
Serial Number – 884
Manufactured – March 18, 1929

Bought new by Pittsburgh Airways Inc. of Pittsburgh, Pennsylvania, March 1929. Sold to Atlantic Airways Inc. of York, Pennsylvania, February 1932. Bought by Harry L. Magee and C. C. Housenick of Bloomsburg, Pennsylvania, May 1932. Sold to Bloomsburg Flying Club, Inc. of Bloomsburg, Pennsylvania, July 1932. Bought by Queen City Flying Service, Inc. of Cincinnati, Ohio, April 1934. Sold to Johnson Flying Service of Missoula, Montana, October 1939. In 1944 the original J-6-9 was replaced with a Wright R-975 and updates were made to make the plane a model 6B. In 1940 Dick Johnson used this airplane to drop the first Region 1 smokejumpers to a wildland fire. In April 1956 the plane was flown on a charter by Bob Fogg to scatter the ashes of well-known western writer Bernard DeVoto (DeVoto was an authority on Lewis and Clark, and requested his ashes be spread across the Lolo Trail). Bought by Dolph Overton of Mullins, South Carolina, May 1965. Sold to Central Flying Service, Inc. of Little Rock, Arkansas, December 1981. Bought by Pleasant Aviation, LLC of Mt. Pleasant (Scott Glover), Texas, August 2008.

NC8865 in McCall circa 1996.

NC8865

Model – S6000B
Serial Number – 986
Manufactured – April 1, 1929

Bought new by S.A.T. Flying Service, Inc. of Fort Worth, Texas, April 1929. Sold to Texas Air Transport, Inc. of Dallas, Texas, October 1930. Bought by Sheldon T. Shoff of Lubbock, Texas, February 1931. Sold to L. Morganstern of Hartford, Connecticut, July 1934. Bought by Harold L. Crawford and Charles G. Mazza of Hartford, Connecticut, September 1934. Sold to Harold L. Crawford of Hartford, Connecticut, January 1935. Bought by Edward S. Beebe of Norwich, Connecticut, September 1935. While Beebe owned the aircraft the wings, fuselage, and empennage were completely rebuilt. Sold to Wesley N. Raymond (Raymond Aero Service Company) of Macon, Georgia, July 1941. Bought by Bradley Mining Company of San Francisco, California, and Boise, Idaho, June 1943. A year after buying, Zimmerly Air Transport located in Lewiston, Idaho, went through the whole airplane, completely disassembling, stripping, and rebuilding. Sold to Aircraft Service Company (a division of Bradley Mining Company) of Boise, Idaho, March 1946. The airplane spent much of its time flying supplies and people for the Stibnite, Idaho, mining operation. In 1945 Johnson Flying Service of Missoula, Montana, made major repairs, most likely due to an accident. Bought by Johnson Flying Service, Inc. of Missoula, Montana, May 1958. Sold to Dolph Overton of Mullins, South Carolina, July 1965. Bought by Ernest E. Webb of Charlotte, North Carolina. Sold to D. M. Creech of Pineville, North Carolina, October 1974.

Bought by Virginia Aircraft Sales Company, Inc. of Madison, North Carolina, October 1974. Sold to Morton W. Lester of Madison, North Carolina, August 1979. The airplane once restored was on display in the Staggerwing Museum in Tullahoma, Tennessee. Bought by Michael R. Dorris, James J. Eldredge, and Richard H. Waite (Six Thousand Club Limited Liability) of Twin Falls, Idaho, April 1994. Sold to Richard H. Waite (Six Thousand Club Limited Liability) of Twin Falls, Idaho, June 2008. Waite keeps it in a hangar at the airport in Gooding, Idaho.

NC8879 sunk at Deadwood Reservoir in January 1937.

NC8879

Model – 6000B
Serial Number – 992
Manufactured – April 15, 1929

Bought new by Johnson Flying Service Inc. (Robert R. Johnson) of Missoula, Montana, April 1929. This was Johnson's first cabin airplane and provided him with the real start to his legendary business. Harry Gerard was Johnson's major financial backer for the airplane. As a tribute to his efforts the plane was dubbed the "Mae Gerard" in honor of Gerard's wife, Mae.

On January 12, 1937 with just a little over 2,000 total airframe hours and two engine rebuilds, the plane, mounted on wheels, went through the ice on Deadwood Reservoir southeast of Cascade, Idaho, while delivering supplies to a nearby mine. The plane piloted by Johnson broke through the ice in a shallow area near the dam and the wheels came to rest about four feet below the surface. Johnson returned days later with mechanic Art Pritzl to recover the airplane. While trying to hoist the aircraft back to the surface the two men melted ice around the plane with a flame driven heater. Somehow the flame came in contact with fumes from one of the Travel Air's fuel tanks. Within minutes the aircraft became engulfed in fire. All that was left of Johnson's prized Mae Gerard was a burnt airframe, charred engine, propeller, and the tail surfaces. The uninsured airplane was a complete loss.

On August 22, 1939, Dick Johnson was dropping cargo for the USFS near Hamilton, Montana, in Roaring Lion canyon within the Bitterroot Mountains. After making several drops he encountered a severe downdraft at an altitude too low to recover and the aircraft was forced into tall timber. Johnson and USFS employee Clarence D. Sutliff were both badly injured but eventually made full recoveries. The plane was declared a complete loss.

The August 1939 Roaring Lion canyon crash of NC9813.

NC623H parked at Big Creek in the early 1940s.

NC9813

Model – S6000B
Serial Number – 1027
Manufactured – May 8, 1929

Bought new by H. C. Lippiatt of Hollywood, California, May 1929. Sold to G. E. Ruckstell of Bel-Air/Los Angeles, California, July 1929. Bought by Frank Muller of Hollywood, California, September 1929. Sold to Roy T. Minor of Van Nuys, California, December 1930. Bought by Aero Brokerage Service Company of Inglewood, California, January 1931. Sold to D. Flynn of Spokane, Washington, January 1931. Flynn operated the aircraft some on Edo K Floats. Sold to Lionel Kay of Boise, Idaho, November 1934. Bought by Thomas McCall of McCall, Idaho, September 1935. Sold to Intermountain Air Transport Company Inc. (Thomas McCall President) of McCall, Idaho, November 1935. Bought by Johnson Flying Service of Boise, Idaho, December 1936. The plane was later registered to Johnson in Missoula, Montana. In June 1939 a replacement Wright R-975D was installed.

NC623H

Model – S6000B
Serial Number – 6B-2001
Manufactured – September 26, 1929

Bought new by Curtiss Flying Service, Inc. of New York City, New York, September 1929. Sold to Curtiss Flying Service of Kansas City, Missouri, November 1929. Bought by Curtiss-Wright Flying Service, Inc. of Oklahoma City, Oklahoma, April 1930. Sold to Curtiss-Wright Flying Service, Inc. of Glendale, California, October 1931. Damaged in a landing accident August 17, 1932. Repairs included a new propeller and fabric work. Bought by Grand Central Air Terminal, Ltd. of Los Angeles, California, November 1932. Sold to Archie J. Sneed Jr. of Los Angeles, California, January 1933. The same year Sneed purchased the aircraft it was completely overhauled. Bought by Ryan School of Aeronautics, San Diego, California, August 1935. Sold to Nagel Flying Service (John H. Nagel) of Los Angeles, California, April 1940. Bought by Johnson Flying Service of Missoula, Montana, July 1940. Johnson rebuilt the airplane in 1942, which included many modifications and the

Bill Yaggy in September 1945.

NC655H at Mackay Bar in the early 1940s.

instillation of a new Wright R-975-E1. In 1943 a regular Wright R-975-E, which weighed thirty pounds less, replaced the previous motor.

The airplane was destroyed February 2, 1946 while on a seeding operation for the BLM. Pilot William "Bill" Bramwell Yaggy was seeding an area north of Mountain Home, Idaho, over a shallow valley that had burned the previous summer. The terrain required Yaggy to make low altitude turns over ridges on both sides. In his final turn he got caught in a downdraft by air spilling over one of the ridges. Complicating the situation were low ceilings and snow squalls. Realizing that he was in trouble in a box canyon, he added full power and initiated a steep turn, but could not avoid the terrain. The plane crashed north of Long Tom Reservoir killing him instantly. However, Robert McBride of McCall who was riding in the right seat survived with a dislocated shoulder. The plane was later recovered and hauled back to Missoula for parts.

NC655H

Model – S6000B
Serial Number – 6B-2008
Manufactured – October 4, 1929

Bought new by Travel Air Company of Wichita, Kansas, October 1929. Sold to Curtiss-Wright Flying Service, Inc. of Glenview, Illinois, May 1930. Bought by Chicago Air Terminals, Inc. of Glenview, Illinois, December 1932. Sold to Earl F. Cranston of Boise, Idaho, October 1933. Bought by C. R. King of Boise, Idaho, December 1933. Sold to Lionel Kay of Boise, Idaho, January 1934. The plane was wrecked on April 4, 1935 in Atlanta, Idaho. Bought by Tom McCall of McCall, Idaho, September 1935. Sold to Intermountain Air Transport Company (Thomas McCall President) of McCall, Idaho, November 1935. Sold to Robert R. Johnson of Boise, Idaho, December 1936 as a wrecked airplane that had not flown since April 1935. The plane was rebuilt at Johnson's Boise facility. Bought by Johnson Flying Service, Inc. of Missoula, Montana, June 1939. The same year the plane was repowered with a 330 horsepower Wright R-975-E1. Destroyed in an accident south of Jackson Hole, Wyoming, March 2, 1945.

Based from Jackson Hole, Dick Johnson was flying Bob Brown, a Wyoming deputy game warden, and Orange Olsen, the Region 4 assistant forester, on a several-day elk counting project. Working in the Moose Creek and Greys River area thirty miles south of Alpine, Wyoming, near the state's border with Idaho, the plane became surrounded in snow squalls. Trying to outfly the weather Johnson found himself in rough air and zero visibility. The right wing of the airplane hit a tree, which sent the plane into a dive causing it to crash nose first into the timber. Johnson and Olsen were killed instantly. Brown was badly injured, but survived. When they did not return a rescue crew started to the area by ground. A call was placed to Johnson Flying Service in Missoula. The next day Johnson's stepson Jack Hughes and brother Bob flew two separate Travel Airs (Hughes in NC447W) to Idaho Falls, Idaho, where they based an aerial search operation. They returned to Missoula three days later with the sad news and Johnson's body.

NC450N on a flight during smokejumper training.

NC450N

Model – 6B
Serial Number – 2029
Manufactured – September 27, 1930

Bought new by Henry L. Lemon, Inc. of Tulsa, Oklahoma, September 1930. Sold to The Frates Company, Trust Estate of Tulsa, Oklahoma, June 1932. In early 1933 this airplane was badly damaged on landing, breaking the fuselage in half behind the aft baggage compartment. In addition, the right axle stub was broken off, the left wing damaged, motor mounts broken, and prop bent. Christopher Airplane Service of Wichita, Kansas, rebuilt the aircraft. Bought by Bennett Griffen Flying Service, Inc. of Oklahoma City, Oklahoma, June 1933. Sold to Aviators Inc. of Tulsa, Oklahoma, August 1934. Bought By Aero Salvage Corp. of Jackson Heights, New York, December 1934. Sold to Nobadeer Flying Service (David Raub and J. Leslie Holm) of Nantucket, Massachusetts, December 1936. Bought by Nobadeer Flying Service (David Raub) of Nantucket, Massachusetts, January 1937. Sold to Charles Miller III of Hollywood, California, February 1937. Bought by Johnson Flying Service Inc. of Missoula, Montana, July 1937. In May 1939 Johnson hung a new Wright R-975, replacing the original Wright J-6-9.

On July 22, 1939 Dick Johnson attempted a takeoff fully loaded with five passengers from Butte, Montana, in windy conditions and went off the runway. Nearly airborne he continued the takeoff and hit a large wooden ramp that was obscured by tall grass. The unmarked wooden ramp had been used earlier in the day as part of an air show. When the aircraft hit the ramp it broke the right landing gear and tor

the wheel off, which caused the plane to skid onto its side. None of the occupants were injured. In the accident report under, "Result of accident to aircraft crew," a notation was typed, "None. Made pilot very unhappy."

The airplane was repaired and almost one year later on July 15, 1940 was destroyed in a fatal accident in the Selway-Bitterroot area (see Selway Lodge section for complete story).

NC447W as it appeared after the Zimmerly rebuild.

NC447W

Model – 6B
Serial Number – 2040
Manufactured – April 10, 1931

Bought new by National Construction Company of Omaha, Nebraska, April 1931. Sold to Sohler Flying Service, Inc. of Bend, Oregon, February 1936. The airplane was involved in an accident while landing in Bend in March 1936. Damage occurred to the fuselage, two windows, both wheels, right landing gear, both wing tips, right wing struts, and the propeller. Bought by Zimmerly Bros. Air Transport (Bert Zimmerly and Fred Zimmerly) of Lewiston, Idaho, January 1939. Sold to Johnson Flying Service, Inc. of Missoula, Montana, June 1941. Bought by Clyde H. Fredrickson Jr. of Hamilton, Montana, September 1972. Sold to C. Leslie DeLine of San Diego, California, October 1974. Bought by Douglas T. Rounds of Zebulon, Georgia, March 1975. In 1981 as Rounds was finishing a restoration on the airplane he changed the registration number to NC452N. The alteration was to pay tribute to friend and pilot Truman Wadlow who flew NC452N (serial number 6B-2037) in the 1930 Ford Air Tour. Sold to Delta Air Lines, Inc. of

Atlanta, Georgia, August 1985. In 1997 Delta Air Transport Heritage Museum changed the registration number to NC8878, which was originally assigned to a Travel Air (serial number S6000B – 988) operated by Delta Air Service.

NC615K parked at McCall in 1937.

NC615K
Model – A6000A
Serial Number – A6A2001
Manufactured – August 14, 1929

Bought new by Dean Banks of San Marino, California, August 1929. Sold to H. C. Lippiatt of Bel Air/Los Angeles, California, December 1929. Bought by Hal Roach Studios, Inc. of Culver City, California, July 1930. Sold to Title Insurance and Trust Company, Receiver for Lockheed Aircraft Company of Burbank, California, January 1932. Bought by Wayne H. Fisher of Los Angeles, California, April 1932. Sold to Henry H. Sharman of Salt Lake City, Utah, August 1933. Bought by Tom McCall of McCall, Idaho, February 1935. Sold to Intermountain Air Transport Company of McCall, Idaho, November 1935. Bought by Johnson Flying Service (Robert R. Johnson) of Boise, Idaho, December 1936. Sold to Wallace Aerial Surveys (Hillford R. Wallace) of Spokane, Washington, August 1937. Wallace installed an aerial camera in the floor. Bought by Bert Ruoff (Bristol Bay Air Service) of Anchorage, Alaska, January 1940. Sold to John W. Moore of Nome, Alaska, April 1942. Bought by Madeleine Moore of Nome, Alaska, May 1942. Sold to Alaska Star Airlines of Anchorage (later Alaska Airlines), Alaska, June 1942. In January 1945, while being piloted by Norman Weaver, the plane broke through shallow ice on a landing area near Stuart Island, Alaska. The minor damages were repaired. In April 1947 the aircraft disappeared en route from Kotzebue, Alaska, to Candle, Alaska.

NC9844 circa 1940 in Lewiston.

Zimmerly Brothers Air Transport

NC9844
Model – S6000B
Serial Number – 1034
Manufactured – May 28, 1928

Bought new by S.A.T. Flying Service, Inc. of Fort Worth, Texas, May 1929. Sold to Central Air Service of Fargo, North Dakota, February 1932. Bought by Central Airways, Inc. of Fargo, North Dakota, August 1932. Under their ownership the plane was repowered from a Wright J-6-9 to a smaller 220 horsepower Wright J-5. Also while at Central Airways the plane flew with a neon sign attached to the bottom of the fuselage advertising for local businesses. Sold to Dan L. Carver of Lidgerwood, North Dakota, March 1934. Bought by De Ponti Aviation Company, Inc. of Minneapolis, Minnesota, June 1935. De Ponti made several modifications to the airplane, including the replacement of the J-5 engine with a 330 horsepower Wright R-975. Sold to Sohler Flying Service, Inc (Myrl P. Hoover) of Bend, Oregon, April 1936. Bought by Zimmerly Bros. Air Transport (Bert and Fred Zimmerly) of Lewiston, Idaho, January 1939. Zimmerly overhauled the engine and made a few repairs to the aircraft such as rebuilding the wings. Zimmerly pilot B. Davis lost control of the aircraft on takeoff at Moose Creek, Idaho, June 1940. No one was injured but the airplane required major repairs. At this time Zimmerly completely overhauled the plane. Sold to Wien Alaska Airlines Inc. (Noel Wien) of Fairbanks, Alaska, September 1941. In 1943 Wien started using the aircraft on Edo Floats. Declared totally destroyed after an accident in July 1948.

NC9842 with spray booms.

NC9842
Model – S6000B
Serial Number – 1036
Manufactured – May 15, 1929

Bought new by S.A.T. Flying Service of Fort Worth, Texas, May 1929. Sold to Peter J. Klimek of Minneapolis (Baudette), Minnesota, March 1932. Bought by Kurtzer Flying Service (Lana R. Kurtzer) of Seattle, Washington, June 1936. While with Kurtzer the plane was operated on Edo K floats. Sold to Zimmerly Air Transport of Lewiston, Idaho, March 1943. Shortly after purchasing it, Zimmerly completely rebuilt the aircraft, adding many modifications. The plane was finished in a silver paint scheme with black stripes. A large portion of the plane was rebuilt again in 1947 after an accident occurred on landing. Not only did Zimmerly rebuild the plane more than once, the company also went through several motors on the craft. In 1948 they installed a 420 horsepower version of the Wright Whirlwind (R-975-E-3). In May 1949 the airplane was mounted with spray booms and a single tank for agricultural work. This system was used until 1952 when it was retrofitted with dual one-hundred-gallon tanks. Bought by Hillcrest Aircraft Company of Lewiston, Idaho, March 1953. Sold to Linn Emerich of Mercer Island, Washington, March 1962. Aircraft declared destroyed after an accident on March 4, 1966 near Ellensburg, Washington. Howard E. and Kelly H. Mason of Arlington, Washington, bought the wreckage, mainly consisting of a data plate and rudder in September 1993. Sold to Michael L. Daacke of Phoenix, Arizona, July 1995. Bought by Philip L. Taylor of Seattle, Washington, July 1996. Taylor has plans to rebuild the aircraft.

NC656H
Model – S6000B
Serial Number – 2009
Manufactured – August 27, 1929

Bought new by Travel Air Company of Wichita, Kansas, August 1929. Sold to Curtiss Flying Service Inc. of New York City, New York, October 1929. Bought by Curtiss Wright Flying Service Inc. of Baltimore, Maryland, November 1929. Sold to Charles F. Thompson of Baltimore, Maryland, January 1933. Bought by David H. Whiteley III and Charles F. Thompson of Baltimore, Maryland, January 1935. Sold to J. Frank Wilson of Boiling Springs, Pennsylvania, March 1936. Bought by Newark Air Service Inc. of Newark, New Jersey, February 1937. In April 1937 the airplane was completely overhauled and recovered by the company. Sold to Emile H. Burgin of New Egypt, New Jersey, April 1940. Bought by Clinton H. Housel of Maplewood, New Jersey, May 1940. Sold to Donald O. and Marjorie E. Whitworth of Newark, New Jersey, May 1941. Bought by Zimmerly Bros. Air Transport (Bert and Fred Zimmerly) of Lewiston, Idaho, October 1941. Sold to E. W. Elliott of Seattle, Washington, August 1942. Bought by Al Jones of Bethel, Alaska, August 1944. In December 1947 documentation was filed from Al Jones stating, "The aircraft has been permanently retired from service and I request that the registration be canceled."

NC447W
Model – 6B
Serial Number – 2040
Manufactured – April 10, 1931
(See Johnson Flying Service)

Bennett Air Transport Company

NC9084
Model – 6000
Serial Number – 865
Manufactured – January 8, 1929
(See Johnson Flying Service)

NC411N
Model – S6000B
Serial Number – 2024
Manufactured – November 23, 1929

Bought new by Travel Air Company of Wichita, Kansas, November 1929. Sold to Aircraft Sales Corporation (D. H. Davis) of Atlanta, Georgia, February 1930. Later registered under Davis Airlines Incorporated. Bought by Southern Airways Inc. of Augusta, Georgia, October 1930. Sold to Clare G. Richmond of Montpelier, Ohio, July 1934. Bought by K-T Flying Service Limited (Robert Tyce and Charles B. Knox) of Chula Vista, California, October 1934. In 1937 the airplane was shipped and used in Honolulu, Hawaii. A major overhaul occurred after shipment to Hawaii. Sold to David C. Brewer of Menlo Park, California, July 1945. Bought by Intermountain Aeromotive (Eugene O. Frank) of Boise, Idaho, February 1946. Under Frank's ownership the plane was partially rebuilt, including a new engine. Sold to General Aircraft Company Inc. (Frank Medlin) of Boise, Idaho, May 1946. Bought by J. C. Medlin of Boise, Idaho, February 1947. Sometime during the plane's life in Boise it was flown regularly by Bennett. In May 1947 Central Aircraft Company of Yakima, Washington, installed twin one-hundred-gallon spray tanks and booms. In late 1947 the airplane was severely damaged due to a forced landing in Bryce Canyon, Utah. A major rebuild followed in the early winter of 1948. Sold to Donald D. Brisco of Boise, Idaho, August 1950. Bought by Paul A. Abbott (Aircraft Supervisor for Harrah's Club) of Reno, Nevada, June 1964. Sold to Harrah's Club of Reno, Nevada, July 1964. Bought by J. L. Terteling of Boise, Idaho, September 1981. Sold to Heritage Aircraft Inc. of Fort Washington, Pennsylvania, September 1986. Later the company was re-located to Ambler, Pennsylvania, and then to Chalfont, Pennsylvania.

Aircraft Service Company/ Bradley Mining Company

NC8865
Model – S6000B
Serial Number – 986
Manufactured – April 1, 1929
(See Johnson Flying Service)

Bill Woods

NC9846
Model – 6000B
Serial Number – 1038
Manufactured – Records for this aircraft no longer exist.

In the early 1930s the aircraft was owned by Bill Gowen of Boise, Idaho. It was later operated by Bill Woods of Boise, Idaho. The aircraft was last recorded in Anaconda, Montana. Registration was canceled October 1951.

Johnson Flying Service Ford Tri-Motor NC9642 on takeoff with Bob Johnson and Bob Fogg at the controls.

CHAPTER 13

FORD TRI-MOTORS OF THE IDAHO BACKCOUNTRY

An Informal List and History of the Known Ford Tri-Motors Flown in the Idaho Backcountry by Operator

Along with the Travel Air 6000s the Ford Tri-Motors came to be the epitome of the commercial workhorse in the early years of Idaho backcountry aviation. Also similar to the Travel Air 6000s, they were first sold as luxury aircraft. Most Tri-Motors were primarily sold to large commercial operators and used to carry passengers. Unbeknownst to many, the Ford Tri-Motor came in several different sizes and models. The main production models were the smaller 4-AT version that weighed a little over 10,000 pounds on average at gross weight and the larger 5-AT variation that weighed 13,500 pounds on average at gross weight. The 5-AT also carried thirteen passengers instead of the 4-AT's eleven-passenger capability.[1]

From 1926 through 1929 seventy-eight 4-AT model Fords were built. While the production of the smaller Fords ended, the company turned to constructing the larger models. Between 1928 and the end of 1933, 117 of the 5-ATs were built. The aircraft originally carried hefty price tags ranging from $40,000 to $50,000 and were sold all over the globe. However, the prices were affected by the Great Depression and fell rapidly. Although the all-metal airplane was not revolutionary in the aviation field, its construction was rugged and durable compared to other aircraft of the time. The Fords were powered in many different ways, not to mention small variations from one serial number to another. By the mid-1930s the Ford lost popularity in the industry to the sleeker and faster Boeing 247s, Douglas DC-2s, and Douglas DC-3s.[2]

The Ford then became popular with smaller air carriers for hauling passengers and especially freight. From the beginning their design was well suited to the demanding flying required in the Idaho backcountry. Nick Mamer of Spokane, Washington, brought the first Ford Tri-Motors to the Idaho backcountry when he purchased two of them directly from the factory (NC9612 and NC8403). Influenced by Mamer, Johnson Flying Service acquired its first of eight used Fords in 1934, and flew them commercially longer than any other operator in the United States, through the end of the 1960s. Similar to the Travel Airs, Johnson's ownership of many Fords was due to the fact that he lost five of them to accidents. Johnson's initial Ford (NC435H) was the most unique model operated in the backcountry. It was equipped with three Pratt & Whitney Wasp 450 horsepower engines, speed ring cowlings, engine cooling rings, and a higher wing. It became known in the area simply as "The Wasp Ford."

While Johnson Flying Service used their Fords for a wide variety of operations, from agricultural work to passenger hauling, other Fords listed in this section had more singular functions. For example the Fords used by Robert W. Waltermire, owner and operator of Northwest Agricultural Aviation Corporation of Choteau, Montana, were really only used for spray projects in the backcountry.

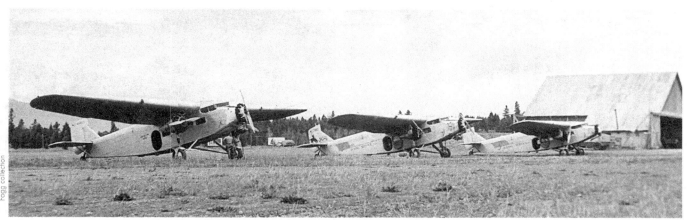

Three Johnson Flying Service Fords lined up at McCall in the early 1950s (l to r): NC8400, NC7861, and NC9642.

Mamer Flying Service

NC9612
Model – 4-AT-E
Serial Number – 4-AT-55
Manufactured – January 15, 1929

NC9612 at the Chamberlain airstrip in the early 1930s with Mamer's logo on the side.

Bought new by Mamer Flying Service of Spokane, Washington, March 1929. Mamer named the plane the "West Wind I." Sold to Reginald Pattinson and Wayne Parmenter of St. Elmo, Illinois, October 1936. Bought by K-T Flying Service of Honolulu, Hawaii, August 1940. The plane was at a field near Pearl Harbor during the December 7, 1941 Japanese attack (evidence of bullet holes were later found in the airplane during a restoration). Sold to Clinton Arthur Johnson of Mt. Shasta City, California. He leased the plane to TWA for a twentieth anniversary celebration of the airline in July 1949. Bought by William Hadden of Orofino, Idaho, January 1952. During this time it was flown often by Abe Bowler, and brought back to the Idaho backcountry, flying USFS contracts as well as spray operations. Sold to Johnson Flying Service of Missoula Montana, October 1957. Bought by Jack Adams Aircraft Sales of Walls, Mississippi, February 1969. Sold to Dolph Overton of Santee, South Carolina, February 1969. Bought by Dolph Overton Wings and Wheels of Orlando, Florida, April 1981. Throughout Overton's ownership the plane under went a complete restoration. Sold at a Barrett-Jackson automobile auction to Collectible Aircraft LLC of Missoula, Montana, January 2009.

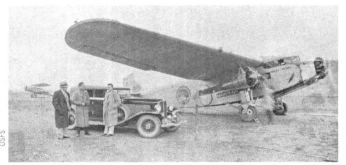

NC8403 most likely at Spokane circa 1932.

NC8403

Model – 4-AT-E
Serial Number – 4-AT-65
Manufactured – May 1, 1929

Bought new by Mamer Flying Service of Spokane, Washington, July 1929. Mamer named the plane the "West Wind II." Sold to Tom Marshall Kester and Edward H. Groenendyke of Pasadena, California, April 1934. The plane was operated by Ptarmigan Airlines and renamed "Ptarmigan II." In October 1934 while on a mission for the airline, it was destroyed in an accident at Flat, Alaska. The Alaska Aviation Heritage Museum of Anchorage, Alaska, acquired the remains in 1989. More recently Greg Herrick of Jackson, Wyoming, obtained the aircraft.

Johnson Flying Service

NC7861

Model – 4-AT-E
Serial Number – 4-AT-46
Manufactured – October 9, 1928

Kept at the factory after being completed and updated with larger engines. Bought new by Union Electric Light and Power Company of St. Louis, Missouri, April 1930. Sold to William A. Monday "Flying Cowboy" of Cody, Wyoming, March 1937. Bought by Johnson Flying Service of Missoula, Montana, September 1939. Sold to Dexter D. Coffin Jr. of Palm Beach, Florida, April 1969. Donated to Naval Aviation Museum of Pensacola, Florida, 1970s. It is on display wearing a military paint scheme.

NC9612

Model – 4-AT-E
Serial Number – 4-AT-55
Manufactured – January 15, 1929
(See Mamer Flying Service)

Starting NC9642 at the Salmon airport in 1949.

NC9642

Model – 4-AT-E
Serial Number – 4-AT-58
Manufactured – January 29, 1929

Bought new by Mohawk Airways of Schenectady, New York, April 1929. Under their ownership it was leased to United Air Service and named "Miss Albany." Sold to J. A. Haraden and John Kovacs of Schenectady, New York, March 1936. Bought by Link Aeronautical Corporation, Endicott, New York, April 1936. Sold to Johnson Flying Service of Missoula, Montana, April 1939. In May 1950 it was modified for use as a sprayer. Destroyed in a crash near Townsend, Montana, on June 19, 1957.

The plane, piloted by Penn Stohr Sr. and Bob Vallance, was being used on a sagebrush spray project. There is a fair amount of speculation as to the cause of the accident, as Stohr was a well-experienced pilot in agricultural spray work. It is believed that the spray machine, which was a separate motor in the rear of the fuselage, became jammed. It was common practice for one of the pilots to climb into the back and fix the problem. Based on where the bodies were found, Stohr who was probably flying from the left seat, got up to fix the malfunction while Vallance continued to fly the plane from the right (copilot) seat. While maneuvering away from a hillside at low altitude the plane's left wing dug in and the aircraft cartwheeled killing both pilots. The wreckage was hauled back to

Missoula and used for parts.

Evergreen Helicopters of McMinnville, Oregon, acquired the wreckage when they purchased Johnson Flying Service in 1975. Bought by Kal Aero of Kalamazoo, Michigan, April 1979. Kal Aero employee Maurice Hovious (Hov-Aire Inc.) of Vicksburg, Michigan, acquired the aircraft remains and paperwork in the mid-1980s and has started a restoration.

NC8400
Model – 4-AT-E
Serial Number – 4-AT-62
Manufactured – April 13, 1929

Bought new by Curtiss Publishing Company of Philadelphia, Pennsylvania, July 1929. Sold to Arthur H. Kudner of New York City, New York, July 1931. Bought by Despatch Corporation of New York City, New York, July 1933. Sold to C. M. Ewan of New York City, New York, February 1936. Bought by Manitowoc Air Service of Manitowoc, Wisconsin, June 1936. Sold to Holland G. Bryan of Paducah, Kentucky, November 1936. Bought by Keith G. Cantine of Detroit, Michigan, June 1937. Sold to Mary Cantine of Akron, Ohio, June 1938. Bought by Johnson Flying Service of Missoula, Montana, March 1941. Destroyed in a crash near Boulder, Montana, July 14, 1953 while on a spray project.

Pilot Jim Dillon and mechanic Dick Duffield were in a tight turn headed back for another spray run when they flew into a set of static cables used to keep tension on nearby high voltage lines. The previous evening Dillon had scouted the run in a Curtiss Air Sedan and had noted the obstacles. For whatever reason he hit the lines while flying the Ford the following day. The quarter inch steel cable wrapped around the nose engine and pulled it in on top of the two pilots. The cable broke loose from its attachments and draped over the main wing, whipping behind the aircraft, but somehow the cable missed the outboard engines entirely. With the two outboard motors running at high power, Dillon began a slow maneuver back to the airstrip, dragging the lines hanging from the aircraft through the streets of Wisdom, Montana. After a long struggle with the airplane he managed to line up on a final approach to the airport. His efforts were cut short when one of

the trailing static lines somehow wrapped around a telephone pole and yanked the entire tail section off the airplane, causing it to smash to the ground upside down, killing both men. The wreckage was hauled back to Missoula and used for parts. Evergreen Helicopters of McMinnville, Oregon, acquired the wreckage when they purchased Johnson Flying Service in 1975. Bought by Kal Aero of Kalamazoo, Michigan, April 1979. Kal Aero employee Maurice Hovious (Hov-Aire Inc.) of Vicksburg, Michigan, acquired the aircraft remains and paperwork in the mid-1980s and has started a restoration.

NC8407
Model – 4-AT-E
Serial Number – 4-AT-69
Manufactured – January 15, 1929
(See Aircraft Service Company)

NC9684
Model – 5-AT-B
Serial Number – 5-AT-40
Manufactured – April 9, 1929

Bought new by Cia Mexicana de Aviacion of Mexico City, Mexico, April 1929. Sold to Pan American Airways of New York City, New York, November 1936. Bought by Cia Nacional Cubana de Aviacion S. A. of Havana, Cuba, June 1938. Sold to Air Tours of Put-in-Bay, Ohio, July 1946. The plane lost its original registration and was reassigned N69905. Under their ownership the plane became highly modified. The engines were uniquely replaced with three R-975-28s, instead of the standard Pratt & Whitneys seen on other 5-AT models. Bought by Charles F. "Frenny" Frensdorf of Orofino, Idaho, August 1952. Sold to Johnson Flying Service of Missoula, Montana, August 1953. Destroyed on takeoff from Spotted Bear airstrip located in the Flathead NF, Montana, August 17, 1953.

Pilot Ken Roth was flying a load of seven Missoula smokejumpers to a fire near Montana's Hungry Horse Reservoir on the Flathead NF. Gusting winds in the vicinity of the fire prevented the drop from being made. Instead of returning home Roth opted to wait the winds out at the nearby Spotted Bear airfield. Hours later Roth decided to give the drop another try. After takeoff and only about 150' in the air, the

NC8419 at the Moose Creek Ranger Station in 1958.

The 1953 wreck of NC9683 (N69905) at Spotted Bear.

plane's three engines began acting up. One engine's RPM would drop off completely and then would come back, while another one would then drop off. Unable to out climb the terrain or turn back to the strip, Roth maintained forward directional control and flew the plane into the tops of the oncoming trees. Everyone aboard survived, but the plane was demolished. The cause of the accident was determined to be the wrong carburetors, which required fuel pumps instead of the original gravity feed system. When the plane's tanks were full of gas there was enough volume and pressure to push the fuel into the carburetors. However, when Roth departed Spotted Bear the tanks had considerably less fuel. The plane was later salvaged and transported back to Missoula. Evergreen Helicopters of McMinnville, Oregon, acquired the wreckage when they purchased Johnson Flying Service in 1975. Bought by Kal Aero of Kalamazoo, Michigan, April 1979. Kal Aero employee Maurice Hovious (Hov-Aire Inc.) of Vicksburg, Michigan, acquired the aircraft remains and paperwork in the mid-1980s. In 2004 Hovious donated the airplane to the Tri-Motor Heritage Foundation of Port Clinton, Ohio. The group has the goal of making the aircraft airworthy.

NC8419

Model – 5-AT-C
Serial Number – 5-AT-58
Manufactured – June 29, 1929

Bought new by Ford Motor Company of Dearborn, Michigan, July 1929. Sold to Northwest Airways of St. Paul, Minnesota, January 1931. Bought by Northern Air Transport of Fairbanks, Alaska, September 1935. Sold to Wien Alaska Airlines of Fairbanks, Alaska, November 1936. Bought by Kenneth Neese of Anchorage, Alaska, June 1940. Sold to Star Air Lines of Anchorage, Alaska, June 1940. Bought by Monroe Airways of Monroe, Michigan, June 1945. Under their ownership the plane was completely rebuilt. Sold to G and G Airlines of Tucson, Arizona, November 1946. Bought by Johnson Flying Service of Missoula, Montana, June 1951. Johnson leased the aircraft to Northwest Airlines in 1956 for commemorative flights. The plane was destroyed in an accident at Moose Creek, August 4, 1959 (see Moose Creek section for complete story). Valuable pieces of the wreckage were salvaged and transported to Missoula and used for parts. Other smaller worthless pieces of the airplane were buried near the accident site and are still evident today. Evergreen Helicopters of McMinnville, Oregon, acquired the wreckage when they purchased Johnson Flying Service in 1975. Bought by Kal Aero of Kalamazoo, Michigan, April 1979. The plane unfortunately was not given an authentic restoration. Not only does the entire cockpit have the appearance of a relatively new airplane but it was painted in an army paint scheme. The paint choice was particularly odd since military Fords were produced using 4-AT models. The plane did fly in 1991 and was piloted by former Johnson Flying Service employee Penn Stohr Jr. It has been on display at the Kalamazoo Aviation History Museum, Kalamazoo, Michigan, since January 1992.

NC435H preparing for takeoff in the mid-1930s.

The 1938 wreck of NC435H at Big Prairie.

NC435H
Model – 5-AT-D
Serial Number – 5-AT-102
Manufactured – April 17, 1931

Bought new by Pacific Air Transport of Oakland, California, April 20, 1931. The transport company dubbed it "Olympia." Sold to National Air Transport, Chicago, Illinois, March 1932. Bought by United Airlines, Chicago, Illinois, April 1933. Sold to Johnson Flying Service (Robert Johnson) of Missoula, Montana, September 1934. Destroyed in a landing accident at Big Prairie, Montana, September 3, 1938.

Dick Johnson was at the controls of the airplane when it crashed. Many people have speculated the cause of the accident, but a common thread in the various stories is that Johnson encountered a large downdraft during landing and the plane was slammed to the ground. On impact the left strut collapsed which caused the Ford to veer off the runway. The plane came to a rest off to the side of the airstrip in some trees. Johnson was knocked unconscious in the accident and fuel began to leak everywhere, but no fire ensued. The plane sat propped up on its right main strut, which saved the right outboard motor from damage. When the crew from the Big Prairie Ranger Station rushed to help Johnson, the right motor was still running at a fairly high RPM, and they did not have the knowledge to shut it down. The engine eventually ran out of gas. Johnson survived the crash and made a full recovery. Most of the valuable parts were salvaged from the plane by Johnson Flying Service and transported back to Missoula. The fuselage and various other scraps were left behind. Circa 2000 the Museum of Mountain Flying located in Missoula obtained ownership of the wreckage. However, the Big Prairie airstrip, which lies within the Bob Marshall Wilderness, is closed. Wilderness Watch, an extremist wilderness organization, has blocked efforts to retrieve the wreckage with a helicopter.

Northwest Agricultural Aviation Corporation

NC9606
Model – 5-AT-4
Serial Number – 5-AT-4
Manufactured – October 24, 1928

Bought new by Transcontinental Air Transport (TAT) of New York City, New York, November 1928. The plane, named the "City of Columbus," was used by Charles Lindbergh to help map TAT's transcontinental route. When the company merged with Transcontinental & Western Air in April 1931 the plane was renamed "City of New York." Sold to William Keith Scott of Los Angeles, California, February 1935. Bought by Fairchild Aerial Surveys of Los Angeles, California, May 1939. Sold to Texas Petroleum Company of New York City, New York, May 1940. Bought by TACA Nicaragua and exported. Sold to James C. Pippinger and Allen A. Crane of Caracas, Venezuela, July 1948. Bought by Sky-Ads Inc. of Miami, Florida, October 1951. Sold to Northwest Agricultural Aviation Corporation (Robert W. Waltermire) of Choteau, Montana. Destroyed on takeoff at Choteau, Montana, April 6, 1953.

NC9683 at Orofino in the summer of 1955 registered as N1124N.

NC9683
Model – 5-AT-B
Serial Number – 5-AT-39
Manufactured – April 6, 1929

Bought new by Southwest Air Fast Express (Earl P. Halliburton) of Tulsa, Oklahoma, April 1929. Sold to Southern Air Fast Express of Dallas, Texas, November 1930. Bought by Colonial Air Transport of Newark, New Jersey, April 1931. Sold to American Airways of Chicago, Illinois, April 1933. Bought by Aviation Manufacturing Corporation of Chicago, Illinois, April 1936. Sold to TACA of Tegucigalpa, Honduras, June 1936. Bought by TACA Nicaragua, January 1942. Sold to Miguel A. Zuniga, Mexico City, Mexico, March 1946. Bought by Raul Fierro Villalobos of Guadalajara, Mexico, August 1953. Sold to Robert W. Waltermire (Northwest Agricultural Aviation Corporation) of Choteau, Montana, November 1953. Waltermire ferried it out of Mexico with foreign registration and was re-assigned United States registration N1124N when he returned. Bought by Gerald D. Wilson of Orofino, Idaho, April 1955. Sold to E. W. Brown III of Orange, Texas, September 1956. Bought by Aircraft Hydroforming of Gardena, California, December 1957. Sold to American Airlines, New York City, New York, September 1962. Bought by the National Air &

Space Museum, Smithsonian Institution, Washington, D.C., November 1973. Currently hanging on display.

NC414H
Model – 5-AT-CS
Serial Number – 5-AT-74
Manufactured – September 4, 1929

Bought new by the Ford Motor Company of Dearborn, Michigan, and used for demonstrations including experimental flights on floats through 1932. Sold to Pan American Airways, New York City, New York, November 1932. Bought by Cia Mexicana de Aviacion, Mexico City, Mexico, March 1935. Sold to Pan American Airways, New York City, New York, November 1936. Bought by Cia Mexicana de Aviacion, Mexico City, Mexico, March 1940. Sold to Cia Guatemalteca de Aviacion of Guatemala City, Guatemala, May 1941. Bought by Robert W. Waltermire (Northwest Agricultural Aviation Corporation) of Choteau, Montana, March 1950. Sold to Lawrence L. Alzheimer of Collins, Montana. Bought by Jack A. Adams of Memphis, Tennessee, October 1956. Sold to C. M. Dunham of Haines City, Florida, April 1958. Bought by Mary Jane Bergerson of Crystal River, Florida, April 1959. Sold to John M. and Katherine M. Louck of Monmouth, Illinois, October 1959. Bought by American Airlines of New York City, New York, February 1965. Sold to John E. Burkdoll and Charles A. LeMaster of Ottawa, Kansas, November 1972. Bought by Burkdoll-LeMaster Inc. of Ottawa, Kansas, July 1973. Sold to LeMaster Inc. of Ottawa, Kansas, October 1973. Bought by Commuter Investment and Development Corporation (John R. Seibold) of Las Vegas, Nevada, August 1977. Sold to Scenic Airlines (John R. Seibold) of Las Vegas, Nevada, September 1985.

Harrah's Club

NC9645
Model – 5-AT-B
Serial Number – 5-AT-8
Manufactured – December 1, 1928

Bought new by Transcontinental Air Transport (TAT) of New York City, New York, January 1929.

Sold to G. E. Ruckstell, Grand Canyon Airlines of Grand Canyon, Arizona, July 1935. Bought by Grand Canyon-Boulder Dam Tours of Boulder City, Nevada, December 1932. Sold to TACA of Tegucigalpa, Honduras, December 1937. Bought by Ricardo Nevarez Izurieta of Campeche, Mexico, January 1946. Sold to Arturo D' Argence of Compeche, Mexico, August 1950. The plane was completely overhauled in 1951 and the corrugated skin was replaced with duralumin skin. For many years this Ford became known as the "Smooth Skin Ford." Bought by Augusto D' Argence of Compeche, Mexico, July 1953. Sold to Frank D. Oergel of Burbank, California, May 1955. Oergel purchased the airplane as a wreck and his son Frank Oergel Jr. of Mexico City, Mexico, somehow became involved. Bought by Eugene Frank of Caldwell, Idaho, November 1955. Frank returned it to the United States and registered it as N58996. Frank used it as an agricultural sprayer in Idaho's Treasure Valley. Sold to Harrah's Club of Reno, Nevada, July 1964.

Under Harrah's ownership the airplane was completely rebuilt to factory specifications. The plane was to be used for transportation to his Middle Fork Lodge along the Middle Fork of the Salmon River at Thomas Creek. However, the aircraft was flown very little for this activity (see Thomas Creek section for more information).

Bought by Gary Norton of Athol, Idaho, June 1986. Sold to Norton Aero Ltd. of Athol, Idaho, July 1986. Bought by Evergreen Aviation of McMinnville, Oregon, March 1990.

The airplane was trimmed in Evergreen colors and flown frequently. Evergreen pilots Penn Stohr Jr. and Doug Smuin flew it to several smokejumper reunions and other events around Oregon, Washington, Montana, and Idaho. This was the last Ford Tri-Motor known to have landed in the Idaho backcountry (see Moose Creek section for more information). The aircraft is currently on display at the Evergreen Aviation & Space Museum in McMinnville, Oregon.

Aircraft Service Company

NC8407
Model – 4-AT-E
Serial Number – 4-AT-69
Manufactured – January 15, 1929

Bought new by Eastern Air Transport of Brooklyn New York, November 1929. Sold to Intercontinent Aviation of New York City, NY. Bought by Rex Williams of Phoenix, Arizona, February 1950. In May 1954 three Pratt & Whitney Wasp engines were hung on the aircraft with the nose engine developing 550 horsepower and the outboard engines developing 450 horsepower each. This made it the highest horsepower 4-AT model flown. Sold to David Callender of Eagle, Idaho, February 1955. Bought by Aircraft Service Company of Boise, Idaho, July 1955. Sold to Johnson Flying Service, of Missoula, Montana, April 1958. Bought by LeMaster-Glenn Aerial Spraying of Ottawa, Kansas, March 1963. Sold to Ford Tri-Motor Inc. of Ottawa, Kansas, July 1964. Bought by Ford Tri-Motor Inc. of Lawrence, Kansas, February 1966. Sold to Experimental Aircraft Association (EAA) Air Museum Foundation of Hales Corners, Wisconsin, July 1973. The EAA bought the wreckage of the aircraft after it was badly damaged in a windstorm in June 1973. Bought by EAA Air Museum Foundation, Wittman Field, Oshkosh, Wisconsin, February 1985. After a complete restoration the airplane flew again in July 1985 and continues to be a flying airplane.

Unloading supplies from NC8407 circa 1956.

NOTES

CHAPTER 1 AN OVERVIEW

1 A. E. Briggs, O - Improvements - Landing Fields - Idaho - Memo. For Supervisor, 30 April 1930.

2 Elers Koch, "The Passing of the Lolo Trail," *Journal of Forestry 33* (2), 1935, 99-104.

3 Kevin R. Marsh, *Drawing Lines in the Forest: Creating Wilderness Areas in the Pacific Northwest*, (Seattle, WA: University of Washington Press, 2007), 23.

4 Gerald W. Williams, *The Forest Service: Fighting for Public Lands*, (Westport, CT: Greenwood Press, 2007), 177-78.

5 Harry C. Shellworth Personal Papers (held by his family).

6 R. H. Rutledge and H. C. Shellworth, Governor's Committee on the Proposed Primitive Area, 20 December 1930, 2.

7 Harry C. Shellworth Personal Papers (held by his family).

8 Harry C. Shellworth, Photo Album - Borah's August 2, 1927 Trip. Idaho State Historical Society, G35(63-219).

9 S. C. Scribner, *Idaho Primitive Area Report*, (USDA, Forest Service: 17 March 1931), 2.

10 Tom Parker, *Proposed Backcountry Ranch Management*, (Boise, ID: Idaho Department of Fish & Game, 1991).

11 Mark Harvey, *Wilderness Forever: Howard Zahniser and the Path to the Wilderness Act*, (Seattle, WA: University of Washington Press, 2005), 202.

12 *Selway-Bitterroot Wilderness Management Plan: Nezperce, Clearwater, Bitterroots, and Lolo National Forests*, (Missoula, MT: United States Department of Agricultural, Forest Service, 1976).

13 William L. Smallwood, *McClure of Idaho*, (Caldwell, ID: Caxton Press, 2007), 390.

14 Ted Trueblood, "How They're Won," *Field & Stream*, January 1981.

15 Ted Trueblood, "Help A Chunk of Your Wilderness Is Up For Grabs," *True's Hunting Yearbook*, 1974.

16 Frank Church, Letter to Clem L. Pope, 19 December 1979. *Frank Church Collection*. Special Collections, MSS 56. Albertsons Library, Boise State University, Boise, ID.

17 Dick Williams, Personal Communication, 10 October 2011.

CHAPTER 2 MIDDLE FORK OF THE SALMON RIVER

1 Elizabeth M. Smith, *History of the Boise National Forest 1905-1976*, (Boise, ID: Idaho Sate Historical Society, 1983), 93.

2 Bear Valley Minerals Inc., Bill Harris, USA, BLM General Land Office Records.

3 Bear Valley Minerals Inc., Bill Harris, USA, BLM General Land Office Records.

4 Bear Valley Minerals Inc., Bill Harris, USA, BLM General Land Office Records.

5 Private Edgar Hoffner, *Journal of the Sheepeater Campaign, May to Oct 1879*, (W. C. Brown Collection, University of Colorado at Boulder Archives), 23 August 1879, 8.

6 Lt. A. G. Forse, *Diary of LT. A. G. Forse, 1st Cavalry, Tuesday July 29, 1879 to Friday Sept. 19, 1879* (Sheepeater Campaign), (Idaho State University Archives), 23 August 1879, 4.

7 Richa Wilson, *"Like Places to US" Administrative Facilities of the Salmon-Challis National Forest, 1905–1960*, (Ogden, UT: USDA Intermountain Region, 2011), 159-60.

8 Ken Rogers, *Interview with F. W. Hamner*, (USDA, Forest Service,

Cobalt Ranger District, 1984), 2.

9 "Decide to Buy Salmon Airport," *Recorder Herald*, 14 June 1944.

10 Grant Havemann, Personal Communication, 13 February 2011.

11 Jim Eldredge, Personal Communication, 27 April 2011.

12 Harold Dougal, *Adventures of an Idaho Mountain Pilot*, (Boise, ID: Self-published, 2009), 154.

13 Dougal, 154.

14 Norman Brown, Personal Communication, 24 November 2010.

15 Brown, Personal Communication.

16 Brown, Personal Communication.

17 Smith, 25.

18 Idaho Department of Aeronautics, General Bruce Meadows Correspondence Folder, Accessed 30 June 2010.

19 Bob Fogg, *Fogg Scrapbook*.

20 Fogg, *Fogg Scrapbook*.

[21] Fogg, *Fogg Scrapbook.*

[22] Fogg, *Fogg Scrapbook.*

[23] Idaho Department of Aeronautics, General Cape Horn Correspondence Folder, Accessed 30 June 2010.

[24] Richa Wilson, *History of the Challis National Forest: A Compilation*, (Challis, ID: USDA Forest Service Intermountain Region, 2009), 83.

[25] Chet Moulton, *Idaho Airport Facilities*, (Boise, ID: Department of Aeronautics State of Idaho, 1950).

[26] Chet Moulton, *Idaho Airport Facilities*, (Boise, ID: Department of Aeronautics State of Idaho, 1964).

[27] Idaho Department of Aeronautics, General Cape Horn Correspondence Folder, Accessed 30 June 2010.

[28] William T. Burns, BLM General Land Office Records.

[29] Gerry (Fox) Turner, Personal Communication, 7 April 2011.

[30] Turner, Personal Communication.

[31] Johnny Carrey and Cort Conley, *The Middle Fork: A Guide*, (Cambridge, ID: Backeddy Books, 1992), 171.

[32] Carrey and Conley, 171.

[33] Tom Parker, *Proposed Backcountry Ranch Management*, (Boise, ID: State of Idaho Department Fish and Game, 1991).

[34] Norman Guth, Personal Communication, 20 July 2010.

[35] N. Guth, Personal Communication.

[36] N. Guth, Personal Communication.

[37] Carrey and Conley, 230.

[38] Bill Guth Jr., Personal Communication, 11 February 2011.

[39] Bert Zimmerly Jr., Personal Communication, 11 February 2011.

[40] "Flew Bull Rake to Middle Fork," *Recorder Herald*, 21 June 1944.

[41] Ed Burnet, Personal Communication, 29 March 2011.

[42] Jim Rearden, *Alaska's First Bush Pilots, 1923–30: And the Winter Search in Siberia For Eielson and Borland*, (Missoula, MT: Pictorial Histories Publishing Company, Inc., 2009), 31–32.

[43] Steve Smith, *Fly the Biggest Piece Back*, (Missoula, MT: Pictorial Histories Publishing Company, 1994), 101–08.

[44] Burnet, Personal Communication.

[45] Burnet, Personal Communication.

[46] Burnet, Personal Communication.

[47] Leila Jarvis, Personal Communication, 14 July 2011.

[48] Jarvis, Personal Communication.

[49] Dick Williams, Personal Communication, 9 May 2011.

[50] Harold Dougal, Personal Communication, 18 July 2011.

[51] Gar Thorsrude, Personal Communication, 10 February 2011.

[52] Thorsrude, Personal Communication.

[53] Dick Karr, Personal Communication, 20 February 2011.

[54] Karr, Personal Communication.

[55] Phil Sullivan, Personal Communication, 10 February 2011.

[56] P. Sullivan, Personal Communication.

[57] P. Sullivan, Personal Communication.

[58] P. Sullivan, Personal Communication.

[59] Tom Sullivan, Personal Communication, 10 February 2011.

[60] T. Sullivan, Personal Communication.

[61] T. Sullivan, Personal Communication.

[62] T. Sullivan, Personal Communication.

[63] T. Sullivan, Personal Communication.

[64] B. Guth Jr., Personal Communication.

[65] Idaho Department of Aeronautics, General Hoodoo Correspondence Folder, Accessed 30 June 2010.

[66] Idaho Department of Aeronautics, General Hoodoo Correspondence Folder, Accessed 30 June 2010.

[67] Mike Dorris, Personal Communication, 25 March 2009.

[68] Dick Williams, Personal Communication. 24 March 2011.

[69] Williams, Personal Communication.

[70] Carrey and Conley, 133.

[71] R. Wilson, 130.

[72] R. Wilson, 120.

[73] Richa Wilson, Personal Communication, 14 January 2013.

[74] Idaho Department of Aeronautics, General Indian Creek Correspondence Folder, Accessed 30 June 2010.

[75] Jim Moorhead, Personal Communication, 30 June 2011.

[76] Ted Anderson, Personal Communication, 3 March 2011.

[77] B. Guth Jr., Personal Communication.

[78] R. Wilson, *"Like Places to US" Administrative Facilities of the Salmon-Challis National Forest*, 1905-1960, 102.

[79] Kenneth D. Smith, *Before the Idaho Public Utilities Commission – Application of Key Transportation, Inc., DBA Sun Valley Key Airlines For Temporary Authority To Provide Daily Scheduled Service From Boise And Sun Valley/Haily To Salmon, Stanley, Indian Creek, And McCall...,"* 3 April 1975. Idaho Department of Aeronautics, *General Indian Creek Correspondence Folder*, Accessed 30 June 2010.

[80] K. Smith.

[81] K. Smith.

[82] Dougal, Personal Communication.

[83] R. Wilson, *History of the Challis National Forest: A Compilation*, 240.

[84] *Report of Investigation Aircraft (Beechcraft) Accident Boise National Forest*, 9 July 1965.

[85] Ronald J. Maki, *Smokejumper, Payette National Forest, About the Forest Service Aerial Accident of July 9, 1965*, 12 July 1965, 1. On file at the Payette National Forest Heritage Program.

[86] Maki, 2.

[87] Michael Kohlhoff, *Norton Creek Fire – 7/9/1965*, 12 July 1965.

[88] Bob Fogg, *July 9, 1965 Johnson Flying Service Accident*, July 1965.

[89] Dorris, Personal Communication.

[90] Jim Mizer, Personal Communication, 25 March 2011.

[91] Mizer, Personal Communication.

[92] Kenneth Cameron, BLM General Land Office Records.

[93] Carrey and Conley, 169.

[94] Parker.

[95] S. O. Scribner, Improvement Landing Fields – Memo for Regional Forester, 26 July 1933. On file at the Payette National Forest Heritage Program.

[96] Sherrill G. Benham, Personal Communication, 30 June 2011.

[97] Pat Armstrong, Personal Communication, 9 April 2011.

[98] Armstrong, Personal Communication.

[99] Armstrong, Personal Communication.

[100] Armstrong, Personal Communication.

[101] Armstrong, Personal Communication.

[102] Armstrong, Personal Communication.

[103] Armstrong, Personal Communication.

[104] Armstrong, Personal Communication.

[105] Armstrong, Personal Communication.

[106] Carrey and Conley, 99.

[107] James M. Fuller, BLM General Land Office Records.

[108] Allen and Mary Dee Dodge, Personal Communication, 6 March 2011.

[109] Dodge, Personal Communication.

[110] Dodge, Personal Communication.

[111] Dodge, Personal Communication.

[112] Dodge, Personal Communication.

[113] Dodge, Personal Communication.

[114] Dodge, Personal Communication.

[115] Dodge, Personal Communication.

[116] Dodge, Personal Communication.

[117] Dodge, Personal Communication.

[118] Dodge, Personal Communication.

[119] Dodge, Personal Communication.

[120] Dodge, Personal Communication.

[121] Dodge, Personal Communication.

[122] Dodge, Personal Communication.

[123] Dodge, Personal Communication.

[124] Dodge, Personal Communication.

[125] Dodge, Personal Communication.

[126] Carrey and Conley, 127.

[127] George L. Risley, BLM General Land Office Records.

[128] Dougal, Personal Communication.

[129] Dougal, 84.

[130] Dougal, Personal Communication.

[131] Dougal, Personal Communication.

[132] Dougal, Personal Communication.

[133] Dougal, Personal Communication.

[134] Dougal, Personal Communication.

[135] Patricia (Hornback) Vance, Personal Communication, 12 July 2010.

[136] Baxter, Personal Communication.

[137] Vance, Personal Communication.

[138] Baxter, Personal Communication.

[139] Patricia (Hornback) Vance, Personal Communication, 25 April 2011.

[140] Carrey and Conley, 99.

[141] Dick L. Johnson, *Pilot's Logbook January 1, 1937 to August 7, 1939.*

[142] "Primitive Area Rancher Presents $668 Hay Bill To Game Department," *Cascade News*, 23 September 1938.

[143] Patricia (Hornback) Vance, Personal Communication, 12 July 2010.

[144] Vance, Personal Communication.

[145] Vance, Personal Communication.

[146] Vance, Personal Communication.

[147] Vance, Personal Communication.

[148] Carrey and Conley, 105.

[149] Vance, Personal Communication.

[150] Carrey and Conley, 106.

[151] Bill Woods, Letter to State Aeronautical Department – Chet Moulton, April 1955, 1.

[152] Woods, 2–3.

[153] Woods, 3.

[154] Barbara Hornback, 1959 Hornback Christmas Letter, 6 January 1960.

[155] Hornback, 1959 Hornback Christmas Letter.

[156] Hornback, 1959 Hornback Christmas Letter.

[157] Carrey and Conley, 143.

[158] Dick L. Johnson, *Pilot's Logbook – January 1, 1937 to August 7, 1939*, 8 August 1937.

[159] "Lone Huntress Bags Deer On Expedition Into Wilds Of Idaho," *The Idaho Statesman*, 11 October 1937.

[160] "Challis Game Head Delays Lady Hunter," *The Challis Messenger*, 13 October 1937.

[161] Norman Guth, Personal Communication, 13 July 2010.

[162] Idaho Department of Aeronautics, General Thomas Creek Correspondence Folder, Accessed 30 June 2010.

[163] Bill Guth Jr., Personal Communication, 9 July 2010.

[164] N. Guth, Personal Communication.

[165] B.Guth, Personal Communication.

166 B. Guth Jr., Personal Communication.

167 B. Guth Jr., Personal Communication.

168 N. Guth, Personal Communication.

169 N. Guth, Personal Communication.

170 N. Guth, Personal Communication.

171 N. Guth, Personal Communication.

172 B. Guth Jr., Personal Communication.

173 B. Guth Jr., Personal Communication.

174 N. Guth, Personal Communication.

175 N. Guth, Personal Communication.

176 N. Guth, Personal Communication.

177 N. Guth, Personal Communication.

178 Lloyd Dyer, Personal Communication, 17 May 2010.

179 Dyer, Personal Communication.

180 Dyer, Personal Communication.

181 Dyer, Personal Communication.

182 Idaho Department of Aeronautics, General Thomas Creek Correspondence Folder, Accessed 30 June 2010.

183 Bill Blackmore, Personal Communication, 23 July 2010.

184 Guth Jr., Personal Communication.

185 Blackmore, Personal Communication.

186 Penn Stohr Jr., Personal Communication.

187 Fogg, *Fogg Scrapbook.*

188 Blackmore, Personal Communication.

189 Blackmore, Personal Communication.

190 Blackmore, Personal Communication.

191 Blackmore, Personal Communication.

192 Daryl Drake, Personal Communication, 4 March 2011.

193 Rupert L. Falconbery, BLM General Land Office Records.

194 Jack Ferguson, BLM General Land Office Records.

195 Rupert L. Falconbery, BLM General Land Office Records.

196 George Frinklin, BLM General Land Office Records.

197 E. E. McKee, Letter to Mr. R. L. Falconbery from Forest Supervisor – L – Uses Challis 2/4/1920 – Special Use Permit, 2 December 1937.

198 "R. L. Falconberry Dies On Monday," *The Challis Messenger*, 16 October 1939.

199 J. Mark Hatch, Personal Communication, 22 March 2011.

200 H. M. Shank, *Letter to F.W. Woods – Horace Ralph – Landing Field Estimates*, 31 August 1942, 2. On file at the Payette National Forest Heritage Program.

201 Hatch, Personal Communication.

202 Hatch, Personal Communication.

203 Hatch, Personal Communication.

204 Charles and Karen Wilson, Personal Communication, 22 March 2011.

205 Hatch, Personal Communication.

206 R. Wilson, 117.

207 Hatch, Personal Communication.

208 Hatch, Personal Communication.

209 Hatch, Personal Communication.

210 Dick Waite, Personal Communication, 24 March 2011.

211 Hatch, Personal Communication.

212 Hatch, Personal Communication.

213 Hatch, Personal Communication.

214 Hatch, Personal Communication.

215 Hatch, Personal Communication.

216 Steve Mulberry, Personal Communication, 2 April 2011.

217 Hatch, Personal Communication.

218 Mulberry, Personal Communication.

219 Mulberry, Personal Communication.

220 Hatch, Personal Communication.

221 Hatch, Personal Communication.

222 John S. Hatch, M.D., *Letter to Mr. Darrell V. Manning, Director Idaho Transportation Department Division of Aeronautics and Public Transportation*, 29 May 1980.

223 J. Mark Hatch, Personal Communication, 24 March 2011.

224 Robert Lee Ramey, BLM General Land Office Records.

225 Carrey and Conley, 183–84.

226 Carrey and Conley, 184.

227 Anderson, Personal Communication.

228 "Trapper Killed In Plane Crash En Route To Hospital," *Payette Lakes Star*, 11 June 1942.

229 "Trapper Killed In Plane Crash En Route To Hospital," *Payette Lakes Star*, 11 June 1942.

230 Penn Stohr, , *Pilot's Log Book – August 12, 1940 to December 28, 1942*, 10 June 1942.

231 Anderson, Personal Communication.

232 Anderson, Personal Communication.

233 Tom Parker, *Proposed Backcountry Ranch Management*, (Boise, ID: State of Idaho Department of Fish & Game, 1991).

234 Blackmore, Personal Communication.

235 Dick Williams, Personal Communication, 3 March 2011.

236 Scott Farr, Personal Communication, 16 October 2010.

237 Farr, Personal Communication.

238 Farr, Personal Communication.

239 Farr, Personal Communication.

240 Farr, Personal Communication.

241 Greg Painter, Personal Communication, 22 April 2011.

242 Kirk Braun, Personal Communication, 23 November 2011.

[243] Horace W. Johnson, BLM General Land Office Records.

[244] Bob Johnson, "Love of Outdoors, Flying Keep Mike Loening in the West," *The Idaho Statesman*, 25 November 1975.

[245] Bill Scherer, Personal Communication, 15 December 2010.

[246] Johnson.

[247] Scherer, Personal Communication.

[248] Marilyn Sword, Personal Communication, 7 November 2011.

[249] Steve Nelson, Personal Communication, 7 March 2011.

[250] Nelson, Personal Communication.

[251] Scherer, Personal Communication.

[252] Scherer, Personal Communication.

[253] Ken Burrows, "In Utah Plane Crash Boise Pilot, Son Killed," *The Idaho Statesman*, 1 March 1977.

[254] Ken Burrows, "Crash Victims Died of Exposure," *The Idaho Statesman*, 1 March 1977.

[255] Sword, Personal Communication.

[256] Idaho Department of Aeronautics, General Upper Loon Creek Correspondence Folder, Accessed 30 June 2010.

[257] G. W. Chase, "Loon Creek Taken by Indians: The Town Burned to the Ground," *Idaho World*, 21 March 1879.

[258] Tom Demorest, Personal Communication, 14 February 2011.

[259] Demorest, Personal Communication.

[260] Demorest, Personal Communication.

[261] Demorest, Personal Communication.

[262] Demorest, Personal Communication.

[263] Demorest, Personal Communication.

[264] Demorest, Personal Communication.

[265] Ernest R. Splettstosser, BLM General Land Office Records.

[266] Ted Anderson, Personal Communication, 1 April 2011.

[267] Ramona McAfee, Personal Communication, 24 March 2011.

[268] McAfee, Personal Communication.

[269] McAfee, Personal Communication.

[270] McAfee, Personal Communication.

[271] McAfee, Personal Communication.

[272] McAfee, Personal Communication.

[273] Dick Williams, Personal Communication, 24 March 2011.

[274] McAfee, Personal Communication.

[275] McAfee, Personal Communication.

[276] Andrew E. Lee, BLM General Land Office Records.

[277] William M. Wilson, BLM General Land Office Records.

[278] Ted Strickler, Personal Communication, 30 March 1930.

[279] Strickler, Personal Communication.

[280] Strickler, Personal Communication.

[281] Strickler, Personal Communication.

[282] Strickler, Personal Communication.

[283] Dick Williams, Personal Communication, 28 March 2011.

[284] Strickler, Personal Communication.

[285] Hidden Valley Ranches Inc., BLM General Land Office Records.

[286] Strickler, Personal Communication.

[287] Frank S. Allison, BLM General Land Office Records.

[288] Bob G. Waite, *Zane Grey and Thunder Mountain*, (McCall, ID: USDA, Forest Service, Payette National Forest, Heritage Program, 1996), 2.

[289] Waite, 2-3.

[290] Waite, 2.

[291] Ethel Kimball, "Trail to Thunder Mountain," *True West: No Fiction*, March-April 1973, 28.

[292] Kimball, 44.

[293] Elmer Keith, *"Hell, I Was There!,"* (Los Angles, CA: Petersen Publishing Company, 1979), 138-40.

[294] Kimball, 46.

[295] Ken Armstrong, Personal Communication, 14 February 2011.

[296] Armstrong, Personal Communication.

[297] Armstrong, Personal Communication.

[298] Armstrong, Personal Communication.

[299] Armstrong, Personal Communication.

[300] R. Lee Ramey, BLM General Land Office Records.

[301] Max Oyler, BLM General Land Office Records.

[302] Ted Anderson, Personal Communication, 23 March 2011.

[303] Preston Dixon, Personal Communication, 5 March 2011.

[304] Berend Friehe, Personal Communication, 5 March 2011.

[305] Wilbur Wiles, Personal Communication (Letter to author), 4 February 2011.

[306] Fouch, 2.

[307] Adelia Parke, *Memoirs of An Old Timer*, (Weiser, ID: Signal-American Printers, 1955), 51.

[308] Francis W. Woods, *Landing Strips in Central Idaho 1943*.

[309] Earl Dodds, Personal Communication June 19, 2010.

[310] Earl Dodds, Photograph Collection and Archives, Dated September 1958.

[311] Fouch, 3.

[312] Orlando M. Abel, BLM General Land Office Records.

[313] Elizabeth Bellingham, BLM General Land Office Records.

[314] Archie C. Bacon, BLM General Land Office Records.

[315] Wayne Minshall, Personal Communication, 21 June 2010.

[316] Noel Routson, *Memoirs of an Old Prospector*, (Self-published, written circa 1980), 13.

[317] Routson, 13.

[318] Routson, 13.

[319] Routson, 14.

[320] Merl Wallace, Letter from Merl to wife Jean Wallace, 14 August 1932.

[321] Merl Wallace, Letter from Merl to wife Jean Wallace, 21 August 1932.

[322] Merl Wallace, Letter from Merl to wife Jean Wallace, 17 April 1933.

[323] Merl Wallace, Letter from Merl to wife Jean Wallace, 21 April 1933.

[324] Merl Wallace, Letter from Merl to wife Jean Wallace, 25 June 1933.

[325] Francis W. Woods, Improvements - Landing Field - Idaho, 2 November 1938.

[326] Merl (Blackie) Wallace and Jean Orr Wallace, *Flying W Ranch (brochure)*, early 1930s.

[327] Minshall, Personal Communication.

[328] Cathy Kough, Personal Communication, 31 January 2012.

[329] Catherine Gillihan, Personal Communication, 29 June 2010.

[330] Earl Dodds, Personal Communication, 22 January 2010.

[331] Cathy Kough, Personal Communication, 26 February 2012.

[332] Kough, Personal Communication.

[333] Kough, Personal Communication.

[334] Kough, Personal Communication.

[335] Valley County Courthouse, Accessed 22 January 2010.

[336] Kough, Personal Communication.

[337] Catherine Gillihan, Personal Communication, 2 March 2011.

[338] Gillihan, Personal Communication.

[339] Blackmore, Personal Communication.

[340] Gillihan, Personal Communication.

[341] N. Guth, Personal Communication.

[342] Dyer, Personal Communication.

[343] Nels Jensen, Personal Communication, 7 February 2011.

[344] Gillihan, Personal Communication.

[345] W. B. Sendt (Payette NF Supervisor), Letter to Mr. Joseph C. Greenley, Director Idaho Fish and Game Department concerning future management plans for the Flying W Ranch, 20 March 1975.

[346] Pat Armstrong, Personal Communication, 9 April 2011.

[347] Armstrong, Personal Communication.

[348] Armstrong, Personal Communication.

[349] Parke, *Memoirs of An Old Timer*

[350] Valley County Courthouse Records, Accessed 22 January 2010.

[351] Virginia Moore, Letter to Jean Wallace, 20 April 1953.

[352] Jennifer Haskell, Letter from Idaho State Brand Recorder Jennifer Haskell to Richard Holm Jr., 19 September 2011.

[353] Dick Waite, Personal Communication, 24 March 2011.

[354] Dodds, Personal Communication.

[355] David Neider, Inter-Department Memo Letter to Dick Norell, 9 November 1965, Mile High Ranch General Lease History File, Idaho Fish & Game, Southwest Region Office.

[356] Valley County Courthouse Records, Accessed 22 January 2010.

[357] "Former Big Creek Man Dies," *Star News*, 3 June 1976.

[358] Dorris, Personal Communication.

[359] Valley County Courthouse Records, Accessed 22 January 2010.

[360] Emma Cox, *Idaho Mountains Our Home: The Life Story of Lafe and Emma Cox*, (Cascade, ID: VO Ranch Books, 1997), 99.

[361] Cox, 45.

[362] Cox, 75.

[363] Cox, 115-16.

[364] Warren Ellison, Personal Communication, 28 July 2004.

[365] Ellison, Personal Communication.

[366] Ellison, Personal Communication.

[367] Dean Wilson, Personal Communication, 29 March 2009.

[368] Wilson, Personal Communication.

[369] Wilson, Personal Communication.

[370] Wilson, Personal Communication.

[371] Valley County Courthouse, Accessed 22 January 2010.

[372] Penn Stohr Jr., Personal Communication, 2 October 2010.

[373] Stohr, Personal Communication.

[374] Mile High Ranch General Lease History File, Idaho Fish & Game, Southwest Region Office.

[375] Mile High Ranch General Lease History File.

[376] Cecil D. Andrus, Letter to Mr. Rex Lanham, 11 September 1975, Mile High Ranch General Lease History File, Idaho Fish & Game, Southwest Region Office.

[377] Mile High Ranch General Lease History File.

[378] Mile High Ranch General Lease History File.

[379] Mike Dorris, Personal Communication, 25 September 2010.

[380] Dorris, Personal Communication.

[381] Dorris, Personal Communication.

[382] Dorris, Personal Communication.

[383] Dorris, Personal Communication.

[384] Jerry Lockhart, Letter to Dale VonSteen, Stacy Gebards, and Ray Lyon - Memorandum - Mile High Airstrip, 19 July 1988, Mile High Ranch General Lease History File, Idaho Fish & Game, Southwest Region Office.

[385] Stacy Gebhards, Letter to Jerry Jeppson - Mile High Outfitters, 2 August 1989, Mile High Ranch General Lease History File, Idaho Fish & Game, Southwest Region Office.

[386] Roy A. Elliot, BLM General Land Office Records.

[387] Wilbur Wiles, Personal Communication, 15 October 2010.

[388] H. M. Shank, Improvement - Monumental Landing Field - Idaho, 27 June 1939. On file at the Payette National Forest Heritage Program.

[389] Sandy McRae, Personal Communication, 17 June 2010.

[390] McRae, Personal Communication.

[391] Gil McCoy, BLM General Land Office Records.

[392] Francis W. Woods, *Landing Strips in Central Idaho 1943*.

[393] Ervin K. Bobo, *D-8 Field Notes,* 15 September 1955.

[394] Payette National Forest, Heritage Program, McCoy Ranch, File PY-464.

[395] Earl Dodds, Personal Communication, 2 June 2010.

[396] Wiles, Personal Communication.

[397] George Dovel, Personal Communication, 4 April 2009.

[398] Dovel, Personal Communication.

[399] Dovel, Personal Communication.

[400] Dovel, Personal Communication.

[401] Dovel, Personal Communication.

[402] Valley County Courthouse Records, Accessed 22 January 2010.

[403] Dovel, Personal Communication.

[404] Ray Hamell, Personal Communication, 4 April 2011.

[405] Hamell, Personal Communication.

[406] Hamell, Personal Communication.

[407] Hamell, Personal Communication.

[408] Hamell, Personal Communication.

[409] Valley County Courthouse Records, Accessed 22 January 2010.

[410] Earl Dodds, Personal Communication, 29 March 2011.

[411] Ray Arnold, Personal Communication, 29 March 2011.

[412] Wiles, Personal Communication.

[413] Dovel, Personal Communication.

[414] Dovel, Personal Communication.

[415] Dovel, Personal Communication.

[416] Clem Pope, Personal Communication, 29 March 2010.

[417] Private Edgar Hoffner, *Journal of the Sheepeater Campaign, May to Oct 1879,* (W. C. Brown Collection, University of Colorado at Boulder Archives), 19 August 1879, 6-7.

[418] Col. W. C. Brown, *The Sheepeater Campaign 1879*, (Boise, ID: Tenth Biennial Report, Idaho State Historical Society), 38

[419] Hoffner, 7.

[420] Harry Eagan Burial File, National Archives, RG92, Stack Area 3/70, Row 65, Compartment 11, Shelf 7, Box 1458.

[421] David Lewis, Letter to Col. W. C. Brown, 1 February 1925. (W. C. Brown Collection, University of Colorado at Boulder Archives).

[422] Eagan Burial File.

[423] Eagan Burial File.

[424] Eagan Burial File.

[425] Eagan Burial File.

[426] Dan LeVan Jr., *LeVan Family Scrapbook.*

[427] Merl Wallace, Letter from Merl to wife Jean Wallace, 17 April 1933.

[428] LeVan, *LeVan Family Scrapbook.*

[429] Hank M. Shank, Improvement - Idaho Landing Fields - Memo for Supervisor, 11 August 1932. On file at the Payette National Forest Heritage Program.

[430] H. M. Shank, O - Improvement - Airplane Landing Fields - Idaho, 3 June 1935. On file at the Payette National Forest Heritage Program.

[431] Bill Little, *Gypsies in the Wilderness: Some Mostly True Tales of Adventures in the Idaho Primitive Area,* (Self-published manuscript, 2011), 65.

[432] Liter Spence, Personal Communication, 19 November 2011.

[433] Bob Nicol, Personal Communication (letter to author), 19 January 2010.

[434] Nicol, Personal Communication.

[435] Nicol, Personal Communication.

[436] Nicol, Personal Communication.

[437] Nicol, Personal Communication.

[438] Nicol, Personal Communication.

[439] Nicol, Personal Communication.

[440] Nicol, Personal Communication.

[441] G. Wayne Minshall, Personal Communication, 27 March 2012.

[442] James Akenson, *Ninety Years of Taylor Ranch History,* (Unfinished manuscript, 1991), 3.

[443] David Lewis, BLM General Land Office Records.

[444] Harry C. Shellworth, Letter to Stanly A. Easton, President, Bunker Hill and Sullivan Mining and Concentration Co., Kellogg, Idaho, 17 May 1937, 3.

[445] R. H. Rutledge and H. C. Shellworth, Governor's Committee on the Proposed Primitive Area, 20 December 1930.

[446] Jim Akenson, Personal Communication, 16 January 2010.

[447] Stan Potts, Personal Communication, 10 March 2011.

[448] Robert Diers Jr., Personal Communication, 28 March 2011.

[449] Potts, Personal Communication.

[450] Potts, Personal Communication.

[451] Potts, Personal Communication.

[452] Wiles, Personal Communication.

[453] Potts, Personal Communication.

[454] Potts, Personal Communication.

[455] Potts, Personal Communication.

[456] Potts, Personal Communication.

[457] Potts, Personal Communication.

[458] Potts, Personal Communication.

[459] Robert M. Loveland, Jess Taylor Interview - Taylor Ranch, 25, 29, August 1971. On file at the Payette National Forest Heritage Program.

[460] Potts, Personal Communication.

[461] Loveland, 41.

462 Maurice Hornocker, Personal Communication, 25 March 2011.

463 Hornocker, Personal Communication.

464 John C. Seidensticker IV, Maurice G. Hornocker, Richard R. Knight, Steven L. Judd, *Equipment and Techniques for Radiotracking Mountain Lions and Elk*, (Moscow, ID: Forest, Wildlife and Range Experiment Station Bulletin No. 6, 1970).

465 Hornocker, Personal Communication.

466 Mike Dorris, Personal Communication, 5 April 2011.

467 Dorris, Personal Communication.

468 Doug Gadwa, Personal Communication, 11 April 2011.

469 Nicol, Personal Communication.

470 Wayne Minshall, Personal Communication, 16 November 2011.

471 Valley County Courthouse Records, Accessed 22 January 2010.

472 Maurice Hornocker, Personal Communication, 2 April 2010.

473 Hornocker, Personal Communication.

474 Hornocker, Personal Communication.

475 Mike Jager, Personal Communication, 29 March 2010.

476 Earl Dodds, Personal Communication, 17 January 2010.

477 Hornocker, Personal Communication.

478 Wiles, Personal Communication.

479 Hornocker, Personal Communication.

480 Jager, Personal Communication.

481 Earl Dodds, Personal Communication, 26 December 2009.

482 Dodds, Personal Communication.

483 Mike Dorris, Personal Communication, 25 March 2009.

484 Valley County Courthouse Records, Accessed 22 January 2010.

CHAPTER 3 SOUTH FORK OF THE SALMON RIVER

1 Payette National Forest, Heritage Program, Rains Ranch, File PY-222.

2 "Letter from N. B. Willey – Full Particulars of the Killing of Rains near Warrens," *Idaho Tri-Weekly Statesman*, 2 September 1879.

3 Payette National Forest, Heritage Program, Freeman Nethkin Homestead Records.

4 Payette National Forest, Heritage Program, Freeman Nethkin Homestead Records.

5 Idaho County Courthouse Records, Accessed 7 June 2010.

6 Payette National Forest, Heritage Program, Adrian Carlson Homestead Records.

7 Payette National Forest, Heritage Program, Rains Ranch, File PY-222.

8 Idaho County Courthouse Records, Accessed 7 June 2010.

9 D. Tice, Personal Communication.

10 D. Tice, Personal Communication.

11 D. Tice, Personal Communication.

12 D. Tice, Personal Communication.

13 Ken Roth, Personal Communication, 19 June 2004.

14 Sheila D. Reddy, *Wilderness Of The Heart: An early history of the land and the people of the Frank Church – River of No Return Wilderness*, (McCall, ID: Payette National Forest USDA, 1995), 29.

15 Idaho County Courthouse Records, Accessed 7 June 2010.

16 Dorris, Personal Communication.

17 Bob Dodge, Personal Communication, 12 April 2011.

18 Dodge, Personal Communication.

19 Dodge, Personal Communication.

20 Dorris, Personal Communication.

21 Dorris, Personal Communication.

22 Ben Salmon, "Plane Crash Victim Rescued After Two Days Alone, Injured," *The Star News*, 1 May 2003.

23 Salmon.

24 Salmon.

25 Payette National Forest, Heritage Program Archives BB#29.

26 Chas C. Randall, BLM General Land Office Records.

27 Chas C. Randall, BLM General Land Office Records.

28 Ruth Knight, *Molly of the Mountains*, (Unpublished Manuscript, 1947), 5-7. On file at the Payette National Forest Service Heritage Program.

29 "Land Case of WM. Kessler, vs. DA Robnett, Was Tried," *Cascade News*, 20 May 1915.

30 Daniel G. Drake, BLM General Land Office Records.

31 Daniel G. Drake, BLM General Land Office Records.

32 Jerri Montgomery, "History Tied to the Mines," *Star News*, 8 June 1979.

33 LeRoy Meyer, *Warm Lake Area History (Timeline)*, (Garden City, ID: Self-published, 2003), 10.

34 Dick L. Johnson, *Pilot's Log Book – January 1, 1937 to August 7, 1939*.

35 Meyer, 13-14.

36 Penn Stohr Sr., *Pilot's Log Book – November 30, 1938 to August 25, 1942*.

37 "Giant Airliner Lands Safely At Cascade Airport," *Cascade News*, 29 March 1935.

38 Knight, 9.

39 Knight, 9.

40 Payette National Forest, Heritage Program, Krassel Guard Station, File PY-584.

41 Payette National Forest, Heritage Program, Krassel Guard Station, File PY-584.

42 Payette National Forest, Heritage Program, Krassel Guard Station, File PY-584.

43 Idaho National Forest, "Krassel Landing Strip – Repair Estimate," 1939. On file at the Payette National Forest Service Heritage Program.

44 Idaho Department of Aeronautics, General Krassel Correspondence Folder, Accessed 30 June 2010.

45 Payette National Forest, Heritage Program, Krassel Guard Station, File PY-584.

46 Larry Swan, Personal Communication, 26 February 2011.

47 Swan, Personal Communication.

48 Linda Cross, Personal Communication, 8 October 2011.

49 Reddy, 33.

50 Bailey O. Dustin, BLM General Land Office Records.

51 Reddy, 33-34.

52 Hockaday, 104.

53 John Carrey, *Sheepeater Indian Campaign: Chamberlain Basin Country*, (Grangeville, ID: Idaho County Free Press, 1968), 38.

54 Julie Schwane, Personal Communication, 30 January 2011.

55 Schwane, Personal Communication.

56 Schwane, Personal Communication.

57 Schwane, Personal Communication.

58 Schwane, Personal Communication.

59 Schwane, Personal Communication.

60 Schwane, Personal Communication.

61 Schwane, Personal Communication.

62 Schwane, Personal Communication.

63 Mike Dorris, Personal Communication, 27 January 2011.

64 Dorris, Personal Communication.

65 Dorris, Personal Communication.

66 Dorris, Personal Communication.

67 Dorris, Personal Communication.

68 Tom and Jeanette Roberts, Personal Communication, 29 January 2011.

69 Payette National Forest, Heritage Program, Reed Ranch, File PY-336.

70 Kathy Deinhart Hill, *The Legacy of William "Deadshot" Reed*, (McCall, ID: Big Mallard Books, 2003), 65-67.

71 Hill, 71.

72 Hill, 89-91.

73 Hill, 91-92.

74 Hill, 101-02.

75 Payette National Forest, Heritage Program, C. F. "Frank" Smith Homestead, File PY-612.

76 Reddy, 31.

77 Doris C. Thompson-Johnston, *Tommy: The Autobiography of Doris "Tommy" Thompson*, (Kick the Can Productions, 2007), 38.

78 Charlotte McDowell Coombes, Personal Communication, 20 January 2011.

79 Coombes, Personal Communication.

80 Coombes, Personal Communication.

81 Larry Hettinger Jr., Personal Communication, 2 February 2011.

82 Ted W. Koskella, O – Inspection, GII, Warren Ranger District, 31 October 1958, 17. On file at the Payette National Forest Service Heritage Program.

83 Hettinger, Personal Communication.

84 Hettinger, Personal Communication.

85 Hettinger, Personal Communication.

86 Penn Stohr Sr., *Pilot's Log Book – November 30, 1938 to August 25, 1942*.

87 Elizabeth M. Smith, *History of the Boise National Forest 1905–1976*, (Boise, ID: Idaho Sate Historical Society, 1983), 127.

88 Smith, 25.

89 Smith, 56-57.

90 Payette National Forest, Heritage Program, Willey Homestead, File PY-643.

91 Payette National Forest, Heritage Program, Willey Homestead, File PY-643.

92 Payette National Forest, Heritage Program, Willey Homestead, File PY-643.

93 Coombes, Personal Communication.

94 Joyce Lukecart, Personal Communication, 2 February 2011.

95 Lukecart, Personal Communication.

96 Lukehart, Personal Communication.

97 Lukehart, Personal Communication.

98 Arnold, Personal Communication.

99 Arnold, Personal Communication.

100 Dorris, Personal Communication.

101 Dorris, Personal Communication.

102 Dorris, Personal Communication.

103 Dorris, Personal Communication.

104 Lukecart, Personal Communication.

105 Dorris, Personal Communication.

106 Dorris, Personal Communication.

107 Dorris, Personal Communication.

[108] Lukecart, Personal Communication.

[109] Dorris, Personal Communication.

[110] Stella Anderson, BLM General Land Office Records.

[111] Linda Cross, Personal Communication, 6 October 2011.

[112] Cross, Personal Communication.

[113] Cross, Personal Communication.

[114] Valley County Courthouse Records, Accessed 22 January 2010.

[115] Dorris, Personal Communication.

[116] Valley County Courthouse Records, Accessed 22 January 2010.

[117] Jay and Floy Hester, Personal Communication, 3 February 2011.

[118] Dorris, Personal Communication.

[119] Hester, Personal Communication.

[120] Hester, Personal Communication.

[121] Jim Eldredge, Personal Communication, 27 April 2011.

[122] Hester, Personal Communication.

[123] Hester, Personal Communication.

CHAPTER 4 **EAST FORK OF THE SOUTH FORK OF THE SALMON RIVER**

[1] Ernest Oberbillig, "More on Al Hennessey," *Yellow Pine, Idaho*, Compiled by Nancy G. Sumner, (Tucson, AZ: Self-published, 1981), 19-20.

[2] M. Barry Bryant, Personal Communication, 24 May 2011.

[3] Nancy G. Sumner, *Yellow Pine, Idaho*, (Tucson, AZ: Self-published, 1981), 2-3.

[4] Bryant, Personal Communication.

[5] Idaho Department of Aeronautics, General Johnson Creek Correspondence Folder, Accessed 30 June 2010.

[6] Emma Cox, *Idaho Mountains Our Home: The Life Story of Lafe and Emma Cox*, (Cascade, ID: VO Ranch Books, 1997), 99.

[7] Cox, 116.

[8] Idaho Department of Aeronautics, General Johnson Creek Correspondence Folder, Accessed 30 June 2010.

[9] Duane Peterson, *Valley County: The Way it Was,* (Cascade, ID: D&D Books, 2002), 114.

[10] Idaho Department of Aeronautics, General Johnson Creek Correspondence Folder, Accessed 30 June 2010.

[11] "Fliers to Construct Facilities At New Johnson Creek Airstrip," *Idaho Daily Statesman*, 5 June 1959.

[12] Idaho Department of Aeronautics, General Johnson Creek Correspondence Folder, Accessed 30 June 2010.

[13] Bryant, Personal Communication.

[14] Bryant, Personal Communication.

[15] Bryant, Personal Communication.

[16] M. Barry Bryant, Personal Communication, 12 June 2011.

[17] Francis W. Woods, *Landing Strips in Central Idaho 1943*, (Ogden, UT: USDA, 1943).

[18] Dick L. Johnson, *Pilot's Logbook - January 1, 1937 to August 7, 1939*, 18 August 1937.

[19] Chet Moulton, Idaho Airport Facilities, (Boise, ID: Department of Aeronautics State of Idaho, 1950).

[20] Idaho Department of Aeronautics, General Landmark Correspondence Folder, Accessed 30 June 2010.

[21] H. D. Bailey, *Stibnite Idaho*, (Boise, ID: Self-published, 1977), 1.

[22] Bailey, 4-9.

[23] Bailey, 9-14.

[24] Bailey, 17-25.

[25] "Ingenuity Rescued Homes of Stibnite," *Star News*, 23 October 1980.

[26] Dr. Robin McRae, Personal Communication, 7 February 2011.

[27] McRae, Personal Communication.

[28] J. R. Clarkson, *A Breif History Of Flying In The Idaho Primitive Area*, (Boise, ID: Self-published, 1946), 1.

[29] Clarkson, 2.

[30] Dan Stohr, Personal Communication, 15 January 2008.

[31] Warren Ellison, Personal Communication, 28 July 2004.

[32] Ellison, Personal Communication.

[33] Ellison, Personal Communication.

[34] Harold Dougal, Personal Communication, 8 February 2011.

[35] "New Airplane," *Stibnite Miner*, 22 March 1944.

[36] Dougal, Personal Communication.

[37] McRae, Personal Communication.

[38] Dougal, Personal Communication.

[39] McRae, Personal Communication.

[40] McRae, Personal Communication.

[41] "Small Plane Crashes Into Tailings Dyke In Attempting Takeoff," *Stibnite Miner*, 16 September 1942.

[42] McRae, Personal Communication.

[43] McRae, Personal Communication.

[44] Ray Arnold, Personal Communication, 8 February 2011.

[45] Arnold, Personal Communication.

[46] Jerry McCauley, Personal Communication, 8 February 2011.

47 Sumner, 1–13.

48 Francis W. Woods, *Landing Strips in Central Idaho 1943*.

49 McRae, Personal Communication.

50 Dick L. Johnson, *Pilot's Logbooks – May 19, 1942 through January 23, 1945*.

51 H. C. Hoffman, Improvements Payette – Idaho – Yellow Pine Landing Field, 5 June 1942. On file at the Payette National Forest Heritage Program.

CHAPTER 5 CHAMBERLAIN BASIN

1 Payette National Forest, Heritage Program, Chamberlain Guard Station, File PY–467.

2 Payette National Forest, Heritage Program, Chamberlain Guard Station, File PY–467.

3 Payette National Forest, Heritage Program, Chamberlain Guard Station, File PY–467.

4 Payette National Forest, Heritage Program, Chamberlain Guard Station, File PY–467.

5 Lawrence Kingsbury, *Chamberlain Guard Station: A Property Listed on the National Register of Historic Places*, (McCall, ID: USDA, Forest Service, Payette National Forest, 2004).

6 Kingsbury.

7 Kingsbury.

8 Glenn A. Thompson, Letter to Big Creek District Ranger Earl Dodds – discussing history of aviation and Chamberlain Ranger Station, 16 February 1968. On file at the Payette National Forest Heritage Program.

9 Clair A. Hartnett, Letter to Big Creek District Ranger Earl Dodds – discussing history of aviation and Chamberlain Ranger Station, 27 January 1968. On file at the Payette National Forest Heritage Program.

10 Chet Moulton, *Idaho Airport Facilities*, (Boise, ID: Department of Aeronautics State of Idaho, 1950).

11 S. O. Scribner, Improvement Landing Fields – Memo for Regional Forester, 26 July 1933. On file at the Payette National Forest Heritage Program.

12 H. M. Shank, Improvements – Landing Fields – Idaho, 2 November 1938. On file at the Payette National Forest Heritage Program.

13 Thompson, Letter to Big Creek District Ranger Earl Dodds. On file at the Payette National Forest Heritage Program.

14 Thompson, Letter to Big Creek District Ranger Earl Dodds. On file at the Payette National Forest Heritage Program.

15 Earl Dodds, Personal Communication, 22 January 2010.

16 Ted Koskella (Ed. Richard H. Holm Jr.), *General Ridgway's Elk Hunt on the Payette: Chamberlain Basin 1954*, (McCall, ID: USDA, Forest Service, Payette National Forest, Heritage Program, 2006), 2.

17 Ted Koskella, Personal Communication, 9 April 2011.

18 Ken Roth, 8 mm Home Movies – with narration.

19 Koskella, 2.

20 Koskella, 2–3.

21 Wilbur Wiles, Personal Communication – Letter to Author, 28 November 2009.

22 Gordon Fouch, *5700 Air Operations: Idaho Primitive Area Study*, (McCall, ID: USDA, Forest Service, Payette National Forest, 1971), 1.

23 Fouch, 2.

24 Fouch, 2.

25 Fouch, 2.

26 Al Stillman, "Flying One Wing Low (Not a Chinese Proverb)," *McCall Smokejumpers: And There We Were .. Memoirs from Boise, Idaho City, and McCall Smokejumpers*, (McCall, ID: Fire Dog Press), 21.

27 Payette National Forest, Heritage Program, August Hotzel Ranch, File PY-1257.

28 Payette National Forest, Heritage Program, August Hotzel Ranch, File PY-1257.

29 Glenn A. Thompson, Letter to Payette National Forest Supervisor William B. Sendt, 27 February 1971. On file at the Payette National Forest Heritage Program.

30 A. C. McCain, Idaho – O – Supervision inspection – Memorandum For Lands, 1 September 1915. On file at the Payette National Forest Heritage Program.

31 Thompson, Letter to Big Creek District Ranger Earl Dodds. On file at the Payette National Forest Heritage Program.

32 Idaho County Courthouse Records, Accessed 17 February 2011.

33 Tom Parker, *Proposed Backcountry Ranch Management*, (Boise, ID: State of Idaho Department of Fish and Wildlife, 1991).

34 Hotzel Ranch General Lease History File, Idaho Fish & Game, Southwest Region Office.

35 Stan Potts, Personal Communication, 29 August 2010.

36 Potts, Personal Communication.

37 Potts, Personal Communication.

38 Potts, Personal Communication.

39 Potts, Personal Communication.

40 Potts, Personal Communication.

41 Scott Farr, Personal Communication, 16 October 2010.

42 Farr, Personal Communication.

43 Farr, Personal Communication.

44 Farr, Personal Communication.

45 Farr, Personal Communication.

46 Farr, Personal Communication.

47 Hotzel Ranch General Lease History File, Idaho Fish & Game, Southwest Region Office.

48 Peggy McCallum, Letter to Mr. Earl Kimball, District Ranger Krassel Ranger District, 23 July 1985, Hotzel Ranch General Lease History File, Idaho Fish & Game, Southwest Region Office.

49 Hotzel Ranch General Lease History File, Idaho Fish & Game, Southwest Region Office.

50 Hotzel Ranch General Lease History File, Idaho Fish & Game, Southwest Region Office.

51 John C. Gosling, "Chamberlain: Heart of Idaho's Primitive Area," *The AOPA Pilot*, June 1971.

52 Ed Allen, Personal Communication, 8 December 2008.

53 Ray Arnold, Personal Communication, 12 October 2009.

54 Jack Trueblood, Personal Communication, 24 August 2010.

55 Mary Carter-Hepworth, Sarah B. Davis, and Alan Virta, *The Ted Trueblood Collection at Boise State University: A Guide to the papers of one of America's foremost outdoor writers and conservationists*, (Boise, ID: Boise State University, 2000).

56 Nick Long, Personal Communication, 28 July 2010.

57 Ted Trueblood, The Ted Trueblood Hunting Treasury, (New York: David McKay Company, Inc., 1978).

58 J. Trueblood, Personal Communication.

59 Ted Trueblood, Letter to River of No Return Wilderness Council, 1 August 1975. *Ted Trueblood Collection*. Special Collections, MSS 124. Albertsons Library, Boise State University Boise State University, Boise, ID.

60 Long, Personal Communication.

61 Long, Personal Communication.

62 Long, Personal Communication.

63 Frank Church, Letter to Ted Trueblood, 25 June 1982. *Ted Trueblood Collection*. Special Collections, MSS 124. Albertsons Library, Boise State University Boise State University, Boise, ID.

64 Glenn A. Thompson, Letter to Payette National Forest Supervisor Mr. William B. Sendt, 27 February 1971. On file at the Payette National Forest Heritage Program.

65 Lawrence Kingsbury, Cold Meadows Guard Station: *A Property Listed on the National Register of Historic Places*, (McCall, ID: USDA, Forest Service, Payette National Forest, 1994).

66 Hank M. Shank, Improvement - Idaho Landing Fields - Memo for Supervisor, 11 August 1932. On file at the Payette National Forest Heritage Program.

67 C. A. Stowell, Improvements - Cold Meadows Landing Field, 28 November 1955. On file at the Payette National Forest Heritage Program.

68 A. L. Anderson, Improvements - Landing Fields (Cold Meadows Landing Field), 19 August 1955. On file at the Payette National Forest Heritage Program.

69 Warren Ellison, Personal Communication, 28 July 2004.

70 Cecil A. Stowell, Improvements - Cold Meadows Landing Field and G.S. Buildings, 12 July 1957. On file at the Payette National Forest Heritage Program.

71 Earl Dodds, Personal Communication, 23 January 2010.

72 Clair Melvin, Landing Adjustment - Idaho - Hida Creek Landing Field Administrative Site, 17 October 1936. On file at the Payette National Forest Heritage Program.

73 H. M. Shank, Improvements - Landing Fields - Idaho, 8 October 1938. On file at the Payette National Forest Heritage Program.

74 Doug Tims, Personal Communication, 8 March 2011.

75 Francis W. Woods, *Landing Strips in Central Idaho 1943*, (Ogden, UT: USDA, Forest Service, 1943).

76 Francis W. Woods, *Landing Strips in Central Idaho 1943*.

77 Richard H. Holm Jr., *Points of Prominence: Fire Lookouts of the Payette National Forest*, (Scotts Valley, CA: Createspace, 2009), 80.

78 Penn Stohr Sr., *Pilot's Logbook – November 30, 1938 to August 25, 1943*.

79 Jim Larkin, Personal Communication, 3 June 2004.

80 Mike Dorris, Personal Communication, 27 December 2009.

81 Clair Melvin, Landing Adjustment - Idaho - Hungry Creek Landing Field Administration Site, 17 October 1936. On file at the Payette National Forest Heritage Program.

82 Francis W. Woods, *Landing Strips in Central Idaho 1943*.

83 Glenn A. Thompson, Letter to Payette National Forest Supervisor William B. Sendt, 27 February 1971. On file at the Payette National Forest Heritage Program.

84 Francis W. Woods, E - Improvements - Idaho Landing Fields - Ramey Meadows Landing Strip, 26 January 1943. On file at the Payette National Forest Heritage Program.

85 Francis W. Woods, E - Improvements - Idaho Landing Fields - Ramey Meadows Landing Strip, 26 January 1943. On file at the Payette National Forest Heritage Program.

86 Francis W. Woods, *Landing Strips in Central Idaho 1943*.

87 Reddy, 44.

88 Kathy Deinhardt Hill, *Spirits of the Salmon River*, (Cambridge, ID: Backeddy Books, 2001), 57-58.

89 Idaho County Courthouse Records, Accessed 7 June 2010.

90 Dan LeVan Jr., Personal Communication, 18 February 2011.

91 Adelia Parke, *Memoirs of An Old Timer*, (Weiser, ID: Signal-American Printers, 1955), 40-41.

92 Idaho County Courthouse Records, Accessed 7 June 2010.

93 May Mann, "Wally (Wally Beery) took me fishing: Movie cameras just have to wait where those big Mackinaws start leaping," *Outdoor Life's Anthology of Fishing Adventures: The World's Best Stories of Fishing Adventures*, (New York: NY, 1945), 9.

94 Edward H. Phillips, *Travel Air: Wings Over the Prairie*, (Eagan, MN: Flying Books International, 1994), 52-54.

95 Idaho County Courthouse Records, Accessed 7 June 2010.

96 Bill Guth Jr., Personal Communication, 11 February 2011.

97 Guth Jr., Personal Communication.

98 Guth Jr., Personal Communication.

99 Ken Roth, 8 mm Home Movies - with narration.

100 Jim Larkin, Personal Communication, 13 July 2004.

[101] Larkin, Personal Communication.

[102] Larkin, Personal Communication.

[103] Larkin, Personal Communication.

[104] Larkin, Personal Communication.

[105] Larkin, Personal Communication.

[106] Idaho County Courthouse Records, Accessed 7 June 2010.

[107] Bill Scherer, Personal Communication, 15 December 2010.

[108] Bill Bernt, Personal Communication, 20 December 2012.

[109] Bernt, Personal Communication.

[110] Stan Potts, Personal Communication, 26 January 2011.

[111] Potts, Personal Communication.

[112] Idaho County Courthouse Records, Accessed 7 June 2010.

[113] Guth Jr., Personal communication.

[114] Pat Murphy, "Mountain Flying Demands Skill: For Pilots, Idaho Backcountry Can Be A Killer," *Idaho Mountain Express And Guide*, 20 August 2004.

[115] Murphy.

[116] G. W. Otterson, BLM General Land Office Records.

[117] George W. Otterson, BLM General Land Office Records.

[118] W. A. Stonebraker, BLM General Land Office Records.

[119] A. C. McCain, Idaho – O – Supervision inspection – Memorandum For Lands, 1 September 1915. On file at the Payette National Forest Heritage Program.

[120] W. A. Stonebraker, BLM General Land Office Records.

[121] "Big Game Hunting By Aeroplane, Now," *Idaho County Free Press October*, 8 October 1925.

[122] Jay Stewart, Letter to Mr. Al Stonebraker from Jay Stewart of Stewart Lumber Company Incorporated, Brooklyn, New York, 13 August 1930.

[123] Paul Patton, Letter to Mr. W. A. Stonebraker from Paul Patton of The Paul Patton Company Contractors Kansas City, Missouri, 11 August 1932.

[124] Larkin, Personal Communication.

[125] "Geo. Stonebraker Purchases Bellanca Plane," *Cascade News*, 31 October 1930.

[126] "Airplane Crash Claims Life of Pilot Ray Fisher," *Cascade News*, 16 January 1931.

[127] "Widow Innocent Male Jury Finds," *The Spokesman-Review*, 21 June 1945.

[128] Idaho County Courthouse Records, Accessed 17 February 2011.

[129] Jim McGoldrick, *One Man's Opinion of The Spokane Aviation Story (Volume I – 1911–1941)*, (Fairfield, WA: Ye Galleon Press), 153.

[130] Idaho County Courthouse Records, Accessed 17 February 2011.

[131] William Schulze, "The Saga of the Sun God," *Seattle Post – Intelligencer*, 26 January 1964, 8.

[132] Schulze, 8.

[133] Schulze, 8.

[134] Schulze, 8.

[135] McGoldrick, 194.

[136] "Mamer's Big Hop 25 Years Old," *The Spokesman-Review*, 29 August 1954.

[137] Schulze, 8.

[138] Harry C. Shellworth, Letter to Mr. J. O. Stewart, 28 October 1932. Harry C. Shellworth Personal Papers (held by his family).

[139] Idaho County Courthouse Records, Accessed 17 February 2011.

[140] *The Idaho Primitive Area*, (Ogden, UT: USDA, Forest Service, 1951), 43.

[141] Earl Dodds, Personal Communication, 14 April 2012.

[142] Dick Tice, Personal Communication, 10 December 2011.

[143] D. Tice, Personal Communication.

[144] D. Tice, Personal Communication.

[145] D. Tice, Personal Communication.

[146] D. Tice, Personal Communication.

[147] Stonebraker Ranch General Lease History File, Idaho Fish & Game, Southwest Region Office.

[148] Stonebraker Ranch General Lease History File, Idaho Fish & Game, Southwest Region Office.

[149] Stonebraker Ranch General Lease History File, Idaho Fish & Game, Southwest Region Office.

[150] Dennis Hardy, Personal Communication, 20 October 2011.

[151] Hardy, Personal Communication.

[152] Jim Larkin, Personal Communication, 3 June 2004.

[153] Harold Dougal, *Adventures of an Idaho Mountain Pilot*, (Boise, ID: Self-published, 2009), 147–48.

[154] Dougal, 148–49.

[155] Dougal, 150.

CHAPTER 6 MAIN SALMON RIVER

[1] Johnny Carrey and Cort Conley, *River of No Return*, (Cambridge, ID: Backeddy Books, 1978), 140.

[2] Samuel Myers, BLM General Land Office Records.

[3] Marian S. Sweeney, *Gold At Dixie Gulch*, (Kamiah, ID: Clearwater Valley Publishing Company Inc., 1982), 117.

[4] Idaho County Courthouse Records, Accessed 7 June 2010.

[5] Carrey and Conley, 141.

[6] Harold E. Thomas, Personal Communication, 3 October 2011.

[7] Thomas, Personal Communication.

[8] Idaho County Courthouse Records, Accessed 7 June 2010.

[9] Harold E. Thomas, Personal Communication, 21 July 2010.

[10] Thomas, Personal Communication.

[11] Idaho County Courthouse Records, Accessed 7 June 2010.

[12] Thomas, Personal Communication.

[13] Thomas, Personal Communication.

[14] Thomas, Personal Communication.

[15] Thomas, Personal Communication.

[16] Thomas, Personal Communication.

[17] Thomas, Personal Communication.

[18] Thomas, Personal Communication.

[19] Thomas, Personal Communication.

[20] Thomas, Personal Communication.

[21] Ernest F. Sillge, BLM General Land Office Records.

[22] Doug Tims, Personal Communication, 8 March 2011.

[23] Doug Tims, Personal Communication.

[24] Ernest F. Sillge, BLM General Land Office Records.

[25] Robert A. Hilands, BLM General Land Office Records.

[26] Tims, Personal Communication.

[27] Tims, Personal Communication.

[28] Carol Furey-Werhan, *Haven in the Wilderness: The Story of Frances Zaumiller Wisner of Campbell's Ferry, Idaho,* (Parks, AZ: Carol Furey-Werhan, 1996), 76–77.

[29] Tims, Personal Communication.

[30] Carol Furey-Werhan, 99.

[31] Frank Crowe, Personal Communication, 8 March 2011.

[32] Crowe, Personal Communication.

[33] Crowe, Personal Communication.

[34] Carol Furey-Werhan, 117.

[35] Carol Furey-Werhan, 125.

[36] Carol Furey-Werhan, 157.

[37] Carol Furey-Werhan, 207–09.

[38] Tims, Personal Communication.

[39] Mike Dorris, Personal Communication, 25 March 2009.

[40] Tims, Personal Communication.

[41] Tims, Personal Communication.

[42] Tims, Personal Communication.

[43] Tims, Personal Communication.

[44] Crowe, Personal Communication.

[45] Crowe, Personal Communication.

[46] Crowe, Personal Communication.

[47] Bill Fogg, Personal Communication, 25 January 2010.

[48] Mel Guerrera, Personal Communication, 8 March 2011.

[49] Don Micknak, Personal Communication, 8 March 2011.

[50] Micknak, Personal Communication.

[51] Micknak, Personal Communication.

[52] Carrey and Conley, 165–66.

[53] Cindy Schacher, Personal Communication, 15 February 2011.

[54] H. W. Higgins, Letter to Forest Supervisor, Nezperce National Forest – Withdrawls – Nezperce – Jim Moore Landing Field (Proposed), 21 February 1958. On file at the Nez Perce National Forest Heritage Program.

[55] A. W. Blackerby, Letter to Regional Forester – Withdrawls – Nezperce – Jim Moore Landing Field (Proposed), 24 February 1958. On file at the Nez Perce National Forest Heritage Program.

[56] Ernest V. Andersen, Letter to Robert O. Rehfeld, Forest Supervisor – Jim Moore Administrative Site – 109526, 9 April 1971. On file at the Nez Perce National Forest Heritage Program.

[57] Cindy Schacher, *Jim Moore: An Early 20th Century Salmon River Rancher,* (Grangeville, ID: Nez Perce National Forest, 2011), 3.

[58] Arthur W. Pope, BLM General Land Office Records.

[59] Walter J. Smith, BLM General Land Office Records.

[60] Stan Potts, Personal Communication, 24 August 2011.

[61] Potts, Personal Communication.

[62] Potts. Personal Communication.

[63] Potts, Personal Communication.

[64] Fred Porter, Personal Communication, 10 August 2011.

[65] Porter, Personal Communication.

[66] Bruce Crofoot, BLM General Land Office Records.

[67] Carrey and Conley, 137.

[68] Idaho County Courthouse Records, Accessed 7 June 2010.

[69] Sue Hanson, Personal Communication, 21 January 2012.

[70] Melissa Wolff, Personal Communication, 26 January 2012.

[71] Hanson, Personal Communication.

[72] Snider, Personal Communication.

[73] Hanson, Personal Communication.

[74] Hanson, Personal Communication.

[75] William H. Dorris, *Pilot's Log Book – August 22, 1955 to June 26, 1963,* May 1962.

[76] Hanson, Personal Communication.

[77] William H. Dorris, *Pilot's Log Book – February 28, 1963 to October 31, 1970.*

[78] Wolff, Personal Communication.

[79] Hanson, Personal Communication.

[80] Idaho County Courthouse Records, Accessed 7 June 2010.

[81] Don Biddison, Letter to Idaho Transportation Department Division of Aeronautics from Nezperce National Forest Supervisor, 24 July 1979.

[82] Thomas, Personal Communication.

[83] Wolff, Personal Communication.

[84] H. M. Shank, Improvements – Landing Fields – Idaho, 8 October 1938. On file at the Payette National Forest Heritage Program. On file at the Payette National Forest Service Heritage Program.

[85] Payette National Forest, Heritage Program, Elk Meadows Cabin and Airfield, File PY-856.

[86] Francis W. Woods, *Landing Strips in Central Idaho 1943*, (Ogden, UT: USDA, 1943).

[87] Payette National Forest, Heritage Program, Elk Meadows Cabin and Airfield, File PY-856.

[88] Mike Dorris, Personal Communication.

[89] Kenneth Ray Walters, BLM General Land Office Records.

[90] Ken Walters, Personal Communication, 1 July 2011.

[91] Ray Hamell, Personal Communication, 1 July 2011.

[92] Hamell, Personal Communication.

[93] Carrey and Conley, 203.

[94] Dr. Howard Adkins, Personal Communication, 31 January 2011.

[95] Adkins, Personal Communication.

[96] Sue Anderson, Personal Communication, 7 July 2011.

[97] Ray Arnold, Personal Communication, 31 January 2011.

[98] Anderson, Personal Communication.

[99] Anderson, Personal Communication.

[100] William M. Mackay, BLM General Land Office Records.

[101] Idaho County Courthouse Records, Accessed 7 June 2010.

[102] Robert G. Bailey, *River of No Return: A Century of Central Idaho and Eastern Washington History and Development*, (Lewiston, ID: Bailey-Blake Printing Company, 1935), 458.

[103] Betty Penson, "Dude Ranch in the Wilderness: Mackay Bar Ranch Story Spans Century of History." *The Idaho Statesman*, 22 August 1971.

[104] "Airplane Service to Mackay Bar Now on Weekly Basis," *Idaho County Free Press*, 3 May 1934.

[105] Philip J. Shenon and John C. Reed, "Down Idaho's River of No Return," *The National Geographic Magazine*, vol. 70, no.1. (1936): 98.

[106] Shenon and Reed, 117.

[107] Dick L. Johnson, *Pilot's Log Book – May 15, 1928 to January 26, 1937*, 13 October 1935.

[108] Dick L. Johnson, *Pilot's Log Book – May 15, 1928 to January 26, 1937*, 13 October 1935.

[109] Dan Stohr, Personal Communication, 4 October 2011.

[110] Stohr, Personal Communication.

[111] D. Tice, Personal Communication.

[112] D. Tice, Personal Communication.

[113] D. Tice, Personal Communication.

[114] Dougal, Personal Communication.

[115] Bill Humphreys, "Bad Bear: Finding a place to put down amid that vertical real estate is tough enough, but then to find a . . . big bad bear on the runway!" *Private Pilot*, August 1969, 69–74.

[116] "Two Boise Men Die In Back-Country Crash," *Payette Lakes Star*, 3 July 1963.

[117] Steve Burak, Personal Communication, 29 December 2010.

[118] Norm Close, Personal Communication, 24 November 2010.

[119] Mary Jane (Tice) Brown, Personal Communication, 15 December 2010.

[120] D. Tice, Personal Communication.

[121] D. Tice, Personal Communication.

[122] D. Tice, Personal Communication.

[123] D. Tice, Personal Communication.

[124] Brown, Personal Communication.

[125] Brown, Personal Communication.

[126] D. Tice, Personal Communication.

[127] Brent Lloyd, Personal Communication, 3 October 2010.

[128] Klara Hansberger, Personal Communication, 10 December 2010.

[129] D. Tice, Personal Communication.

[130] Close, Personal Communication.

[131] Hansberger, Personal Communication.

[132] Lloyd, Personal Communication.

[133] Lloyd, Personal Communication.

[134] Harold Dougal, Personal Communication, 12 January 2011.

[135] Lloyd, Personal Communication.

[136] Sharon Ann Murray, *The Marshall Lake Mines (A Thesis)*, (Moscow, ID: University of Idaho Graduate School, 1979), 2-3.

[137] Murray, 47-65.

[138] Murray, 74.

[139] Murray, 74.

[140] Jerry Robinson, Personal Communication, 18 April 2012.

[141] Murray, 89.

[142] Carrey and Conley, 206-8.

[143] Charles W. Shepp, BLM General Land Office Records.

[144] Cort Conley, Personal Communication, 9 June 2011.

[145] Carrey and Conley, 215.

[146] Carrey and Conley, 215.

[147] Carrey and Conley, 216-17.

[148] Conley, Personal Communication.

[149] Cort Conley, Personal Communication, 7 June 2011.

[150] Conley, Personal Communication.

[151] "Five Die in Plane; Blame Pilot Error," *Idaho County Free Press*, 29 September 1966.

[152] Conley, Personal Communication.

[153] Lynn Demerse, Personal Communication, 17 September 2011.

[154] Conley, Personal Communication.

[155] Conley, Personal Communication.

156 Conley, Personal Communication.

157 Conley, Personal Communication.

158 Conley, Personal Communication.

159 Sheila D. Reddy, Warrens, *The Mountain Dream: A History of Early Mining and Ethnic Diversity in the Idaho Territory*, (McCall, ID: USDA, Forest Service, Payette National Forest, 1993).

160 Idaho Gold Dredging Co., Warren Dredging Co., and Warren Creek Dredging Co., BLM General Land Office Records.

161 "Landing Field At Warren" *Idaho County Free Press*, 19 November 1931.

162 J. R. Clarkson, *A Brief History of Flying in the Idaho Primitive Area*, (Self-published, 1946).

163 Dorris, Personal Communication.

164 J. G. Kooch, Cooperation – Landing Fields (Warren) State of Idaho –Letter to Mr. Chet Moulton, Director Department of Aeronautics State of Idaho, 23 September 1953.

165 Hank M. Shank, Improvement – Airplane Landing Fields Idaho – Memo for Supervisor, 3 June 1935. On file at the Payette National Forest Heritage Program.

166 Shank, 3 June 1935.

167 Kooch, 23 September 1953.

168 H. M. Shank, Improvements – Landing Fields Idaho – Memo to Regional Forester, 8 October 1938. On file at the Payette National Forest Heritage Program.

169 H. M. Shank, Improvements – Landing Fields Idaho – Letter to Mr. Ed. M. Bryan Director of Aeronautics Boise, Idaho, 2 November 1938. On file at the Payette National Forest Heritage Program.

170 Francis W. Woods, Improvements – Idaho Landing Field – Letter to Division of Engineering, 18 January 1943. On file at the Payette National Forest Heritage Program.

171 Jim Newcomb, Personal Communication, 21 February 2011.

172 J. Newcomb, Personal Communication.

173 J. Newcomb, Personal Communication.

174 Russell Newcomb, Personal Communication, 24 February 2011.

175 J. Carroll Cons (Assistant Director of Aeronautical Inspector), *Letter to Robert R. Johnson, President of Johnson Flying Service*, (concerning the purchase of Intermountain Air Transport aircraft), 16 February 1937.

176 R. Newcomb, Personal Communication.

177 Stohr, Personal Communication, 28 March 2011.

178 "Boisean Dies In Crash Of Airliner; Capt. McCauley Pilots Big Plane On Fatal Flight," *The Idaho Daily Statesman*, 11 January 1945.

179 Carrey and Conley, 157–58.

180 Carrey and Conley, 159.

181 Cindy Schacher, Personal Communication, 3 October 2011.

182 Idaho County Courthouse Records, Accessed 7 June 2010.

183 Glen Baxter, Personal Communication, 13 July 2010.

184 Baxter, Personal Communication.

185 Baxter, Personal Communication.

186 Baxter, Personal Communication.

187 Baxter, Personal Communication.

188 Zeke West, Personal Communication, 13 July 2010.

189 West, Personal Communication.

190 Steve Shotwell, Personal Communication, 15 October 2011.

191 Shotwell, Personal Communication.

192 Alice Rickman, Personal Communication, 11 July 2010.

193 Rickman, Personal Communication.

194 D. Tice, Personal Communication.

195 D. Tice, Personal Communication.

196 D. Tice, Personal Communication.

197 Dougal, Personal Communication.

198 D. Tice, Personal Communication.

199 Frank O. Schumaker and James E. Dewey, *A History of the Salmon River Breaks Primitive Area*, (Bitterroot and Nezperce National Forests, 1970), 24.

200 Truman G. Thomas, BLM General Land Office Records.

201 Carrey and Conley, 142–44.

202 Carrey and Conley, 144–47.

203 Carrey and Conley, 149–51.

204 Idaho County Courthouse Records, Accessed 7 June 2010.

205 Warren Harrington Brown, *It's Fun To Remember: A King's Pine Autobiography*, (McCall, ID: Warren H. Brown, 1999), 36–37.

206 Brown, 37.

207 Jack Hughes, *Pilot's Log Book – August 8, 1945 to February 7, 1948*.

208 Frank Brown, Personal Communication, 6 January 2012.

209 Brown, 37.

210 Leonard Wallace, Personal Communication, 22 July 2010.

211 Wallace, Personal Communication.

212 Brown, 40.

213 Mike Stewart, "Plane crash kills McCall man, 2 others," *The Central Idaho Star-News*, 21 November 1984.

214 Sue Anderson, Personal Communication, 21 July 2011.

215 Anderson, Personal Communication.

216 Anderson, Personal Communication.

[1] Ron Gustin, Personal Communication, 21 June 2011.

[2] Gustin, Personal Communication.

[3] George Dorris, Personal Communication, 19 April 2011.

[4] Dorris, Personal Communication.

[5] Dorris, Personal Communication.

[6] Dorris, Personal Communication.

[7] Dorris, Personal Communication.

[8] Steve Passmore, Personal Communication, 29 February 2012.

[9] Passmore, Personal Communication.

[10] Cindy Schacher, Personal Communication, 11 February 2011.

[11] Harold Thomas, Personal Communication, 3 October 2011.

[12] Idaho County Courthouse Records, Accessed 17 February 2011.

[13] "Air Crash Takes Guide On Mountain Near Home," *Idaho County Free Press*, 28 May 1964.

[14] Harold Thomas, Personal Communication, 21 July 2010.

[15] Thomas, Personal Communication.

[16] Thomas, Personal Communication.

[17] Don Eberle, Personal Communication, 2 March 2011.

[18] Eberle, Personal Communication.

[19] Marian S. Sweeney, *Gold at Dixie Gulch,* (Kamiah, ID: Clearwater Valley Publishing Company-Inc., 1982), 1.

[20] Sweeney, 104.

[21] Sweeney, 104.

[22] Sweeney, 125.

[23] Jerry McCullough, Personal Communication, 12 February 2011.

[24] McCullough, Personal Communication.

[25] Evan W. Kelley, Airplane Landing Fields: *U.S. Department of Agriculture Forest Service Region One*, (Missoula, MT: USDA Region One Division of Engineering, 1939).

[26] Idaho Department of Aeronautics, General Elk City Correspondence Folder, Accessed 17 February 2011.

[27] Idaho County Courthouse Records, Accessed 17 February 2011.

[28] Idaho Department of Aeronautics, General Elk City Correspondence Folder, Accessed 17 February 2011.

[29] Paul O. Filer, Letter to Chet Moulten Department of Aeronautics, 14 February 1949.

[30] Elvia B. Fisher, "Elk City Airport Seeing Good Use," *Idaho County Free Press*, 3 November 1949.

[31] Idaho Department of Aeronautics, General Elk City Correspondence Folder, Accessed 17 February 2011.

[32] "Pilot Stricken While in Air; Dies," *Idaho County Free Press*, 16 August 1956.

[33] Penn Stohr Jr., Personal Communication, 9 February 2011.

[34] Jack Demmons, "Pilots, jumpers survive close call when engine falls from Tri-motor," *Seeley Swan Pathfinder*, 15 April 1993, 9.

[35] Demmons, 9.

[36] Demmons, 9.

[37] Demmons, 9.

[38] Demmons, 9.

[39] Robert G. Bailey, *River of No Return: A Century of Central Idaho and Eastern Washington History and Development*, (Lewiston, ID: Bailey-Blake Printing Company, 1935), 95-96.

[40] Bailey, 98-99.

[41] Marion G. Jungert, Letter to Co-Owners – Idaho Mining & Milling, Inc., 19 March 1960.

[42] James Heid, *Cultural Resource Evaluation of the Florence Basin – Nez Perce National Forest*, 1989.

[43] "Ten-Acre Mining Claim," *Wall Street Journal*, 22 July 1964.

[44] Heid.

[45] George M. Annable, BLM General Land Office Records.

[46] Herman Konrad, Personal Communication, 9 February 2011.

[47] William M. Logan, BLM General Land Office Records.

[48] Jim Babb, Personal Communication, 28 February 2011.

[49] Babb, Personal Communication.

[50] Albert N. Cochrell, *A History of the Nezperce National Forest*, (Missoula, MT: USDA Forest Service, 1970), 40.

[51] Idaho Department of Aeronautics, General Orogrande Correspondence Folder, Accessed 22 February 2011.

[52] Cindy Schacher, *Walker Cabin History*, (Grangeville, ID: USDA Forest Service, 2011), 1.

[53] Schacher, 1.

[54] John R. Milodragovich, Letter from Forest Supervisor J. R. Milodragovich to Regional Forester – Organization (Air Operations) (Transportation System), 2 July 1962. On file at the Nez Perce National Forest Heritage Program.

[55] Milodragovich.

[56] Milodragovich.

[57] S. K. Skoblin, Improvements – Nezperce – Landing Fields – Shissler – Report on Reconnaissance Survey of Potential Airport Site, 28 September 1946. On file at the Nez Perce National Forest Heritage Program.

[58] S. K. Skoblin, Improvements – Nezperce – Landing Fields – Galena Cr. Site – Reconnaissance Survey Report, 21 May 1946. On file at the Nez Perce National Forest Heritage Program.

[59] S. K. Skoblin, Improvements – Nezperce – Landing Fields – Red River – Report on Reconnaissance Survey of Potential Airport Site, 28 September 1946. On file at the Nez Perce National Forest

Heritage Program.

[60] Idaho County Courthouse Records, Accessed 17 February 2011.

[61] Mullins, Personal Communication.

[62] Mullins, Personal Communication.

[63] Mullins, Personal Communication.

CHAPTER 8 SELWAY-BITTERROOT WILDERNESS

[1] William Reap, BLM General Land Office Records.

[2] Jean Carroll and Borg Hendrickson, *I Never Felt Poor Except In Town: Selway Saga 1932–1948*, (Kearney, NE: Morris Publishing, 2003), 15.

[3] Carroll and Hendrickson, 15–16.

[4] Idaho County Courthouse Records, Accessed 7 June 2010.

[5] Jim Renshaw, Personal Communication, 26 May 2010.

[6] Renshaw, Personal Communication.

[7] Bob Black, Personal Communication, 13 January 2011.

[8] Dick Walker, Personal Communication, 1 June 2010.

[9] Black, Personal Communication.

[10] Donald Denton Sr., Personal Communication, 1 June 2010.

[11] Sister M. Alfreda Elsensohn, *Pioneer Days In Idaho County Volume II*, (Cottonwood, ID: The Idaho Corporation of Benedictine Sisters, 1971), 370.

[12] Francis M. Horrace, BLM General Land Office Records.

[13] Idaho County Courthouse Records, Accessed 7 June 2010.

[14] Loren L. Newman, Personal Communication (letter to author), 4 June 2010.

[15] Newman, Personal Communication.

[16] Newman, Personal Communication.

[17] Newman, Personal Communication.

[18] Newman, Personal Communication.

[19] Newman, Personal Communication.

[20] Black, Personal Communication.

[21] Idaho County Courthouse Records, Accessed 7 June 2010.

[22] Dr. Maurice Hornocker, Personal Communication, 1 June 2010.

[23] Hornocker, Personal Communication.

[24] Idaho County Courthouse Records, Accessed 7 June 2010.

[25] Jim Eldredge, Personal Communication, 20 December 2011.

[26] Eldredge, Personal Communication.

[27] Eldredge, Personal Communication.

[28] Eldredge, Personal Communication.

[29] Eldredge, Personal Communication.

[30] Thomas H. Maugh II, "Robert Iacono, 55, Practitioner of Radical Surgery for Parkinson's, Is Killed in Crash," *Los Angeles Times*, 26 June 2007.

[31] Maugh II.

[32] Carole Simon Smolinski and Don Biddison, *Moose Creek Ranger District Historical Information Inventory and Review*, (Clarkston, WA: Northwest Historical Consultants, 1988), 52.

[33] Renshaw, Personal Communication.

[34] Carroll and Hendrickson, 6.

[35] Carroll and Hendrickson, 8.

[36] Charles Duus, *Soaring With Eagles*, (Missoula, MT: Pictorial Histories Publishing Company, Inc., 2001), 112.

[37] Jean Carroll, Personal Communication, 23 January 2013.

[38] Carroll and Hendrickson, 69–70.

[39] Renshaw, Personal Communication.

[40] Carroll and Hendrickson, 70–71.

[41] Renshaw, Personal Communication.

[42] Renshaw, Personal Communication.

[43] Renshaw, Personal Communication.

[44] Renshaw, Personal Communication.

[45] Allen Renshaw, Personal Communication, 1 May 2012.

[46] Jerry Hinkle, Personal Communication, 13 January 2011.

[47] Hinkle, Personal Communication.

[48] Hinkle, Personal Communication.

[49] Hinkle, Personal Communication.

[50] Black, Personal Communication.

[51] Renshaw, Personal Communication.

[52] Hinkle, Personal Communication.

[53] Black, Personal Communication.

[54] Black, Personal Communication.

[55] Black, Personal Communication.

[56] Black, Personal Communication.

[57] Dick Waite, Personal Communication, 2 June 2010.

[58] Rolla Briggs, Personal Communication, 3 June 2010.

[59] Waite, Personal Communication.

[60] Renshaw, Personal Communication.

[61] Waite, Personal Communication.

[62] Black, Personal Communication.

[63] Waite, Personal Communication.

[64] Idaho County Courthouse Records, Accessed 7 June 2010.

65 Waite, Personal Communication.

66 Idaho County Courthouse Records, Accessed 7 June 2010.

67 Dick Williams, Personal Communication, 29 January 2013.

68 Virginia Rhinehart, Personal Communication, 9 July 2010.

69 Rhinehart, Personal Communication.

70 Rhinehart, Personal Communication.

71 Rod Nielsen, Personal Communication, 2 July 2010.

72 Jerry McCauley, Personal Communication, 8 June 2010.

73 Smolinski and Biddison, 50.

74 Idaho County Courthouse Records, Accessed 7 June 2010.

75 Cindy Schacher, Personal Communication, 27 May 2010.

76 Renshaw, Personal Communication.

77 Clarence C. Strong, Improvement - Bitterroot - Shearer Landing Field, 3 August 1935. On file at the Nez Perce National Forest Heritage Program.

78 Renshaw, Personal Communication.

79 Carroll and Hendrickson, 73-74.

80 Jim Renshaw, Personal Communication, 29 January 2013.

81 Renshaw, Personal Communication.

82 Bert Zimmerly Jr., Personal Communication, 28 March 2010.

83 Penn Stohr Jr., Personal Communication, 28 May 2010.

84 H. R. Jones, Inspection - Bitterroot - Shearer Landing Field, 17 July 1952. On file at the Nez Perce National Forest Heritage Program.

85 Schacher, Personal Communication.

86 Arnie Brandt, Personal Communication, 11 May 2010.

87 Brandt, Personal Communication.

88 Brandt, Personal Communication.

89 Warren Ellison, Personal Communication 6 June 2004.

90 Brandt, Personal Communication.

91 Julie Hauger, Shearer Airfield: Briefing Package, (Grangeville, ID: U.S. Department of Agriculture, F, 1987).

92 Hauger, Shearer Airfield: Briefing Package.

93 John W. Carothers, BLM General Land Office Records.

94 Jim Renshaw, Personal Communication, 11 May 2010.

95 Renshaw, Personal Communication.

96 Renshaw, Personal Communication.

97 Renshaw, Personal Communication.

98 Renshaw, Personal Communication.

99 Smolinski and Biddison, 23.

100 Robert Printz, Dead Man's Flat, (Self-published, 1940s), 1-2.

101 Printz, 5.

102 Printz, 7-9.

103 Idaho County Courthouse Records, Accessed 7 June 2010.

104 Renshaw, Personal Communication, 10 June 2010.

105 Zimmerly, Personal Communication.

106 Zimmerly, Personal Communication.

107 Zimmerly, Personal Communication.

108 Zimmerly, Personal Communication.

109 Zimmerly, Personal Communication.

110 Renshaw, Personal Communication, 26 May 2010.

111 Renshaw, Personal Communicaiton.

112 Stan Hepler, Personal Communication, 11 May 2010.

113 Zimmerly, Personal Communication.

114 Zimmerly, Personal Communication.

115 Hepler, Personal Communication.

116 Hepler, Personal Communication.

117 Thurman H. Trosper, Improvements - Bitterroot - Moose Creek Landing Field Memorandum, 12 December 1955. On file at the Nez Perce National Forest Heritage Program.

118 Hepler, Personal Communication.

119 Dave Medel, "Downed Aircraft Discovered, 1948 Mystery May Be Solved," Idaho County Free Press. 8 April 1987.

120 Dave Medel, "Plane Remains Identified as 1948 Crash," Idaho County Free Press. 15 April 1987.

121 Penn Stohr Jr., Personal Communication, 18 January 2011.

122 Stohr, Personal Communication.

123 Bob Olesen, "Moose Creek Lodge Helps The West Stay Wild," Lewiston Morning Tribune, 11 May 1958.

124 Idaho County Courthouse Records, Accessed 7 June 2010.

125 Olesen.

126 Zimmerly, Personal Communication.

127 Renshaw, Personal Communication.

128 Renshaw, Personal Communication.

129 Olesen.

130 "Moose Creek Ranch Now a Memory; Torch is Set," Idaho County Free Press, 1 September 1966.

131 Penn Stohr Jr., Personal Communication, 4 June 2010.

132 "Moose Creek Ranch Now a Memory; Torch is Set."

133 Ray Rice, "Wilderness Beauty as Seen from Aerial Viewpoint," Idaho County Free Press, 6 October 1966.

134 Smolinski and Biddison, 23-24.

135 Smolinski and Biddison, 24-25.

136 Smolinski and Biddison, 27.

137 K. Wolfe, Letter to Regional Forester, 14 June 1930. On file at the Nez Perce National Forest Heritage Program.

138 E. J. Jost, Fire-Air Patrol Moose Creek Landing Field Memorandum, 2 July 1931. On file at the Nez Perce National Forest Heritage Program.

139 E. J. Jost, Fire-Air Patrol Moose Creek Landing Field Memorandum (additional handwritten follow up notes made 6 July

139 1931 on document), 2 July 1931. On file at the Nez Perce National Forest Heritage Program.

140 H. Neff, Moose Creek Airport Selway N.F. – Memorandum For O. Improvement, 22 August 1934. On file at the Nez Perce National Forest Heritage Program.

141 Stan Cohen, A Pictorial History of Smokejumping, (Missoula, MT: Mountain Press Publishing Co., 1983), 26–29.

142 Cohen, 16.

143 Dick L. Johnson, Pilot's Log Book – August 1, 1938 to May 18, 1942, 12 July 1940.

144 Earl Cooley, Trimotor and Trail, (Missoula, MT: Mountain Press Publishing Co., 1984), 22–23.

145 Cooley, 24–25.

146 Dick L. Johnson, Pilot's Log Book – August 1, 1938 to May 18, 1942, 12 July 1940.

147 Cohen, 98.

148 Renshaw, Personal Communication.

149 Stephen F. Roberts, Final Construction Report Moose Creek Landing Field Contract No. 12–11–261–829, (Grangeville, ID: Forest Service – Region One – Department of Agriculture, 1958), 5. On file at the Nez Perce National Forest Heritage Program.

150 "Planes Give Bulldozers Lift To Build Moose Creek Strip," Lewiston Morning Tribune. 10 November 1957.

151 Renshaw, Personal Communication.

152 Roberts, 2.

153 Roland M. Stoleson, Personal Communication, 11 January 2013.

154 Stoleson, Personal Communication.

155 Roland M. Stoleson, Personal Communication, 13 January 2013.

156 Stoleson, Personal Communication.

157 Stoleson, Personal Communication.

158 Memorial: A Tribute to Forest Service Employees Who Perished at Moose Creek August 4, 1959, (Grangeville, ID: USDA, Forest Service, Nez Perce National Forest, 1989).

159 Stohr, Personal Communication.

160 Stohr, Personal Communication.

161 Stohr, Personal Communication.

162 Stohr, Personal Communication.

163 Stohr, Personal Communication

164 Dick Hughes, Personal Communication, 27 January 2011.

165 Hughes, Personal Communication.

166 Hughes, Personal Communication.

167 Black, Personal Communication.

168 Black, Personal Communication.

169 Jack R. Hughes, Pilot's Log Book – April 21, 1948 to April 12, 1950.

170 Smolinski and Biddison, 111.

171 Rod Snider, Personal Communication, 12 June 2010.

172 Snider, Personal Communication.

173 Snider, Personal Communication.

174 Deane Hess, Personal Communication, 15 October 2010.

175 Hess, Personal Communication.

176 Snider, Personal Communication.

177 Snider, Personal Communication.

178 Snider, Personal Communication.

179 Snider, Personal Communication.

180 Snider, Personal Communication.

181 Snider, Personal Communication.

182 Snider, Personal Communication.

183 Snider, Personal Communication.

184 Snider, Personal Communication.

185 Snider, Personal Communication.

186 Snider, Personal Communication.

187 Snider, Personal Communication.

188 Snider, Personal Communication.

189 Snider, Personal Communication.

190 Thurman H. Trosper, Improvements – Bitterroot – Moose Creek Landing Field Memorandum, 12 December 1955. On file at the Nez Perce National Forest Heritage Program.

191 Brandt, Personal Communication.

192 Renshaw, Personal Communication.

193 Renshaw, Personal Communication.

194 "Gregory Franklin Hill (Obituary)," Idaho County Free Press, 26 November 1986.

195 Dave Medel, "Moose Cr. Airplane Crash Claims Life of Local Pilot," Idaho County Free Press, 26 November 1986.

196 Medel.

197 Medel.

198 Medel.

199 Black, Personal Communication.

200 Ty Edling, Personal Communication, 19 April 2011.

201 Black, Personal Communication.

202 Black, Personal Communication.

203 Penn Stohr Jr., Personal Communication, 16 November 2011.

204 Stohr, Personal Communication.

205 Stohr, Personal Communication.

206 Stohr, Personal Communication.

207 Stohr, Personal Communication.

208 Glenn P. Haney, Aircraft Accident Investigation Report DC-3 Crash June 11, 1979, (Missoula, MT: U.S. Department of Agriculture – Forest Service, 1979), 9.

209 Haney, 26.

210 Haney, 26.

211 Hal Blegen, Personal Communication, 29 March 2010.

212 Haney, 27.

213 Blegen, Personal Communication.

214 Blegen, Personal Communication.

215 Blegen, Personal Communication.

216 "10 feared dead but two survive place crash in Northern Idaho," *The Spokesman-Review*, 12 June 1979.

217 James M. Fazio, "A Lasting Memorial – Care of the Wilderness," *The Forester*, (Moscow, ID: University of Idaho, 1980).

218 Haney, 19.

219 Haney, 21.

220 Haney, 24.

221 Haney, 25.

222 Haney, 24.

223 Haney, 21.

224 Haney, 23.

225 Albert N. Cochrell, *A History of the Nezperce National Forest*, (Missoula, Mt: U.S. Department of Agriculture Forest Service, 1970), 24.

226 Idaho County Courthouse Records, Accessed 7 June 2010.

227 Renshaw, Personal Communication.

228 Dale Richardson, Personal Communication, 11 May 2010.

229 Richardson, Personal Communication.

230 Richardson, Personal Communication.

231 Brandt, Personal Communication.

232 Richardson, Personal Communication.

233 Idaho County Courthouse Records, Accessed 7 June 2010.

234 Robert "Bob" and Robin Griffiths, Personal Communication, 4 February 2013.

235 Griffiths, Personal Communication.

236 Griffiths, Personal Communication.

237 Renshaw, Personal Communication.

238 Griffiths, Personal Communication.

239 Jerry V. Adelblue, Letter to Nezperce National Forest Supervisor J. E. Sanderson – Wilderness and Primitive Areas (Selway-Bitterroot Wilderness), 30 August 1967. On file at the Nez Perce National Forest Heritage Program.

240 Griffiths, Personal Communication.

241 Griffiths, Personal Communication.

242 Griffiths, Personal Communication.

243 Griffiths, Personal Communication.

244 Joe Rimensberger, Personal Communication, 31 January 2013.

245 Rimensberger, Personal Communication.

246 Rimensberger, Personal Communication.

247 Rimensberger, Personal Communication.

248 Griffiths, Personal Communication.

249 Griffiths, Personal Communication.

250 Fae Smith, BLM General Land Office Records.

251 Smolinski and Biddison, 58.

252 Louis F. Hartig, *Lochsa: The Story of a Ranger District and its People in Clearwater National Forest*, (Dubuque, IA: Kendall/Hunt Publishing Company, 1989), 24.

253 Hartig, 23.

254 Hartig, 22.

255 Jim Renshaw, Personal Communication, 7 January 2011.

256 Renshaw, Personal Communication.

257 Renshaw, Personal Communication.

258 Renshaw, Personal Communication.

259 Renshaw, Personal Communication.

260 Renshaw, Personal Communication.

261 Renshaw, Personal Communication.

262 Stohr, Personal Communication.

263 Stohr, Personal Communication.

264 Stohr, Personal Communication.

265 Stohr, Personal Communication.

266 Renshaw, Personal Communication.

267 Renshaw, Personal Communication.

268 Renshaw, Personal Communication.

269 Renshaw, Personal Communication.

270 Renshaw, Personal Communication.

271 Renshaw, Personal Communication.

272 Renshaw, Personal Communication.

273 Renshaw, Personal Communication.

274 Renshaw, Personal Communication.

275 Renshaw, Personal Communication.

276 Renshaw, Personal Communication.

277 Renshaw, Personal Communication.

278 Renshaw, Personal Communication.

279 Renshaw, Personal Communication.

280 Renshaw, Personal Communication.

281 Renshaw, Personal Communication.

282 Renshaw, Personal Communication.

283 Renshaw, Personal Communication.

[1] "Lesley 'Billie' Eva Brakel Oberbillig Schwab [Obituary]," *The News Times*, (Newport, Oregon), 5 August 2009.

[2] "Lesley 'Billie' Eva Brakel Oberbillig Schwab [Obituary]."

[3] Carol Arnold, Personal Communication, 15 December 2011.

[4] C. Arnold, Personal Communication.

[5] C. Arnold, Personal Communication.

[6] C. Arnold, Personal Communication.

[7] C. Arnold, Personal Communication.

[8] C. Arnold, Personal Communication.

[9] Mila Alvarez, *The State of America's Forests*, (Bethesda, MD: Society of American Foresters, 2007), 43.

[10] Malcolm M. Furniss, *Entomological Aspects of the 1955 Spruce Budworm Control Project in Southern Idaho*, (Ogden, UT: Intermountain Forest And Range Experiment Station, 1955).

[11] Robert D. Beeman, "Big Game Salting in Idaho," *Idaho Wildlife Review*, September–October 1957, 3.

[12] Beeman, 3–4.

[13] Beeman, 4.

[14] Levi Mohler, Wesley Shaw, and Dr. Paul Dalke, "Elk and Elk Hunting in Idaho," *Wildlife Review*, May–June 1959, 5.

[15] Beeman, 4.

[16] Martel Morache, *Fifty Years of Game Management (1938–1988) in Idaho*, (Boise, ID: Idaho Fish & Game Department, 1988), 2.

[17] James O. Beck, *Twenty-First Biennial Report Fish & Game Department Of The State Of Idaho*, (Boise, ID: Idaho Fish & Game, 1945–1946), 37.

[18] Morache, 1–2.

[19] "Furbearers Dropped to New Homes in Wilderness Areas," *Idaho Wildlife Review*, August 1949, 7.

[20] Morache, 2.

[21] Stacy Gebhards, *Wild Thing: Backcountry Tales and Trails*, (Pullman, WA: WSU Press, 1999), 27.

[22] Leon Murphy, "Mountain Lakes Fisheries Management," *Idaho Wildlife Review*, March–April 1956, 3–4.

[23] Thelma Anne Dean, *Fish Planting by Airplane in Idaho*, (Self-published, 1977).

[24] Forrest Hauck, "Mountain Lakes Beckon Idaho Anglers Into Remote Backcountry for Summer's Fishing," *Idaho Wildlife Review*, April–May 1950, 10.

[25] "Pilot Joins Department On a Part-time Basis," *Idaho Wildlife Review*, December 1948, 2.

[26] "Aerial Fish Planting Program Stocks High Mountain Waters," *Idaho Wildlife Review*, October–November 1949, 8.

[27] "Mt. Lakes Receive Aerial Plant," *Idaho Wildlife Review*, September-October 1951, 3.

[28] Murphy, 3.

[29] Murphy, 4–5.

[30] "Helicopter Used to Plant Trout," *Idaho Wildlife Review*, January-February 1959, 12.

[31] Stacy Gebhards, "Bottled Fish and Mountain Lakes," *Wildlife Review*, January–February 1963, 10.

[32] Stacy Gebhards, "Mountain Lakes . . . A Challenge to Man, Beast and Machines," *Wildlife Review*, March–April 1965, 10.

[33] Gebhards, 12.

[34] Gebhards, 12.

[35] Mike Dorris, Personal Communication, 18 January 2012.

[36] Dorris, Personal Communication.

[37] Steve Kammeyer, Personal Communication, 19 January 2012.

[38] Steve Passmore, Personal Communication, 23 September 2011.

[39] Kammeyer, Personal Communication.

[40] Kammeyer, Personal Communication.

[41] Passmore, Personal Communication.

[42] Dorris, Personal Communication.

[43] Dorris, Personal Communication.

[44] Dorris, Personal Communication.

[45] Passmore, Personal Communication.

[46] James O. Beck, *Nineteenth Biennial Report Of The Fish & Game Department Of The State Of Idaho*, (Boise, ID: Idaho Fish & Game, 1941-1942), 13.

[47] Beck, 11–12.

[48] James O. Beck, *Twentieth Biennial Report Of The Fish & Game Department Of The State Of Idaho*, (Boise, ID: Idaho Fish & Game, 1943-1944), 23.

[49] Beck, 23–24.

[50] James O. Beck, *Twenty-First Biennial Report Fish & Game Department Of The State Of Idaho*, (Boise, ID: Idaho Fish & Game, 1945-1946), 30.

[51] Beck, 31.

[52] Dick L. Johnson, *Pilot's Logbooks – April 17, 1928 through January 23, 1945*.

[53] Bill Scherer, Personal Communication, 6 November 2011.

[54] Jim Newcomb, Personal Communication, 4 November 2011.

[55] Mike Dorris, Personal Communication, 15 November 2011.

[56] Ray Arnold, Personal Communication, 11 December 2011.

[57] Jim Renshaw, Personal Communication, 11 December 2011.

[58] Penn Stohr Jr., Personal Communication, 8 January 2012.

[59] Stohr, Personal Communication.

[60] Stohr, Personal Communication.

[61] Sue Hart, "'Eye to See': The Writers of Eastern Montana." *In Writing Montana: Literature Under the Big Sky*, edited by Rick

Newby and Suzanne Hunger, (Helena, MT: Falcon Press, 1996), 47-48.

[62] Dana Odessey, Personal Communication, 5 March 2012.

[63] Bill Woods, *Wood's Scrapbook*.

[64] Gene Nora Jessen, "Idaho Plane Talk: Floating Feather Airport Founder Laughs Retelling Airport's Colorful Past," *The Idaho Statesman*, 14 February 1969.

[65] "Army Airmen Perish When Big Bomber Crashes Near Boise: Burning Aircraft Falls to Earth At Floating Feather Airport, Causing Hangar and Range Fires," *The Idaho Daily Statesman*, 30 June 1944.

[66] Odessey, Personal Communication.

[67] *Wood's Scrapbook*.

[68] "Veteran Pilot Solos His 500th Aviation Student," *The Idaho Sunday Statesman*, 26 August 1945.

[69] *Wood's Scrapbook*.

[70] Randy Woods, Personal Communication, 20 February 2012.

[71] Odessey, Personal Communication.

[72] Woods, Personal Communication.

[73] *Wood's Scrapbook*.

[74] *Wood's Scrapbook*.

[75] Woods, Personal Communication.

[76] *Wood's Scrapbook*.

[77] Odessey, Personal Communication.

[78] Edited by Edward A. Johnson, Kiyoko Miyanishi, *Forest Fires: Behavior and Ecological Effects*, (San Diego, CA: Academic Press, 2001), 383-85.

[79] Donald M. Fuquay and H. J. Wells, *The Project Skyfire: Cloud-Seeding Generator*, (Ogden, Utah: Intermountain Forest and Range Experiment Station, Forest Service, USDA, 1957).

[80] Penn Stohr Jr., Personal Communication, 25 March 2010.

[81] Stohr, Personal Communication.

[82] Johnson and Miyanishi, 385.

[83] Penn Stohr Jr., Personal Communication, 23 December 2009.

[84] Stohr, Personal Communication.

[85] C. B. Walker Jr., Letter to Mr. Worthie M. Rauscher, Administrator – Idaho Division of Aeronautics and Public Transportation, 1 November 1976.

[86] Peter Mourtsen, Personal Communication, 29 January 2011.

[87] Mourtsen, Personal Communication.

[88] Peter Mourtsen, *Visitor Use Survey*, (McCall, ID: Big Creek Ranger District – Payette National Forest, 1975).

[89] Mourtsen, Personal Communication.

CHAPTER 10 # A GLIMPSE AT BACKCOUNTRY FLYING IN FILM

[1] Dick L. Johnson, *Pilot's Log Books – August 1, 1938 through May 18, 1942*.

[2] "Local Pilots Perform for Paramount Film," *The Payette Lakes Star*, 23 October 1941.

[3] "Local Pilots Perform for Paramount Film," *The Payette Lakes Star*, 23 October 1941.

[4] David Richards, Personal Communication, 21 August, 2011.

[5] Richards, Personal Communication.

[6] Richards, Personal Communication.

[7] Richards, Personal Communication.

[8] Richards, Personal Communication.

[9] Richards, Personal Communication.

[10] "Obituary – George Oliver Smith," *Idaho Statesman*, 16 May 2005.

[11] Bruce Reichert and Pat Metzler, "Vanishing Idaho," *Outdoor Idaho*, (Boise, ID: Idaho Public Television, 1995), DVD.

[12] Reichert and Metzler.

[13] Rod Snider, Personal Communication, 19 July 2010.

[14] Dan Vichorek, "One More Try," *Montana Magazine*, September 1981.

[15] Vichorek.

[16] Bob Nicol, Personal Communication, 9 March 2011.

[17] Dick Williams, Personal Communication, 10 October 2011.

[18] Williams, Personal Communication.

[19] Williams, Personal Communication.

CHAPTER 11 WORLD WAR II MILITARY AIRPLANE CRASHES IN THE BACKCOUNTRY

1 Anthony J. Mireles, *Fatal Army Air Forces Aviation Accidents In The United States 1941–1945*, (Jefferson, NC: McFarland & Company, Inc., 2006).

2 Craig Fuller, Personal Communication (Aviation Archeological Investigation & Research), 4 January 2012.

3 Captain Charles A. Leidy, *War Department U.S. Army Air Forces Report of Aircraft Accident, B-23 39-052*, 22 February 1943, 1. Declassified military documents.

4 Gloria Freeborg, Personal Communication, 22 October 2001.

5 Paul Loewen, *Untitled manuscript concerning the crash at Loon Lake*, (Ault, CO: Self-published, 1988), 1.

6 Loewen, 1.

7 Loewen, 1.

8 Lieutenant Robert R. Orr, *Report on Crash B-23 #9052* January 29, 1943, 29 February 1943, 1. Declassified military documents.

9 Orr, 1.

10 Edward M. Freeborg, *Crash in the Hills*, (Portland, OR: Self-published, 1943), 1.

11 Leidy, 1.

12 Orr, 1.

13 Orr, 2.

14 Orr, 2.

15 2nd Lieutenant James V. Kelly, *Report on Crash B-23 #9052 January 29, 1943*, 29 February 1943, 1. Declassified military documents.

16 Corporal Earl J. Beaudry, *Report on Crash B-23 AC #9052 January 29, 1943*, 29 February 1943, 1. Declassified military documents.

17 Loewen, 4.

18 Loewen, 5.

19 Freeborg, 2.

20 Lloyd Johnson, Personal Communication, 14 January 2007.

21 Loewen, 6.

22 Johnson, Personal Communication.

23 Freeborg, 2.

24 Freeborg, 3.

25 Freeborg, 3.

26 Loewen, 7.

27 Freeborg, 3.

28 Colonel Lyman L. Phillips, *Transmittal of Report of Search for B-23 No. 39052*, 12 February 1943. Declassified military documents.

29 Lyman.

30 Lyman.

31 "Five Fliers Rescued After Being Marooned 16 days Near Cascade," *The Idaho Morning Statesman*, 16 February 1943.

32 Loewen, 6.

33 "Five Fliers Rescued After Being Marooned 16 days Near Cascade," *The Idaho Morning Statesman*, 16 February 1943.

34 Penn Stohr Sr., *Pilot's Logbook – November 30, 1938 to August 25, 1943*, 13 February 1943.

35 Dan Stohr, Personal Communication, 18 July 2002.

36 Loewen, 8.

37 Stohr, Personal Communication.

38 "Idaho's Miracle Pilot," *The Cascade News*, 19 February 1943.

39 "Idaho's Miracle Pilot," *The Cascade News*, 19 February 1943.

40 Penn Stohr Sr., *Pilot's Logbooks – November 30, 1938 to August 25, 1943*, 14 February 1943.

41 Loewen, 10.

42 Penn Stohr Sr., *Pilot's Logbooks – November 30, 1938 to August 25, 1943*, 14 February 1943.

43 Loewen, 10.

44 Lloyd Johnson, Personal Communication, 8 July 2002.

45 Loewen, 10.

46 Gene Powers, Notes on the Loon Lake Rescue, 12 December 1988. On file at the Payette National Forest Heritage Program.

47 Powers.

48 Lloyd Johnson, Personal Communication, 14 January 2007.

49 Dick L. Johnson, *Pilot's Logbooks – May 19, 1942 through January 23, 1945*, 15 February 1943.

50 Powers.

51 "Five Fliers Rescued After Being Marooned 16 days Near Cascade," *The Idaho Morning Statesman*, 16 February 1943.

52 Dan Stohr, Personal Communication, 11 January 2012.

53 Penn Stohr Jr., Personal Communication, 10 January 2012.

54 Freeborg, 3.

55 "Three Army Fliers Safe, Waite Rescue on Sleds," *The Idaho Evening Statesman*, 17 February 1943.

56 Freeborg, 4–6.

57 Freeborg, 6.

58 Edward M. Freeborg, *Ed's Scrapbook* (assembled by his mother), 1943.

59 Freeborg, 8.

60 Freeborg, *Ed's Scrapbook*.

61 Loewen, 1.

[62] Capt. LeRoy G. Heston, *War Department U.S. Army Air Forces Report of Aircraft Accident, B-25D 41-29653 – 29 January 1943*. 3 February 1943. Declassified military documents.

[63] "Idaho Forest Service Men and Penn Stohr Bring In Salvaged Parts From Bomber Crash Scene at Loon Lake," *The Payette Lakes Star*, 4 March 1943.

[64] Dick L. Johnson, *Pilot's Logbooks – May 19, 1942 through January 23, 1945.*

[65] "Idaho Forest Service Men and Penn Stohr Bring In Salvaged Parts From Bomber Crash Scene at Loon Lake," *The Payette Lakes Star*, 4 March 1943.

[66] Terry Aitken, Personal Communication, 17 July 2002.

[67] Stohr, Personal Communication.

[68] Stohr, Personal Communication.

[69] Billie Orr Larson, Personal Communication, 19 July 2002.

[70] Robert K. Ellison, Letter to Mrs. Orr, 1 December 1944.

[71] Major Elliott T. Pardee, *War Department U.S. Army Air Forces Report of Aircraft Accident, B-24J 42-72980*, 19 November 1944, 1–7. Declassified military documents.

[72] Jan Schermerhorn, Personal Communication, 5 August 2002.

[73] Gloria Freeborg, Personal Communication, 29 March 2002.

[74] Penn Stohr Sr., *Stohr Scrapbook.*

[75] Lorren Loewen, Personal Communication, 13 January 2012.

[76] "Survivor of 1943 place crash returns to Loon Lake site," *The Star-News*, 7 August 1969.

[77] Loewen, 4.

[78] L. Loewen, Personal Communication.

[79] Freeborg, Personal Communication.

[80] Freeborg, Personal Communication.

[81] Freeborg, Personal Communication.

[82] Edward Freeborg, *A Crash Survivor Returns to Bomber at Loon Lake*, (Self-published, 1992), 2.

[83] Freeborg, Personal Communication.
[84] Freeborg, *Ed's Scrapbook.*

[85] Freeborg, *Ed's Scrapbook.*

[86] Freeborg, *Ed's Scrapbook.*

[87] Richard S. Cayo, Use Application and Report – Treasure Salvors LTD., 7 September 1997. On file at the Payette National Forest Heritage Program.

[88] Payette National Forest, Heritage Program, Loon Lake B-23 Crash Site, File PY-843.

[89] Payette National Forest, Heritage Program, Loon Lake B-23 Crash Site, File PY-843.

[90] Lt. Col. John C. Covington, *War Department U.S. Army Air Forces Report of Aircraft Accident, B-17F 42-29514*, 5 May 1943, 3. Declassified military documents.

[91] Covington, 3.

[92] George W. Smith, *Survivor*, (Carlsbad, CA: Self-published, 1993), 1.

[93] Flight Officer Harold E. Thompson, *Statement By Flight Officer Harold E. Thompson on the Crash of B-17F 42-29514*, April 1943, 1. Declassified military documents.

[94] 2nd Lt. Joseph R. Brensinger, *Statement of Pilot B-17F 42-29514*, 14 April 1943, 1. Declassified military documents.

[95] Thompson, 2.

[96] 2nd Lt. George W. Smith, *Statement of Bombardier B-17F 42-29514*, 14 April 1943, 1. Declassified military documents.

[97] Thompson, 2.

[98] M. G. Markle, Letter to John N. Kinney, A. R. F. – O – Supervision – Challis, Airplane Crashes of March 30 and April 8, 20 April 1943.

[99] John P. Ferguson, *Search For the Downed*, (McCall, ID: Payette National Forest USDA, 1996), 2.

[100] "Big Bomber Crashes Near Challis: Searching Party Finds No Life In Plane's Ruins," *The Idaho Daily Statesman*, 1 April 1943.

[101] "Planes Still Search for Bomber Crew," *The Challis Messenger*, 7 April 1943.

[102] "Five Missing Airmen Reach Ranger Cabin High on Idaho Peak," *The Idaho Daily Statesman*, 6 April 1943.

[103] Ferguson, 5.

[104] Ferguson, 6.

[105] Harvey R. Wiegand, *Statement By Sgt. Harvey R. Wiegand on the Crash of B-17F 42-29514*, April 1943, 1. Declassified military documents.

[106] Wiegand, 1.

[107] 2nd Lt. Austin Finley, *Statement By 2nd Lt. Austin Finley on the Crash of B-17F 42-29514*, April 1943, 1. Declassified military documents.

[108] Wiegand, 2.

[109] Ferguson, 9.

[110] "Idaho Mountain Fliers Rescue Five Of Ill-Fated Flying Fortress Crew," *The Idaho Daily Statesman*, 7 April 1943.

[111] Dick L. Johnson, *Pilot's Logbooks – May 19, 1942 through January 23, 1945.*

[112] Smith, 10.

[113] "Idaho Mountain Fliers Rescue Five Of Ill-Fated Flying Fortress Crew," *The Idaho Daily Statesman*, 7 April 1943.

[114] Smith, 11.

[115] Smith, 11.

[116] Smith, 5–6.

[117] Smith, 7–11.

[118] Smith, 12.

[119] Smith, 14.

[120] Smith, 15.

[121] Smith, 15–16.

[122] Smith, 15.

[123] Smith, 2.

[124] Covington, 4.

[125] Covington, 2–3.

[126] Maj. James E. Blount, *War Department U.S. Army Air Forces Report of Aircraft Accident, B-17F 42-5305 – 24 October 1943*, 2 November 1943. Declassified military documents.

[127] Dick L. Johnson, *Pilot's Logbooks – May 19, 1942 through January 23, 1945*.

[128] Smith, 20.

[129] Smith, 22.

[130] Smith, 18–19.

[131] Jeraldine K. Smith, Personal Communication, 11 February 2002.

[132] Smith, Personal Communication.

[133] Smith, 25.

[134] Smith, 21.

[135] Harold Dougal, *Adventures of an Idaho Mountain Pilot*, (Boise, ID: Self-published, 2009), 174–75.

CHAPTER 12 TRAVEL AIR 6000S OF THE IDAHO BACKCOUNTRY

[1] Hank Galpin, "Travel Air 6000s – Ten Years Later," *The Travel Air Log: Travel Air Restorers Association*, Volume 16, No. 1, March 2009.

[2] Hank Galpin, Personal Communication, 1 April 2011.

[3] Galpin, Personal Communication.

CHAPTER 13 FORD TRI-MOTORS OF THE IDAHO BACKCOUNTRY

[1] William T. Larkins, *The Ford Tri-Motor 1926–1992*, (West Chester, PA: Schiffer Publishing Ltd., 1992).

[2] Larkins.

INDEX

X

Y

Z

Richard H. Holm Jr. - a historian, commercial pilot, outdoor enthusiast, and a third generation Idahoan has a profound fascination with the state's history, especially topics related to the remote central region of the state. After graduating from the University of Idaho in 2005, Holm has written numerous pieces related to the backcountry, including his last book *Points of Prominence: Fire Lookouts of the Payette National Forest*. When not collecting information for the latest project, Holm resides in Boise and McCall with his wife.

CPSIA information can be obtained
at www.ICGtesting.com
Printed in the USA
LVHW022255010623
748676LV00008B/217